HOW TO PAINT
Watercolor Flowers

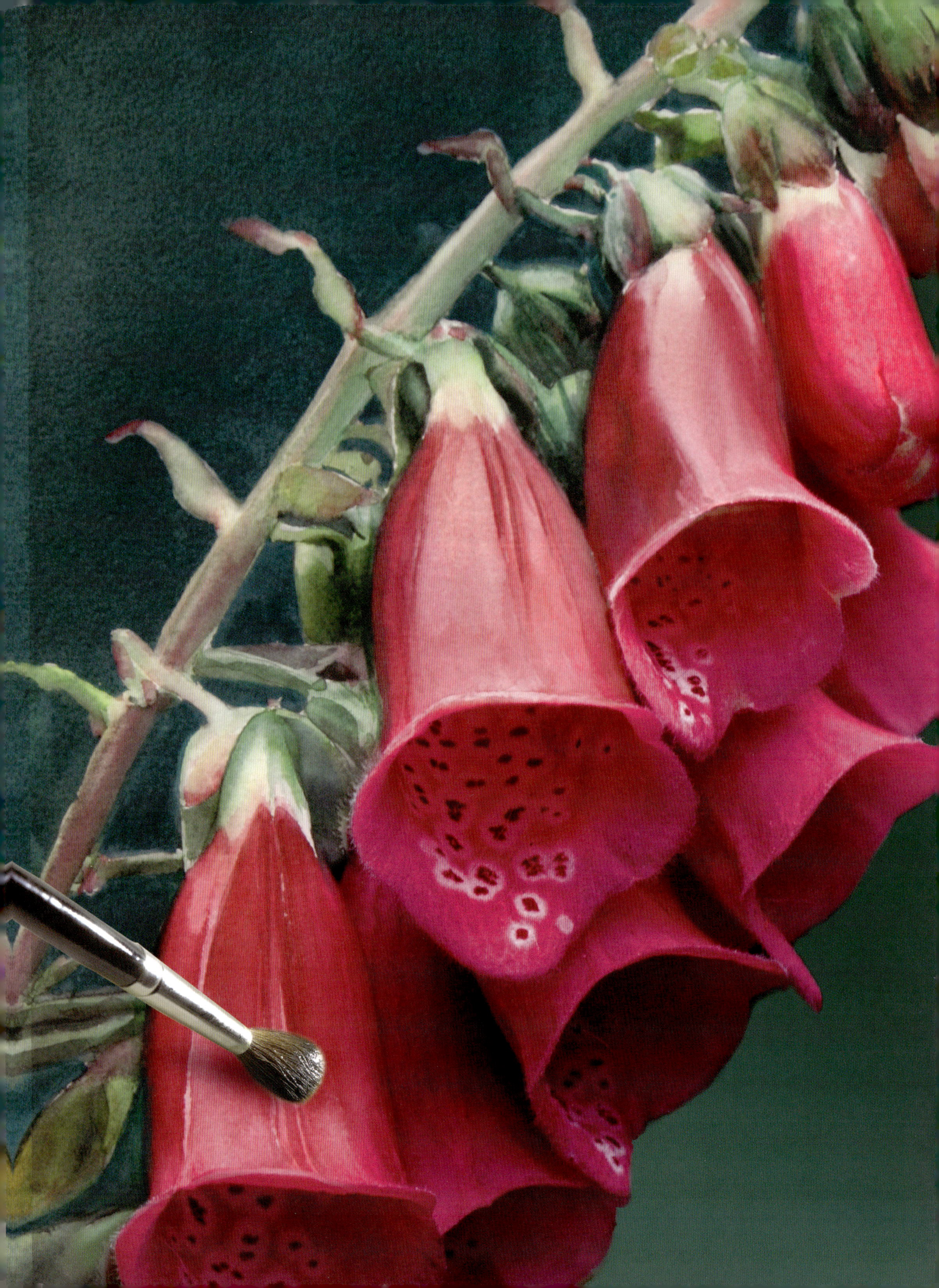

HOW TO PAINT

Watercolor Flowers

Create Your Own Masterpiece in 6 Easy Steps

Robin Berry

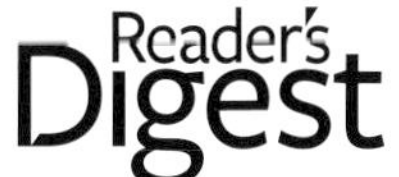

The Reader's Digest Association, Inc.
Pleasantville, New York/Montreal/Sydney/Mumbai/Singapore

A READER'S DIGEST BOOK

This edition published by The Reader's Digest Association, Inc., by arrangement with Quarto Inc.

QUAR.MPWF

Conceived, designed, and produced by
Quarto Publishing plc
The Old Brewery
6 Blundell Street
London N7 9BH

FOR QUARTO
Senior Editor **Katie Crous**
Designer **Louise Clements**
Design Assistant **Saffron Stocker**
Copy Editors **Diana Chambers and Liz Dalby**
Author's Photographer **Vicki Madsen**
Photographer **Phil Wilkins**
Proofreader **Claire Waite Brown**
Indexer **Ann Barrett**
Art Director **Caroline Guest**
Creative Director **Moira Clinch**
Publisher **Paul Carslake**

FOR READER'S DIGEST
U.S. Project Editor **Siobhan Sullivan**
Canadian Project Manager **Pamela Johnson**
Project Designer **Jennifer Tokarski**
Senior Art Director **George McKeon**
Executive Editor, Trade Publishing **Dolores York**
Associate Publisher, Trade Publishing **Rosanne McManus**
President and Publisher, Trade Publishing **Harold Clarke**

Library of Congress Cataloging-in-Publication Data:
Berry, Robin, 1942-
How to paint watercolor flowers: create your own masterpiece in 6 easy steps / Robin Berry. -- 1st ed. p. cm.
"A Reader's Digest book."
ISBN 978-1-60652-168-7
1. Flowers in art. 2. Watercolor painting--Technique. I. Title. II. Title: Create your own masterpiece in 6 easy steps.
ND2300.B47 2011
751.42'24343--dc22
2010017323

ISBN: 978-1-60652-168-7

We are committed to both the quality of our products and the service we provide to our customers. We value your comments, so please feel free to contact us.
The Reader's Digest Association, Inc.
Adult Trade Publishing
Reader's Digest Road
Pleasantville, NY 10570-7000

For more Reader's Digest products and information, visit our website:
www.rd.com (in the United States)
www.readersdigest.ca (in Canada)
www.readersdigest.com.au (in Australia)
www.readersdigest.co.nz (in New Zealand)

Color separation by Modern Age
Printed in China by Toppan Leefung Printing Ltd.

10 9 8 7 6 5 4 3 2 1

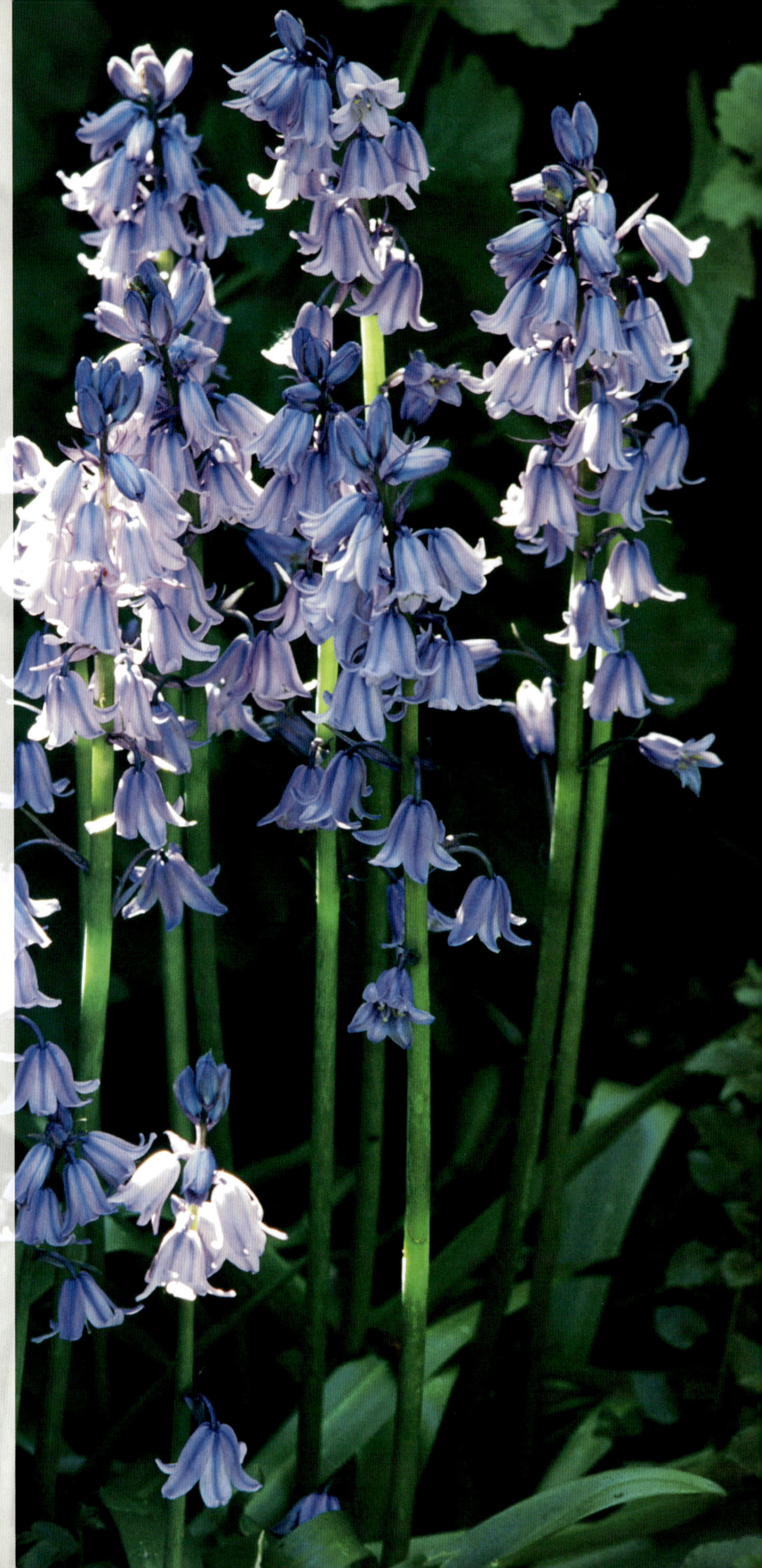

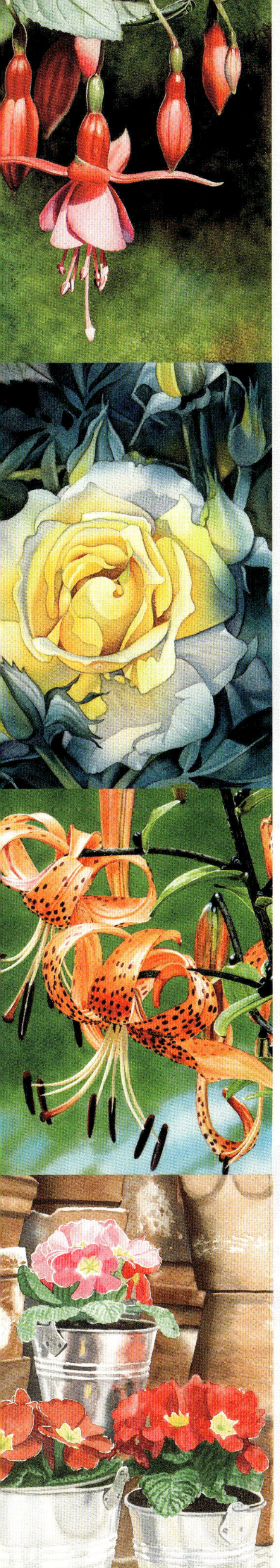

Contents

Before You Begin

The core of this book is a series of 55 stunning photographs of flowers—a virtual library of flower photography. Each photograph occupies a whole page and is accompanied by a step-by-step demonstration of a watercolor treatment on the opposite page. Copy the watercolor demonstration or use it for reference, interpreting the subject in your own way.

How to Use This Book

Before rushing for your paints and brushes, take a look at the first section of this book to read about supplies, skills, and techniques that will give flight to your imagination. If you are a beginner, this introductory information is indispensable; if you are an experienced painter, you will find new and exciting ways to enhance your approach to flower painting and reference materials that will help you throughout your painting experience.

THE FLOWERS

The flower photographs and their associated step-by-step paintings are divided into portrait and landscape formats. The portrait-format subjects are featured on pages 36–107 and include five steps to guide you through the painting; landscape-format subjects are featured on pages 108–145 and include six steps. Within these two formats, the flowers are loosely grouped into three categories: Single Specimens, Floral Still Life, and Flowers Outdoors. Each open page, or spread, is one complete project.

ARTIST'S INTERPRETATION

All the demonstrations in this book have been specially commissioned from a team of professional watercolor artists, each of whom has an individual style and way of working. If you find you respond strongly to one artist's interpretation of a subject, you might want to try a mix-and-match approach, choosing a photograph that appeals to you and painting it first in the style of the associated artist and then in another. Trying out different methods is an important step toward finding your own style.

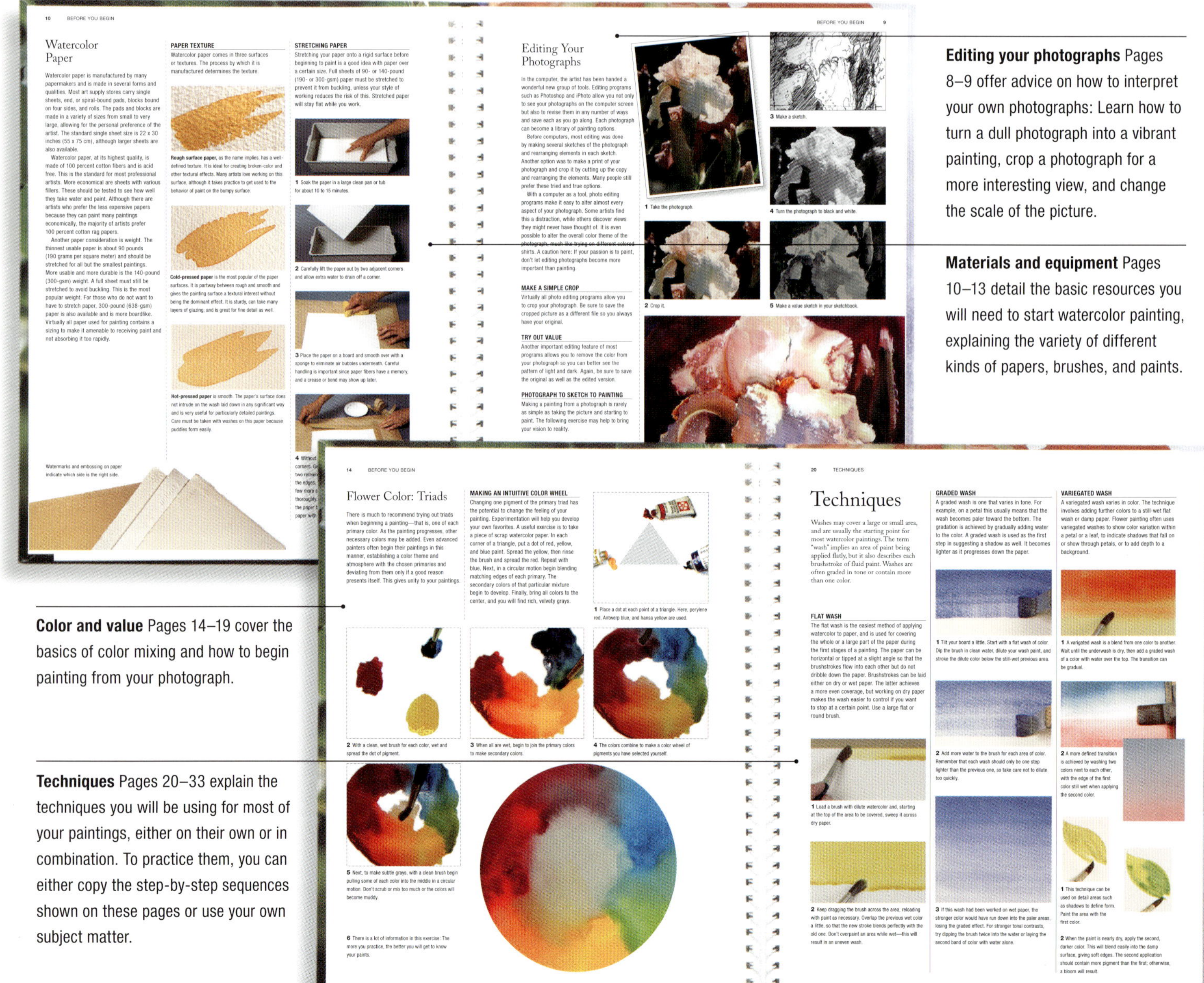

Editing your photographs Pages 8–9 offer advice on how to interpret your own photographs: Learn how to turn a dull photograph into a vibrant painting, crop a photograph for a more interesting view, and change the scale of the picture.

Materials and equipment Pages 10–13 detail the basic resources you will need to start watercolor painting, explaining the variety of different kinds of papers, brushes, and paints.

Color and value Pages 14–19 cover the basics of color mixing and how to begin painting from your photograph.

Techniques Pages 20–33 explain the techniques you will be using for most of your paintings, either on their own or in combination. To practice them, you can either copy the step-by-step sequences shown on these pages or use your own subject matter.

The Projects

Look through all the projects before you decide on your first choice. There is an array of compositions, colors, and styles to consider. Each painting project includes a list of the paints, tools and materials, and techniques you will need.

Techniques used The methods used by the artist are listed and cross-referenced to the Techniques pages at the front of this book so that you can refresh your memory if needed.

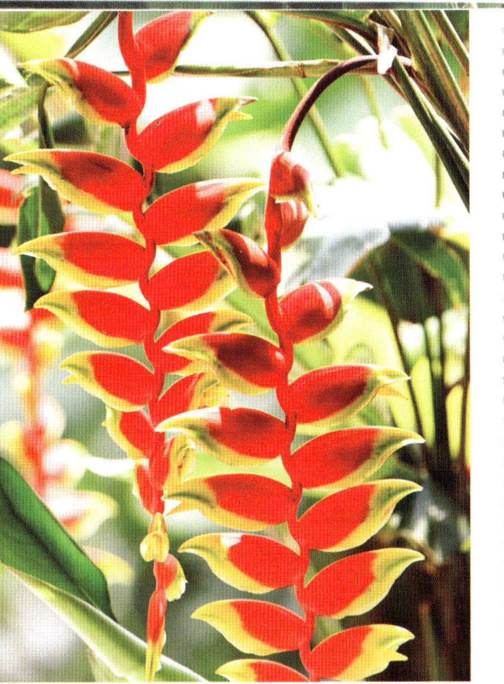

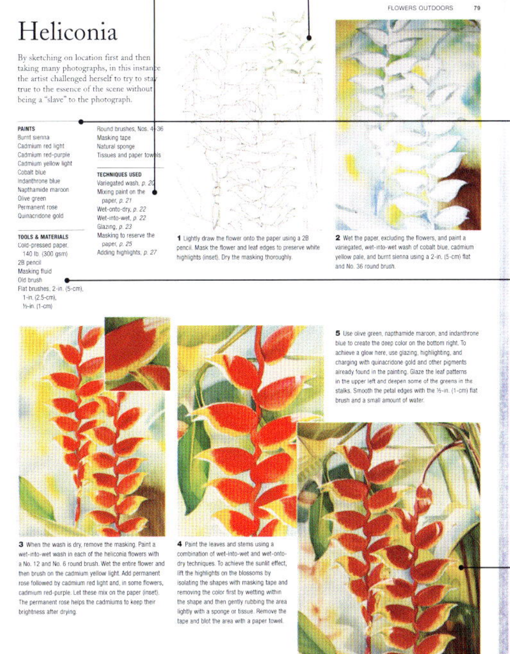

Details These additional images allow you to "look over the artists' shoulders" as they use specific techniques.

Paints Colors are listed in alphabetical order. Note that names can vary according to manufacturer.

Tools and materials The paper, brushes, and other equipment used by the artist are listed in order of use.

Final painting The finished painting is shown in the final step.

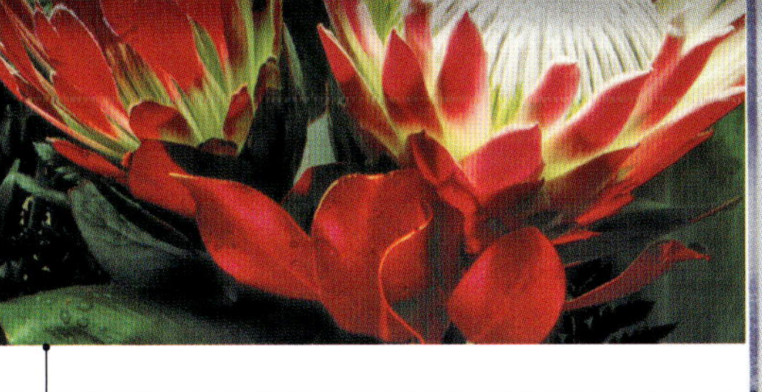

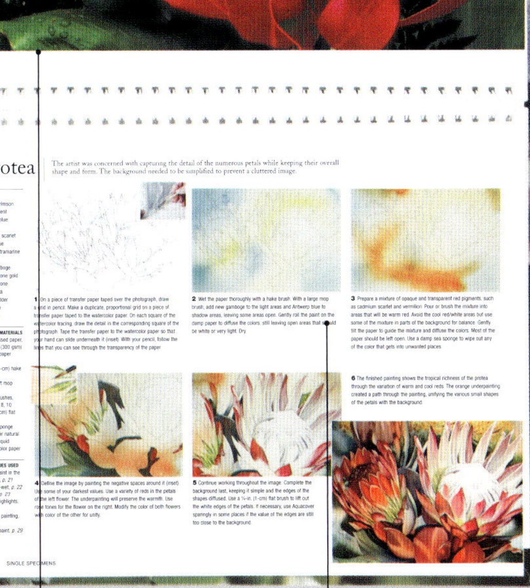

The photograph The floral subject is shown in a large, high-quality image for you to use as a reference.

Step-by-step sequences Follow the steps to see how the artist builds up a painting from start to completion.

In Detail

Pages 146–157 feature selected projects on a larger scale and up close.

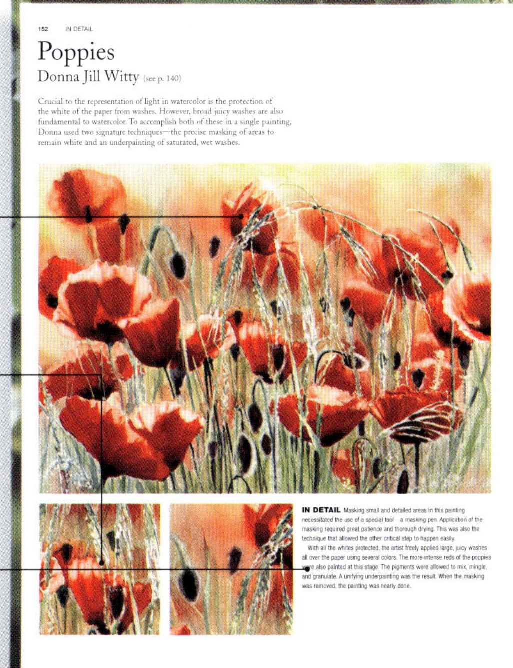

Final painting Shown in a larger size, it is possible to see the full effect of the artist's work.

Details Certain techniques and elements of particular interest are shown close up.

Analysis The effect of specific techniques is explained.

The "Eye" of the Camera

With the coming of the digital age, almost everyone has the ability to take a picture—with a cell phone, digital point-and-shoot camera, or more traditional equipment. And every artist who has done this has discovered that the resulting photograph, though it records the scene or the flower, rarely shows what was in the mind's eye. Therefore, try different views of the same thing, or make a sketch with a few notes to go along with the shot.

In photographs, color is not always true. It may be too blue, have a yellow cast, or be washed out. Shadows are often opaque and detail is missing. You are the artist and can take away or add detail, lighten or darken, brighten, or mute as you choose. The camera is another tool to help you bring your vision alive. It can help you to imagine, or simply record what you see in the moment.

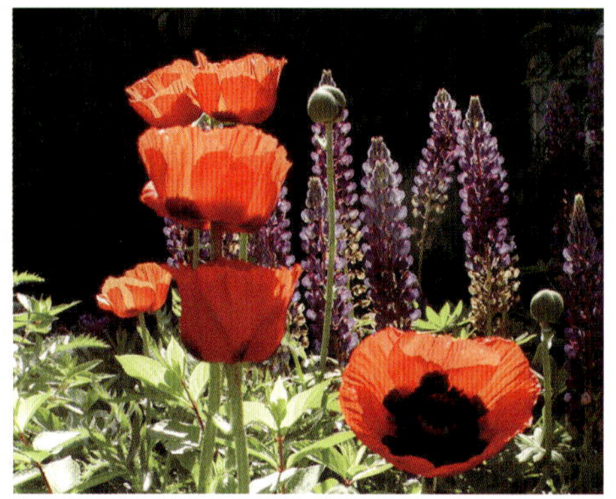

Horizontal format.

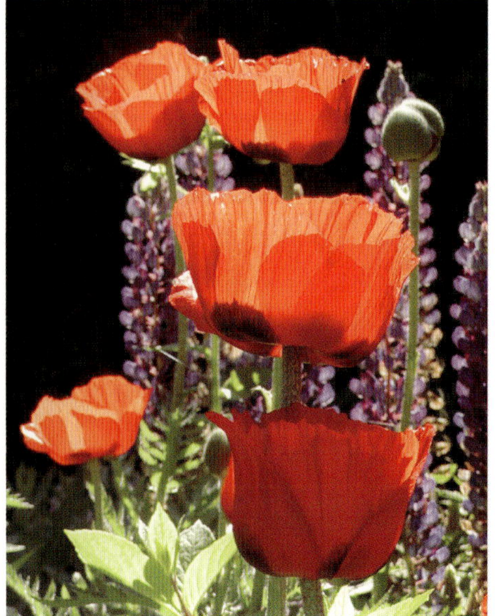

Vertical format.

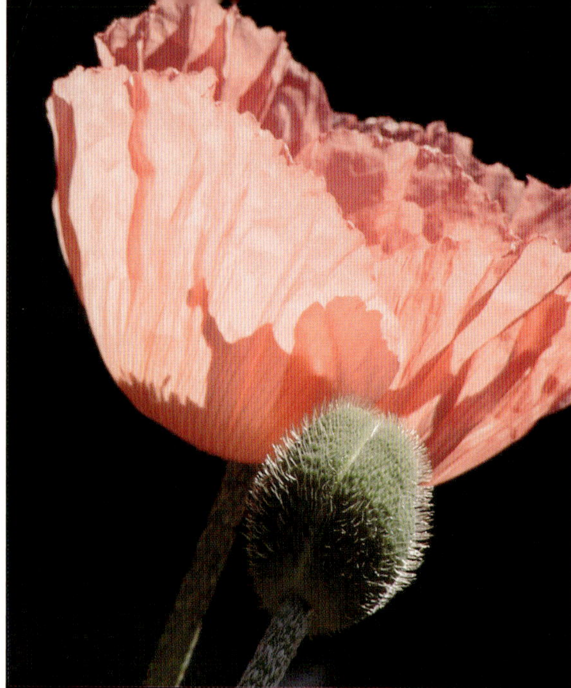

1 Choose your photograph (left).

2 Make a sketch (below). It will help you remember how you felt at the moment.

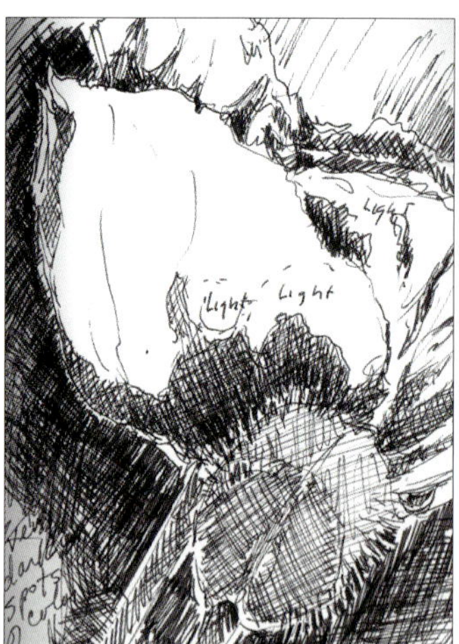

TRY DIFFERENT VIEWS

When approaching your subject, a quick way to begin focusing on a possible subject for painting is to turn your camera, or even to turn yourself.

MAKE A SKETCH

When you find something that excites you, take a few minutes to make a sketch, and make notes so you don't forget what went through your mind when you shot the photograph.

YOUR PHOTOGRAPH IS ONLY A GUIDE

Most flower painters take hundreds of photographs. Some may be works of art all by themselves but, more likely, they are only meant as a guide to the flower's form or some other aspect the artist noticed at the time.

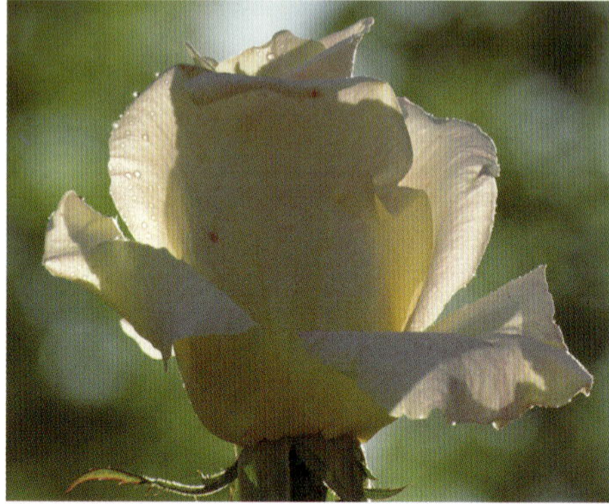

The backlit aspect of this rose captured the artist's imagination, but the photograph is underexposed.

The final painting, though dramatically different from the photograph, retains the backlighting and shadows.

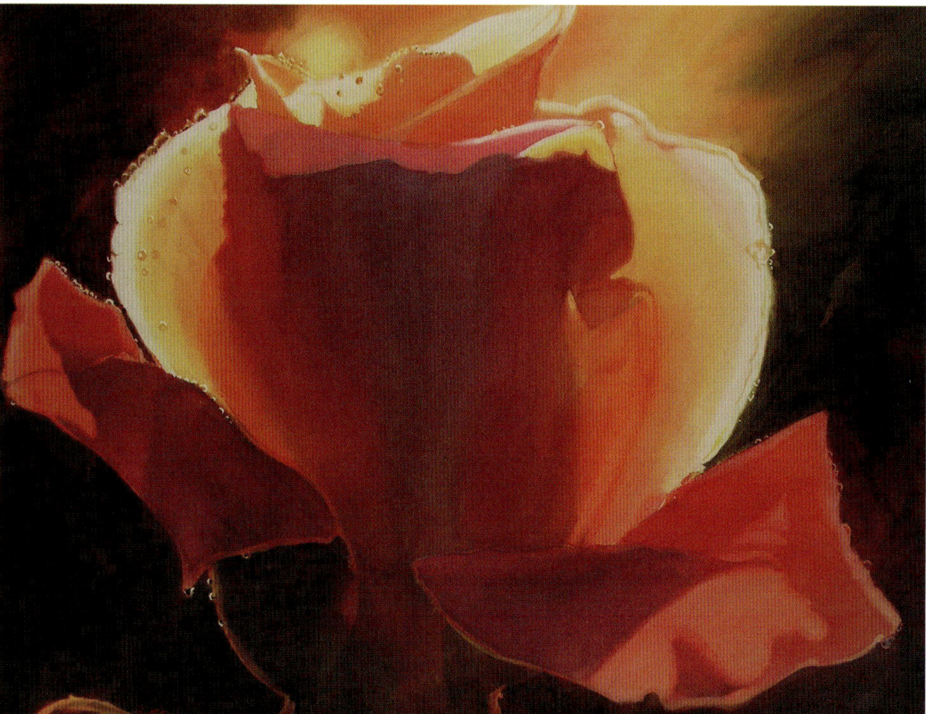

Editing Your Photographs

In the computer, the artist has been handed a wonderful new group of tools. Editing programs such as Photoshop and iPhoto allow you not only to see your photographs on the computer screen but also to revise them in any number of ways and save each as you go along. Each photograph can become a library of painting options.

Before computers, most editing was done by making several sketches of the photograph and rearranging elements in each sketch. Another option was to make a print of your photograph and crop it by cutting up the copy and rearranging the elements. Many people still prefer these tried and true options.

With a computer as a tool, photo editing programs make it easy to alter almost every aspect of your photograph. Some artists find this a distraction, while others discover views they might never have thought of. It is even possible to alter the overall color theme of the photograph, much like trying on different colored shirts. A caution here: If your passion is to paint, don't let editing photographs become more important than painting.

MAKE A SIMPLE CROP

Virtually all photo editing programs allow you to crop your photograph. Be sure to save the cropped picture as a different file so you always have your original.

TRY OUT VALUE

Another important editing feature of most programs allows you to remove the color from your photograph so you can better see the pattern of light and dark. Again, be sure to save the original as well as the edited version.

PHOTOGRAPH TO SKETCH TO PAINTING

Making a painting from a photograph is rarely as simple as taking the picture and starting to paint. The following exercise may help to bring your vision to reality.

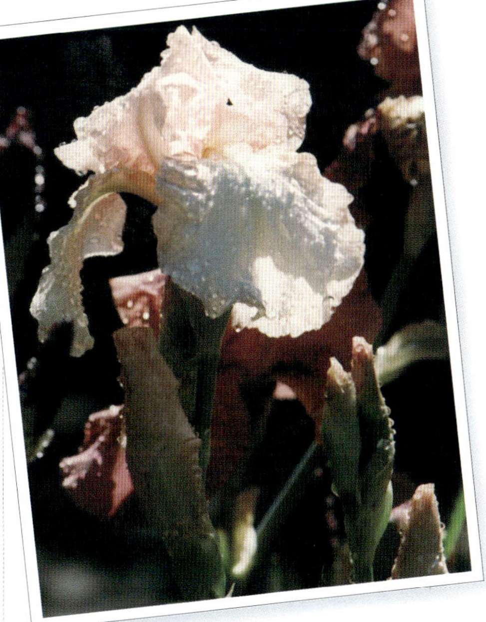

1 Take the photograph.

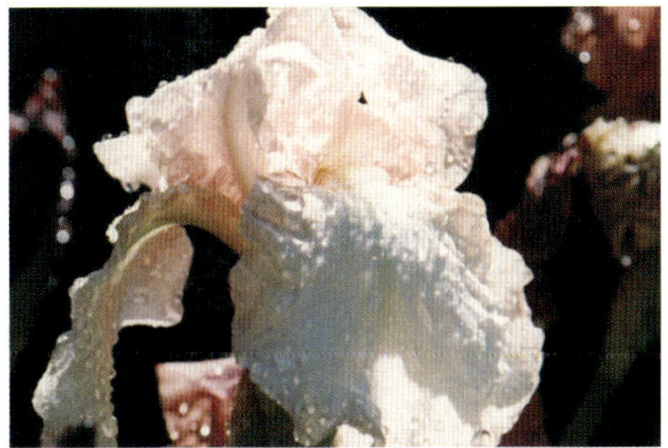

2 Crop it.

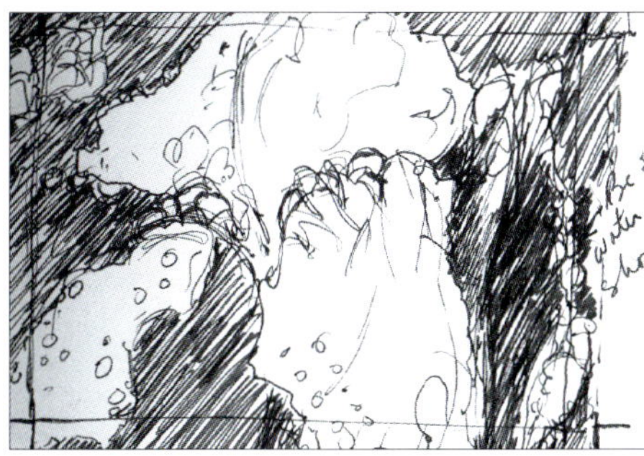

3 Make a sketch.

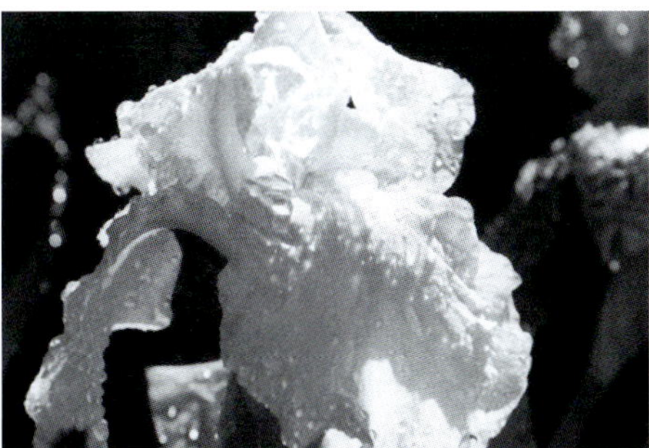

4 Turn the photograph to black and white.

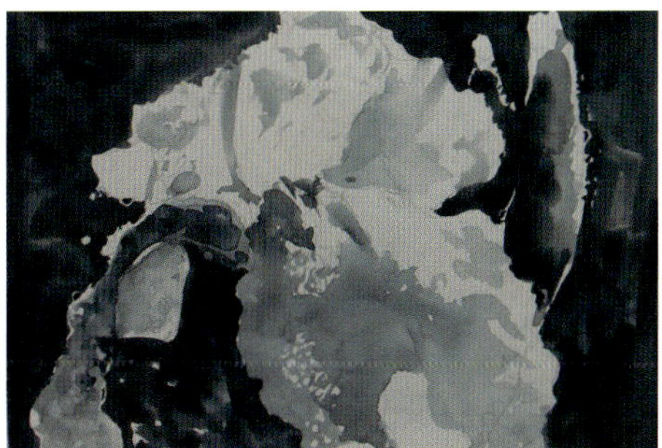

5 Make a value sketch in your sketchbook.

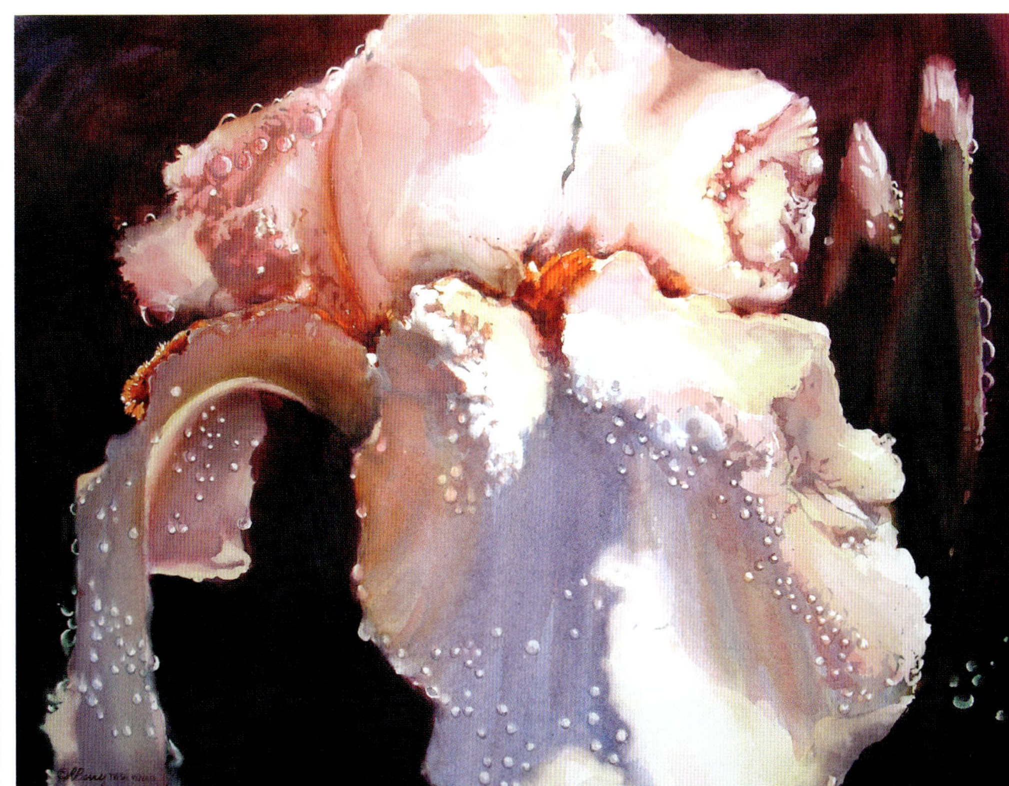

6 Make your full painting—by now you will know your subject well.

Watercolor Paper

Watercolor paper is manufactured by many papermakers and is made in several forms and qualities. Most art supply stores carry single sheets, end, or spiral-bound pads, blocks bound on four sides, and rolls. The pads and blocks are made in a variety of sizes from small to very large, allowing for the personal preference of the artist. The standard single sheet size is 22 x 30 inches (55 x 75 cm), although larger sheets are also available.

Watercolor paper, at its highest quality, is made of 100 percent cotton fibers and is acid free. This is the standard for most professional artists. More economical are sheets with various fillers. These should be tested to see how well they take water and paint. Although there are artists who prefer the less expensive papers because they can paint many paintings economically, the majority of artists prefer 100 percent cotton rag papers.

Another paper consideration is weight. The thinnest usable paper is about 90 pounds (190 grams per square meter) and should be stretched for all but the smallest paintings. More usable and more durable is the 140-pound (300-gsm) weight. A full sheet must still be stretched to avoid buckling. This is the most popular weight. For those who do not want to have to stretch paper, 300-pound (638-gsm) paper is also available and is more boardlike. Virtually all paper used for painting contains a sizing to make it amenable to receiving paint and not absorbing it too rapidly.

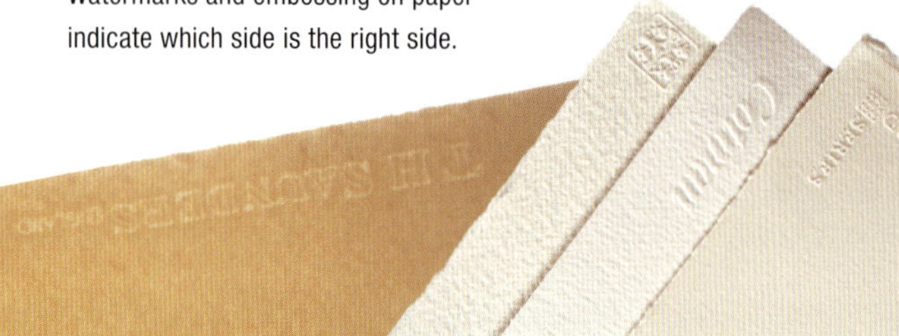

Watermarks and embossing on paper indicate which side is the right side.

PAPER TEXTURE

Watercolor paper comes in three surfaces or textures. The process by which it is manufactured determines the texture.

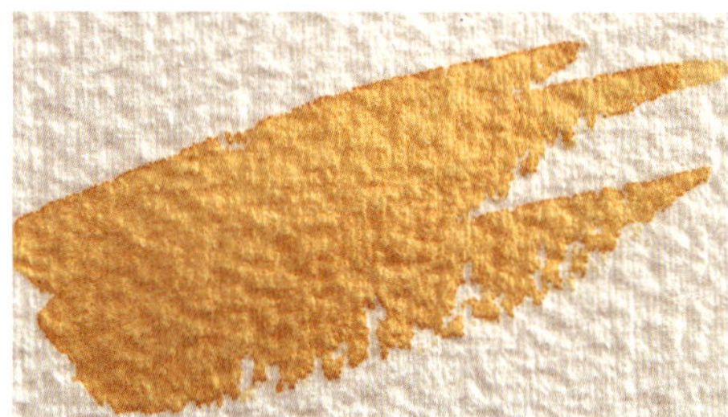

Rough surface paper, as the name implies, has a well-defined texture. It is ideal for creating broken-color and other textural effects. Many artists love working on this surface, although it takes practice to get used to the behavior of paint on the bumpy surface.

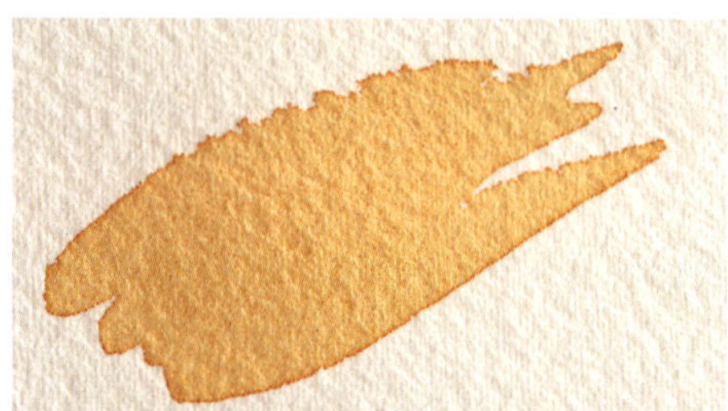

Cold-pressed paper is the most popular of the paper surfaces. It is partway between rough and smooth and gives the painting surface a textural interest without being the dominant effect. It is sturdy, can take many layers of glazing, and is great for fine detail as well.

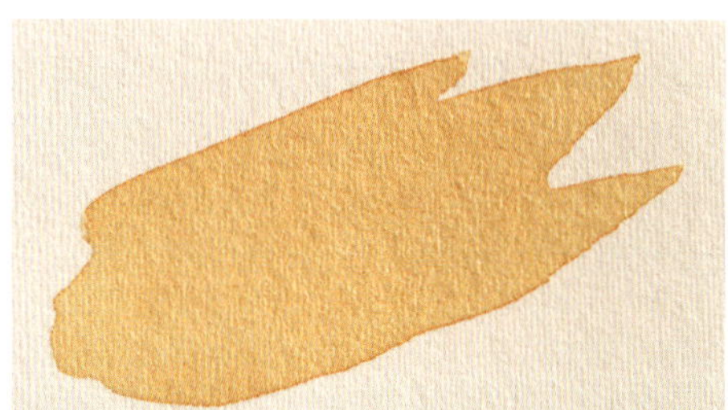

Hot-pressed paper is smooth. The paper's surface does not intrude on the wash laid down in any significant way and is very useful for particularly detailed paintings. Care must be taken with washes on this paper because puddles form easily.

STRETCHING PAPER

Stretching your paper onto a rigid surface before beginning to paint is a good idea with paper over a certain size. Full sheets of 90- or 140-pound (190- or 300-gsm) paper must be stretched to prevent it from buckling, unless your style of working reduces the risk of this. Stretched paper will stay flat while you work.

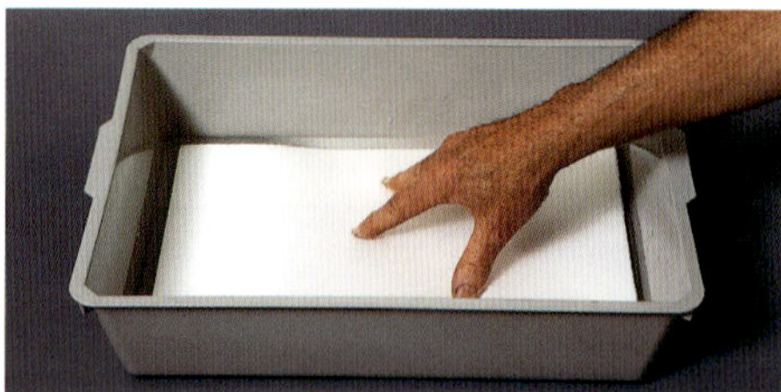

1 Soak the paper in a large clean pan or tub for about 10 to 15 minutes.

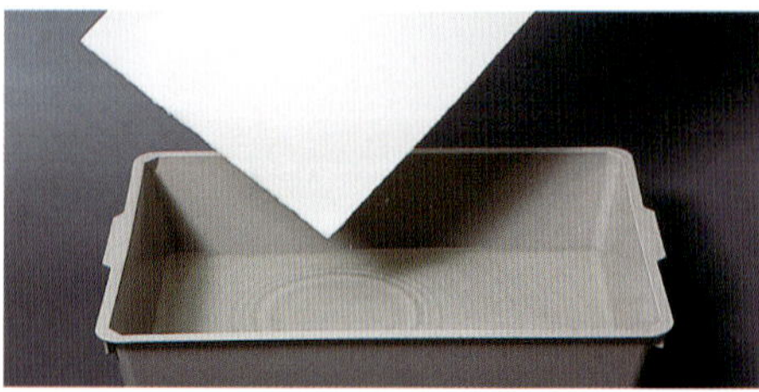

2 Carefully lift the paper out by two adjacent corners and allow extra water to drain off a corner.

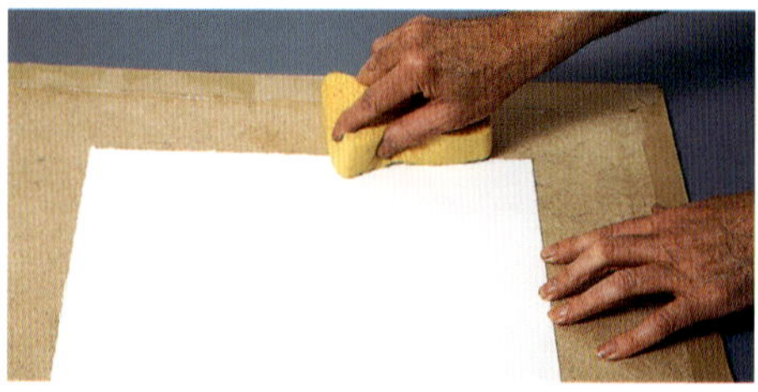

3 Place the paper on a board and smooth over with a sponge to eliminate air bubbles underneath. Careful handling is important since paper fibers have a memory, and a crease or bend may show up later.

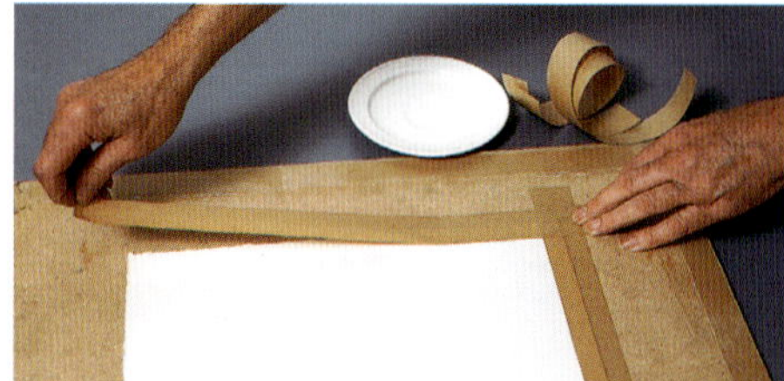

4 Without overstretching, place a staple in two adjacent corners. Gently pull the unstapled end and staple the two remaining corners. Place wetted brown tape around the edges, overlapping the board and the paper. A few more staples will secure it well. Allow it to dry thoroughly. A border of white artist's tape that overlaps the paper by half an inch (1.25 cm) will surround your paper with a cleanable frame.

Brushes and Other Equipment

The world of brushes is a study in itself, and although this section is confined to the most common watercolor brushes, it is recommended that you spend time looking at various styles in an art supply store or online. Brushes vary from the tiniest 000 sable brush to the giant 10-inch (25-cm) wide hake brush, with hundreds in between.

The hairs of watercolor brushes range from sable to bristle to synthetic. The cost varies greatly and most stores stock a wide variety. Sable brushes are not essential, as there are excellent, less expensive alternatives.

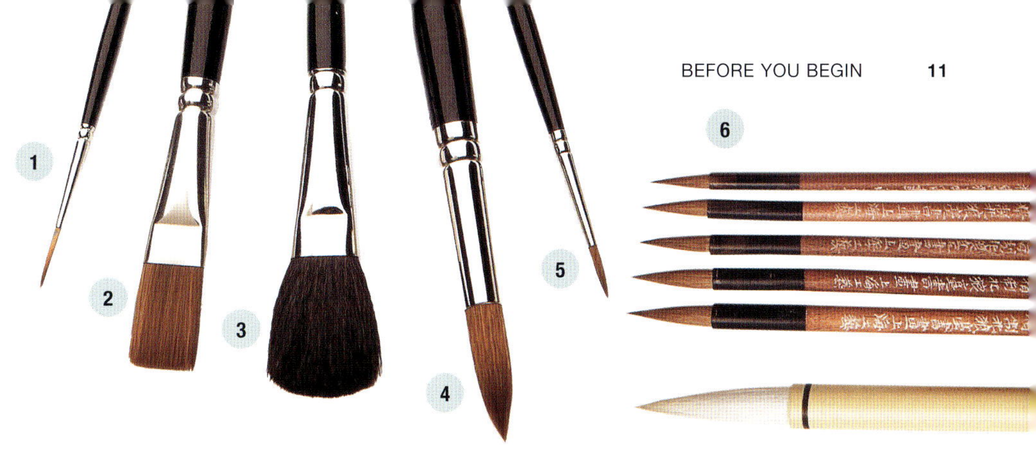

The most common brushes for use with watercolor are round, sizes 6 to 24, and flat, sizes ½ inch (1.25 cm) to 3 inches (7.5 cm). (If you can afford only three, consider a No. 12 round with a good point, a 1-inch (2.5-cm) flat, and a rigger or liner—a longhair pointed brush for detail.)

Brushes (from left to right):
1 Rigger
2 Flat
3 Wash
4 & 5 Round
6 You will find an affordable tool in Chinese brushes. Far less expensive than most, they are very versatile, forming a fine point but with a full "belly" to hold a great deal of paint.

ADDITIONAL EQUIPMENT

1 Paper towel Essential for cleaning up or dabbing the brush, or lifting clouds or highlights. Bathroom tissues work well, too, and you might want both.

2 Water containers Some artists keep one for the first rinse and a second with clean water.

3 Masking fluid For saving the white of the paper in watercolor. It is applied with a brush, but always use either a cheap or old brush, dunked in dishwashing detergent and wiped off first. Always clean the brush immediately after use to prevent the masking fluid from drying in the bristles.

4 Masquepen A great asset to the flower artist, which enables you to "paint" very accurately by reserving the fine veins or details on petals and leaves. Available in two nib widths of fine and super fine.

5 Masking tape or artist's white tape Most commonly used to tape down your paper or mask straight shapes. It may also be torn to form a jagged or rippled edge to save light on a flower.

6 Gummed brown paper tape For stretching paper.

7 Sponges Natural sponges are great for dabbing on foliage or lifting paint. Common kitchen sponges are useful to wipe off an overwet brush or an overly messy painting surface.

8 Drawing board, gator board, or plywood For support or stretching your paper.

9 Pencils and erasers Use a B or HB pencil to draw on watercolor paper. A soft nonabrasive eraser, if used gently, will not harm the surface of the paper.

10 Palettes For tube paints there are many variations on a theme of the covered plastic palette, with wells for the paint and large mixing spaces. A cover is desirable to keep your paints clean and moist. That the palette is white is essential so you see your colors accurately.

You will find that, over time, your painting area will fill up with other useful equipment you have discovered. Such items as plastic plates, squirt bottles, scrapers, other media, towels, and hair dryers are all useful.

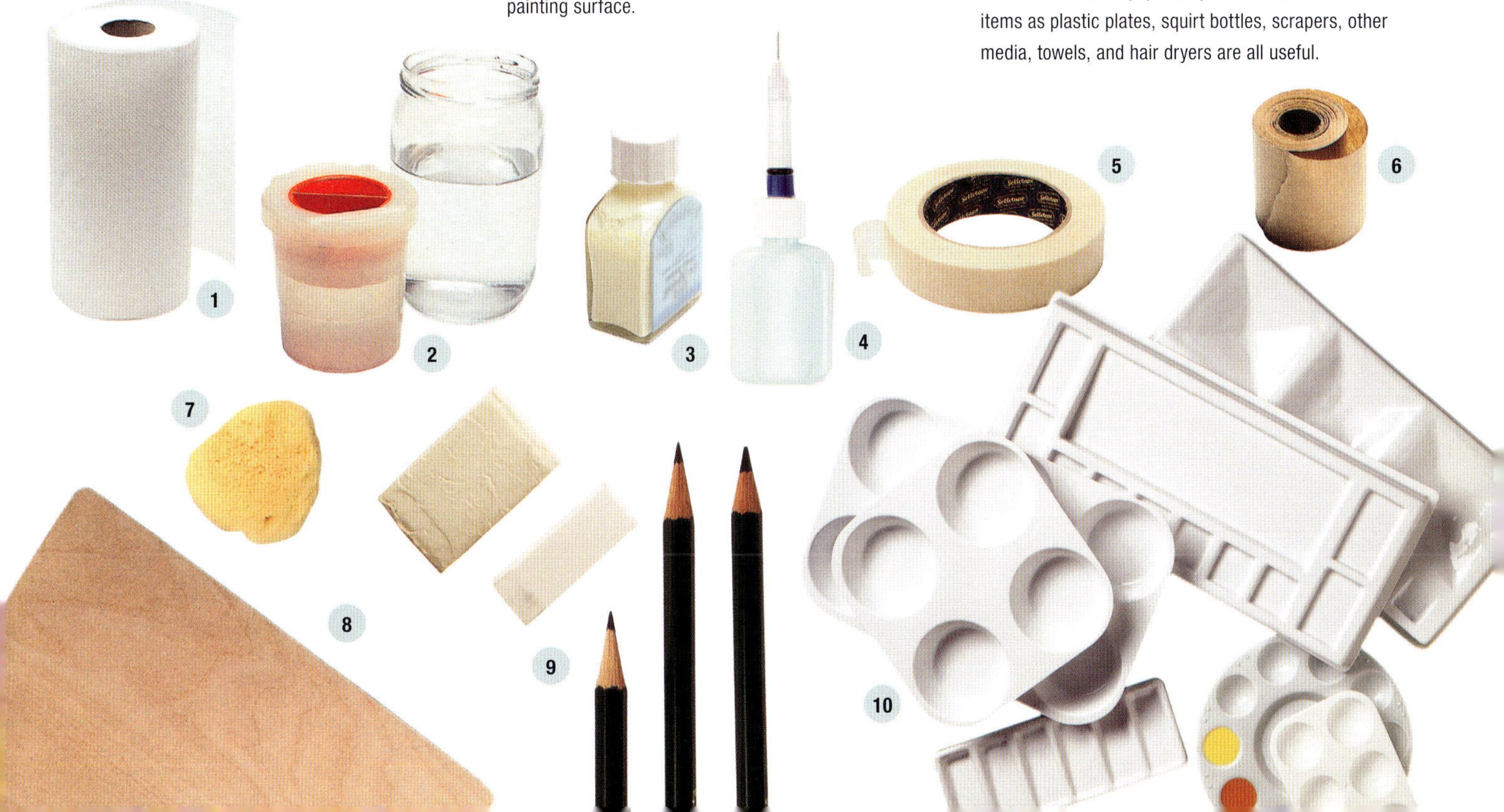

Watercolor Choices

Some watercolor pigments are more expensive than others. Each pigment is derived from its own specific source, which may not have changed for centuries. For example, lamp black is made from soot. Its history can be traced back to cave paintings dated 35,000 years ago.

Watercolors are available in two qualities: student and artist grade. Student grade is less expensive but contains less pure pigment and more filler. It will not achieve the brilliance of color that the pure artist pigments do.

Many companies manufacture watercolor. Most artists have favorites but often use more than one brand.

TUBES OR PANS?

Paint comes in dried blocks or pans, and in tubes. The dried blocks fit into pans that close and are useful for travel. The tube paint is easier to use since it comes from the tube wet. Watercolor pigment is now available in sticks, crayons, and pencils as well, all of which make paint when wet.

You will find varieties of watercolor that are pure and transparent; opaque, called gouache; mixed with a milk binder, called casein; and mixed with a plastic binder, called acrylic. All have the potential to spark your imagination and add brilliant color to your flower paintings.

WHICH COLORS?

Watercolor manufacturers produce such a large range of colors that the artist can always find a palette of colors to fit a particular style or subject. Below are suggestions for basic palettes and other colors you may like to add. The key is to have a balanced palette that will give you a good mixing range. The one pigment that most artists use is aureolin, a clear, cool transparent yellow. You would then choose a warmer yellow or gold, such as cadmium yellow, to give a good spectrum of yellows. A balanced palette also needs at least two reds, such as a warm cadmium red, and a cool alizarin crimson. Common blue pigments are cobalt blue and French ultramarine blue. Most colors can be mixed with these.

But flower painters, drawn to the endless variation in flower colors with their highlights and shadows, and preferring the relative purity of color as it comes from the tube, will often have many more pigments with subtle changes in hue (color). The important thing that these colors have in common is transparency, for unless one is drawn to a more opaque vision of flowers, it is the light—as it shines on and through the flower, as it penetrates upward from the paper, as it brings the pigments to life—that gives watercolor flower painting its appeal.

Below you will find a typical flower painter's palette. With only a couple of exceptions, these are primary and secondary colors—a variety of yellows, reds, and blues, as well as oranges, greens, and violets.

As you work with a basic palette, you may find something missing and begin a search for new colors, adding an emerald green or a turquoise, a neutral tint (dark gray), or Payne's gray. The exploration of color is half the fun for a flower painter. Useful tools in this search are art supply catalogs, manufacturers' catalogs, and books on color.

A caution: Try adding only one or two pigments at a time. The temptation to add everything at once can be almost irresistible.

Cadmium red
Alizarin crimson
Cadmium yellow
Ultramarine
Lemon yellow
Winsor blue

Warm and cool primaries

Tube sizes vary from small finger-size tubes to more economical large tubes. As long as the tube is not left uncapped, the paint will stay moist for a long time.

How you organize your palette comes down to personal preference. One suggestion is to arrange the colors as the color wheel, thereby limiting the effect of any one color flowing over to the next.

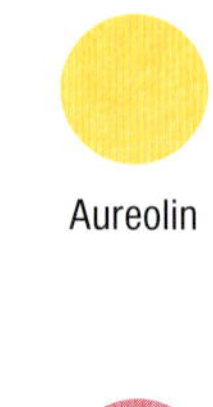
Aureolin

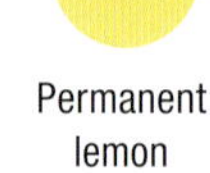
Permanent lemon yellow

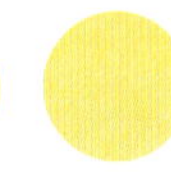
Cadmium yellow

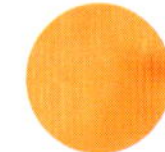
Permanent orange

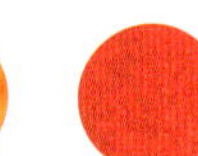
Quinacridone coral

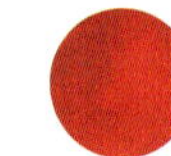
Quinacridone red

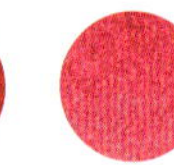
Quinacridone magenta

Opera

Cobalt blue

French ultramarine blue

Cobalt turquoise light

Viridian

Phthalo green

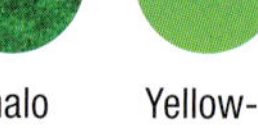
Yellow-green

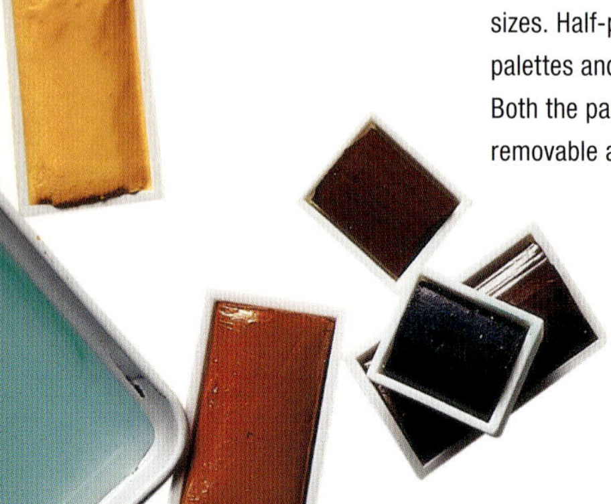
Pans can be bought in whole or half-pan sizes. Half-pans fit in smaller travel-size palettes and are more readily available. Both the paint and the pan it fits in are removable and replaceable.

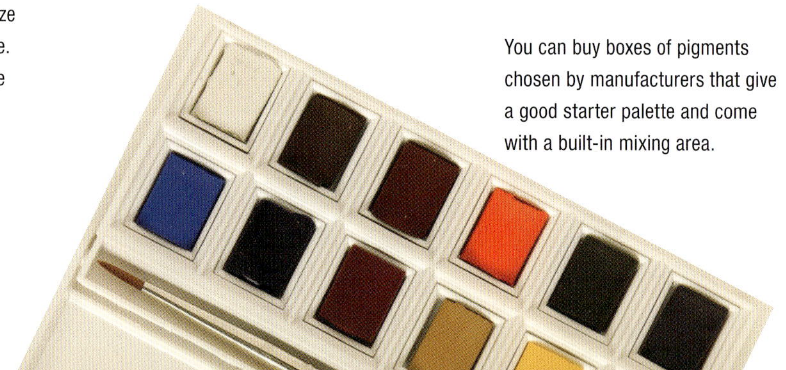
You can buy boxes of pigments chosen by manufacturers that give a good starter palette and come with a built-in mixing area.

Understanding the Color Wheel

The color wheel will help you understand how to mix colors for your flower paintings. For example, it shows you how to achieve the brightest pinks and oranges or the best shadowy muted background colors. It is a good idea to paint swatches for your own wheel with your bought colors and add any subsequent purchases; in this way you can assess how warm or cool the color is, and how it will mix with other colors.

A primary color can't be mixed from any other colors. The three primaries are red, yellow, and blue. You can see these, right, at the points of the solid triangle. When two primaries are mixed together, the result is a secondary color—orange, green, or violet (the gray dotted triangle). And when a secondary color, such as orange, is mixed with a primary color, such as red, the result is a tertiary color—red-orange.

One of the things that makes colors so different from one another is "temperature." Some colors are perceived as "warm" and others as "cool," and red, yellow, and blue have both warm and cool versions. When mixing secondary colors, it is important to choose the right primaries. For example, alizarin crimson and ultramarine blue are both warm and slightly purple in color, so a mixture of these will make a bright purple, whereas a mix of cadmium red and Prussian or Winsor blue will result in a muddy brown—the result of cadmium red having an orange cast.

Cool colors—those with more blue or green—tend to recede, while warm colors—those with more red and yellow—come to the fore. Warm colors also appear larger and far more energetic. For this reason flower painters typically use cooler colors for the background of a painting—to produce a sense of depth—and warmer colors in the foreground.

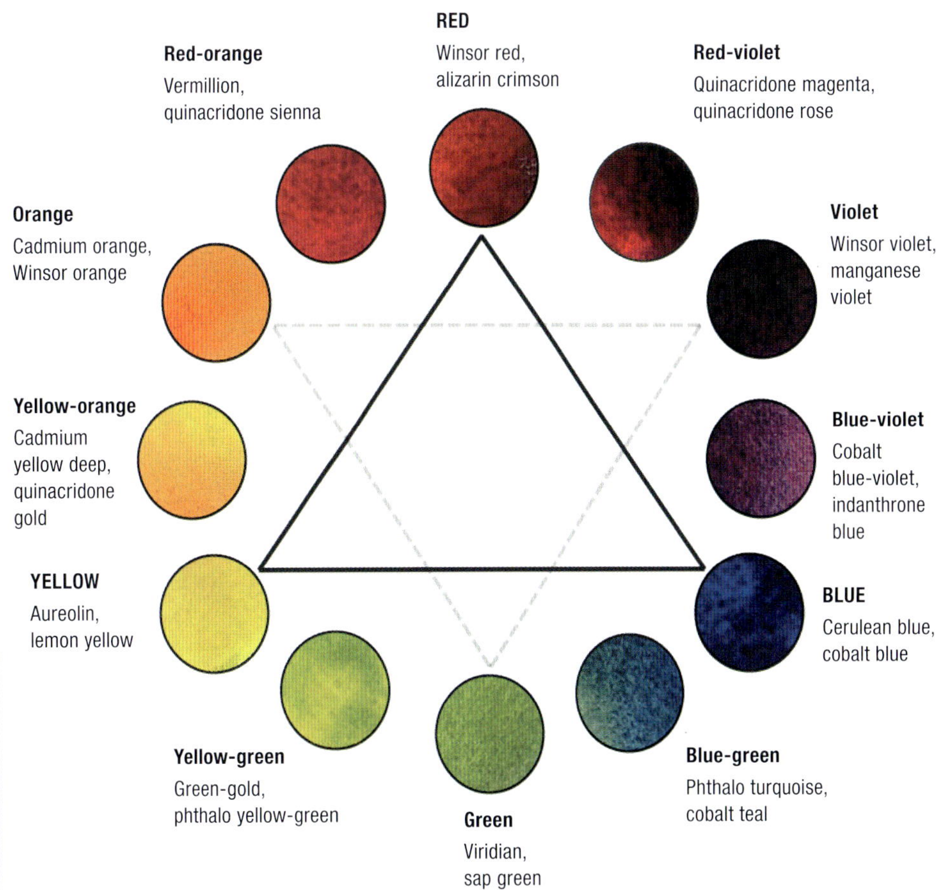

Indispensable guide
The color wheel suggests possibilities for both experimentation and for individualizing your palette. Not only is it a guide to the colors you can mix to make another color, it is a visual demonstration of analogous and complementary colors.

Mixing from one wheel
The same wheel as featured opposite is used here to show how to mix bright, intense secondaries with muted, subtle ones.

1 Cadmium red (yellow bias)
2 Alizarin crimson (blue bias)
3 Ultramarine blue (red bias)
4 Winsor blue (yellow bias)
5 Lemon yellow (blue bias)
6 Cadmium yellow (red bias)

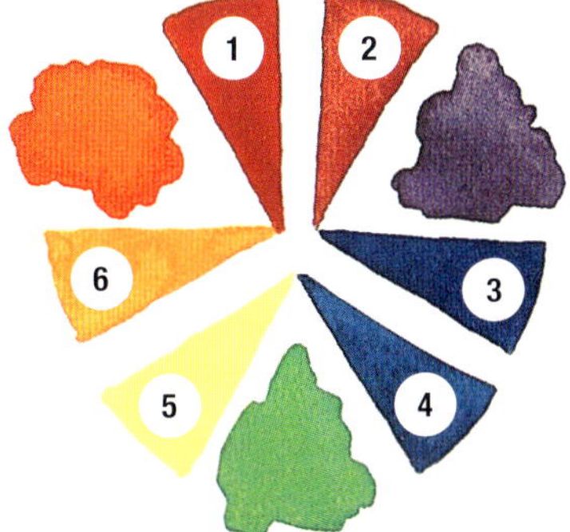

Intense secondaries
Here the colors closest together on the wheel have been mixed to produce intense secondaries. The blue-and-yellow mix, green, is cool, and the other two are warm.

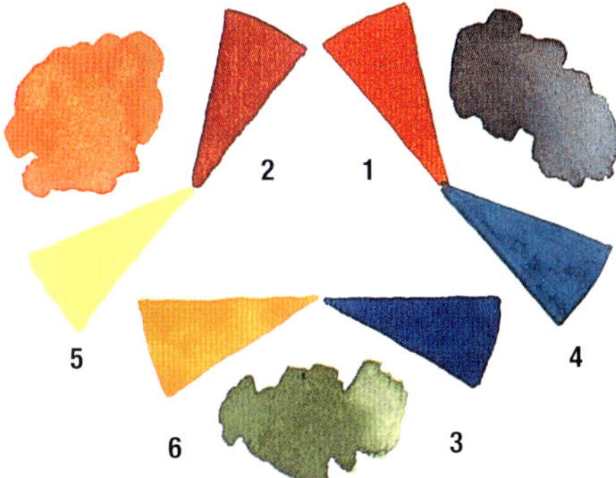

Muted secondaries
The primary colors farthest apart create more muted mixtures, which could be useful for creating shadows.

Flower Color: Triads

There is much to recommend trying out triads when beginning a painting—that is, one of each primary color. As the painting progresses, other necessary colors may be added. Even advanced painters often begin their paintings in this manner, establishing a color theme and atmosphere with the chosen primaries and deviating from them only if a good reason presents itself. This gives unity to your paintings.

MAKING AN INTUITIVE COLOR WHEEL

Changing one pigment of the primary triad has the potential to change the feeling of your painting. Experimentation will help you develop your own favorites. A useful exercise is to take a piece of scrap watercolor paper. In each corner of a triangle, put a dot of red, yellow, and blue paint. Spread the yellow, then rinse the brush and spread the red. Repeat with blue. Next, in a circular motion begin blending matching edges of each primary. The secondary colors of that particular mixture begin to develop. Finally, bring all colors to the center, and you will find rich, velvety grays.

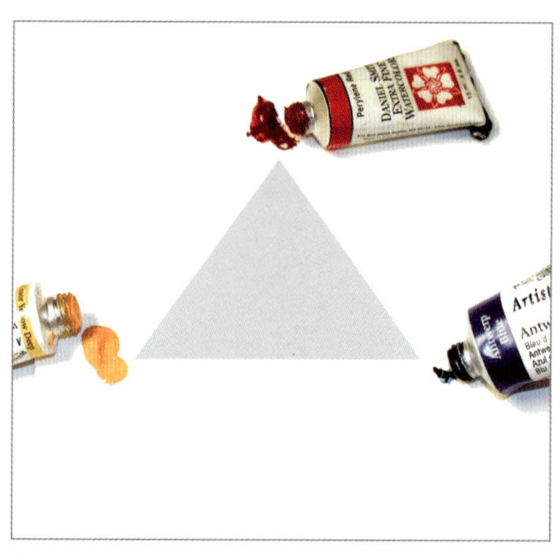

1 Place a dot at each point of a triangle. Here, perylene red, Antwerp blue, and hansa yellow are used.

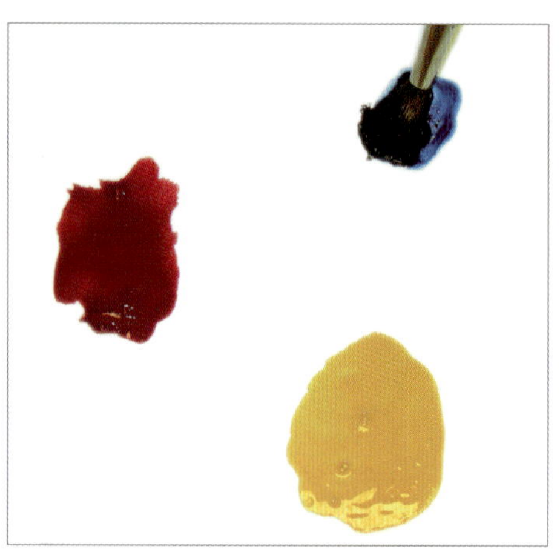

2 With a clean, wet brush for each color, wet and spread the dot of pigment.

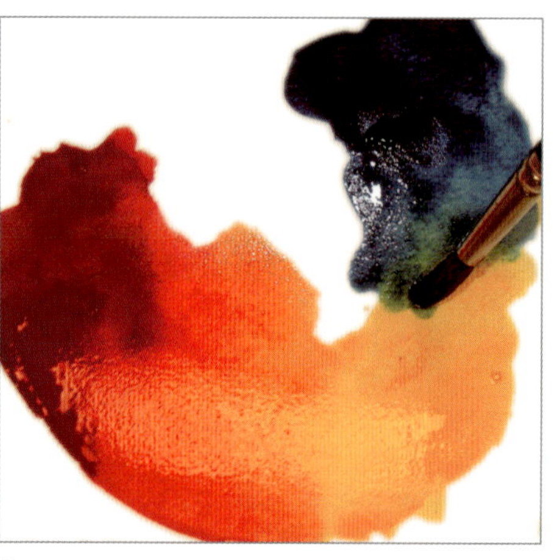

3 When all are wet, begin to join the primary colors to make secondary colors.

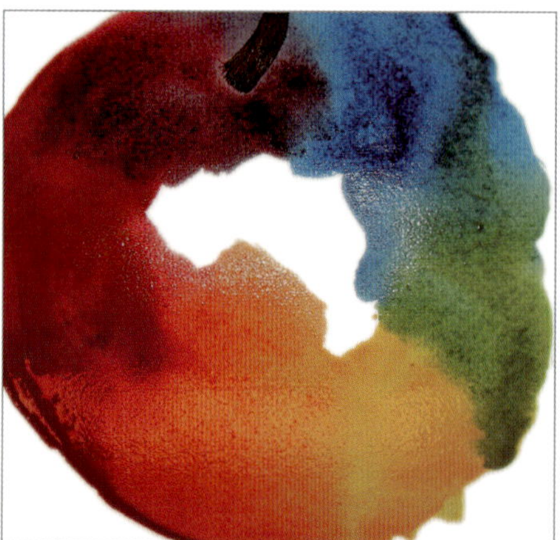

4 The colors combine to make a color wheel of pigments you have selected yourself.

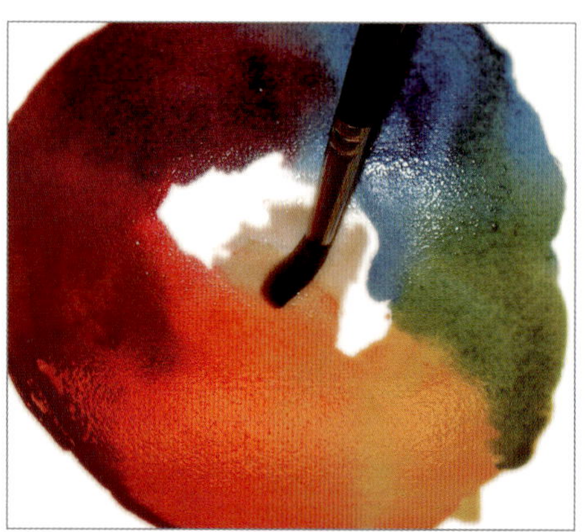

5 Next, to make subtle grays, with a clean brush begin pulling some of each color into the middle in a circular motion. Don't scrub or mix too much or the colors will become muddy.

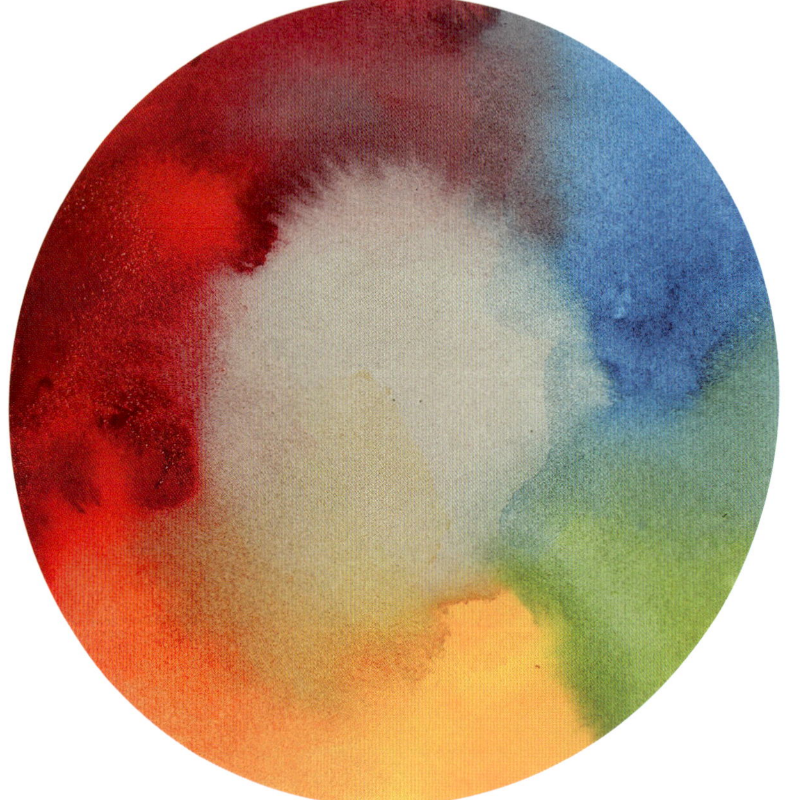

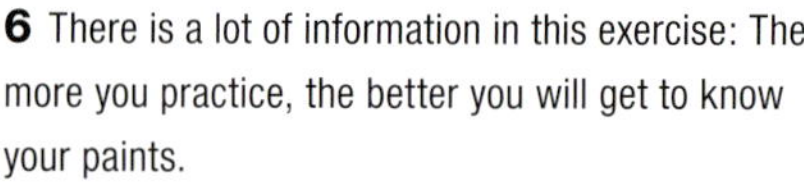

6 There is a lot of information in this exercise: The more you practice, the better you will get to know your paints.

GET TO KNOW THE TRIADS

Experiment with other triads to see the different secondary and tertiary mixes. For example, the cool triad makes the brightest greens, whereas the warm triad makes mossy greens; the best oranges come from the warm triad.

Quinacridone coral

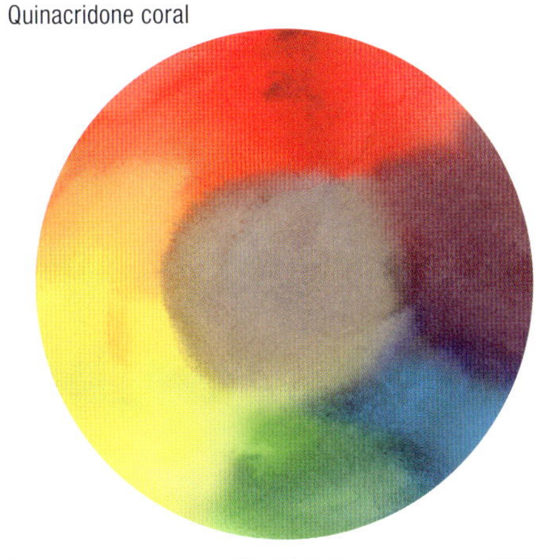

Lemon yellow | **Cool triad** | Winsor blue

Quinacridone red

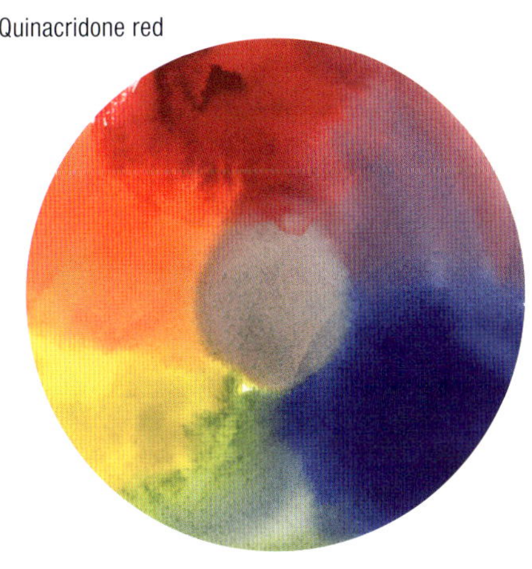

Aureolin | **Neutral triad** | French ultramarine blue

Quinacridone magenta

Winsor yellow deep | **Warm triad** | Cobalt blue

Warm and cool

These two poppy paintings demonstrate the benefit of understanding the principle of the triads. You can use them individually, or, as here, mix them for different elements of your painting.

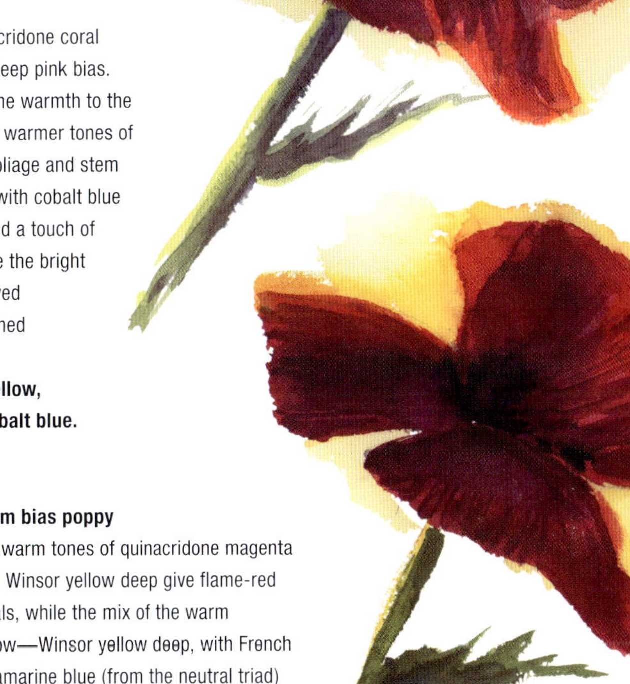

Cool bias poppy

Lemon yellow and quinacridone coral give these red petals a deep pink bias. The artist brought in some warmth to the shadow tones, using the warmer tones of cobalt blue. The green foliage and stem were similarly modified with cobalt blue (from the warm triad) and a touch of quinacridone coral, since the bright green that can be achieved using the cool triad seemed too artificial.

Colors used: Lemon yellow, quinacridone coral, cobalt blue.

Warm bias poppy

The warm tones of quinacridone magenta with Winsor yellow deep give flame-red petals, while the mix of the warm yellow—Winsor yellow deep, with French ultramarine blue (from the neutral triad) create a mossy mix for the stem and foliage color.

Colors used: Winsor yellow deep, quinacridone magenta, French ultramarine blue.

Mixing grays from complementary colors

Colors opposite each other on the color wheel are called "complementary colors." When complements are mixed, a soft gray color is the result. A whole range of warm or cool colorful grays can be mixed in this way. The more the mixture uses equal parts of both colors, the closer it will get to neutral, but mixing more of one shade or another will push it to a warmer or cooler gray.

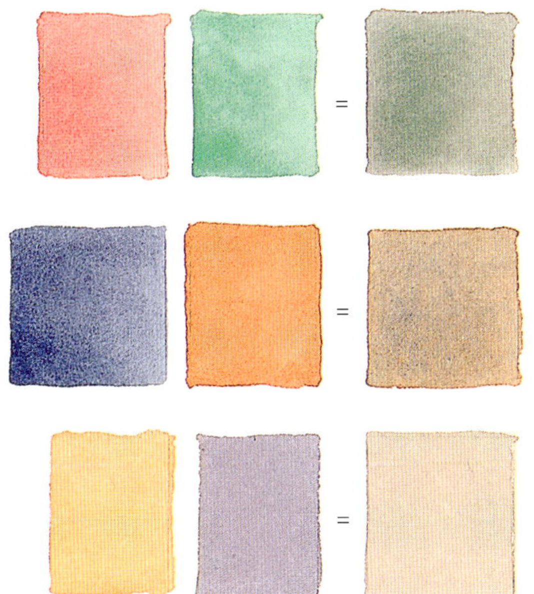

Color Mixing

Watercolor dries lighter than the shade you see in your palettes, because the white of the paper shows through the paint in transparent watercolor. Try out a color on a scrap of the same paper until your results are reliable. It is always easier to darken a color with another wash of paint if what you have laid down looks too light. At the same time, the more layers of paint you put down, the greater the risk of losing the translucence of light reflected upward from the paper. Practice will help you find the desired color in only one or two washes.

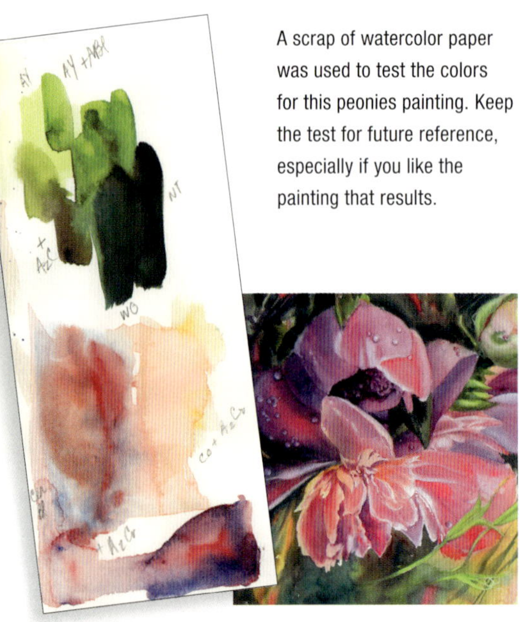

A scrap of watercolor paper was used to test the colors for this peonies painting. Keep the test for future reference, especially if you like the painting that results.

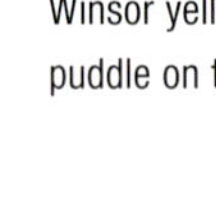

Winsor yellow deep puddle on the palette.

Single passage. Note how much lighter it is in the center where it is dry.

Another glaze of the same color approximates the color in the puddle. It is closer because less of the white paper shows through.

STAINING AND NON-STAINING COLORS

Some pigments sit on the surface of the paper and are easily removed even when dry. These are non-staining colors. They are transparent and ideal for glazing one layer upon another.

Other pigments stain the paper because they sink into its fibers. Unless freshly laid down, these are difficult to remove. Practice in using these brilliant hues is rewarding since the majority of paints stain the paper to some degree. Although they can be intimidating, persistence is rewarded with glowing results.

Staining **Non-staining**

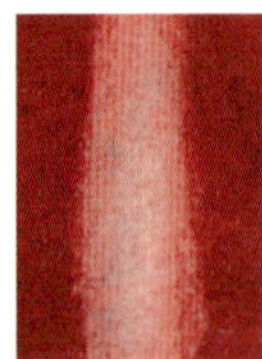

Left alizarin crimson **Right** rose madder genuine

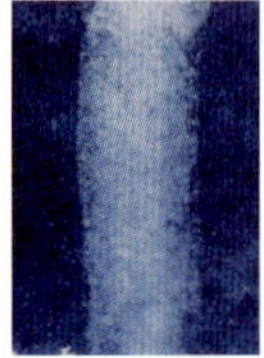

Left phthalo blue **Right** cobalt blue

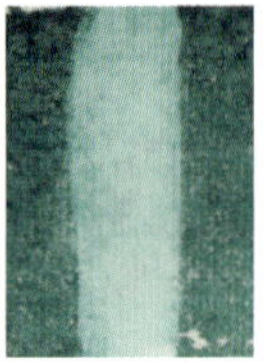

Left phthalo green **Right** viridian

"MUD" VS. NEUTRAL

Not all brown or gray color is mud. Here is an example of the difference.

When ultramarine blue, burnt sienna, and cadmium yellow are mixed in the palette, the result is a dull, lifeless brown.

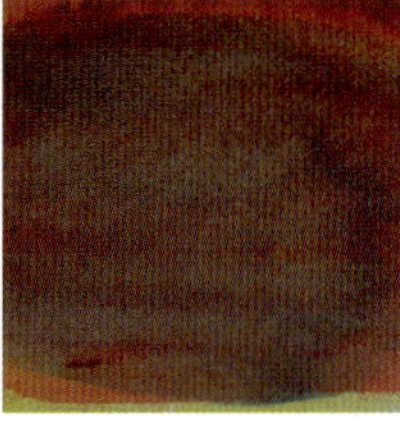

However, when the same pigments are laid down a layer at a time over a dried layer below, a lively color is the result.

MULTIPLE MIXES

The freshest color is the simplest color. Try not to mix more than three colors, and use only two if possible; overmixing can produce muddy hues. Remember, you will continue to mix colors as you work.

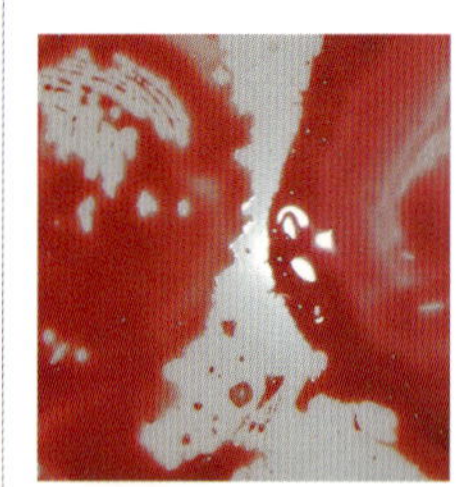

In the palette these two mixtures look the same, but on paper the combination of three colors is darker and less translucent.

Cadmium red—the mix on the left of the picture above.

Quinacridone coral, cadmium orange, and Winsor red—the mix on the right.

SEDIMENTARY OR GRANULATING COLORS

Sedimentary colors are those denser pigments that have larger particles suspended in the paint that separate out when laid down on the paper. They add texture and interest to the wash. Many artists find these pigments preferable for the interest their texture adds.

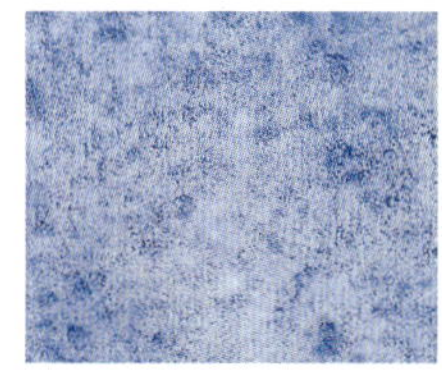

Cobalt blue

Phthalo blue

Flower Mixing: Darks

Most watercolorists have no trouble painting the light and transparent washes necessary in flower painting. More challenging is creating the rich darks necessary to turn on the lights. There are plenty of dark colors that come in tubes and can be used directly, however, many artists prefer to mix their darks from some of the richer colors available. Some of these colors are alizarin crimson, quinacridone violet, burnt sienna, phthalo blue, Antwerp blue, and phthalo green. A note of caution: Do not mix more than three transparent pigments together or a muddy color may result. Two in a mixture is ideal.

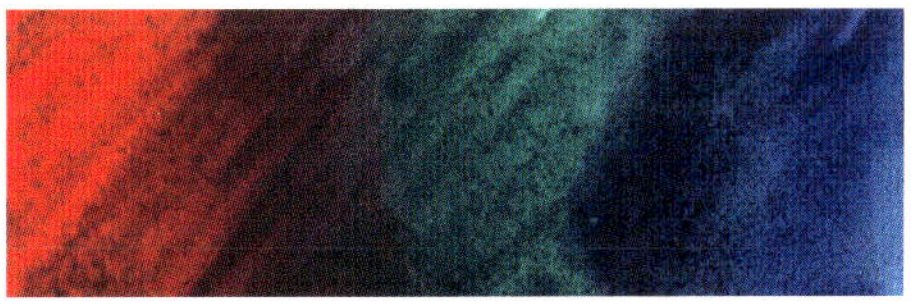

Alizarin crimson (left) blended into phthalo green (center). Phthalo green is blended into phthalo blue. These three pigments are so transparent that they can readily be mixed to form an almost-black color.

Quinacridone violet blended with phthalo green. The two together make a very deep navy. Quinacridone violet is not quite as transparent as alizarin crimson, so be careful not to make it thick or it will be chalky.

Burnt sienna blended with Antwerp blue. In dense mixtures, together they appear greenish black. They also make an excellent natural deep green.

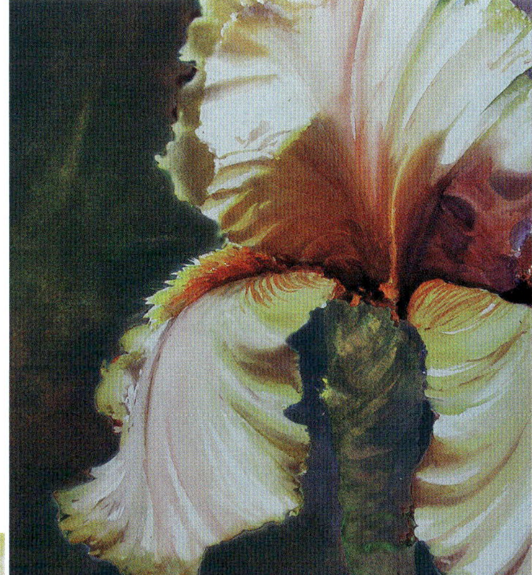

This painting makes use of a triad consisting of quinacridone rose, quinacridone gold, and Antwerp blue, with spots of orange on the iris beards. You can see it would be a very different painting if the darks were washed out. The inset image has been edited in Photoshop to illustrate this.

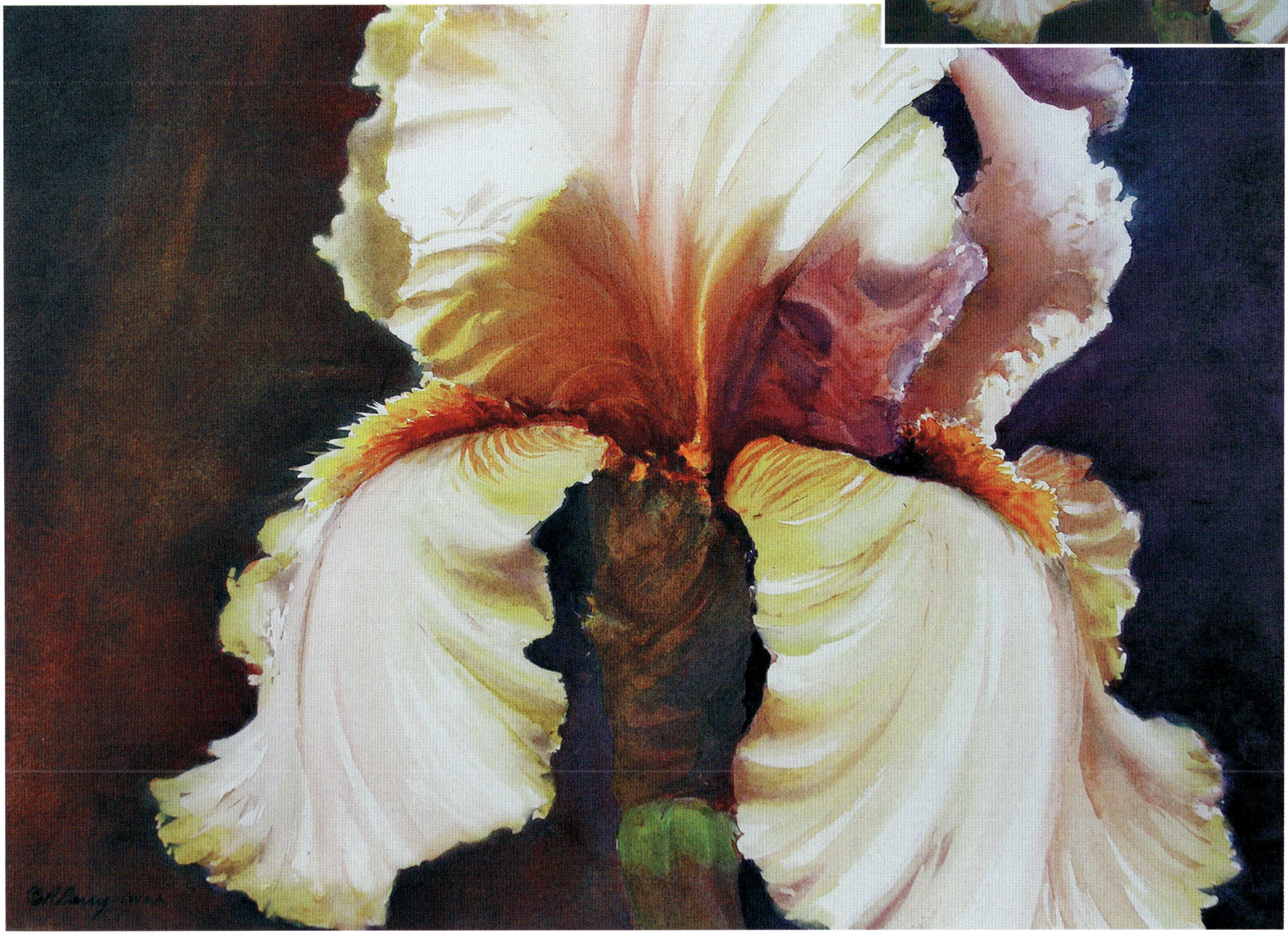

The Value of Color

Gray scale
This chart shows how some common pigments compare on the gray scale.

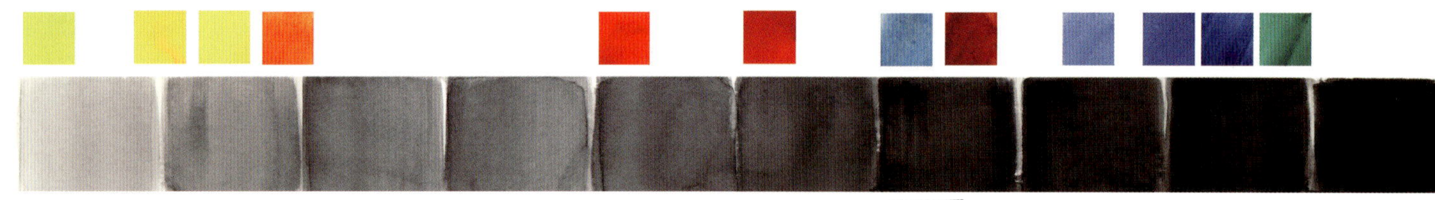

Tonal value refers to the continuum of white to black and all gradations of gray in between. In traditional transparent watercolor, tonal value is not only an element of design but also the critical element to the creation and maintaining of light in the design. In a flower painting, value can tell the time of day, the position of the sun, atmosphere, and weather. A strong value design can bring a dramatic emphasis, leading the viewer's eyes to your focal point. Light in your painting is thus expressed in light values, and dark objects and shadows in dark values. It is the latter, the darkest values, that make the lightest values glow, and thus the designing of these lights and darks is crucial to the success of the painting.

GRAY SCALE

In the chart above, you can see that although most pigments are in the middle, a few are almost black in value, and a few are near white. It is no accident that the yellows and golds are often used to indicate light and the blues to indicate shadow.

HOW TO SEE VALUE

There are several photographic ways to see value in a picture. In each example to the right, two values become immediately apparent. The light on the petals is clear, and the darks are easy to see. Which of these methods you prefer may depend on where your paintings fall on the value scale above. Try them all. Each step you take to know your subject better will show in your final painting. When this is clear, move on to the next phase of getting to know your subject (see opposite).

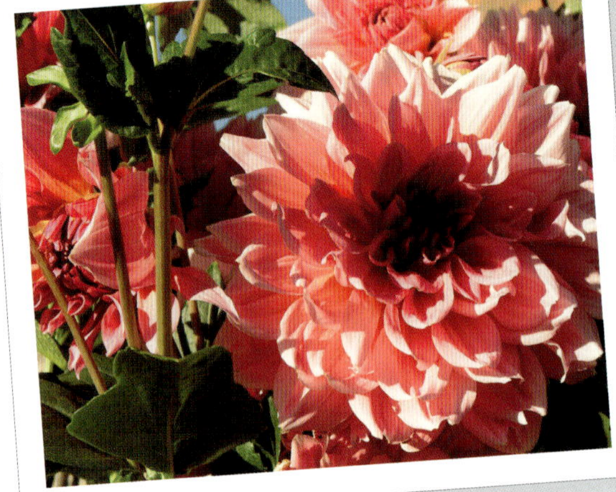

Original photograph, as shot.

Make a black-and-white photocopy of your photograph.

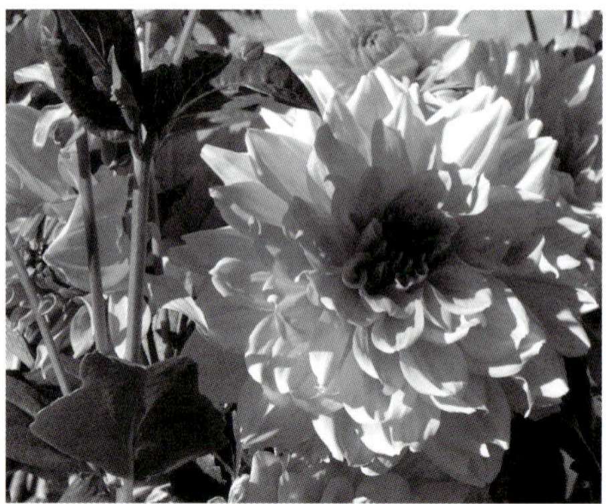

On your computer's photo editing program (see p. 9) turn it to gray scale.

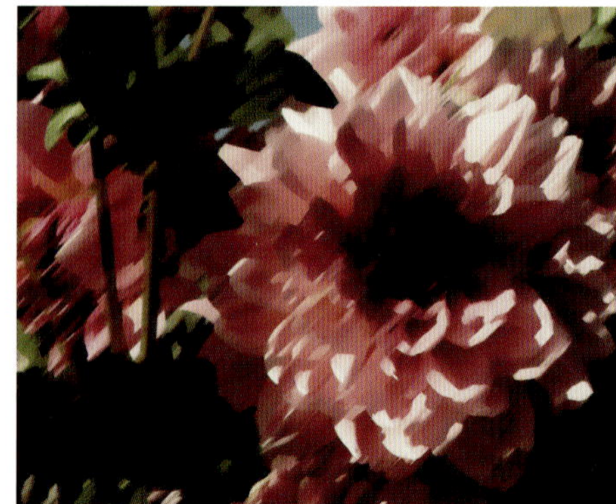

Squint at your photograph or blur it in a photo editing program. You will lose saturation, and the values will be clear.

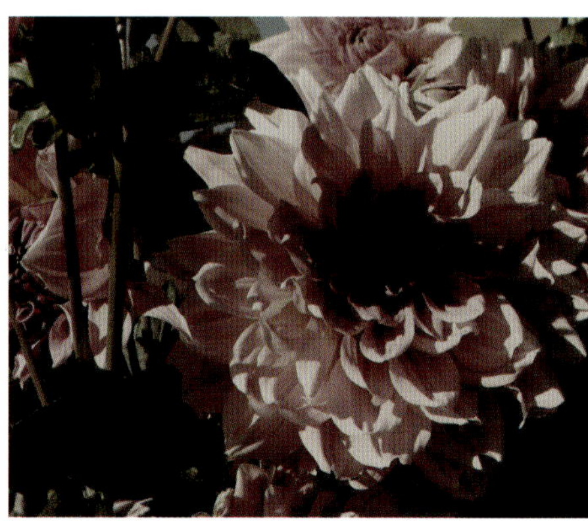

Look at your photograph in dim light. It will lose saturation and the whites will pop out.

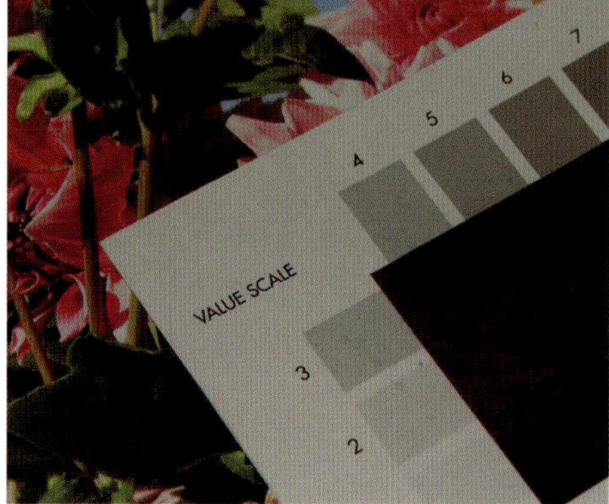

Use a red cellophane value viewer. Hold it to your eyes and view the photograph through it. This will show you the relative tones.

SKETCHING

Sketching brings your focus into the present and lets you get to know your subject intimately. Whether you are a beginner or an advanced artist, a sketchbook is your most important tool. Through it you can learn to see flowers in a new way.

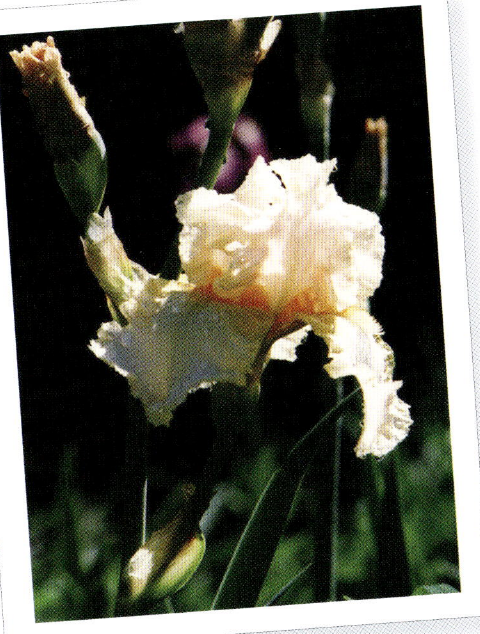

1 Original photograph: inspiration. A photograph of a beautiful flower. Ask what draws you to this particular flower. Explore the possibilities through drawing.

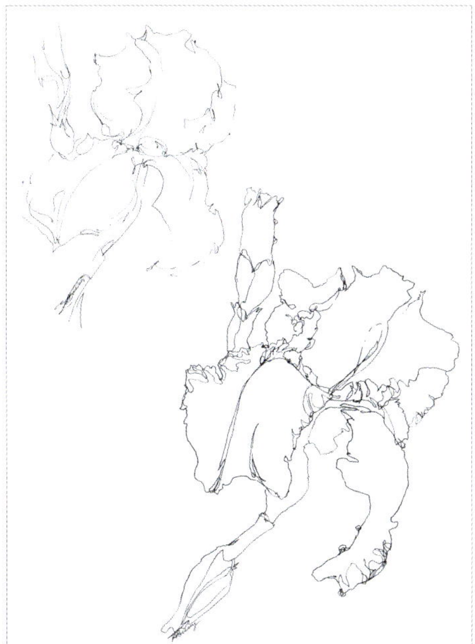

2 Contour drawing: slow, careful exploration. Place your pencil on the paper but look at the flower. As your eyes follow the edges, not just the outline, your pencil moves as well. Don't watch your drawing.

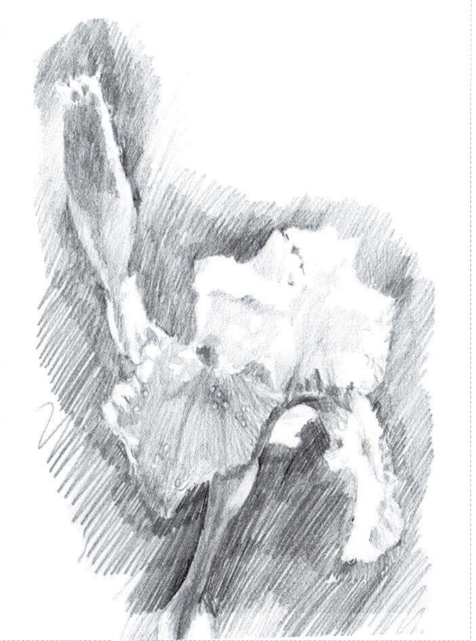

3 Tone drawing: explores mass and surface. A tonal drawing avoids lines but uses light and shading to sculpt the three-dimensionality of the flower. Use the side of your pencil lead for this. Build up the darks gradually. To shade with a pen, use cross-hatching or stippling to build up your dark areas. This is a studied and slow procedure.

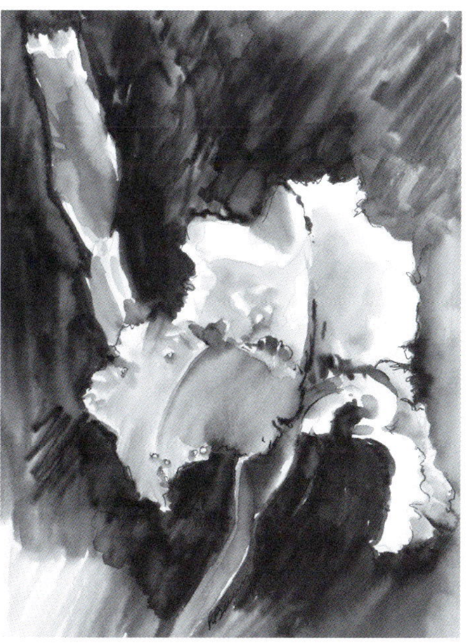

4 Wash: value sketch. Line and wash can put the entire form and attitude of the flower together. Begin with a light gesture, drawing to get all aspects of the flower correct. Use contour drawing to define the form and tones, created with paint or ink wash, to fill out the mass and value. This should also reflect how you would like to paint the flower in color.

5 Final painting: interpretation. The finished painting should reflect a new vision that the drawing process has given you. More than just copying a photograph, you have the opportunity to emphasize the things you love most, eliminate extraneous detail, and create a flower that moves not only you but all who see it.

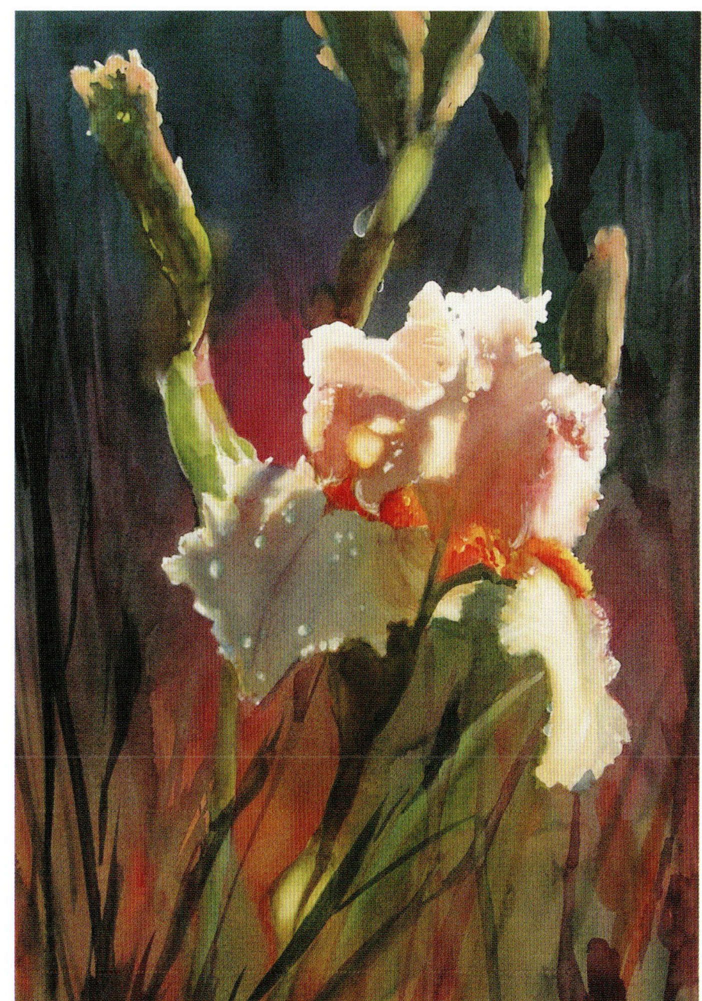

Techniques

Washes may cover a large or small area, and are usually the starting point for most watercolor paintings. The term "wash" implies an area of paint being applied flatly, but it also describes each brushstroke of fluid paint. Washes are often graded in tone or contain more than one color.

FLAT WASH

The flat wash is the easiest method of applying watercolor to paper, and is used for covering the whole or a large part of the paper during the first stages of a painting. The paper can be horizontal or tipped at a slight angle so that the brushstrokes flow into each other but do not dribble down the paper. Brushstrokes can be laid either on dry or wet paper. The latter achieves a more even coverage, but working on dry paper makes the wash easier to control if you want to stop at a certain point. Use a large flat or round brush.

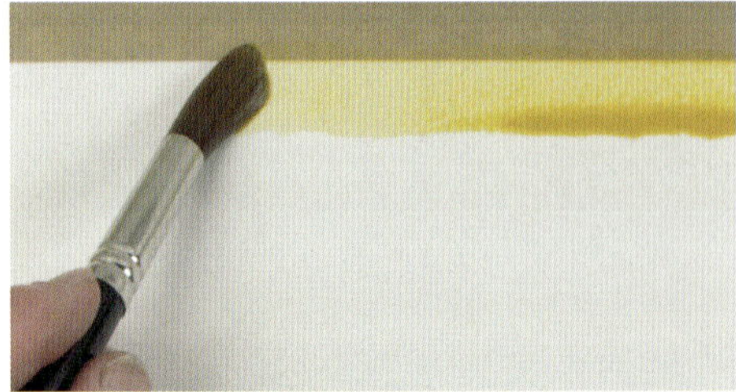

1 Load a brush with dilute watercolor and, starting at the top of the area to be covered, sweep it across dry paper.

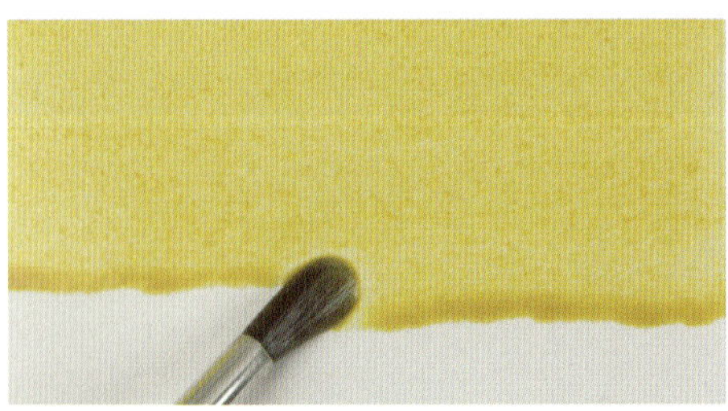

2 Keep dragging the brush across the area, reloading with paint as necessary. Overlap the previous wet color a little, so that the new stroke blends perfectly with the old one. Don't overpaint an area while wet—this will result in an uneven wash.

GRADED WASH

A graded wash is one that varies in tone. For example, on a petal this usually means that the wash becomes paler toward the bottom. The gradation is achieved by gradually adding water to the color. A graded wash is used as the first step in suggesting a shadow as well. It becomes lighter as it progresses down the paper.

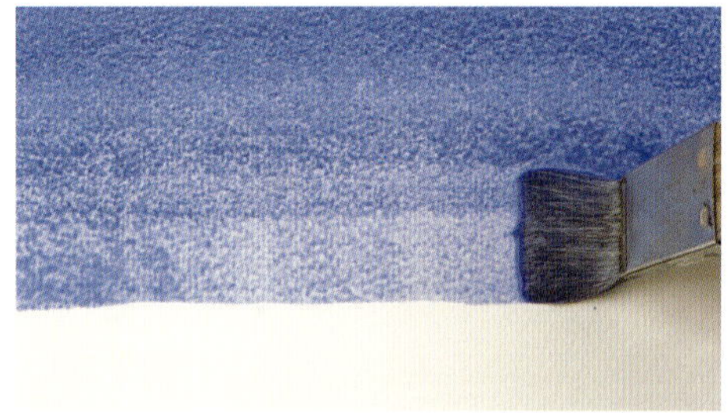

1 Tilt your board a little. Start with a flat wash of color. Dip the brush in clean water, dilute your wash paint, and stroke the dilute color below the still-wet previous area.

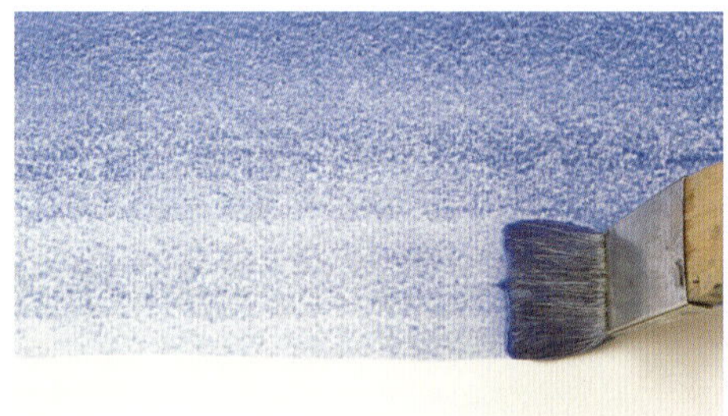

2 Add more water to the brush for each area of color. Remember that each wash should only be one step lighter than the previous one, so take care not to dilute too quickly.

3 If this wash had been worked on wet paper, the stronger color would have run down into the paler areas, losing the graded effect. For stronger tonal contrasts, try dipping the brush twice into the water or laying the second band of color with water alone.

VARIEGATED WASH

A variegated wash varies in color. The technique involves adding further colors to a still-wet flat wash or damp paper. Flower painting often uses variegated washes to show color variation within a petal or a leaf, to indicate shadows that fall on or show through petals, or to add depth to a background.

1 A varigated wash is a blend from one color to another. Wait until the underwash is dry, then add a graded wash of a color with water over the top. The transition can be gradual.

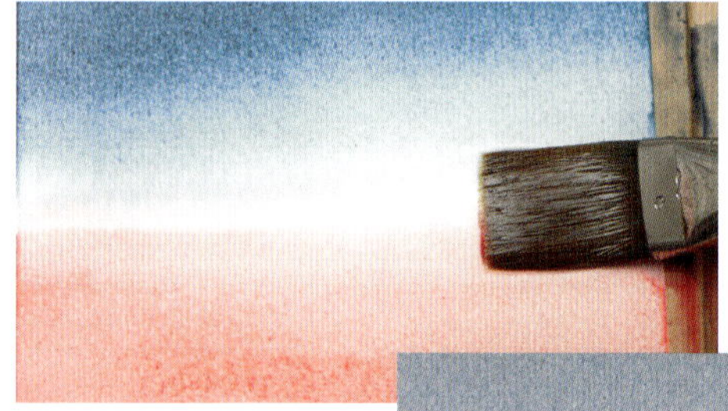

2 A more defined transition is achieved by washing two colors next to each other, with the edge of the first color still wet when applying the second color.

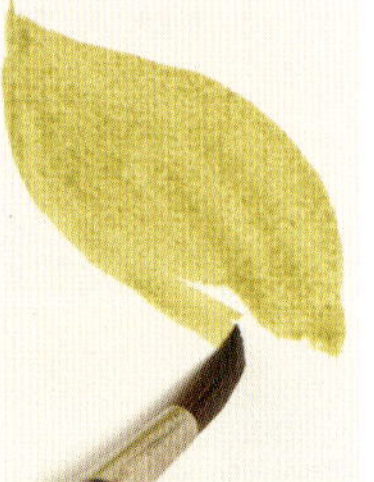

1 This technique can be used on detail areas such as shadows to define form. Paint the area with the first color.

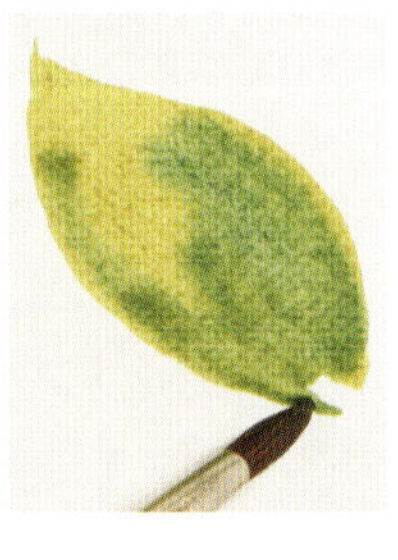

2 When the paint is nearly dry, apply the second, darker color. This will blend easily into the damp surface, giving soft edges. The second application should contain more pigment than the first; otherwise, a bloom will result.

MIXING PAINT IN THE PALETTE

When mixing colors in the palette, begin by making sure your wells of paint are moist and you are able to get a strong color. Begin with the lightest color. Once you have an adequate puddle of paint, rinse your brush well, wipe it on a towel or tissue, and bring a little of the darker color to your mix. Continue this process until the desired color is achieved. Note: Don't start with a strong dark color, such as phthalo blue, and attempt to mix a lighter color, such as aureolin, into it. You could use a whole tube of the latter and still not achieve a spring green. Test your mix on a scrap of paper if you are unsure.

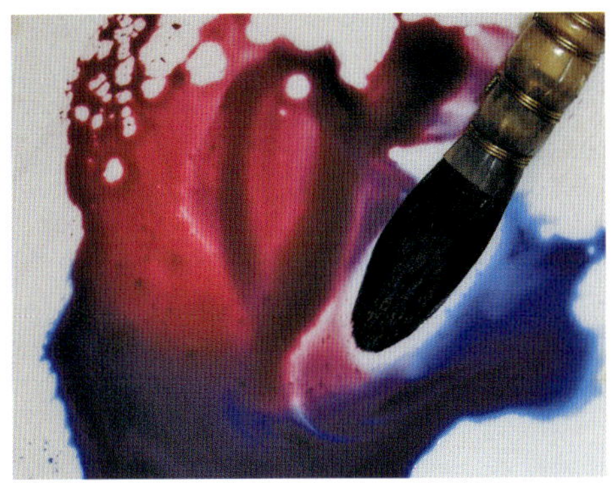

1 Use your brush to carry paint to be mixed to a clean area of the palette. Make a note of the individual character of both colors.

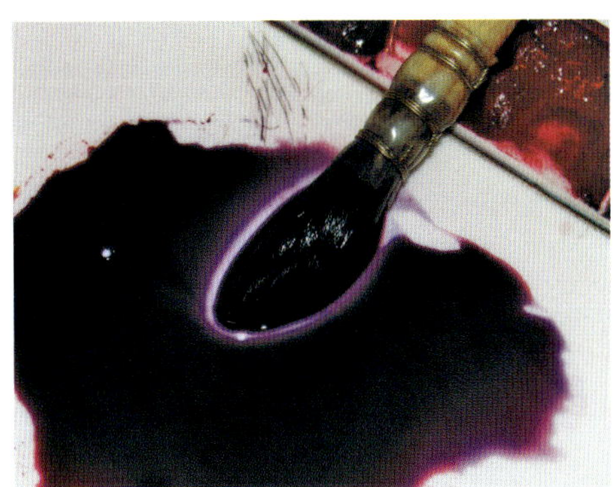

2 If mixed too thoroughly, you may achieve your desired color, but you will also lose the individual color personalities.

MIXING PAINT ON THE PAPER

Different color mixing effects can be created by letting the colors blend on the paper surface, rather than mixing them in the palette. They do not mix as thoroughly, but each color retains its identity. This is known as "wet-into-wet" (see p. 22). Tipping the painting surface controls the direction of the flow in the blending pigments.

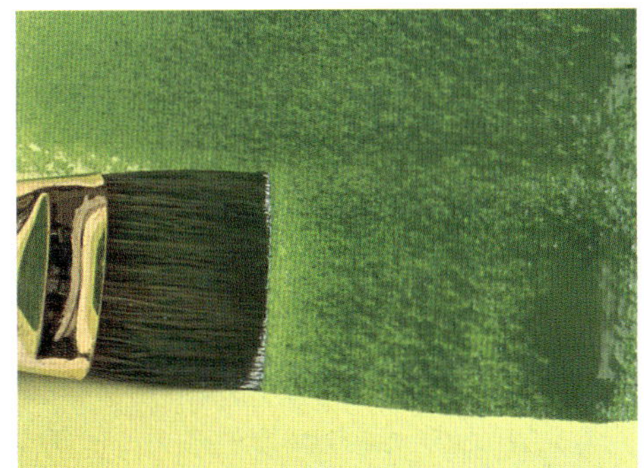

Color mixing by glazing (see p. 23) a blue over a yellow. The yellow is still visible under the blue, a combination that forms green.

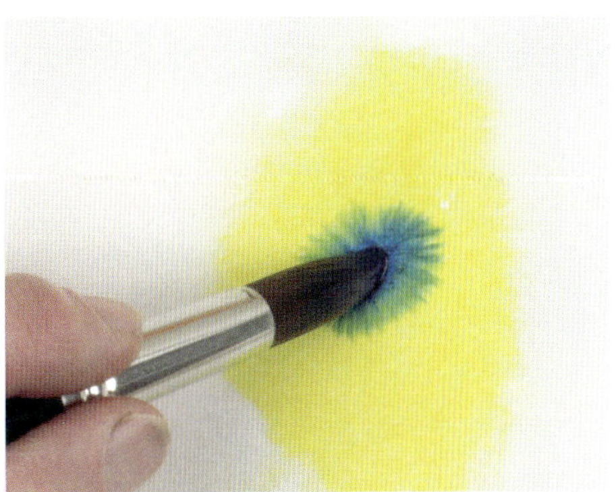

1 Color mixing through working wet-into-wet (see p. 22). The still-wet paint allows the second color to bleed into the first.

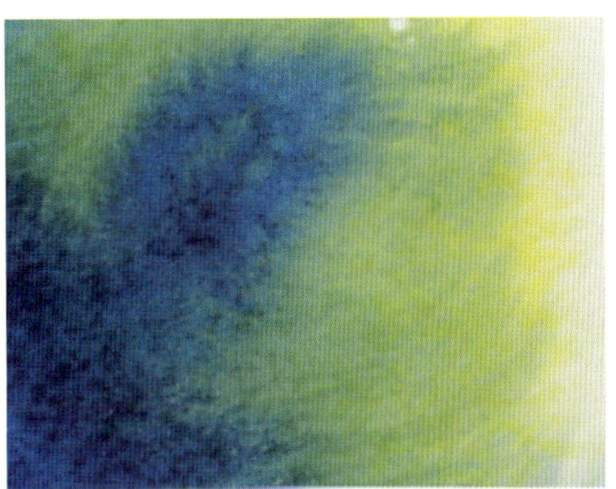

2 The blue and yellow merge magically to create green. As in the glazing method above, the integrity of the original is still obvious, which can create a more interesting and varied green than a palette mix or a green straight from the tube.

DROPPING IN COLOR

You can drop a pure color into a wet wash and, depending on the nature of each pigment and the wetness of the wash, exciting effects can be achieved. The colors retain their individual characteristics and blend as their nature determines. Other than to deliver the color, you do little with the brush.

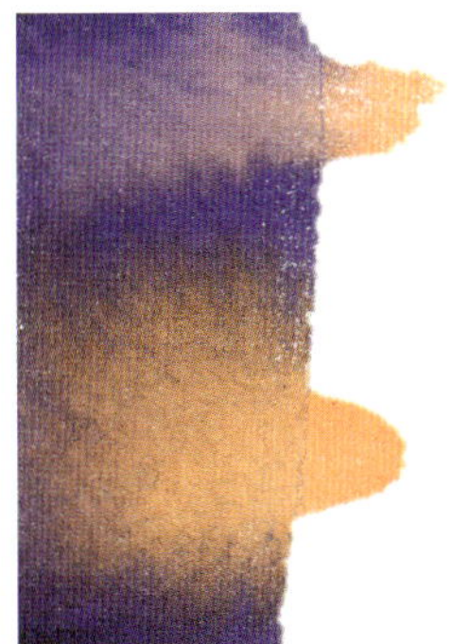

Quinacridone gold dropped into carbazole violet. A "blast" of light appears.

Ultramarine blue dropped into carbazole violet. The colors blend and form a shadow effect.

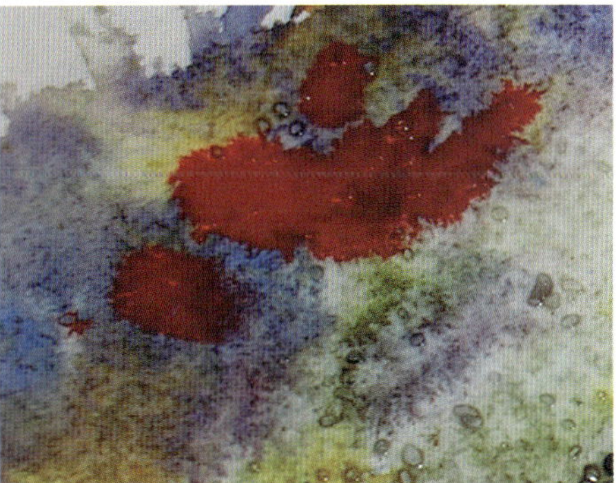

To create the "chaos" of a garden in full bloom, drop red into a green and gold mixture to indicate poppies, and blue to indicate bachelor's buttons.

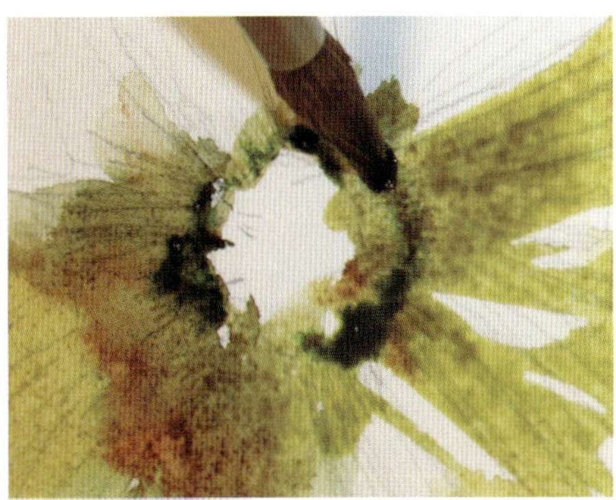

To form shadows of stamen in the center of a flower (here, a hollyhock), drop in small amounts of phthalo green with the tip of a brush. Leave to dry before painting the center.

WET-ONTO-DRY

The technique of applying watercolor to dry paper or over a layer of paint that has been left to dry is used in most paintings, and it allows you to take as much time as you need to consider your next step.

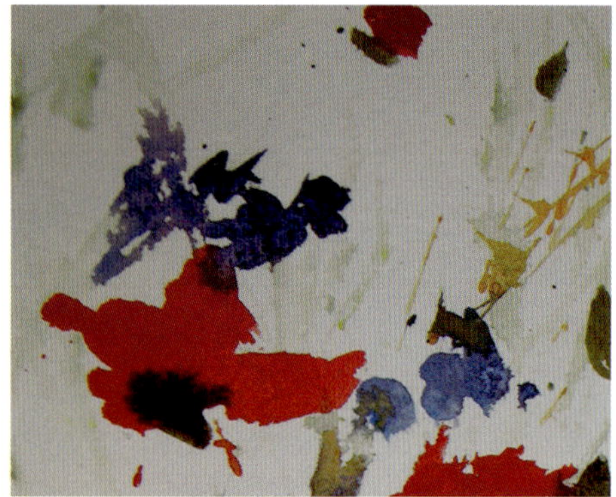

Poppies and bachelor's buttons applied on dry paper. The crisp edge is achieved as the paint dries almost immediately on the dry paper.

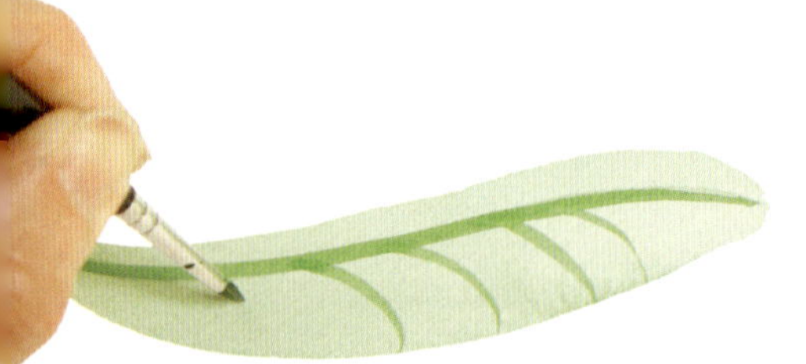

Linear marks for details or explaining shape can be painted with a small brush working wet-onto-dry. When painting veins on leaves or petals (above) work from the center vein out toward the edge of the leaf, since the paint tends to thin out toward the end of the stroke, giving a natural effect. Stamen and markings on throats of flowers can also be painted using this technique (below).

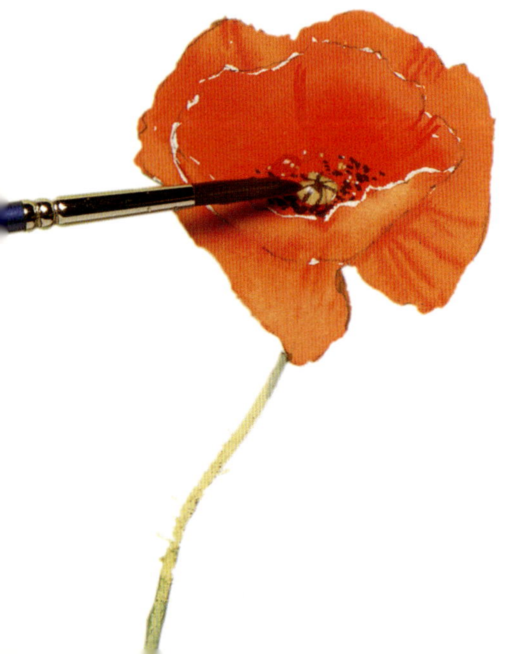

WET-INTO-WET

Painting wet paint shapes onto wet paper or wet paint is the technique that gives watercolor its reputation as a soft, juicy medium. No other medium has the ability to flow like watercolor.

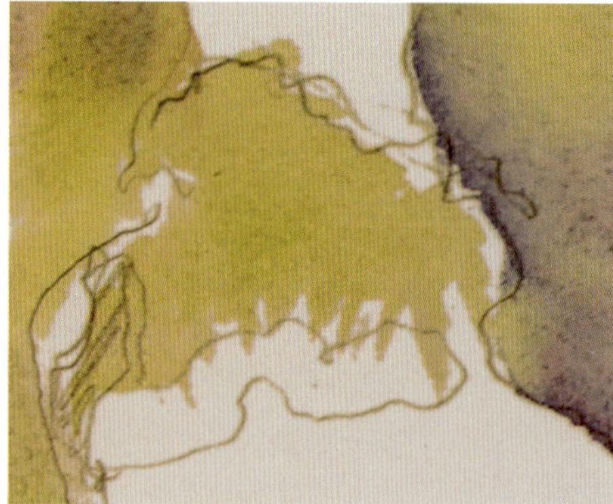

To apply paint to one area and save the white of the paper in another, wet the area to receive paint. Gently apply the color(s) to the wet area and allow them to blend and run. They will stop at the dry edge.

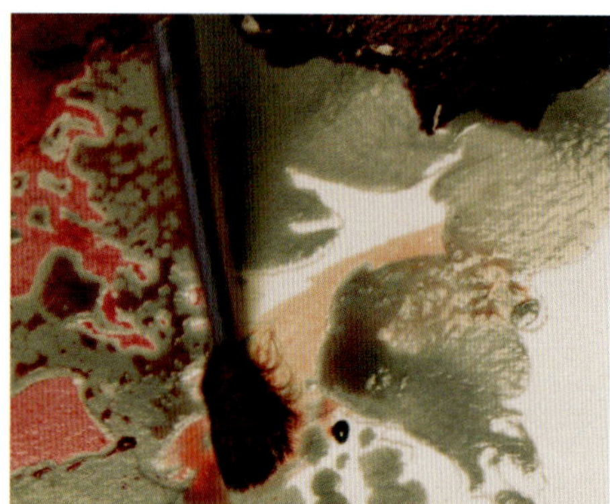

If you have masked the whites (see p. 25), wet as much of the paper as you need and freely apply colors, letting them blend together.

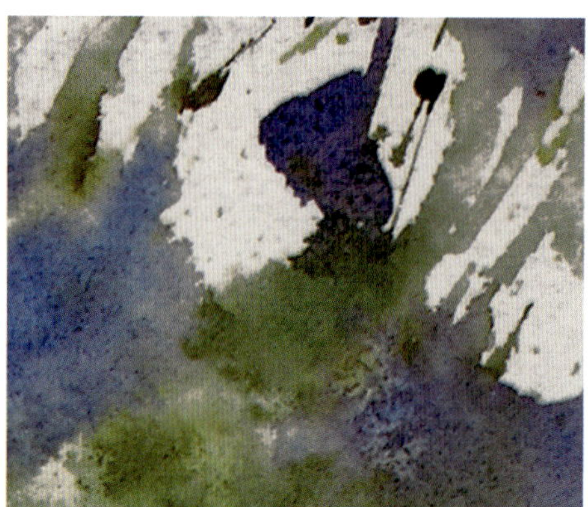

As you work wet-into-wet, some parts of the paper will begin to dry and give you contrasting soft and hard edge forms (see p. 24).

COMBINED WET-INTO-WET AND WET-ONTO-DRY

Most paintings use both wet-into-wet and wet-onto-dry passages to achieve the desired effect. Where wet-into-wet gives a feeling of mystery, wet-onto-dry gives the effect of clarity.

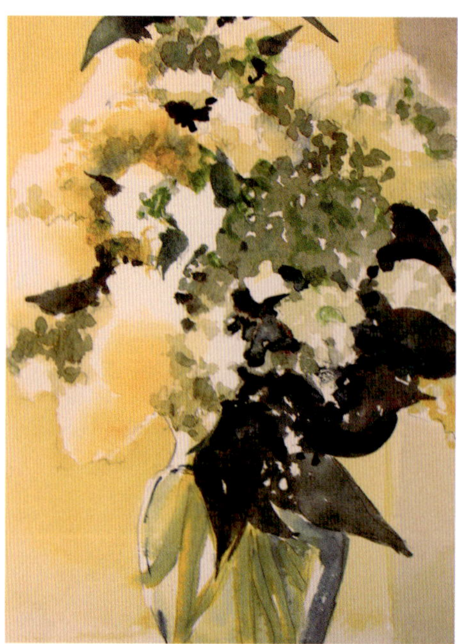

The combined techniques give this vase of flowers a realistic look, forming the rounded bunches of lilacs and the misty glass vase, set off by the harder-edged, dark leaves.

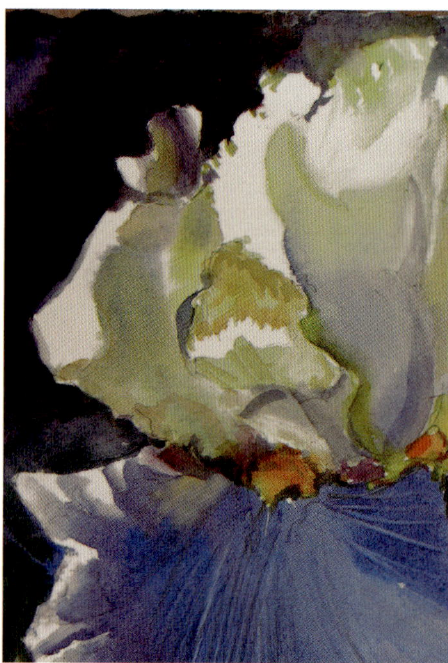

Contrast for emphasis: The hard edge of the background defines the edge of the petal, while the shapes within the petal are softer-edged to create texture.

PAINT LIGHT TO DARK

Traditionally, transparent watercolor is painted light to dark because light transparent color has no density to cover a darker color. You can gradually "feel your way" into the shapes of the painting, using pale colors first. The technique is "akin" to glazing (right)—in which the color layers shine through each other to create transparent luminescent layers. By following this well-worn path, many problems can be avoided.

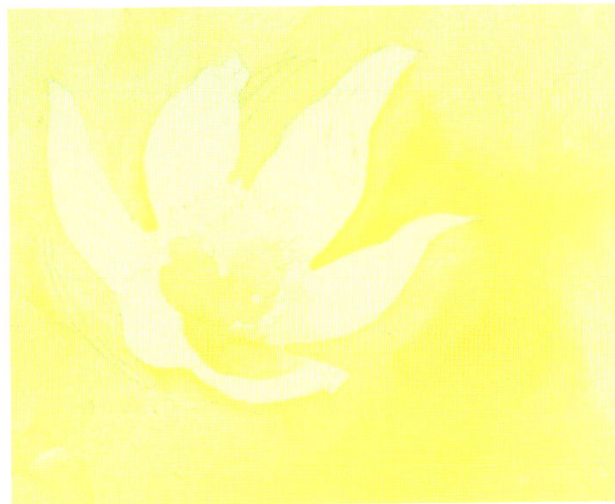

1 Establish the light tones of the painting with a wash of yellow, applied everywhere except where the white is to be saved. Most of this will be painted over with the subsequent transparent glazes.

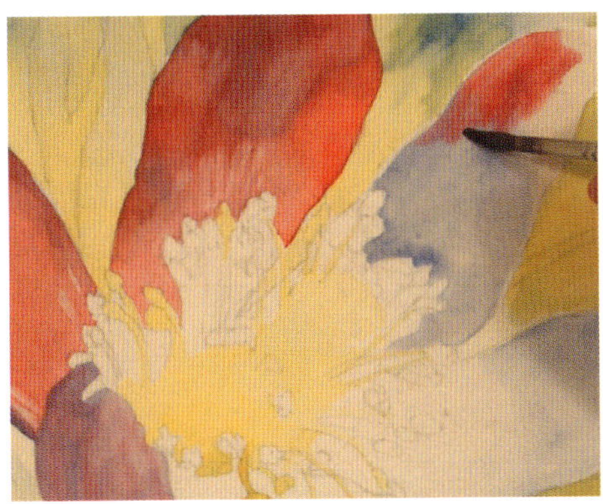

3 Add the strong tones of the magenta petals. The petals represent what will be the midtones of the final painting.

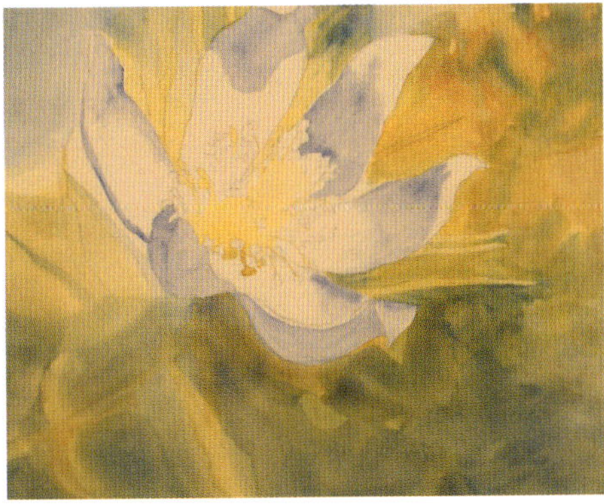

2 Wash blue into the background areas and onto the shadow area of the petals. This starts to define the mid and dark areas and mixes with the yellow to create foliage colors.

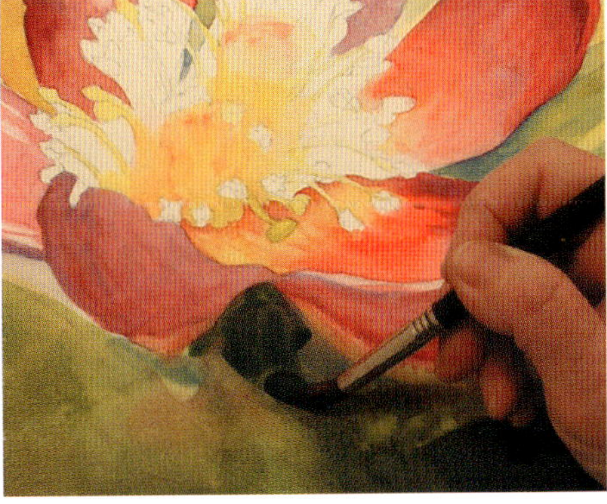

4 Wash in mixes of blue and violet to create the dark tones. The basic light to dark tones of the painting are now established. All the final details and adjustments can now be painted (see below).

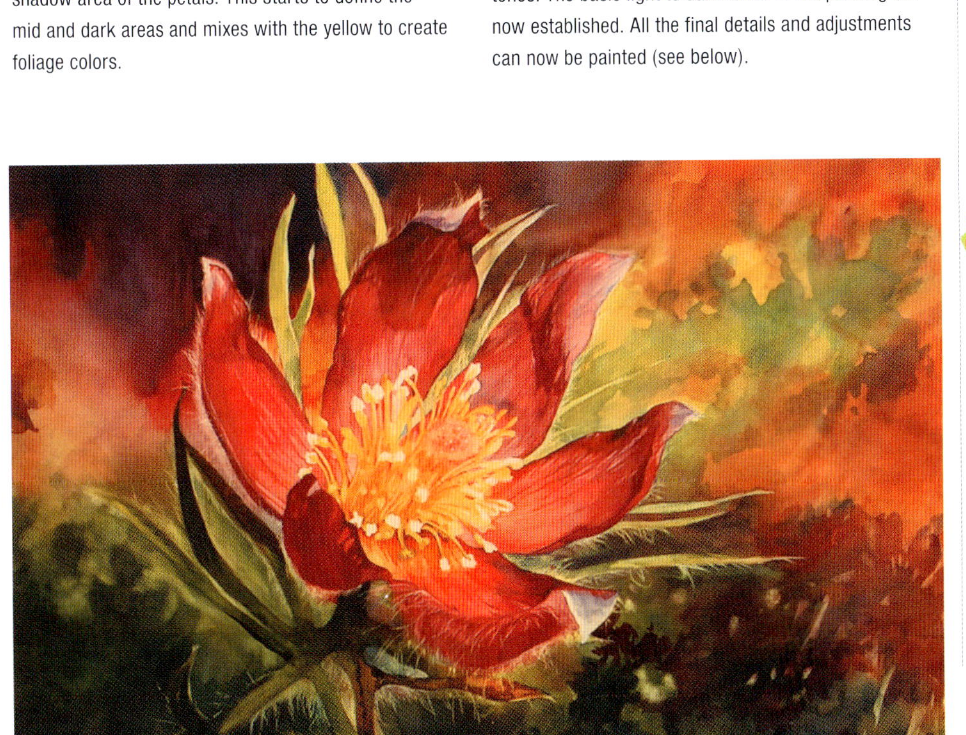

GLAZING

Glazing goes hand in hand with working wet-onto-dry and light to dark. It is a way of achieving maximum control while creating a transparent, glowing effect. This demonstration shows a test strip for a coral rosebud.

1 Paint a yellow base. Putting yellow under the other colors will add an upward glow through the painting.

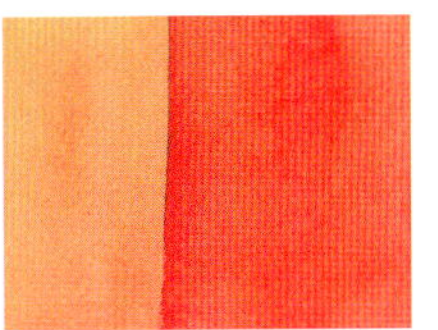

2 When the yellow is completely dry, apply a tea-strength glaze of quinacridone coral and, for the leaf color, a mixture of aureolin and phthalo yellow-green. When dry, add quinacridone burnt sienna to the coral for the deeper colors of the flowers, and paint another layer of the green mixture to deepen the green.

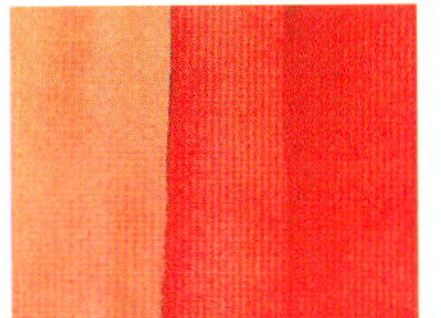

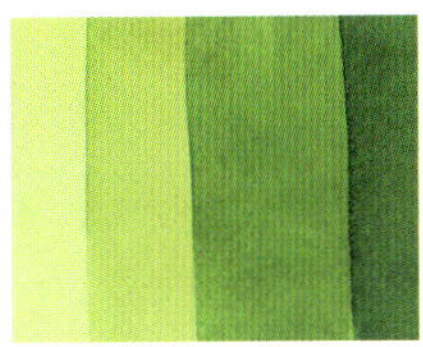

3 Mix a milk-strength puddle of quinacridone red and burnt sienna for the deepest corals and another layer of green for the deepest greens.

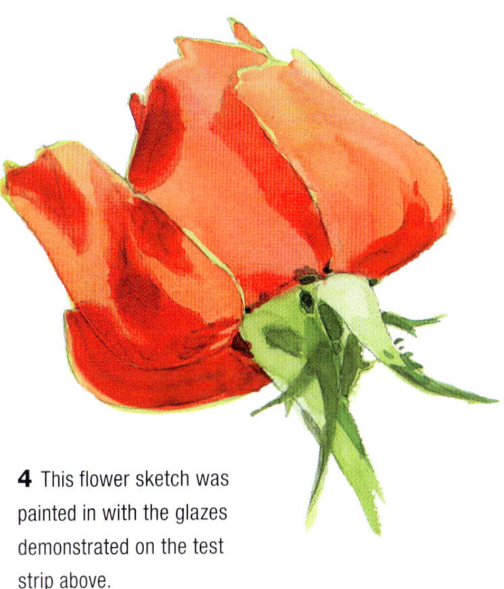

4 This flower sketch was painted in with the glazes demonstrated on the test strip above.

BLENDING

To avoid hard lines or edges with paint that has been laid down wet-onto-dry (see p. 20), try blending.

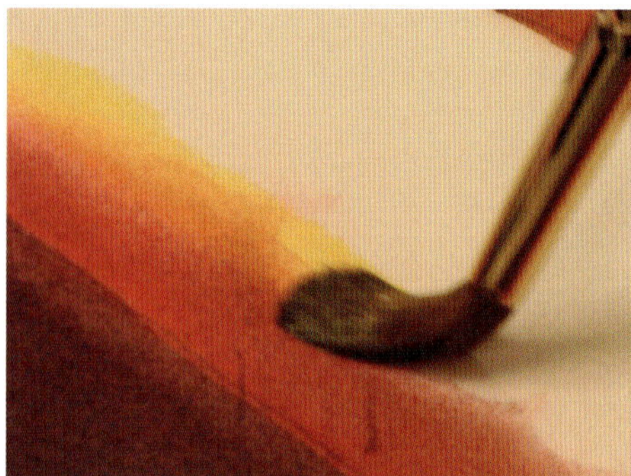

1 Place one color next to another.

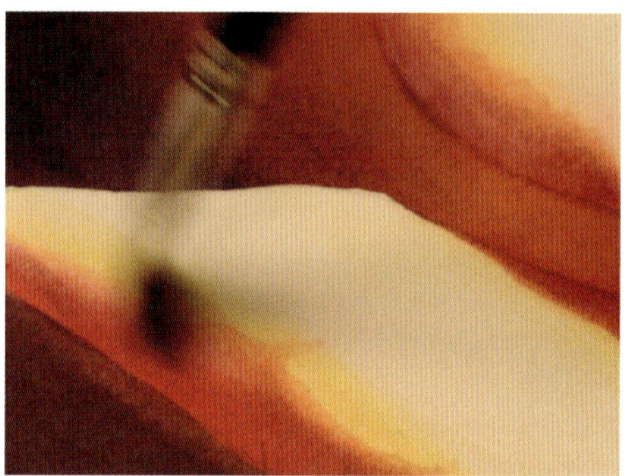

2 Blend the new color into the old color using rapid, light, back and forth movements with a dry or very thirsty brush.

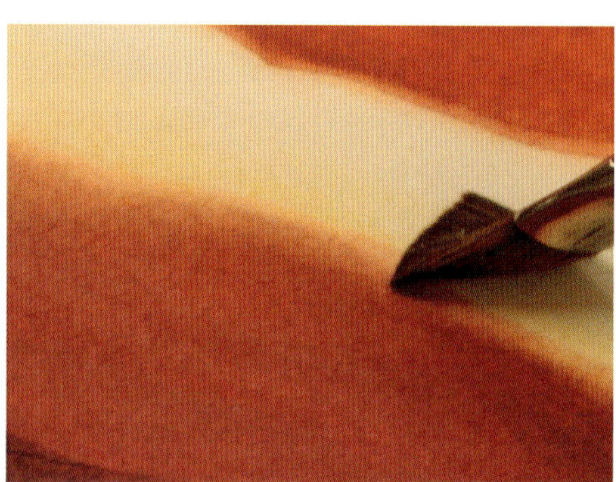

3 A natural softness is the result.

LOST AND FOUND EDGES

Lost edges and found edges can be painted separately, but it is useful to paint them at the same time since one can define the other. Paint a wash with a defined edge on one side and a fade on the other. The technique is useful for defining the hard edge of a shape that then fades into the background. By blending both edges, soft transitions from one object to another, or into the background, can be achieved without any visible lines. Lost edges connect areas of light, shadow, and color.

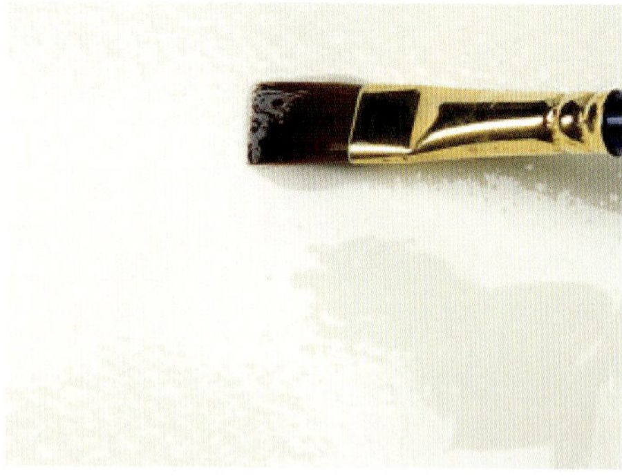

1 To create a shape with hard and soft edges, paint a layer of clear water (no puddles) onto white paper. Wait until the water has sunk in but there is still a sheen.

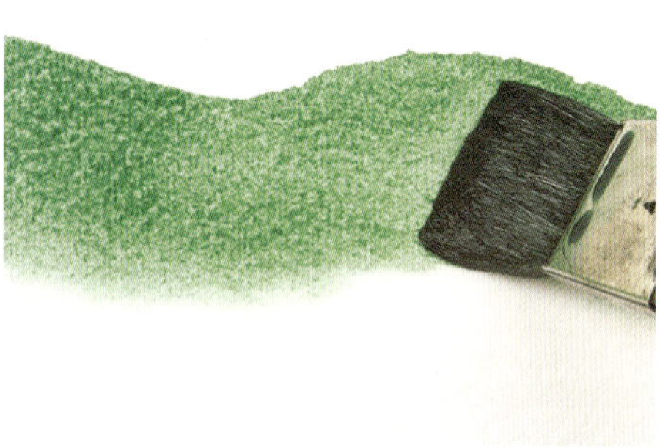

2 Using a flat or large round brush, paint color up to one of the edges of the wet area, allowing the other edge to bleed into the damp paper.

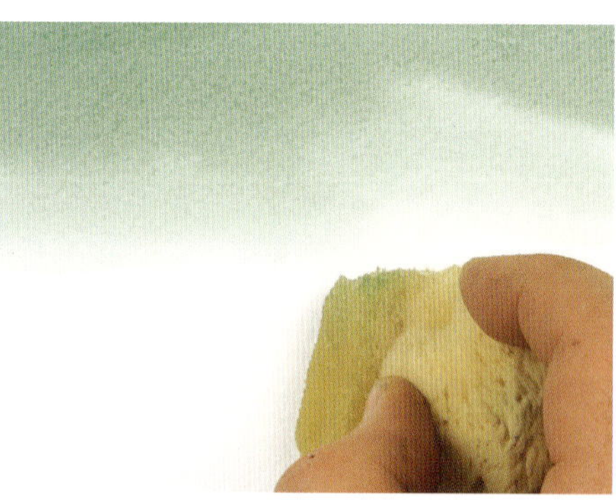

3 Soft edges are also the way in which one color meets another: They appear to blend. Use a natural sponge to intensify this effect.

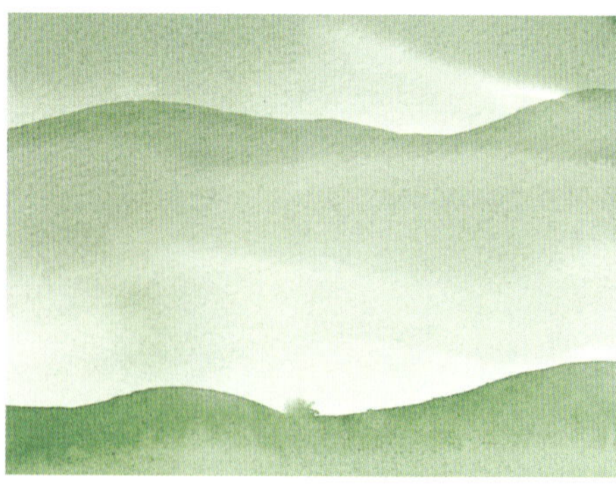

4 Soft edges give the sense of motion. In a garden, the breeze may stir the flowers, and it may be that feeling you want to capture. Hard edges are more fixed and defined.

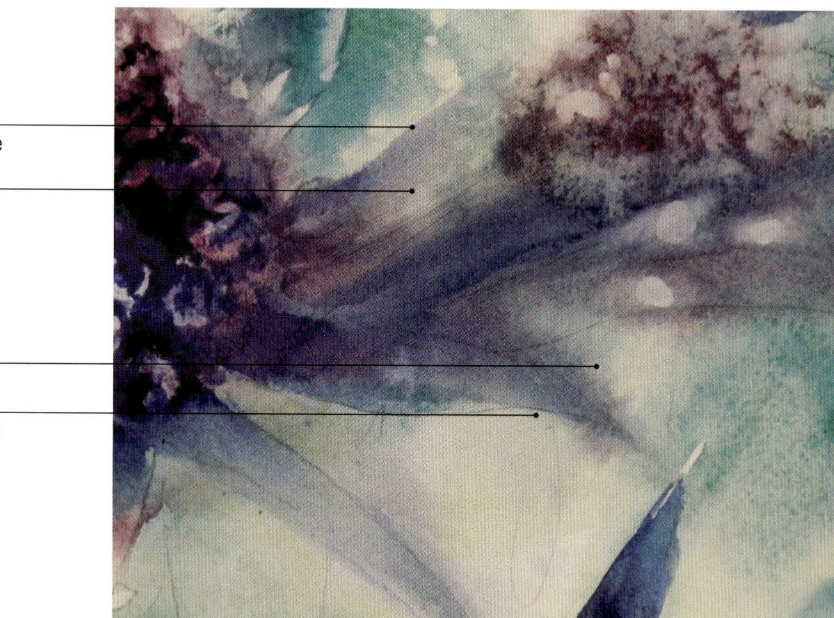

MASKING TO RESERVE THE PAPER

Masking fluids form a waterproof seal that protects the paper underneath, enabling washes to be painted over without having to carefully leave tiny areas white.

1 To apply masking fluid to all the white areas of a flower, such as this backlit magnolia, use an old synthetic fiber brush. Dipping it in dishwashing detergent first and then wiping it will help you clean it after use.

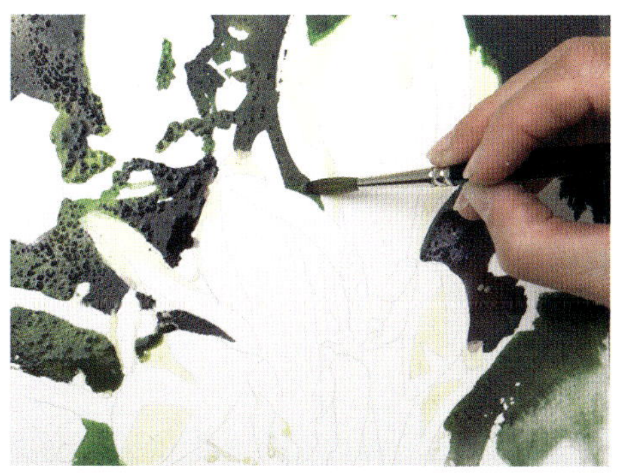

2 You can now apply paint speedily and fluidly. Once the shadows have been painted and allowed to dry, rub or peel off the masking, revealing the white paper underneath.

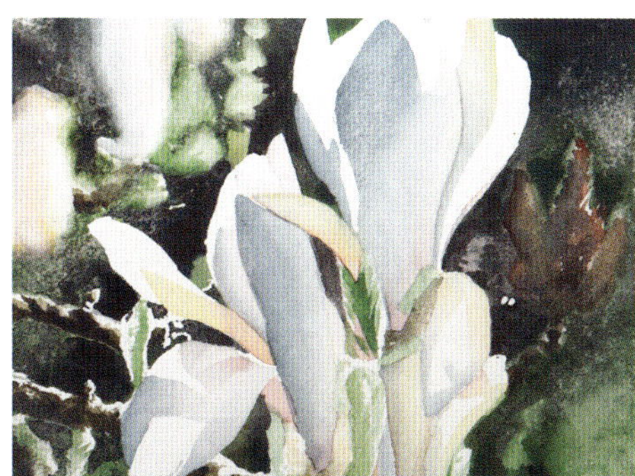

3 You now have white areas you can work into. If the paper appears too white when the fluid is removed, lightly color the area. In this case, the pure whites are ideal for the subject.

MASKING FOR DETAILS

The best method of reserving intricate highlights is to use masking fluid before painting.

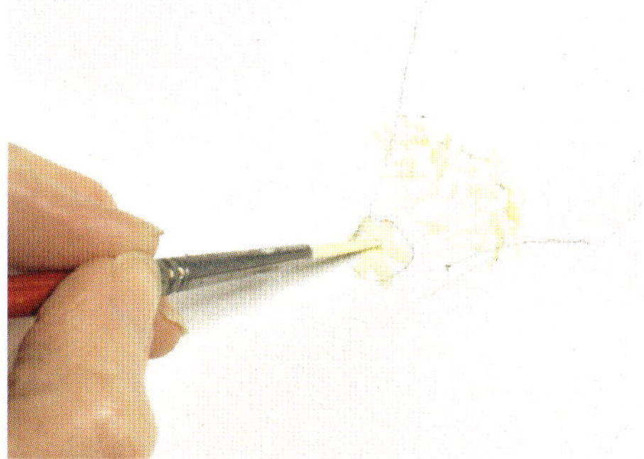

1 To reserve stamens, such as these poppy stamens, paint with masking fluid using an old synthetic fiber brush. Wash the brush out immediately with warm, soapy water.

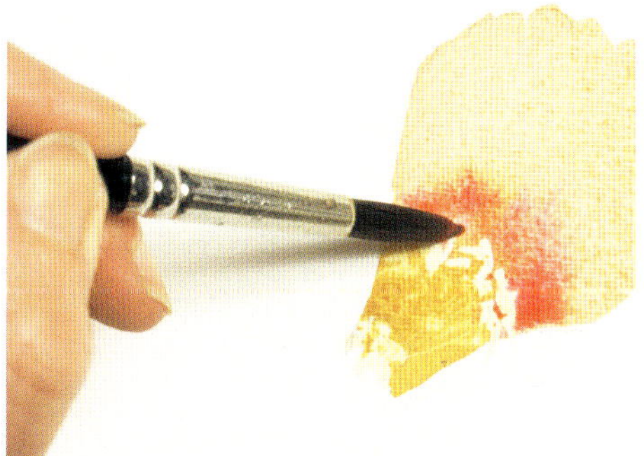

2 When the masking fluid is dry, you can paint freely over it because it acts as a block to the paint. Here new gamboge and permanent rose are used to complete the petal washes.

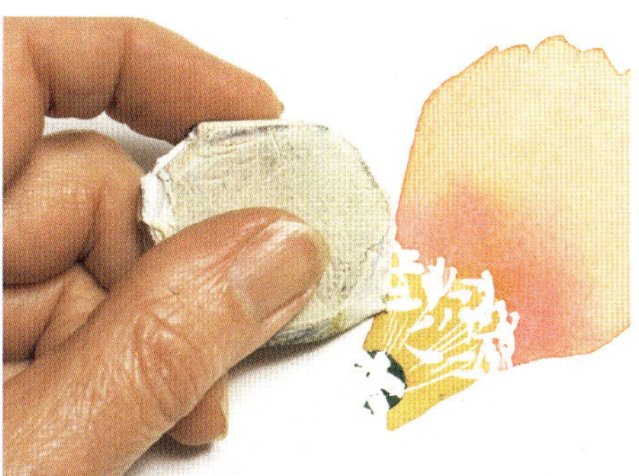

3 When the paint has dried, remove the masking by gently rubbing with a finger or a soft eraser to reveal clean, white paper. If the highlights are a pale color rather than pure white, they can be tinted in the final stages.

SOFTENING MASKED EDGES

As useful as masking fluid is to the flower painter, when it is removed, the edges left are unnaturally hard and unpleasing.

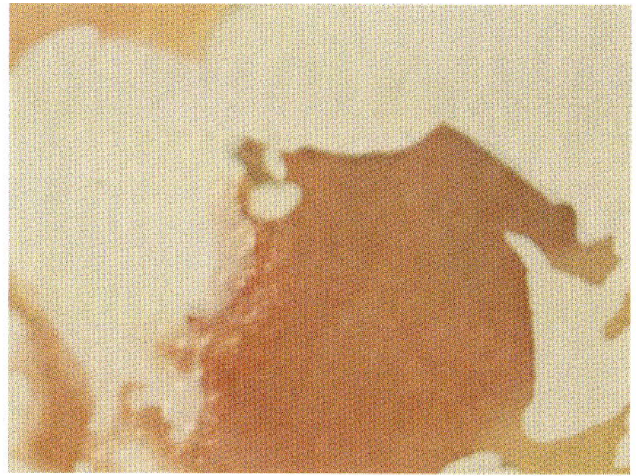

1 Remove the masking. The protected edge of the highlight will never be perfect and will require touching up. Evaluate which edges you would like hard and which you would like soft.

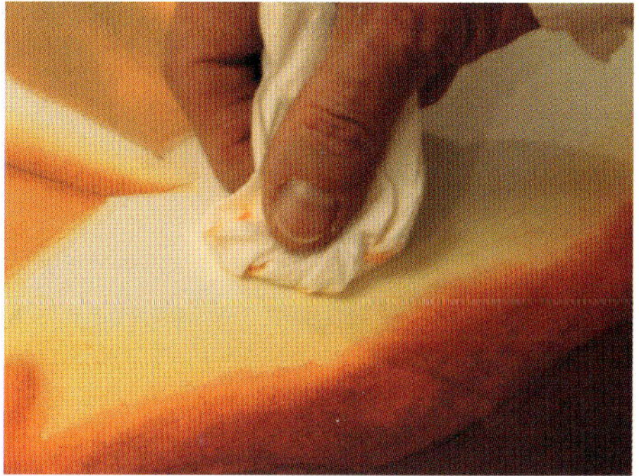

2 In the case of edges you want to leave almost as is, paint a thin line of water along the edge; dabbing with a tissue may be all that is needed to blend the color into the white highlight area.

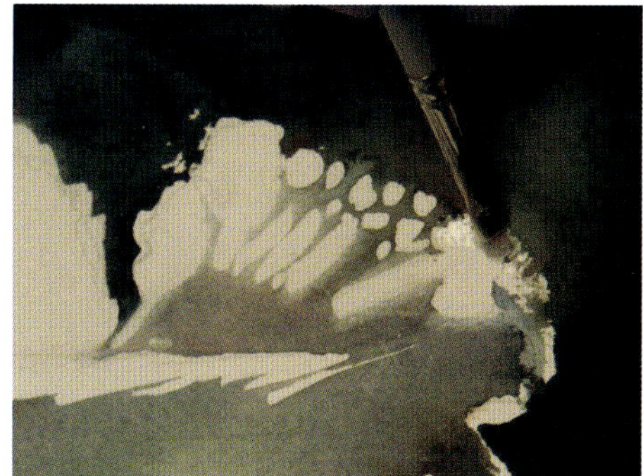

Alternative for small areas: Run a wet scrubber carefully along the edge to be softened. Dab with tissue.

MAKE SOFTENED EDGES GLOW

Once your masked edges are softened, you may want to add a glow to them. Notice that the edges of shadows in bright sunlight often have a golden edge. Recreating this can give warmth to your flower.

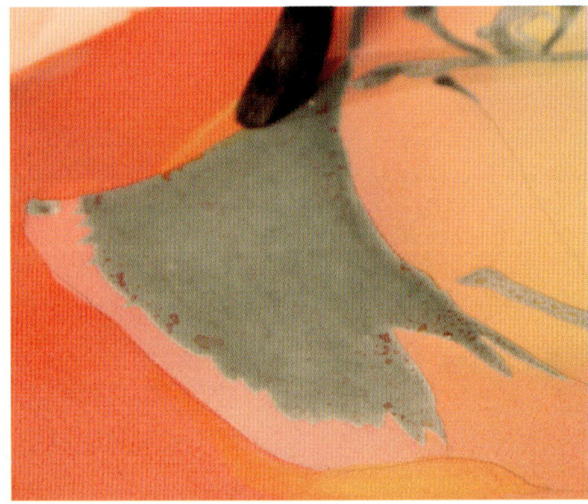

1 Before removing the masking, you may want to glaze around it with a deep yellow. Even if it fades into a darker background, there will be a glow.

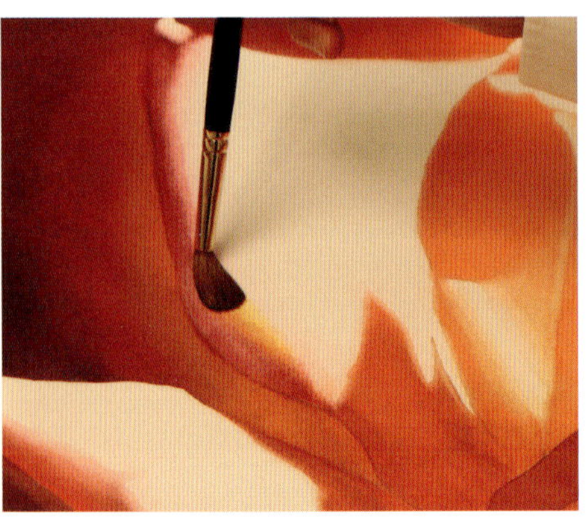

2 Once the masking is removed and the edges are softened, paint a yellow or golden almost-dry wash along the edge.

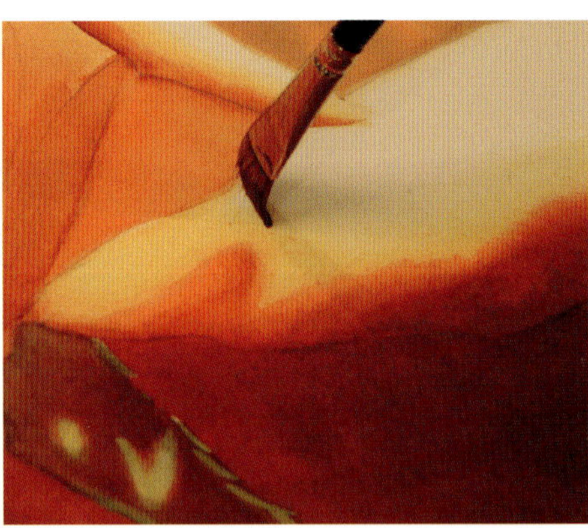

3 Blend the yellow into the white and shadow color (see p. 28). At the center of interest, paint more golden color and blend.

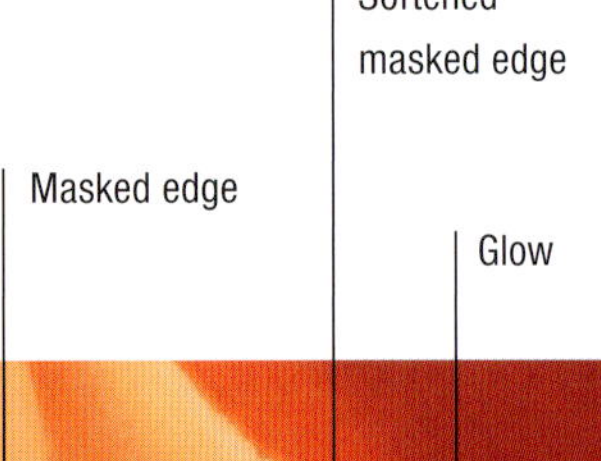

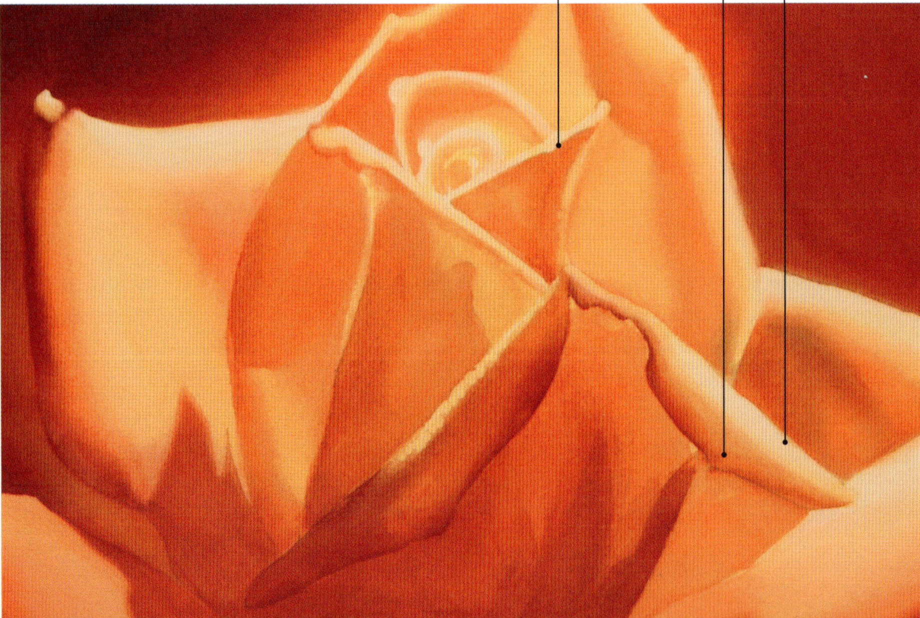

WHITE OF THE PAPER

In traditional transparent watercolor, it is the white of the paper that gives the painting its translucence and freshness. White paint is not usually used, although there are nonpurist artists who find it useful at times.

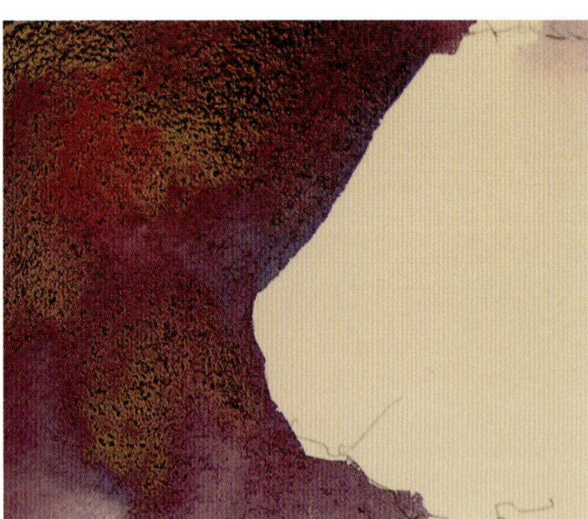

To reserve white highlight areas of paper, paint clear water washes on the areas to be colored. When paint is applied to the wet area, it bleeds up to the edge of the dry area.

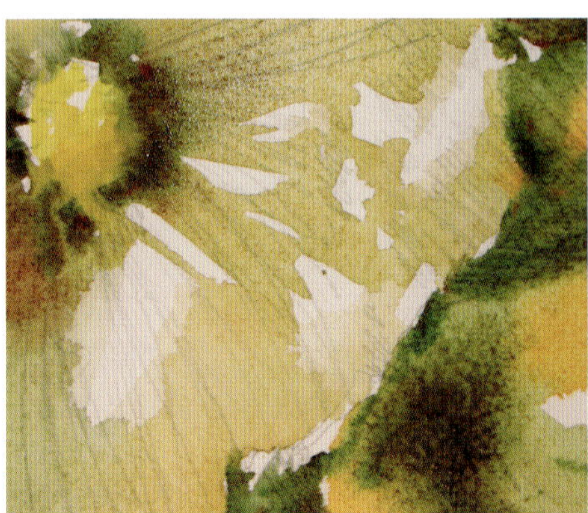

Hard-edge highlights on an open hollyhock. The technique detailed above can be applied to small areas as well as large.

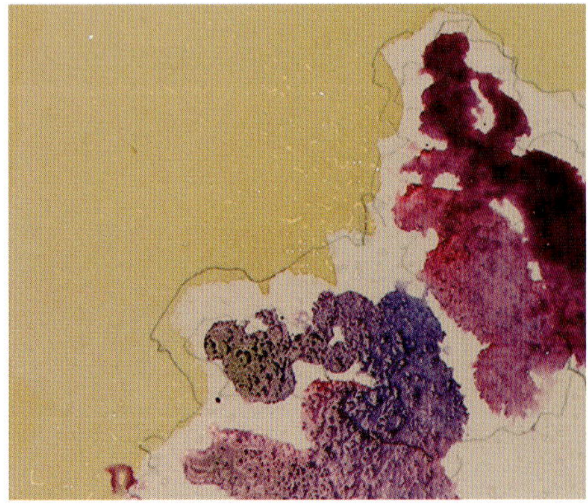

Create a backlit situation once a background is painted by leaving a white edge as you paint the inside of the flower (here in soft ocher).

WHITE-ON-WHITE

There are many colors or tones of white. In bright light, white is simply white, but white objects in white surroundings will take on light shades or values of other colors due to the influence of the surrounding area.

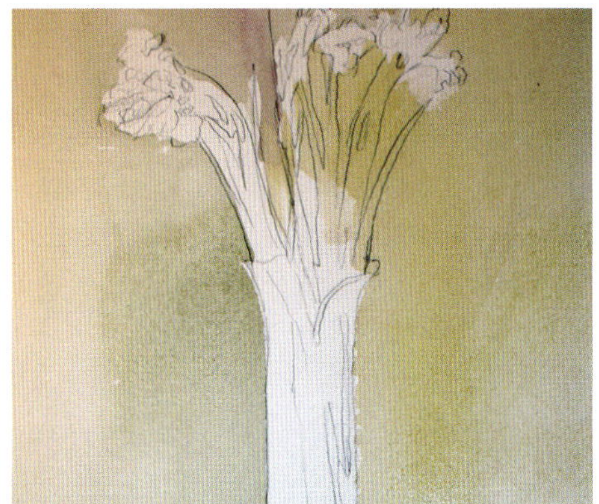

1 A drawing of blue flags in a white vase, on a white mantle, against a white wall. Pale background washes establish the basic shape.

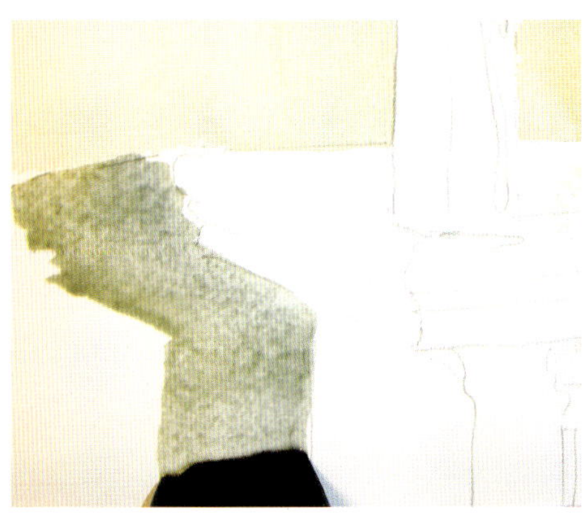

2 To establish the range of values in the painting, the midrange values are painted first.

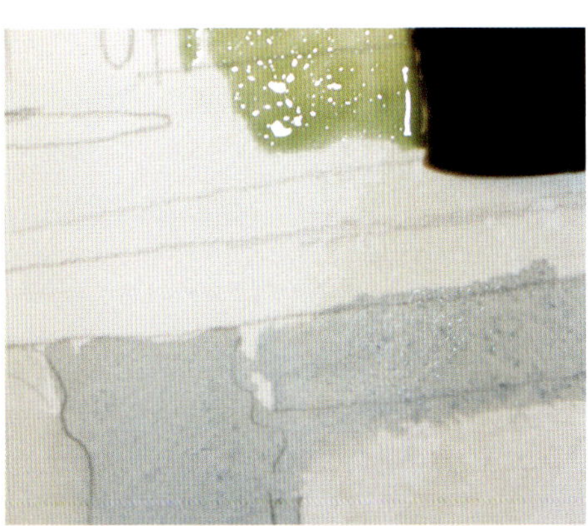

3 These midrange tones define the white light even further. A cooler middle value has also been added to imply cast shadow.

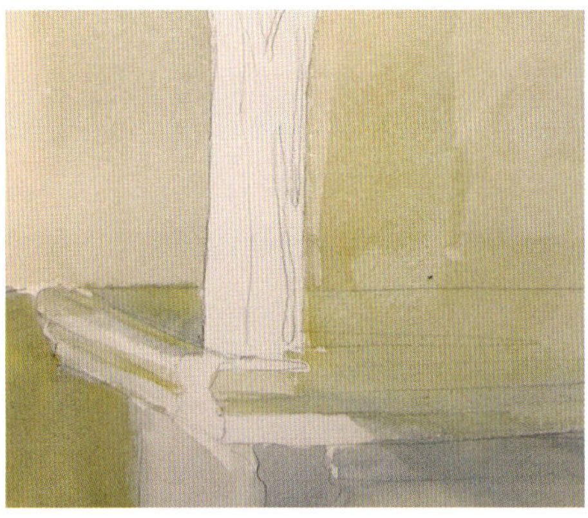

4 With the surrounding whites in place, paint the vase and flowers. The light source is from the left and goes behind the vase as well.

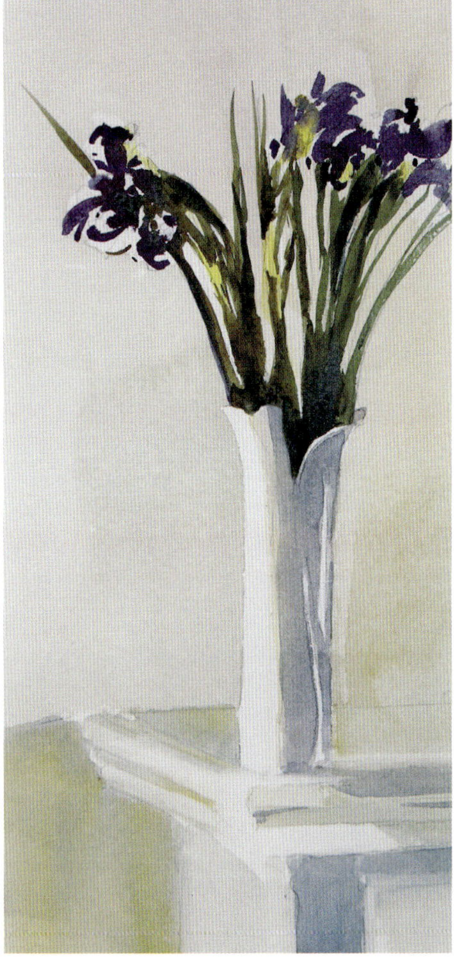

5 With the vase painted and all the highlights preserved, there is a realistic look to this white-on-white painting.

ADDING HIGHLIGHTS

There are many ways to add highlights and glitter to a painting without using masking fluid or white paint.

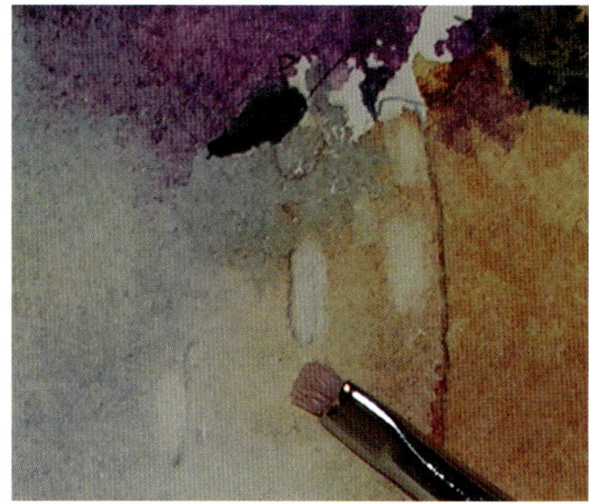

Scrubber: Use a firm synthetic brush, called a scrubber, to gently wipe away small spots of light. Take care not to overuse the scrubber and go through the paper.

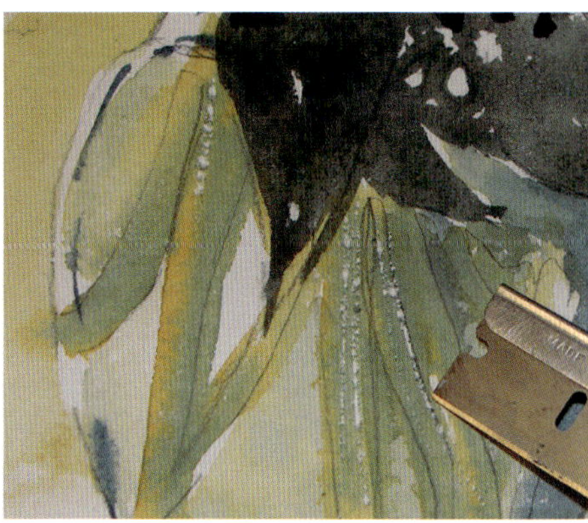

Razor blade: Use a single-edge razor blade to recover dots of white by removing tiny "divots" of painted paper.

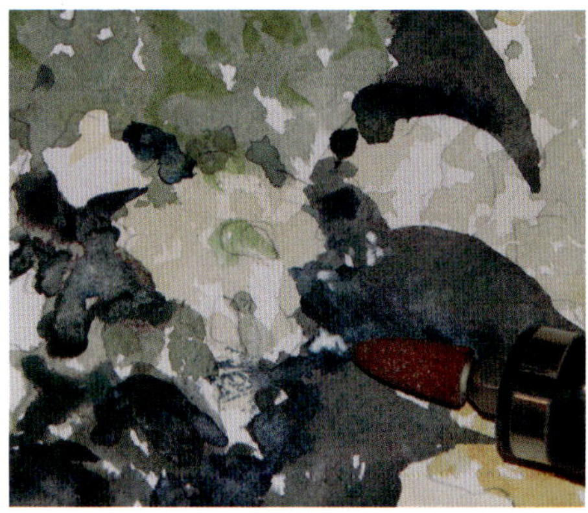

Dremel tool: Another way to achieve the same effect—but use extreme caution—is with a light touch from a Dremel tool with a sanding bit.

SHADOWS

Nothing brings out the light in a flower painting more than the presence of deep darks and shadows. These shadows “turn on the lights.”

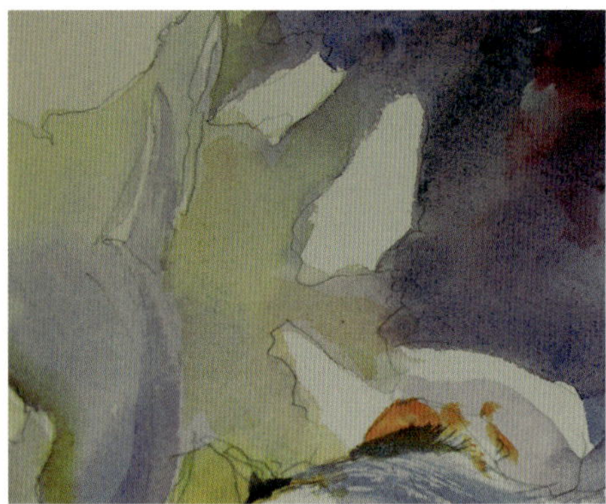

1 Paint a blue-and-white iris against a warm medium background, which emphasizes the predominantly cool colors of the flower. It will look a little washed out.

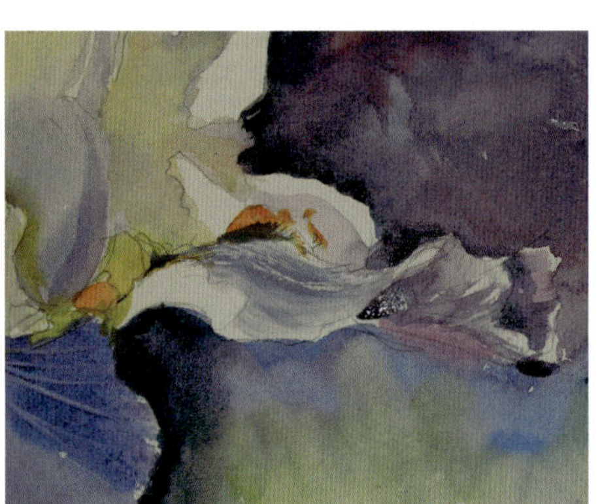

2 Add some very dark color along the edge to make that part of the flower stand out.

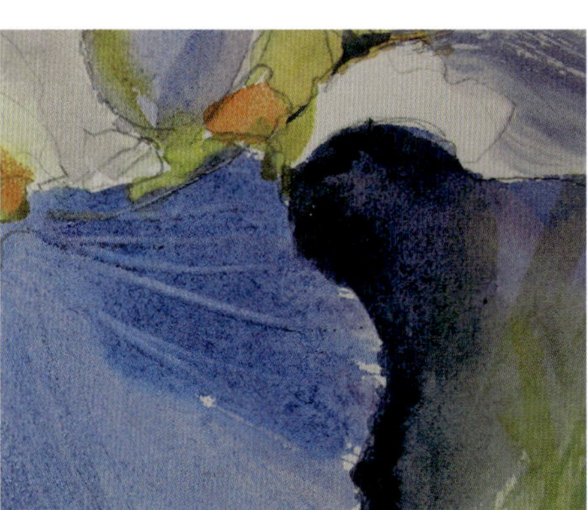

3 Continue to paint the dark outward, producing an even stronger effect.

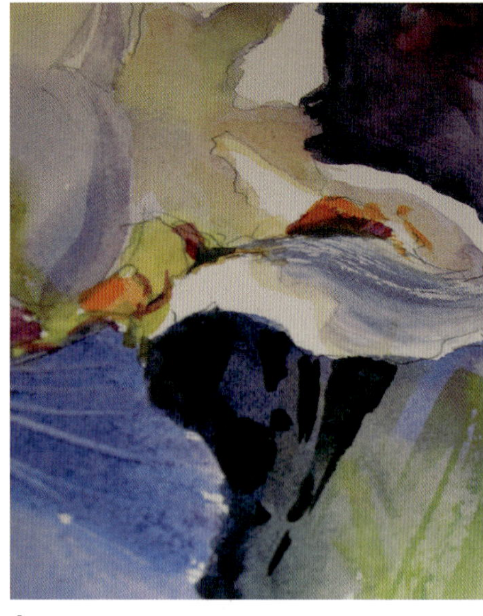

4 This application of dark leads into the negative painting of the flower's background. Glaze the violet above to a deeper value as well.

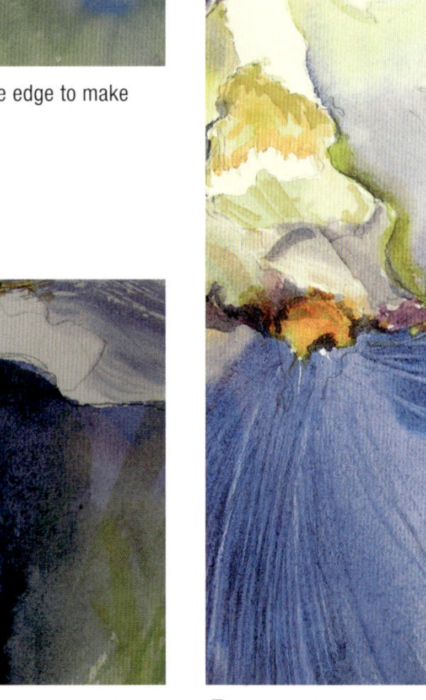

5 The iris stands out from the background due to the colorful shadows in the white of the flower and the rich dark that surrounds the flower.

NEGATIVE PAINTING

Negative painting is a way of painting into a shape to create the illusion of depth and the feeling that something is happening back there. Look carefully at the background in your photographs and you will find a jumble of abstract shapes that, from a distance, forms garden foliage.

1 First paint the positive shapes of the leaves, leaving (or reserving) the white of the paper for the pale flowers and the background areas.

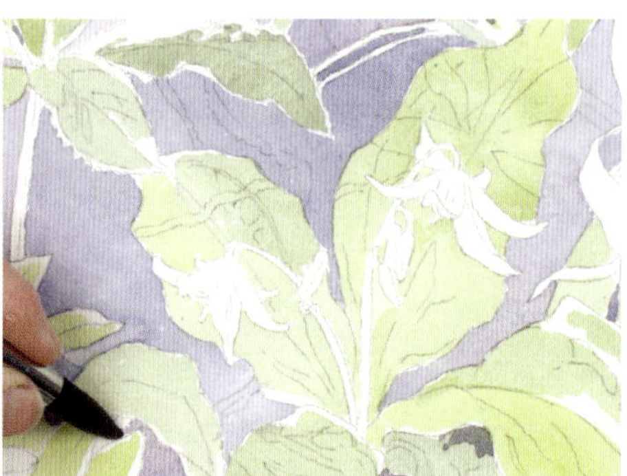

2 Paint the negative shapes of the background in a cool recessive wash.

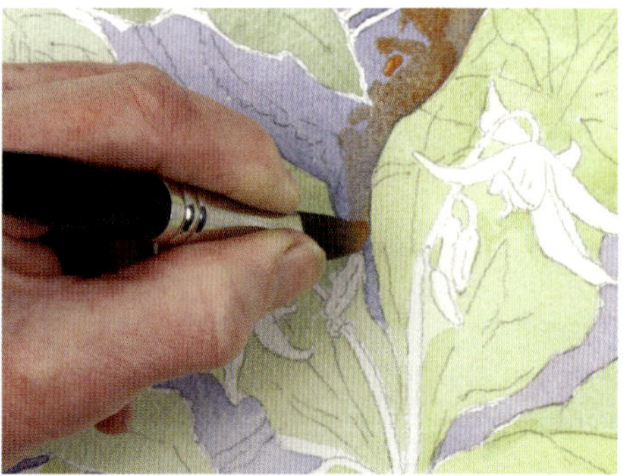

3 Pursue the tangle of shapes and shadows in the background, adding a glaze of orange to create interesting colors in the shadowy background.

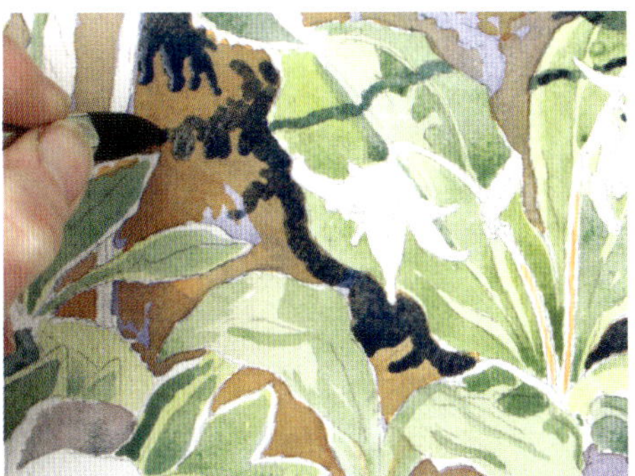

4 Add a darker blue to define the negative background area. Also add cast shadows on the leaves using the same blue.

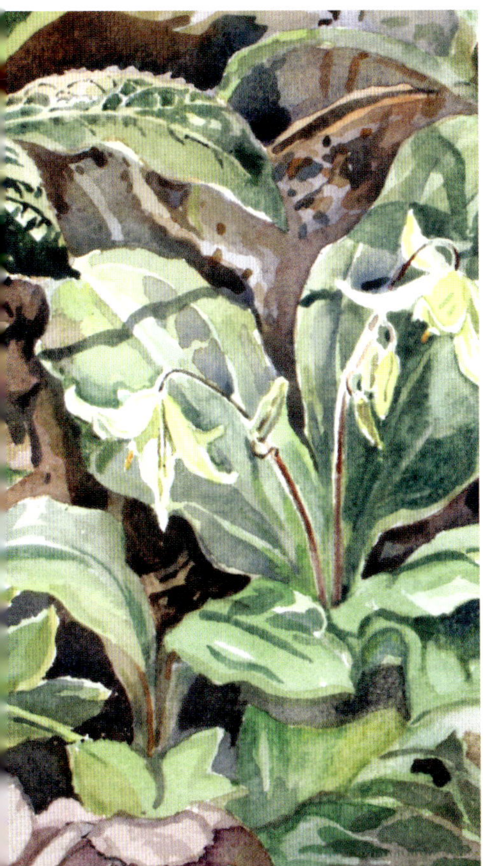

5 Every layer you paint into the negative space around the flower and leaves adds depth and interest to the entire painting. Notice these marks are simply abstract shapes.

POURING PAINT

Paint is often poured onto a painting, especially in the early stages, and also as an underpainting. This bottom layer will affect everything on top of it and can provide a warm or cool base from which to start. It gives unity to the whole painting. Generally a technique used for large paintings, you will need to stretch your paper to board first, because this will give you better control.

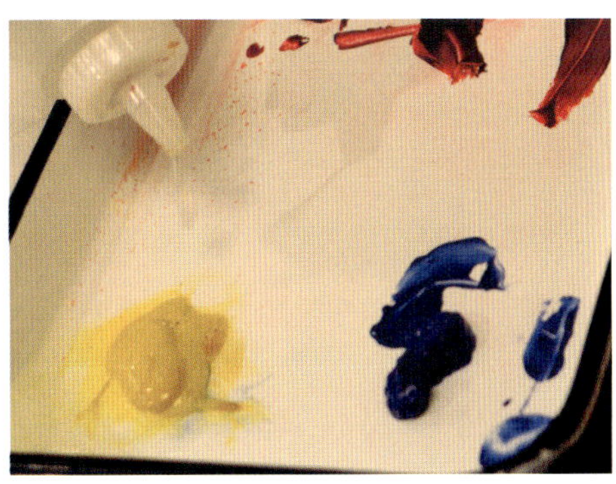

1 In a cup or the corner of a butcher tray, add clean water, with the tray tilted to keep it in the corner. Mix the first color—usually yellow—into a creamy mixture.

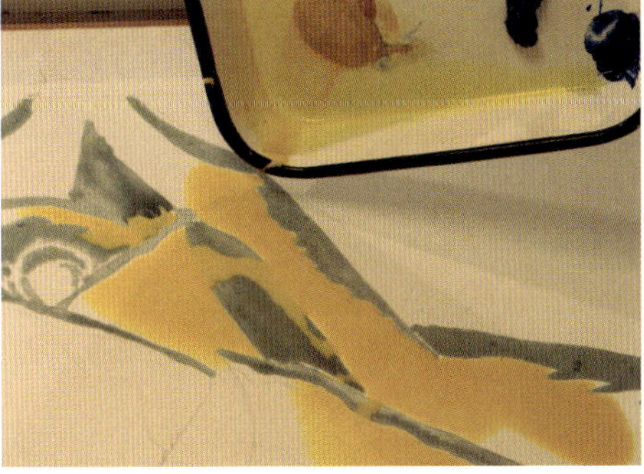

2 Paint the areas of highlights with masking fluid, allow to dry, then wet the paper with water. Pour the mixture onto the desired area. The paint will bleed into the wet paper—drag it into areas requiring the base.

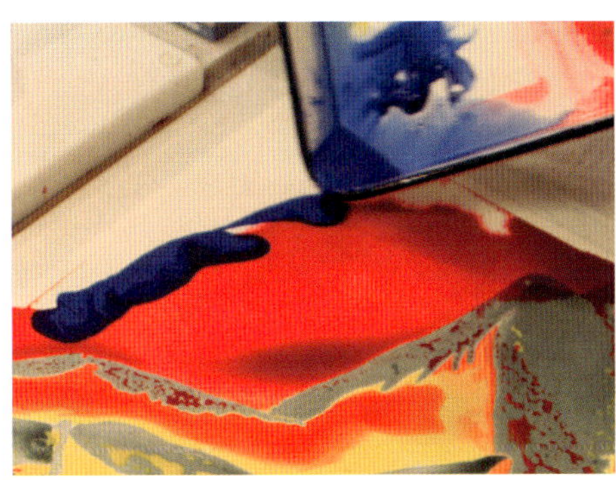

3 Repeat the process with red and blue.

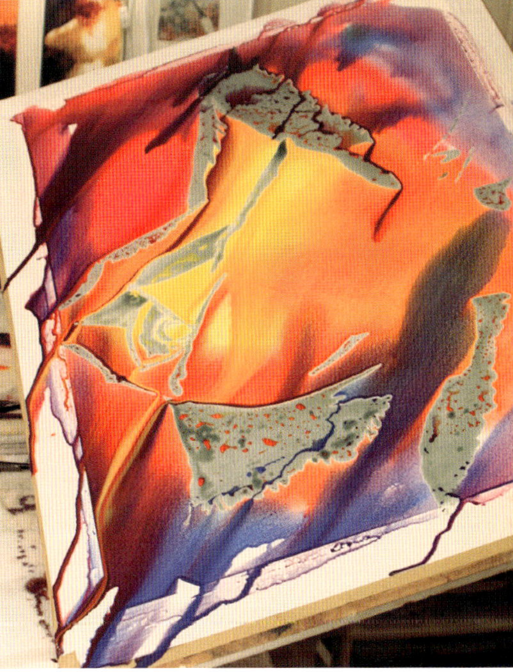

4 Tilt the board in all directions, letting the paint run until you are pleased with the look. Place the board on a flat surface and allow to dry. You can repeat this process. The result is a luminous, rich layer of color.

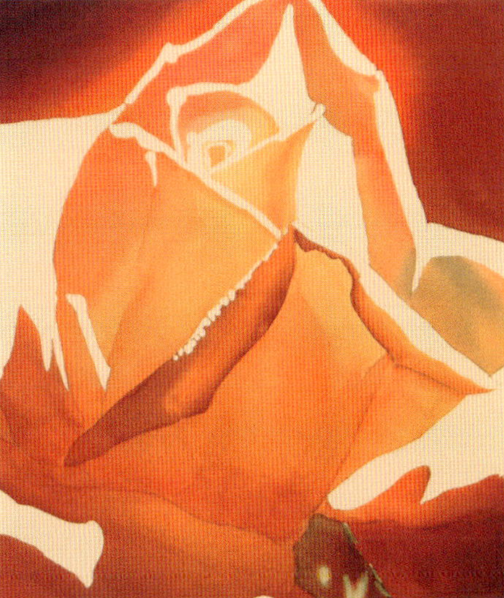

5 Remove the masking fluid to reveal the final effect of the pouring. (See p. 26 for the final painting.) See how the red has dominated the purple.

SALT

Use of table salt and kosher salt is one of the most common ways to create texture in a painting. Because it is used so often, it is wise to combine it with other techniques to avoid looking clichéd.

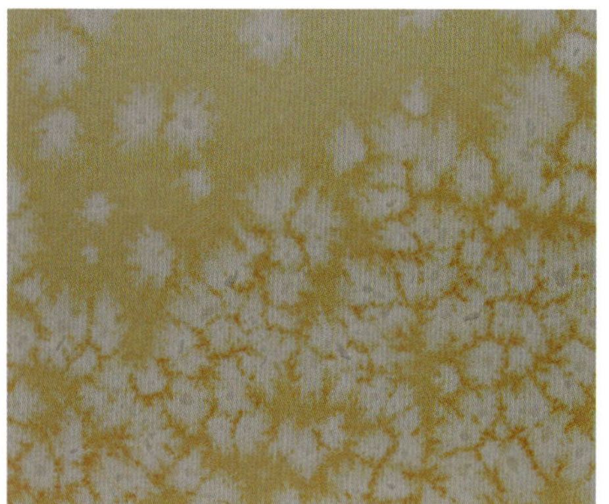

Kosher (coarse grind) salt applied to a wet wash. Note how the paint is absorbed and repelled by the salt.

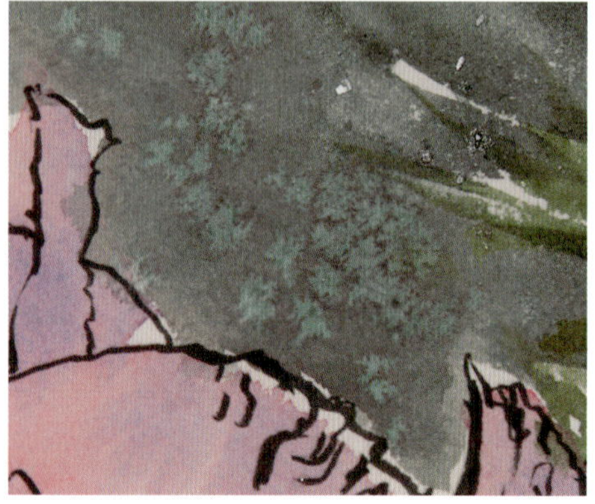

Salt applied to a mixture of two colors, at least one of which is a staining pigment, will allow the staining color to remain in the paper.

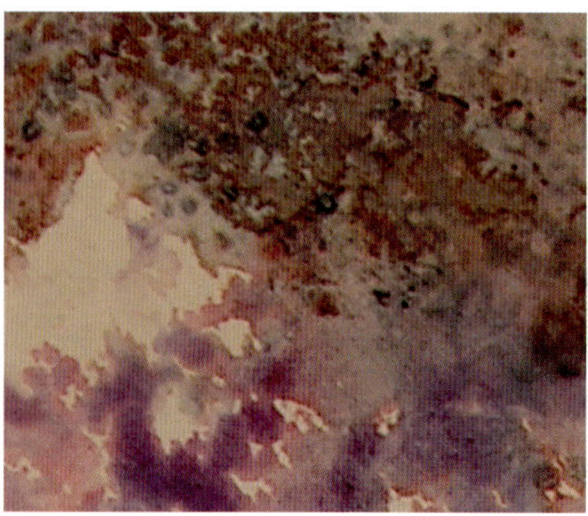

Lightly spritzing with water (see right) will also avoid the "salt only" look.

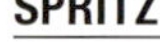

SPRITZ

Spritzing is a light spray of water from a pump or trigger spray bottle. A pump bottle is easier to control. The distance from which you spray determines the texture; spritzing close to the painting will create large water drops.

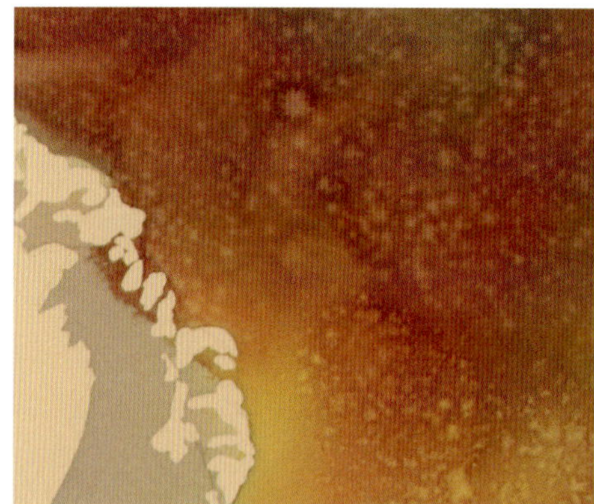

Spraying the background from between 18 inches and 24 inches (45 cm and 61 cm) produces a condensed texture.

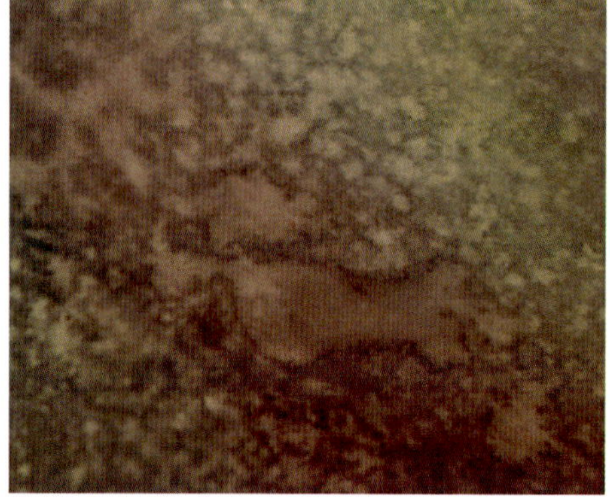

Spritzing with a pump bottle from 12 inches (30 cm) or so gives a varied pattern.

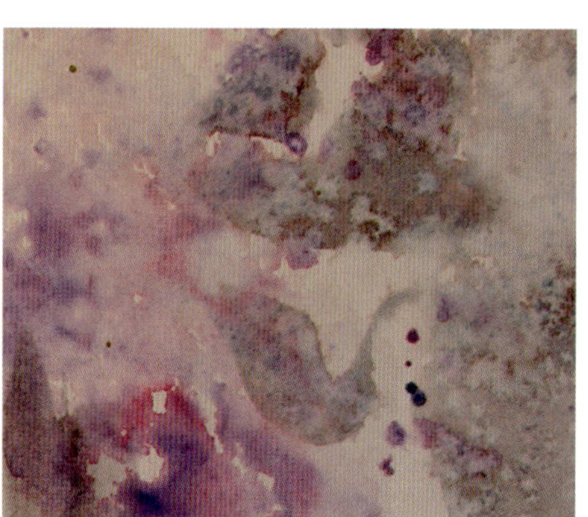

Spritzing combined with salt can give an interesting texture and is ideal for making lilacs.

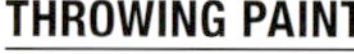

THROWING PAINT

Throwing paint is a controlled way to mimic foliage and branches. It works best with an oriental brush. Note: This is messy. Put up barriers, such as cardboard, to keep your area clean when you are "throwing."

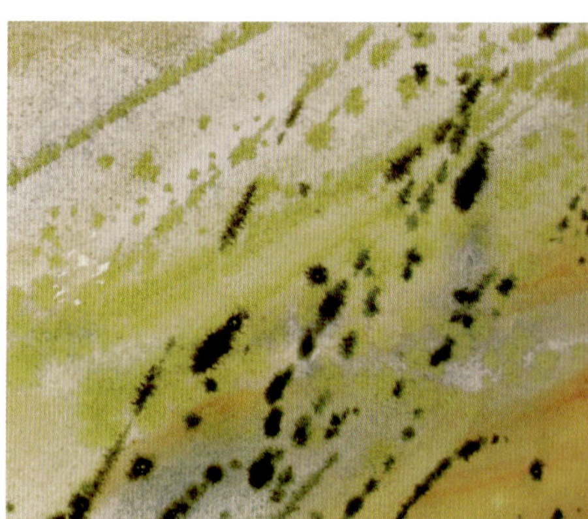

1 First, spritz the paper in the area to be covered. Then, protecting the uninvolved parts of the painting with paper towel, gently flick the brush at the angle you want the paint to land. This takes practice.

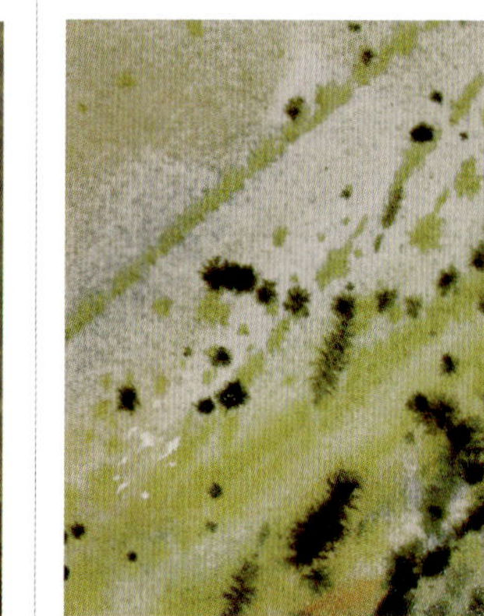

2 It may take several throws to produce the required effect.

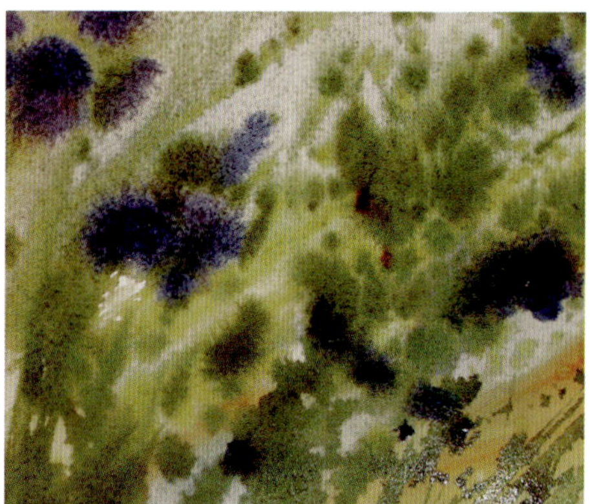

3 Here you can see that the thrown paint has blended and bachelor's buttons have been dropped in as well.

PENCIL AND WASH

For an artist wanting to sketch outdoors and carry only a sketchbook and pencil, this technique combines pencil drawing, done on site in detail, with a watercolor wash applied at a later time.

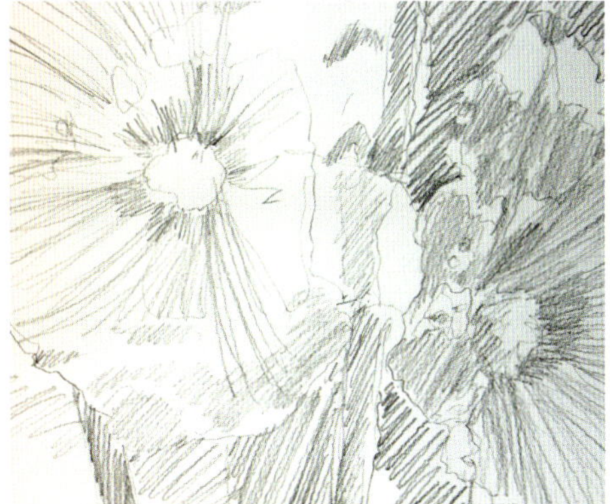

1 Draw a complete tonal drawing. The single hatched lines radiating from the flower provide detail of the shape and angle of the petals.

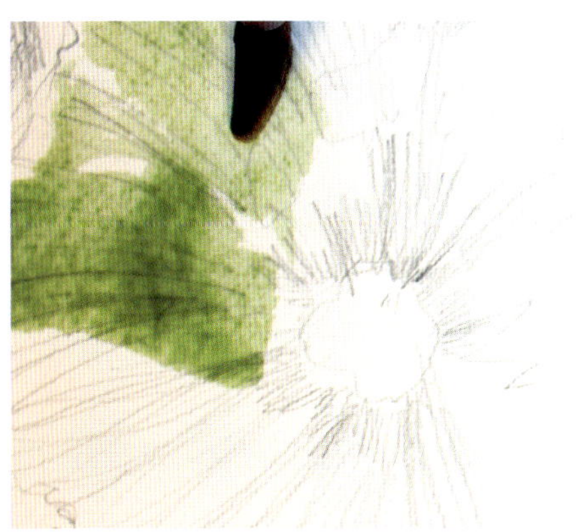

2 Keep washes fairly thin so the texture of the pencil shows through. Begin to lay in the color.

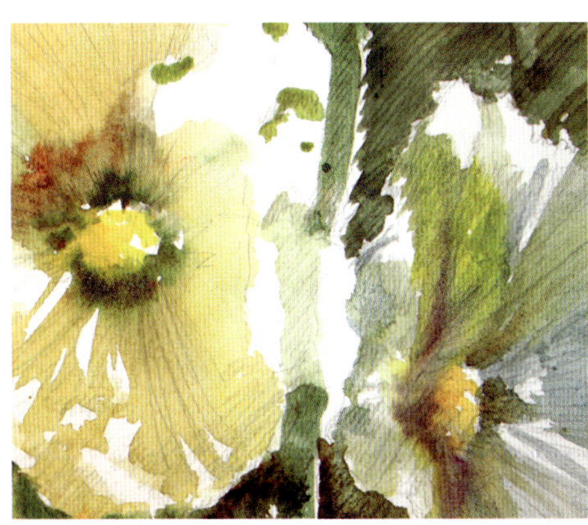

3 Maintaining transparency, move through the flower, dropping color into wet washes. Let the pigments flow into each other and outside the lines.

PEN AND WASH

Similar to pencil and wash, and generally employed for the same reasons, pen and wash also offers slightly different attributes. You can use permanent ink that will not run later when the wash is applied (below left), or you can use an ink pen that will run and join in the complete effect (below right).

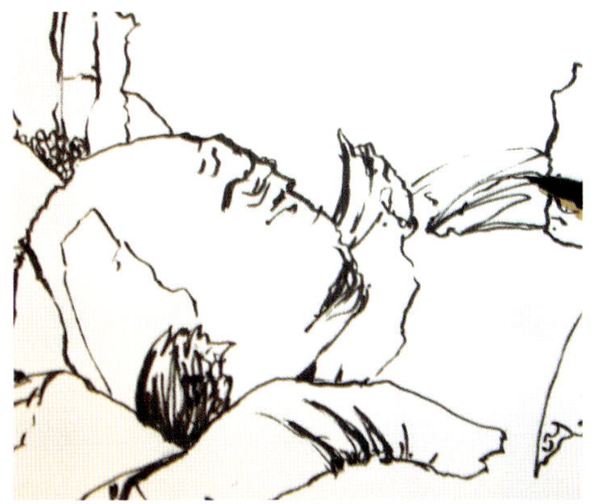

Permanent ink

1 Draw your flower with permanent ink and in as much detail as you would like. To include shading, use hatching or cross-hatching.

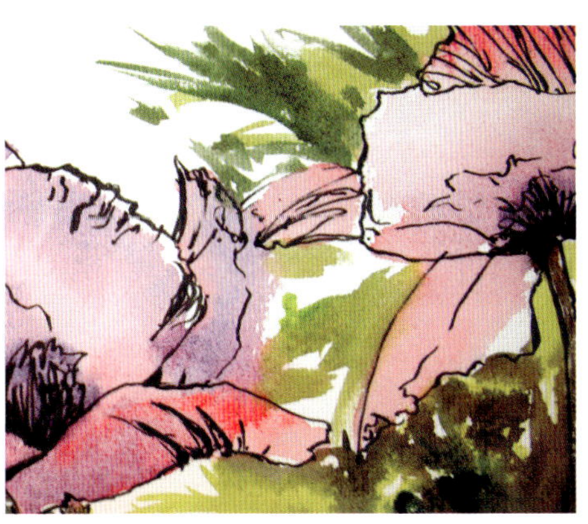

2 Paint in the color. You can see there is a slight "cartoon" look.

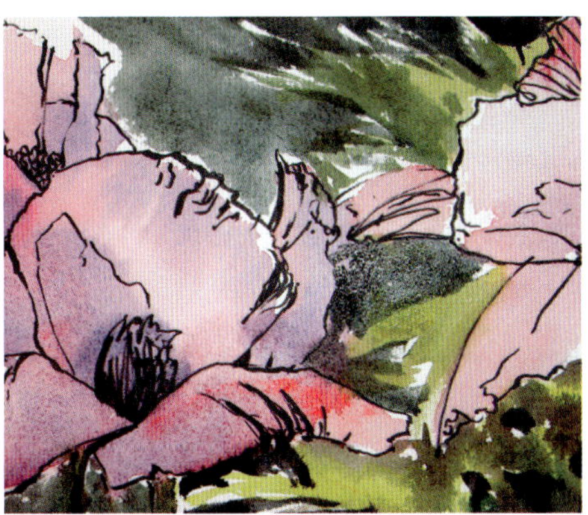

3 In the end, when the darkest values are applied, some or all of the cartoon look can disappear by use of dark washes.

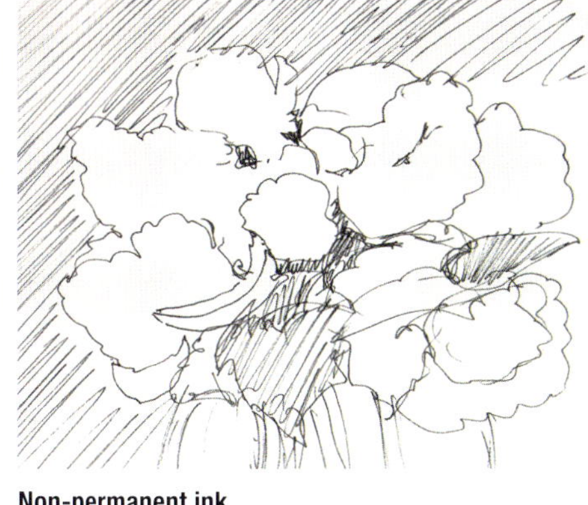

Non-permanent ink

1 Draw your flowers with a regular, non-permanent ink pen.

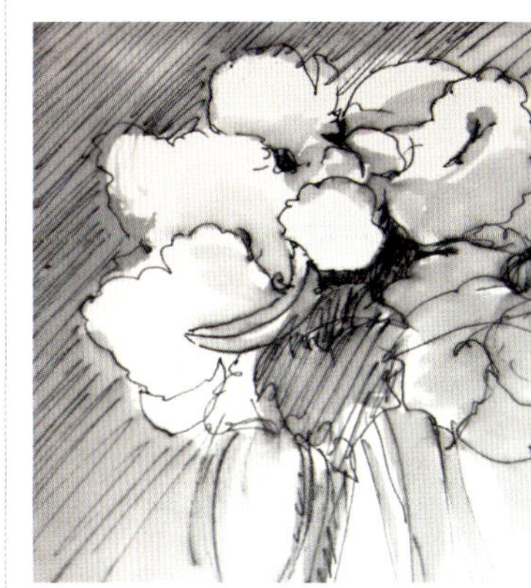

2 When the ink is dry, use a brush wet with only water to rewet the ink and shade the drawing with the dissolving ink.

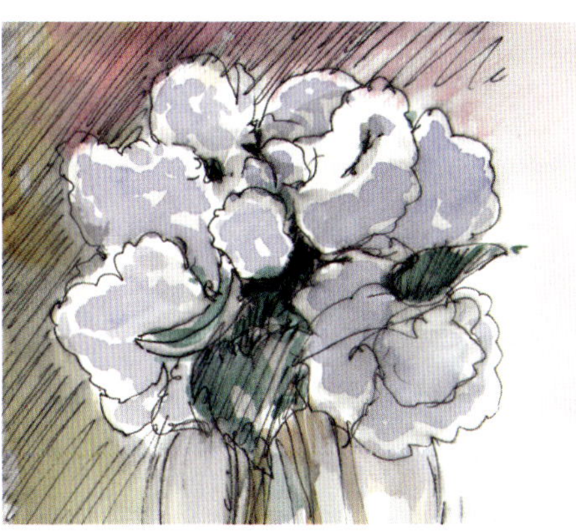

3 When the tonal drawing is dry, apply a watercolor wash, producing a subtle sketch of the flowers.

WATERCOLOR AND PASTEL

Pastel is pure pigment compressed to chalklike sticks. When pastel is used with watercolor, it has the effect of intensifying those areas by bringing pure and undiluted pigment to them. Breathing pastel dust is hazardous, so wear a protective mask and gloves.

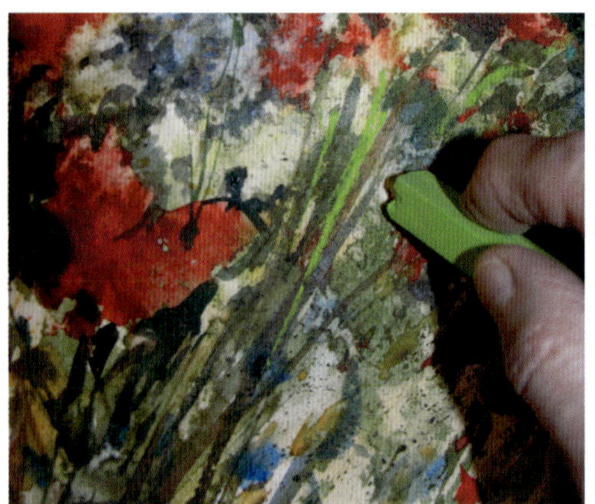

1 Use pastel as a simple stroke.

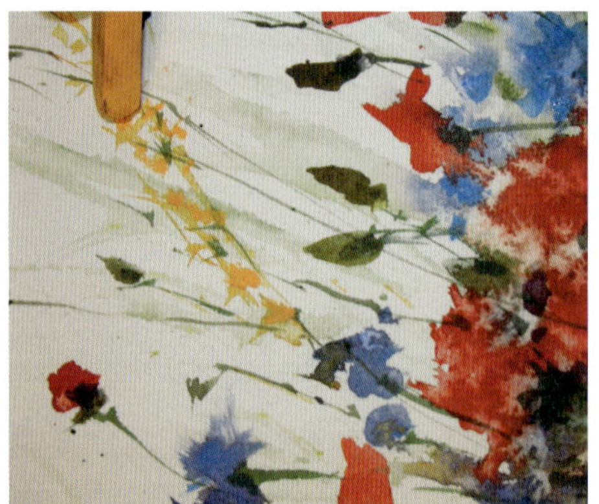

2 Use it to indicate tiny flowers that would get lost in a diluted wash.

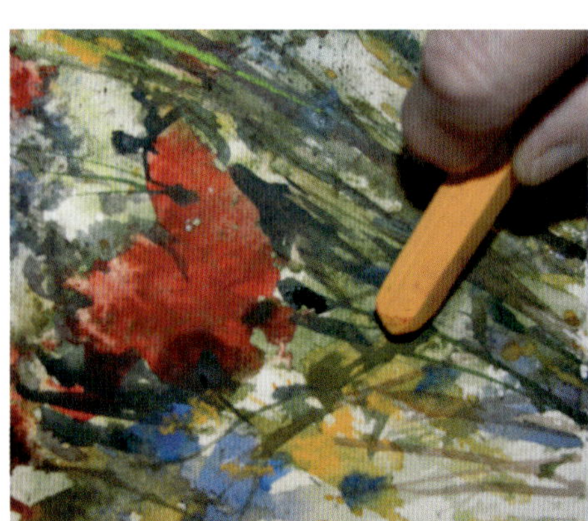

3 Use pastel's intensity to draw the viewer's eye to certain spots in the painting.

WATERCOLOR AND GOUACHE

Gouache is opaque watercolor; the same pigment as its transparent version with an opacifier added. It means that light colors can be painted over dark. It can be used for tiny details or highlights. Some artists use the opaque nature of gouache to produce body color mixes (a color mixed with white gouache), which can be laid over areas of the painting in flat or semi-opaque washes to produce a chalky effect.

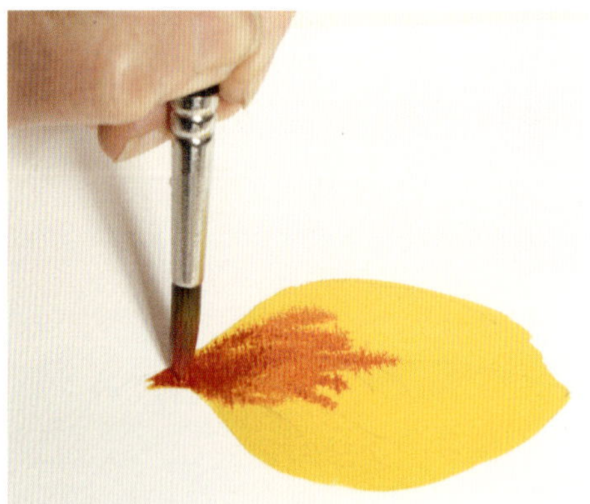

Gouache for details

1 Paint the petal with yellow and, when nearly dry, paint the petal markings with a darker red.

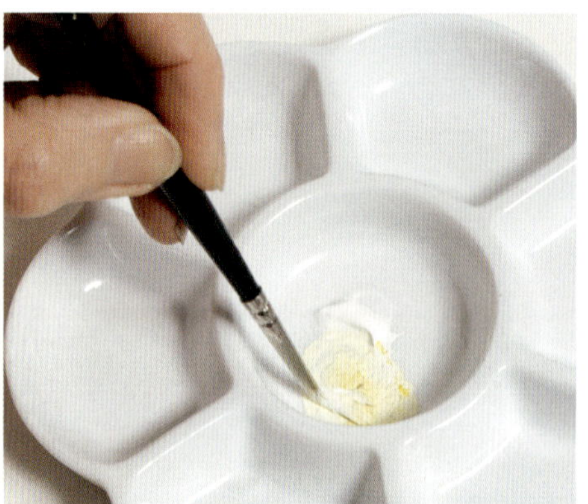

2 If tinting white gouache, avoid diluting the gouache too much; otherwise, it will not cover the earlier colors—you need only enough dilution to produce a painting consistency.

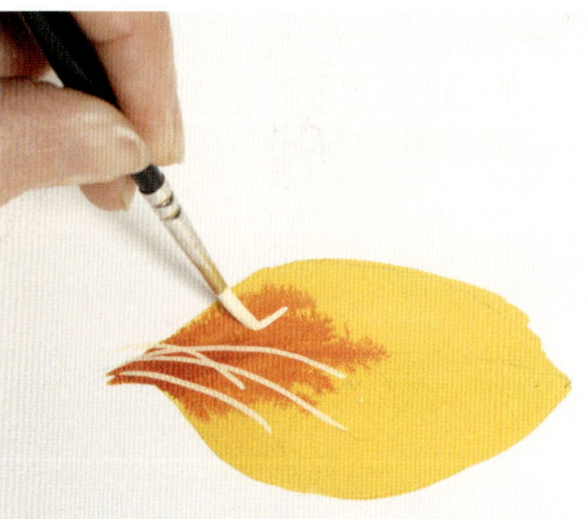

3 Paint in the stamen stalks with a small brush, using the body color sparingly, because gouache has a matte surface that can look dull and out of place beside a watercolor wash.

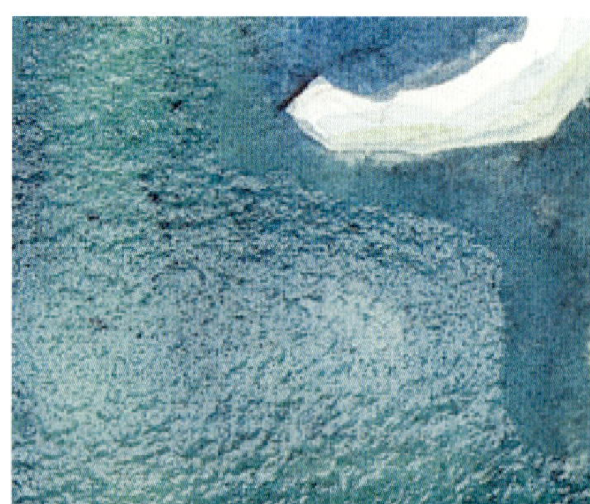

Gouache for highlights

1 Glaze washes of aureolin yellow, phthalo blue, and indigo over each other to create a dark background.

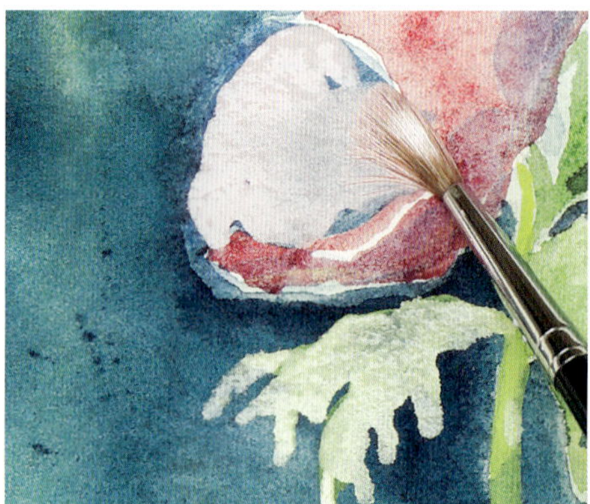

2 In a palette, mix watercolors with white gouache to create two colors, for the leaves and petals. The colors need to be much lighter than required because they will sink into the wash background once applied.

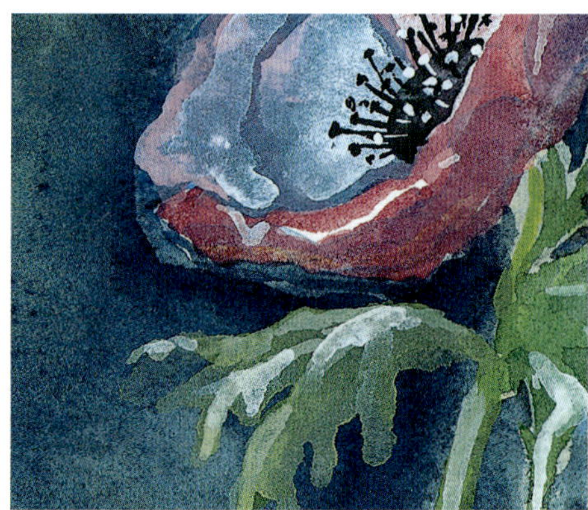

3 The technique would not be used over the whole painting. Here, the chalky highlights on the petals and leaves fade into the background, giving a sense of form.

WATERCOLOR PENCIL

Watercolor pigment also comes in pencil form, either as traditional pencils or as solid sticks of hardened pigment. In either form, pencils are great for drawing or painting while traveling or outdoors. The drawing can be wet at any time later, and a painting will result.

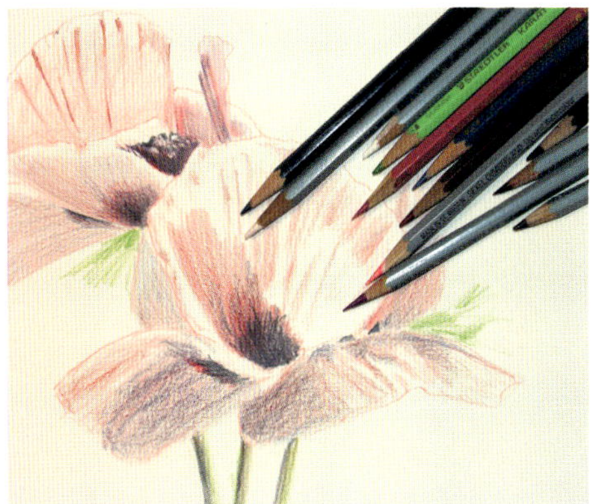

1 Choose a selection of pencils and then make a tonal drawing.

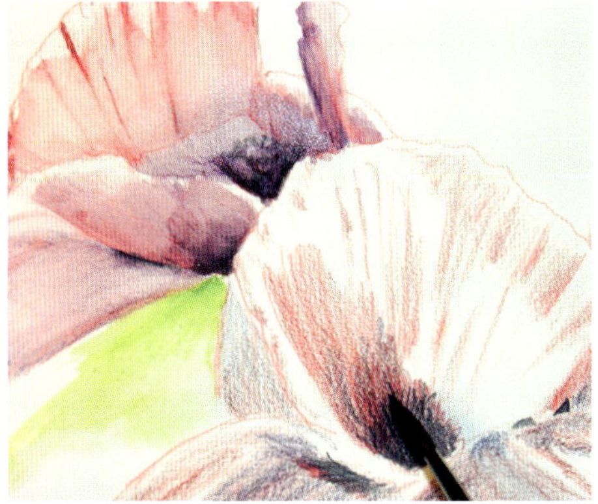

2 When the drawing is complete, use a brush with plain water to turn the drawing into a painting.

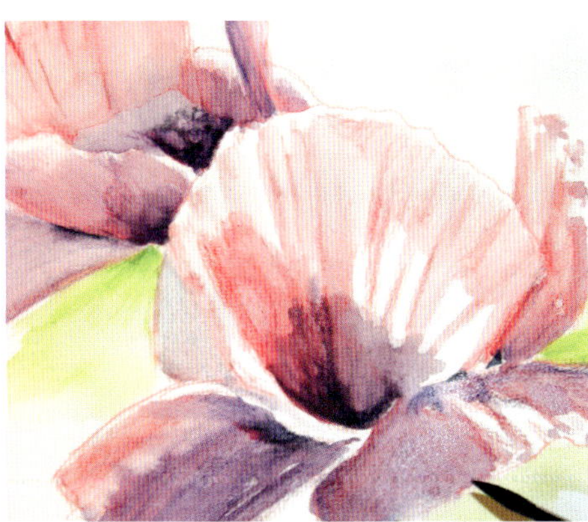

3 A second layer of pencil on the dry painting deepens the value in some areas.

WATERCOLOR CRAYON

Although similar to watercolor pencils, watercolor crayons look and feel like those colored sticks you used as a child. They have a waxy feel when applied but are water-soluble and can be used in the same way as the watercolor pencils.

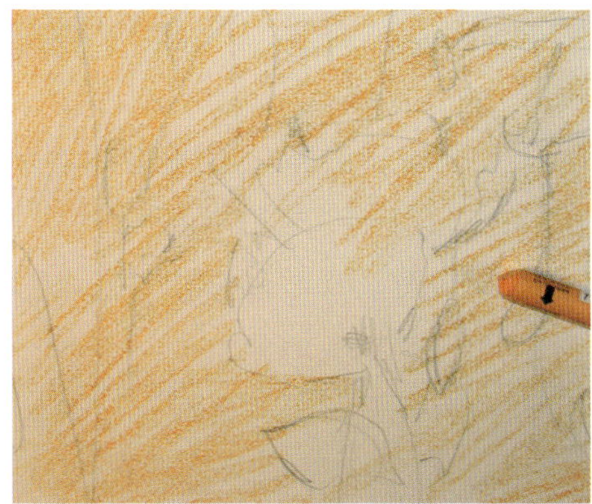

1 Call out all the elements to be drawn with a quick pencil sketch. Cover the drawing in scribbled crayon.

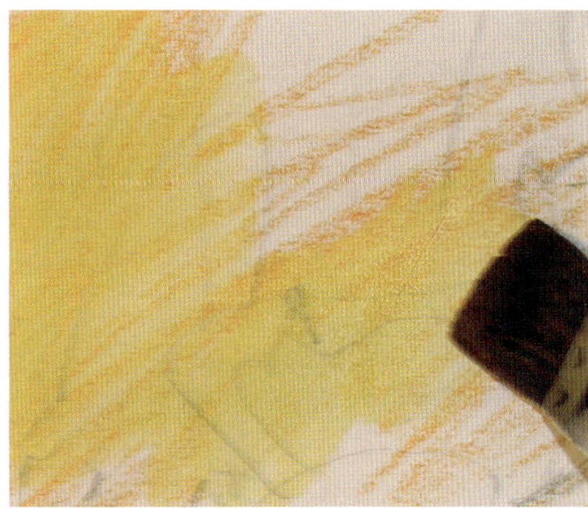

2 Use a wet brush to turn the scribble into rich color.

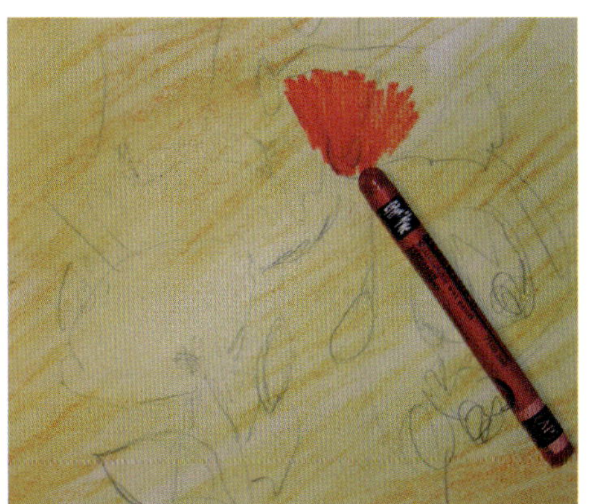

3 While the yellow is wet, draw right into it with a red crayon. An intense color will result.

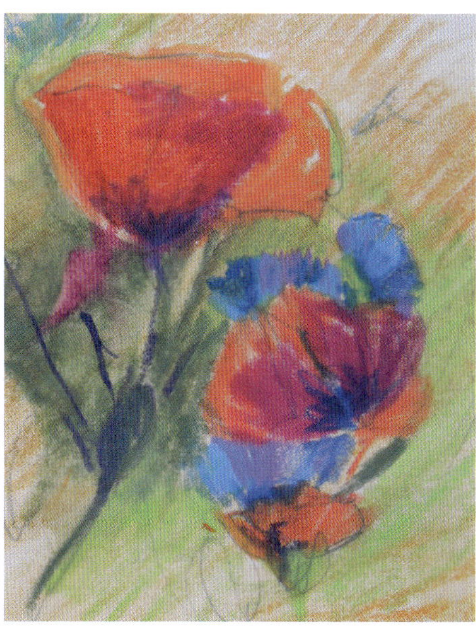

4 Finish the sketch. All of this can be drawn dry and painted later.

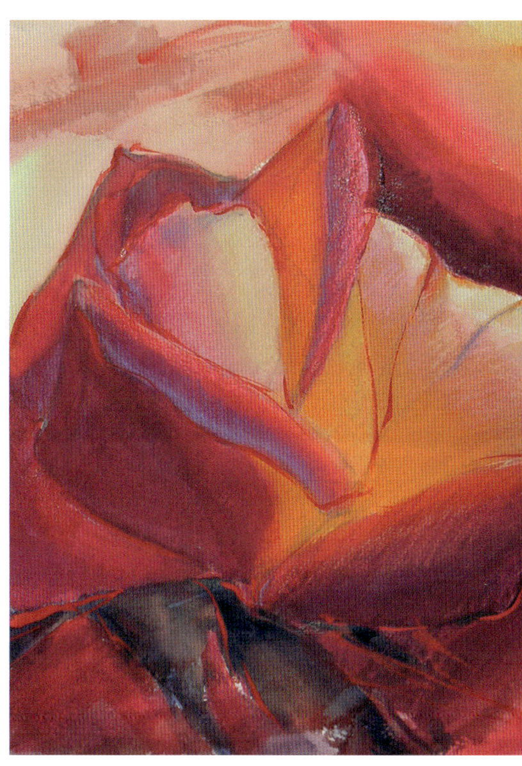

A painting with washes of transparent watercolor and lines of gouache. When these lines were almost dry, watercolor crayon was used to heighten the color and gouache to heighten the detail.

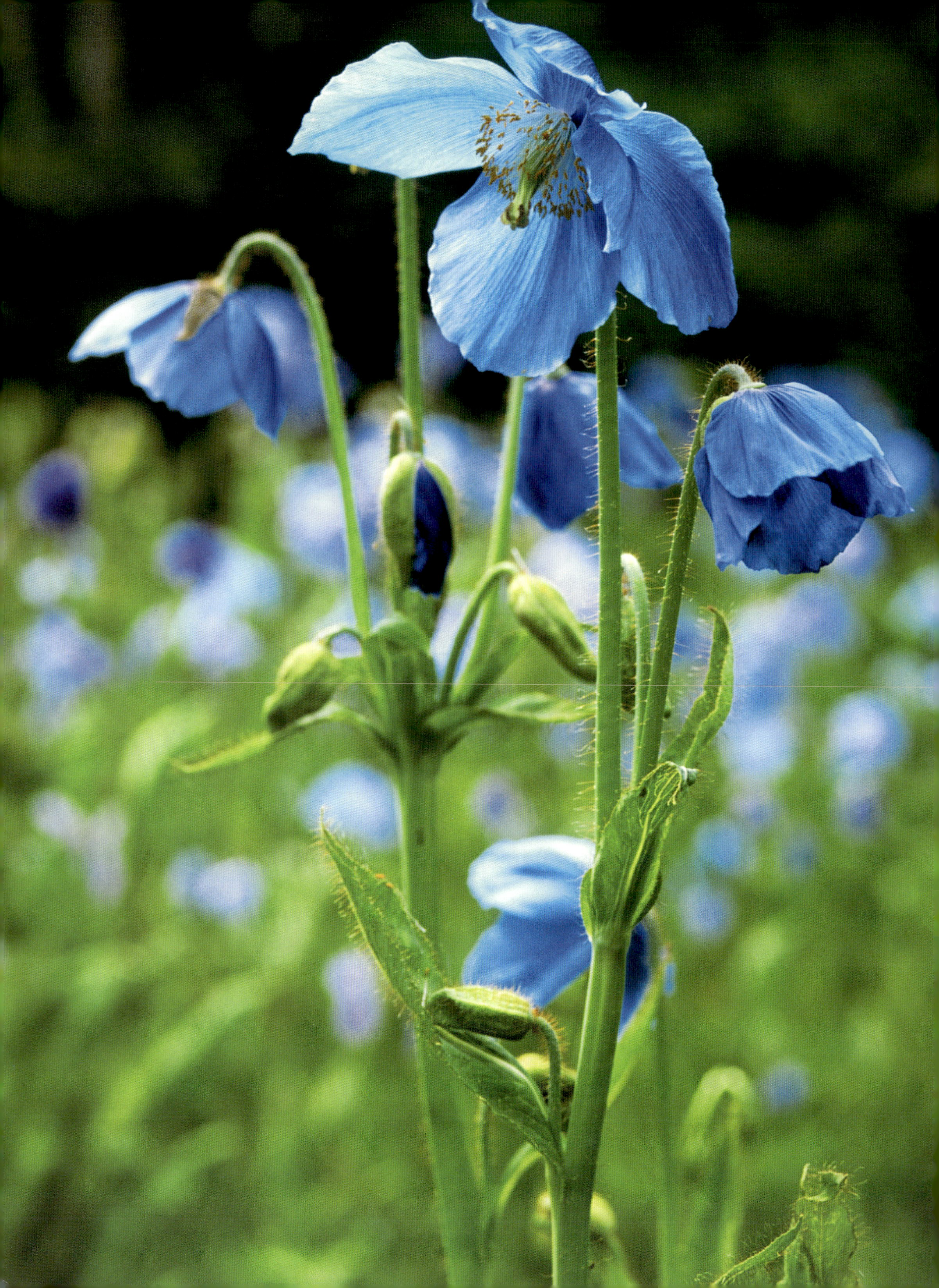

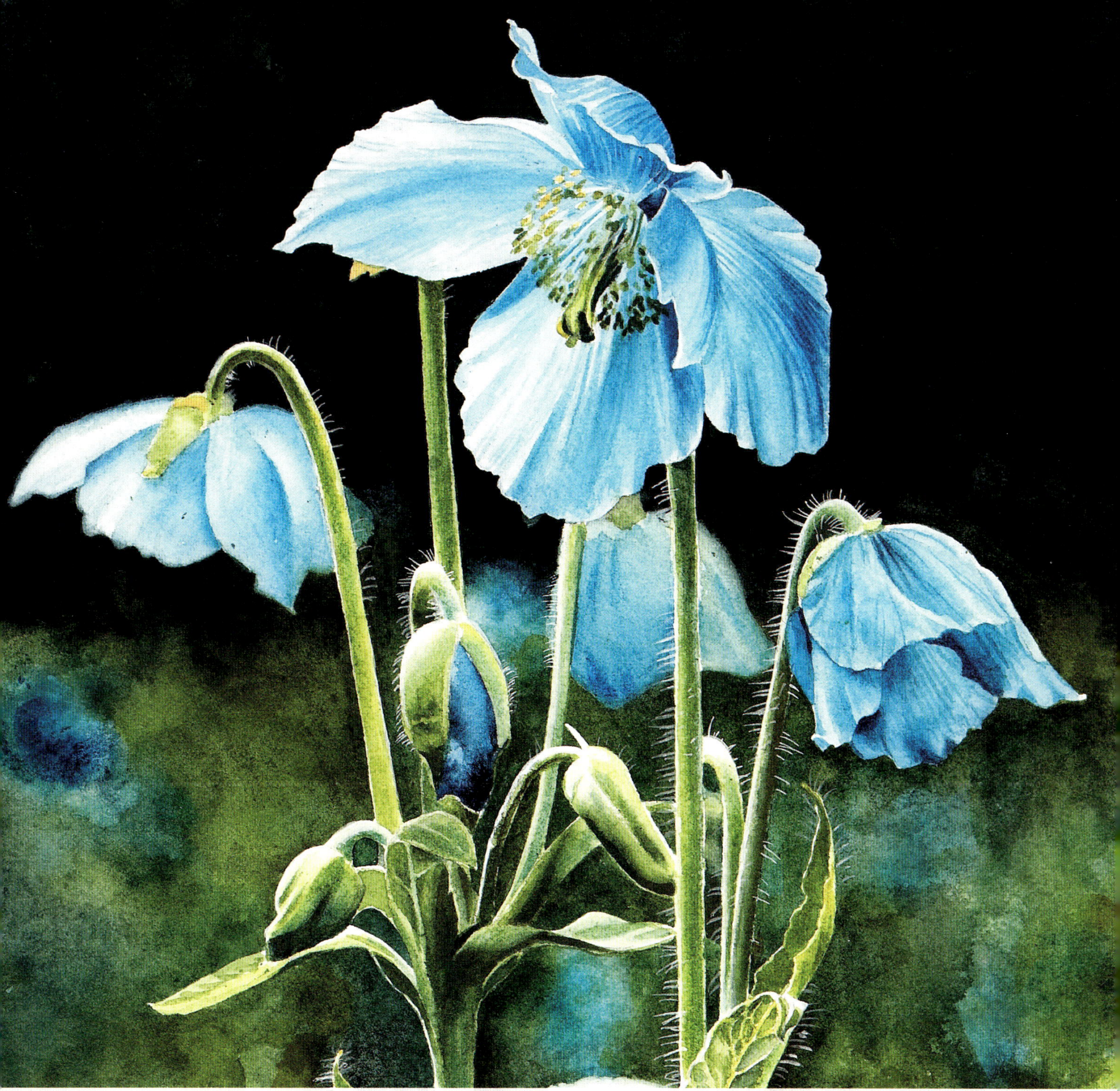

Projects

The flower photographs and their associated step-by-step paintings are divided into portrait and landscape formats. Within these two formats, the flowers are loosely grouped into three categories—Single Specimens, Floral Still Life, and Flowers Outdoors—so that you can find quickly and easily the right subject for your painting.

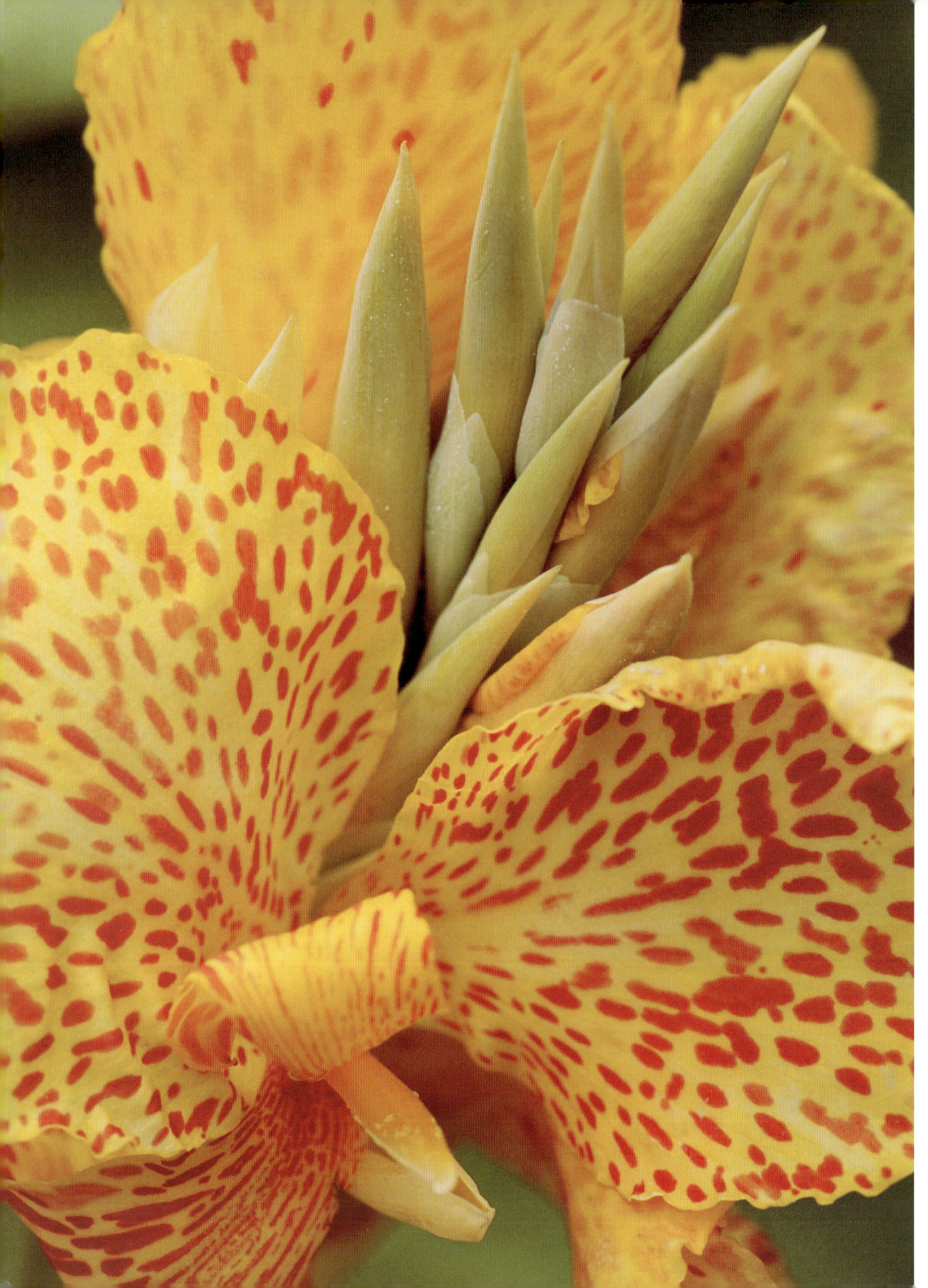

Indian Reed Lily

A high-key painting dominated by light values presents a challenge—incorporating interesting dark values without creating harsh contrasts.

PAINTS
Aureolin
Hansa yellow medium
New gamboge
Organic vermilion
Perylene red
Phthalo blue
Phthalo green
Quinacridone rose
Sap green

TOOLS & MATERIALS
Cold-pressed paper, 140 lb. (300 gsm)
HB drawing pencil
Masquepen
Round brushes, Nos. 6, 8, 10
Tissues
½-in. (1-cm) flat chisel brush
Soft-bristled scrubber
Rigger

TECHNIQUES USED
Variegated wash, *p. 20*
Mixing paint in the palette, *p. 21*
Mixing paint on the paper, *p. 21*
Dropping in color, *p. 21*
Wet-onto-dry, *p. 22*
Wet-into-wet, *p. 22*
Glazing, *p. 23*
Masking for details, *p. 25*
Softening masked edges, *p. 25*
Adding highlights, *p. 27*
Shadows, *p. 28*

1 Make an accurate drawing of the flower. Sketched lines should be faint or easily lightened with an eraser before painting over them. Use a Masquepen to draw a thin line of masking fluid along the lightest edge of each bud and petal (inset). Let the masking fluid dry completely before beginning to paint.

2 When using yellow pigments, maximum value contrast can be achieved with multiple thin glazes of color. To avoid lifting the initial layers when applying subsequent glazes, paint wet-into-wet. With a No. 10 brush, apply water to a petal. When the sheen has disappeared, brush on another thin wash of water. For a variegated wash, drop in aureolin for the cool, light value areas, and Hansa yellow medium and new gamboge for darker values.

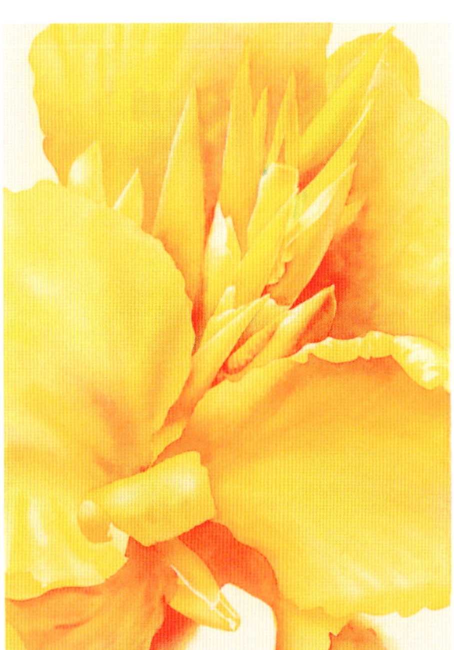

3 Remove the masking fluid. Soften the masked edges by stroking a wet No. 6 round brush over the edge and blotting with a tissue. Similarly, ease out and lift any paint buildup along the edges. With a No. 8 brush, use wet-into-wet with only one glaze of water to lay in two to three thin washes of color. Add a touch of cool phthalo green to the light side of the buds and warm sap green to the shadowed side. Introduce organic vermilion on the shadowed petals and between the buds.

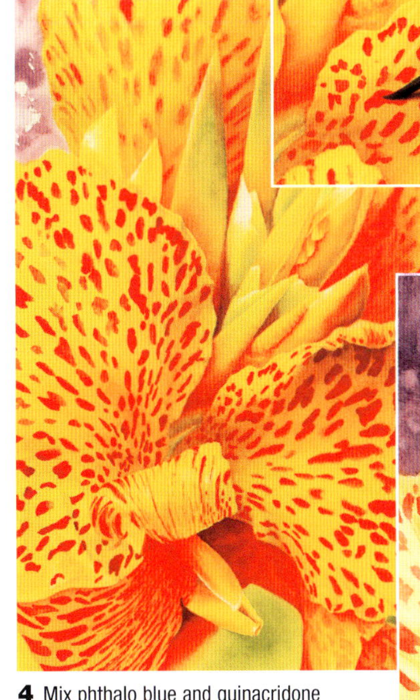

4 Mix phthalo blue and quinacridone rose for the upper background and drop wet-into-wet with a No. 10 brush. Use a watery sap green and new gamboge mix for a subtle shadow color. Paint the bold red lines and splashes with organic vermilion and perylene red with a No. 6 brush (inset). When dry, apply a second glaze. Deepen the shadows between the buds using sap green and vermilion.

5 Use a ½ in. (1 cm) damp chisel brush and scrubber to lift paint from the light edges. Create fine striations on the buds with varying mixes of sap green, new gamboge, and organic vermilion. Using a rigger, lightly paint the lines wet-on-dry with sweeping strokes. Apply a second layer to the lines in shadowed area.

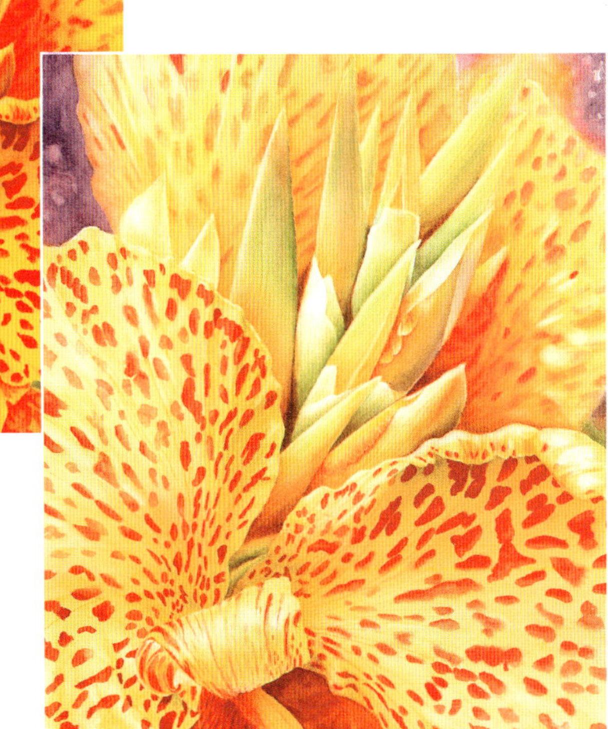

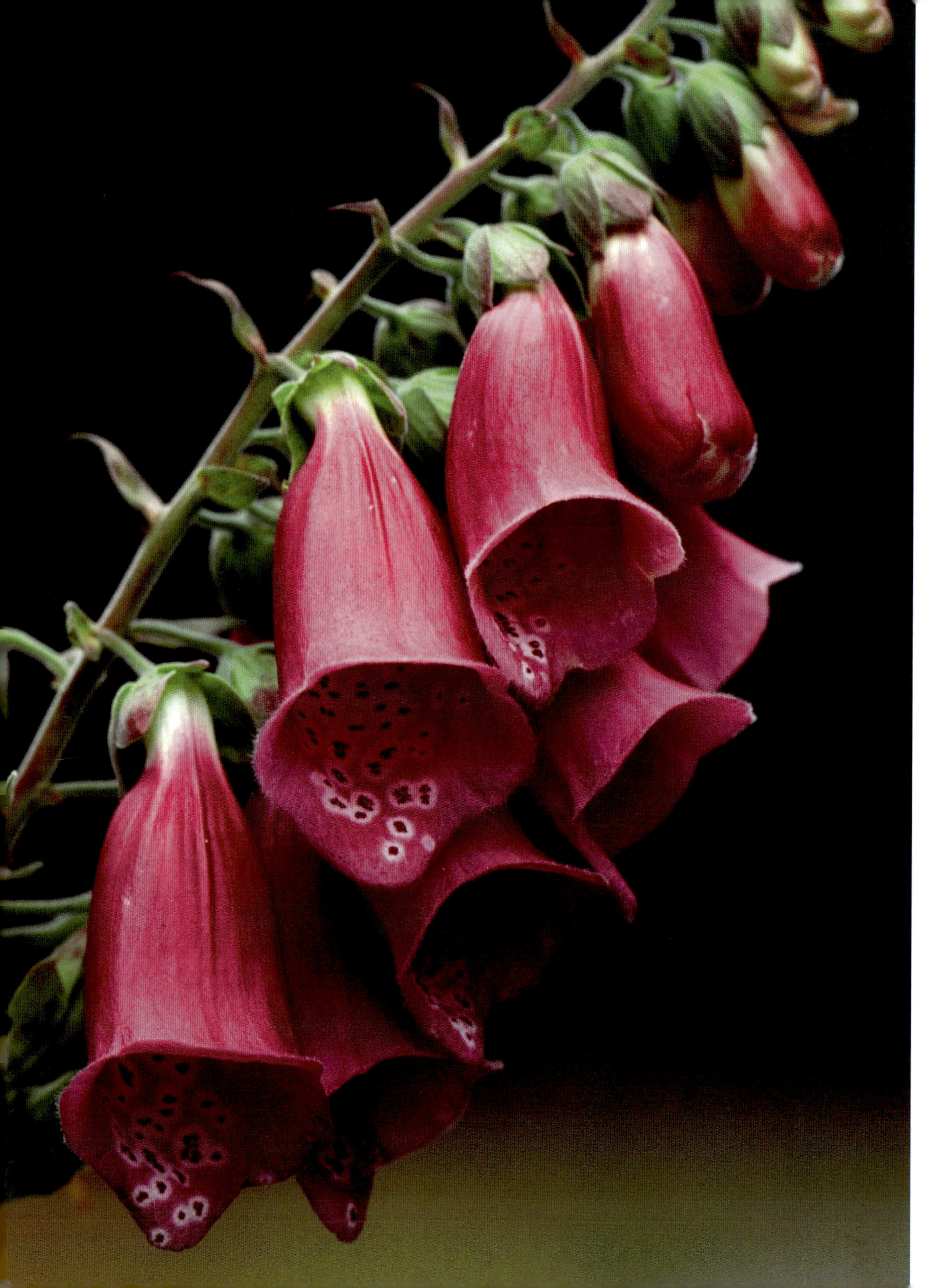

Foxglove

The artist was drawn to the startling complementary play between the multiple greens and the rose-magenta colored flowers. Very little artistic alteration was made to the photograph.

PAINTS
Cobalt blue
French ultramarine blue
Phthalo green
Quinacridone burnt scarlet
Quinacridone coral
Quinacridone gold
Quinacridone magenta
Quinacridone pink
Quinacridone red
Quinacridone rose
Quinacridone violet

TOOLS & MATERIALS
Cold-pressed paper, 140 lb. (300 gsm)
Mechanical pencil
Masking fluid
Old brush
Masking film
3-in. (7.5-cm) wash brush
1-in. (2.5-cm) flat brush
Round brushes, Nos. 6, 10, 14
Liner
Fritch scrubber, No. 2
Tissues and paper towels
Sharp tool, such as a seam ripper

TECHNIQUES USED
Graded wash, *p. 20*
Mixing paint in the palette, *p. 21*
Dropping in color, *p. 21*
Wet-onto-dry, *p. 22*
Wet-into-wet, *p. 22*
Glazing, *p. 23*
Blending, *p. 24*
Lost and found edges, *p. 24*
Masking to reserve the paper, *p. 25*
Shadows, *p. 28*

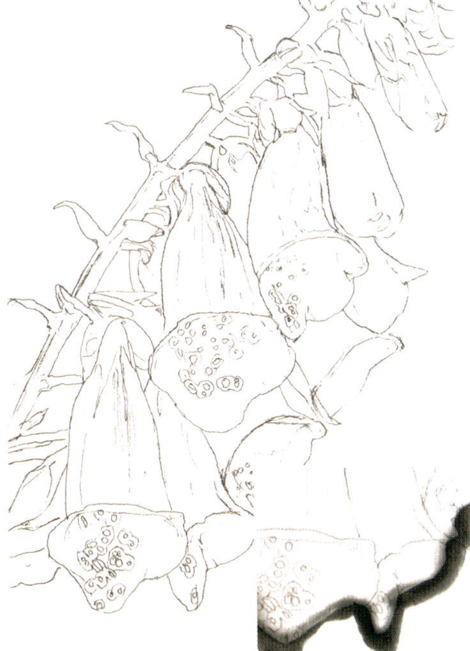

1 Do a detailed drawing from the photograph. Mask over the entire area of flowers including the "holes" in the stem area where the background can be seen. Cut out from masking film an approximate form, leaving ½ in. (1 cm) around the edge. Apply masking fluid to seal the film (inset). Extend it out to the edge of the stem and flowers. When dry, apply a second coat to avoid any seepage.

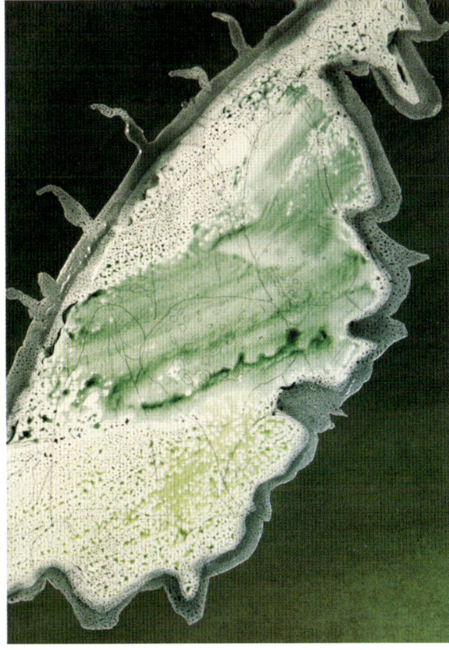

2 With a 3-in. (7.5-cm) wash brush, lay down several layers of graded wash, drying between applications. Begin with a strong yellow. If the first layer dries too light, dry, apply again, and dry. Follow the yellow with a medium-value red. Then mix a natural-looking green to glaze several layers until you achieve the desired depth. Remove masking, mix a green to match the background, and fill in the "holes" with this color.

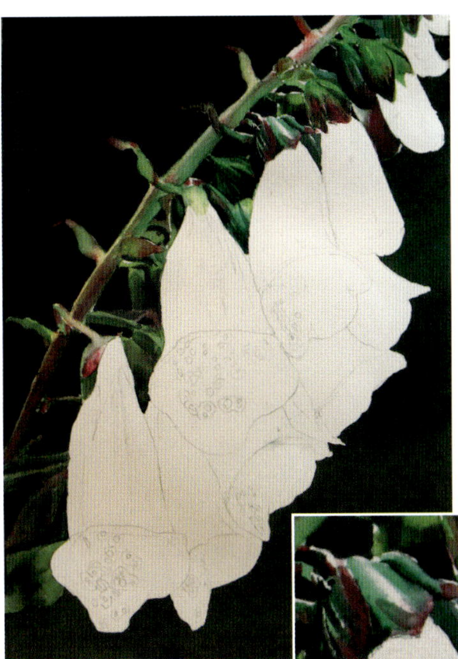

3 Study the photograph to understand the complex layers of stems and leaves that top each flower. Use a green with some cobalt blue to cool it for the deeper layers (the blue makes the stems and leaves recede), and a warmer green with some red and yellow added to it to bring the rest forward (inset). Green and red will make gray if mixed, so when you paint the red variegation in the green areas be sure the green is dry. Choose the appropriate brush size for the size of the area you are painting.

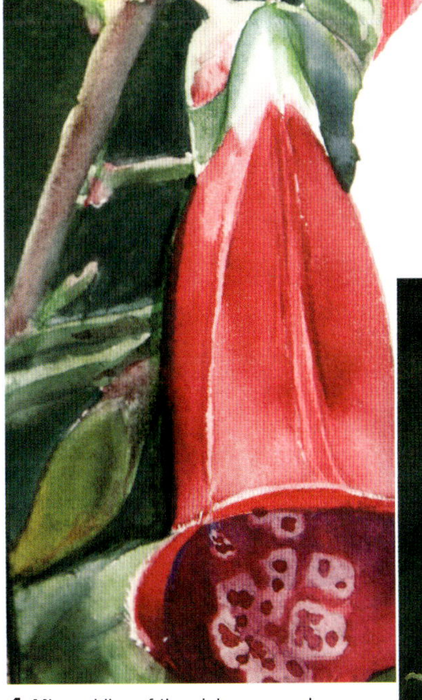

4 Mix puddles of the pink, rose, and magenta quinacridone colors to the consistency of cream. Paint each hanging flower with your 1-in. (2.5-cm) flat brush. Dab in highlights with tissue paper where the light hits the flower. Use violet and cobalt blue for the shadows. Leave the paper white where the bell meets the stem. When dry, use a diluted, warm yellow to warm up the white.

5 Paint around the inside white spots with a deeper mixture of the outside color (by adding blue or quinacridone violet), using a small round brush. When dry, with a damp 1-in. (2.5-cm) flat brush, stroke across the white spots to bring some color across the white. Dry and apply the darker spots with a liner and using quinacridone violet. When the painting is dry, use a sharp tool to scratch the furry edge of the bell.

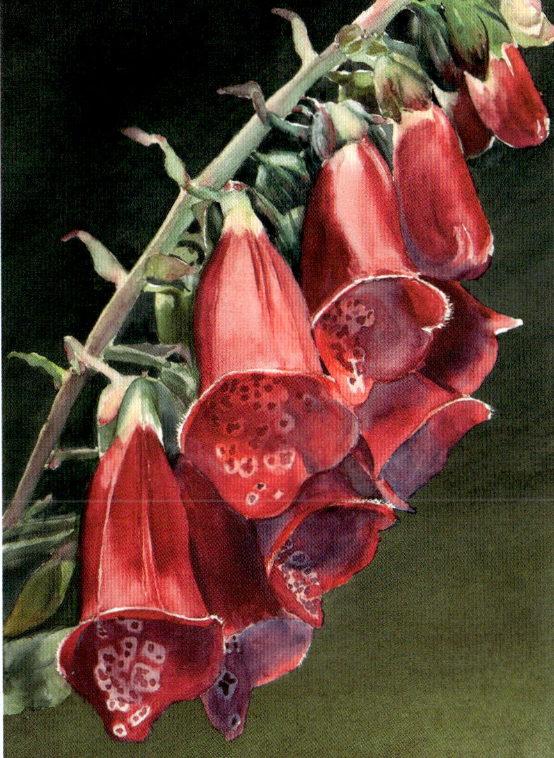

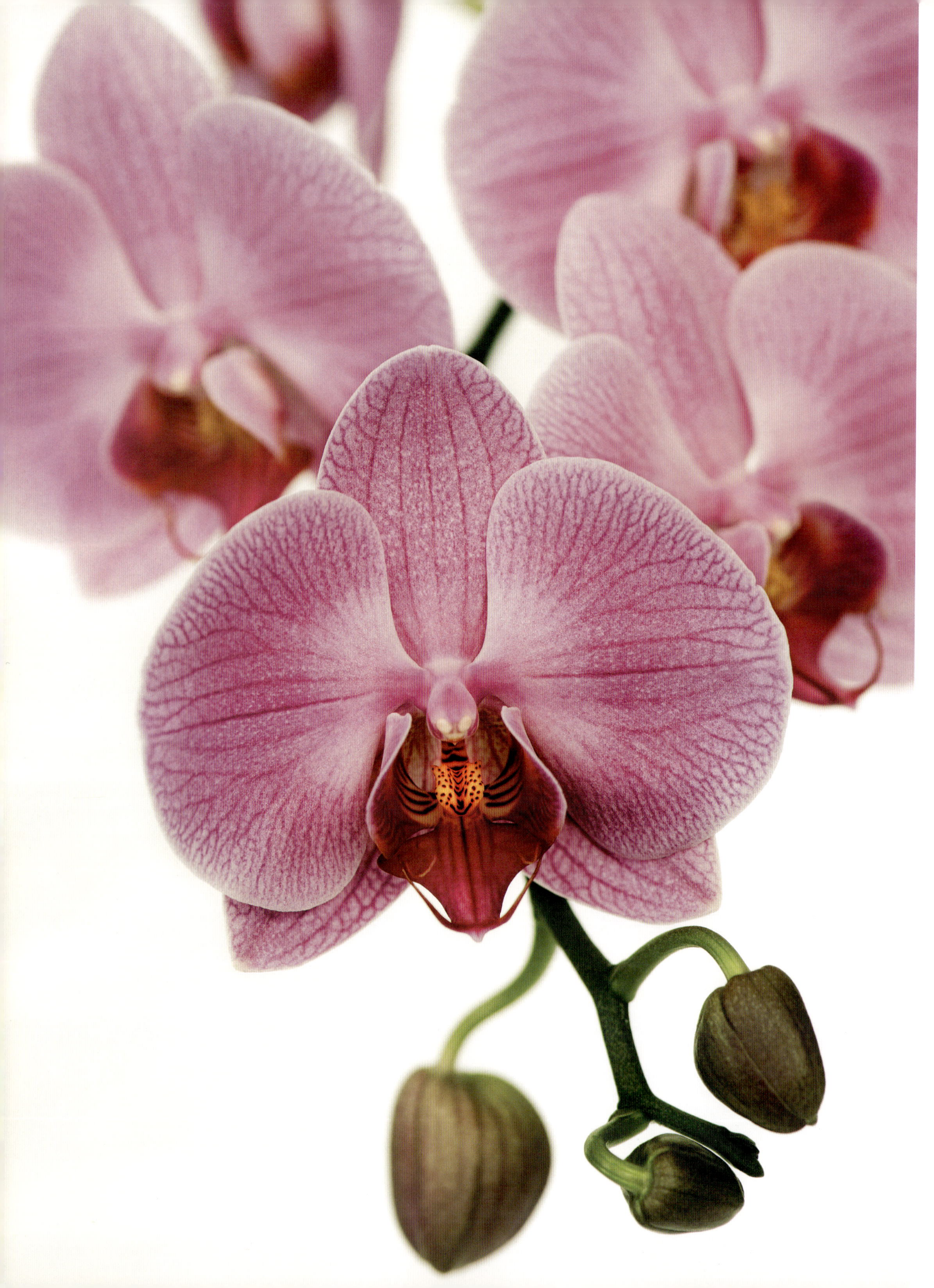

Orchids

The artist's challenge was to find the right combination of pigments that would express the delicate simplicity of the flowers with their brilliant pink color, and that would behave wet-into-wet with just the right amount of movement and blending.

PAINTS
Cobalt blue
French ultramarine blue
New gamboge
Permanent sap green
Purple madder
Quinacridone magenta
Scarlet lake

TOOLS & MATERIALS
Cold-pressed paper, 140 lb. (300 gsm)
HB pencil
Small pointed round brush
Round brush, No. 5
Tissues

TECHNIQUES USED
Mixing paint in the palette, *p. 21*
Mixing paint on the paper, *p. 21*
Wet-onto-dry, *p. 22*
Wet-into-wet, *p. 22*
Lost and found edges, *p. 24*

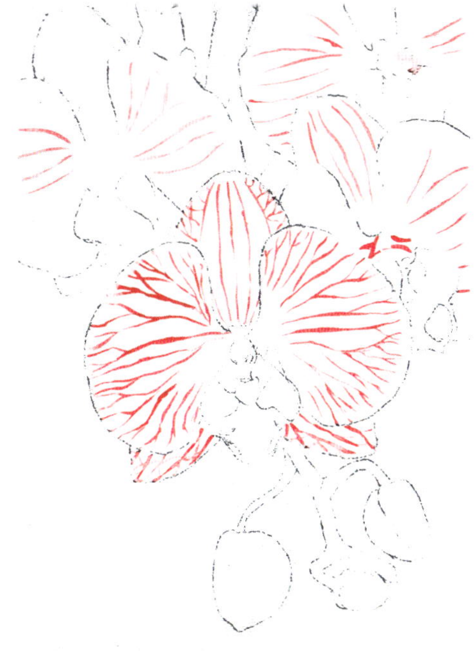

1 Draw the large shapes of the composition on watercolor paper using a soft HB pencil with a light touch. Paint the veins of the petals with a small pointed round brush using a watery mix of purple madder. Paint the veins first so that the next layer of paint will soften them.

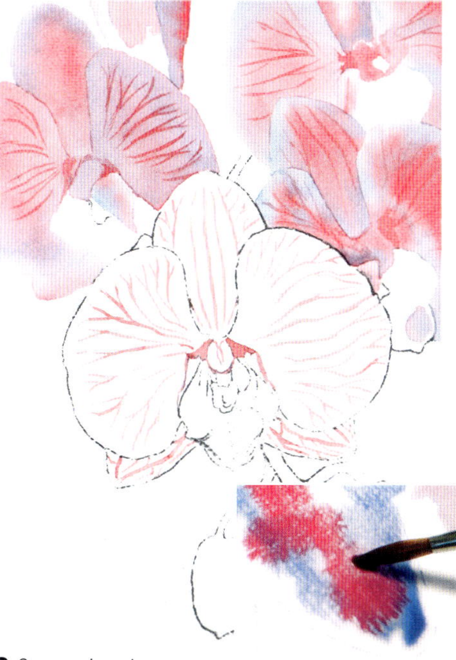

2 Generously wet one background petal so that the surface glistens. Mix cobalt blue and quinacridone magenta each to the consistency of low-fat milk. Apply a line of cobalt blue just inside the perimeter of the petal. Then drop quinacridone magenta into the center of the petal (inset). Tilt the board in different directions to mingle the colors. Repeat for each petal.

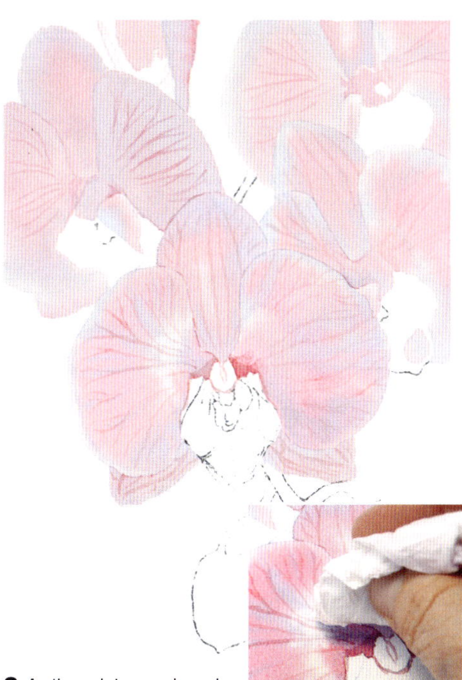

3 As the paint spreads and the moisture evaporates, you may want to lighten some areas. Use a "thirsty" (wiped dry) brush or a tissue to lift some of the paint from those areas (inset). If some areas appear too light, wait until the petal is dry, gently wet the petal again, and drop in a little more paint where needed. Again, dab with a tissue to bring out the highlights.

4 Paint the yellow and red centers of each blossom, using quinacridone magenta beside scarlet lake for the reds, and new gamboge for the yellows. In the background flowers allow the colors to mingle. For the foreground flower, let the red dry before painting the yellow. Mix a nearly black color from purple madder, sap green, and scarlet lake. With the tip of a small round brush, paint in the lines and dots in the center.

5 Paint the stems and buds directly, wet-onto-dry but allowing the colors to touch and blend for the first layer, using sap green with new gamboge for the yellower areas; sap green with French ultramarine blue for the darker areas; quinacridone magenta for the pinker areas, and all the above mixed together for the browner areas.

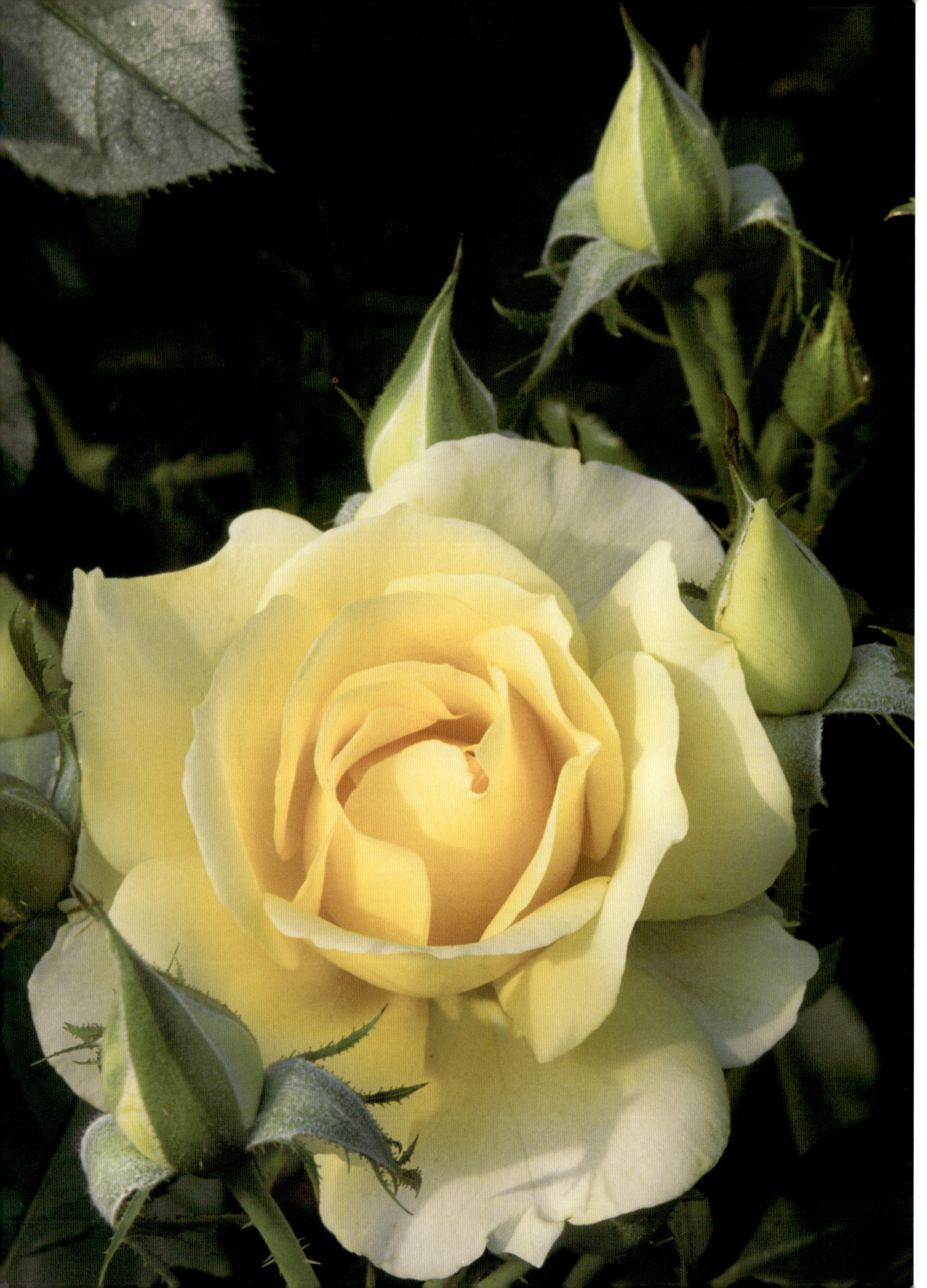

Rose

The artist saw this photograph of a rose as a challenge—to see it in a fresh way and to insert an air of mystery by having the beauty of the image emerge from the deep tones of the background.

PAINTS
Alizarin crimson
Antwerp blue
Aureolin
Cadmium orange
Cadmium yellow light
Cobalt blue
French ultramarine blue
Rose madder genuine

TECHNIQUES USED
Graded wash, *p. 20*
Mixing paint in the palette, *p. 21*
Dropping in color, *p. 21*
Wet-into-wet, *p. 22*
Negative painting, *p. 27*
Pouring paint, *p. 29*
Spritz, *p. 30*

TOOLS & MATERIALS
Cold-pressed paper, 140 lb. (300 gsm)
Clear acetate
HB pencil or pen
3-in. (7.5-cm) hake brush
Large soft mop brush
Natural sponge
Spray bottle
Round brushes, Nos. 4, 8, 10
¼-in. (6-mm) flat brush
½-in. (12-mm) flat brush

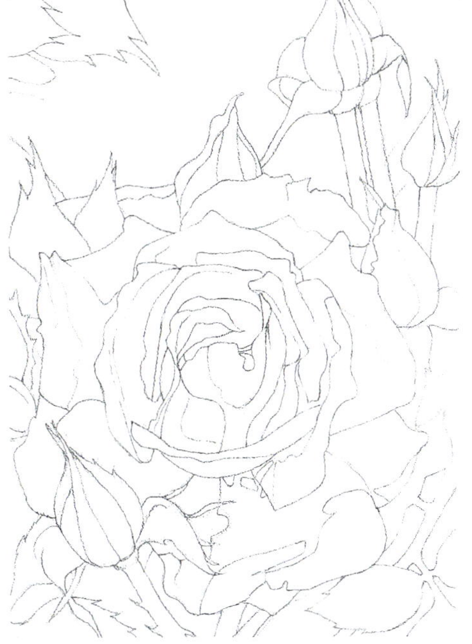

1 On a piece of clear acetate laid on the image, draw a grid dividing the photograph into thirds in each direction, resulting in nine squares. Lightly repeat this grid on your watercolor paper. Methodically transfer the lines in each square in the photograph to the same square on the watercolor paper. The completed drawing should show all necessary detail with lines that are light enough to be erased.

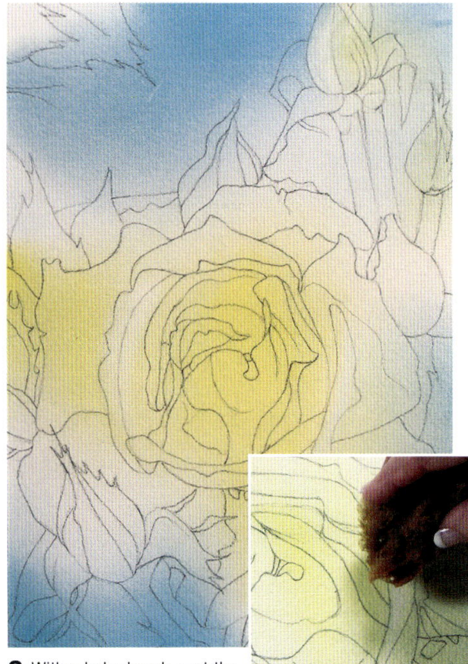

2 With a hake brush, wet the paper and let it relax. Brush using a large mop brush or pour aureolin in areas of light and cobalt blue in areas of shadow. Tilt the paper and let the colors roll. Use transparent pigments to make a soft underpainting. Lift out areas with a damp sponge (inset) or brush to preserve a light value.

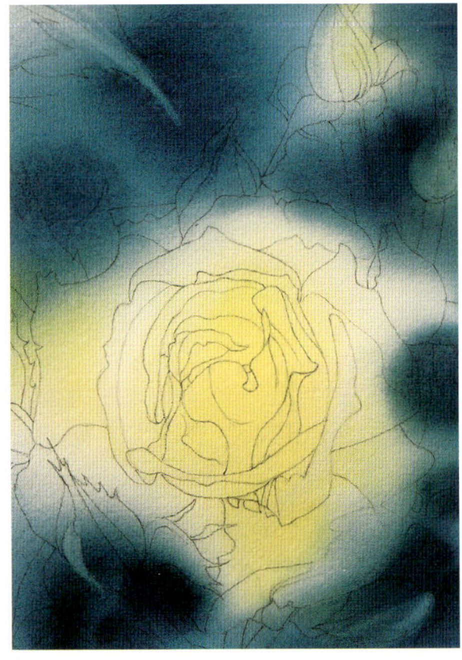

3 This stage is similar to step 2, but this time uses a mixture of opaque and granulating pigments (see p. 16). For this, the mixture should be a dark blue-green placed in the darkest areas of the negative space. Carefully control the mixture by spritzing and rolling. It should have soft graded edges with lots of open space.

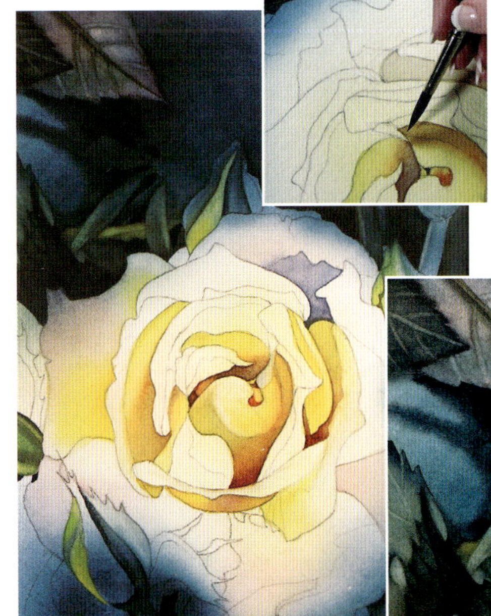

4 Begin to carve the image by painting the dark values behind the back petals with a No. 10 round brush. Next, using a No. 4 and 8 round brushes, paint the dark areas in the rose center to model the image (inset). Play warm yellows against cool ones with the deepest color in the crevice areas. The underpainting intrudes into the petal area in places and softens the image.

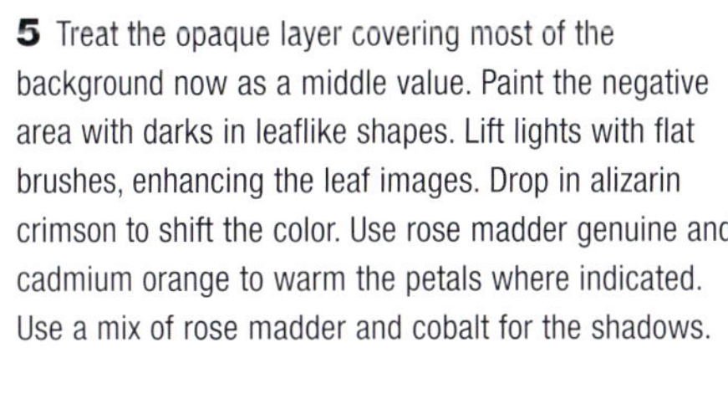

5 Treat the opaque layer covering most of the background now as a middle value. Paint the negative area with darks in leaflike shapes. Lift lights with flat brushes, enhancing the leaf images. Drop in alizarin crimson to shift the color. Use rose madder genuine and cadmium orange to warm the petals where indicated. Use a mix of rose madder and cobalt for the shadows.

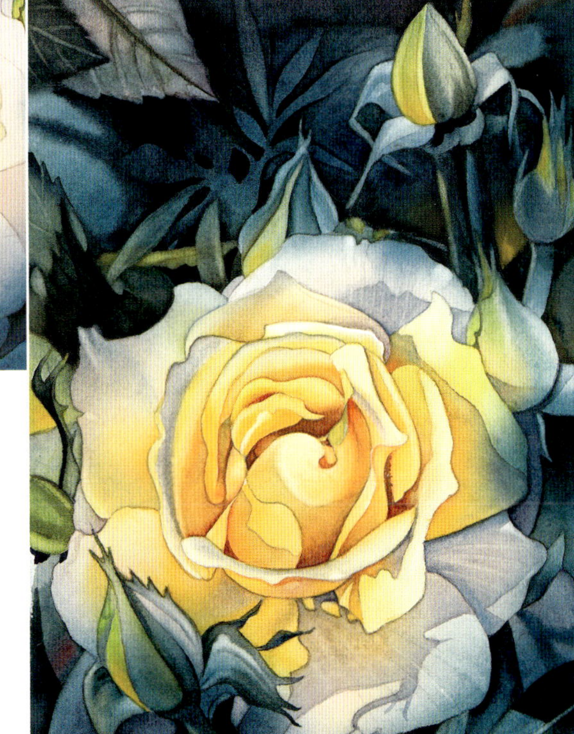

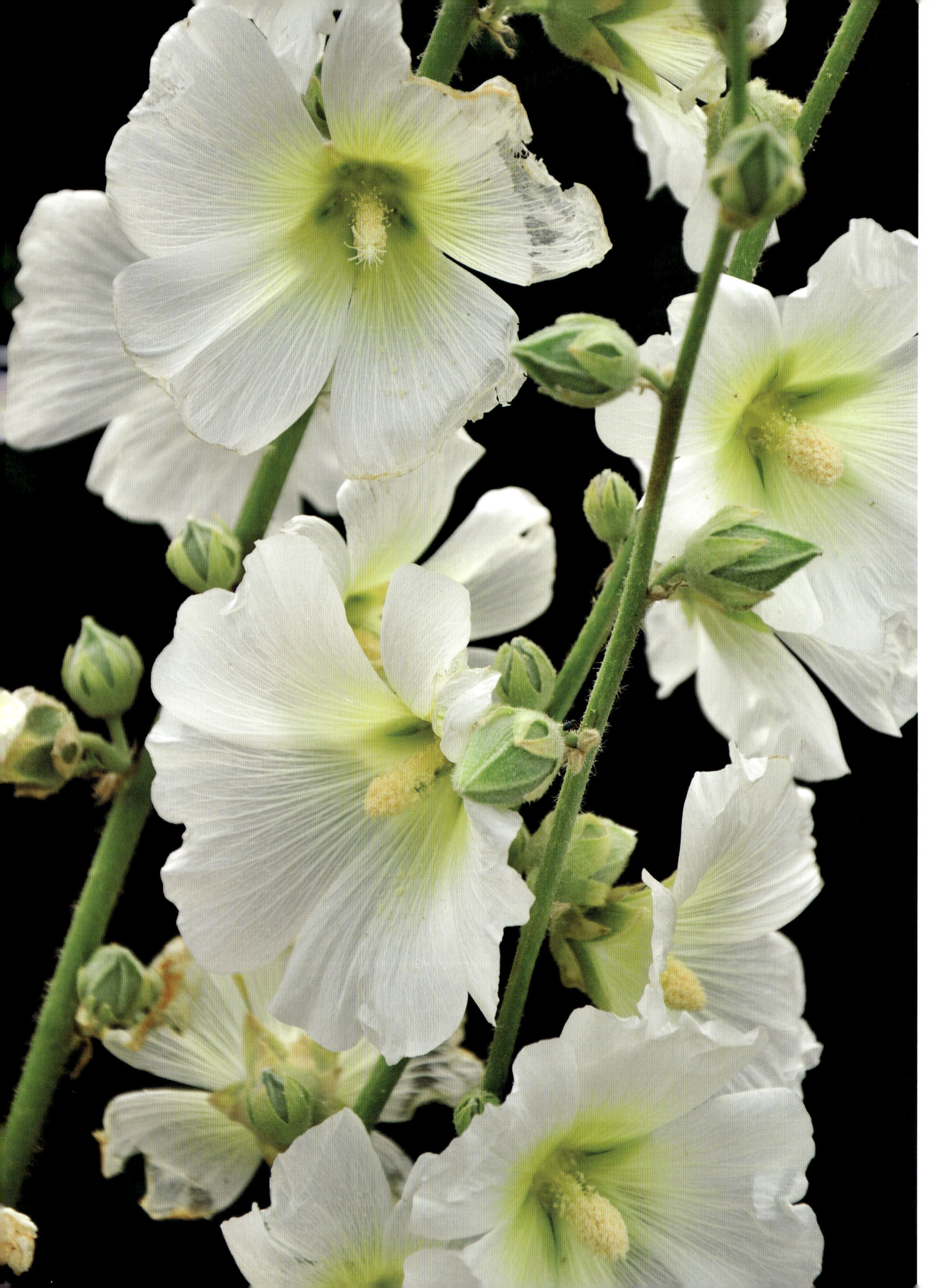

Mallows

The artist found that the veined petals were almost impossible to replicate and were best represented by suggestion only. The subtle color changes in the flower petals and buds were managed carefully to avoid hard contrasts.

PAINTS
Alizarin crimson
Burnt umber
French ultramarine blue
Lemon yellow
Permanent sap green
Prussian blue
Raw sienna

TOOLS & MATERIALS
Cold-pressed paper, 140 lb. (300 gsm)
HB pencil
Round brushes, Nos. 5 or 8 and 10 or 12
Masking fluid
Old brush

TECHNIQUES USED
Mixing paint in the palette, *p. 21*
Dropping in color, *p. 21*
Wet-into-wet, *p. 22*
Paint light to dark, *p. 23*
Lost and found edges, *p. 24*
Masking to reserve the paper, *p. 25*
Masking for details, *p. 25*

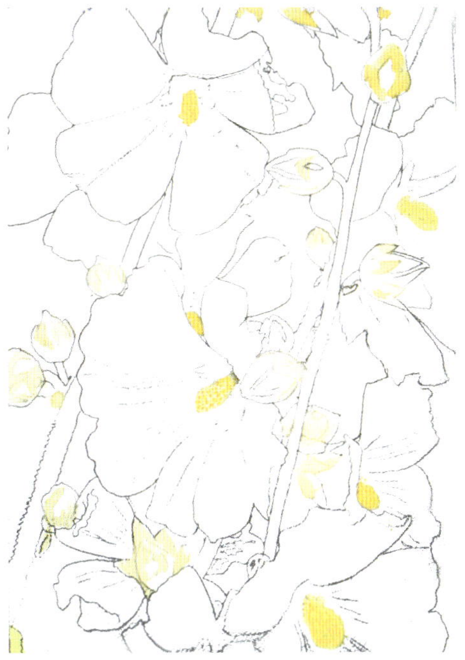

1 Make a detailed drawing of the image. Mix a small puddle of raw sienna and, using a No. 5 or No. 8 round brush, paint each pistil and husk. When dry, use a stronger mixture of the same color and dot a random pattern of tiny spots on each pistil. Dry. Apply a coating of masking fluid, with irregular edges. Also apply dots of masking fluid to indicate the smattering of small specks around the base of each pistil.

2 Using a No. 10 or No. 12 round brush, wet the center of the first flower with water half the distance to the edge of the petals. Introduce lemon yellow, drawing the brush from the center outward, allowing the color to fade toward the edge. When dry, repeat the wetting process over a smaller center and introduce a thin wash of sap green, not completely covering the first yellow wash.

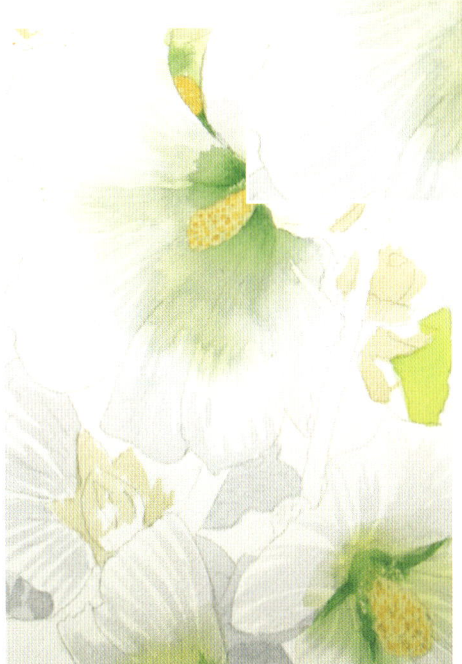

3 Create a weak mixture of alizarin crimson and Prussian blue to add texture and shadows to the white petals (inset). An alternative to replicating the network of veins is to paint fine, sweeping strokes that are irregular in thickness. Be sure to preserve sufficient white between these strokes to indicate the veins. When dry, remove the masking fluid and touch up the color of the pistils.

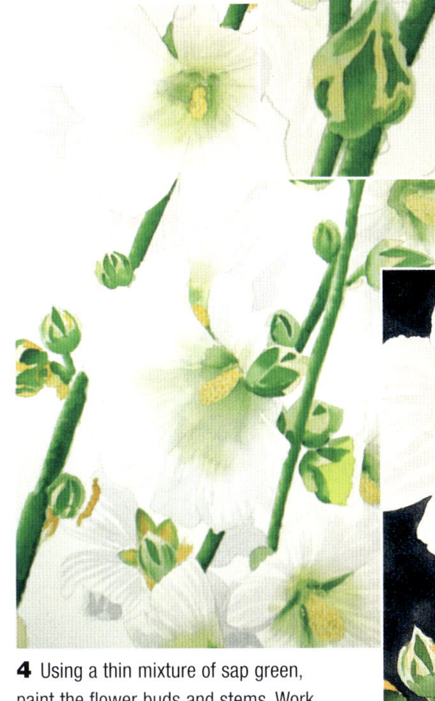

4 Using a thin mixture of sap green, paint the flower buds and stems. Work on small segments at a time and, while still wet, introduce a strong mix of sap green along the shadow side of the stem, allowing it to bleed toward the light side (inset).

5 Mix a large puddle of burnt umber and French ultramarine blue for the background. While the background paint is still wet on the paper, drop in colors such as ultramarine blue, alizarin crimson, or sap green, adding interest. Paint short strokes out from the stems to create the furry look.

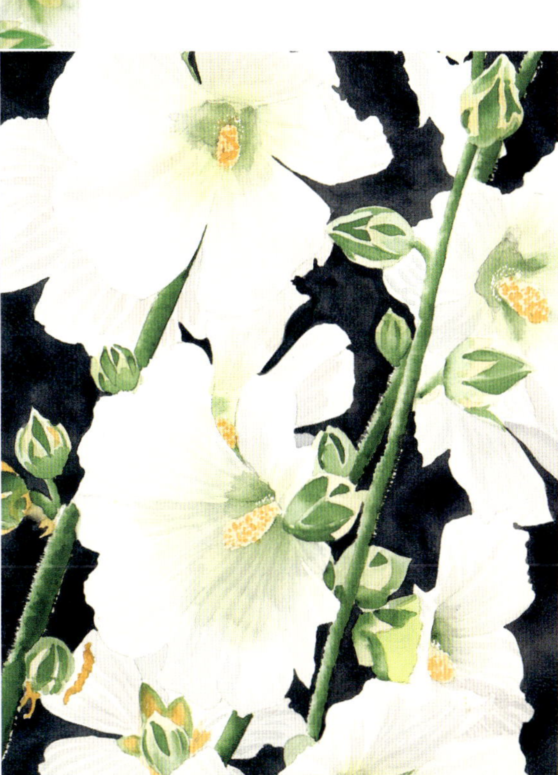

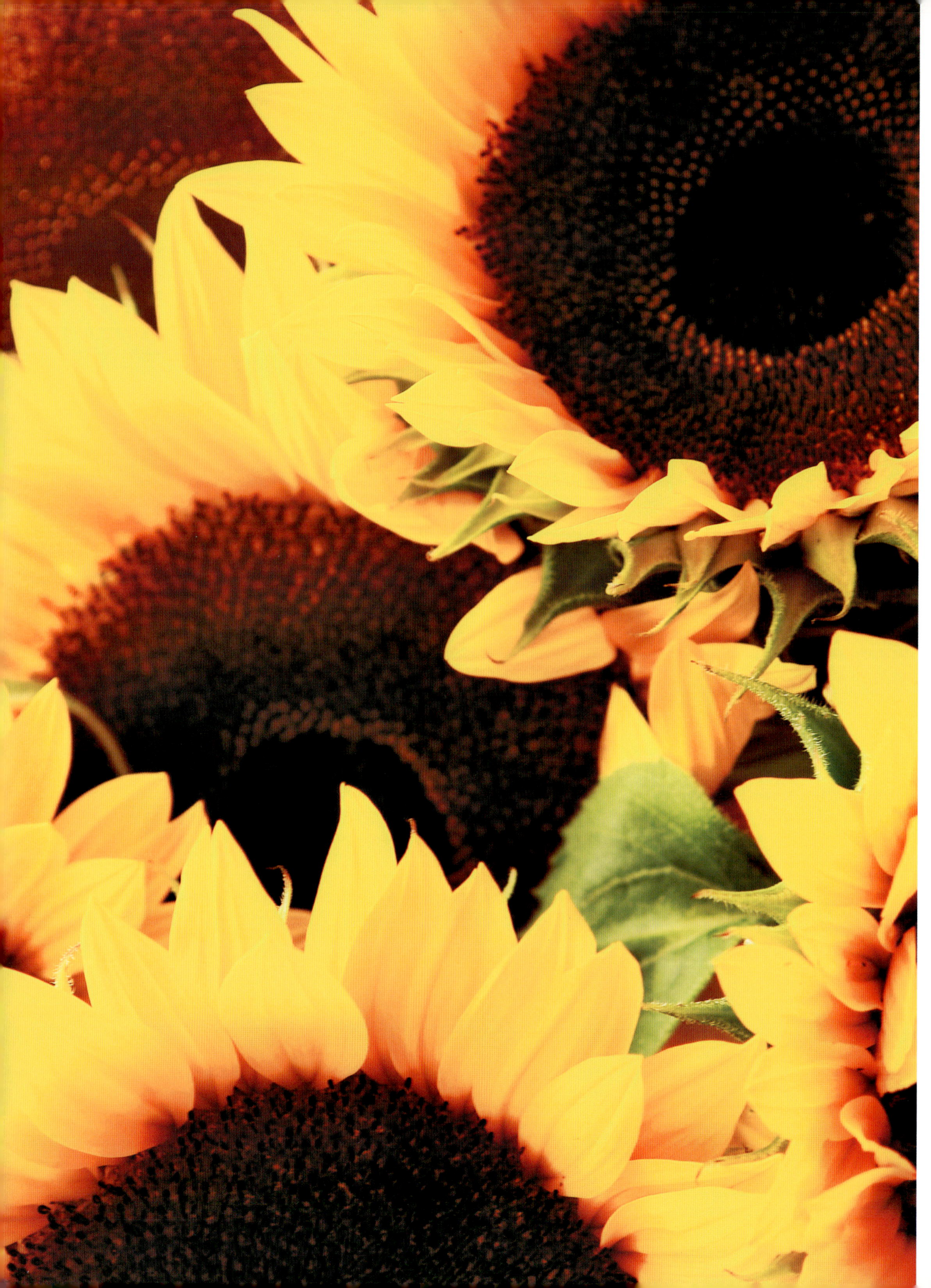

Sunflowers

To create a center of interest in the sunflowers, the artist created a path of light to break up some of the yellow in the petals and to add luminosity to the already radiant flowers.

PAINTS
Aureolin
French ultramarine blue
Hooker's green
Permanent orange
Quinacridone burnt scarlet
Quinacridone burnt sienna
Quinacridone coral
Quinacrindone magenta
Quinacridone violet
Winsor yellow deep

TOOLS & MATERIALS
Cold-pressed paper, 140 lb. (300 gsm)
HB pencil
Round brushes, Nos. 3, 6, 10
Kosher salt
Metal scraper
Masking film or tissue paper
Mouth atomizer
1-in. (2.5-cm) flat brush
Mat knife
Fritch scrubbers, Nos. 2, 12, 16

TECHNIQUES USED
Mixing paint in the palette, *p. 21*
Mixing paint on the paper, *p. 21*
Dropping in color, *p. 21*
Wet-onto-dry, *p. 22*
Wet-into-wet, *p. 22*
Adding highlights, *p. 27*
Salt, *p. 30*

1 Make a detailed drawing with light HB pencil lines, since dark lines will show through the transparent yellow pigments of the petals. (Note that for the purposes of the photograph above, the lines are darker than you should make them.) Working with one flower center at a time, wet the paper in that area with a No. 10 round brush, moving in a circular motion, allowing the wet to extend into the petal area.

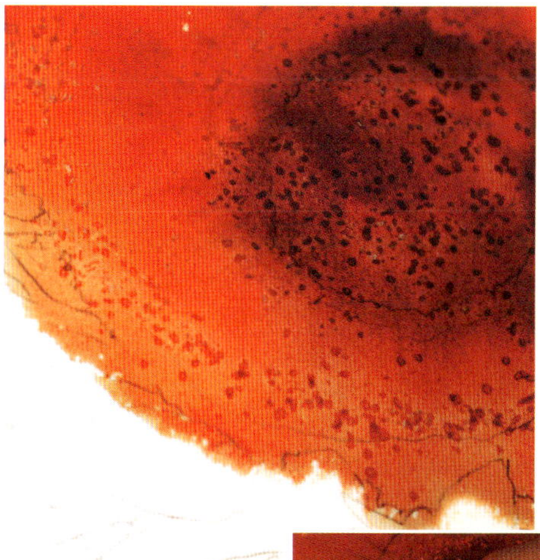

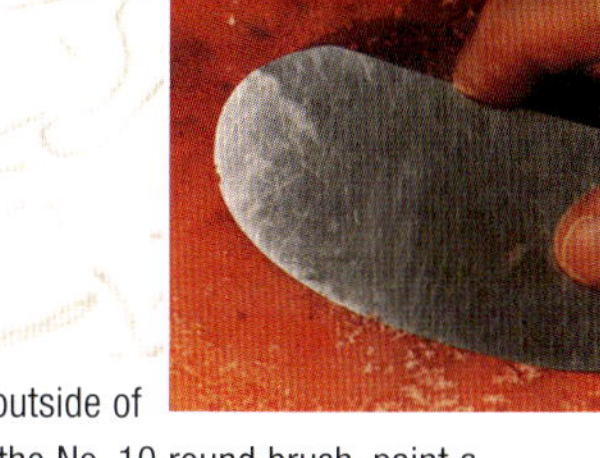

2 Beginning at the outside of the circle, still using the No. 10 round brush, paint a medium value of quinacridone burnt sienna. Then switch to quinacridone burnt scarlet, and, in the center of the flower, mix that with a little quinacridone magenta. Sprinkle kosher salt in the center and in the outer ring. Dry thoroughly and scrape any salt away with a metal scraper (inset).

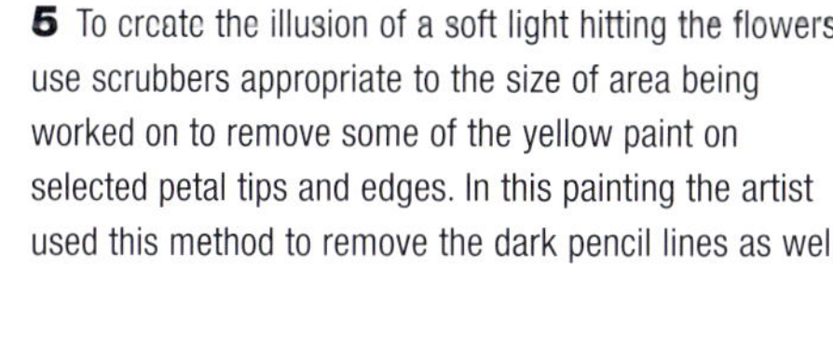

3 Cover all remaining white areas with masking film cut around the petals or with tissue paper. Make a creamy mixture of quinacridone burnt scarlet and water, and a similar mixture of the burnt scarlet mixed with quinacridone violet and Hooker's green. Spatter the flower seed in the center with a mouth atomizer (inset), working first with the red and then with the dark. Do not let any paint pool; otherwise, the texture will be lost. Dry and repeat if necessary.

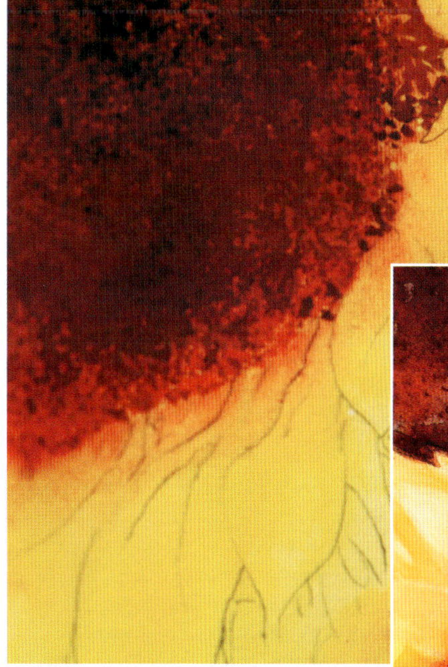

4 Using a No. 6 brush in the larger areas and a No. 3 in the tighter crevices, wet the petals. Drop or paint in aureolin and, at the juncture with the central pod, Winsor yellow deep. Paint the leaves with a mixture of quinacridone gold and French ultramarine blue, using a knife to scrape in veins and highlights.

5 To create the illusion of a soft light hitting the flowers, use scrubbers appropriate to the size of area being worked on to remove some of the yellow paint on selected petal tips and edges. In this painting the artist used this method to remove the dark pencil lines as well.

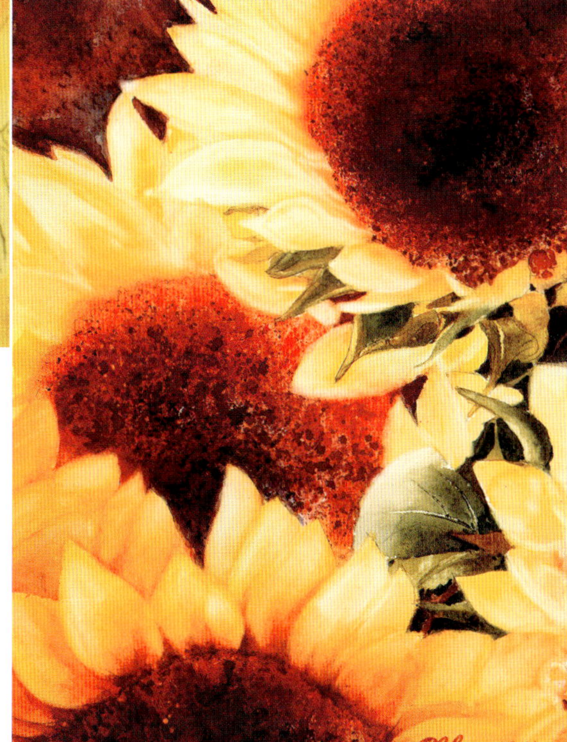

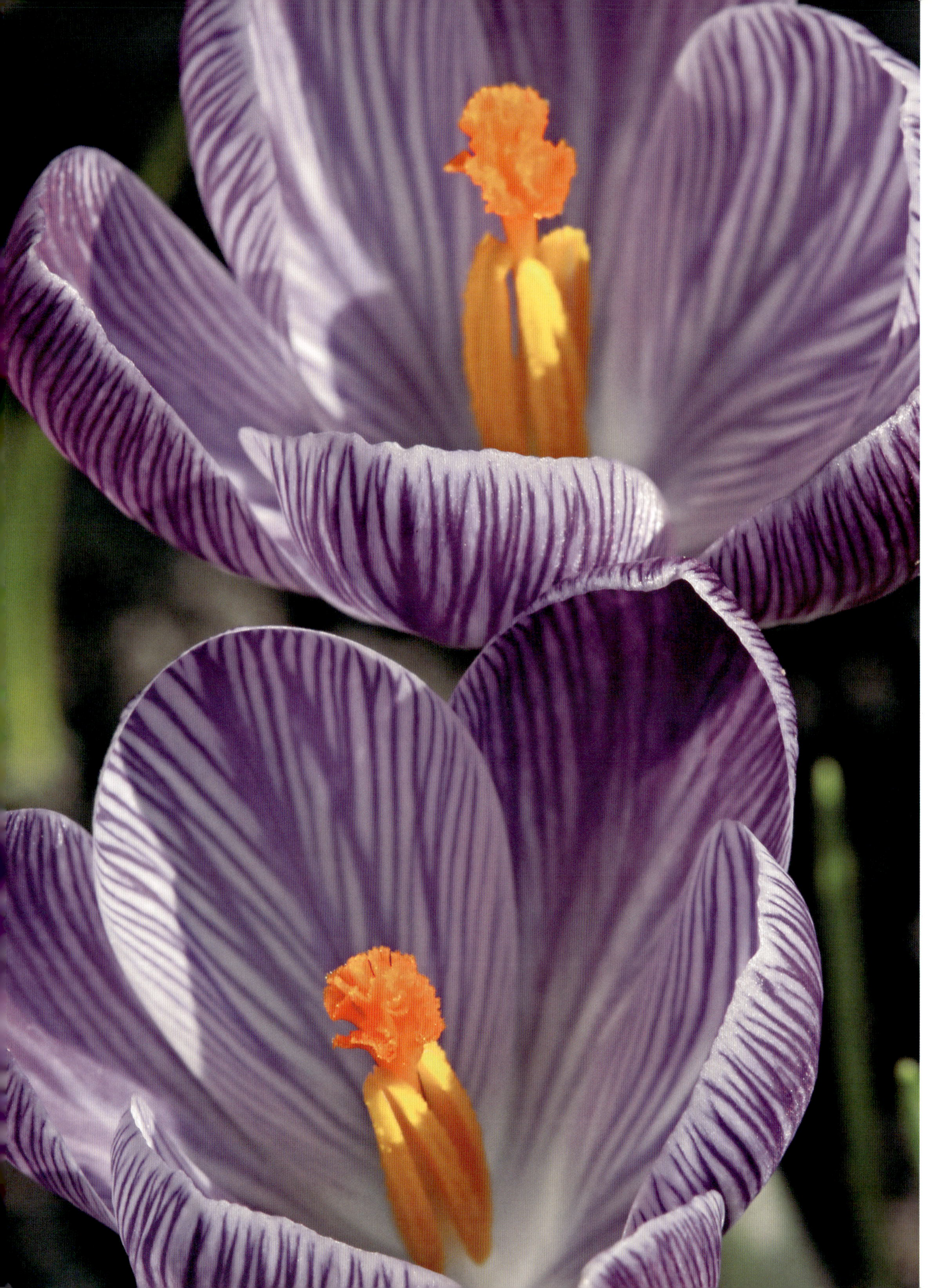

Crocuses

The large scale of this view results in large, even shapes that require variation in color and form. It is important that the veining does not appear too busy.

PAINTS
Antwerp blue
Brilliant purple
Brilliant red-violet
Cadmium scarlet
Cadmium yellow light
French ultramarine blue
New gamboge
Orange lake
Permanent rose
Purple-magenta

TECHNIQUES
Mixing paint in the palette, *p. 21*
Wet-into-wet, *p. 22*
Glazing, *p. 23*
Adding highlights, *p. 27*

TOOLS & MATERIALS
Cold-pressed paper, 140 lb. (300 gsm)
Transfer paper
Pencil
3-in. (7.5 cm) hake brush
Soft mop brush
Round brushes, Nos. 4, 8, 10
¼-in. (6-mm) flat brush

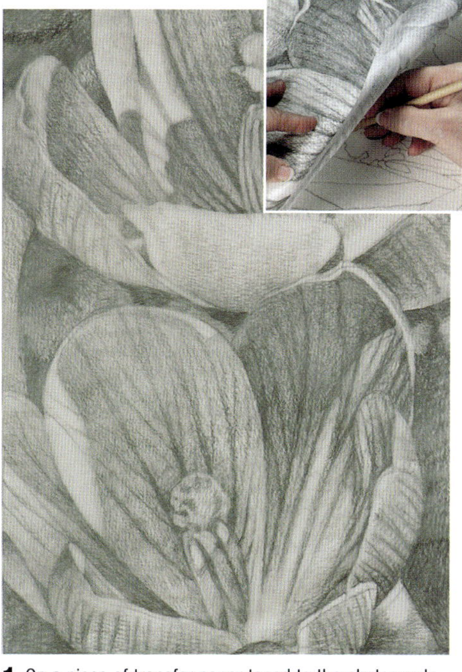

1 On a piece of transfer paper taped to the photograph, make a drawing of the flower, shading in the dark areas and noting where you will save the light. Next, tape the transfer paper to the watercolor paper so that your hand can slide underneath it. With your pencil, follow the lines that you can see through the transparency of the paper (inset). Draw in the major shapes, adding details later.

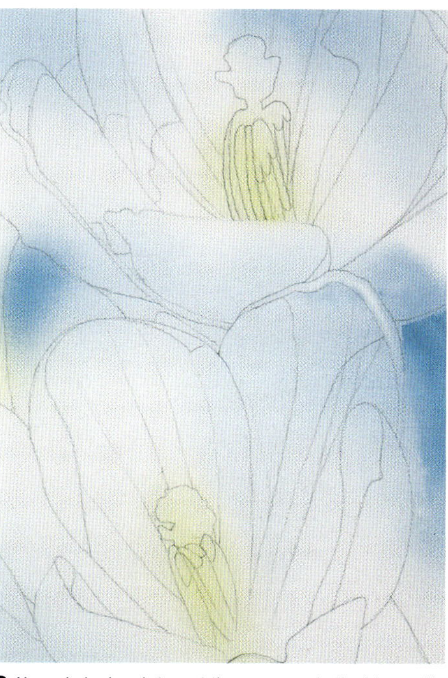

2 Use a hake brush to wet the paper on both sides until limp. With a soft mop brush, add new gamboge to the stamens of the flowers, keeping it away from most areas that will be purple. Brush Antwerp blue into the background area with a No. 10 round brush and let it expand into some of the petal shapes to soften the edges.

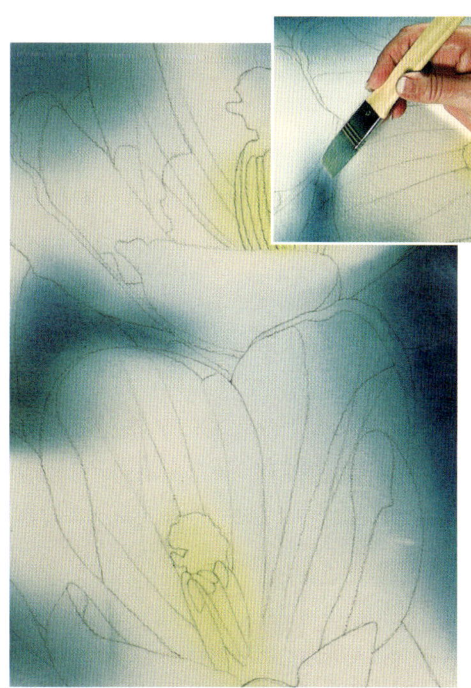

3 Make a mixture of transparent and opaque colors (French ultramarine blue, Antwerp blue, and new gamboge). Use the hake brush to paint the mixture sparingly into areas of the background, intruding into petal areas (inset). Leave some of the previous wash open.

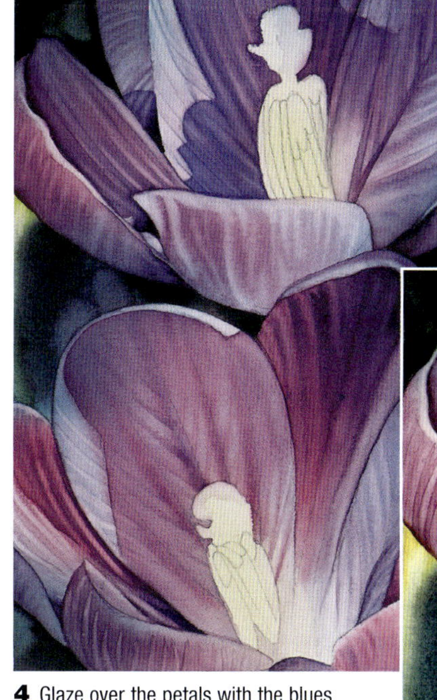

4 Glaze over the petals with the blues already used, permanent rose, purple-magenta, brilliant red-violet, and brilliant purple to produce cool and warm violets. Keep the washes wet and vary the color and value. Dry between glazes. While the washes are damp, use a ¼-in. (6-mm) flat brush to lift out light lines in the direction of the veins. Repeat the process to get the desired colors and values.

5 Add the yellows and oranges of the stamens, using orange lake, cadmium yellow light, and cadmium scarlet. Use a dark purple to add the veins of the flower, varying the values. Soften some of the veins. This is an opportunity to use many beautiful colors. Some of them will stain so they should be painted into wet areas to keep them from being uneven.

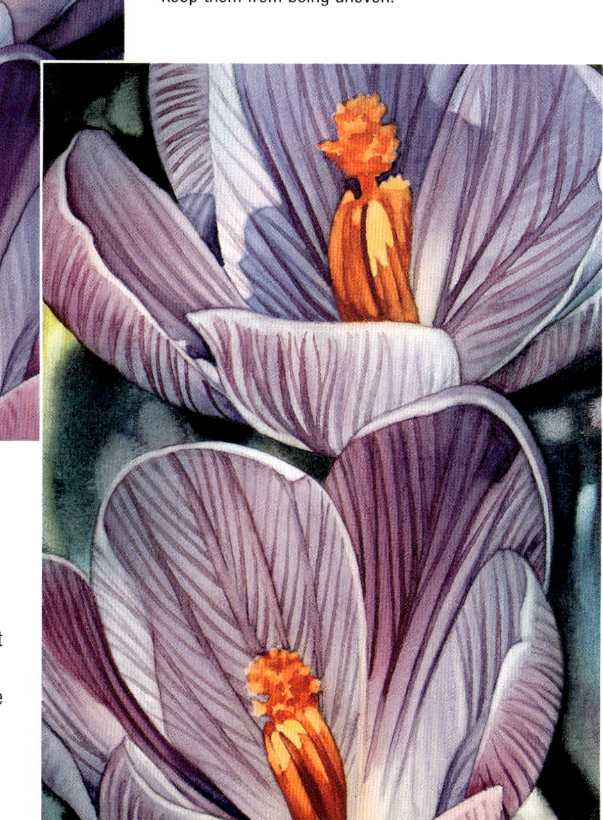

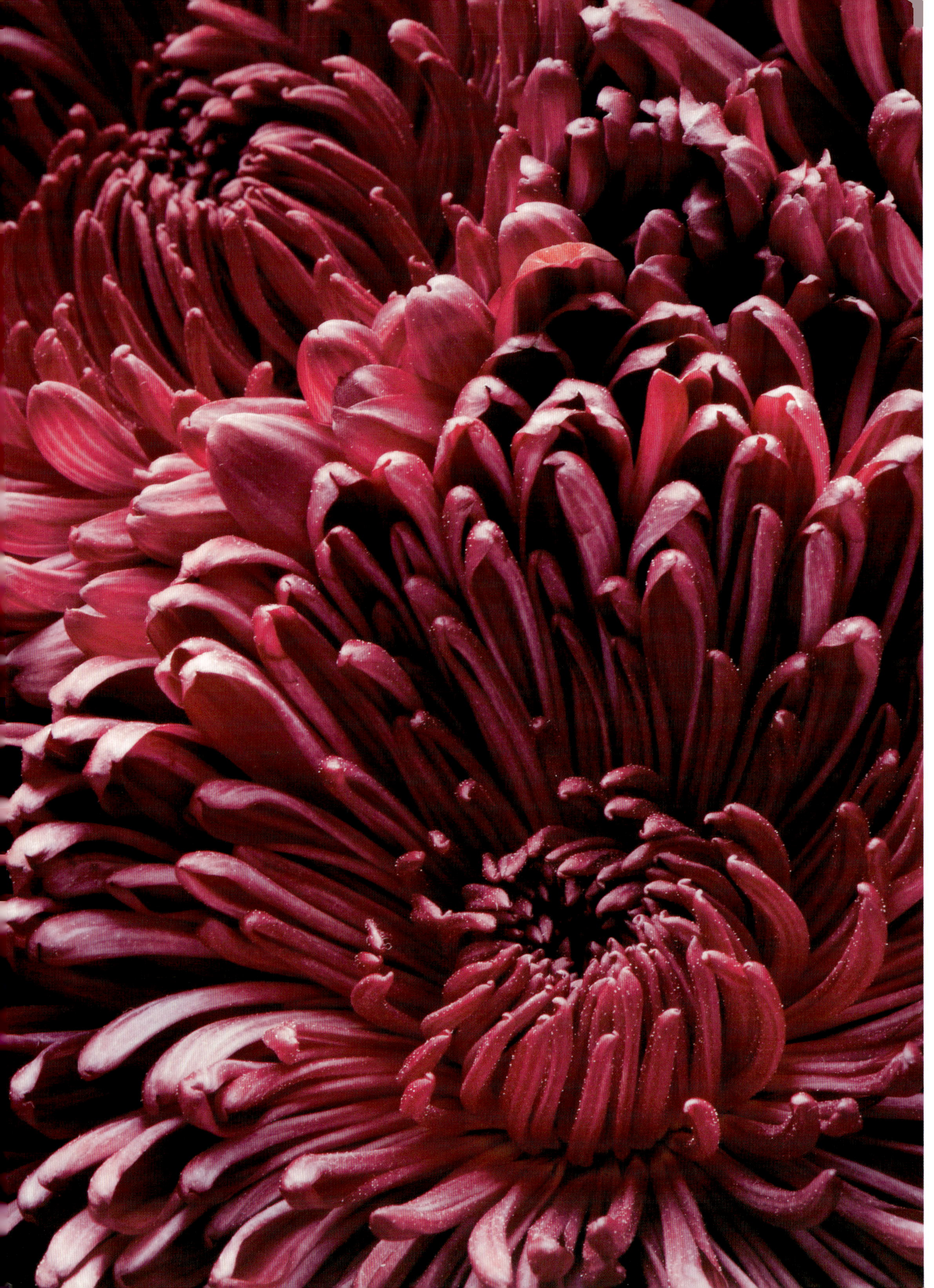

Chrysanthemums

This photograph is all pink! The challenge is to use a variety of tone and the value of a single color. Separating the forms of the foreground, middle ground, and background make it less confusing as an image and more pleasing as a painting.

PAINTS
Cobalt violet
Dioxazine purple
Opera
Permanent alizarin crimson
Permanent rose
Quinacridone rose
Ultramarine blue

TOOLS & MATERIALS
Cold-pressed paper, 140 lb. (300 gsm)
H pencil
Masquepen
Stiff-bristled brush, No. 5
Masking fluid
Spray bottle
Round brushes, Nos. 5, 12, 16
Fritch scrubber, No. 3

TECHNIQUES USED
Mixing paint in the palette, *p. 21*
Wet-into-wet, *p. 22*
Masking to reserve the paper, *p. 25*
Softening masked edges, *p. 25*
Adding highlights, *p. 27*
Spritz, *p. 30*

1 As you begin the drawing, pay attention to the placement of form on the paper. Consider the large flower to be the foreground and place its top edge above the center. The area above it will encompass midground and background. Draw the petal shapes with careful positioning of all highlights.

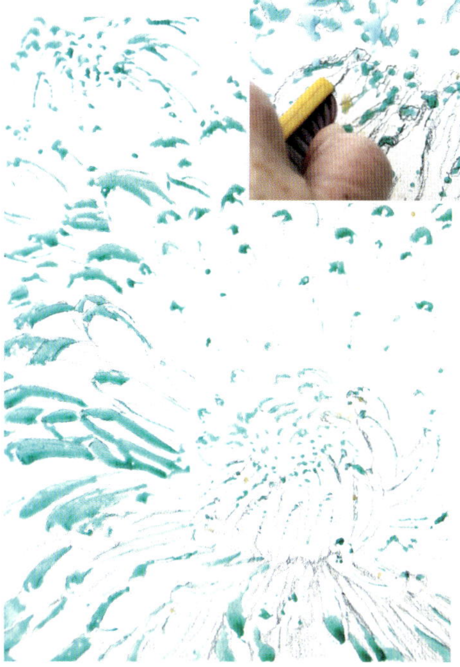

2 Using a Masquepen, apply masking to each shape of light on the petals of the flowers. This pattern of light will define the placement of individual petals. Next, using a stiff-bristled brush, dip the tip into a small pool of masking fluid and, flicking your thumb against the bristles, spritz tiny flecks of mask all around the main flower (inset). Let it dry.

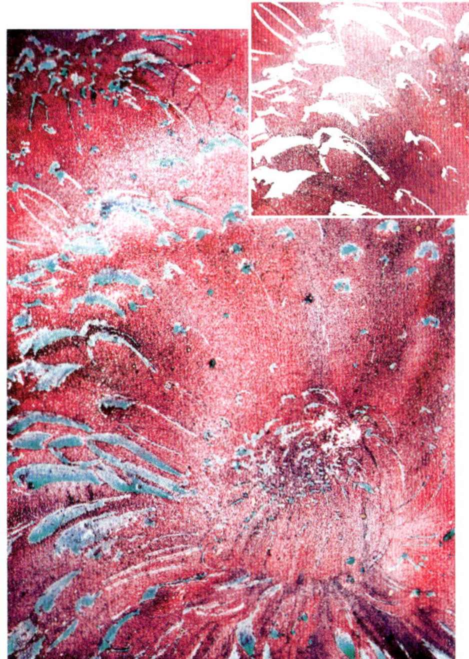

3 Squeeze onto your palette quinacridone rose, permanent rose, cobalt violet, opera, and dioxazine purple. With a spray bottle, thoroughly spritz the entire sheet. Working wet-into-wet with a No. 16 sable brush, flow mixtures of color and value. Pay attention to the reference photograph. Be aware of lights and darks, pinks and purples as you add color. Leave the painting to dry before removing the masking (inset).

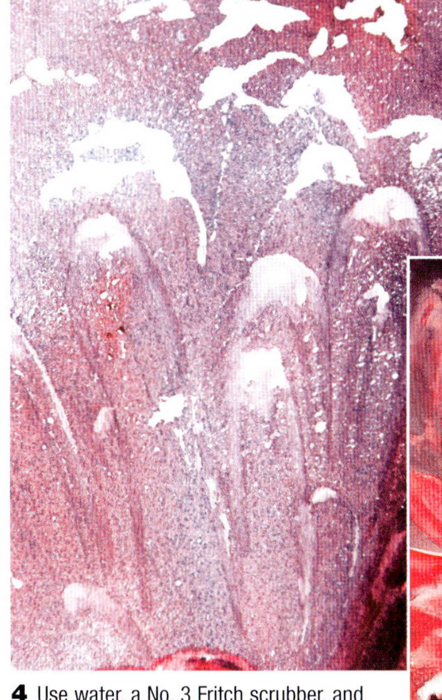

4 Use water, a No. 3 Fritch scrubber, and a stiff bristle brush to define shapes and soften edges. "Draw" the outline of petal shapes with a No. 5 round brush by softly lifting the pigment. Soften the edges on the highlights with the Fritch scrubber, since leaving the harsh edges would be too distracting.

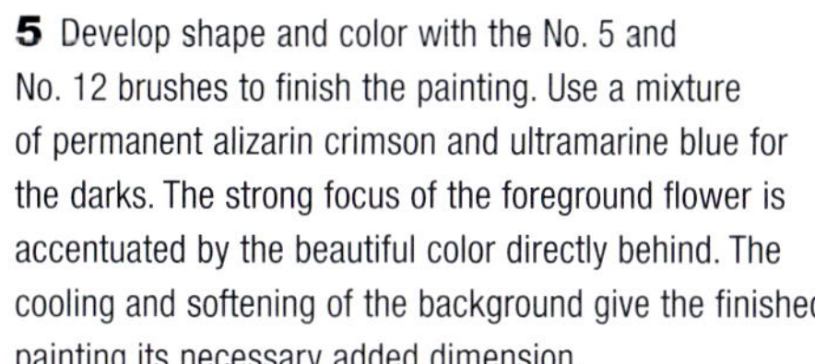

5 Develop shape and color with the No. 5 and No. 12 brushes to finish the painting. Use a mixture of permanent alizarin crimson and ultramarine blue for the darks. The strong focus of the foreground flower is accentuated by the beautiful color directly behind. The cooling and softening of the background give the finished painting its necessary added dimension.

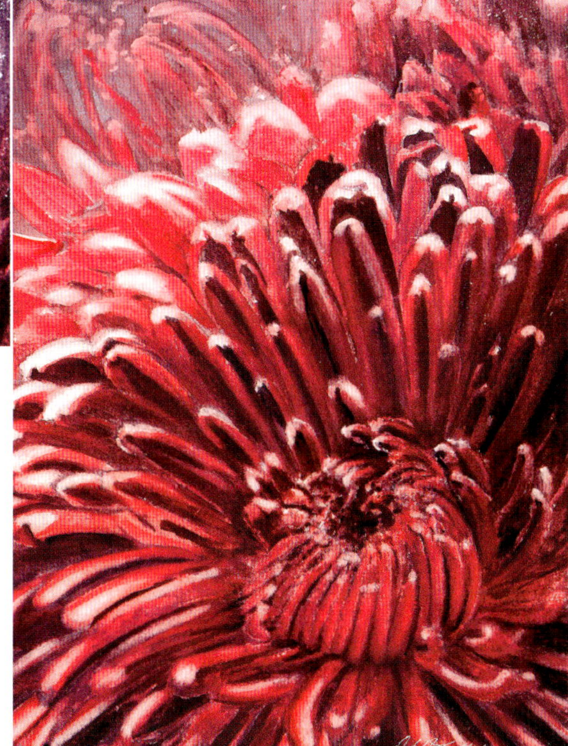

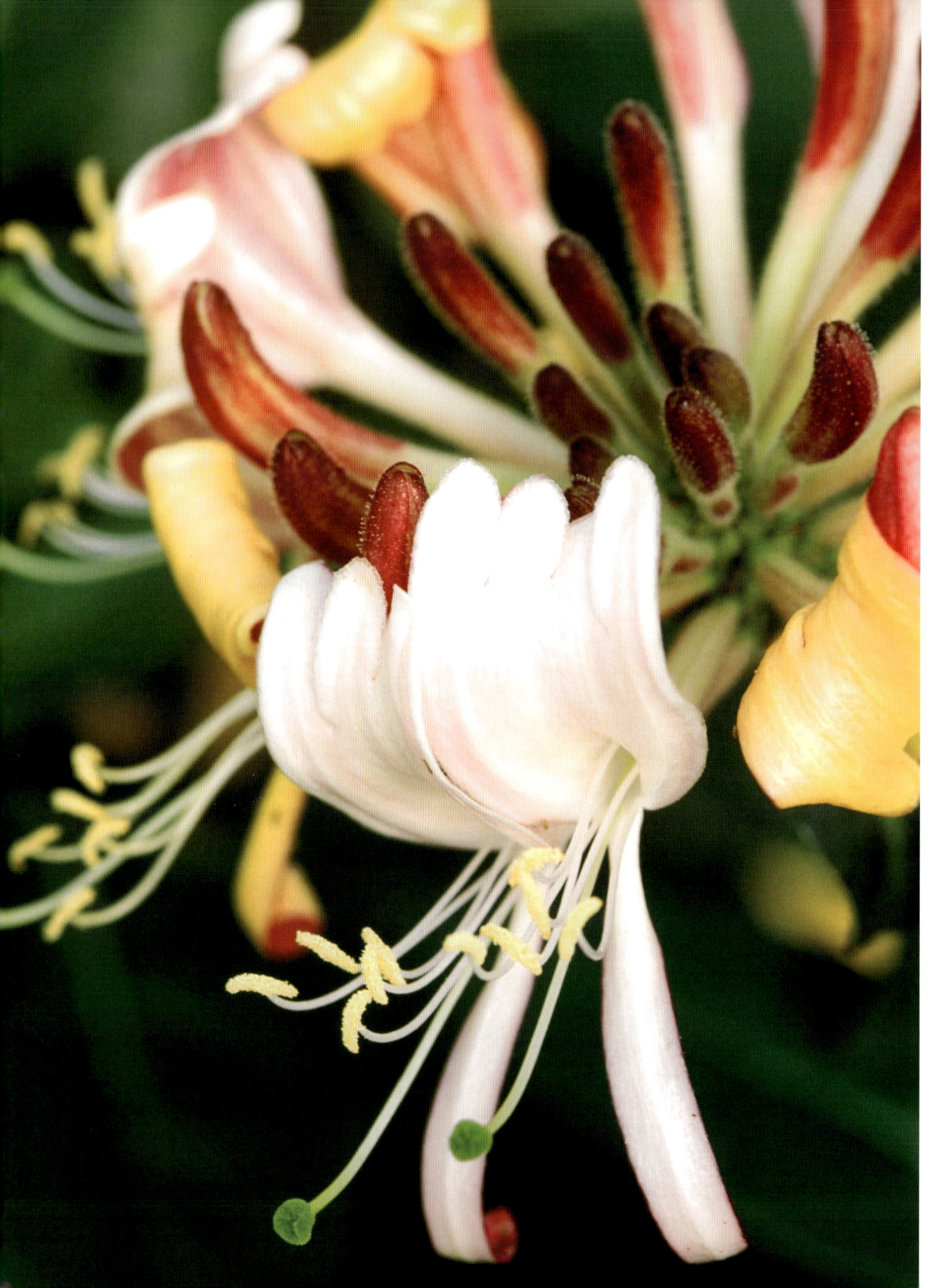

Honeysuckle

The honeysuckle's beauty lies in its delicate curving shapes and warm glowing colors. This was a major consideration when choosing a palette—to create a strong, vibrant painting while retaining the flower's softness.

PAINTS
Aureolin
Indigo
New gamboge
Permanent rose
Perylene maroon
Quinacridone gold
Winsor green

TOOLS & MATERIALS
Hot-pressed paper, 200 lb. (425 gsm)
HB pencil
Masking fluid
Old brush
Round brushes, Nos. 00, 3, 7, 12
Filbert brush

TECHNIQUES
Flat wash, *p. 20*
Mixing paint in the palette, *p. 21*
Mixing paint on the paper, *p. 21*
Dropping in color, *p. 21*
Lost and found edges, *p. 24*
Masking to reserve the paper, *p. 25*
Softening masked edges, *p. 25*

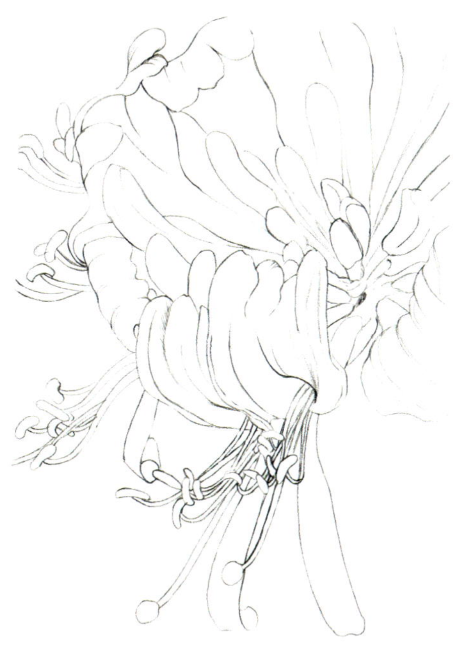

1 Draw the flower lightly onto the watercolor paper with an HB pencil. Put in just the basic shapes, emphasizing curves to strengthen the design. To retain white paper for highlights on the petals, apply masking fluid to those areas with an old brush.

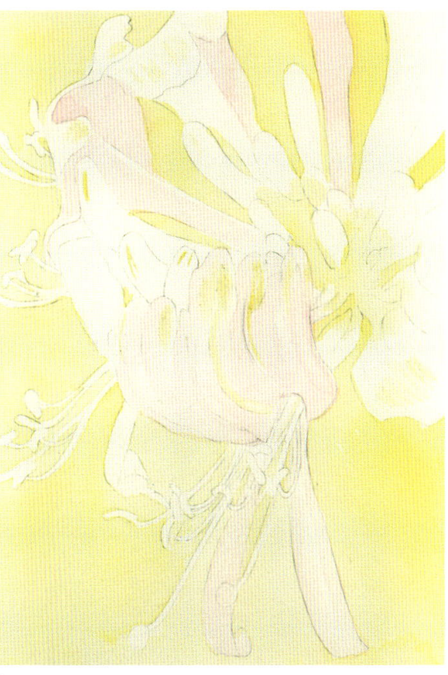

2 Using a No. 12 brush and clean water, wet the background areas, leaving the stamens dry. Apply a dilute wash of new gamboge to the wet areas and let dry. Repeat for the buds and remaining yellow petals. Wet the pink petals and charge lightly with permanent rose, blending to give tonal value and shape.

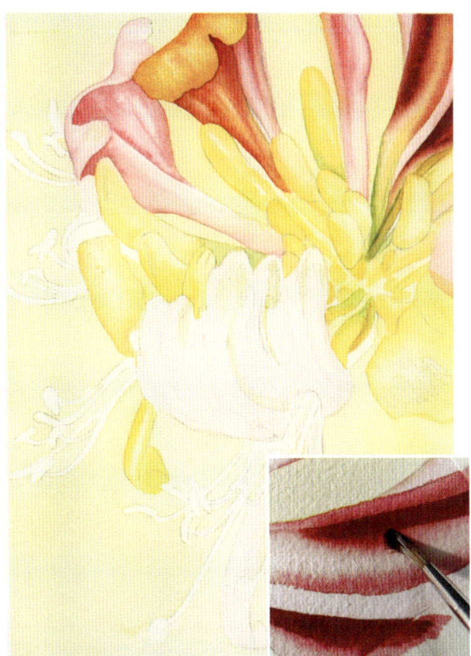

3 For the darker petals, charge with permanent rose and new gamboge, adding more pigment and a touch of perylene maroon for deeper tones (inset). Apply aureolin and Winsor green lightly to the basal areas. With a No. 7 brush continue to build the petals, adding wet-into-wet layers of new gamboge, quinacridone gold, and permanent rose.

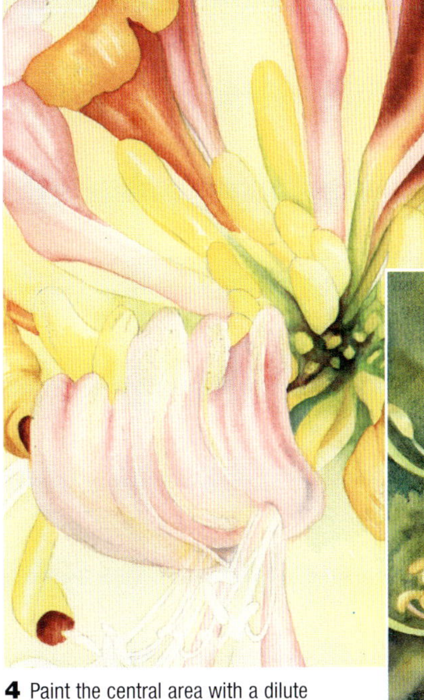

4 Paint the central area with a dilute underpainting of Winsor green and aureolin, dropping in perylene maroon and indigo for the darker areas. Wet the central buds with a No. 3 brush and flood with permanent rose, adding perylene maroon for darker areas. Lift color to preserve highlights.

5 Develop the petal bases with a dilute mix of quinacridone gold and Winsor green. Begin the background by wetting an area using a No. 12 brush. Drop in dark colors from the palette. To finish, paint the stamens, remove the masking fluid, soften and blend hard edges with a filbert brush, and add detail to foreground petals with a No. 00 brush.

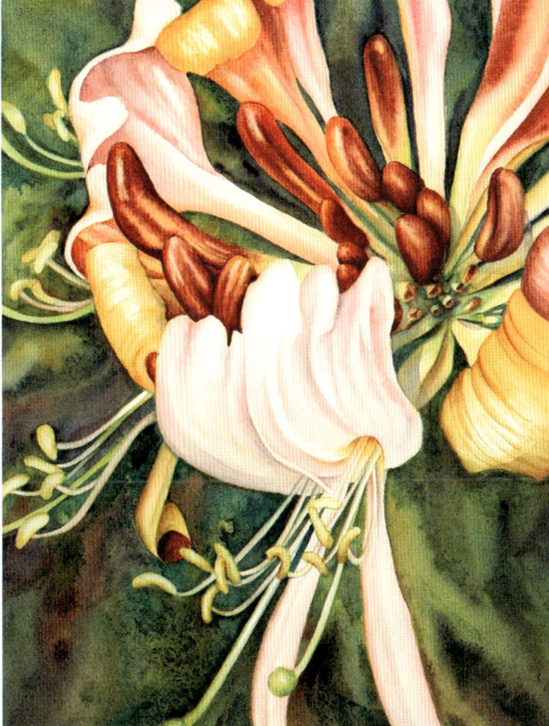

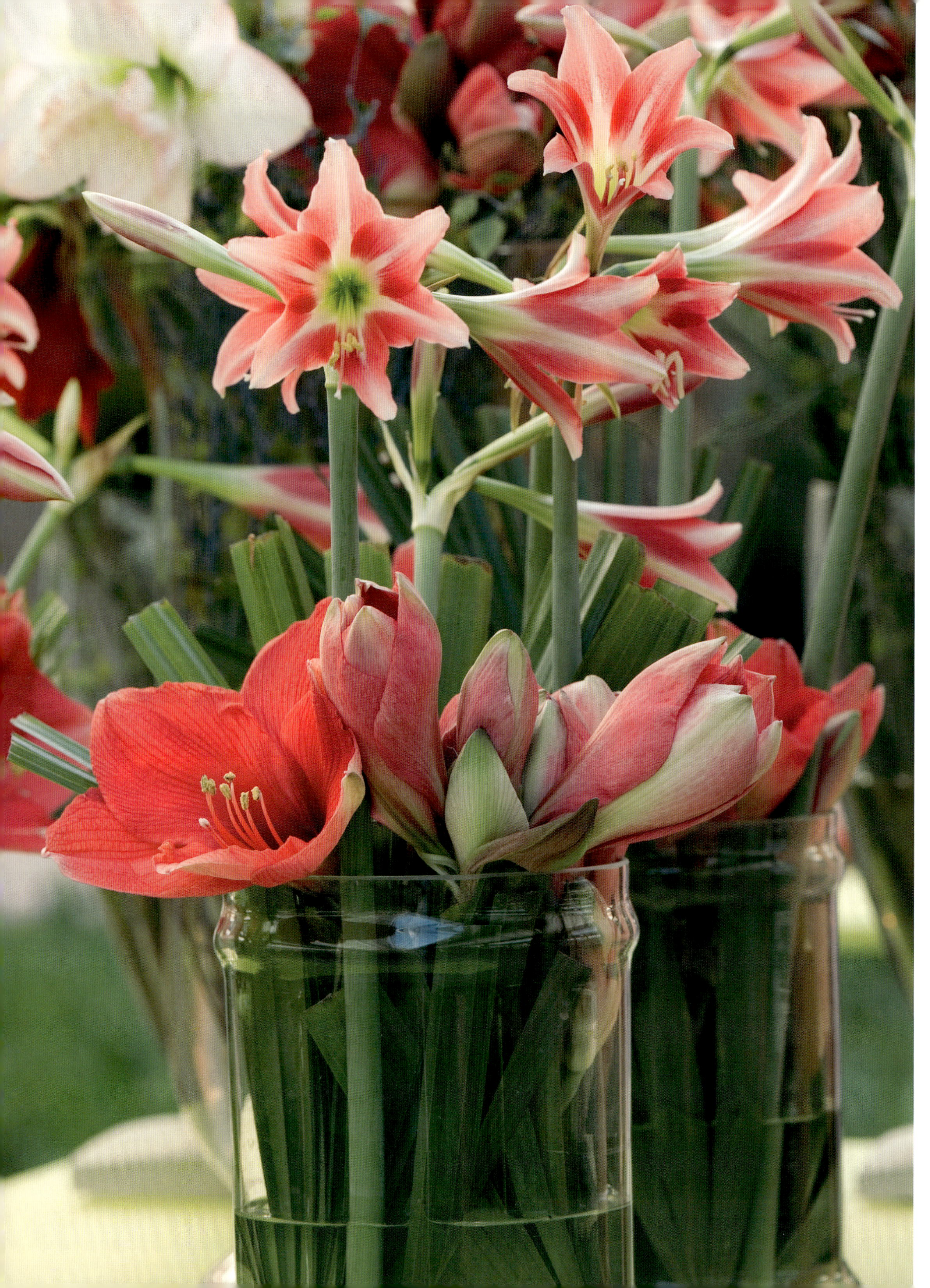

Amaryllis

The artist's initial task was to eliminate some background detail, by adding white areas, in order to improve the overall layout. Overlaying shades of blue and yellow keep the abundant green areas of the painting visually stimulating.

PAINTS
Black
Brilliant cadmium red
Cobalt violet
Gamboge
Phthalo green
Quinacridone magenta
Sap green
Turquoise blue

TOOLS & MATERIALS
Cold-pressed paper, 140 lb. (300 gsm)
2B pencil
Invisible tape
Plastic putty knife
Exacto knife
Incredible Nib
Round brushes, Nos. 3–8
Hair dryer
Rubber cement pickup

TECHNIQUES USED
Mixing paint in the palette, *p. 21*
Wet-onto-dry, *p. 22*
Wet-into-wet, *p. 22*
Blending, *p. 24*
Lost and found edges, *p. 24*
Softening masked edges, *p. 25*
Adding highlights, *p. 27*
Shadows, *p. 28*
Glazing, *p. 31*

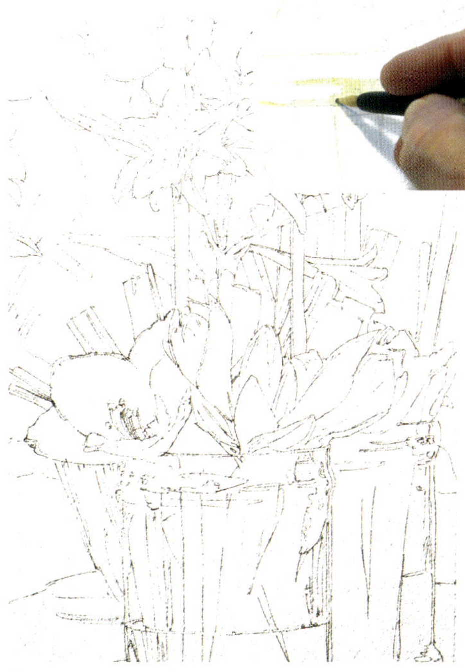

1 Make a drawing of the photograph. Before applying any paint, tape the perimeter of the painting with invisible tape, securing its adhesion by pressing it with a plastic putty knife. (When the painting is completed, the tape releases easily and allows for a crisp, clean edge.) Preplan any small areas that will remain white and apply masking fluid with an Incredible Nib (inset).

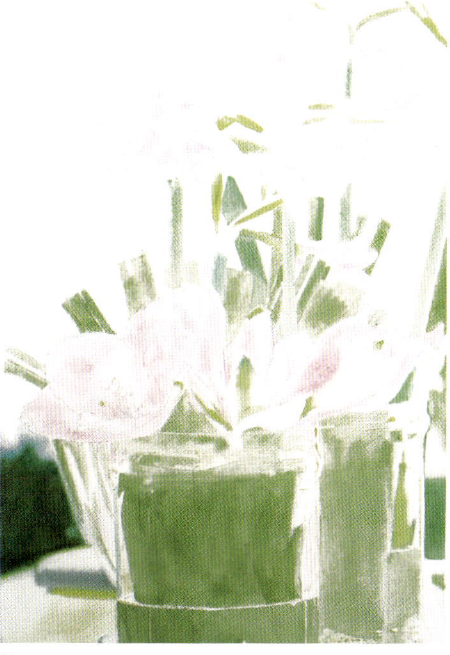

2 To attain definition of the color breakdown and prevent possible color misplacement later, begin painting an overall light wash of sap green mixed with some phthalo green wet-into-wet, using a No. 8 brush for the leaf and stem areas. Dry with a hair dryer in order to proceed more quickly. Apply a mixture of quinacridone magenta and brilliant cadmium red wet-into-wet for the floral area.

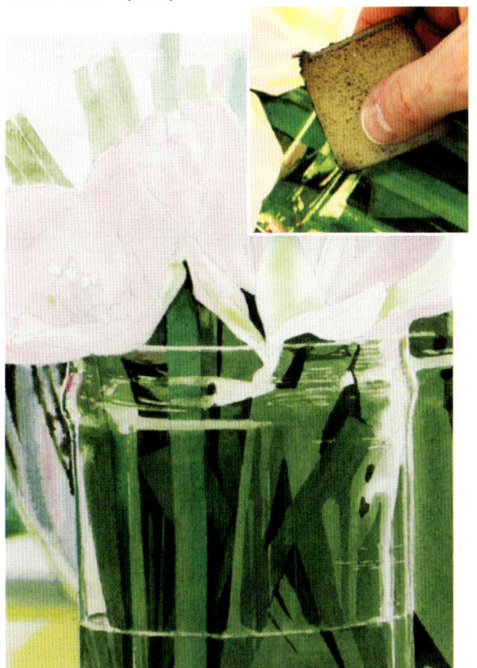

3 Layer the submerged area of the flower stems wet-onto-dry. Use light layers of pigment to avoid overworking. Apply turquoise blue to the stems and vase reflections. Use a light gamboge yellow wet-into-wet for the flower centers and lighter stems. After completing an area, use a rubber cement pickup to pull up the masking fluid (inset). Refine the white areas by softening the edges, allowing a few harsh white areas for impact.

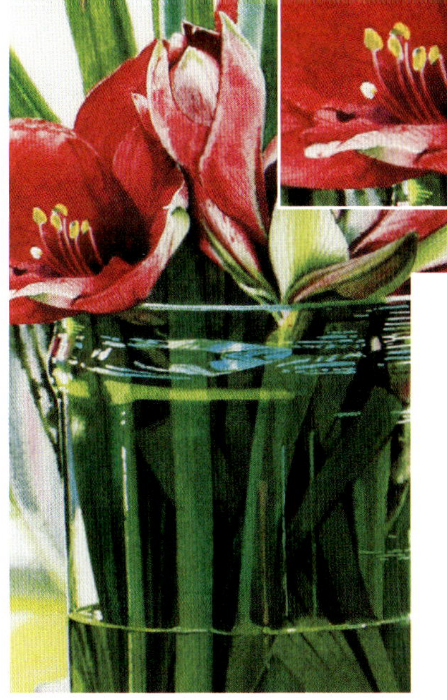

4 Begin detailing the flowers with a wet-into-wet method for more intense color, adding cobalt violet for the shadowed areas. Follow up with a wet-onto-dry technique for detail then wet-into-wet again for finer detail and softening the edges (inset). Complete the taller stemmed flowers in the same layering method described in step 3.

5 Use an Exacto knife to gently scrape the surface of the paper to achieve subtle white highlights on the flowers, leaves, and vase. Add a few out-of-focus leaves by applying light wet-into-wet washes to the background. Mix cobalt violet and quinacridone magenta, and apply light washes to some of the petals.

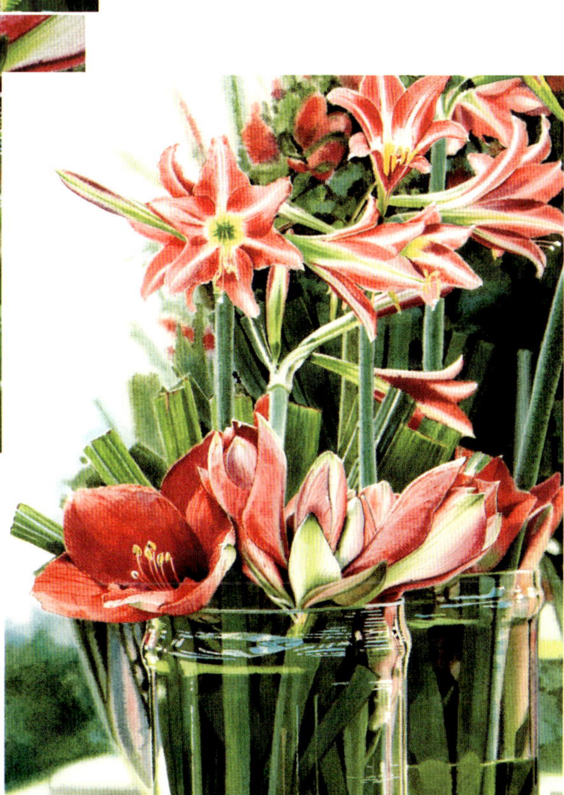

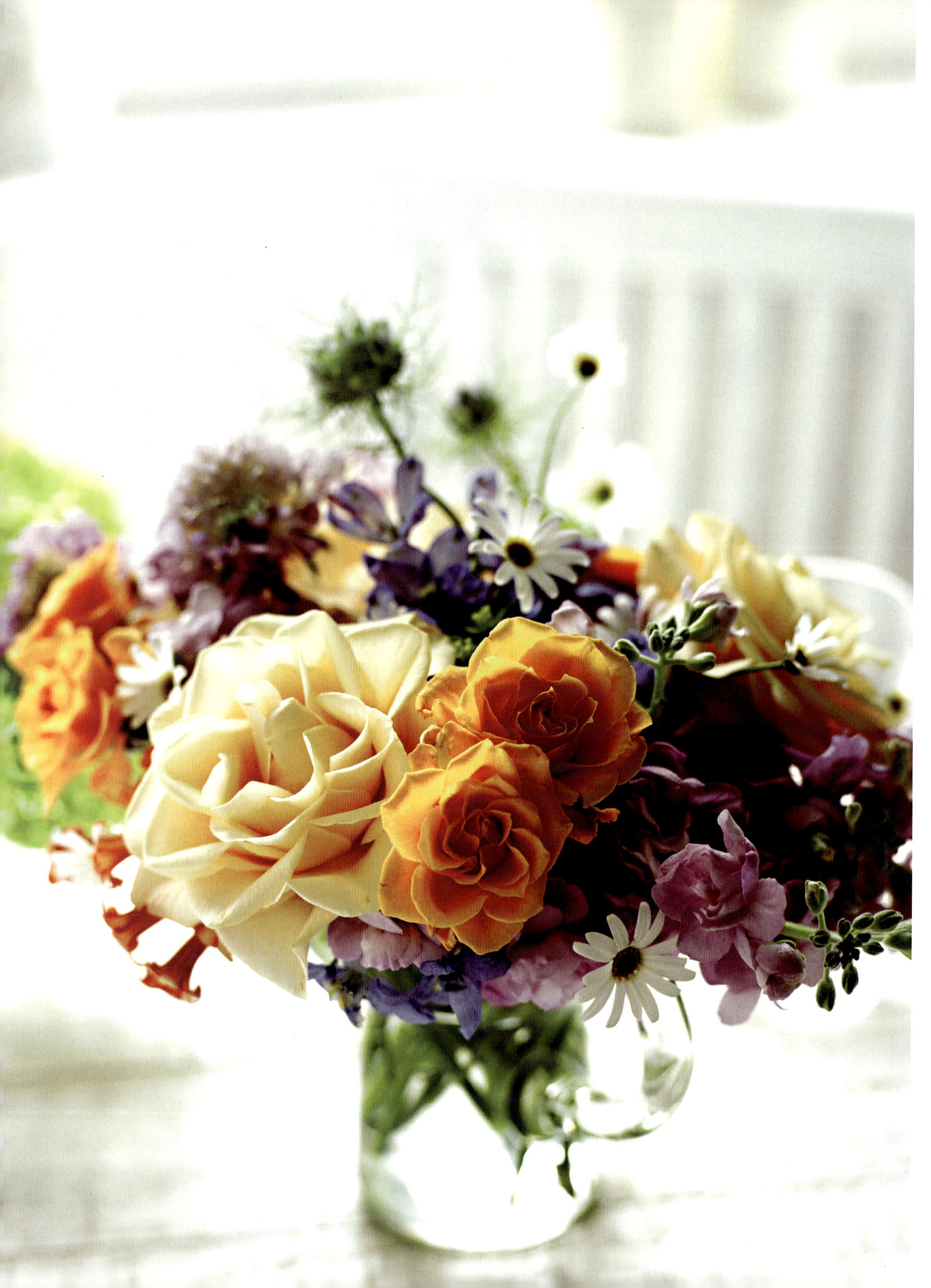

Sunny Bouquet

The artist was drawn to the colorful impressionistic flowers in the center of the photograph and chose to make a painting that was both literal and looser than the original image.

PAINTS
Aureolin
Cadmium orange
Cadmium red
French ultramarine blue
French ultramarine blue-violet
Hooker's green
Naples yellow
Quinacridone coral
Quinacridone rose
Winsor blue
Winsor yellow deep

TOOLS & MATERIALS
Hot-pressed paper, 140 lb. (300 gsm)
HB pencil
Eraser
3-in. (7.5-cm) wash brush
1-in. (2.5-cm) flat brush
Round brushes, Nos. 6, 10, 14

TECHNIQUES USED
Mixing paint in the palette, *p. 21*
Dropping in color, *p. 21*
Wet-onto-dry, *p. 22*
Wet-into-wet, *p. 22*
Glazing, *p. 23*
Blending, *p. 24*
Lost and found edges, *p. 24*

1 Mix a small, creamlike puddle of each of your colors. Use these freely in the following steps, to match the color of the flowers and shadows. Draw the bouquet in more detail than you may need in the final painting, so that you will be able to select as you progress. Keep your lines light, especially in the center of the large white rose on the left. Wet both sides of the paper thoroughly with a 3-in. (7.5-cm) wash brush. This will help the paper to buckle less during painting.

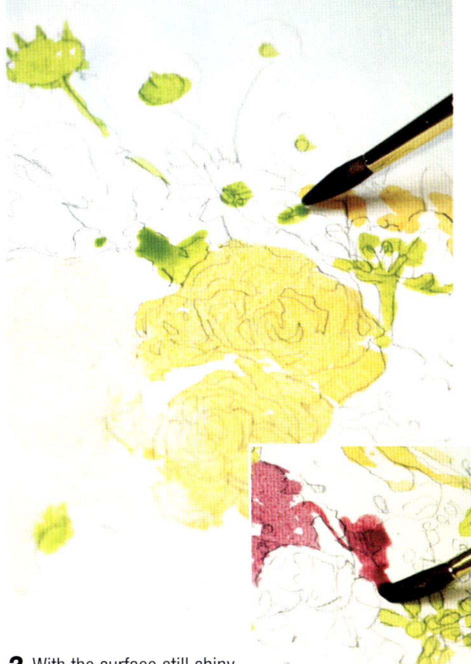

2 With the surface still shiny, but no pooled water, use a 3-in. (7.5-cm) wash brush to apply the background blue (leave the white areas). Take care to paint around the sun-washed daisies. When the paper is dry, if the color is too light, rewet with a light, clean water wash and repeat. Next begin applying blocks of color to the flowers (inset). Work one color at a time all around the painting.

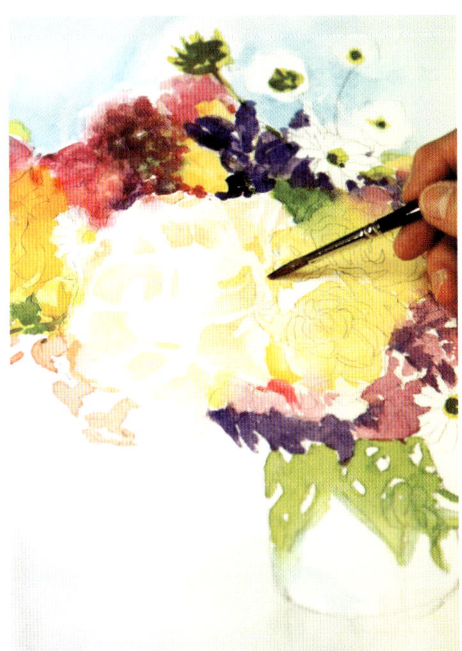

3 When painting the white rose in front left, keep the first petal shadows light (watery) and warm, using a deep gold or grayed orange. Several glazes will bring these shadows to the correct value as the painting progresses. When the shadow is put down, immediately blend the soft end with a thirsty brush where the shadow merges into the light.

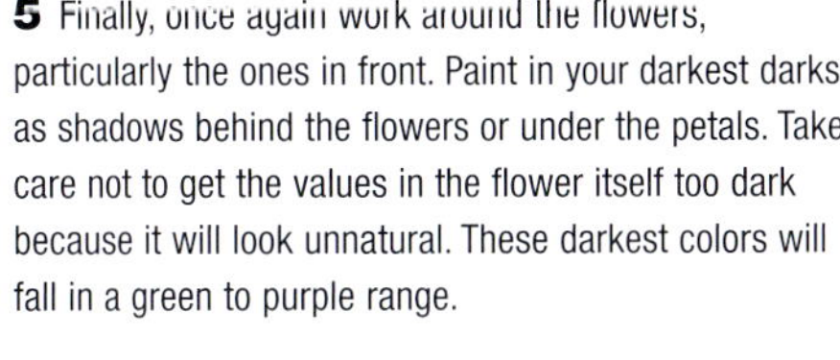

4 Begin to deepen the values of the flower shadows by painting in a darker mixture of the same color you used at first. In the large white rose, glaze in the deepest shadows only in the deepest crevices. Remember to step back from the painting for a perspective on your work.

5 Finally, once again work around the flowers, particularly the ones in front. Paint in your darkest darks as shadows behind the flowers or under the petals. Take care not to get the values in the flower itself too dark because it will look unnatural. These darkest colors will fall in a green to purple range.

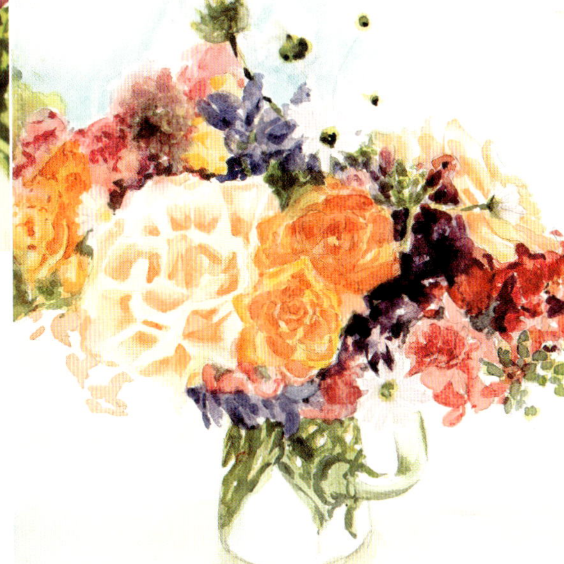

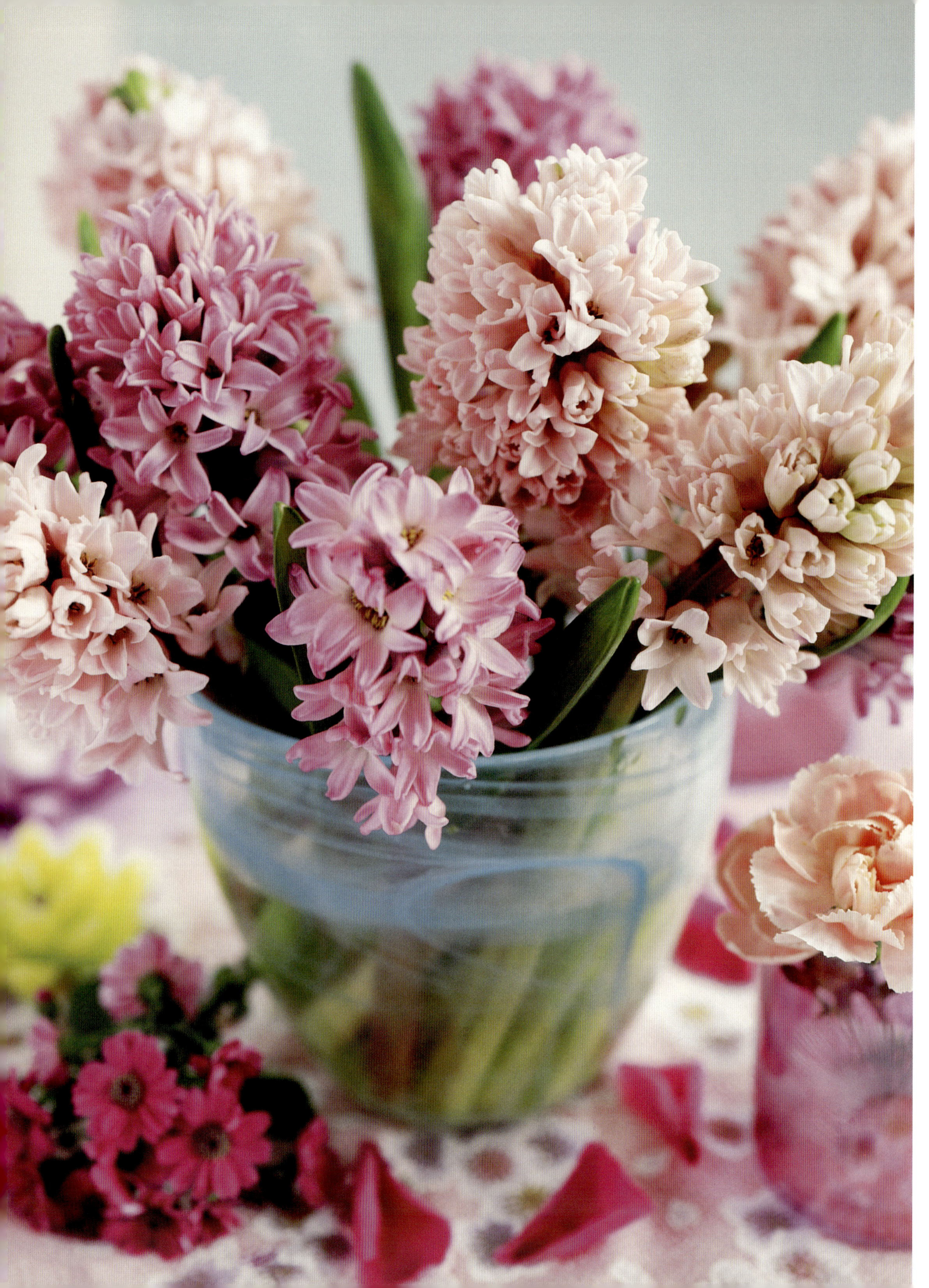

Hyacinths

This painting focuses on color, light, and pattern, with the texture of the flowers contrasting with the softer washes in the bowl.

PAINTS
Cerulean blue
Manganese blue hue
Quinacridone coral
Quinacridone magenta
Quinacridone rose
Winsor yellow

TOOLS & MATERIALS
Cold-pressed paper, 140 lb. (300 gsm)
HB pencil
¾-in. (2-cm) oval brush
Round brush, No. 6
1-in. (2.5-cm) flat brush

TECHNIQUES
Flat wash, *p. 20*
Wet-onto-dry, *p. 22*
Wet-into-wet, *p. 22*
Dropping in color, *p. 21*
Glazing, *p. 23*
Lost and found edges, *p. 24*
Adding highlights, *p. 27*
Negative painting, *p. 28*

1 Draw the flower arrangement onto the watercolor paper using an HB pencil.

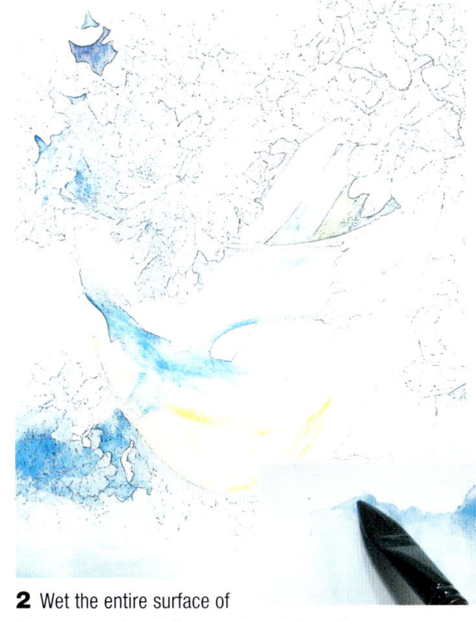

2 Wet the entire surface of the paper and wash in an underpainting of manganese blue hue and Winsor yellow using a ¾-in. (2-cm) oval brush (inset). Let the colors flow together, establishing a strong under-structure where the gray to dark values will be placed. The brush has a point but is also plump and allows a lot of water and pigment to be carried to the paper. The point allows for easy cutting-in where necessary.

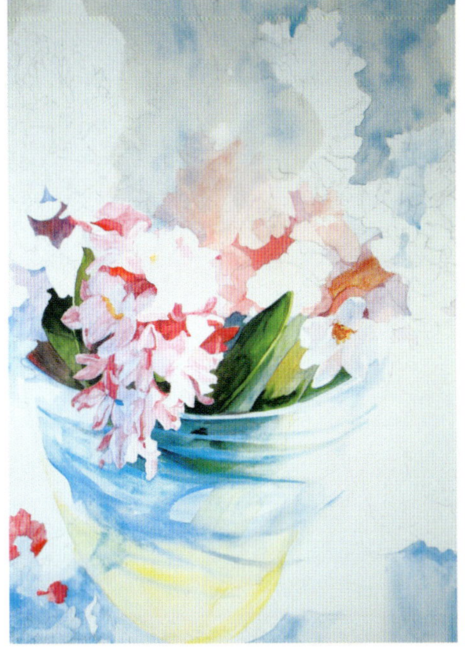

3 When the underpainting has dried, paint the local color of each object. Wash cerulean blue into the background, creating negative spaces around the flowers. Next, with a No. 6 round brush, begin to apply light washes of quinacridone coral and rose. Drop Winsor yellow into the coral wash to produce a glow.

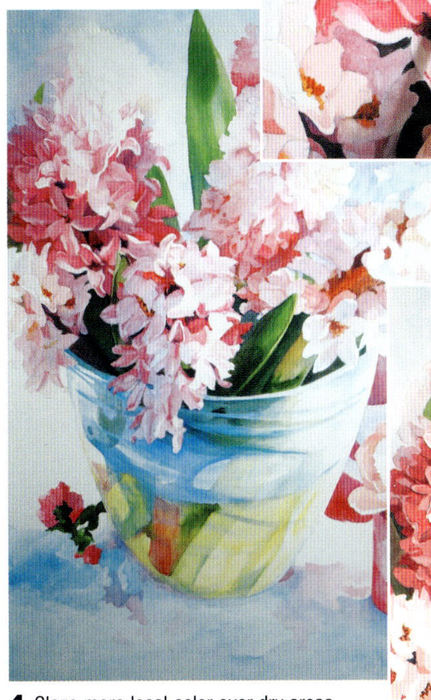

4 Glaze more local color over dry areas and darker values over the flowers using stronger washes of quinacridone coral, rose, and magenta. Dry well between each layer of glazed color. A pattern of light and dark begins to form that helps to carry the viewer's eye through the painting. Using the flat brush, lift back to light values that add detail and dimension to the flowers (inset).

5 Establish soft washes and lost edges using the color lifting technique to contrast with the hard edges and patterns of the flowers. Here, large unifying glazes were pulled over areas in shadow to eliminate detail and to contrast with the lighter areas.

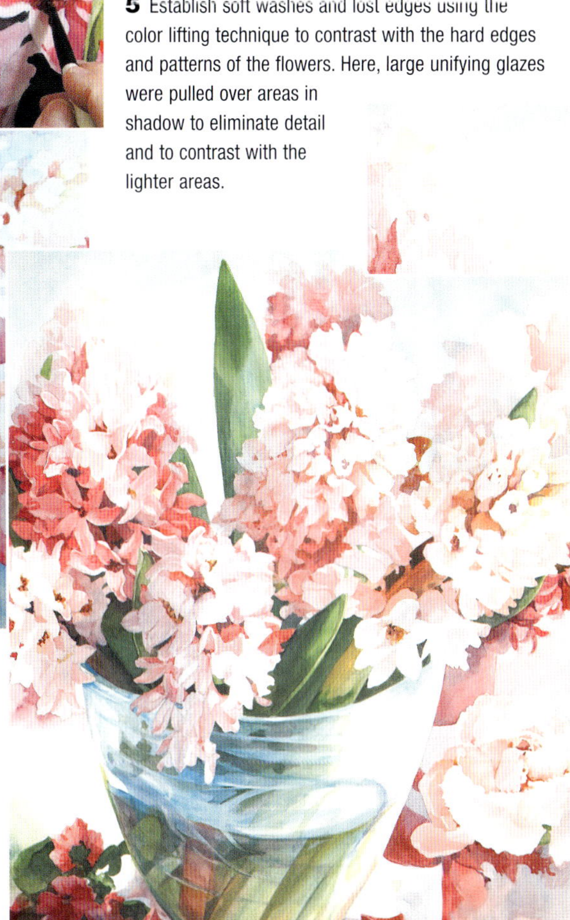

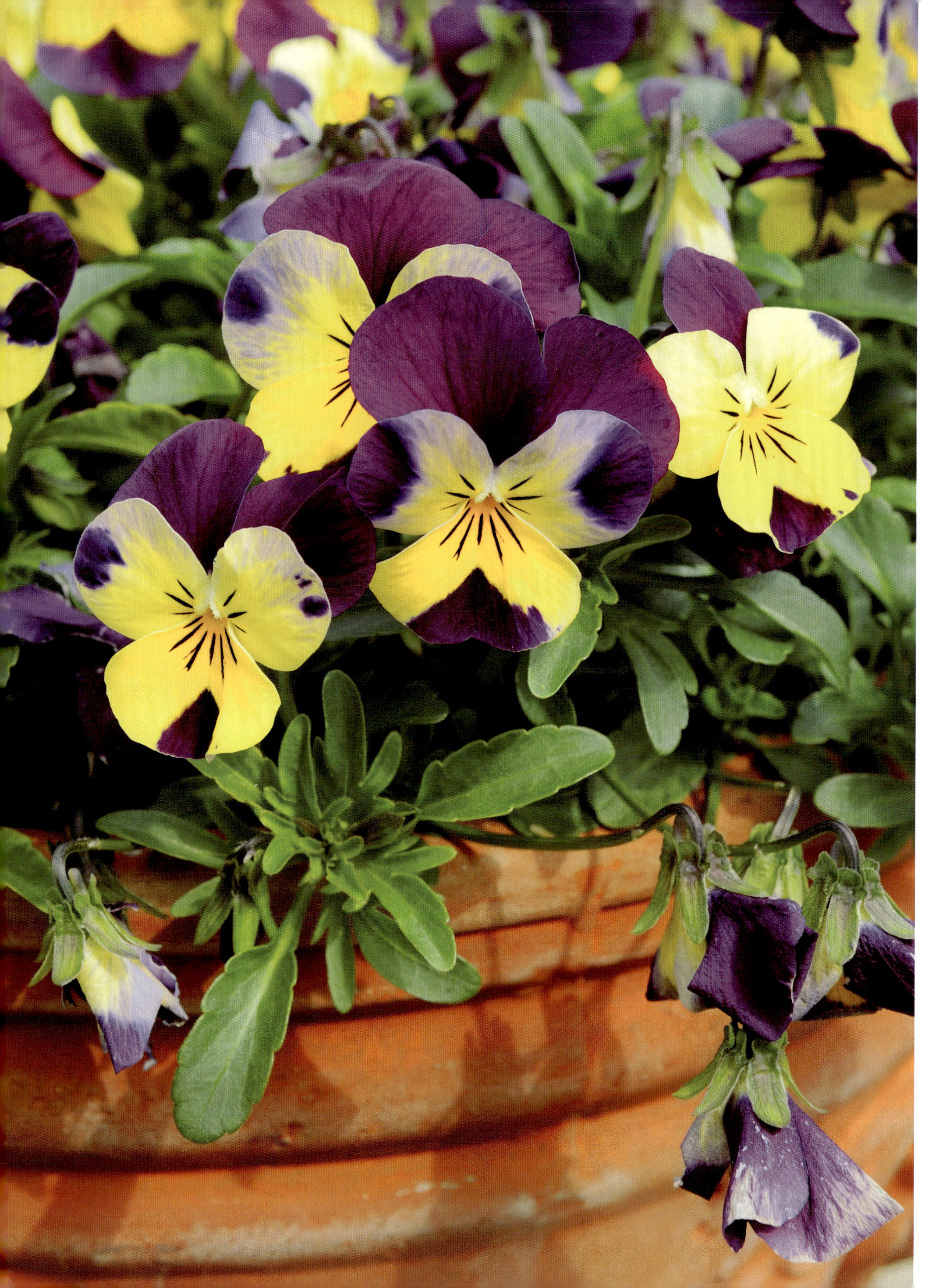

Pansies

Intense, complementary colors and a full range of values from white to deepest green enhance the simple charm of violas. Soft, low-angled light falling on fading blossoms creates unusual shadows.

PAINTS

Aureolin
Hansa yellow medium
Hooker's green
New gamboge
Phthalo blue
Purple magenta
Sap green
Translucent orange

TOOLS & MATERIALS

Cold-pressed paper, 140 lb. (300 gsm)
HB pencil
Masquepen
Round brushes, Nos. 4, 6, 8
Rigger
White watercolor pencil

TECHNIQUES USED

Graded wash, *p. 20*
Mixing paint in the palette, *p. 21*
Wet-onto-dry, *p. 22*
Wet-into-wet, *p. 22*
Glazing, *p. 23*
Masking to reserve the paper, *p. 25*
Masking for details, *p. 25*
Shadows, *p. 28*
Watercolor pencil, *p. 35*

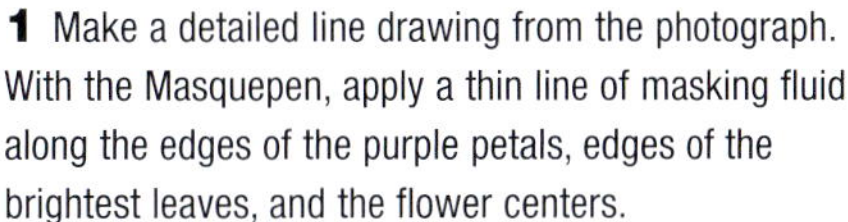

1 Make a detailed line drawing from the photograph. With the Masquepen, apply a thin line of masking fluid along the edges of the purple petals, edges of the brightest leaves, and the flower centers.

2 Using a wet-into-wet technique and a No. 8 round brush, apply a wash of aureolin and Hansa yellow medium to yellow portions of the petals and the leaves. Using a No. 6 round brush, paint a graded wash of phthalo blue on the brightest leaf tips, which reflect the blue sky.

3 Establish the underlying pink glow of the purple petals with two to three graded, wet-into-wet washes of purple magenta applied with a No. 6 brush (inset). With the same technique and brush, lay in graded washes of sap green to the darkest areas of the leaves, stems, and sepals.

4 Mix translucent orange and phthalo blue to create a variety of browns. Use these mixes in graded washes, wet-into-wet with a No. 8 brush, to define the pot. Apply the first of four to five glazes of a purple magenta and phthalo blue mix to the purple petals. Remove the masking. Lay in the veins of the petals, wet-onto-dry, with the purple mix and a rigger.

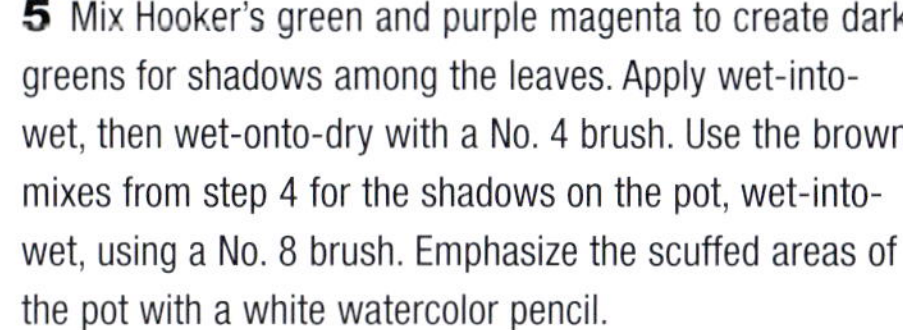

5 Mix Hooker's green and purple magenta to create dark greens for shadows among the leaves. Apply wet-into-wet, then wet-onto-dry with a No. 4 brush. Use the brown mixes from step 4 for the shadows on the pot, wet-into-wet, using a No. 8 brush. Emphasize the scuffed areas of the pot with a white watercolor pencil.

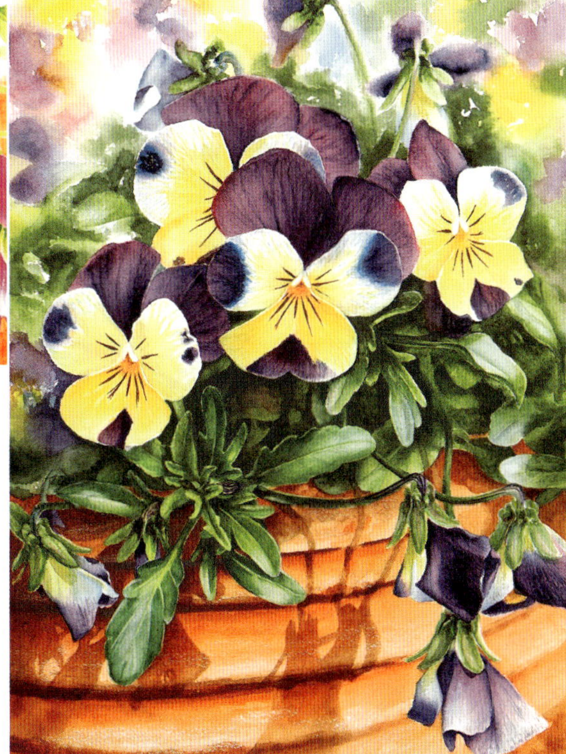

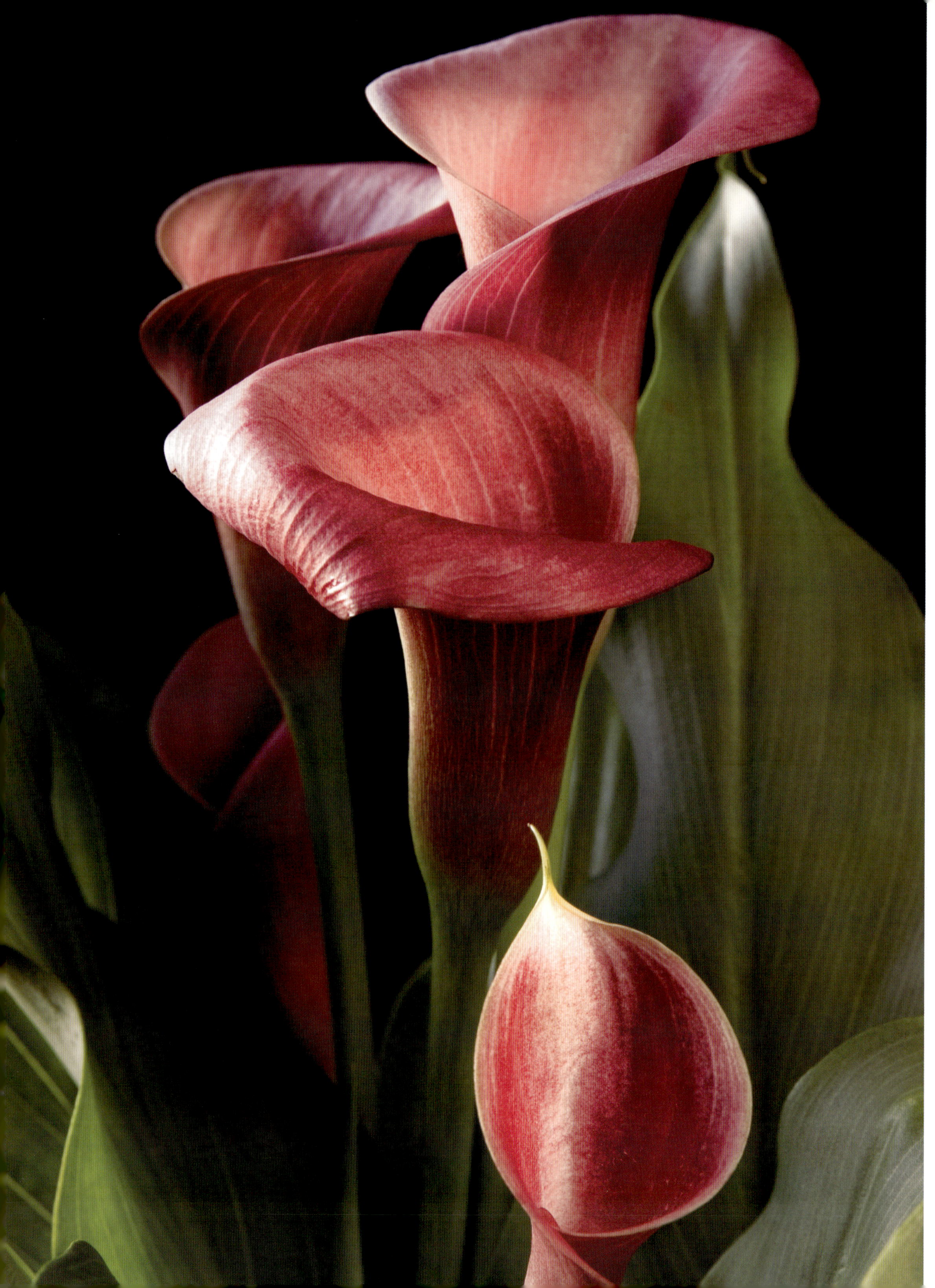

Calla Lilies

The artist was drawn to the extreme value range from white to black, and to the many-hued greens and rose colors in the flowers and leaves.

PAINTS

Aureolin
Cobalt blue
French ultramarine blue
Neutral tint
Phthalo green
Quinacridone burnt scarlet
Quinacridone coral
Quinacridone gold
Quinacridone magenta
Quinacridone rose
Quinacridone violet

TOOLS & MATERIALS

Cold-pressed paper, 140 lb. (300 gsm)
HB pencil
Masking fluid
Old brush
3-in. (7.5-cm) wash brush
1-in. (2.5-cm) flat brush
Round brushes, Nos. 10 and 14
Fritch scrubber, No. 2
Tissues and paper towels

TECHNIQUES USED

Flat wash, *p. 20*
Mixing paint in the palette, *p. 21*
Dropping in color, *p. 21*
Wet-onto-dry, *p. 22*
Wet-into-wet, *p. 22*
Glazing, *p. 23*
Blending, *p. 24*
Lost and found edges, *p. 24*
Masking to reserve the paper, *p. 25*
Masking for details, *p. 25*
Softening masked edges, *p. 25*
Shadows, *p. 28*

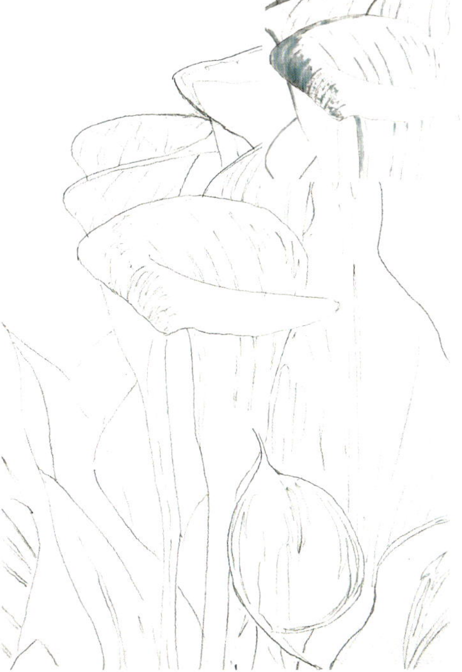

1 Complete a detailed drawing of the calla lilies using the photograph as your reference. Take special care with the veins in the flower and the leaves. Because they are prominent, the accuracy of your drawing is important. Mask the light and white areas. If you choose to mask the veins, make those lines as thin as possible (inset). Dry thoroughly.

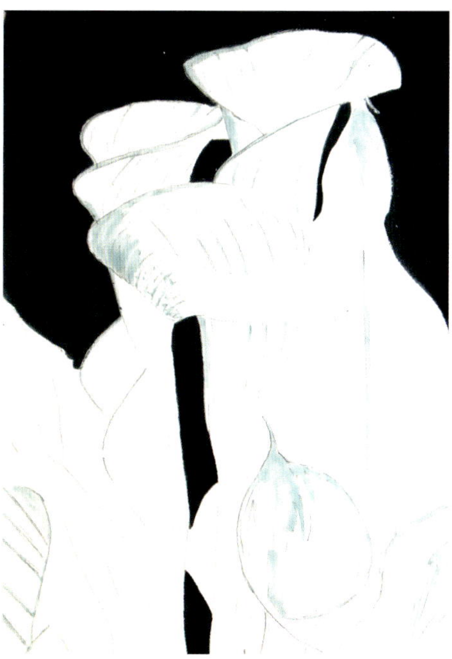

2 Begin glazing the dark background using a mixture of phthalo green and neutral tint using a No. 10 or a No. 14 brush. Keep this mixture on the green side for the first flat wash. To achieve an even wash, turn your painting 180 degrees and tilt it about 45 degrees. This will allow the paint to run down and not jeopardize the flowers with dripping paint. Fill in those spaces between the flowers and leaves where the background shows through.

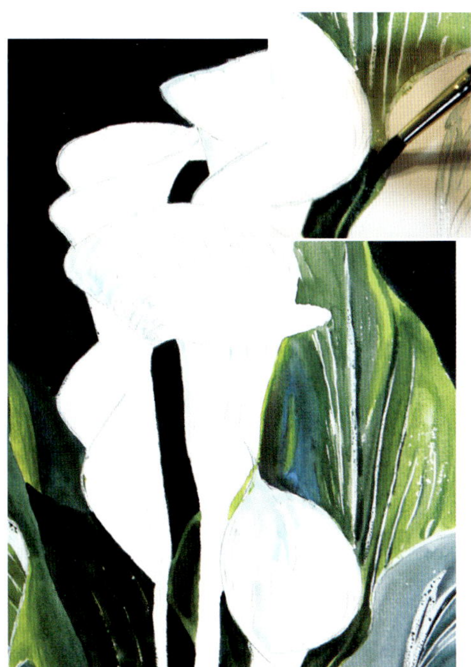

3 In your palette, make creamy puddles of aureolin, cobalt blue, French ultramarine blue, phthalo green, quinacridone gold, magenta, and violet, and neutral tint. With these you should be able to mix all the greens you see in the photograph. As you paint the leaves, bear in mind that the leaves in the background will be cooler in temperature (add cobalt blue) and those in the foreground will be warmer (add yellow). In addition, shaded parts of the leaves will be a darker shade of the green you used in the leaf itself (inset).

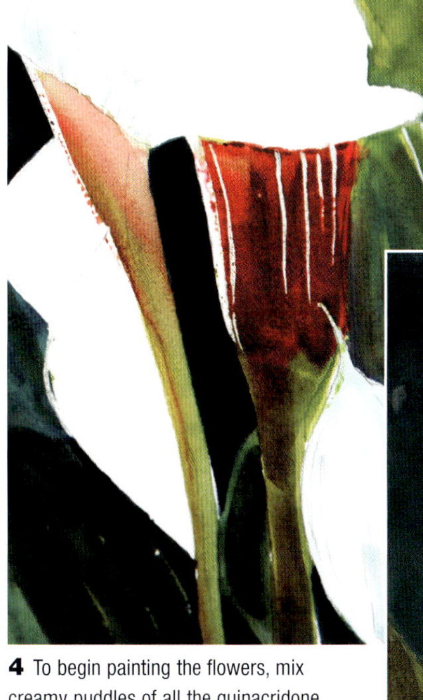

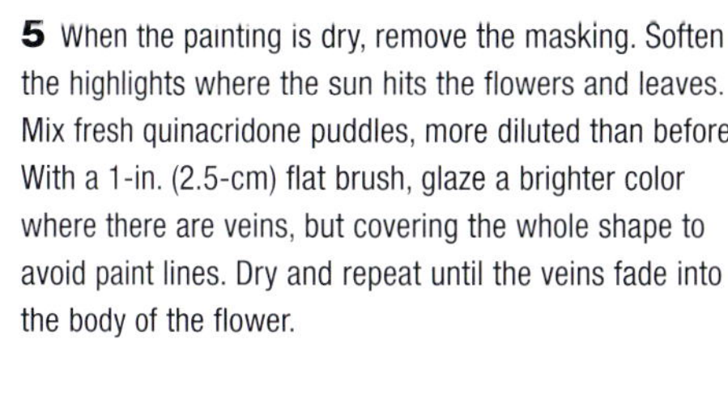

4 To begin painting the flowers, mix creamy puddles of all the quinacridone colors as well as French ultramarine and cobalt blues. With a thirsty 1-in. (2.5-cm) flat brush, blend the grayed underside of the two left calla lilies with the green of the stem. Paint one flower at a time. Once dry, glaze each of the flowers. Continue with successive glazes until the colors look realistic.

5 When the painting is dry, remove the masking. Soften the highlights where the sun hits the flowers and leaves. Mix fresh quinacridone puddles, more diluted than before. With a 1-in. (2.5-cm) flat brush, glaze a brighter color where there are veins, but covering the whole shape to avoid paint lines. Dry and repeat until the veins fade into the body of the flower.

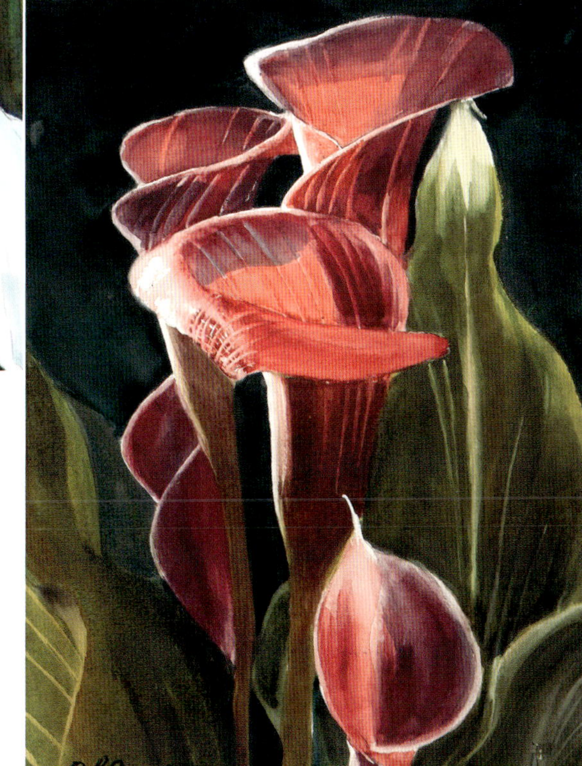

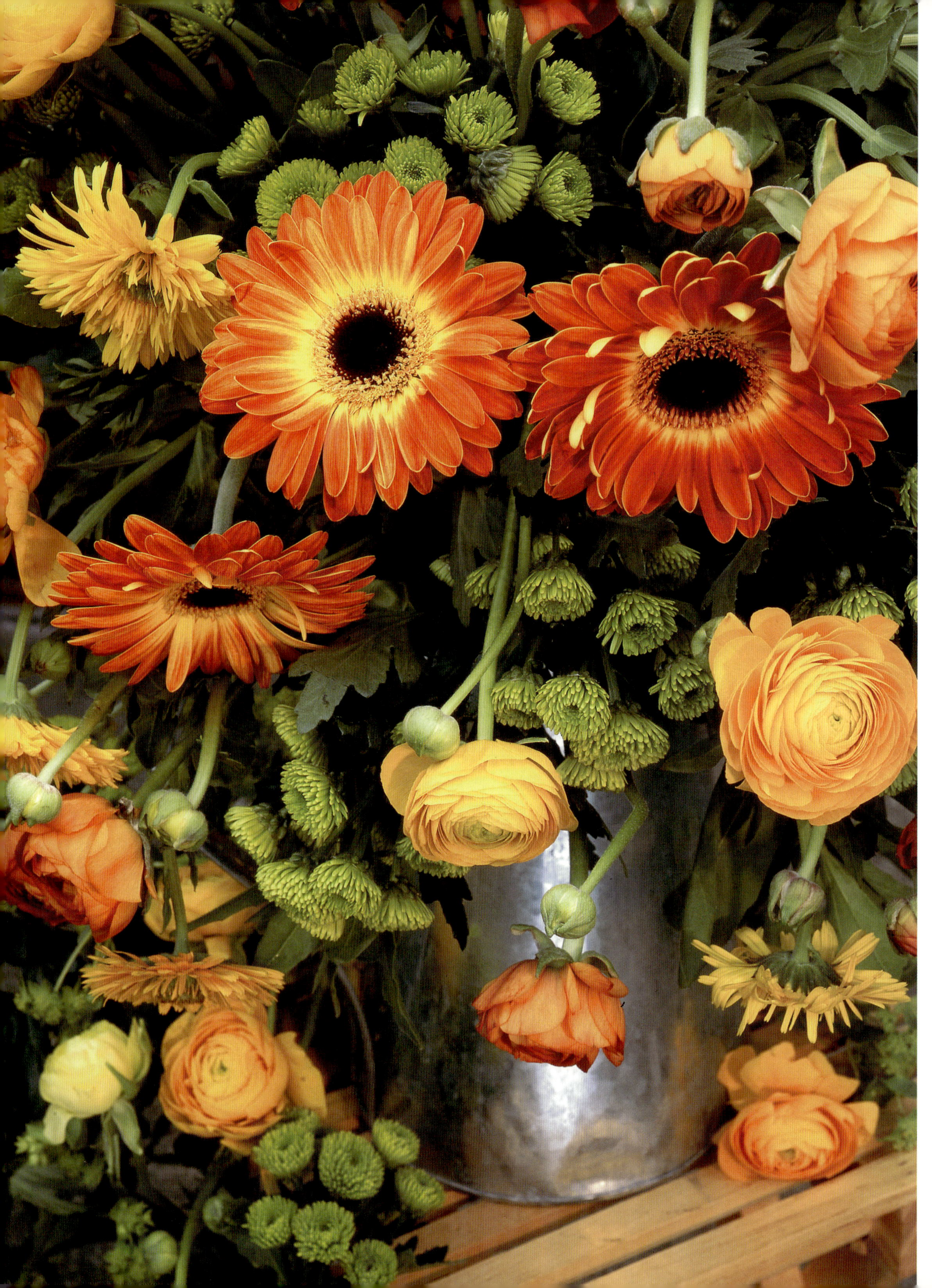

Ranunculus

The artist was drawn to the impact of dark against light, the rich colors, and the complementary color scheme of reds against greens and yellow against violet.

PAINTS
Alizarin crimson
Burnt sienna
Cadmium orange
Cadmium yellow light
Cerulean blue
New gamboge
Permanent rose
Sap green
Ultramarine blue
Winsor green
Winsor violet

TECHNIQUES USED
Mixing paint in the palette, *p. 21*
Wet-onto-dry, *p. 22*
Wet-into-wet, *p. 22*
Paint light to dark, *p. 23*
Masking to reserve the paper, *p. 25*
Negative painting, *p. 28*

TOOLS & MATERIALS
Cold-pressed paper, 140 lb. (300 gsm)
Transfer paper
Invisible tape
Ballpoint pen
Masking fluid
Old brush
Round brushes, Nos. 3, 7, 10

1 Place a sheet of transfer paper on top of your watercolor paper and lay the enlarged print on top. Tape them together at the top of the block to make sure it stays in place. Using a ballpoint pen, trace over the shapes of the flowers, leaves, stems, and shadows to transfer graphite lines from the transfer paper onto the watercolor paper.

2 Use an old brush dipped in masking fluid to mask around the pitcher. When dry, paint the pitcher with ultramarine blue, permanent rose, alizarin crimson, cadmium orange, and sap green wet-into-wet so that the colors blend. When the paint is dry, remove the dried masking. Then paint the wooden slatted table with burnt sienna (mixed with violet for the shadows).

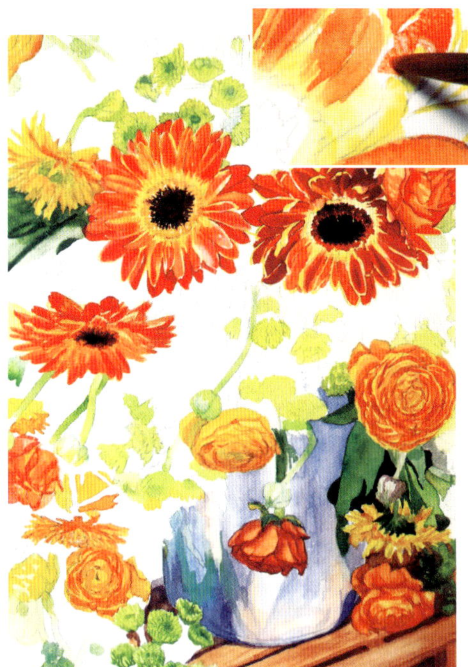

3 Outline the petals and centers of the three large flowers with cadmium yellow light. Apply mixtures of cadmium orange, permanent rose, and new gamboge to each petal (inset), letting it dry before going on to the next. Paint the other yellow and orange flowers, then paint the flowers' middle sections yellow, adding a dark mixture of burnt sienna and violet to the center. Paint the first layer of the yellow-green flowers with cadmium yellow light mixed with a touch of cerulean blue.

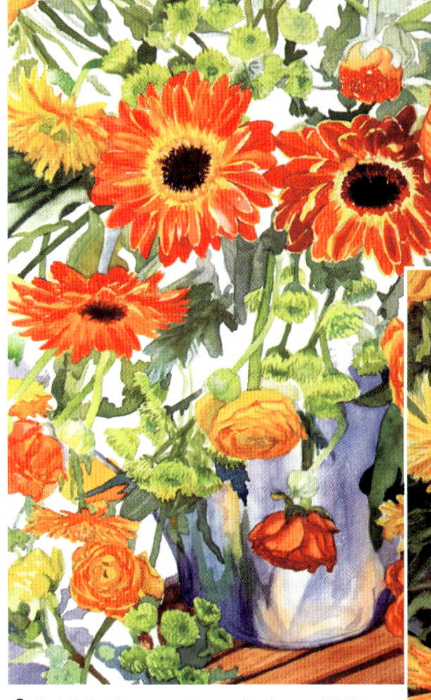

4 Paint the leaves, stems, buds, and little yellow-green flowers using a variety of greens mixed from yellows, blues, and sap green. On the first layers of leaves, add a little burnt sienna to neutralize the color for the grayer greens. Also use a green mixture to add details to the yellow-green flowers you painted in step 3.

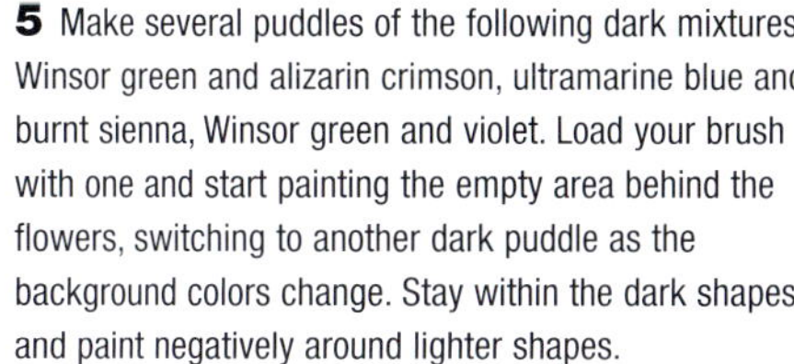

5 Make several puddles of the following dark mixtures: Winsor green and alizarin crimson, ultramarine blue and burnt sienna, Winsor green and violet. Load your brush with one and start painting the empty area behind the flowers, switching to another dark puddle as the background colors change. Stay within the dark shapes and paint negatively around lighter shapes.

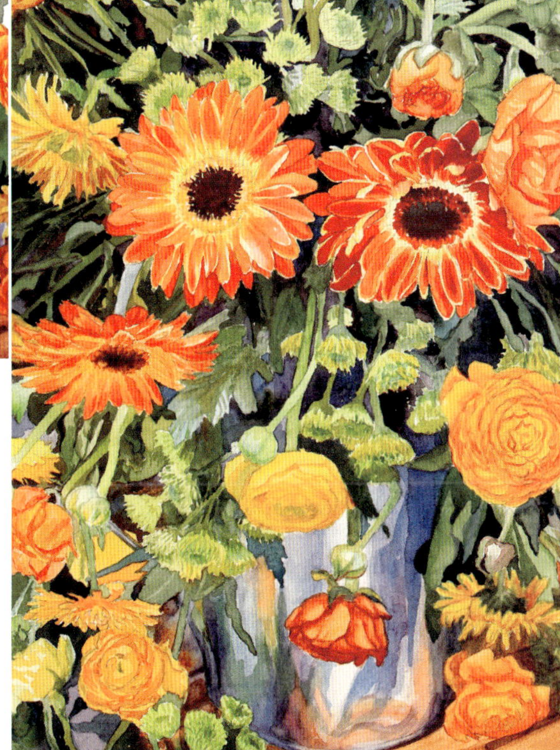

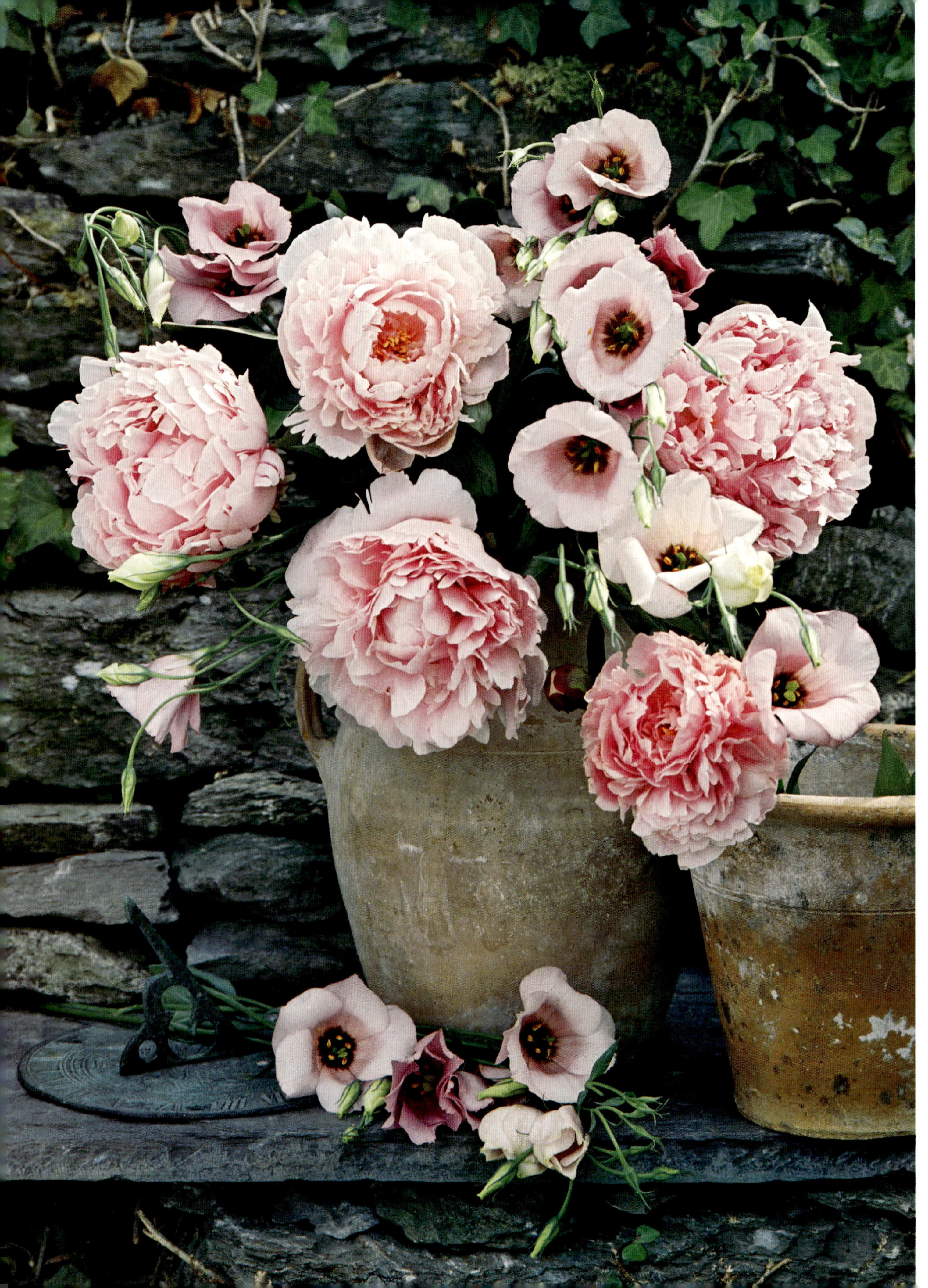

Peonies and Poppies

The artist was intrigued not only by the beautiful lights against the strong darks, but also by the ruffled shapes and the delicacy of the flower petals against the rough textures of the pots and the wall.

PAINTS
Bismuth yellow
Burnt orange
Cadmium scarlet
Cobalt blue
French ultramarine blue
Opera
Permanent rose
Viridian
Winsor green (blue shade)
Winsor red

TOOLS & MATERIALS
Rough paper, 140 lb. (300 gsm)
H pencil
Masking fluid
Old brush
Round brushes, Nos. 2, 4, 12
3-in. (7.5-cm) hake brush
Kosher salt

TECHNIQUES
Flat wash, *p. 20*
Wet-onto-dry, *p. 22*
Wet-into-wet, *p. 22*
Masking to reserve the paper, *p. 25*
Shadows, *p. 28*
Salt, *p. 30*

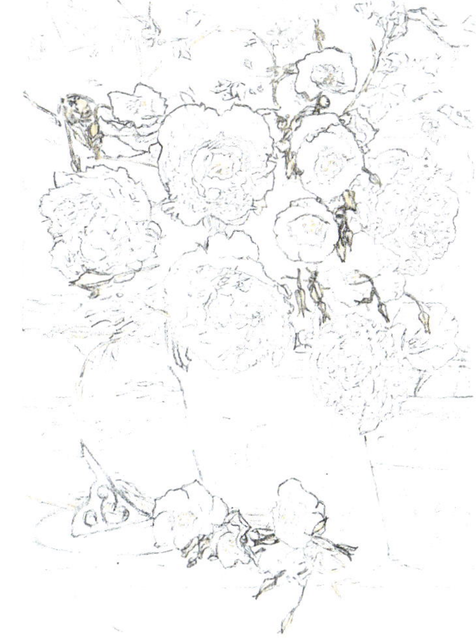

1 Draw out the flowers in pencil on the watercolor paper. Pay attention to the details—include the ruffles in the peonies, the vines, and their buds, as well as the stones and texture in the wall. Indicate the shape of the sundial. Use masking fluid and an old brush to carefully mask only the shapes that fall across the flowers.

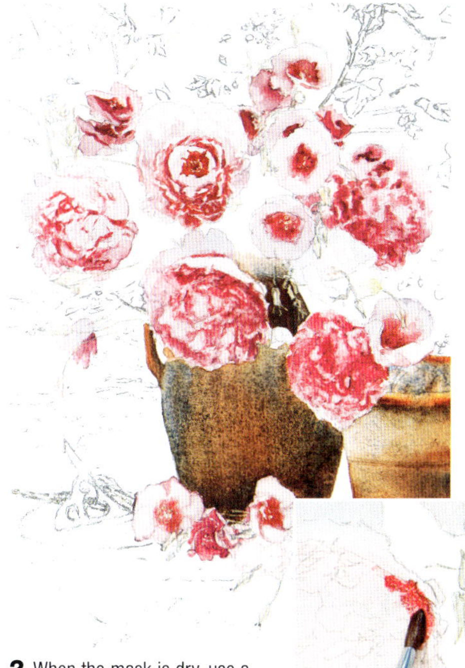

2 When the mask is dry, use a No. 12 brush to run a light pink wash over the flowers and indicate their placement around the painting. Once the wash has dried, begin painting the individual flower shapes, using a No. 4 brush and a variety of pinks and reds (inset). When these are dry, turn your attention to the pots. Use burnt orange and French ultramarine blue to produce granulation and a textured effect.

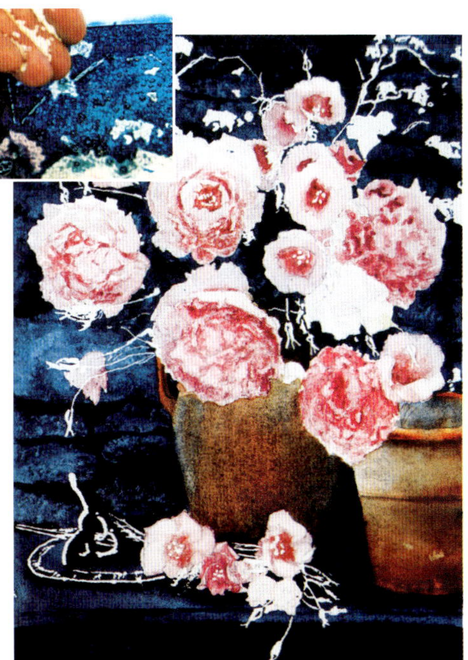

3 Mask the flower shapes and the remaining vines and leaves to protect them from the background wash. Also mask the light parts of the sundial. With a hake brush, run water behind the flowers and around the pots. Paint in the darks with the No. 12 brush then sprinkle with kosher salt for texture (inset). As the dark wash begins to dry, paint shadows to indicate the shapes of the rocks. Make sure all of your shadows are dark enough.

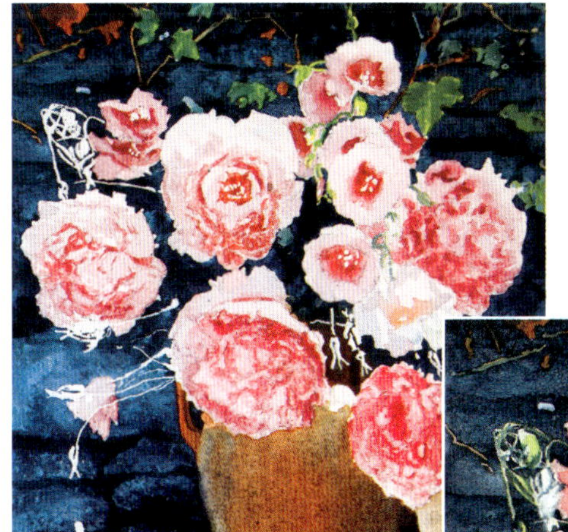

4 When everything is totally dry, remove the mask. Using the No. 4 brush, begin to paint the vines, buds, and leaves into the background, using greens and yellows.

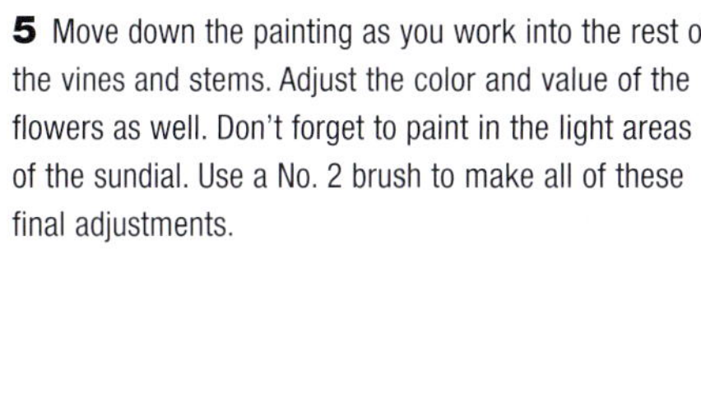

5 Move down the painting as you work into the rest of the vines and stems. Adjust the color and value of the flowers as well. Don't forget to paint in the light areas of the sundial. Use a No. 2 brush to make all of these final adjustments.

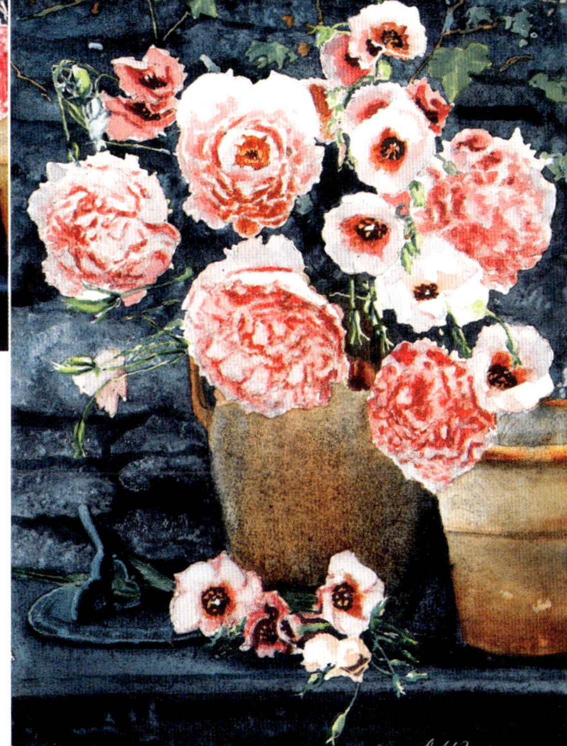

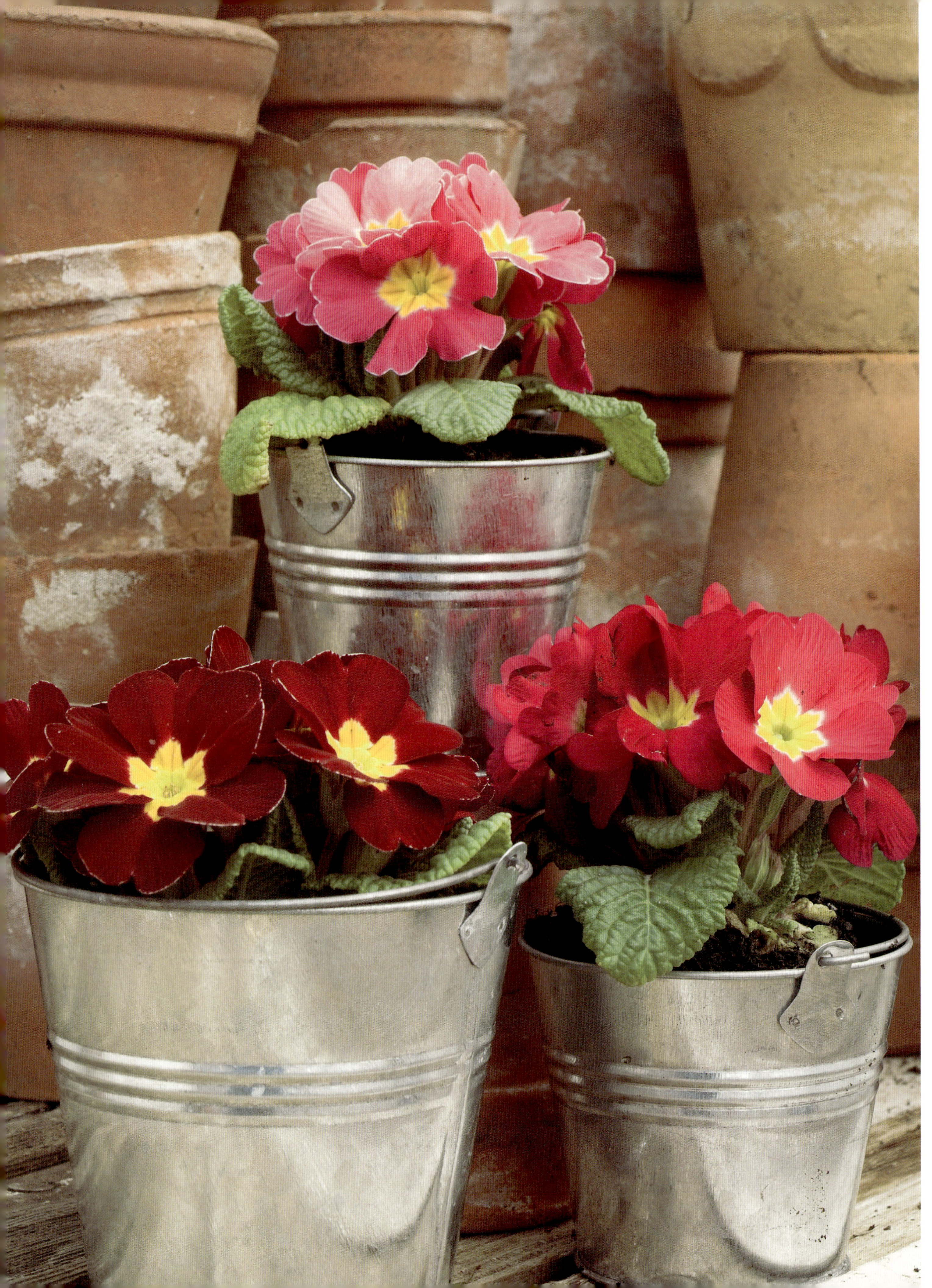

Primroses

These primroses form a very complex image—the greatest challenge lies perhaps in replicating the tin pails to give life to the reflections.

PAINTS

Bright pink
Burnt umber
French ultramarine blue
Hooker's green
New gamboge
Rose madder

TECHNIQUES

Mixing paint in the palette, *p. 21*
Dropping in color, *p. 21*
Wet-into-wet, *p. 22*
Lost and found edges, *p. 24*
Masking for details, *p. 25*

TOOLS & MATERIALS

Cold-pressed paper, 140 lb. (300 gsm)
Mechanical pencil with 5mm HB lead
Masking fluid
Old brush
Round brushes, Nos. 5 or 8 and 10 or 12
Natural sponge

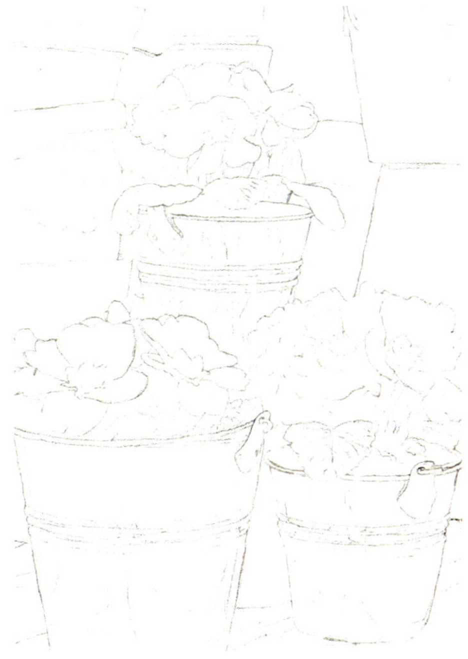

1 Make a detailed pencil drawing on the watercolor paper of the flower to define the light and dark areas. Using masking fluid and an old brush, mask the white edges of the flower petals and the brightest highlights in the metal pails, edges, seams, and ridges.

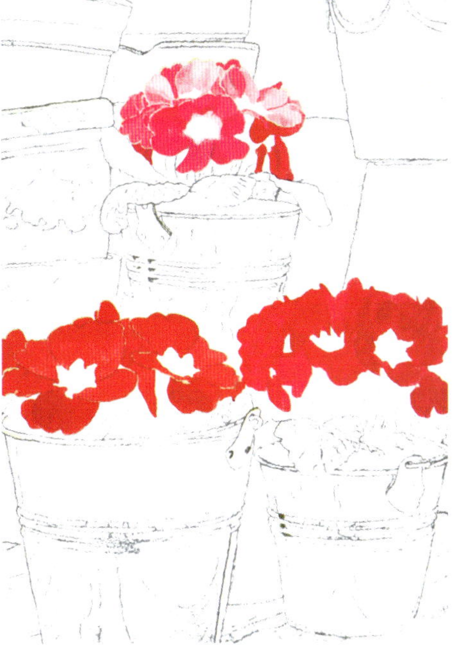

2 Paint the petals of the upper flower in bright pink with a No. 5 or 8 brush. Use the color in varying intensities to differentiate the petals. Mix a second puddle of rose madder for the left-hand flowers and a mixture of bright pink and rose madder for the right-hand flowers. Add French ultramarine blue and new gamboge to the last puddle. Apply to the darkest edge of a shadow and draw it toward the lighter area, using water in your brush to blend the outer edge.

3 Paint the leaves and stems as a single mass in a light shade of Hooker's green. To the Hooker's green, add French ultramarine blue and new gamboge. Use the mix and a No. 5 brush to paint the leaf wrinkles and various shadows that denote the stems and deep shade areas. When dry, apply masking fluid to the outer edge of all painted areas. For the upper pail, using a No. 10 brush, paint a watery mix of French ultramarine blue then, wet-into-wet, add the previous mixtures.

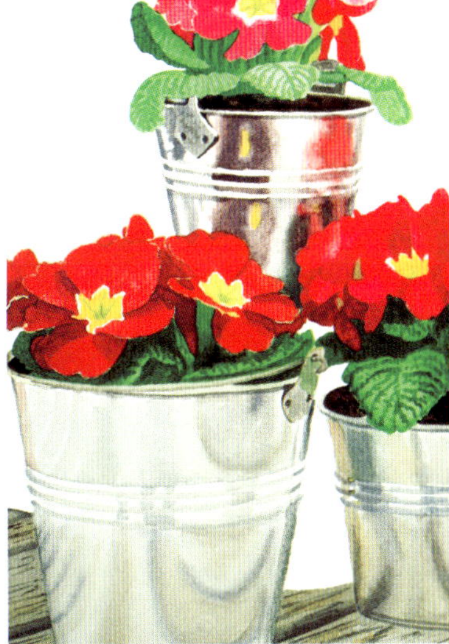

4 Paint the dirt in the pails with burnt umber and French ultramarine blue using a No. 5 brush. For the lower pails, mix French ultramarine blue, rose madder, and new gamboge. Using a No. 10 brush, work in sections, wet-into-wet, blending edges as necessary. Add burnt umber for the reflections. Paint the planks with a mixture of the slate color and then drop in burnt umber, adding detail with a darker shade once dry.

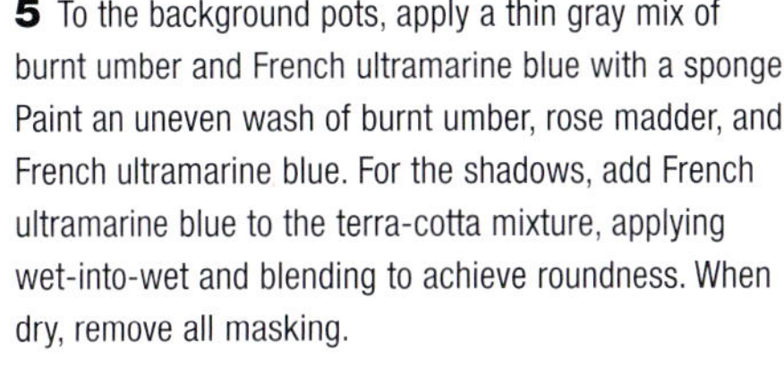

5 To the background pots, apply a thin gray mix of burnt umber and French ultramarine blue with a sponge. Paint an uneven wash of burnt umber, rose madder, and French ultramarine blue. For the shadows, add French ultramarine blue to the terra-cotta mixture, applying wet-into-wet and blending to achieve roundness. When dry, remove all masking.

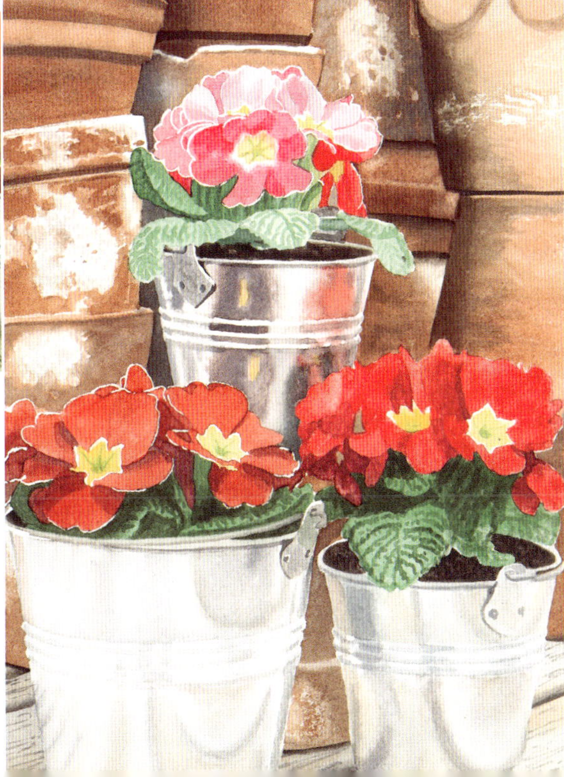

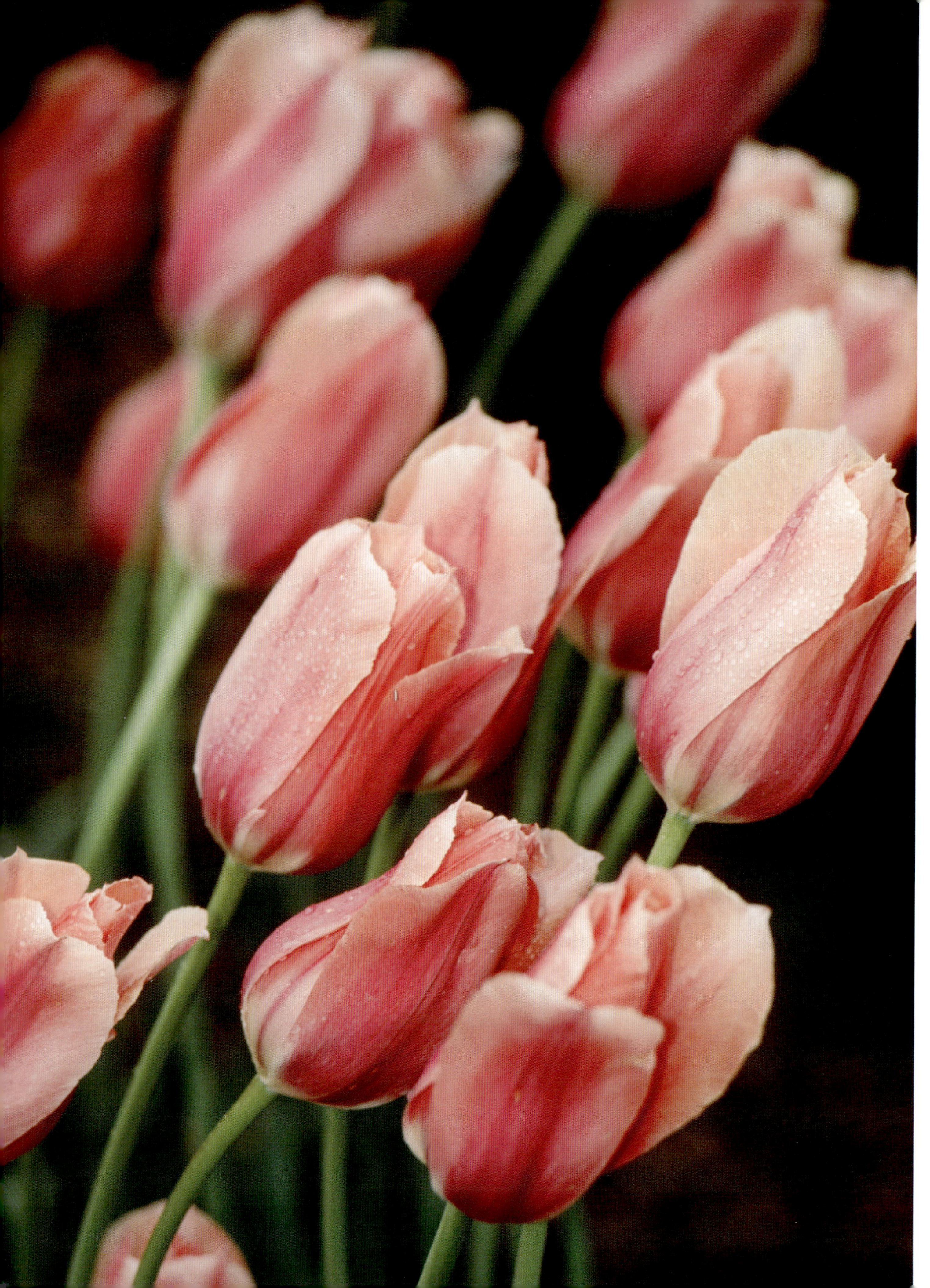

Tulips

This beautiful photograph of wet tulips begs to be painted. Re-creating the water drops is both challenging and fun.

PAINTS
Aureolin
Cobalt blue
Neutral tint
Permanent orange
Phthalo green
Quinacridone coral
Quinacridone magenta
Quinacridone red
Quinacridone rose
Quinacridone violet

TOOLS & MATERIALS
Cold-pressed paper, 140 lb. (300 gsm)
Mechanical pencil
Masking fluid
Old brush
3-in. (7.5-cm) wash brush
Round brushes, Nos. 6 and 10
Fritch scrubber
1-in. (2.5-cm) flat brush
Tissues and paper towels
Dremel tool

TECHNIQUES USED
Flat wash, *p. 20*
Mixing paint in the palette, *p. 21*
Dropping in color, *p. 21*
Wet-onto-dry, *p. 22*
Wet-into-wet, *p. 22*
Glazing, *p. 23*
Lost and found edges, *p. 24*
Masking to reserve the paper, *p. 25*
Masking for details, *p. 25*
Softening masked edges, *p. 25*
Shadows, *p. 28*

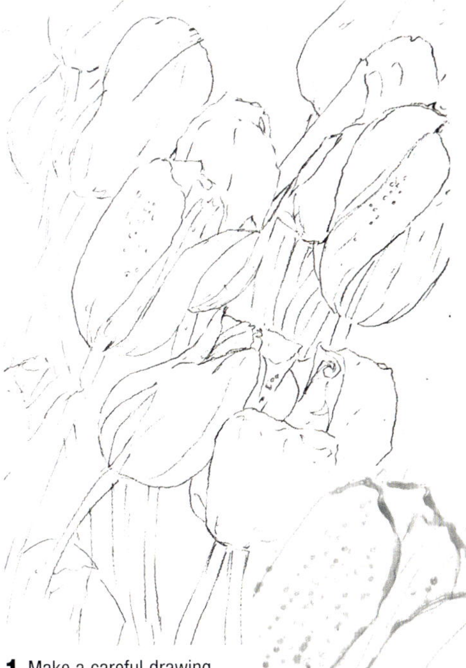

1 Make a careful drawing from the photograph. Use caution when putting in the water drops. Do not make them too large and do not try to put in all of them. Mask the white edges and the water drops (inset). A tiny dot of masking fluid will suffice for the drops. Practice these on a separate sheet of paper before you mask the drawing.

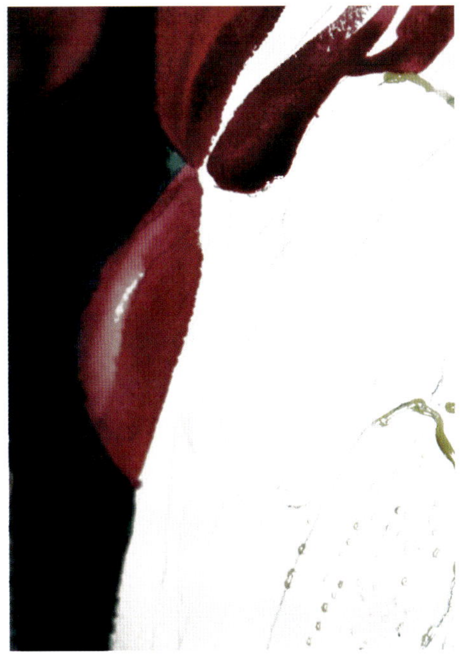

2 Mix a large cream-consistency puddle each of phthalo green, neutral tint, and the quinacridone colors. Begin in the upper left of the painting by wetting the first area to be painted with a No. 10 round brush. Paint in a very dark green (mixing phthalo green and neutral tint), going around the tulips and stems. While the green is wet, paint the flower color right up against the green. Allow them to touch and blend lightly.

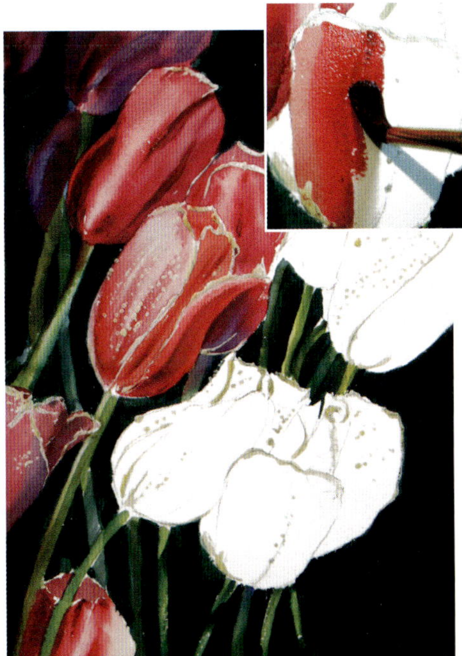

3 Paint the foreground tulips with relatively hard edges using warmer quinacridone mixtures as you move forward in the picture plane (inset). Also paint the stems with a No. 6 brush and with various green and gold mixtures, brushing cobalt blue in shadows across them. Each time you dip your brush, use a different color related to the previous one. This adds more dimension to each object in the painting.

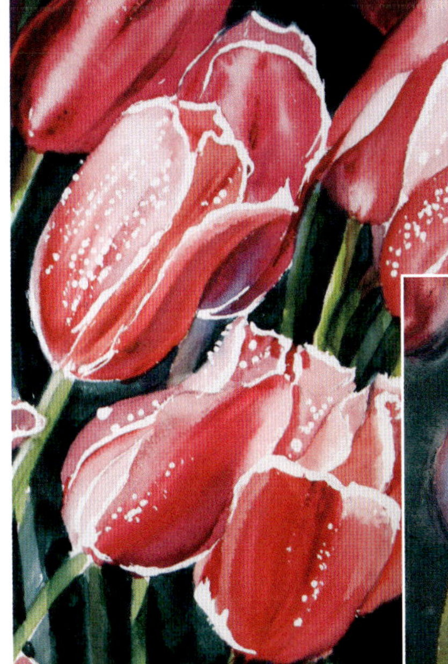

4 When all the tulips are completed and dry, remove the masking, using caution not to smear the green into the protected white area. Using a Fritch scrubber, soften all lines left by the masking but not the water drops. Go deeper into some of the petals, dabbing with tissue to avoid unwanted water lines.

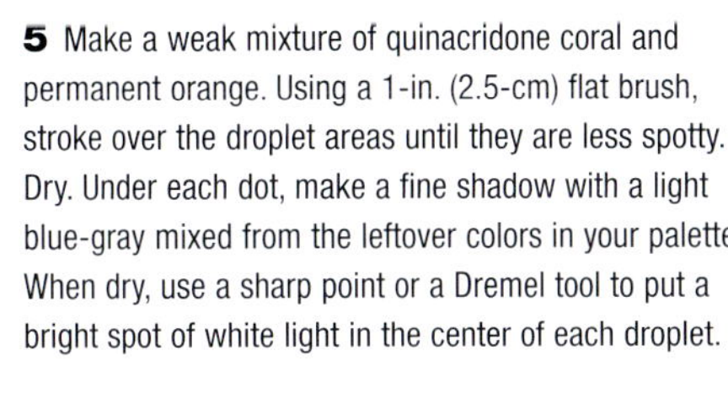

5 Make a weak mixture of quinacridone coral and permanent orange. Using a 1-in. (2.5-cm) flat brush, stroke over the droplet areas until they are less spotty. Dry. Under each dot, make a fine shadow with a light blue-gray mixed from the leftover colors in your palette. When dry, use a sharp point or a Dremel tool to put a bright spot of white light in the center of each droplet.

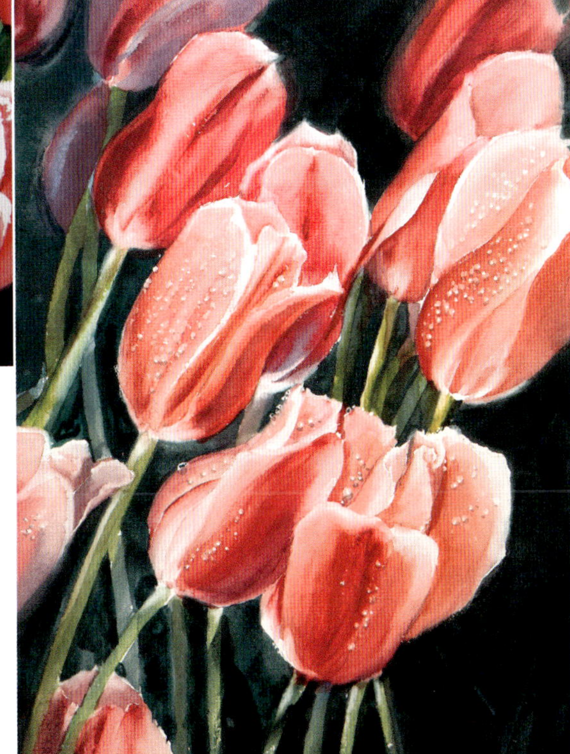

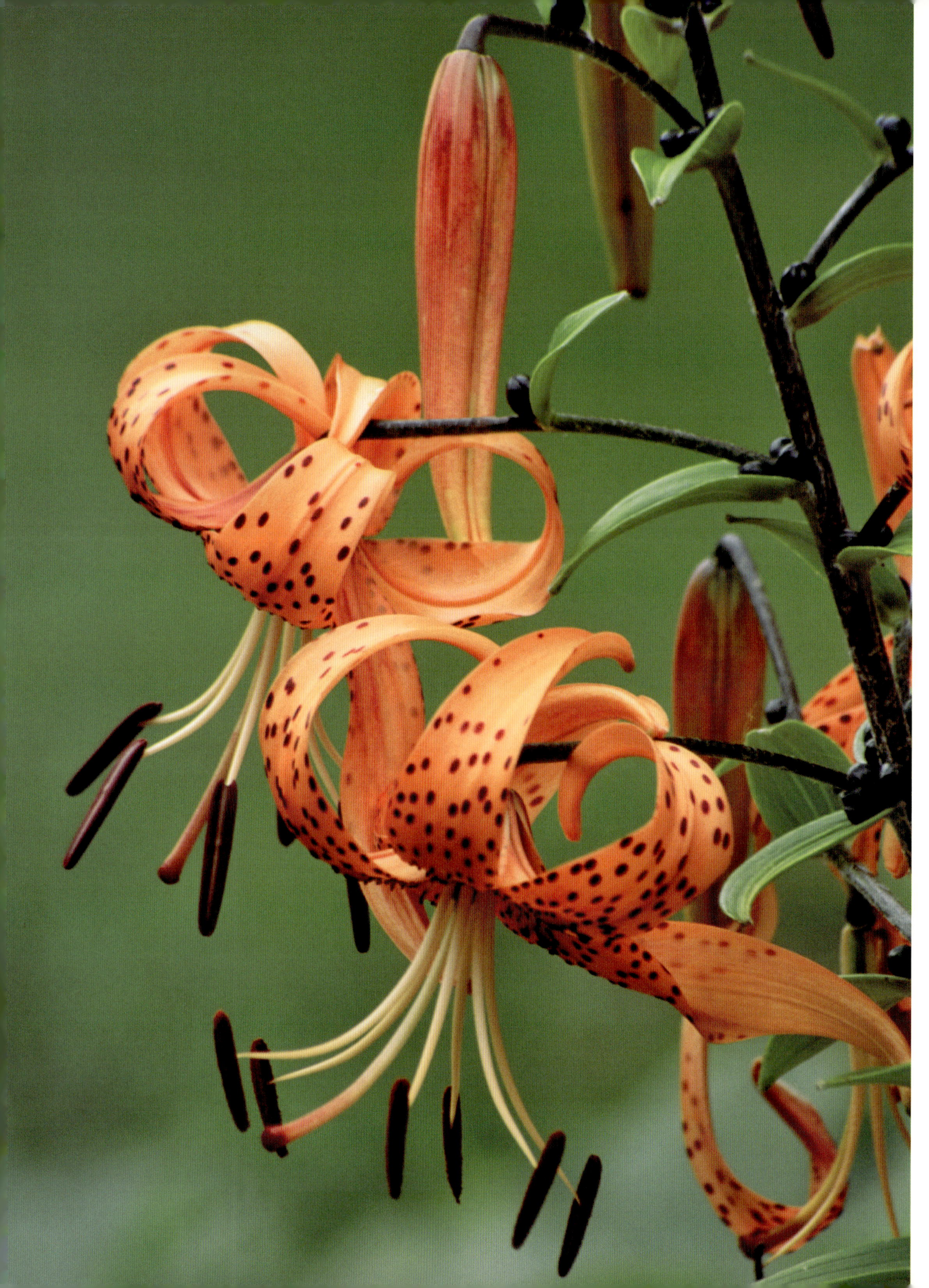

Tiger Lilies

The artistic challenge laid down by this photograph is to make the tiger lilies stand out from the flat green background. The artist added a cleverly chosen color to do this.

PAINTS
Black
Brilliant cadmium red
Chrome yellow
Cobalt violet
French ultramarine blue
Gamboge
Hansa yellow medium
Quinacridone magenta
Sap green
Turquoise blue

TECHNIQUES
Mixing paint in the palette, *p. 21*
Wet-onto-dry, *p. 22*
Wet-into-wet, *p. 22*
Masking to reserve the paper, *p. 25*

TOOLS & MATERIALS
Cold-pressed paper, 140 lb. (300 gsm)
2B pencil
Masking fluid
Incredible Nib
Round brushes, Nos. 3, 5, 12

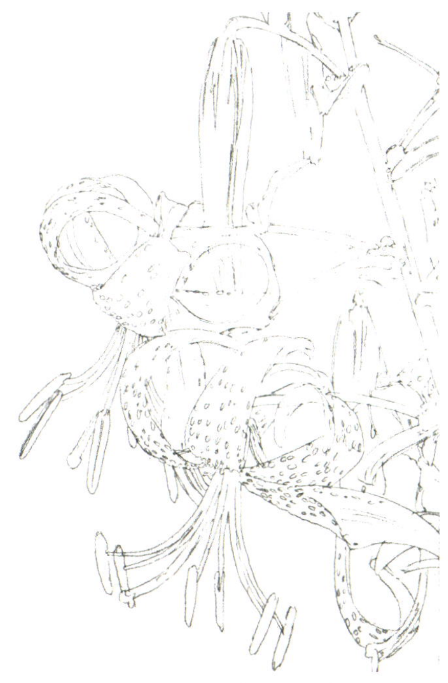

1 Draw the flower in pencil on the watercolor paper. Apply masking fluid with the Incredible Nib to any area of the painting that will remain very light or white. For larger areas of white, don't bother applying masking—work around them.

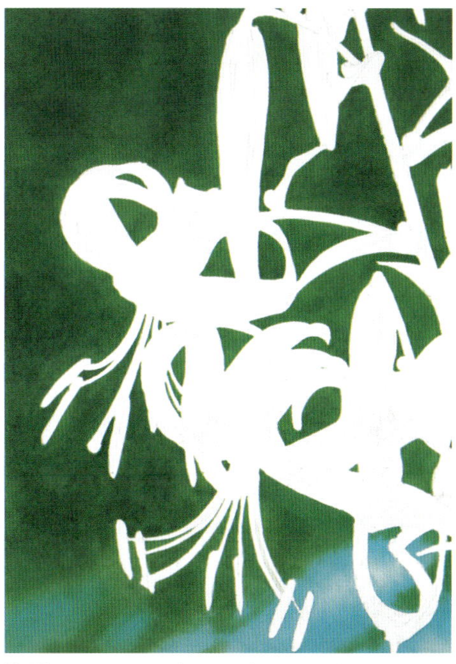

2 Mix sap green, gamboge, and turquoise blue in the palette—enough to complete five layers of the green background. Use a No. 12 brush to paint the larger areas and a No. 5 for smaller areas. Keep the paint moving to achieve an even color. Near the bottom of the painting, apply the turquoise wet-into-wet. Layering wet-onto-dry will ensure an overall balanced color. Paint the larger areas quickly; make at least four layers of background.

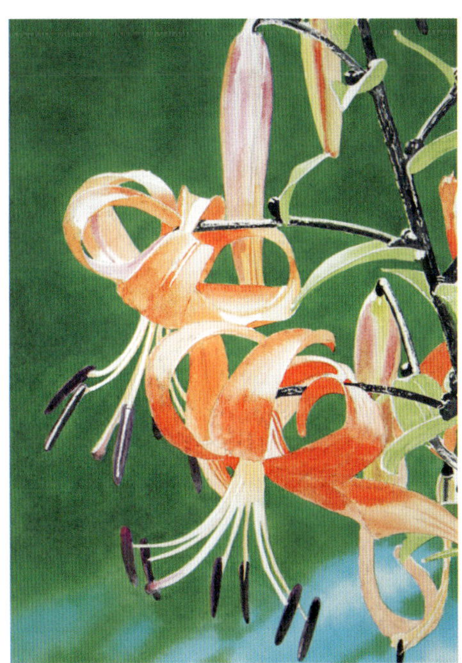

3 With the No. 5 brush, paint all the leaves with a combination of sap green and chrome yellow, using both wet-into-wet and wet-onto-dry techniques. Wet-into-wet, apply a mixture of brilliant cadmium red and chrome yellow to areas of the lily petals. Also apply quinacridone magenta where necessary, for deeper color in the petals. Paint the stems using black and French ultramarine blue. Soften some of the edges of the stems by applying the same paint with a No. 3 brush wet-into-wet.

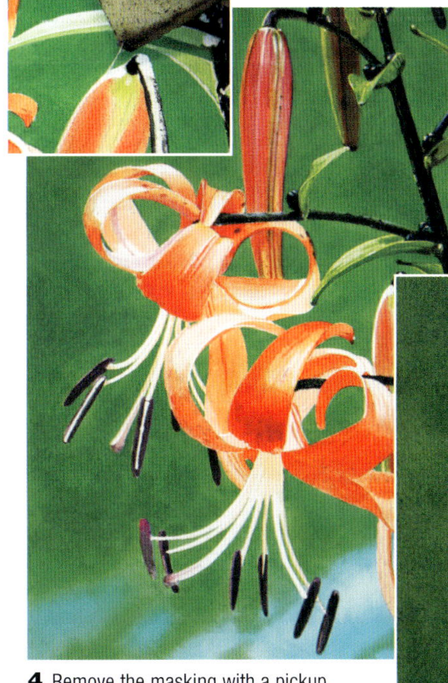

4 Remove the masking with a pickup (inset). Reapply the masking fluid only to areas that are to remain white. Paint over the unmasked areas in the stem using a mixture of sap green, turquoise, and a small amount of black to create the texture on the stems. Starting in the upper right-hand corner, paint one petal and one leaf at a time with a No. 3 brush, focusing on subtle color variations within that area.

5 Reapply the last layer of green background color for a more uniform wash, using the No. 5 and No. 12 brushes, wet-onto-dry, and carefully painting the color to the leaf and petal edges. Remove any remaining masking. The addition of turquoise (a complement of orange) at the bottom of the painting lifts the orange flowers into the spotlight.

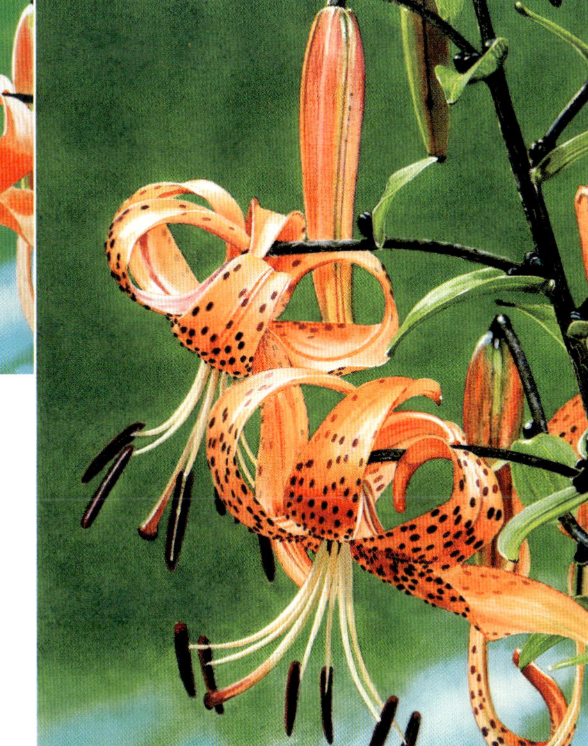

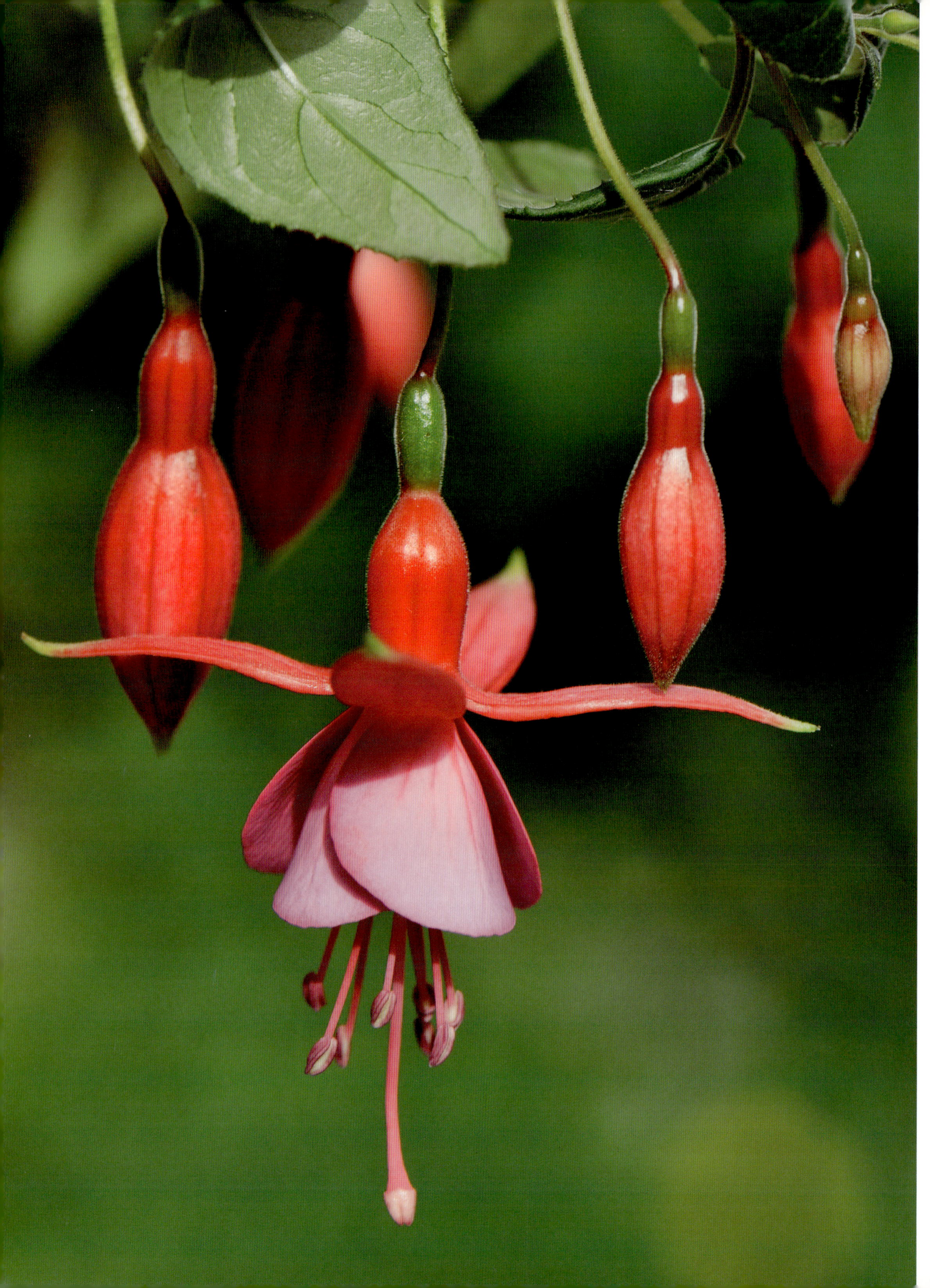

Fuchsia

It is important to have the subject stand away from the background with a three-dimensional effect, and to emphasize the fluorescence of the main flower.

PAINTS

Bright violet
Dioxazine violet
French ultramarine blue
Madder lake
Opera
Orange lake
Permanent rose
Rich green-gold
Sap green
Viridian
Zinc white designers' gouache

TOOLS & MATERIALS

Cold-pressed paper, 140 lb. (300 gsm)
Pencil
Masking fluid
Taper point firm color shaper, No. 0
Flat chisel soft color shaper, No. 2
Natural sponge
Round brushes, Nos. 0, 2, 5, 12
Kosher salt

TECHNIQUES

Variegated wash, *p. 20*
Mixing paint on the paper, *p. 21*
Dropping in color, *p. 21*
Wet-onto-dry, *p. 22*
Wet-into-wet, *p. 22*
Paint light to dark, *p. 23*
Glazing, *p. 23*
Blending, *p. 24*
Lost and found edges, *p. 24*
Masking to reserve the paper, *p. 25*
Softening masked edges, *p. 25*
Salt, *p. 30*
Watercolor and gouache, *p. 32*

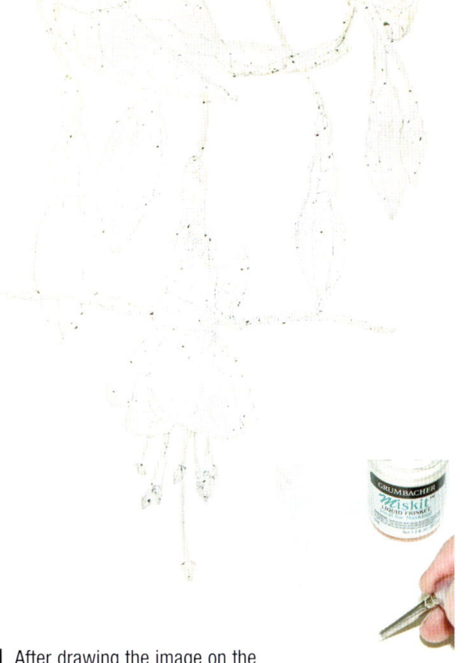

1 After drawing the image on the watercolor paper with a pencil, mask the flower and leaves with the masking fluid, using the color shapers (inset). Dry thoroughly.

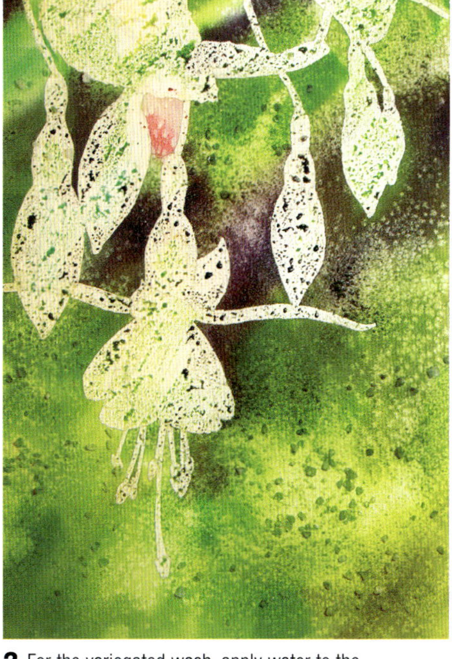

2 For the variegated wash, apply water to the background with a natural sponge. Using a No. 12 round brush, drop and spread blobs of these colors, fully saturated: sap green, viridian, rich green-gold, and dioxazine violet. Take care not to overwork the spreading; you don't want the background to get muddy. Sprinkle kosher salt onto portions of the wet background. When dry, brush all the salt off of the paper, being careful not to disturb the masked areas.

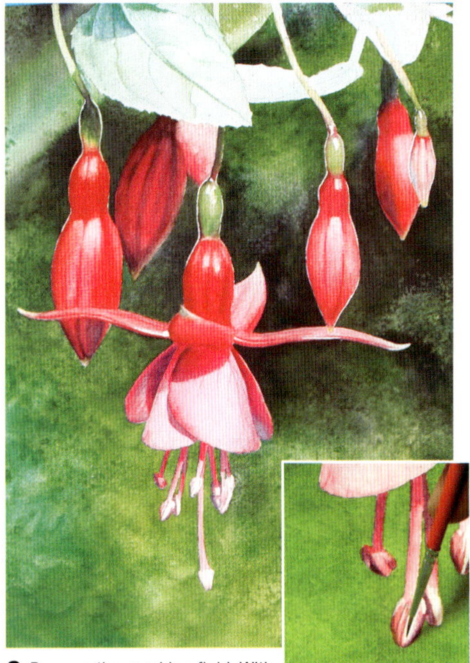

3 Remove the masking fluid. With a No. 5 brush, moisten each area separately, wet-into-wet. Build color depth with several glazings, letting each application dry. Lay in the color, spreading the pigment to the edges. For the top petals, use permanent rose and glaze in madder lake and orange lake. For the bottom petals and sepals, glaze in permanent rose and opera (inset). Use bright violet and French ultramarine blue for shadows. Follow these techniques for the leaves, using the greens, purple, and blue.

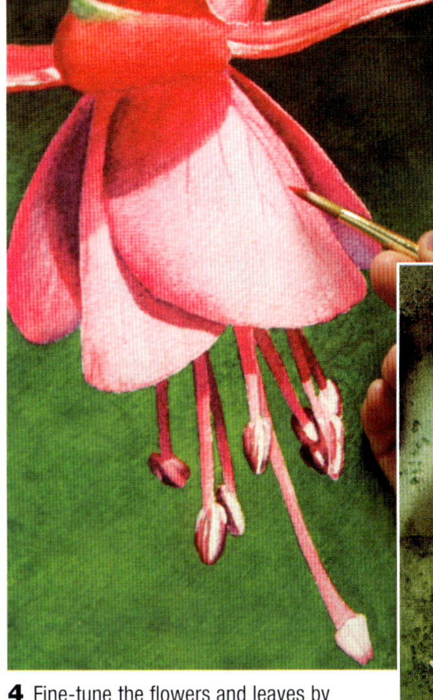

4 Fine-tune the flowers and leaves by glazing using different percentages of saturated color. For the flowers, glaze many layers of the same colors to build the saturation. To paint in the veins, use a No. 2 or a No. 0 round brush.

5 If the background needs to be more saturated, add water to the area with a No. 12 brush, then glaze in saturated color, working the color up to the edge of the water. As you continue add more water to the edges, pulling the pigment into it. Once the background is dry, use white gouache to paint in highlights.

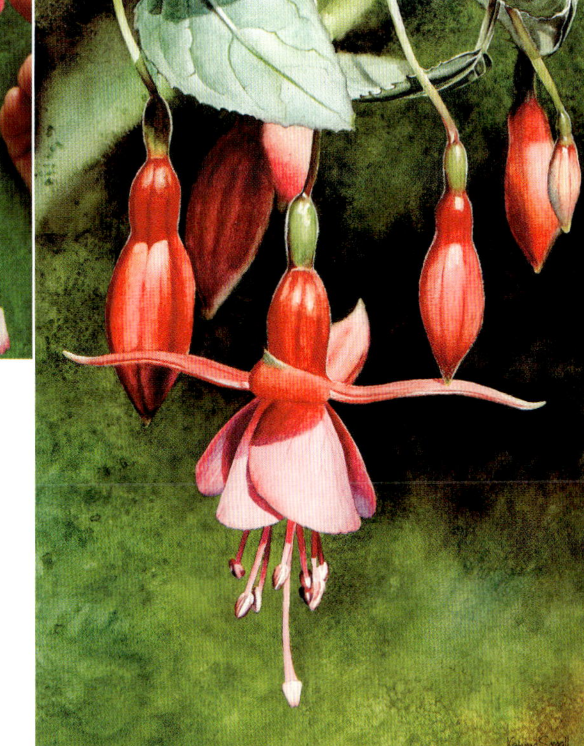

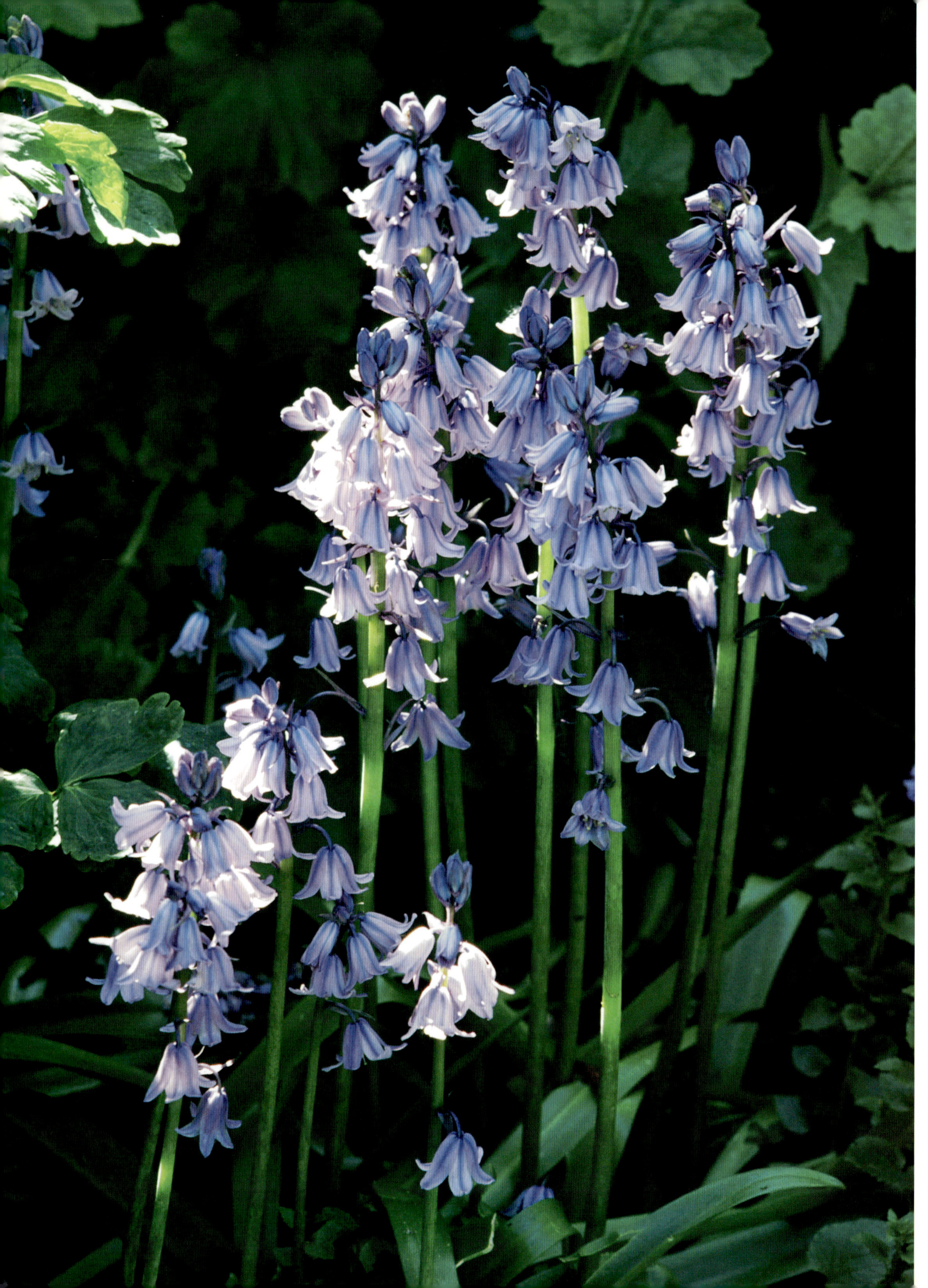

Bluebells

Bluebells generally grow in woodlands, so it is important to capture the dappled light found in these shady environments. To achieve this, a palette of cool colors was selected.

PAINTS

Aureolin
Cobalt blue deep
French ultramarine blue
Indigo
Quinacridone gold
Quinacridone magenta
Winsor green

TOOLS & MATERIALS

Hot-pressed paper, 140 lb. (300 gsm)
HB pencil
Masking fluid
Old brush
Round brushes, Nos. 00, 3, 7, 10
Filbert brush

TECHNIQUES

Flat wash, *p. 20*
Mixing paint in the palette, *p. 21*
Mixing paint on the paper, *p. 21*
Dropping in color, *p. 21*
Wet-onto-dry, *p. 22*
Wet-into-wet, *p. 22*
Blending, *p. 24*
Masking to reserve the paper, *p. 25*
Softening masked edges, *p. 25*
Adding highlights, *p. 27*
Negative painting, *p. 28*

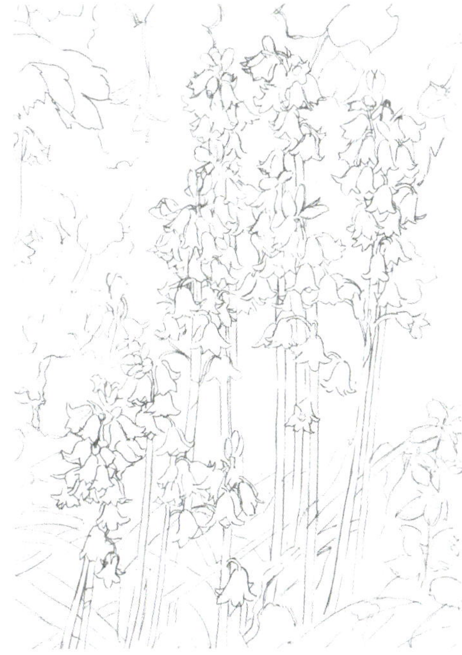

1 Draw the bluebells and leaves lightly onto the watercolor paper with an HB pencil. They are complex flowers, so put in the basic shapes only. To retain white paper for highlights on some of the leaves and petals, apply masking fluid with an old brush.

2 Using a No. 10 brush and clean water, wet the background area, moving carefully around the flowers. Flood diluted washes of aureolin and Winsor green into the wet areas and move the paper, allowing paint to run between the petals. Section the background into smaller areas if necessary. Let dry.

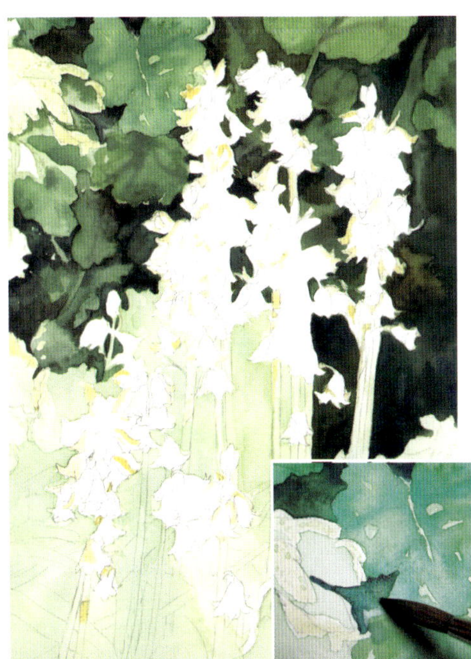

3 Having set the lightest tonal value, continue painting the negative areas of the background by wetting background areas and dropping in stronger mixes of Winsor green, quinacridone gold, aureolin, and indigo for the leaves, adding very light touches of quinacridone magenta with a No. 10 round brush. Use indigo, Winsor green, and quinacridone gold to build up the strong darks for the shadiest areas (inset). Use a smaller brush (No. 7) for smaller spaces.

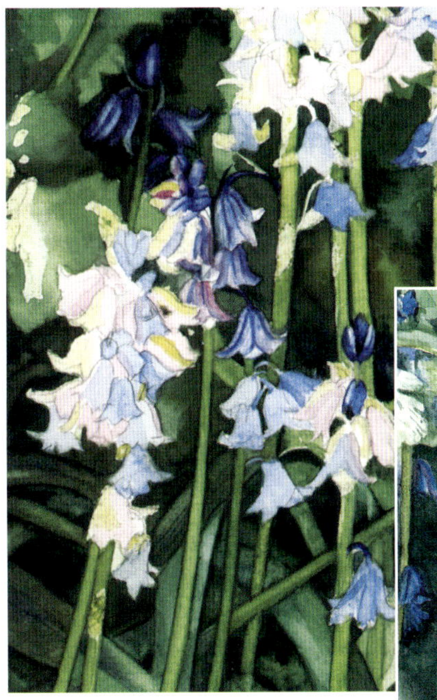

4 Add paint wet-into-wet to the background and soften hard edges. Drop French ultramarine blue into the darks above the lower leaves. Work on the longer leaves and ensure wet areas are not adjacent to one another. With a No. 3 brush, wet individual flowers, charging with cobalt blue deep for the midtones. Dilute quinacridone magenta for the light tones and French ultramarine blue for the darkest.

5 Lift color with a filbert brush to preserve highlights. Remove masking fluid and soften some of the hard edges with the filbert brush. Using French ultramarine blue and a No. 00 brush, add detail to the petals. Increase contrast by darkening the flowers and stems not in dappled light. Blend masked highlights on leaves and add dilute aureolin.

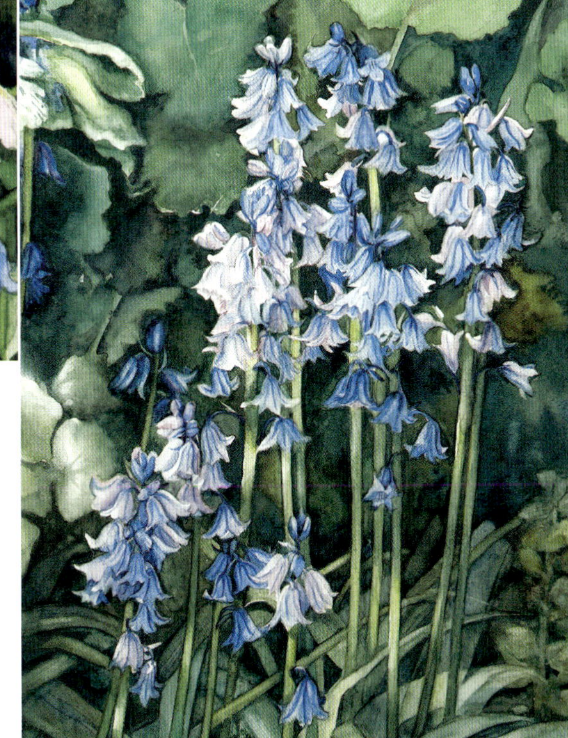

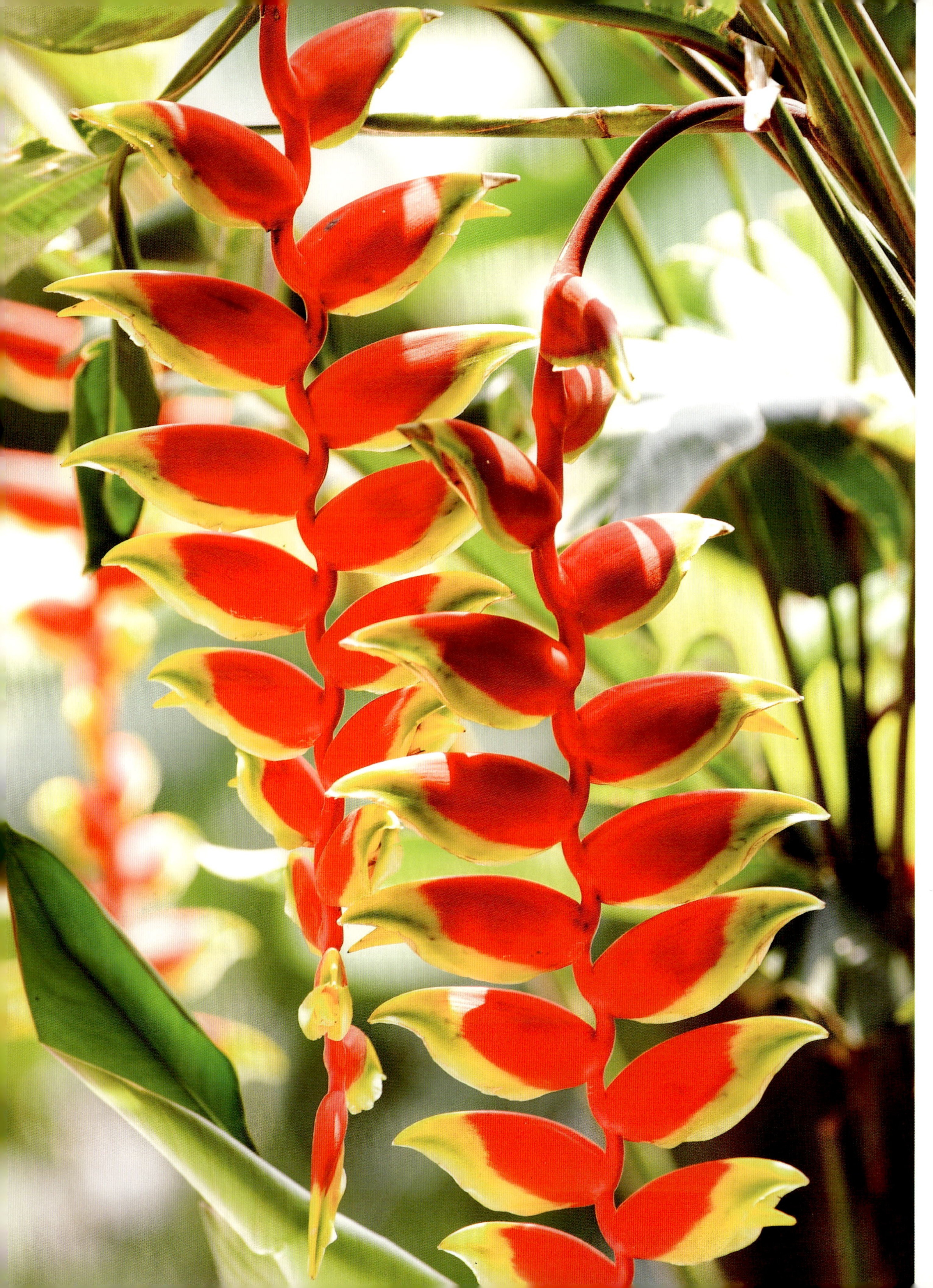

Heliconia

By sketching on location first and then taking many photographs, in this instance the artist challenged herself to try to stay true to the essence of the scene without being a "slave" to the photograph.

PAINTS
Burnt sienna
Cadmium red light
Cadmium red-purple
Cadmium yellow light
Cobalt blue
Indanthrone blue
Napthamide maroon
Olive green
Permanent rose
Quinacridone gold

TOOLS & MATERIALS
Cold-pressed paper, 140 lb. (300 gsm)
2B pencil
Masking fluid
Old brush
Flat brushes, 2-in. (5-cm), 1-in. (2.5-cm), ½-in. (1-cm)
Round brushes, Nos. 4–36
Masking tape
Natural sponge
Tissues and paper towels

TECHNIQUES USED
Variegated wash, *p. 20*
Mixing paint on the paper, *p. 21*
Wet-onto-dry, *p. 22*
Wet-into-wet, *p. 22*
Glazing, *p. 23*
Masking to reserve the paper, *p. 25*
Adding highlights, *p. 27*

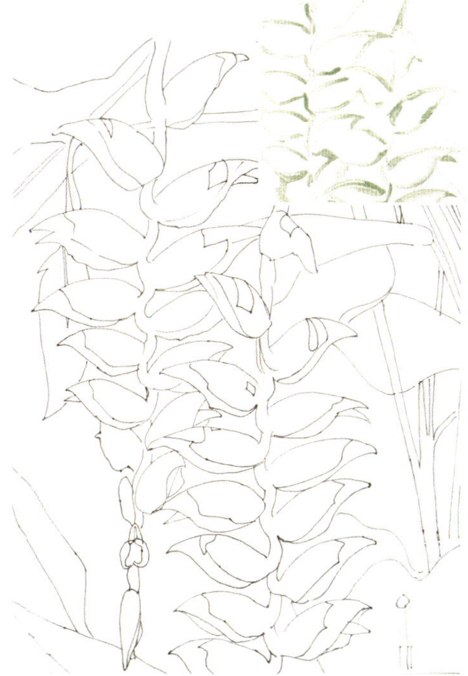

1 Lightly draw the flower onto the paper using a 2B pencil. Mask the flower and leaf edges to preserve white highlights (inset). Dry the masking thoroughly.

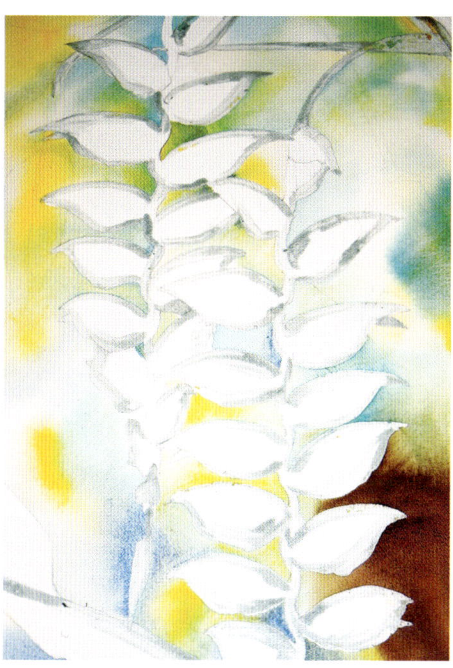

2 Wet the paper, excluding the flowers, and paint a variegated, wet-into-wet wash of cobalt blue, cadmium yellow pale, and burnt sienna using a 2-in. (5-cm) flat and No. 36 round brush.

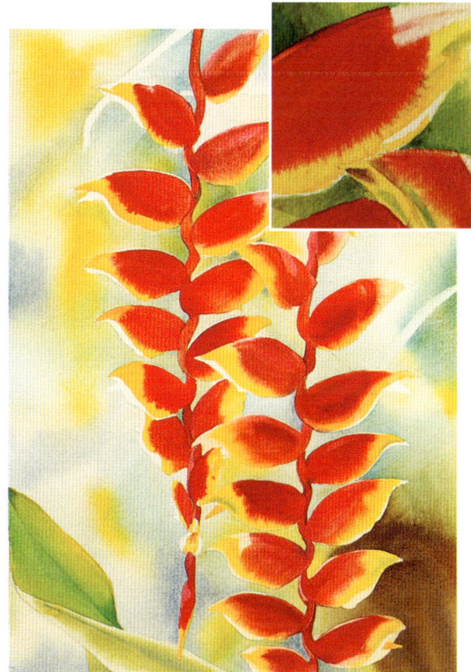

3 When the wash is dry, remove the masking. Paint a wet-into-wet wash in each of the heliconia flowers with a No. 12 and No. 6 round brush. Wet the entire flower and then brush on the cadmium yellow light. Add permanent rose followed by cadmium red light and, in some flowers, cadmium red-purple. Let these mix on the paper (inset). The permanent rose helps the cadmiums to keep their brightness after drying.

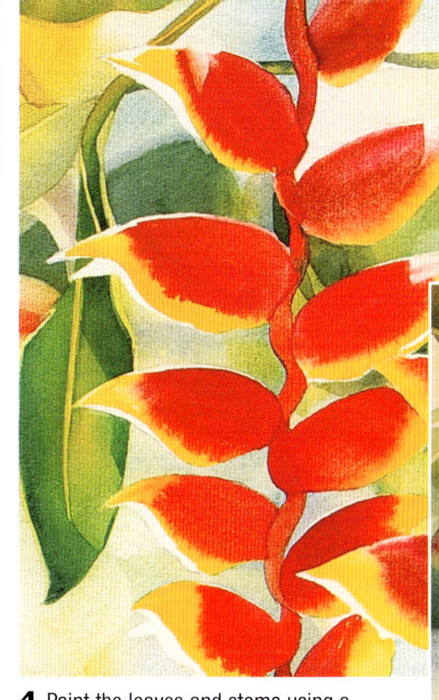

4 Paint the leaves and stems using a combination of wet-into-wet and wet-onto-dry techniques. To achieve the sunlit effect, lift the highlights on the blossoms by isolating the shapes with masking tape and removing the color first by wetting within the shape and then gently rubbing the area lightly with a sponge or tissue. Remove the tape and blot the area with a paper towel.

5 Use olive green, napthamide maroon, and indanthrone blue to create the deep color on the bottom right. To achieve a glow here, use glazing, highlighting, and charging with quinacridone gold and other pigments already found in the painting. Glaze the leaf patterns in the upper left and deepen some of the greens in the stalks. Smooth the petal edges with the ½-in. (1-cm) flat brush and a small amount of water.

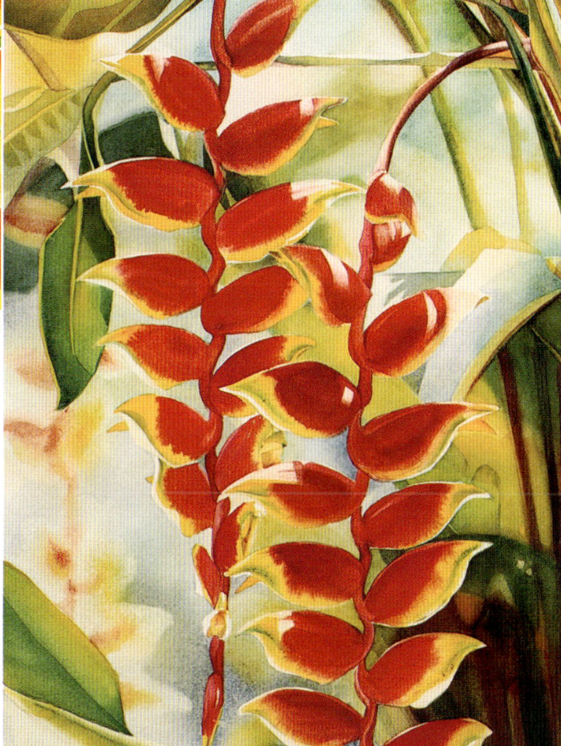

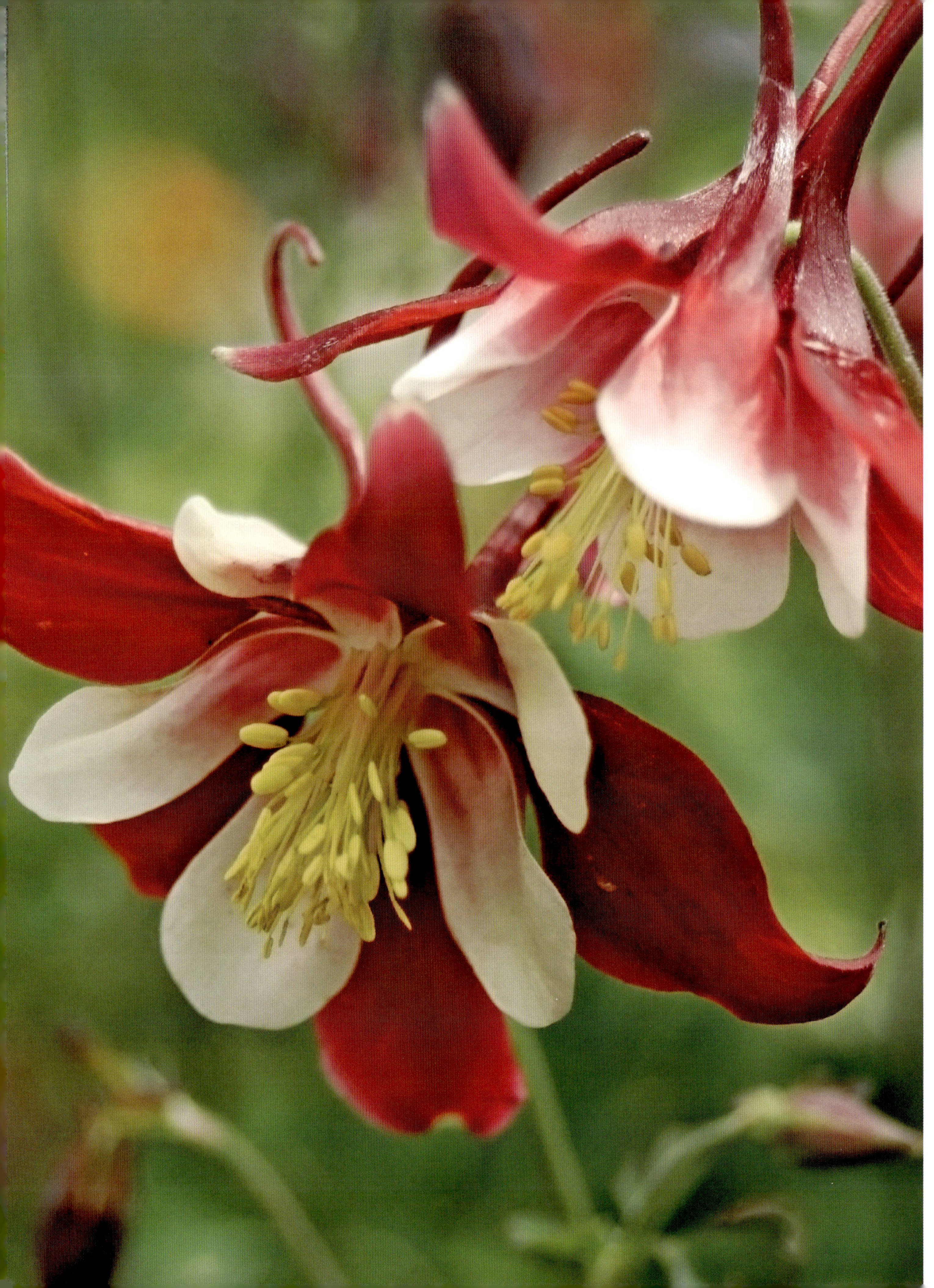

Columbines

The artist made few changes to the photograph in this painting, other than to warm up the entire scene by adding more glowing light.

PAINTS
Aureolin
French ultramarine blue
Quinacridone coral
Quinacridone gold
Quinacridone magenta
Quinacridone pink
Quinacridone red
Quinacridone rose
Quinacridone violet

TOOLS & MATERIALS
Cold-pressed paper, 140 lb. (300 gsm)
HB pencil
Masking fluid
3-in. (7.5-cm) wash brush
Old brush
Kosher salt
1-in. (2.5-cm) flat brush
Round brushes, Nos. 6, 10, 14
Tissues

TECHNIQUES USED
Mixing paint in the palette, *p. 21*
Mixing paint on the paper, *p. 21*
Dropping in color, *p. 21*
Wet-into-wet, *p. 22*
Lost and found edges, *p. 24*
Masking to reserve the paper, *p. 25*
Softening masked edges, *p. 25*
Make softened edges glow, *p. 26*
Shadows, *p. 28*
Pouring paint, *p. 29*
Salt, *p. 30*

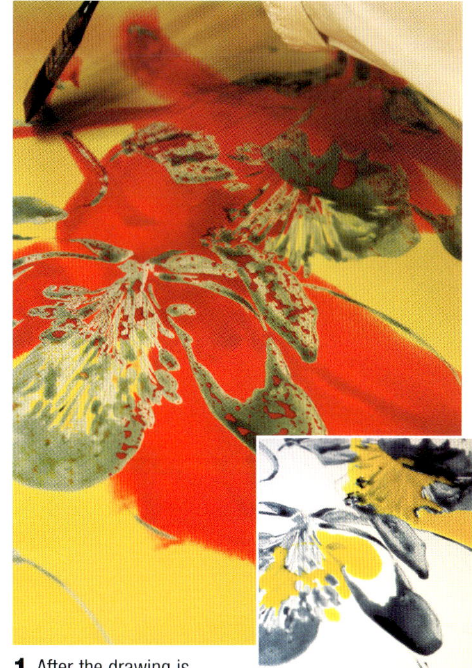

1 After the drawing is completed using an HB pencil, mask all whites, yellows, and areas of light. Dry thoroughly. Pour an aureolin creamlike mixture onto the prewet sheet of watercolor paper (inset), spreading it around the focal area by tilting the board or brushing lightly with a 3-in. (7.5-cm) wash brush. Repeat with quinacridone red and rose, followed by French ultramarine blue.

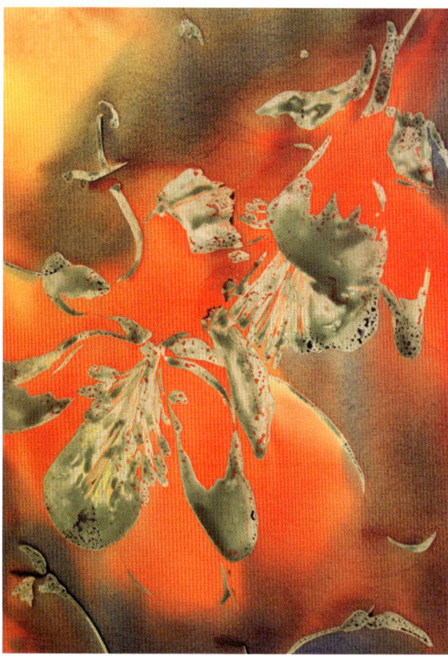

2 Sprinkle kosher salt into the still-wet poured washes of the background area for textural interest. Dry the painting on a flat surface. Remove the salt. Pour a second round of colors to intensify selected areas. Do not pour yellow over any area that is already dark; it will not show and could look muddy. Dry again, preferably overnight.

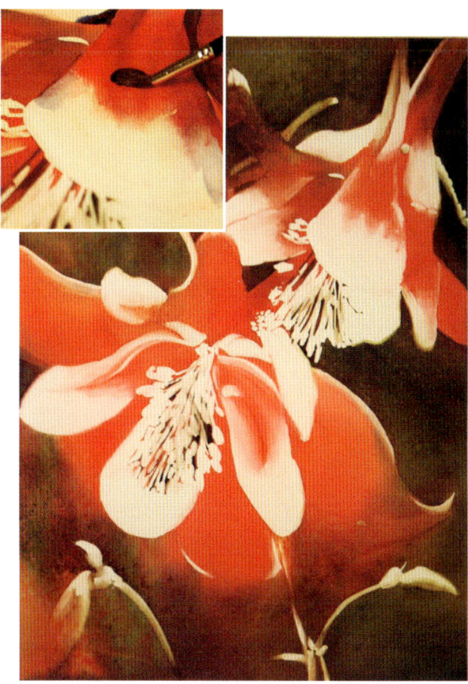

3 Remove the masking and soften the edges. One by one, wet the petals up to the white tip and drop in quinacridone red, coral, and pink (inset). Let the photograph be your guide. Separate the overlapping layers of the flower parts, keeping those in the foreground warm and those in the background cool. In case of shadows, use a darker, cooler color.

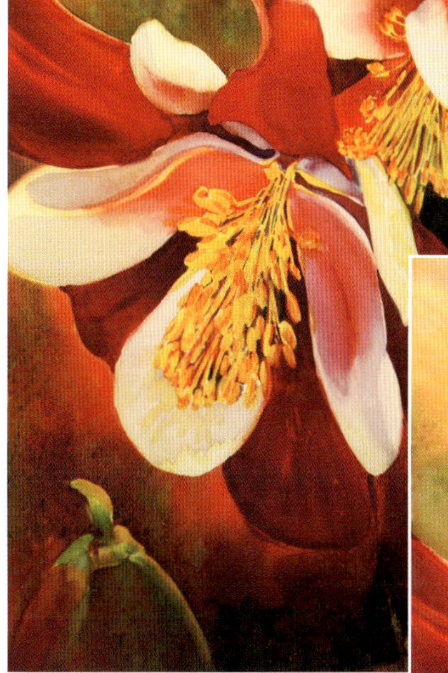

4 Paint the stamens in aureolin and quinacridone gold. Add shadows to the yellow with an orange mix of aureolin and quinacridone red. To show the glow coming down behind the flowers from above, paint a golden yellow-orange at the edge of the lowest petals.

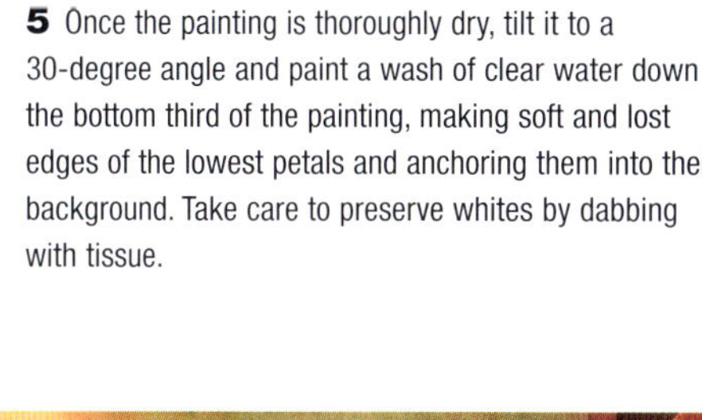

5 Once the painting is thoroughly dry, tilt it to a 30-degree angle and paint a wash of clear water down the bottom third of the painting, making soft and lost edges of the lowest petals and anchoring them into their background. Take care to preserve whites by dabbing with tissue.

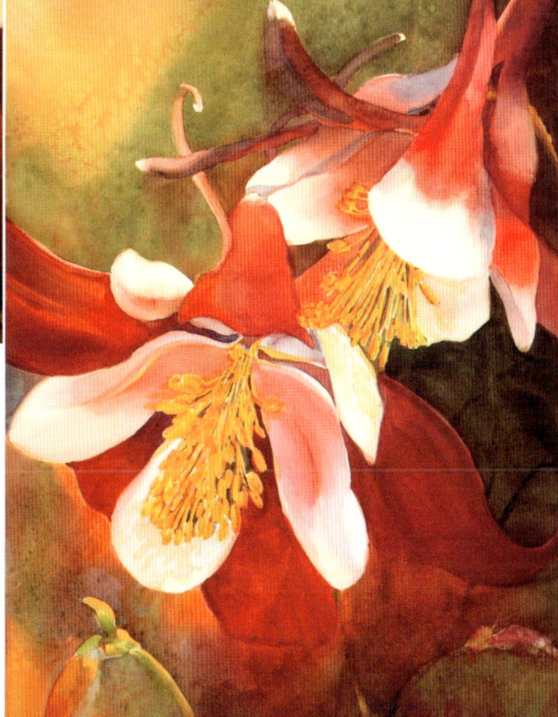

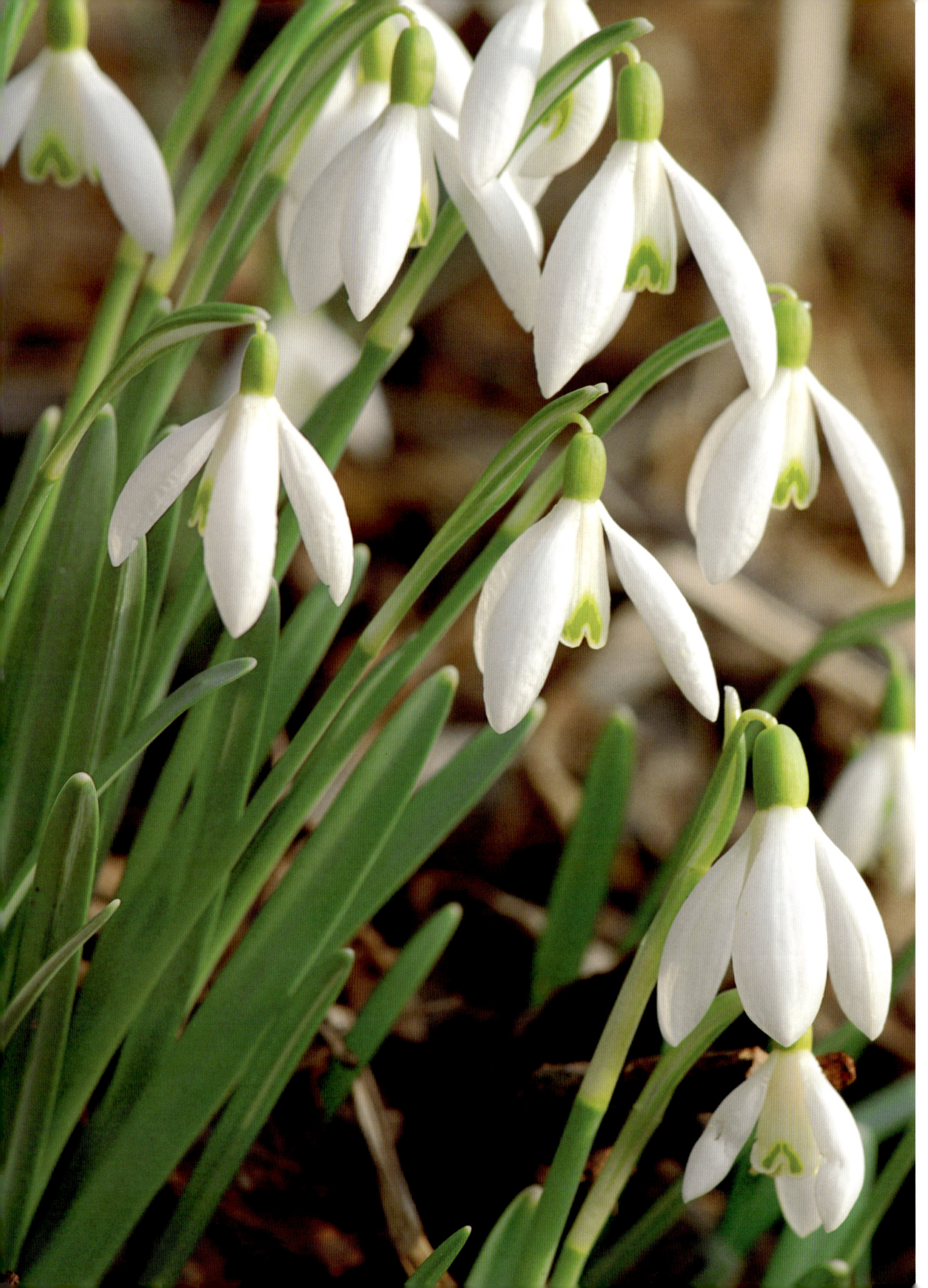

Snowdrops

These small flowers always appear in a cluster; pay attention to the design of negative shapes as well as the positive ones.

PAINTS
Antwerp blue
Burnt sienna
Cadmium scarlet
Cadmium yellow medium
Cerulean blue
Cobalt blue
French ultramarine blue
New gamboge
Perylene maroon
Rich green-gold
Rose madder genuine

TECHNIQUES
Mixing paint in the palette, *p. 21*
Dropping in color, *p. 21*
Wet-into-wet, *p. 22*

TOOLS & MATERIALS
Cold-pressed paper, 140 lb. (300 gsm)
Pencil
3-in. (7.5-cm) hake brush
Soft mop brush
Round brushes, Nos. 4, 8, 10
Natural sponge
¼-in. (6-mm) flat brush

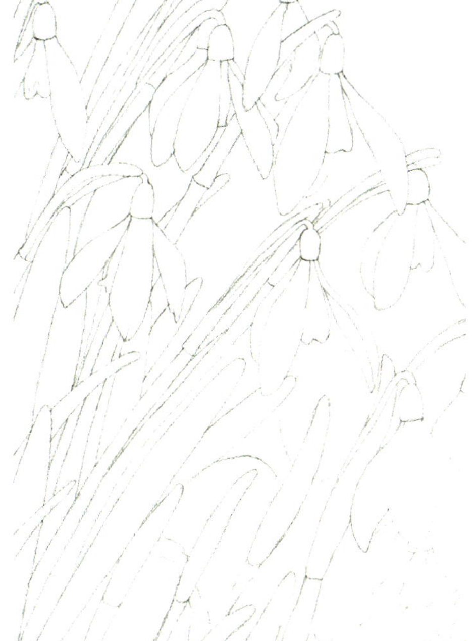

1 Make a careful pencil drawing of the photograph on watercolor paper. Block in the major shapes. As you prefer, details can be added now or later.

2 Use a hake brush to wet the paper on both sides until limp. With a soft mop brush, add new gamboge to the stamen areas of the flowers, keeping it away from most areas of purple. Brush Antwerp blue into the background area and let it expand into some of the petal shapes to soften the edges.

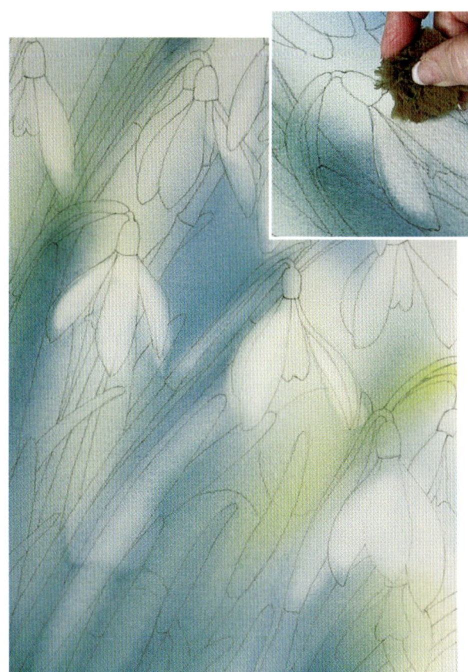

3 Make a mixture of transparent and opaque colors (French ultramarine blue, Antwerp blue, and new gamboge). With a No. 10 round brush, paint into areas where the green leaves will be, keeping the edges soft and diffused. With a damp sponge, keep the white petals wiped out (inset). The edges will be soft.

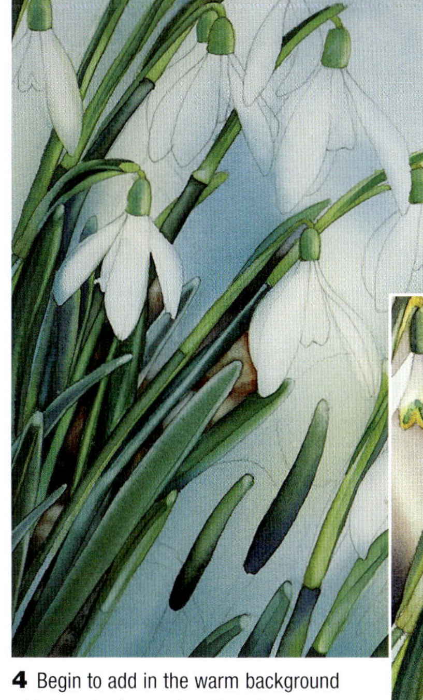

4 Begin to add in the warm background with French ultramarine blue, dropping in burnt sienna. Keep the edges soft. Use the blues and yellows to mix a variety of greens, paying close attention to values. Use the dark colors to set off the white petals.

5 Add form to the petals by wetting each one and brushing on soft grays, being sure to leave open white areas. To add body, use a small amount of cerulean blue in the grays. Restate the greens to keep the color sharp and vibrant and try energizing them by adding slashes of cadmium scarlet.

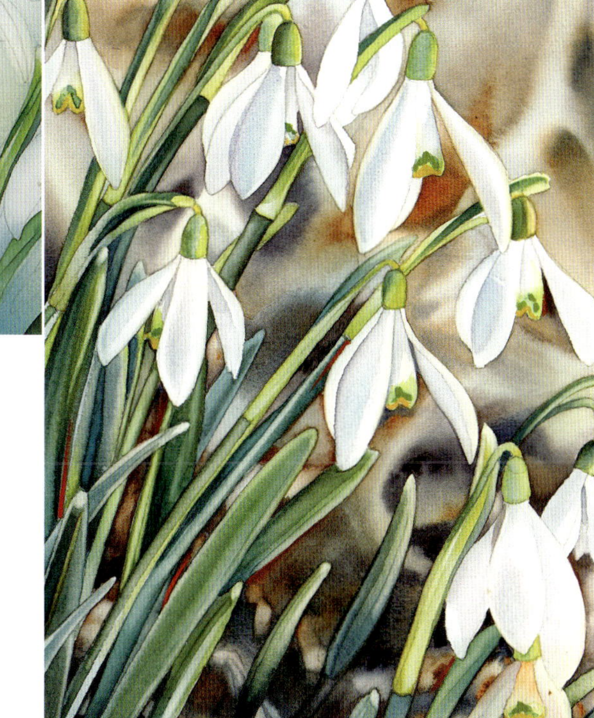

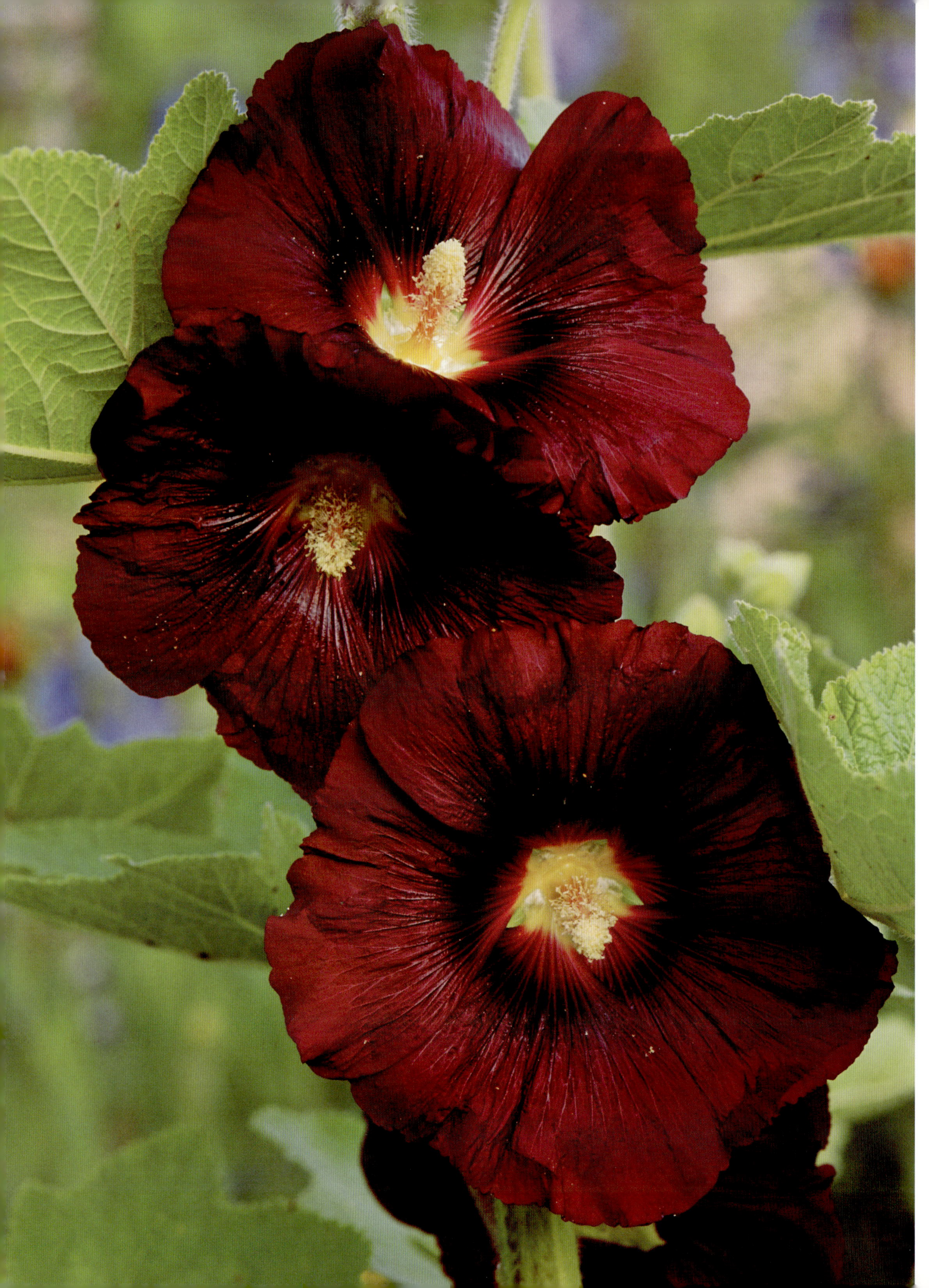

Hollyhocks

In designing the painting of hollyhocks, the artist chose to simplify and abstract the background as well as backlight the flowers. A warm palette with fewer blues and greens was used to create a glow about the flowers and reduce the pull between the red and green complementary colors.

PAINTS
Aureolin
Carbazole violet
Cobalt blue
Hooker's green
Permanent orange
Quinacridone coral
Quinacridone magenta
Quinacridone pink
Quinacridone red
Viridian
Winsor yellow deep

TOOLS & MATERIALS
Cold-pressed paper, 140 lb. (300 gsm)
HB pencil
Masking fluid
Ruling pen
3-in. (7.5-cm) wash brush
Round brushes, Nos. 3, 6, 10
1-in. (2.5-cm) flat brush
Fan brush

TECHNIQUES USED
Mixing paint in the palette, *p. 21*
Dropping in color, *p. 21*
Wet-into-wet, *p. 22*
Glazing, *p. 23*
Lost and found edges, *p. 24*
Masking for details, *p. 25*
Shadows, *p. 28*
Pouring paint, *p. 29*

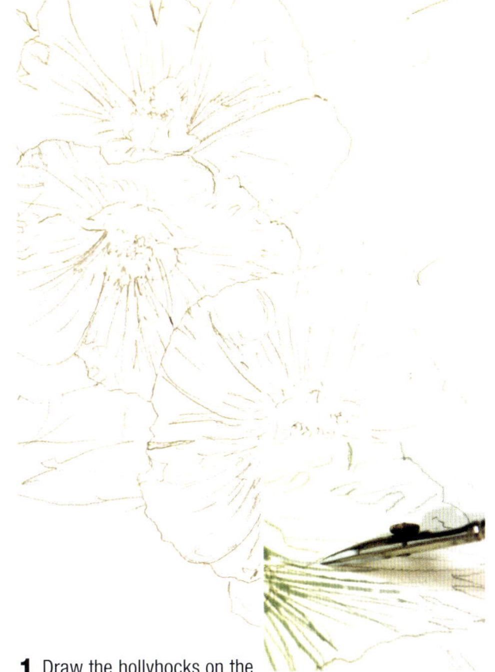

1 Draw the hollyhocks on the paper. Keep the HB pencil lines dark enough to see through several layers of poured pigment. Mask the center area of each flower. A ruling pen—a traditional graphic design tool for making thin, straight lines with ink—was used to apply the masking to the veins in the petals (inset). A very fine brush or sharpened stick could also be used.

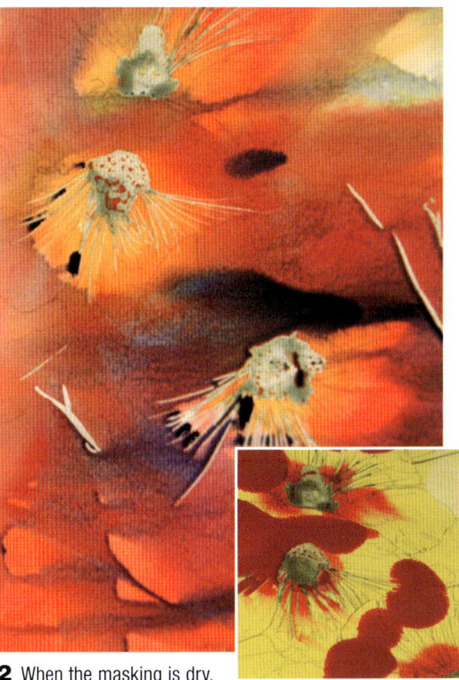

2 When the masking is dry, pour aureolin onto the paper, directing the movement of paint with a 3-in. (7.5-cm) wash brush. While the yellow is wet, pour in red (inset), such as quinacridone coral, quinacridone red, and quinacridone magenta. Tip and tilt your board to blend. Pour cobalt blue in selected areas. Continue tilting and tipping the board until the colors look natural. Let the board dry on a flat surface.

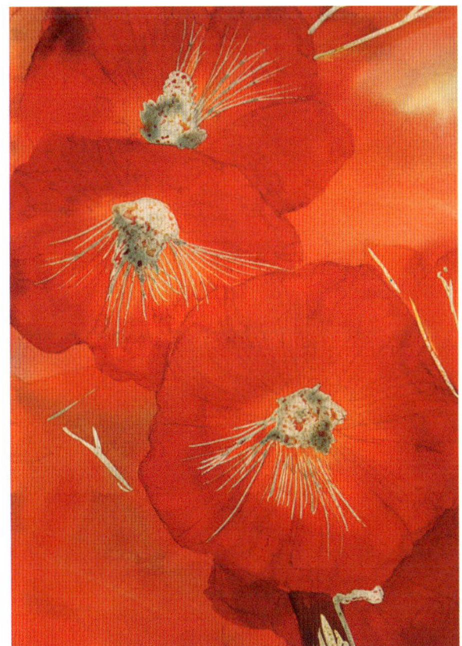

3 Reinforce the glow around the center of each flower by painting around the center with Winsor yellow deep and permanent orange. Use a No. 10 round brush to define the petals and whole flowers, keeping in mind that a value difference can be used to separate the front flower from the one behind it. After each color glaze, allow the paint to dry.

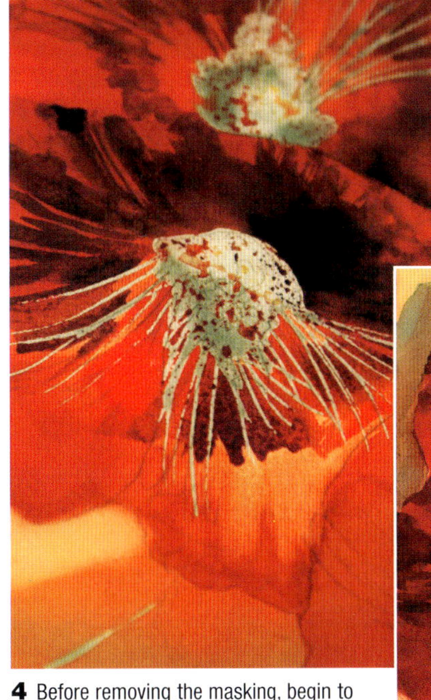

4 Before removing the masking, begin to define the dark areas and shadows of the flower using carbazole violet and working wet-into-wet. As a violet passage is laid down, place a deep quinacridone magenta passage next to it, leaving some lighter red on the petals where the sun comes through. Dry thoroughly and remove the masking.

5 Paint a golden glaze over the white veins with a 1-in. (2.5-cm) flat brush, blending them into the flower with a fan brush. Then paint the center of the flower with aureolin and Winsor yellow deep, and red dots. Add green points, using Hooker's green, viridian, or mixed from Winsor blue and aureolin. To finish the leaves use cobalt blue to add shadows and texture.

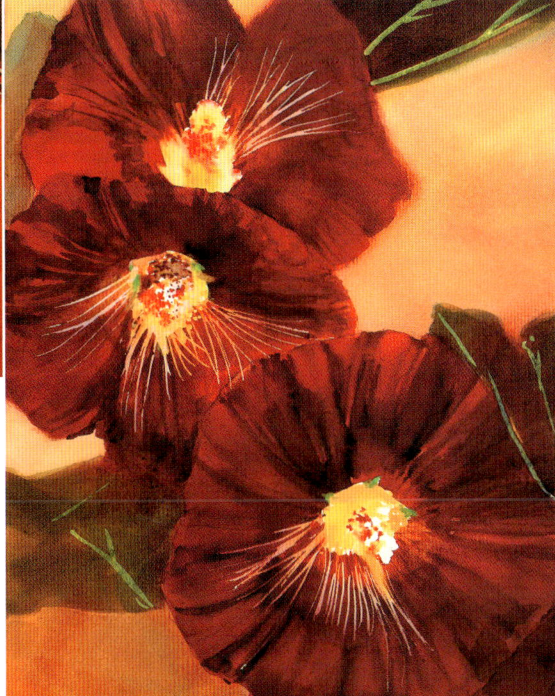

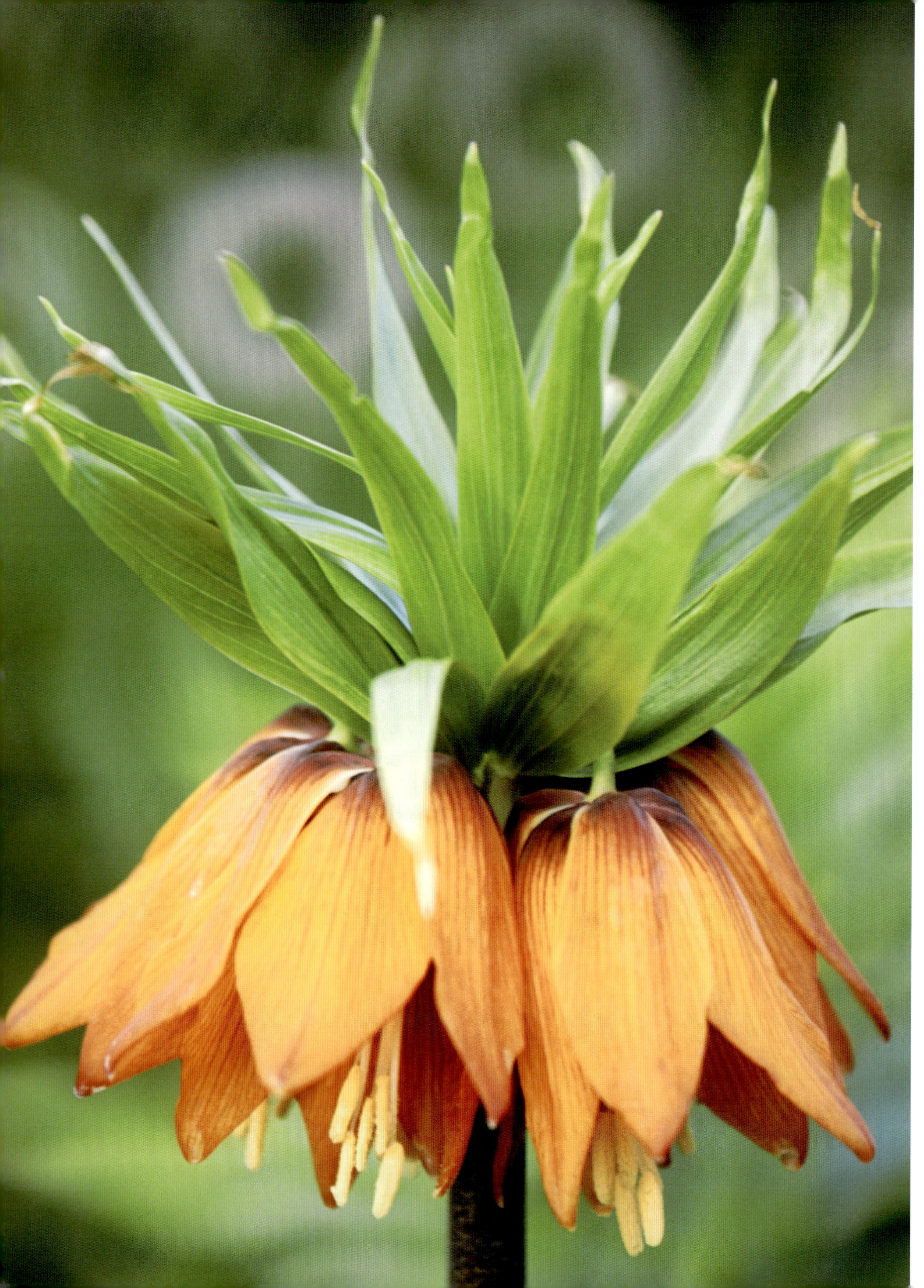

Crown Imperial

This flower is floating on a turquoise background wash. The juxtaposing colors of cool turquoise and hot orange create a wonderful tension.

PAINTS
Aureolin
Burnt sienna
Cadmium orange
Cobalt teal
Green-gold
Mars yellow
Sepia
Winsor green

TECHNIQUES
Graded wash, *p. 20*
Mixing paint in the palette, *p. 21*
Wet-onto-dry, *p. 22*
Wet-into-wet, *p. 22*
Blending, *p. 24*
Masking to reserve the paper, *p. 25*
Adding highlights, *p. 27*

TOOLS & MATERIALS
Cold-pressed paper, 140 lb. (300 gsm)
Pencil
Masking tape
Masking fluid
Small old brush
Round brushes, Nos. 2, 8, 12
2-in. (5-cm) wash brush
Mat knife

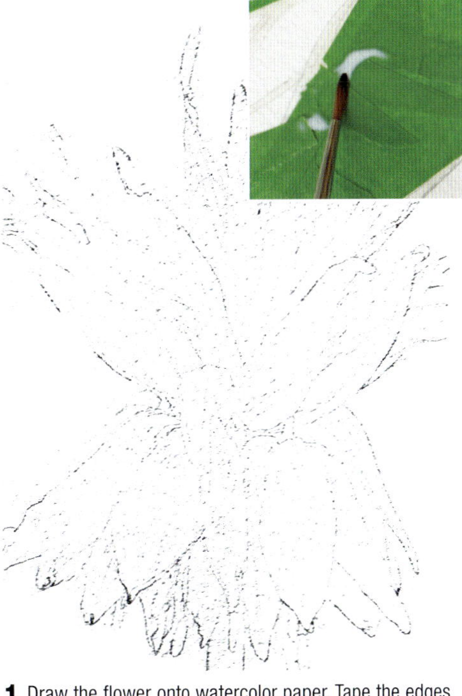

1 Draw the flower onto watercolor paper. Tape the edges of the paper with masking tape for a clean border. Mask the flower with masking fluid, applied with a small old brush, and masking tape. Seal the masking tape with masking fluid (inset).

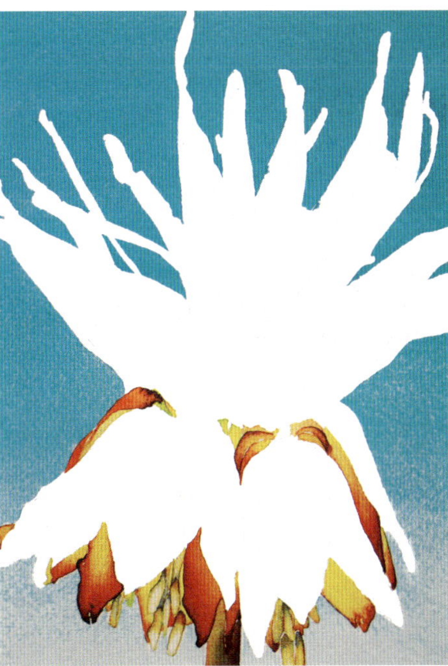

2 Wet the paper with clear water. Using the 2-in. (5-cm) wash brush, paint the background with a graded wash beginning with dark cobalt teal at the top and graduating to a lighter blue. When the background is dry, remove all masking. Begin painting the background petals, keeping colors cool toward the back. Paint wet-into-wet using cadmium orange as the base.

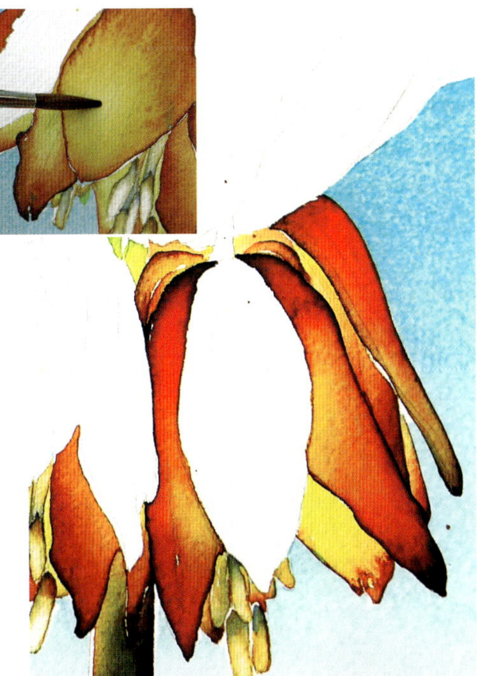

3 Wet each petal shape and float in aureolin and cadmium orange leaving the center of the petal light in value to create luminosity (inset). Use light layers of pigment to avoid overworking. Dry between layers. Using a small brush, outline the petals with burnt sienna and sepia.

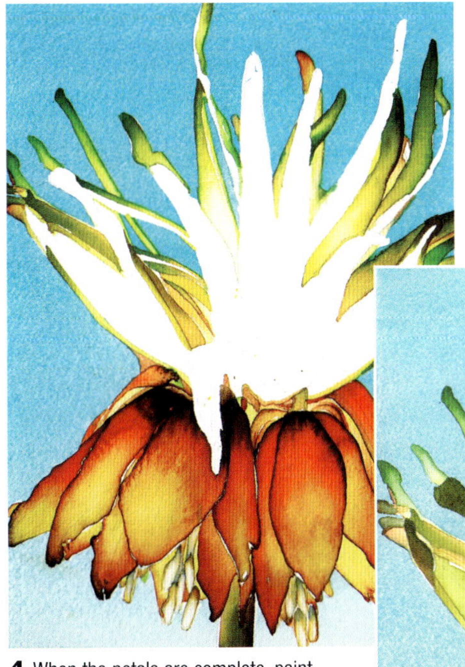

4 When the petals are complete, paint the leaves one by one with a No. 2 brush. Gradate the wash from a soft yellow near the flower to dark green at the tip using mixtures of yellows, green-gold, Winsor green, and sepia. This will keep the values light at the base and retain the glow in the center of the flower.

5 Using a mat knife, scratch out small white highlights. Use sepia at the tips of a few leaves to make some more prominent. Outline the leaves to ensure crisp edges.

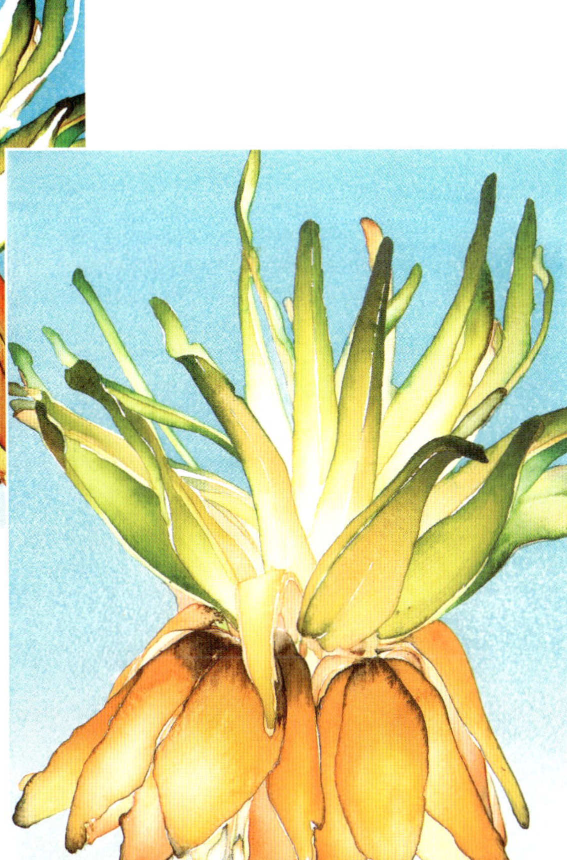

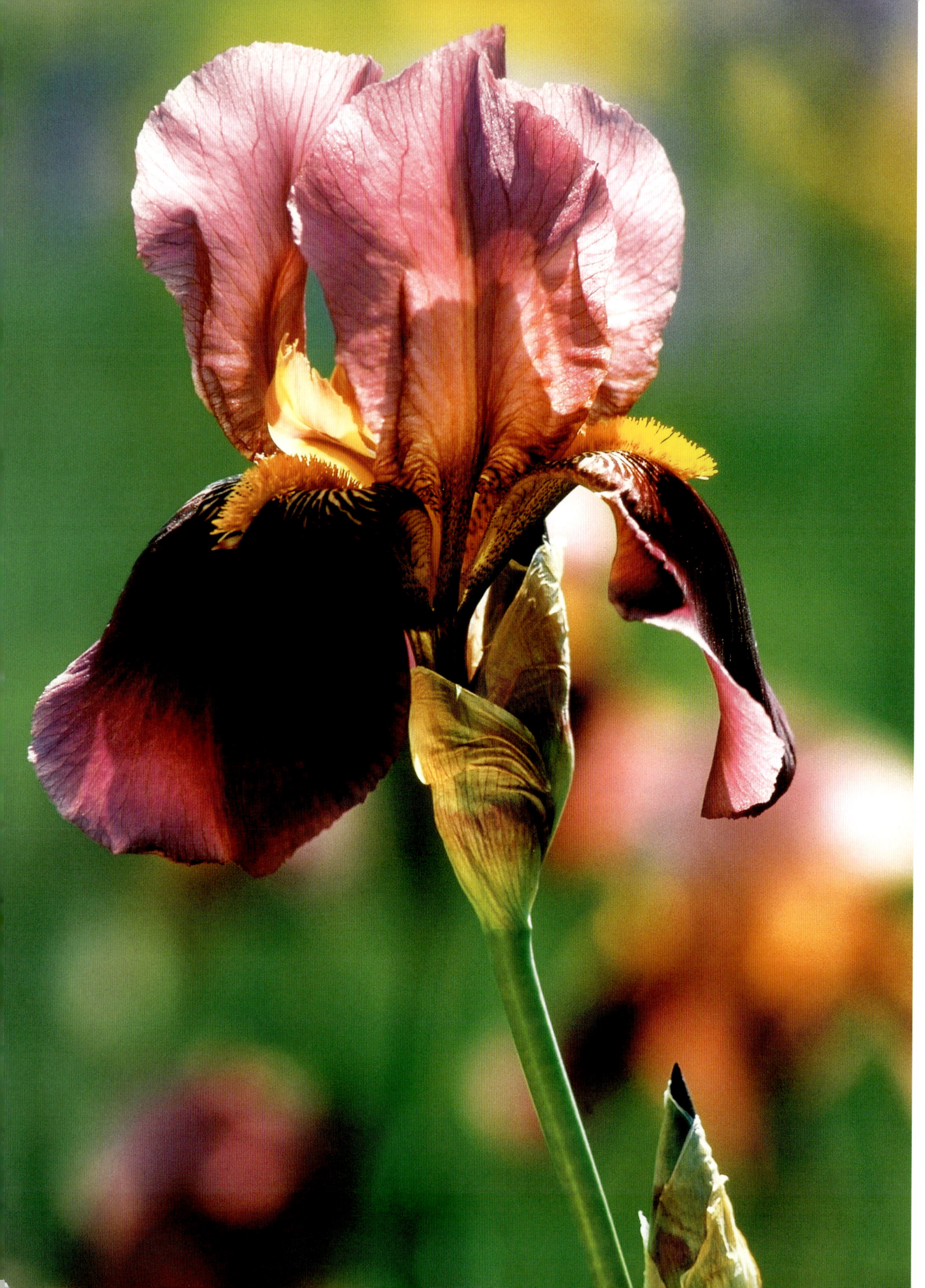

Iris

The artist decided to crop the image and focus on the pattern and intensity of color in the flower head. She created a textured background using the salt spatter technique.

PAINTS
Dioxazine violet
New gamboge
Sap green
Venetian red

TOOLS & MATERIALS
Watercolor board
B or HB pencil
Masking fluid
Old brush
Round brushes, Nos. 6 and 10
Dip pen
Tissues
Scrubber
Kosher salt

TECHNIQUES USED
Flat wash, *p. 20*
Mixing paint in the palette, *p. 21*
Dropping in color, *p. 21*
Wet-onto-dry, *p. 22*
Wet-into-wet, *p. 22*
Masking to reserve the paper, *p. 25*
Shadows, *p. 28*
Salt, *p. 30*

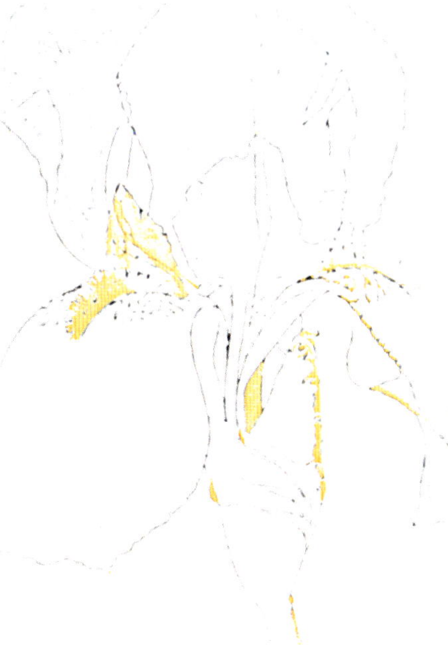

1 Draw the flower on the board, then mask out all the highlights with masking fluid and an old brush.

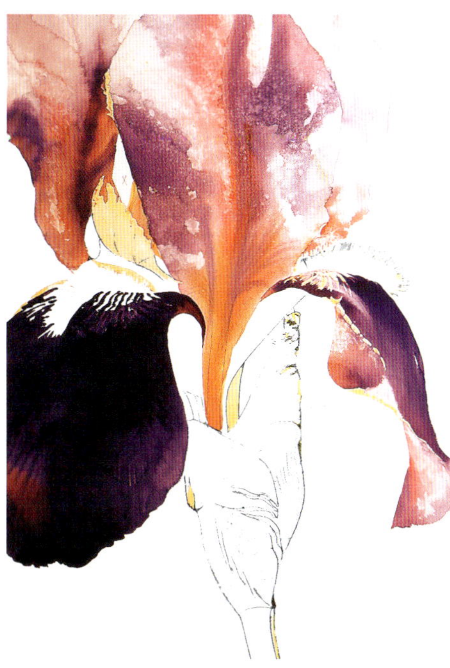

2 Make up a strong mix of dioxazine violet and Venetian red for the dark petals and a more diluted version of the same colors for the lighter ones. Using a No. 10 round brush, work wet-into-wet within the outlines of the petals, dropping touches of the darker mix into the light petals and letting the colors blend.

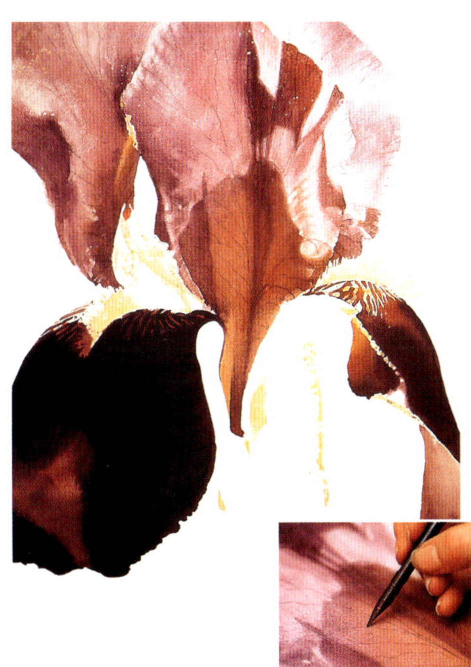

3 Dip a pen into the dark wash and draw in the fine veins of the upper petals (inset). When dry, use a No. 10 round brush to apply further washes of color to each petal, dabbing with a scrunched-up tissue to give a papery texture. Build up with further washes of the light violet-red mix. For the shadow of the opposite petal, apply a warmer wash with a touch more red and new gamboge. Soften the edges with a scrubber.

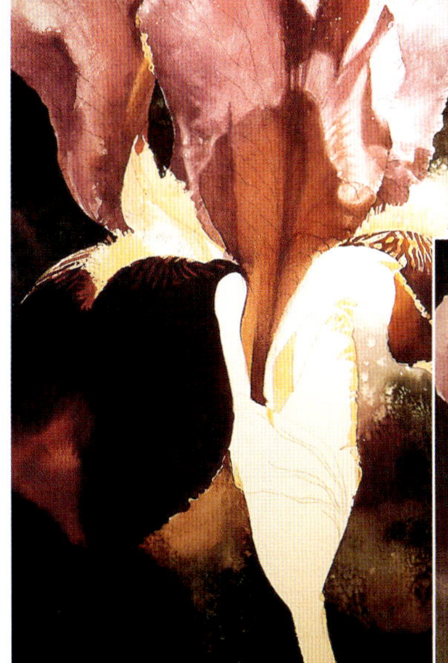

4 Wet the background areas, leaving the petals dry, and apply a dark wash of sap green and dioxazine violet. While wet, sprinkle kosher salt into some areas, and leave to dry before brushing off. Paint the papery-textured sepals wet-into-wet with all the colors used previously. When dry, dip the pen into the dark green-violet wash used for the background, and draw in some linear detail.

5 Remove the mask. Using a No. 6 round brush and thin washes of new gamboge and Venetian red overlaid with violet, work up the details in the heart of the flower. Add the markings at the base of each petal with a green-violet mix. Finally, paint in the stamens with new gamboge.

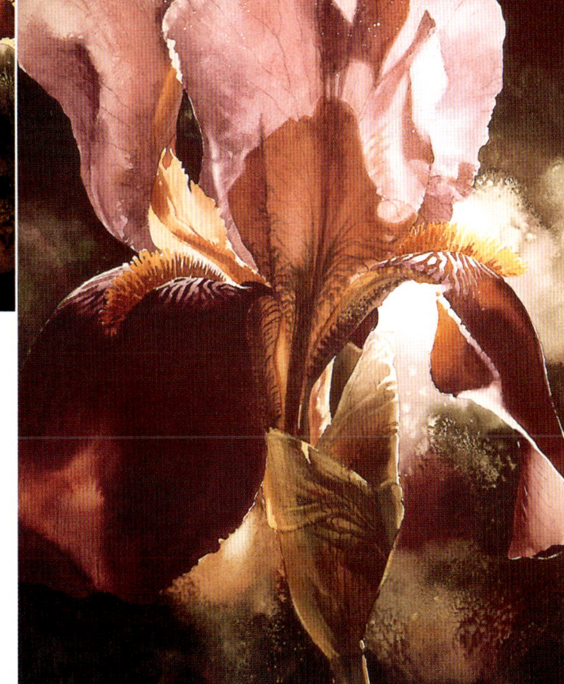

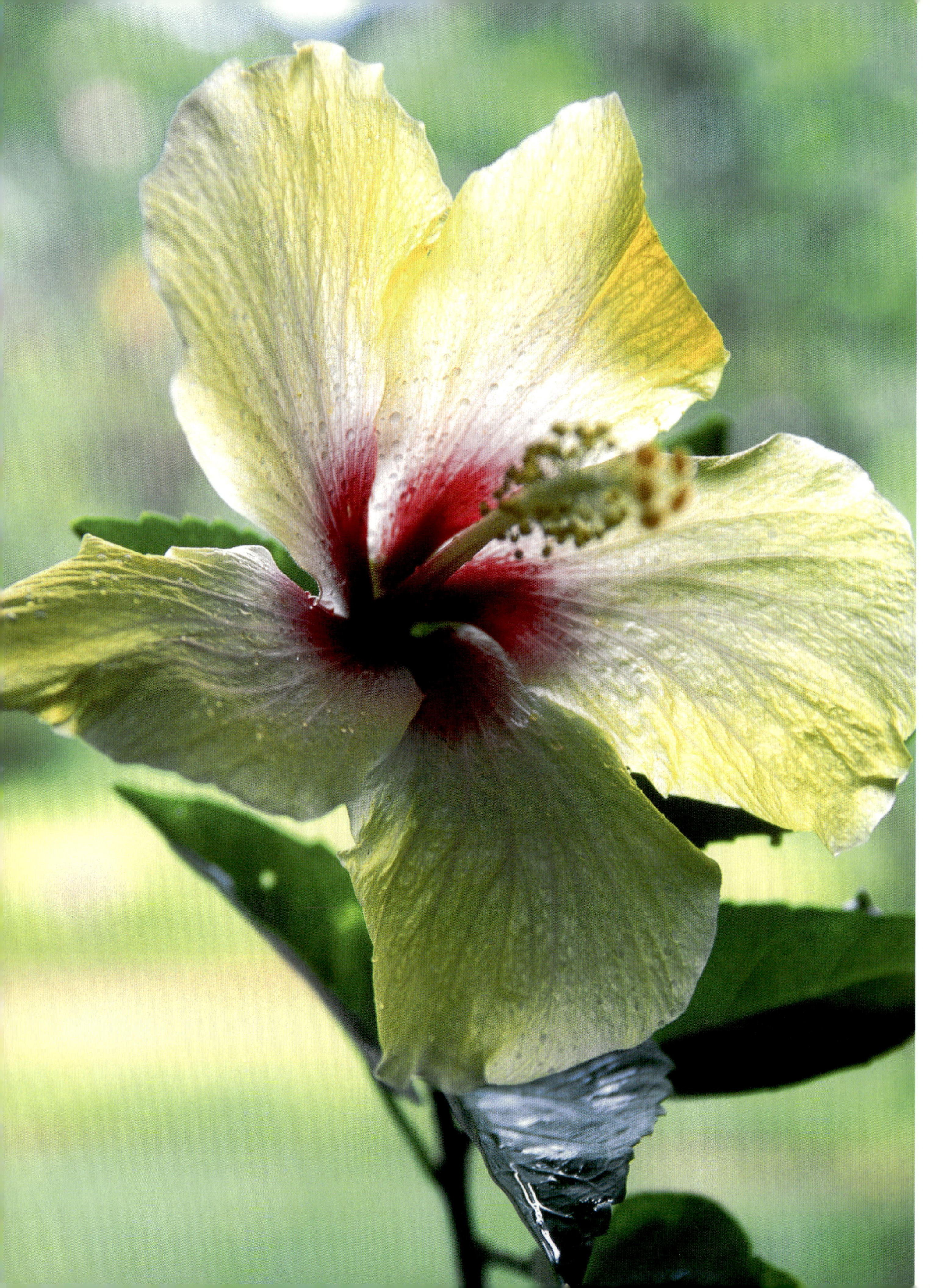

Hibiscus

The way the light passes through the fragile petals and the translucency of the flower attracted the artist to this image. The flower is darker than the background, which allows the light to appear as if it is streaming through.

PAINTS
Alizarin crimson
Aureolin
Bismuth yellow
Cobalt blue
French ultramarine blue
Opera
Permanent rose
Quinacridone gold
Spring green
Winsor green-blue shade

TOOLS & MATERIALS
Cold-pressed paper, 140 lb. (300 gsm)
H pencil
Masquepen
Round brushes, Nos. 4, 10, 12
3-in. (7.5-cm) hake brush
Stiff-bristled brush, No. 5
Masking fluid
Old brush

TECHNIQUES USED
Wet-onto-dry, *p. 22*
Wet-into-wet, *p. 22*
Masking to reserve the paper, *p. 25*
Softening masked edges, *p. 25*

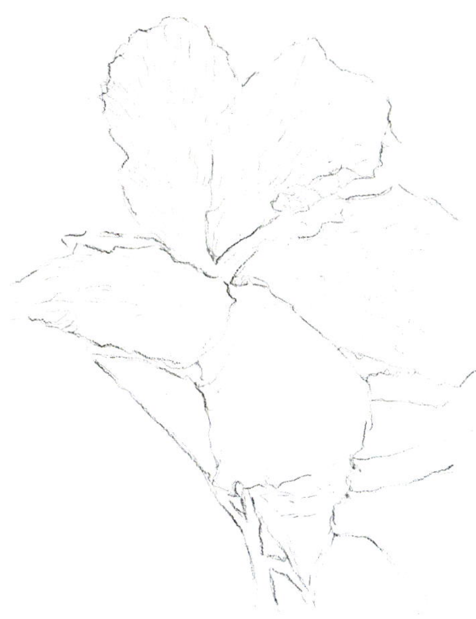

1 Draw the image in H pencil, noticing that the placement of the image causes the form of the flower to touch the edges of the paper on three sides. The top-right petal creates an unusual line.

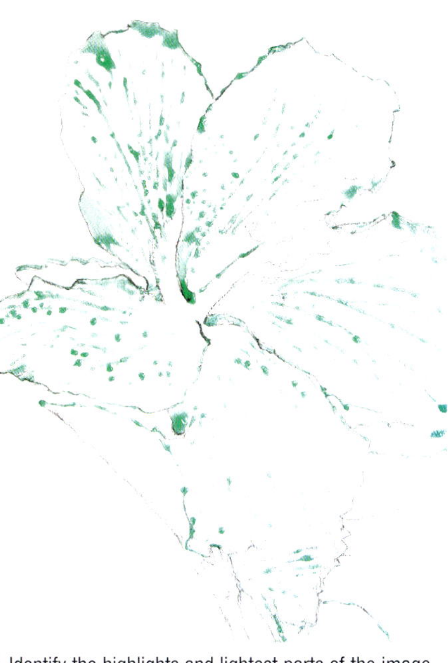

2 Identify the highlights and lightest parts of the image. Carefully apply the mask to protect these light elements. Initially, masking the raindrops allows for the option to retain them or paint them out at a later stage.

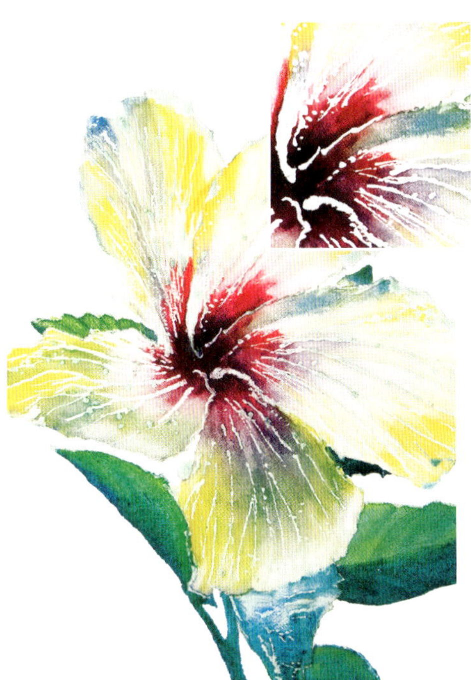

3 Apply initial washes of aureolin onto dry paper with a No. 12 round brush. Switching to a No. 10 brush, drop in light mixtures of cobalt blue and French ultramarine blue to the petal shadows. On sunlit petal tips, paint some light quinacridone gold. Use opera and permanent rose to paint the pink center, gently drawing colors out into the petal veins (inset).

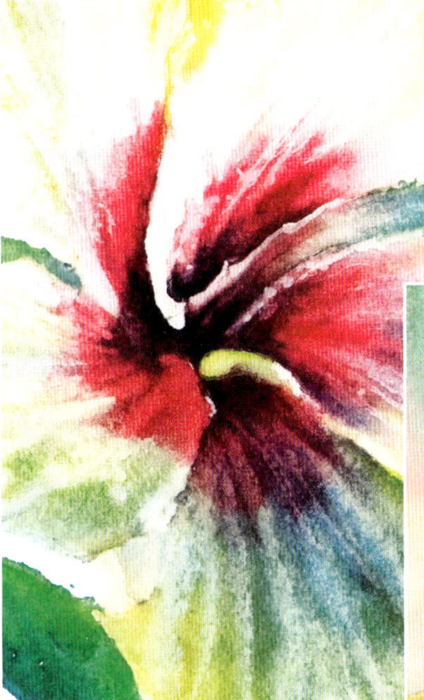

4 Once the painting is completely dry, remove the mask and soften the edges with a stiff-bristled brush and a little water. Let it dry completely and then, using an old brush, mask the entire shape of the flower. White masking fluid allows the image to show through while protecting it from the paint you will apply around it.

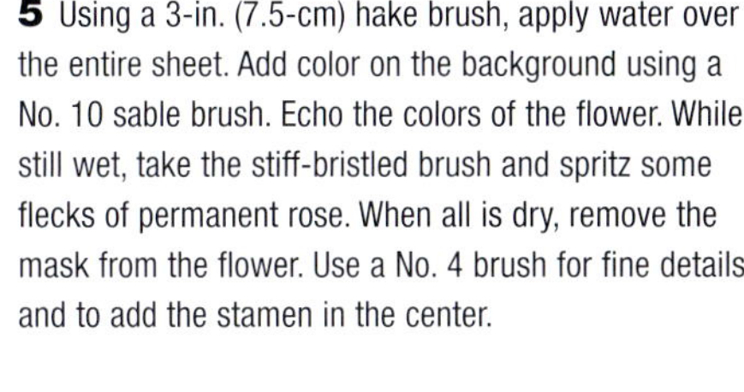

5 Using a 3-in. (7.5-cm) hake brush, apply water over the entire sheet. Add color on the background using a No. 10 sable brush. Echo the colors of the flower. While still wet, take the stiff-bristled brush and spritz some flecks of permanent rose. When all is dry, remove the mask from the flower. Use a No. 4 brush for fine details and to add the stamen in the center.

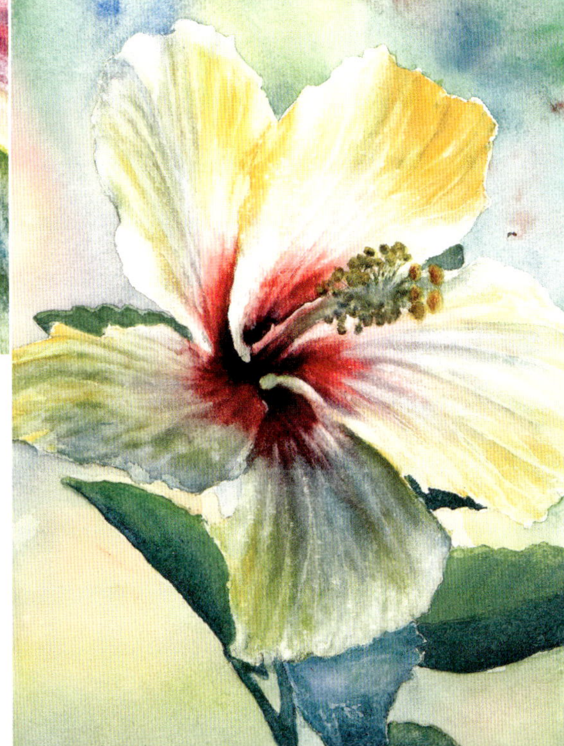

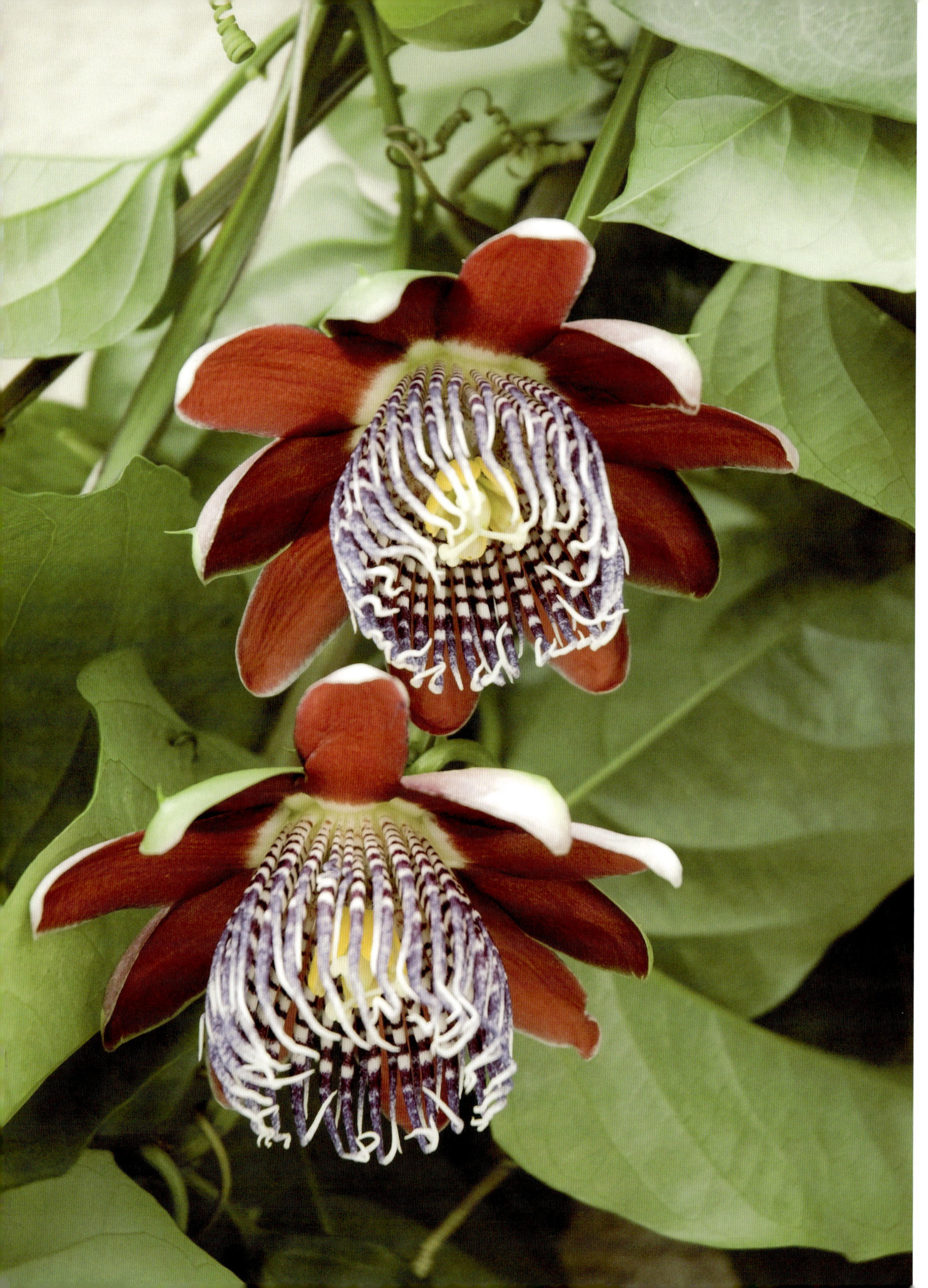

Passion Flowers

A composition featuring two main subjects is a challenge. The artist decided to crop the photograph and alter the background to emphasize a diagonal composition with light coming from the upper left.

PAINTS
Aureolin
Cobalt blue
Indanthrone blue
Nickel azo
Perylene scarlet
Quinacridone magenta
Quinacridone sienna
Ultramarine turquoise

TECHNIQUES
Flat wash, *p. 20*
Mixing paint in the palette, *p. 21*
Wet-onto-dry, *p. 22*
Wet-into-wet, *p. 22*
Glazing, *p. 23*

TOOLS & MATERIALS
Cold-pressed paper, 140 lb. (300 gsm)
H pencil
Large wash brush
1-in. (2.5-cm) flat brush
Round brush, No. 6

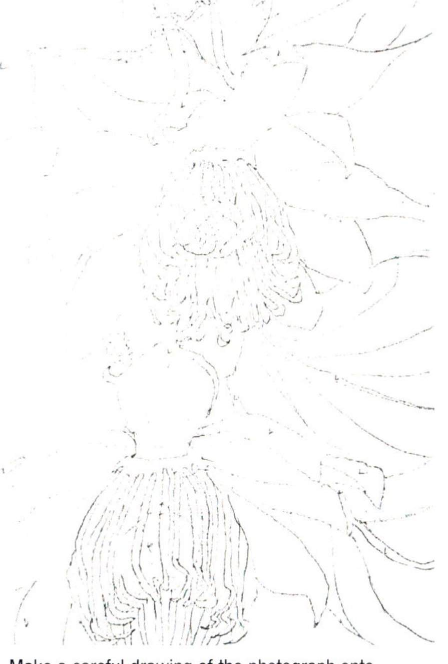

1 Make a careful drawing of the photograph onto the watercolor paper using an H pencil. There is a great deal of detail at the center of this flower that should be addressed in the drawing if the painting is to reflect it accurately.

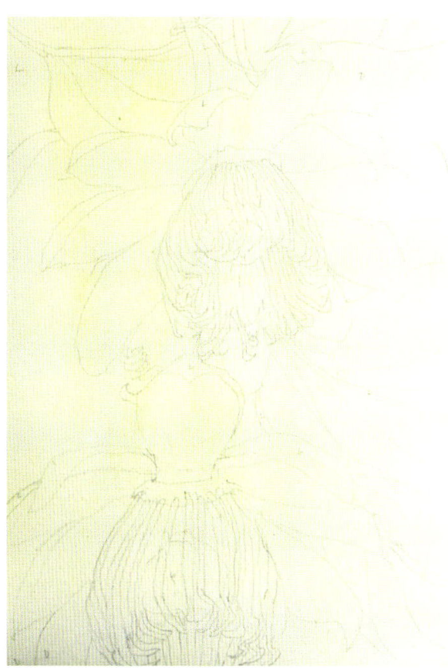

2 Wet the paper with a large wash brush. Use the same brush to paint a wash of aureolin to cover the entire painting, letting it dry completely before proceeding. This will give the painting a general warmth, even under the cooler background colors.

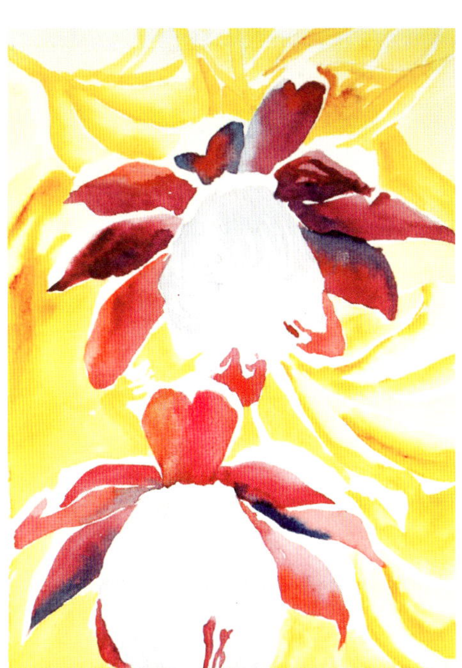

3 Paint in the main colored shapes, still using the wash brush, and using nickel azo as an underlayer. (This area will later be glazed with blues to achieve greens.) Next, with various reds and blues, paint the petals, sepals, and radial filaments. Emphasize the color variations formed by the light and shadows. Stay loosely controlled by using a 1-in. (2.5-cm) flat brush. Mix a pale lavender from cobalt blue and quinacridone magenta for the gestured filaments and paint with a No. 6 round brush.

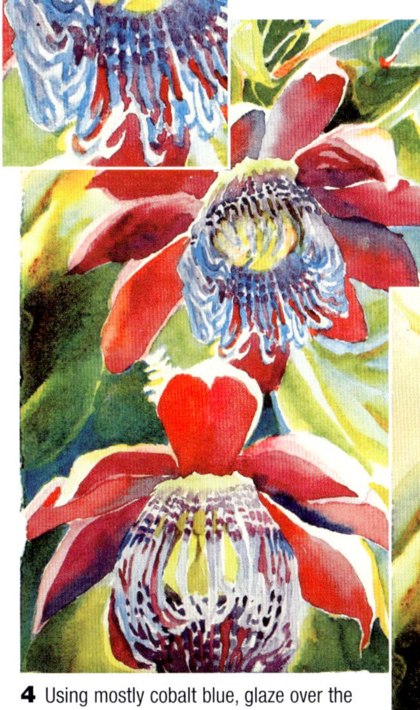

4 Using mostly cobalt blue, glaze over the underlying nickel azo passages in the background. Leave some unpainted areas to connect to the lights throughout the painting. When dry, add some darker mixed greens of ultramarine turquoise and quinacridone sienna. Using quinacridone magenta in varying mixes with indanthrone blue and cobalt blue, paint the filaments with the No. 6 brush (inset).

5 Paint in the deepest and darkest greens to add depth to the background. Deepen the shadows in the petals of the flowers using a mixture of quinacridone magenta and indanthrone blue. Lift a few light spots connecting the two flowers. Add finishing touches using the No. 6 brush.

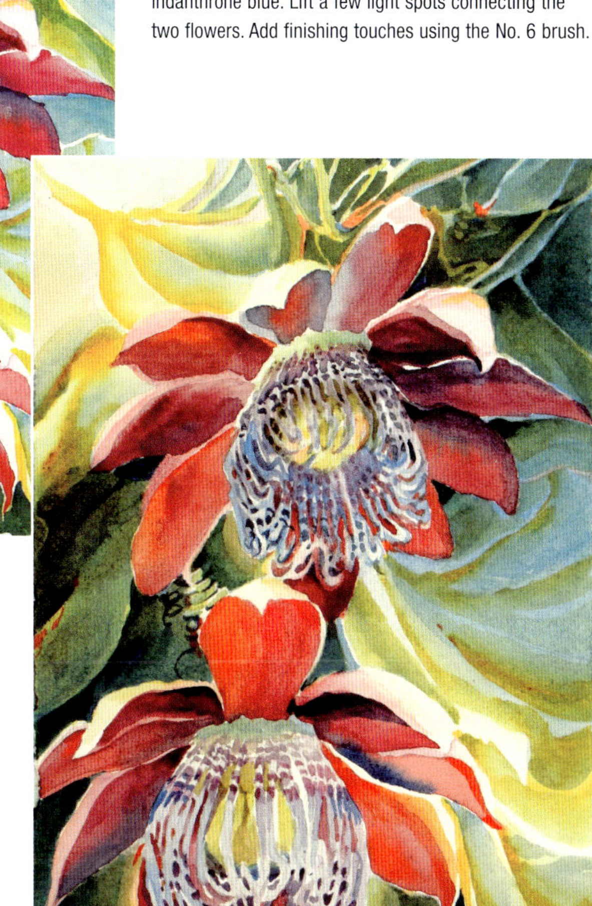

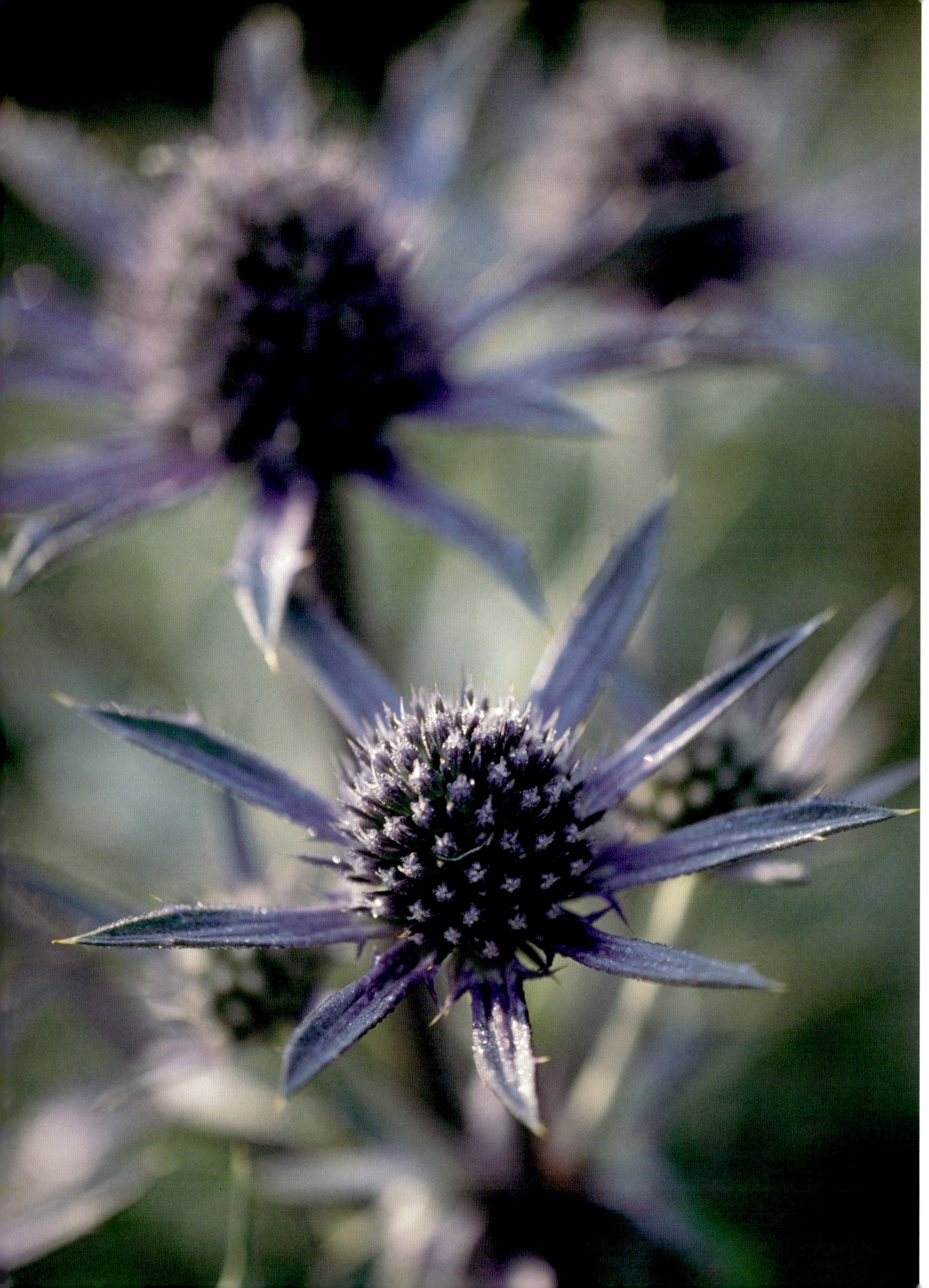

Blue Thistles

The artist chose to follow the photograph closely, adding more light only in the center to increase the backlighting effect.

PAINTS
Carbazole violet
Cobalt blue
Cobalt green
Cobalt turquoise
Cobalt turquoise light
Indanthrone blue
Mineral violet
Phthalo turquoise
Phthalo yellow-green
Ultramarine turquoise

TOOLS & MATERIALS
Hot-pressed paper, 300 lb. (638 gsm)
Pencil
Masking fluid
Old brush
3-in. (7.5-cm) wash brush
Kosher salt
Fritch scrubber, No. 2
Tissues
1-in. (2.5-cm) flat brush
Large round mop brush
Round brushes, Nos. 6, 10, 14

TECHNIQUES USED
Dropping in color, *p. 21*
Wet-onto-dry, *p. 22*
Lost and found edges, *p. 24*
Masking to reserve the paper, *p. 25*
Masking for details, *p. 25*
Softening masked edges, *p. 25*
Salt, *p. 30*
Throwing paint, *p. 30*

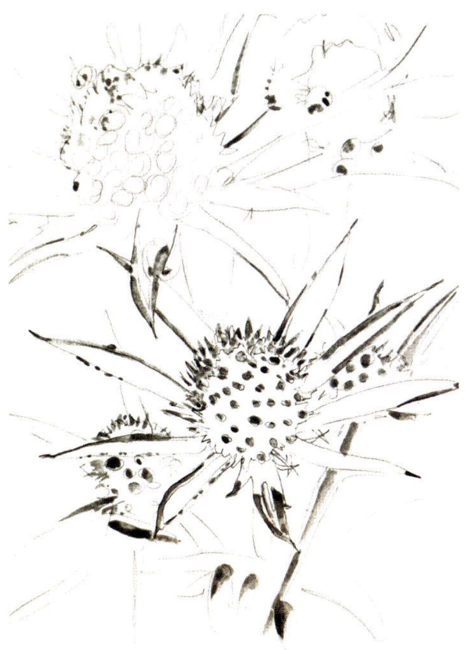

1 Make a detailed drawing from the photograph, being sure to mark a spot of light for masking. Using masking fluid and an old brush, mask any areas of white you would like to preserve, including light flower details, light flares in the photograph, and sunlit edges of the petals. Leave to dry completely.

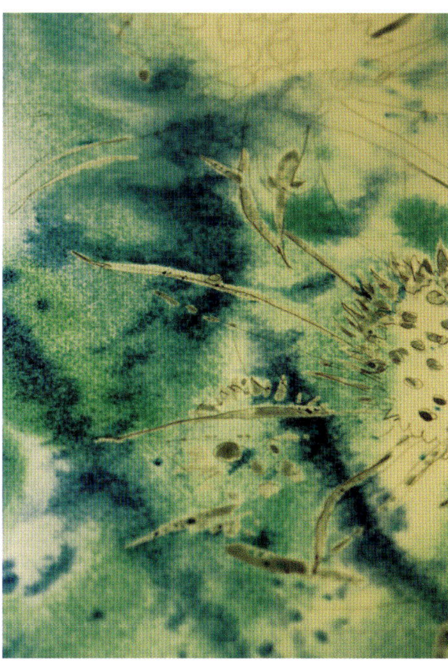

2 Wet the paper on both sides with a 3-in. (7.5-cm) wash brush, so it buckles less during painting. With the surface still shiny, use the wash brush to apply large swatches of cobalt green and turquoise, avoiding the center light area and the backlit area behind the thistles. Spatter or throw mineral violet, cobalt blue, and cobalt turquoise for further textural effects.

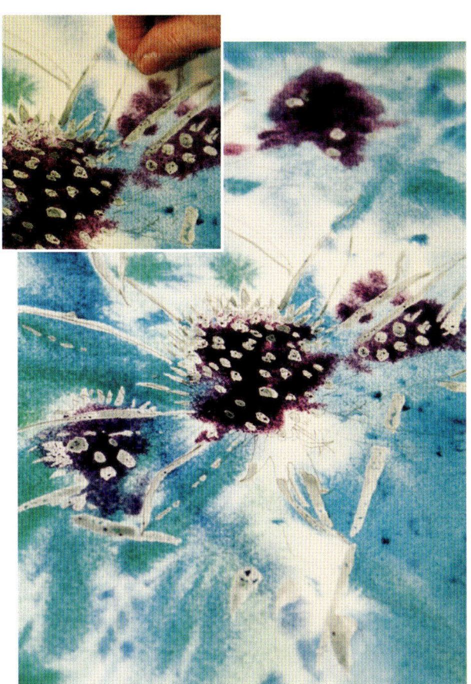

3 While the paper is still wet, paint the center of the flowers with mineral violet and carbazole violet. When the color no longer pools but is still wet, drop grains of kosher salt into the violet at the center of each flower (inset). Dry overnight.

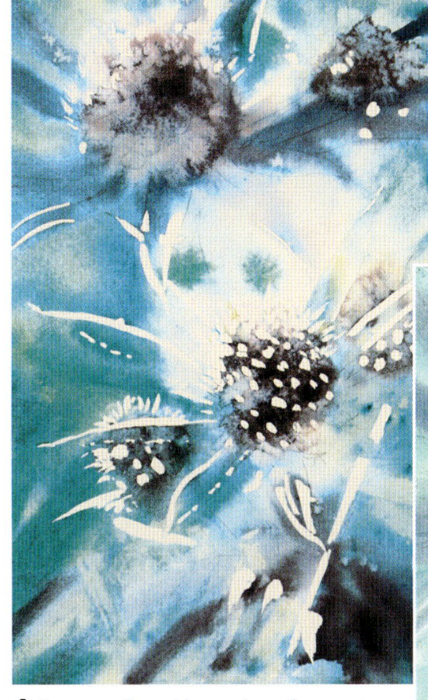

4 Remove all masking and gently scrape away any salt grains. Using a No. 2 Fritch scrubber, soften all edges. This paper is soft, so do not scrub too hard but use plenty of water, dabbing with tissue as you go along.

5 Finish the flowers by painting the centers and petals wet-into-wet using cobalt and indanthrone blues (inset). Let the paint blend. Dab on mineral violet at the top of the flower center, and carbazole violet and indanthrone blue in the shadow. For the in-focus flower use harder edges.

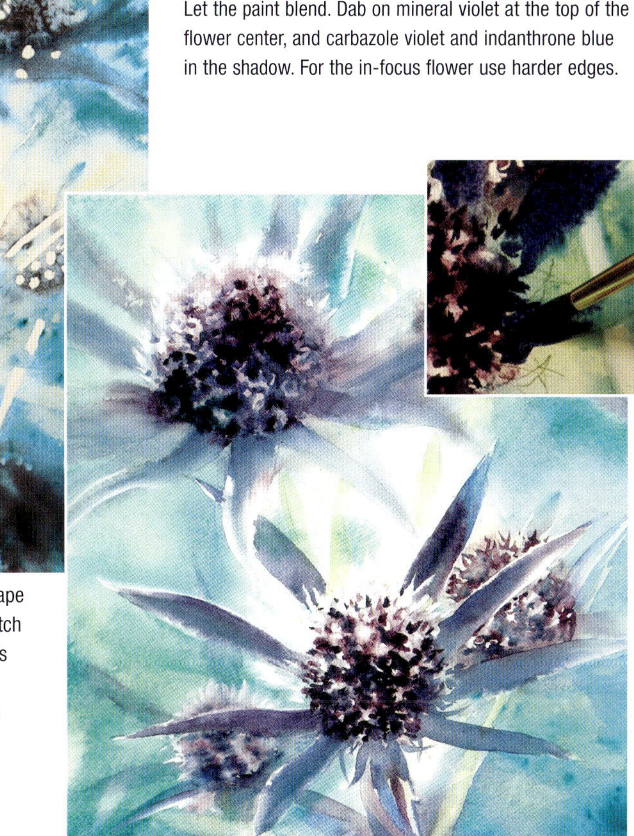

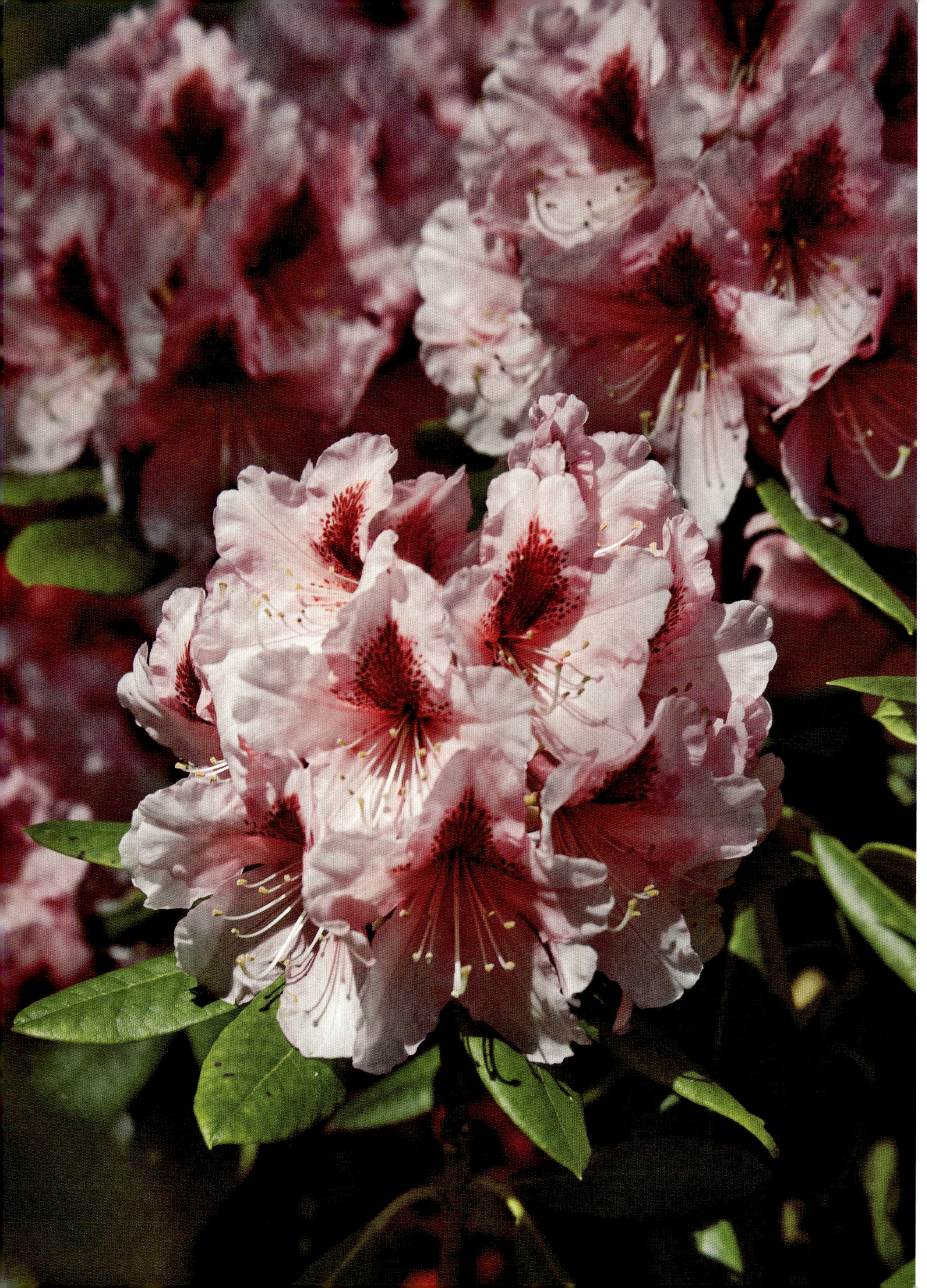

Rhododendron

The velvety surface of hot-pressed paper is perfect for delicately blended shadows and the detailed edges of petals. The ruffles and frills of the flowers are a counterpoint to the thick, smooth-edged leaves.

PAINTS
Hooker's green
New gamboge
Phthalo blue
Purple magenta
Pyrrole orange
Sap green
Translucent orange

TOOLS & MATERIALS
Hot-pressed paper, 140 lb. (300 gsm)
HB pencil
Masking fluid
Old brush
Round brushes, Nos. 4, 6, 8, 10
Scrubber
Tissues

TECHNIQUES
Flat wash, *p. 20*
Mixing paint in the palette, *p. 21*
Wet-onto-dry, *p. 22*
Wet-into-wet, *p. 22*
Glazing, *p. 23*
Blending, *p. 24*
Masking to reserve the paper, *p. 25*
Shadows, *p. 28*

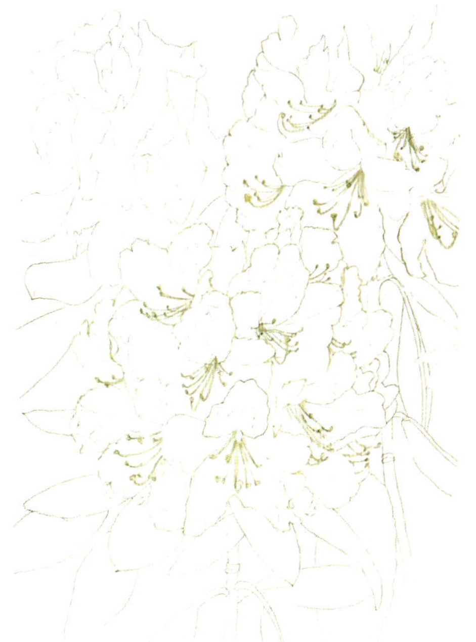

1 Make a detailed drawing of the photograph on the watercolor paper in pencil. Apply a thin line of masking fluid with an old brush along the outside edges of all the petals of the main flower heads, and the stamens. Let dry completely before applying paint.

2 Mix phthalo blue and purple magenta and apply in light washes, wet-into-wet, with No. 6 and No. 8 brushes. Make several mixes ranging from cool blue to warm purple to establish the shadow patterns on the petals and the main leaves. Soften all edges with a damp scrubber and blot with a tissue.

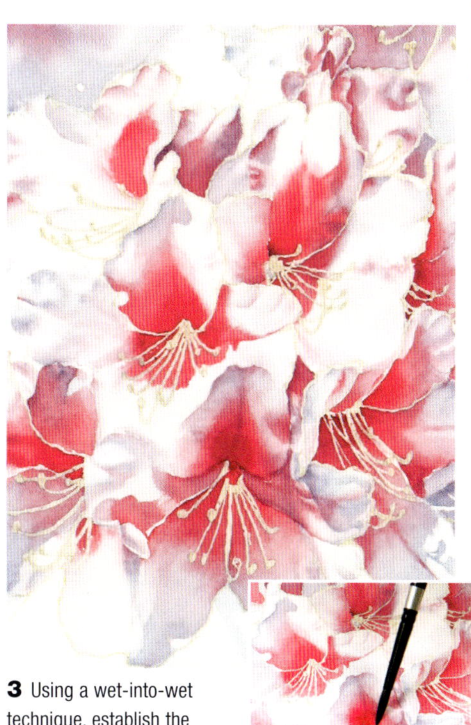

3 Using a wet-into-wet technique, establish the underlying pink in the flower centers with purple magenta and a No. 8 brush (inset). Glaze several layers, allowing the paint to dry between each. Soften and feather all the edges, especially along the lines of masking fluid.

4 Use new gamboge in a wet-into-wet wash with a No. 8 brush as an underlay on the leaves (inset). A glow will result when sap green and Hooker's green, mixed with a touch of purple magenta, are glazed over the top. Apply the greens with No. 6 and No. 8 brushes. Remove the masking.

5 Apply new gamboge, purple magenta, and pyrrole orange wet-into-wet to the background with a No. 8 brush. Use the green mixes from step 4 and a muted mix of purple magenta and Hooker's green to deepen the background wet-onto-dry. Use pyrrole orange wet-into-wet with a No. 6 brush in the flower centers. Mix translucent orange and phthalo blue and apply to the flower centers in a dotted pattern with a No. 4 brush.

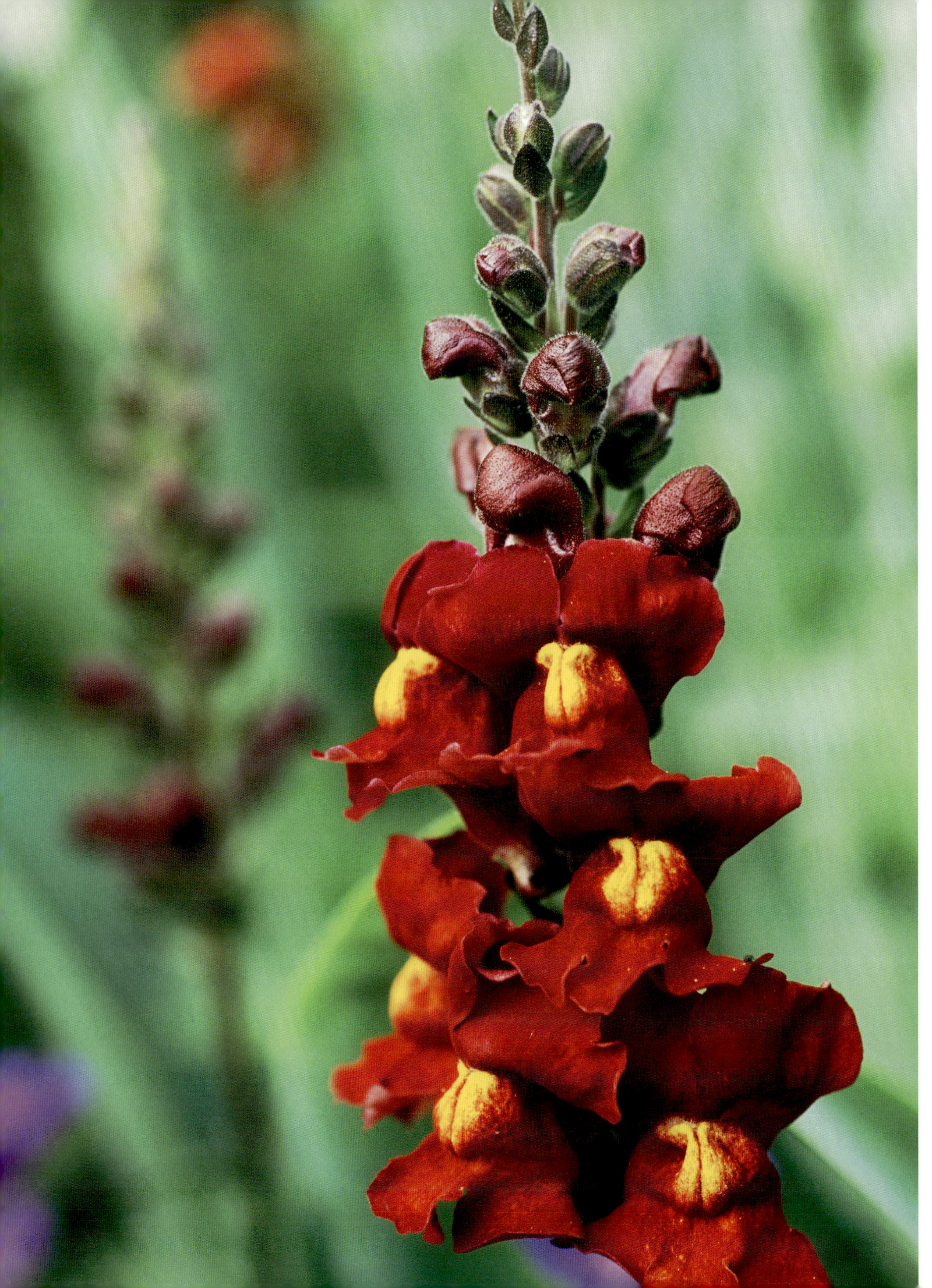

Snapdragon

The artist was drawn to the swirling, brilliant red shapes of each individual snapdragon flower. The opportunity to use beautiful and active reds against a complementary background of variegated greens is always exciting.

PAINTS
Alizarin crimson
Bismuth yellow
Cadmium scarlet
Cadmium yellow
Cobalt blue
French ultramarine blue
Permanent rose
Winsor green (blue shade)
Winsor red

TECHNIQUES
Mixing paint in the palette, *p. 21*
Mixing paint on the paper, *p. 21*
Dropping in color, *p. 21*
Wet-onto-dry, *p. 22*
Wet-into-wet, p. 22
Masking to reserve the paper, *p. 25*
Masking for details, *p. 25*

TOOLS & MATERIALS
Rough watercolor paper, 140 lb. (300 gsm)
H pencil
Masking fluid
Old brush
3-in. (7.5-cm) hake brush
Round brushes, Nos. 4 and 12

1 Make a careful drawing, with pencil on watercolor paper, of the primary snapdragon stalk. Add an additional flower shape at the bottom left to improve the design. (Without the addition of this flower, the stalk would appear top-heavy and wobbly.) The bottom edge should feel solid to avoid creating tension that would draw the eye out of the painting. Lightly sketch in the background image on the left.

2 Precisely mask off the primary snapdragon stalk. Pay attention to the "holes" that separate the individual blossoms and mask around them. Dry the masking before beginning to paint.

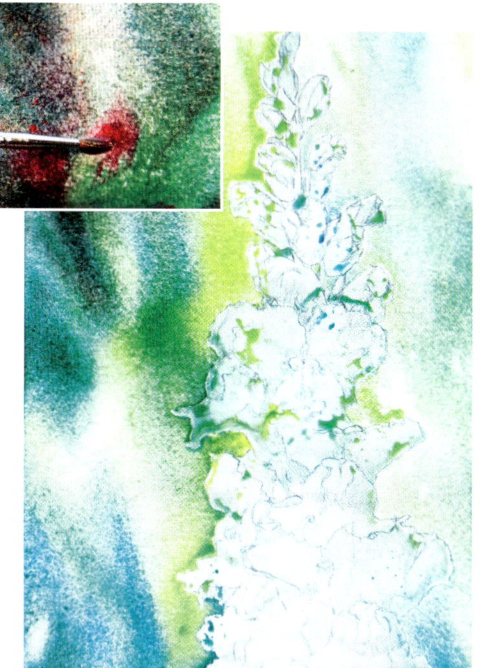

3 With a 3-in. (7.5-cm) hake brush, apply water over the entire painting. Paint strokes of color with a No. 12 round brush, using bismuth yellow, cadmium yellow, cobalt blue, and French ultramarine blue, allowing the colors to mix on the paper to create greens. When all is dry, remove the mask. Lightly re-wet the area of the background image and, using a No. 12 brush, drop in a mixture of Winsor green and alizarin crimson for the rich darks and permanent rose to "cool" the background buds (inset).

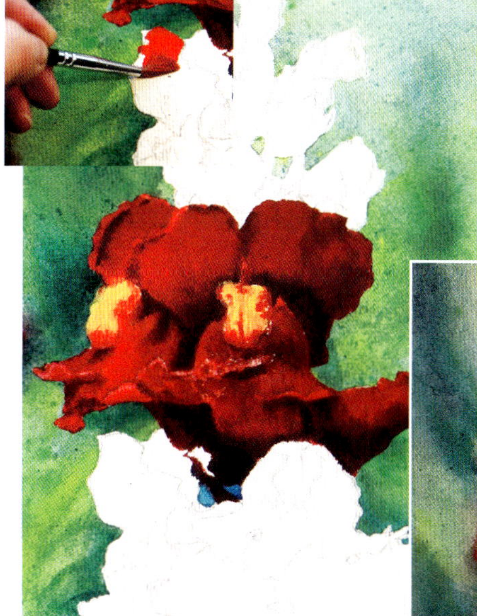

4 Paint the main flowers one by one (inset). Using a No. 4 round brush, build your image with a variety of reds: Winsor red, cadmium scarlet, and alizarin crimson. Use bismuth yellow and cadmium yellow for the centers. A mixture of alizarin crimson and French ultramarine blue will give you a nice dark where required.

5 Finish the upper part of the flower stalk. While these unopened flowers are more magenta than red, if you paint it this way it will visually cut your image in half. In developing the top, add some of the same reds you used before. Make adjustments to color and value all around the painting to bring it to completion.

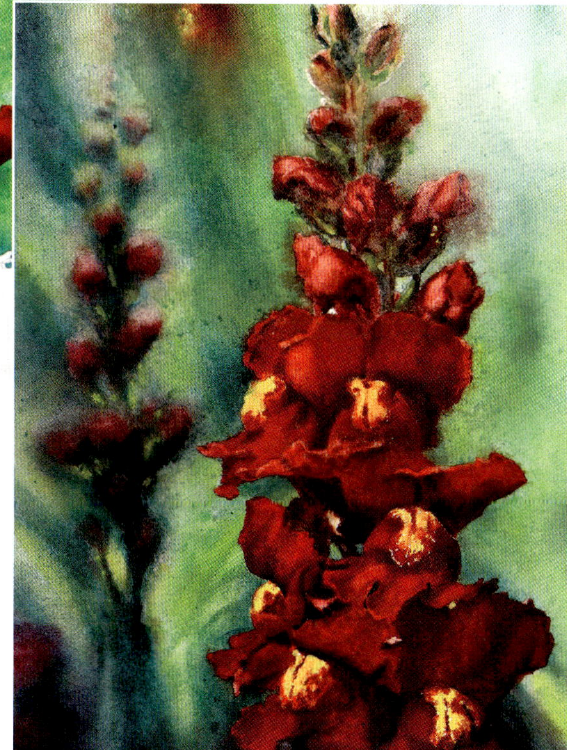

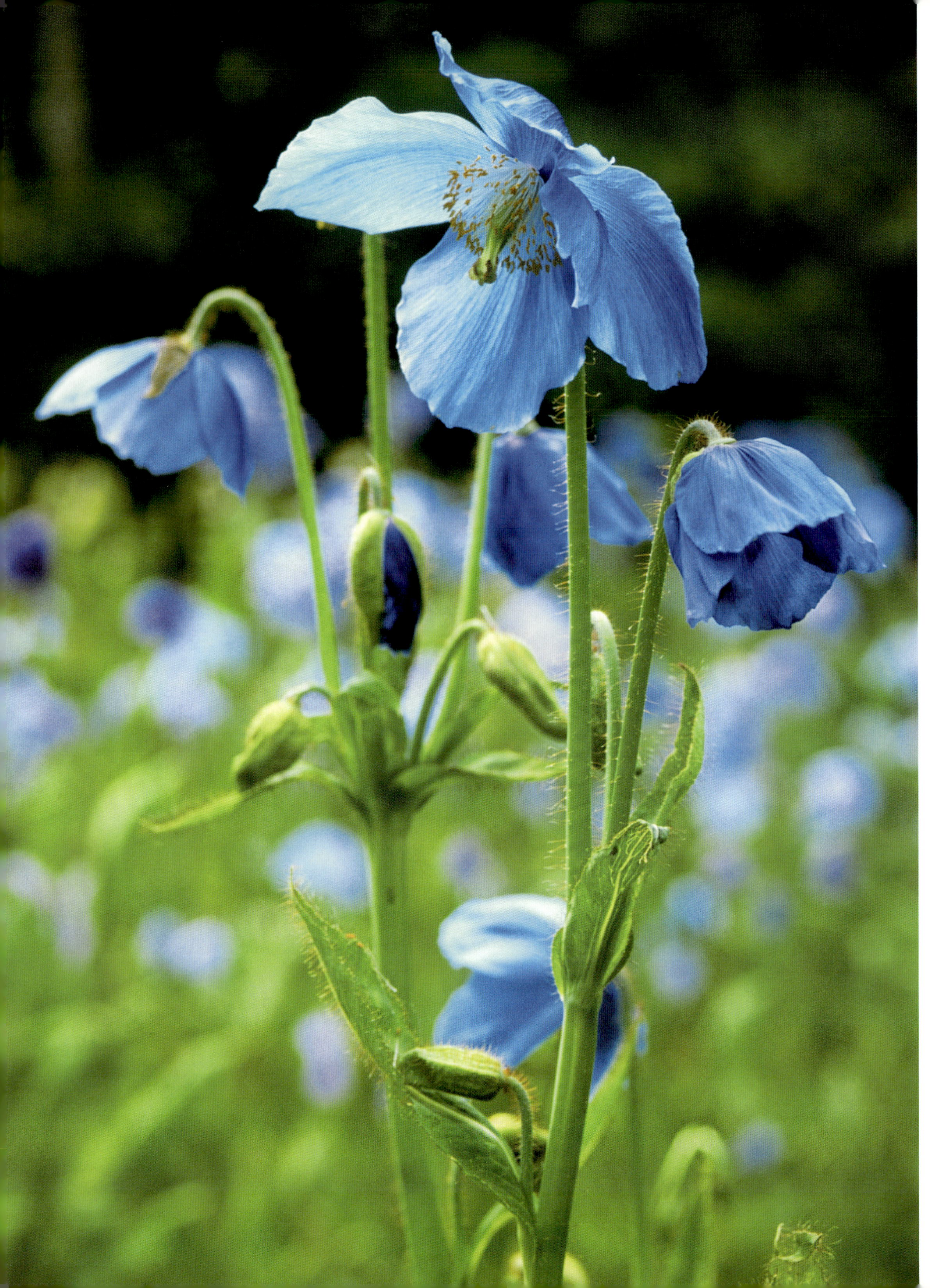

Blue Poppies

The subject here stands away from the background with a three-dimensional effect, with the blue colors emphasized in the main flowers.

PAINTS
Aureolin
Cerulean blue
Cinereous blue
Indigo
Peacock blue
Phthalo blue
Prussian blue
Rich green-gold
Sap green
Viridian
Zinc white designers' gouache

TOOLS & MATERIALS
Cold-pressed paper, 140 lb. (300 gsm)
2H or HB pencil
Masking fluid
Taper point firm color shaper, No. 0
Flat chisel soft color shaper, No. 2
Natural sponge
Round brushes, Nos. 2, 4, 5, 12
Kosher salt

TECHNIQUES
Mixing paint on the paper, *p. 21*
Dropping in color, *p. 21*
Wet-onto-dry, *p. 22*
Wet-into-wet, *p. 22*
Paint light to dark, *p. 23*
Glazing, *p. 23*
Blending, *p. 24*
Lost and found edges, *p. 24*
Masking to reserve the paper, *p. 25*
Softening masked edges, *p. 25*
Shadows, *p. 28*
Salt, *p. 30*
Watercolor and gouache, *p. 32*

1 Draw the image out on watercolor paper in pencil, and mask the flower and leaves with the masking fluid (inset), using the color shapers. Apply water to the background with a natural sponge.

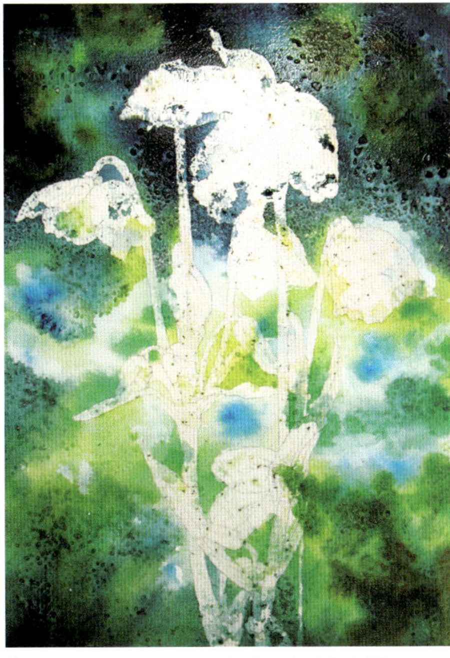

2 Using a No. 12 round brush, drop in phthalo blue, Prussian blue, indigo, cinereous blue, sap green, rich green-gold, and aureolin. Do not overwork, otherwise the paint will get muddy. Sprinkle kosher salt onto portions of the wet background along with drops of water over already saturated areas to produce "blooms" in the color. When dry, brush all the salt off the paper, taking care not to disturb the masked areas.

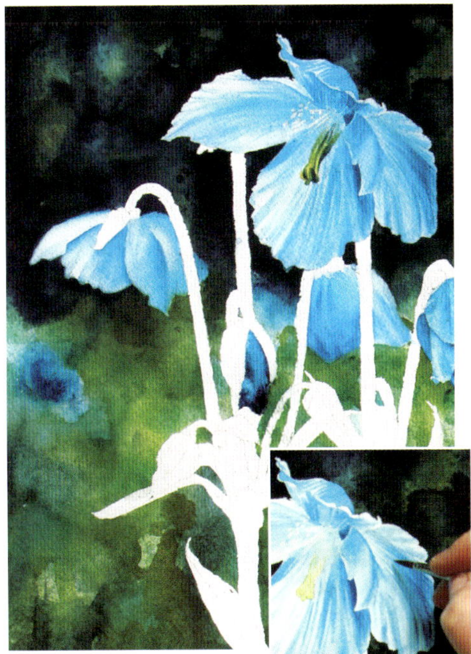

3 Using a No. 5 brush, moisten each petal with water and add color wet-into-wet. With the No. 4 and No. 2 brushes, spread the pigment to the edges. Build the saturation with several glazes, letting each application dry before applying the next. For the petals, use phthalo blue, cinereous blue, and indigo, the last color on the petals for the deepest shadows (inset).

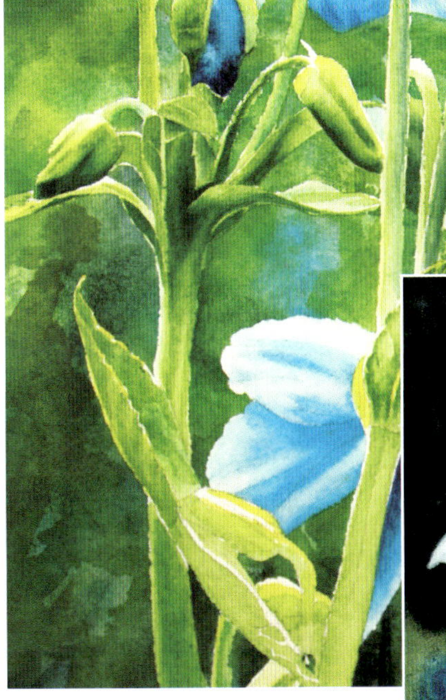

4 Moisten each leaf area and add sap green, rich green-gold, viridian, aureolin, and indigo wet-into-wet with a No. 4 brush. Build the saturation with several glazes, letting each application dry. Fine-tune the flowers and leaves by glazing with different percentages of saturated color. The flowers need to be highly saturated.

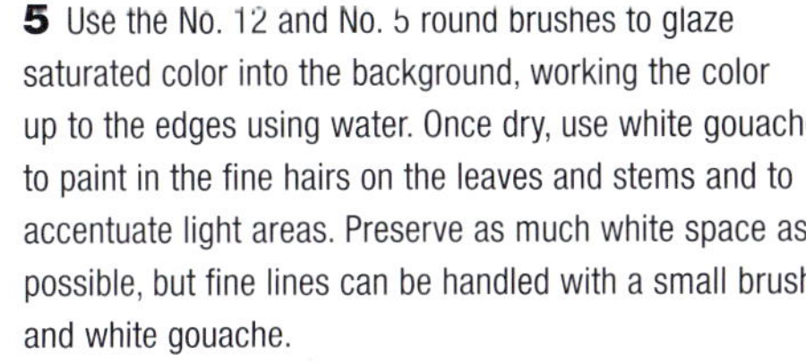

5 Use the No. 12 and No. 5 round brushes to glaze saturated color into the background, working the color up to the edges using water. Once dry, use white gouache to paint in the fine hairs on the leaves and stems and to accentuate light areas. Preserve as much white space as possible, but fine lines can be handled with a small brush and white gouache.

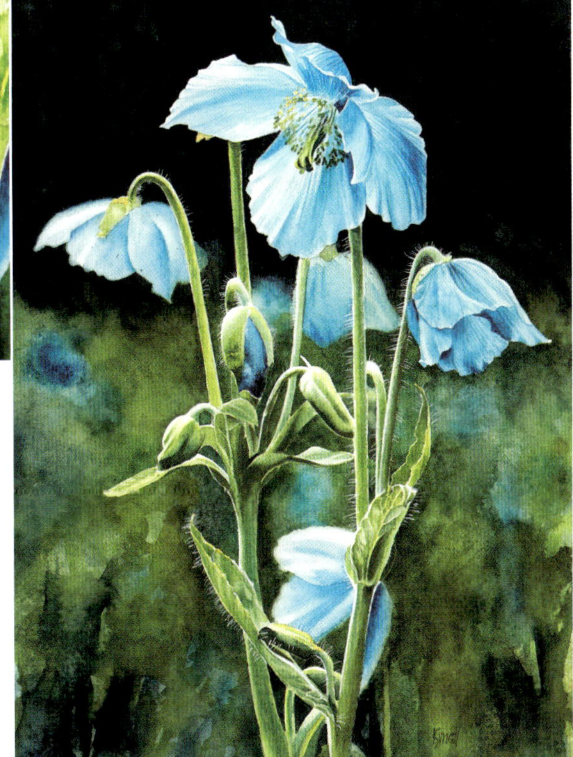

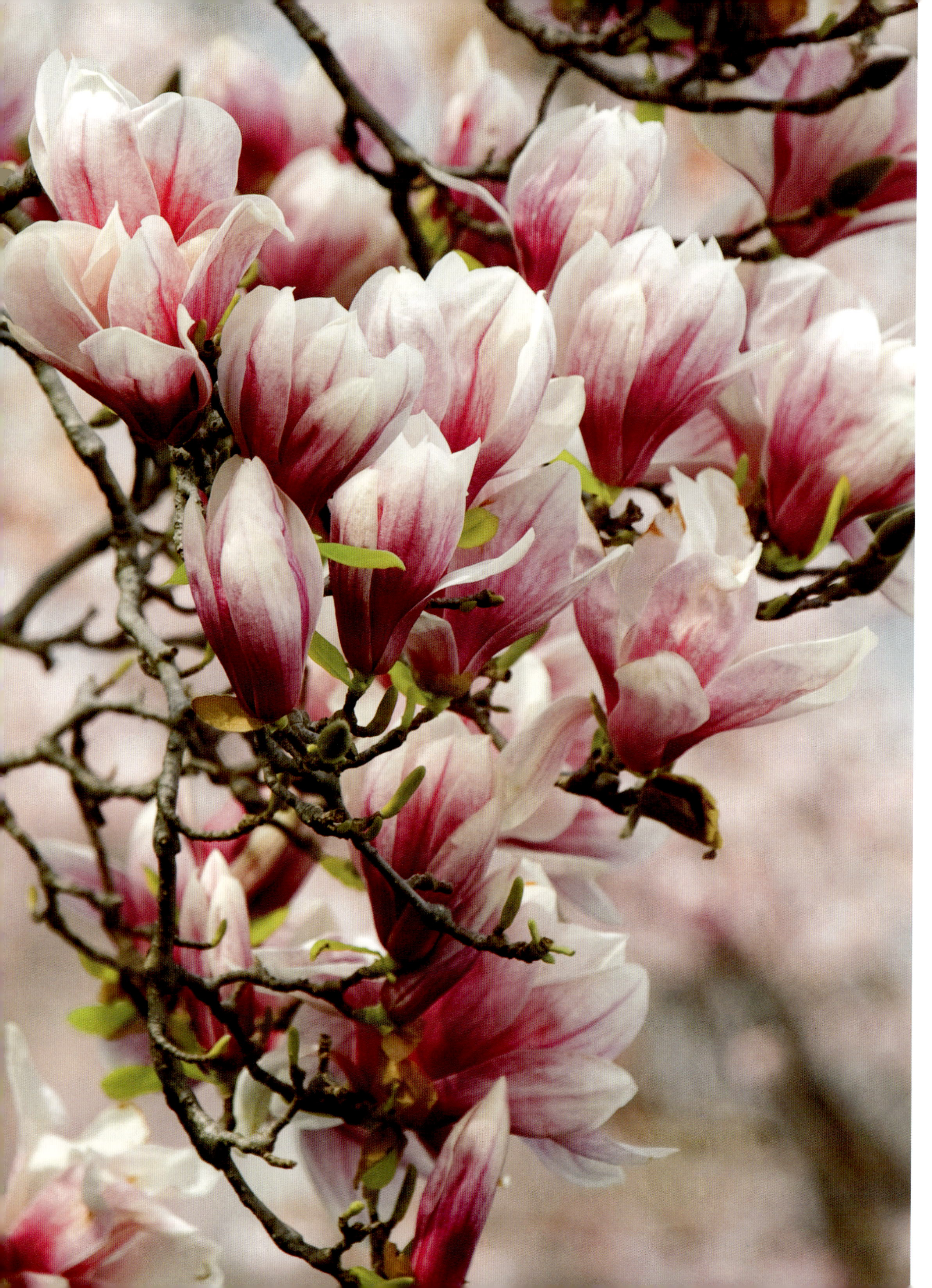

Magnolia Blossom

The artist was drawn to the soft, pillowlike quality of these blossoms.

PAINTS
Aureolin
Cobalt blue
French ultramarine blue
Phthalo blue
Quinacridone coral
Quinacridone magenta
Quinacridone pink
Quinacridone red
Quinacridone rose
Quinacridone violet

TOOLS & MATERIALS
Cold-pressed paper, 140 lb. (300 gms)
Mechanical pencil
Masquepen
Tissues and paper towels
3-in. (7.5-cm) wash brush
1-in. (1.5-cm) flat brush
Round brushes, Nos. 6, 10, 14
Liner
Fritch scrubber

TECHNIQUES USED
Flat wash, *p. 20*
Mixing paint in the palette, *p. 21*
Dropping in color, *p. 21*
Wet-onto-dry, *p. 22*
Wet-into-wet, *p. 22*
Glazing, *p. 23*
Lost and found edges, *p. 24*
Masking to reserve the paper, *p. 25*
Softening masked edges, *p. 25*

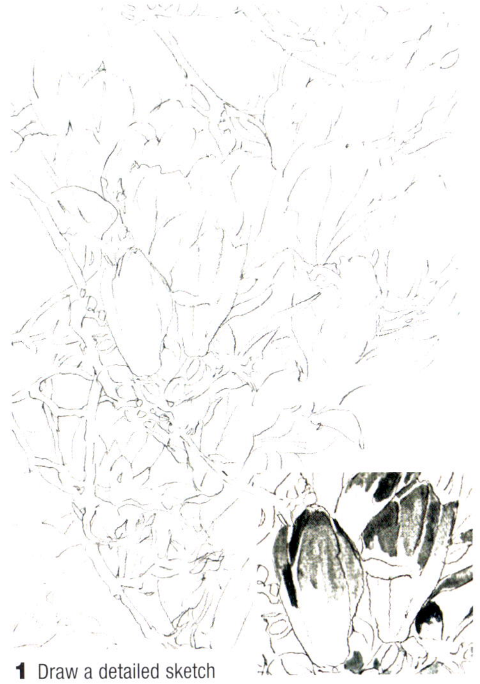

1 Draw a detailed sketch from the photograph. Mask all the in-focus white flower tips (inset). Wet your paper on both sides and then blot away any standing water so the paper is damp.

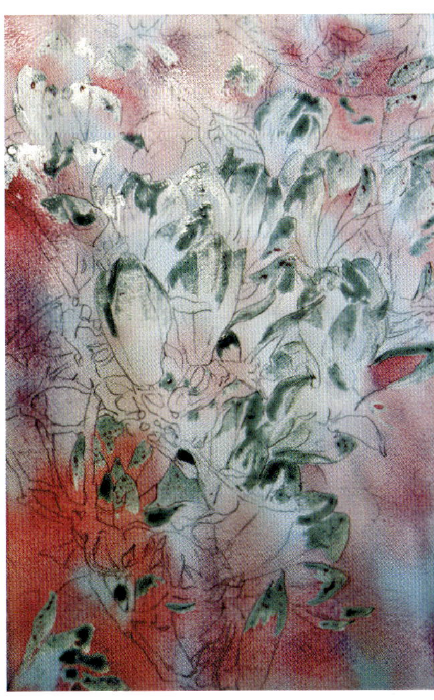

2 With a wide wash brush, paint on cobalt blue diluted to the strength of tea—dark enough to look blue but very transparent. Repeat if the blue is too weak. While the blue is still wet, drop in a slightly stronger mixture of quinacridone pink. Let the colors mingle. Leave some blue areas. You should have a soft background when the paper is dry.

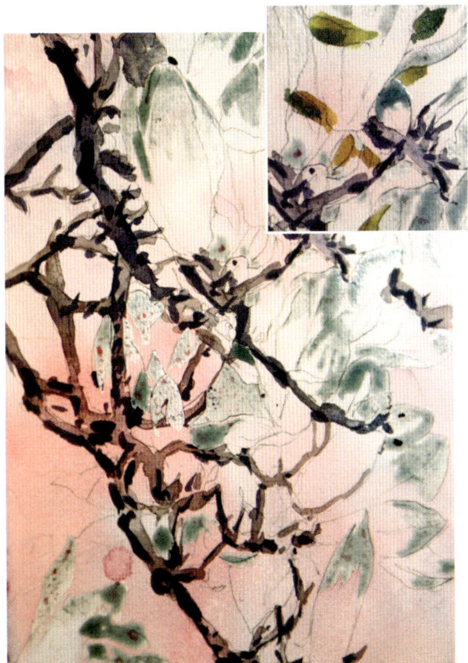

3 To paint the branches, mix a warm gray from aureolin, quinacridone rose, and French ultramarine blue. With a No. 10 brush, wet a line of branch and drop this mixture into the wet stream. Move along the branches and twigs until all are painted and dried. Indicate color irregularities and shadows in the branches with a slightly darker mixture (inset). Dry the branches. From mixtures of aureolin, phthalo blue (very little), and a drop of quinacridone red, mix two or three greens, and paint the small leaves.

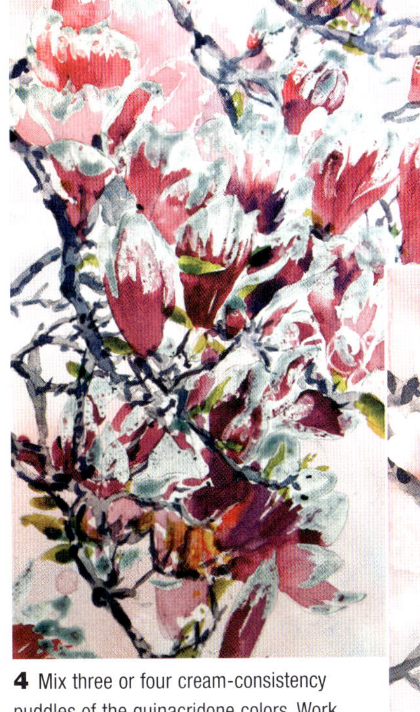

4 Mix three or four cream-consistency puddles of the quinacridone colors. Work your way through the blossoms, noting that the colors become more intense toward the foreground. Each time you dip your brush for a particular blossom, dip it in a different mixture of red so you have variety. Note where the shadows are and touch in cobalt blue. Dry.

5 Remove all the masking. Using a Fritch scrubber, wet the line between the rose and white, and move and blend the paint, filling out the volume and depth of each blossom (inset). Dab with tissue where necessary to recover the white.

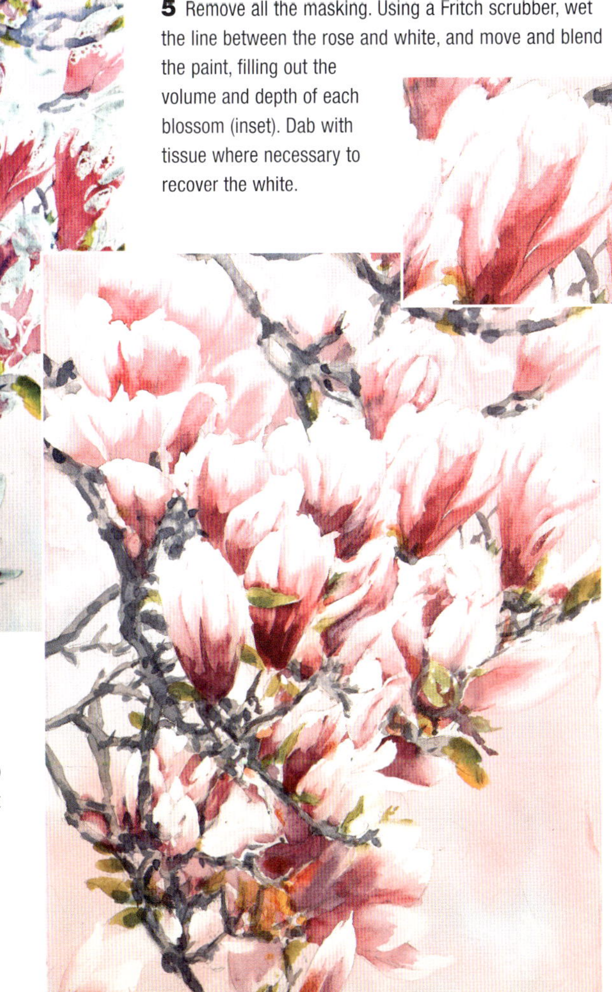

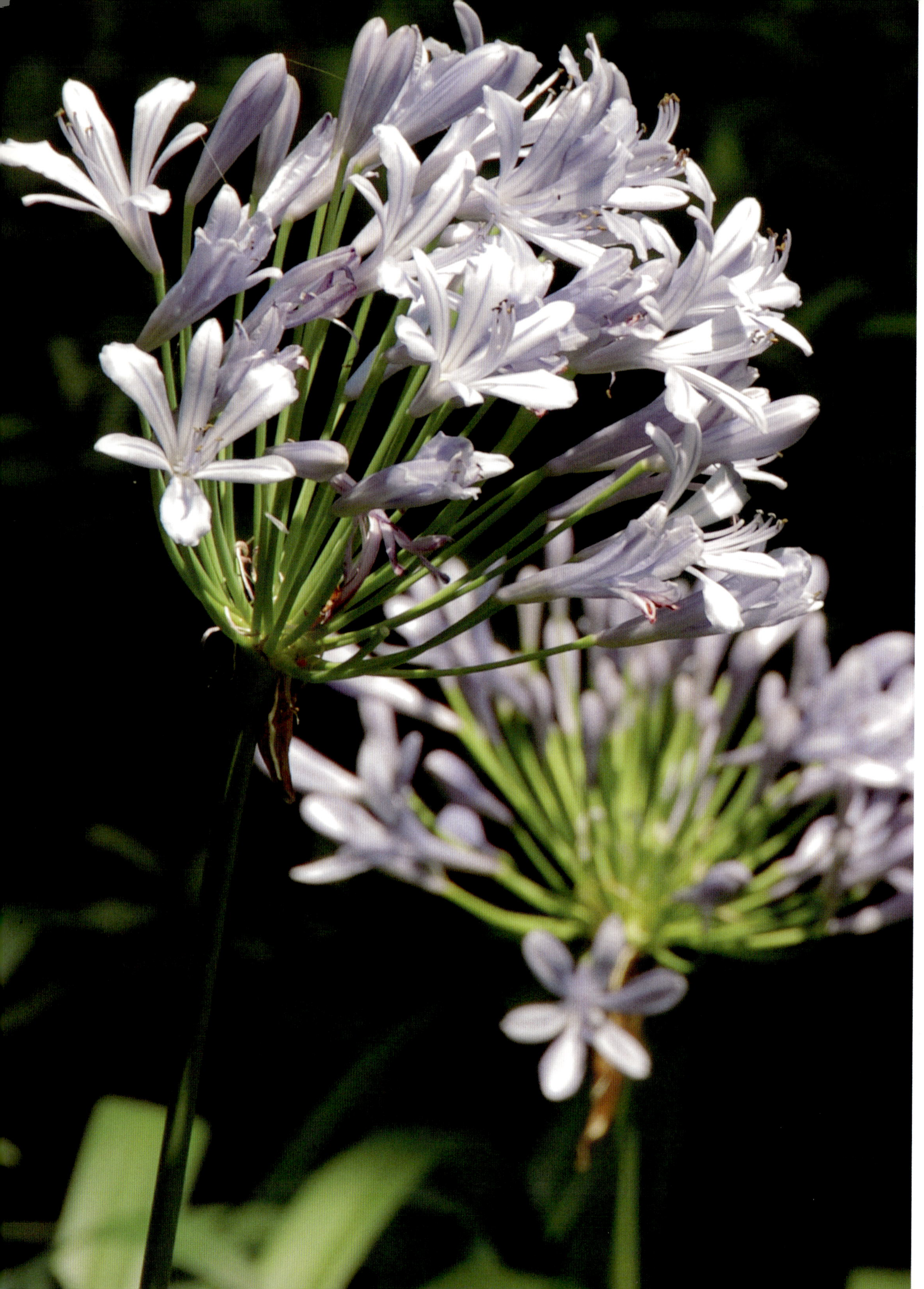

Lilies of the Nile

The artist was challenged by the need to simplify the complex flower pattern while staying true to the form of these sunny agapanthus.

PAINTS
Alizarin crimson
Bismuth yellow
Burnt orange
Cobalt blue
French ultramarine blue
Permanent rose
Winsor green (blue shade)

TECHNIQUES
Mixing paint in the palette, *p. 21*
Mixing paint on the paper, *p. 21*
Wet-onto-dry, *p. 22*
Wet-into-wet, *p. 22*
Masking, *p. 25*

TOOLS & MATERIALS
Cold-pressed paper, 140 lb. (300 gsm)
H pencil
Round brushes, Nos. 4 and 12
Masquepen
3-in. (7.5-cm) hake brush

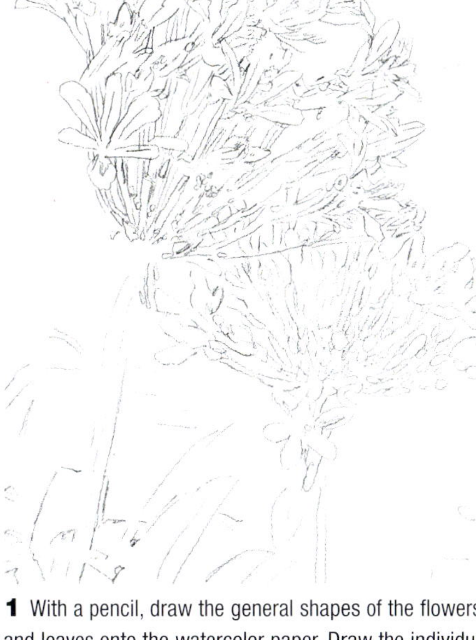

1 With a pencil, draw the general shapes of the flowers and leaves onto the watercolor paper. Draw the individual flower shapes as best you can. There is an area of confusion in the upper right portion of the top flower. Don't worry about this yet.

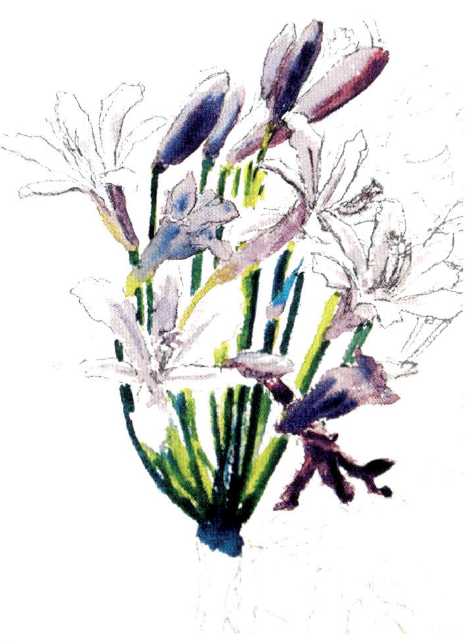

2 Take a No. 4 round brush and begin to paint the individual flowers using mixtures of alizarin crimson, permanent rose, cobalt blue, and French ultramarine blue. When you get to the upper right area on the top flower, pick out complete flower shapes one by one as you work your way around. Don't try to paint everything that is there—edit! Work at making sense of the area.

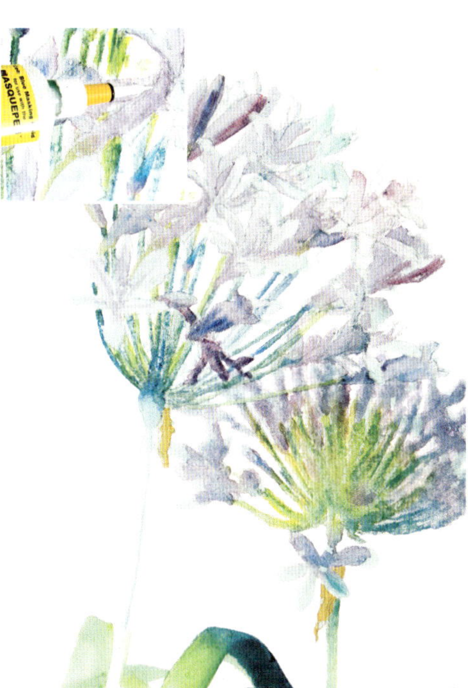

3 When dry, use a Masquepen to mask to the entire area of the foreground flowers. Once this has dried completely you will see how well the design sits on the paper. If you want to add a flower or two, simply "paint" these new shapes using the Masquepen (inset).

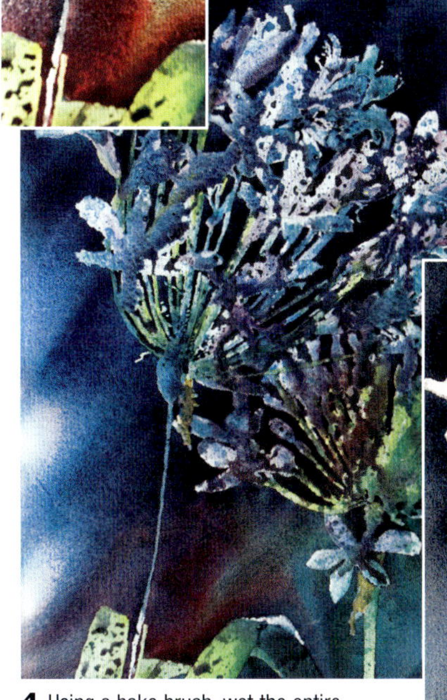

4 Using a hake brush, wet the entire painting with clean water. Begin to paint in the darks with a No. 12 brush. When painting this background wash, the idea is to vary the color across the paper. Create bands of dark blue, alizarin crimson, and dark greens, allowing them to mix and blend slightly (inset). Work to produce a granulating texture.

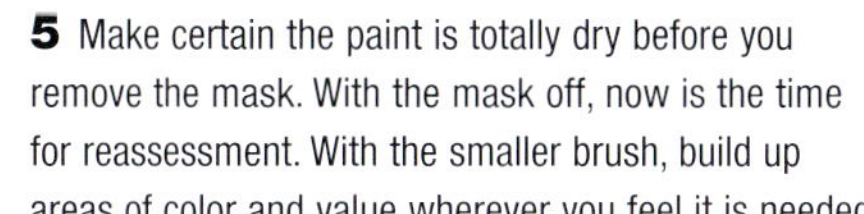

5 Make certain the paint is totally dry before you remove the mask. With the mask off, now is the time for reassessment. With the smaller brush, build up areas of color and value wherever you feel it is needed.

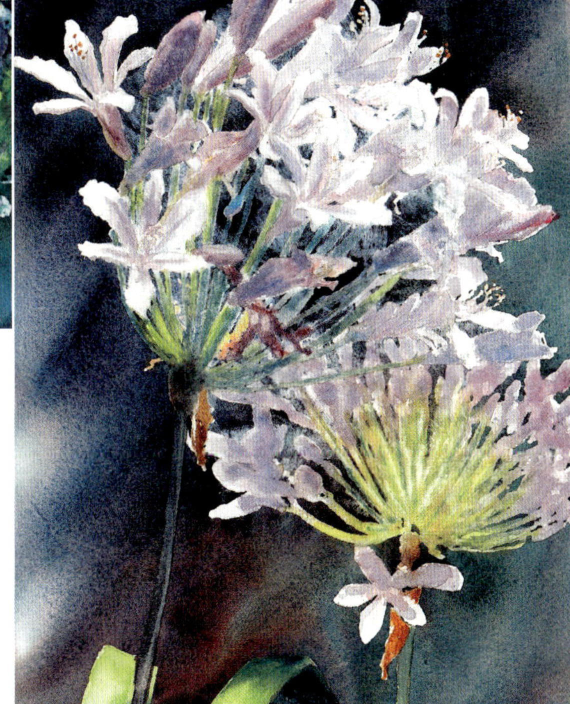

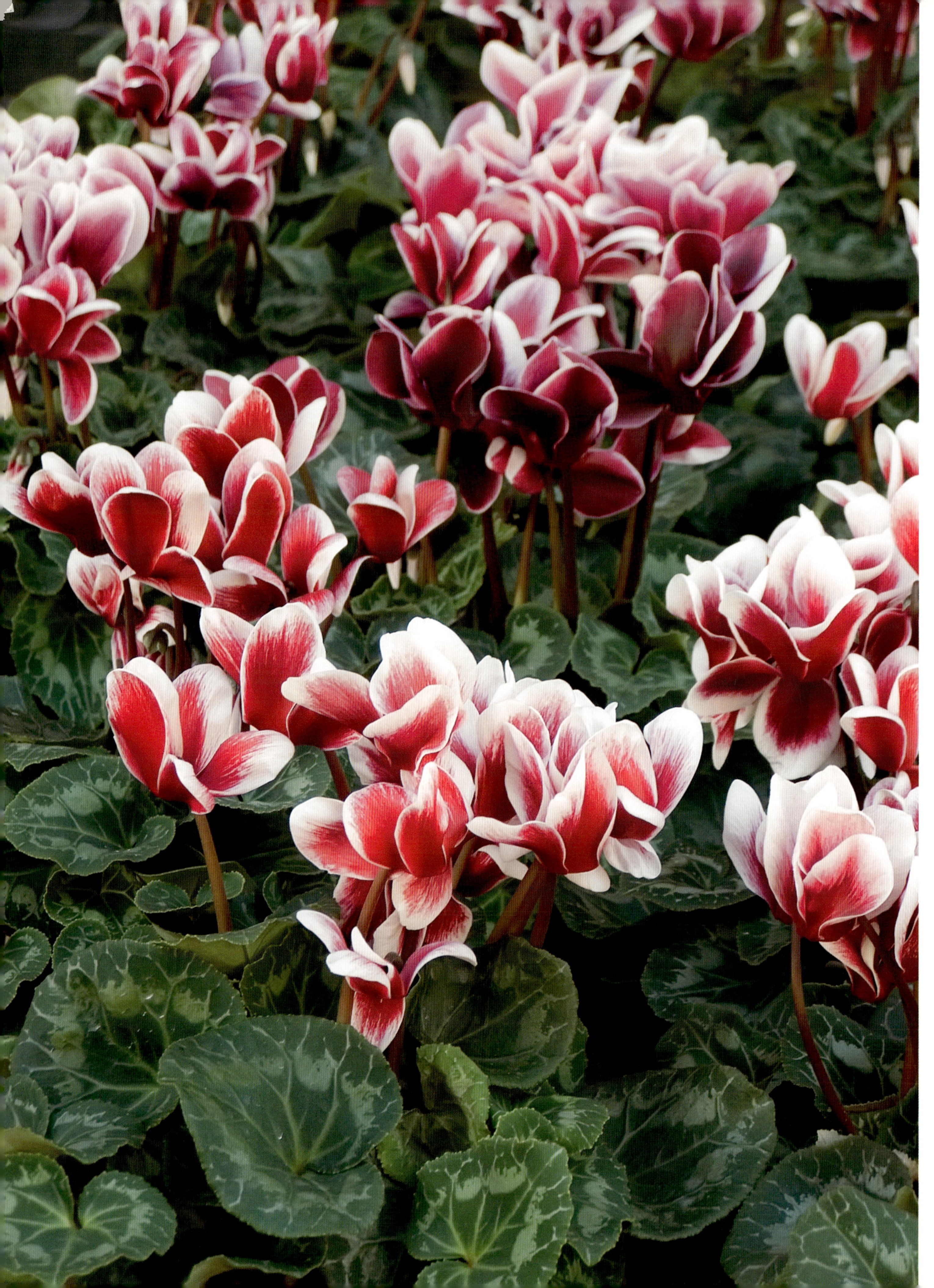

Cyclamen

It is challenging to unify several busy elements into a good composition. Defining the leaf shapes and surface patterns with negative painting is like working a puzzle.

PAINTS

Hansa yellow medium
Hooker's green
Phthalo blue
Purple magenta
Quinacridone red

TOOLS & MATERIALS

Cold-pressed paper, 140 lb. (300 gsm)
HB pencil
Masking fluid
Old brush
Round brushes, Nos. 4, 6, 8
Scrubber
Tissues

TECHNIQUES

Mixing paint in the palette, *p. 21*
Wet-onto-dry, *p. 22*
Wet-into-wet, *p. 22*
Glazing, *p. 23*
Blending, *p. 24*
Masking to reserve the paper, *p. 25*
Softening masked edges, *p. 25*
Shadows, *p. 28*
Negative painting, *p. 28*

1 Draw the design in pencil on the watercolor paper. Apply a thin line of masking fluid using an old brush along the outside edge of each petal and the leaves in the foreground. Let dry completely before applying paint.

2 With a No. 8 brush, apply phthalo blue wet-into-wet to the background leaves and most of the foreground leaves. Use Hansa yellow medium in the bright, warm areas of the foreground leaves. Apply a mix of phthalo blue and purple magenta with a No. 6 brush to the shadowed petal areas.

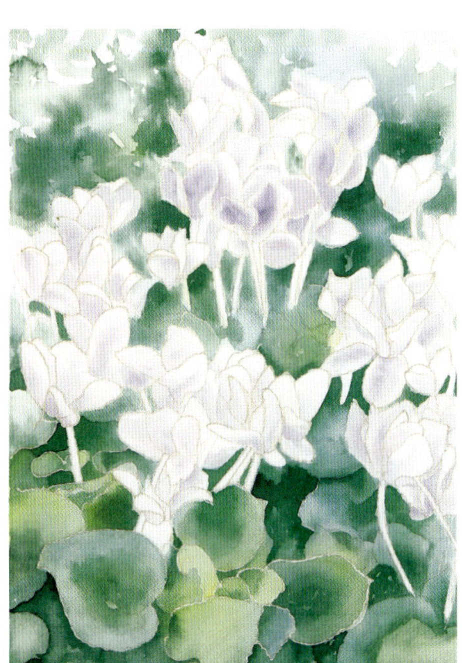

3 Mix Hooker's green and purple magenta and apply wet-into-wet with a No. 8 brush to the shadowed leaf areas. For the darkest shadows, use two or three glazes with a negative painting technique. Soften edges with a damp scrubber, especially where paint builds up along the lines of masking fluid. Blot with tissue.

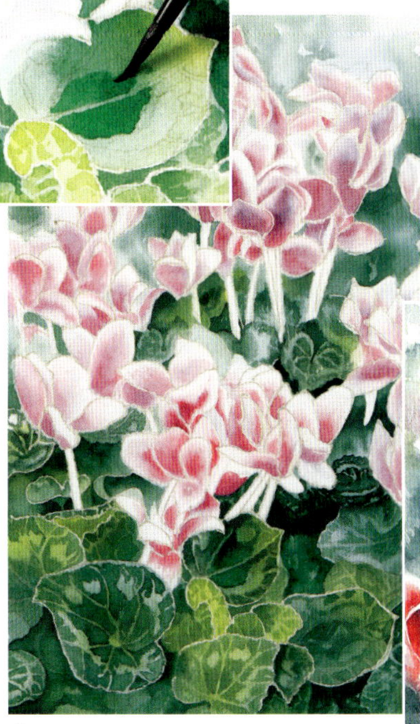

4 With a No. 6 brush and the previous green mix, use negative painting to define the leaf splotches and veins (inset). Working wet-into-wet, use purple magenta alone and with phthalo blue on the petals. Remove the masking and soften the edges with a damp scrubber. Dry-brush quinacridone red with a No. 6 brush on the foreground petals.

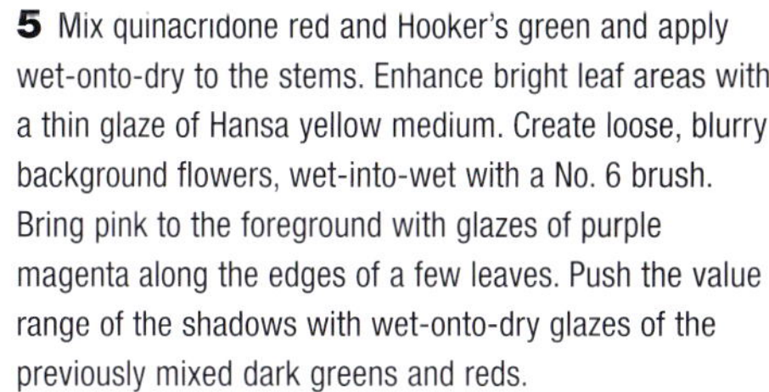

5 Mix quinacridone red and Hooker's green and apply wet-onto-dry to the stems. Enhance bright leaf areas with a thin glaze of Hansa yellow medium. Create loose, blurry background flowers, wet-into-wet with a No. 6 brush. Bring pink to the foreground with glazes of purple magenta along the edges of a few leaves. Push the value range of the shadows with wet-onto-dry glazes of the previously mixed dark greens and reds.

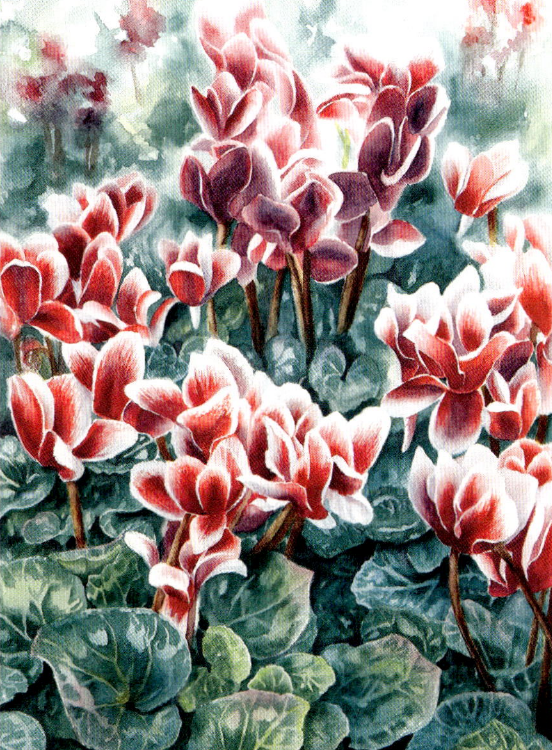

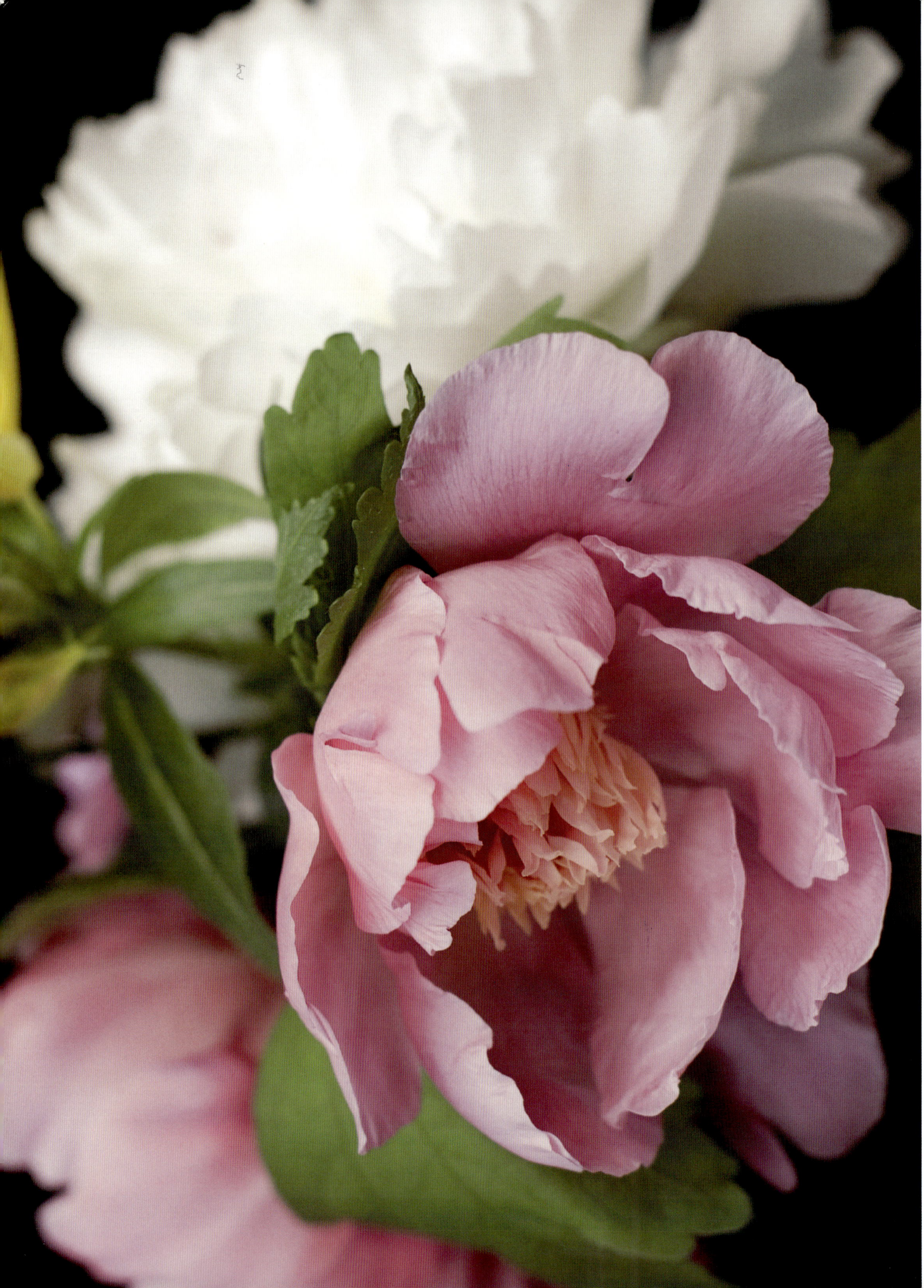

Peonies

The artist made several alterations to the photograph, the most significant of which was to sharpen the focus on the right-hand white peony and lighten the background in that area, giving weight and balance to the composition.

PAINTS
Aureolin
Cobalt blue
Phthalo blue
Quinacridone coral
Quinacridone magenta
Quinacridone pink
Quinacridone red
Quinacridone rose
Quinacridone violet
Winsor yellow deep

TOOLS & MATERIALS
Cold-pressed paper, 140 lb. (300 gsm)
HB pencil
Masking fluid
Old brush
3-in. (7.5-cm) wash brush
Spray bottle
Fritch scrubber
Tissues
Round brushes, Nos. 6, 10, 14
1-in. (2.5-cm) flat brush
Dremel tool

TECHNIQUES USED
Mixing paint in the palette, *p. 21*
Dropping in color, *p. 21*
Wet-into-wet, *p. 22*
Lost and found edges, *p. 24*
Masking to reserve the paper, *p. 25*
Softening masked edges, *p. 25*
Adding highlights, *p. 27*
Shadows, *p. 28*
Pouring paint, *p. 29*
Spritz, *p. 30*

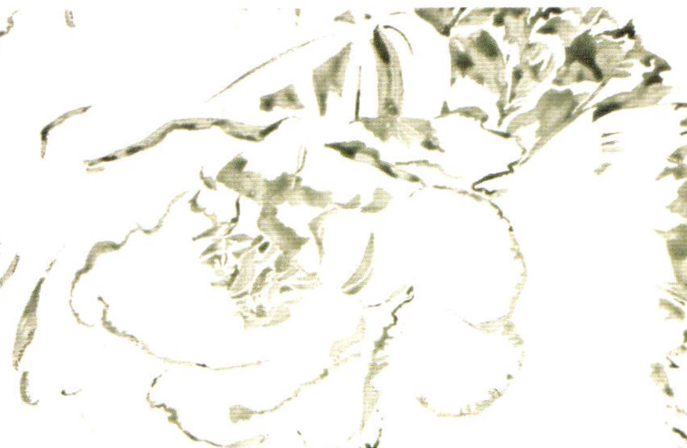

1 Draw the flower with an HB pencil, so that the lines are erasable. Mask all whites, yellows, and spots of light (above). Mix aureolin yellow, quinacridone red, and phthalo blue each to the consistency of cream, ready for pouring. Wet the paper but leave no standing water.

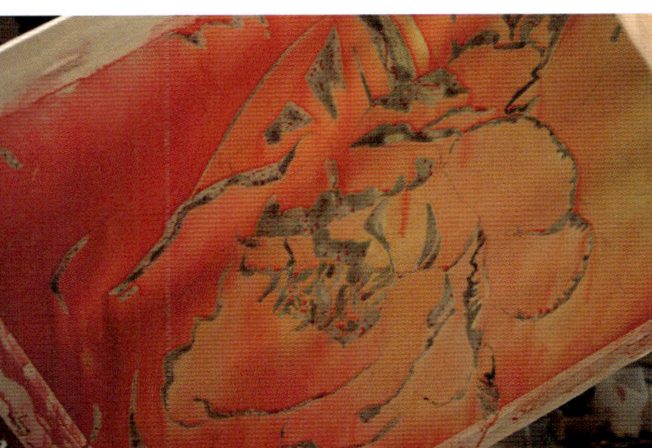

2 Pour the yellow in the center of the flowers. Spread with a 3-in. (7.5-cm) wash brush. Repeat with quinacridone red and phthalo blue. After each pouring, tilt and spritz the painting so the paint runs freely. Keep taped edges wiped to prevent backruns. Dry the painting on a flat surface. If the colors are too weak, repeat this process.

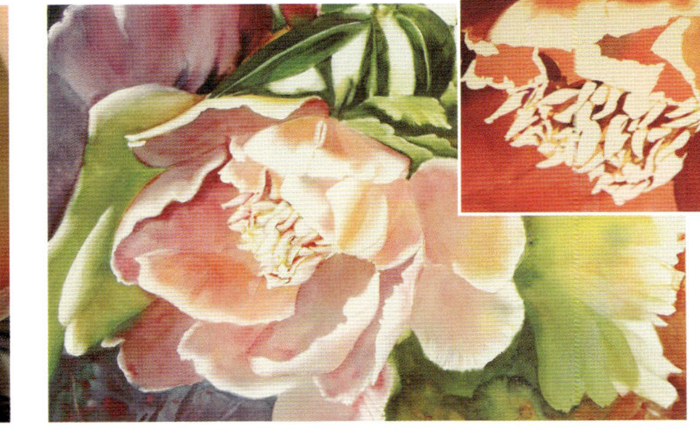

3 Remove the masking and soften all the edges where paint meets white paper with a Fritch scrubber (inset). Use plenty of water and dab with tissue. This is a critical step in pouring color over masking because of the hard lines left when you remove the masking. When softening the lines, use the paint you remove to blend color into the white area, creating a soft transition.

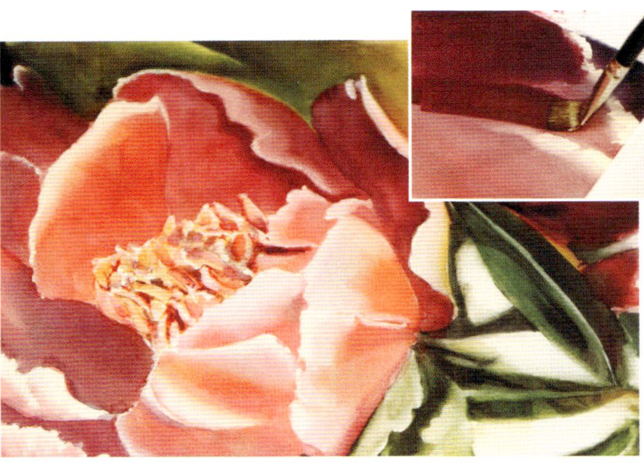

4 Looking at the photograph, place shadows in the deep attachments of the petals to the flower (inset) as well as the background. The color of the shadows should change slightly with the location of the petal. The deepest shadow colors are quinacridone violet mixed with a little phthalo blue. In the brighter areas, eliminate the blue and use only the deeper-colored quinacridone colors. Wet the area close to the white edge, dip your brush in paint, and paint from the center of the flower into the wet. Let it blend then dry.

5 Using a No. 10 or 14 round brush dipped in puddles of cobalt blue, Winsor yellow deep, and quinacridone coral, paint the shadows in the white peony. Begin your stroke at the deepest area and pull the paint outward into the light. Blend with clear water in a damp 1-in. (2.5-cm) flat brush. In the tighter areas use a No. 6 round. Using phthalo blue and quinacridone violet, deepen the darkest areas on the left side of the background.

6 When all the darks have dried, carefully and lightly run a Dremel tool along the edge of the petal, making a clean, white, uneven line. Carefully pick away some highlights along the sunlit edges. Due to the yellow under-wash, the finished painting has a warm, sunlit feeling.

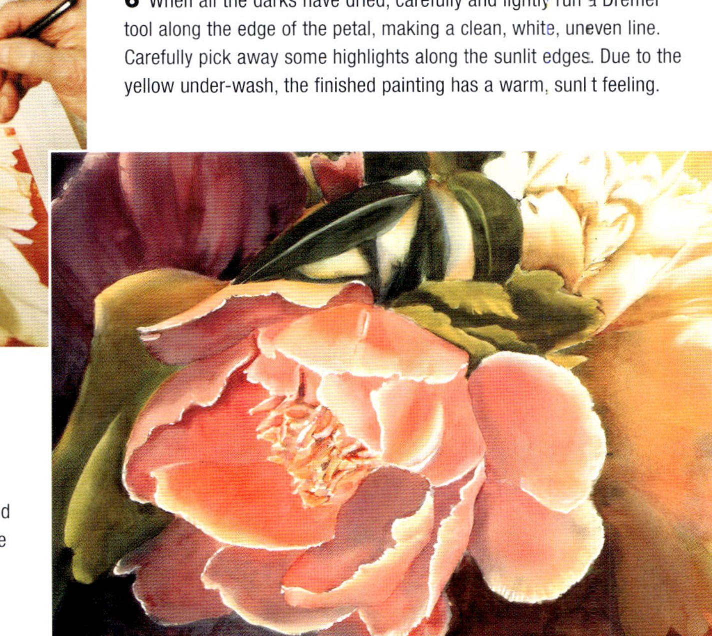

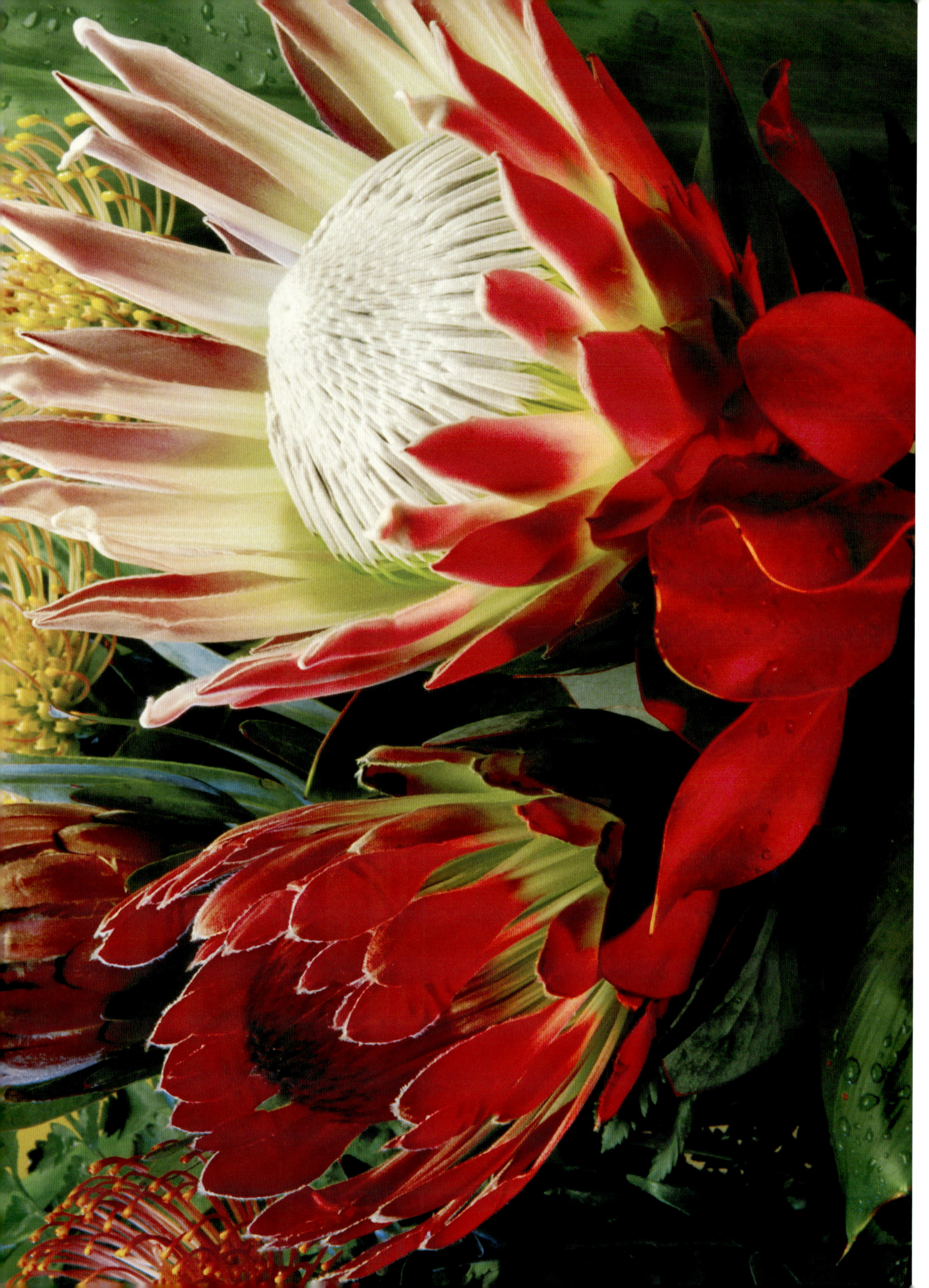

Protea

The artist was concerned with capturing the detail of the numerous petals while keeping their overall shape and form. The background needed to be simplified to prevent a cluttered image.

PAINTS

- Alizarin crimson permanent
- Antwerp blue
- Aureolin
- Cadmium scarlet
- Cobalt blue
- French ultramarine blue
- New gamboge
- Quinacridone gold
- Quinacridone magenta
- Rose madder genuine
- Vermilion

TOOLS & MATERIALS

- Cold-pressed paper, 140 lb. (300 gsm)
- Transfer paper
- Pencil
- 3-in. (7.5-cm) hake brush
- Large soft mop brush
- Round brushes, Nos. 4, 8, 10
- ¼-in. (6-mm) flat brush
- Natural sponge
- Aquacover natural white liquid watercolor paper

TECHNIQUES USED

- Mixing paint in the palette, *p. 21*
- Wet-into-wet, *p. 22*
- Glazing, *p. 23*
- Adding highlights, *p. 27*
- Negative painting, *p. 28*
- Pouring paint, *p. 29*

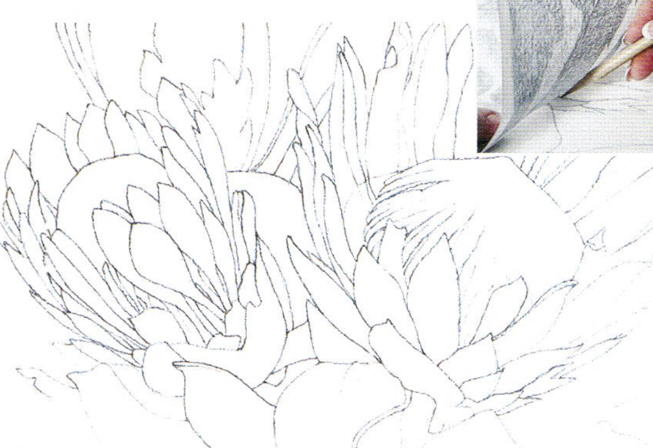

1 On a piece of transfer paper taped over the photograph, draw a grid in pencil. Make a duplicate, proportional grid on a piece of transfer paper taped to the watercolor paper. On each square of the watercolor tracing, draw the detail in the corresponding square of the photograph. Tape the transfer paper to the watercolor paper so that your hand can slide underneath it (inset). With your pencil, follow the lines that you can see through the transparency of the paper.

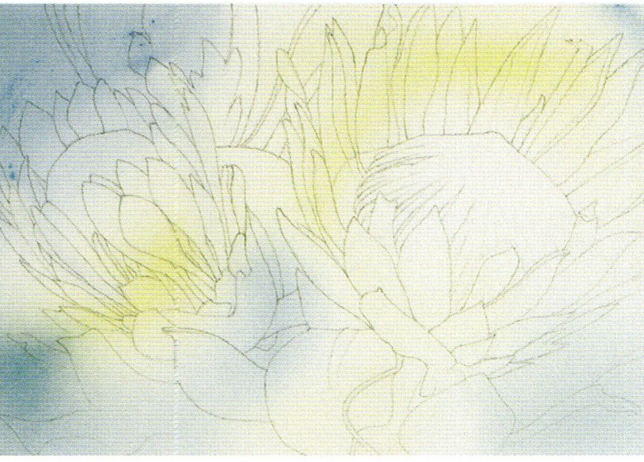

2 Wet the paper thoroughly with a hake brush. With a large mop brush, add new gamboge to the light areas and Antwerp blue to shadow areas, leaving some areas open. Gently roll the paint on the damp paper to diffuse the colors, still leaving open areas that should be white or very light. Dry.

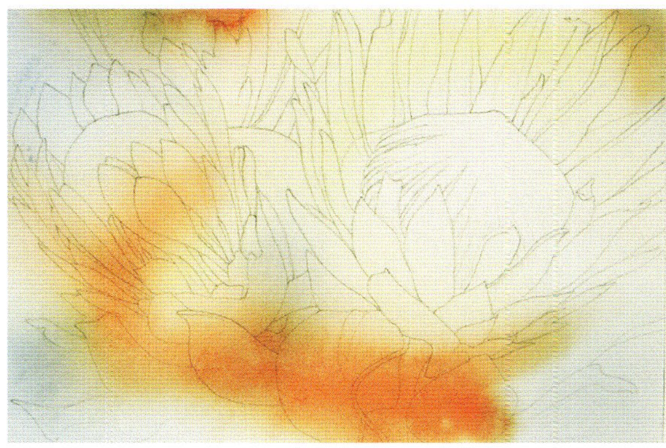

3 Prepare a mixture of opaque and transparent red pigments, such as cadmium scarlet and vermilion. Pour or brush the mixture into areas that will be warm red. Avoid the cool red/white areas but use some of the mixture in parts of the background for balance. Gently tilt the paper to guide the mixture and diffuse the colors. Most of the paper should be left open. Use a damp sea sponge to wipe out any of the color that gets into unwanted places.

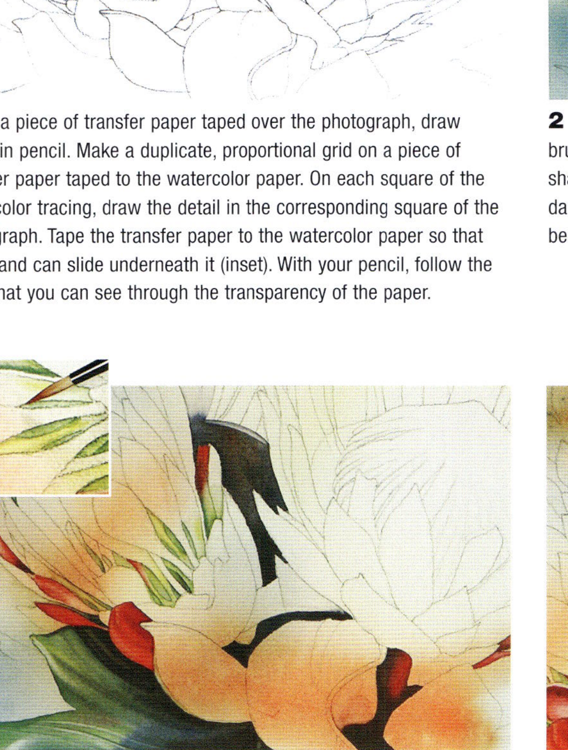

4 Define the image by painting the negative spaces around it (inset). Use some of your darkest values. Use a variety of reds in the petals of the left flower. The underpainting will preserve the warmth. Use rose tones for the flower on the right. Modify the color of both flowers with color of the other for unity.

5 Continue working throughout the image. Complete the background last, keeping it simple and the edges of the shapes diffused. Use a ¼-in. (6-mm) flat brush to lift out the white edges of the petals. If necessary, use Aquacover sparingly in some places if the value of the edges are still too close to the background.

6 The finished painting shows the tropical richness of the protea through the variation of warm and cool reds. The orange underpainting created a path through the painting, unifying the various small shapes of the petals with the background.

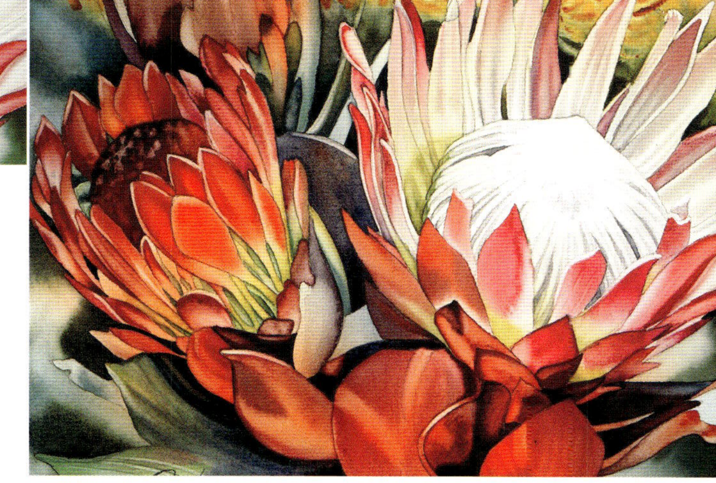

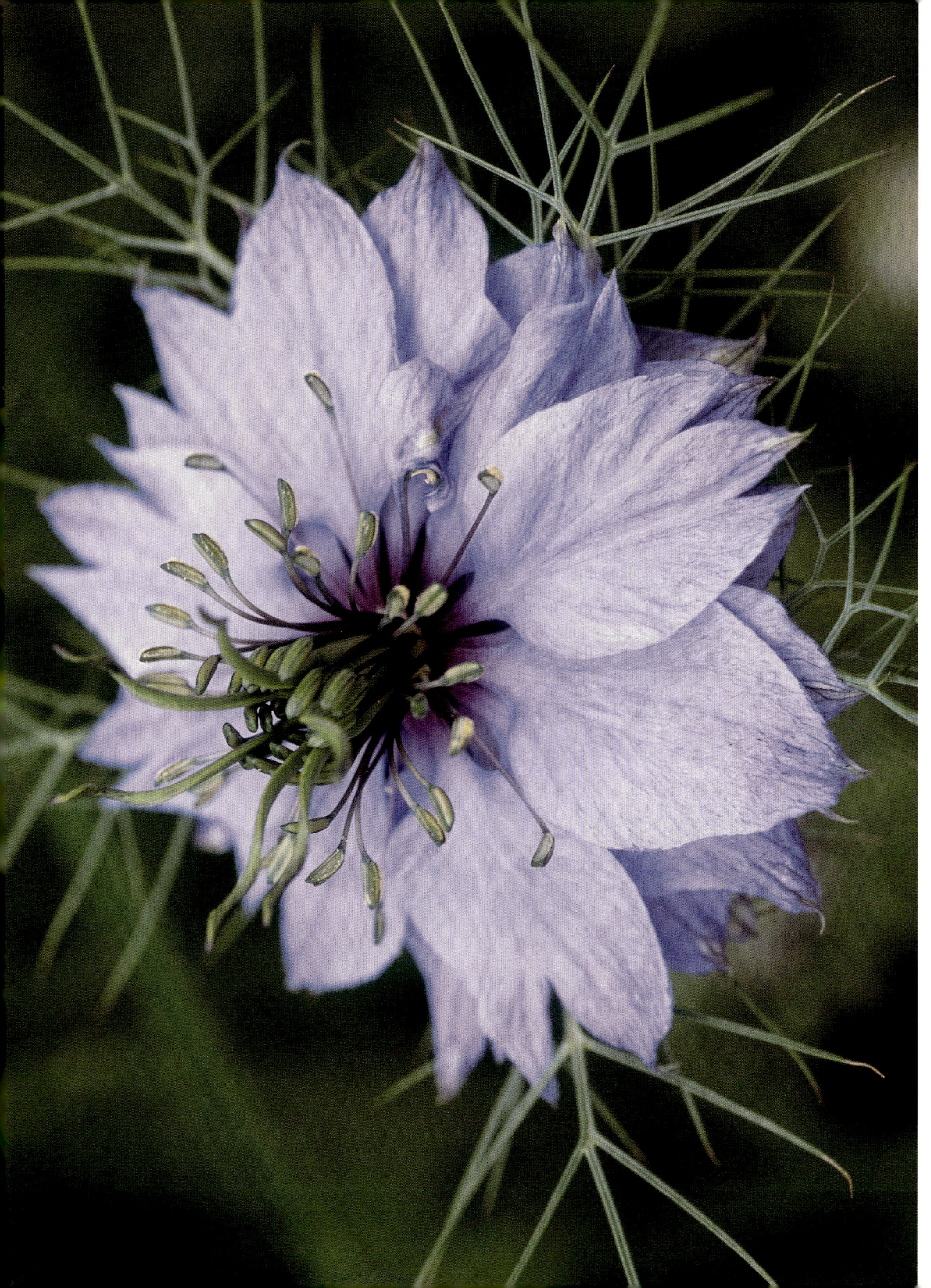

Love in the Mist

The beauty of this flower is heightened by the juxtaposition of the delicate petals and the finely cut leaves (bracts).

PAINTS
Aureolin
Cobalt teal
French ultramarine blue
Green (yellow shade)
Green-gold
Quinacridone burnt orange
Quinacridone magenta
Scheveningen blue light
Sepia
Turquoise blue deep
Winsor green

TOOLS & MATERIALS
Cold-pressed paper, 140 lb. (300 gsm)
Pencil
Masking fluid
Old brush
Round brushes, Nos. 1, 8, 14
Mat knife
Ruby cellophane value screen

TECHNIQUES USED
Variegated wash, *p. 20*
Mixing paint in the palette, *p. 21*
Dropping in color, *p. 21*
Wet-onto-dry, *p. 22*
Wet-into-wet, *p. 22*
Glazing, *p. 23*
Masking for details, *p. 25*
Adding highlights, *p. 27*

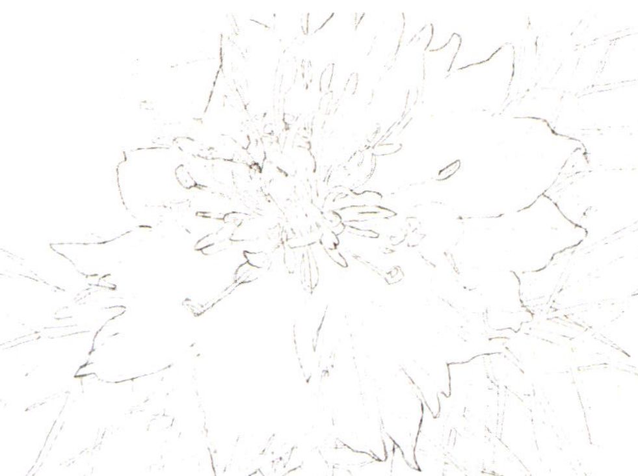

1 Make a detailed drawing of the photograph. The stamens form a very complex cluster—some simplification may be necessary to avoid a cluttered look. However, stay true to the design of the flower. Carefully cover the fine leaves and stamens with masking fluid. Dry the masking fluid completely before starting your washes.

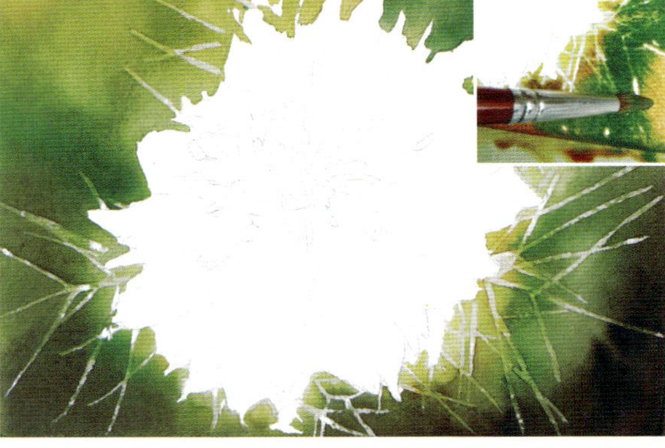

2 Mix puddles of aureolin, quinacridone burnt orange, green (yellow shade), and sepia. Wet the background of the painting surrounding the blossom with clear water. Using a No. 14 round brush, drop in color from the puddles, keeping the lighter areas above the flower (inset). Dry thoroughly. Remove the mask from the fine leaves and paint with lighter value washes of the background colors.

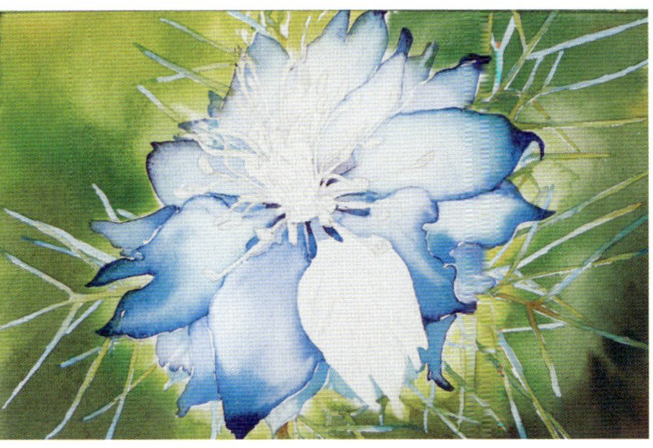

3 With either a No. 14 or No. 8 round brush, paint the petals of the flower from background to foreground using French ultramarine blue, turquoise blue deep, cobalt teal, and Scheveningen blue light. Then with a No.1 brush, paint French ultramarine blue around the outside of the petals to make a crisp edge. Vary the line or make it wet-into-wet to avoid an outlined look.

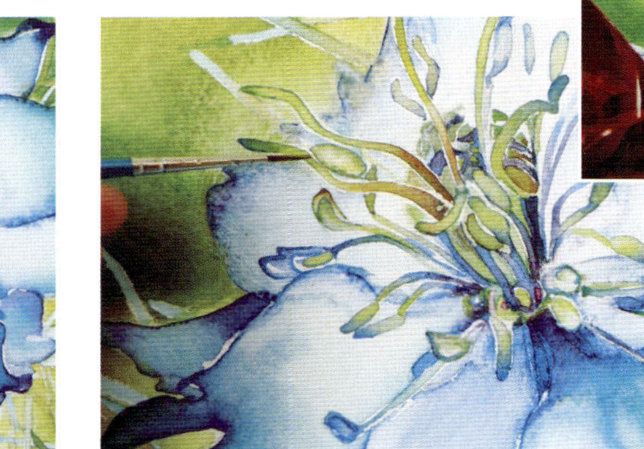

4 Remove the mask from the stamens and paint them with Winsor green, quinacridone magenta, French ultramarine blue, and aureolin. Next, use a small mat knife to scratch out and clarify the whites around the center of the flower—small points of light and the light between the stamens. These crisp whites add more sparkle and life to the flower.

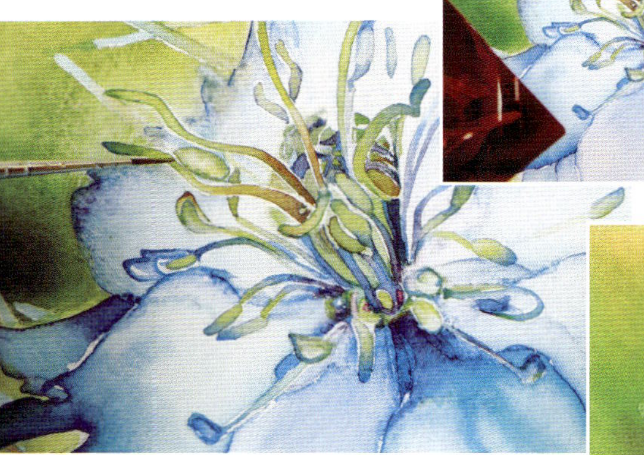

5 Check the values of the painting with a ruby cellophane value screen (inset). This screen shuts out color and allows you to view only the gray-scale value of the work. Compare it with the value of the photograph to check that the darks are dark enough. If not, you can change the value by adding transparent glazes to the area to be darkened. Be sure to dry the area between glazes.

6 You have now called out the most compelling aspects of the photograph for attention: composition and detail. By adding backlight and using only the fringe colors of the petals, the flower is set apart from its background and made to glow, without losing the integrity of the photograph itself.

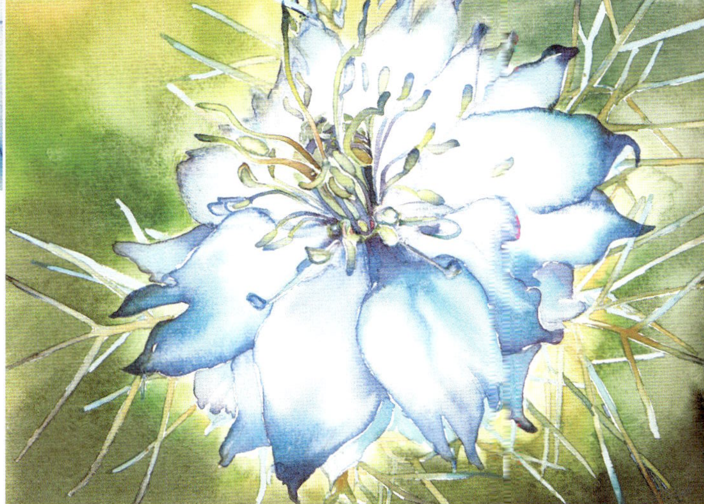

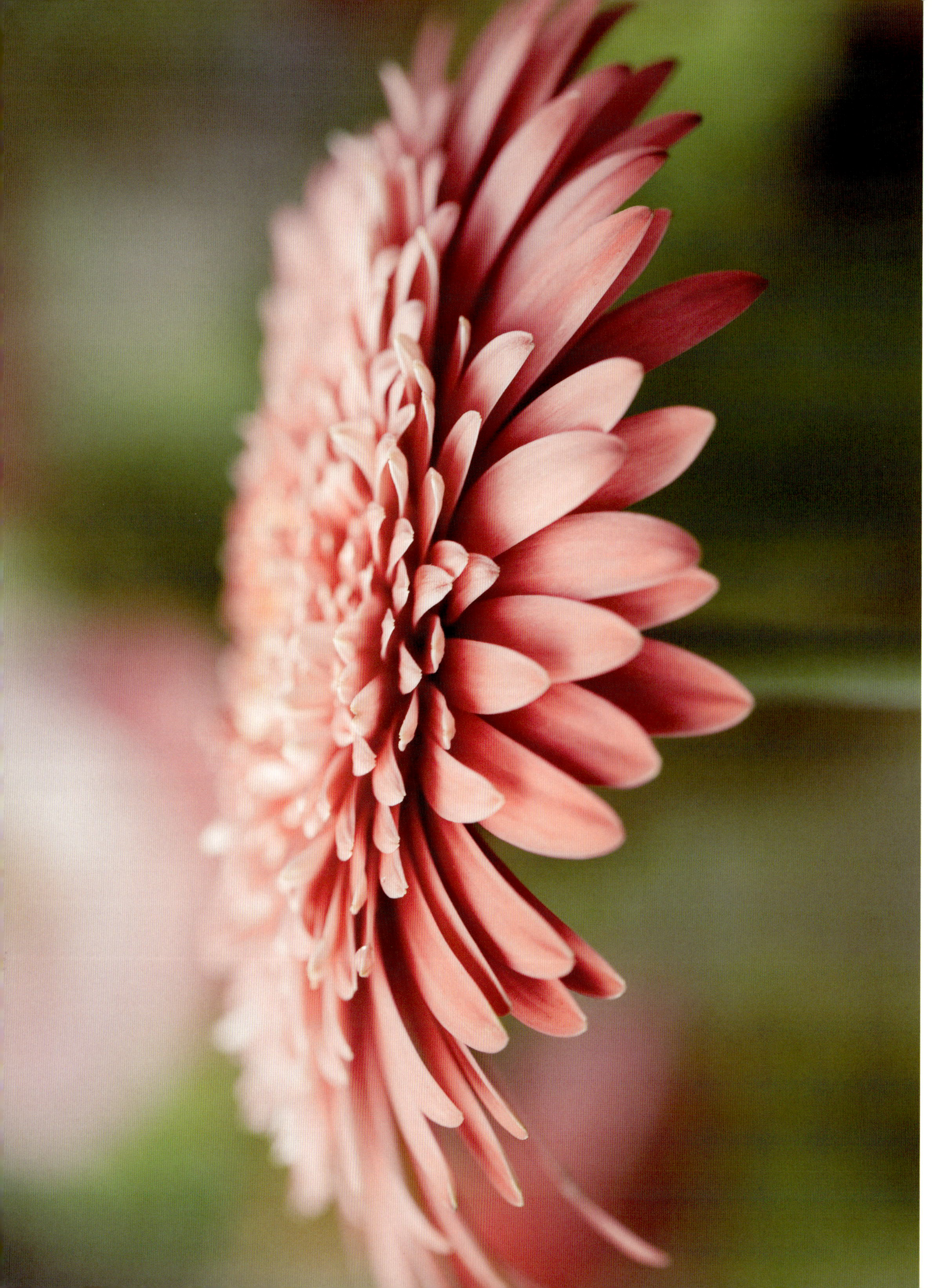

Gerbera Daisy

The petals of this flower are a mix of well-defined and very unstructured shapes that are difficult to replicate and can best be represented by suggestion only.

PAINTS
Brilliant pink
Crimson lake
French ultramarine blue
Quinacridone rose
Sap green

TOOLS & MATERIALS
Cold-pressed paper, 140 lb. (300 gsm)
Mechanical pencil, 5 mm HB lead
Round brushes, Nos. 5 or 6 and 10 or 12

TECHNIQUES USED
Dropping in color, *p. 21*
Mixing paint in the palette, *p. 21*
Wet-into-wet, *p. 22*
Paint light to dark, *p. 23*
Lost and found edges, *p. 24*

1 Make a detailed drawing of the flower to define the light and dark areas. Don't concern yourself with the background since it will be painted last.

2 Wet the upper half of the flower with clear water. Using brilliant pink, slightly thinned, drop the color onto the paper and coax it around with a No. 10 or 12 round brush to approximate the amorphous shapes of the upper petals. As the paper dries, the color will begin to form hard edges. Stop adding the color. If you are not done, you can wait until the paper is totally dry, then rewet it and finish adding the color. Once dry, you may wish to erase the pencil lines in the painted area to lighten them.

3 Still using brilliant pink, paint all the lower petals with strokes emanating at the center of the flower and drawing out toward the tip of each petal. When dry, reduce pencil lines by erasing. With a No. 5 or 6 round brush and using quinacridone rose, begin working into the areas of shadow and use stronger color in the upper petals, gently outlining the shapes. Then, with a brush moderately wet with clear water, draw away the edge of the wet paint to form a soft edge (inset).

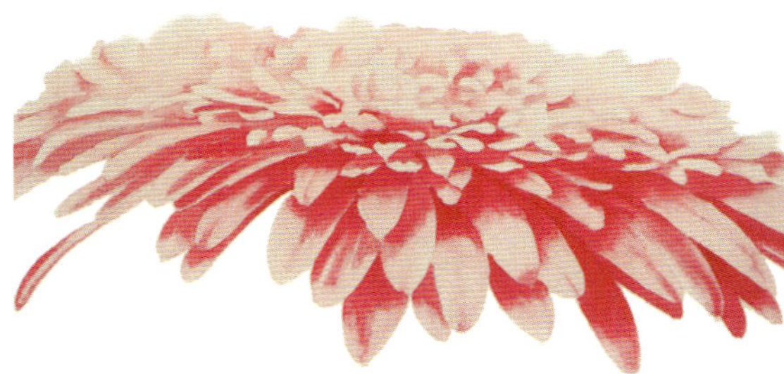

4 With a strong mix of quinacridone rose, begin shading each of the large power petals, starting at the center of the flower and drawing out toward the tip. Where the strong color is to end (based on your drawing), use a clean, moderately wet brush and draw the edge of the quinacridone gently to fade out over the previously painted brilliant pink. Using crimson lake and a small round brush, apply similar techniques to deepen the shadow areas, primarily in the center portion of the flower and the lower petals.

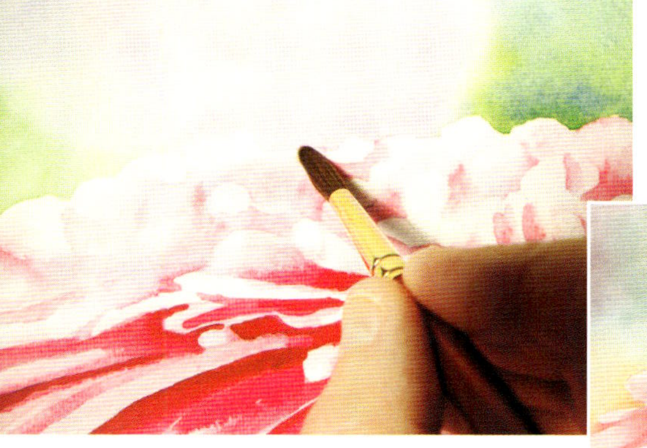

5 The background is a formless, indistinct swirl of colors. In your palette, mix puddles of sap green and French ultramarine blue, and the three "pink" colors. Wet the top half of the background with clear water, being careful to outline the flower petals. Drop the colors in wet-into-wet, allowing them to blend and merge on the paper. Work from the lightest colors to the darkest.

6 The lower background is executed similarly with more emphasis on the darker shades. When dry, paint the stem loosely. The final painting draws the viewer by the subtle flow from the front detail of the flower petals to the swirling background.

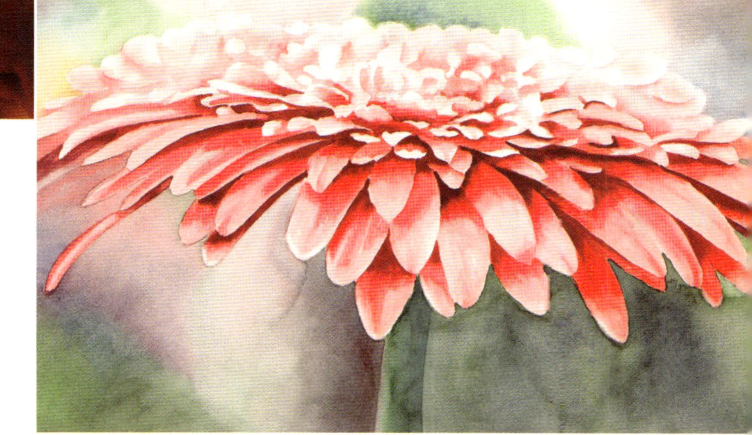

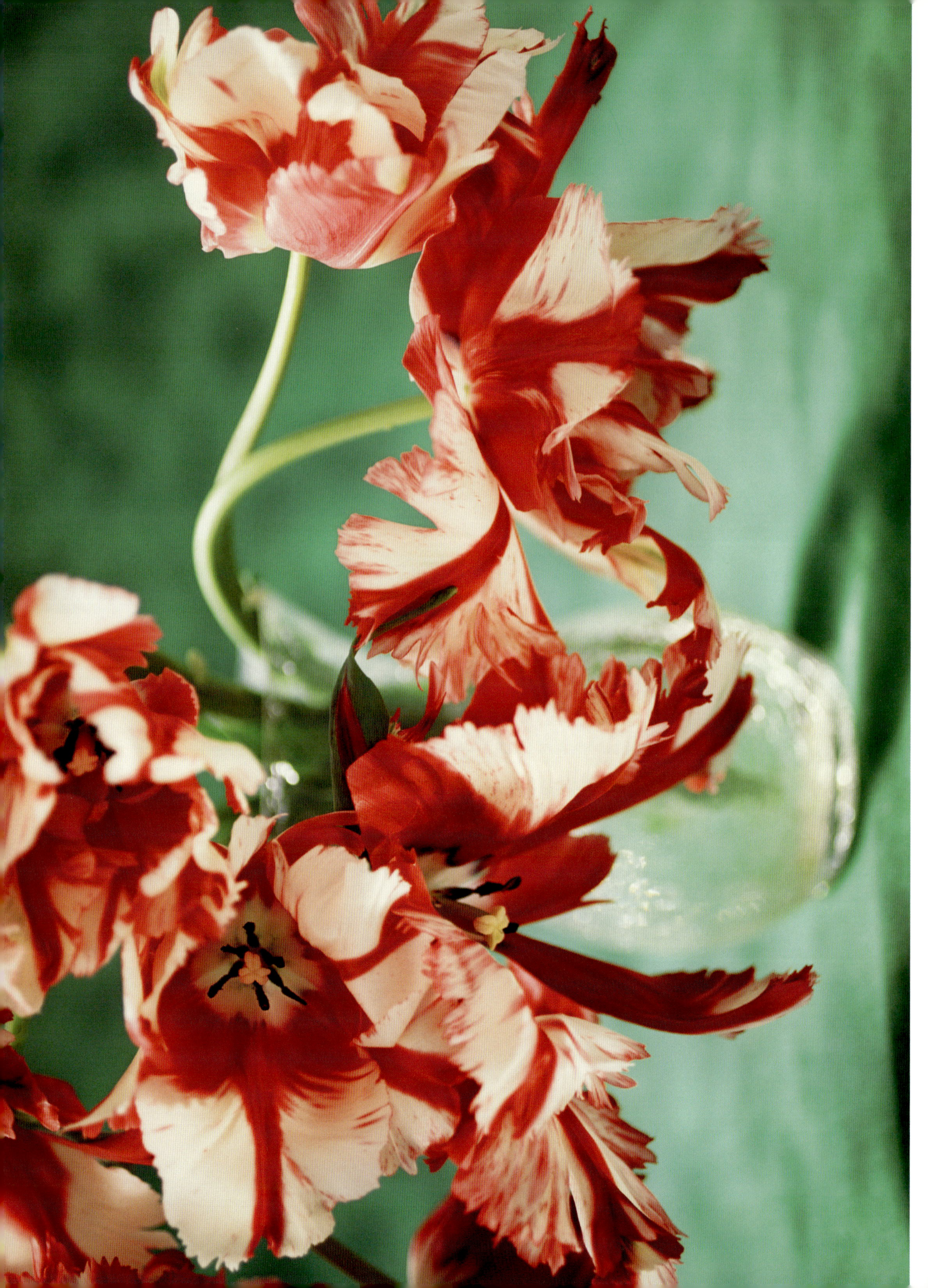

Parrot Tulips

The first glazes, used as an underwash, establish the patterns of dark values in the petals. The rich red hues retain a vivid glow when brushed over the shadows.

PAINTS
Aureolin
Permanent alizarin crimson
Phthalo blue
Phthalo green
Pyrrole orange
Sap green
Scarlet red

TOOLS & MATERIALS
Cold-pressed paper, 140 lb. (300 gsm)
HB pencil
Masking fluid
Old brush
Round brushes, Nos. 4, 6, 8
Scrubber
Tissues

TECHNIQUES
Graded wash, *p. 20*
Variegated wash, *p. 20*
Mixing paint in the palette, *p. 21*
Wet-onto-dry, *p. 22*
Wet-into-wet, *p. 22*
Glazing, *p. 23*
Blending, *p. 24*
Masking to reserve the paper, *p. 25*
Softening masked edges, *p. 25*
Shadows, *p. 28*

1 Draw the design onto the watercolor paper in pencil. Apply a thin line of masking fluid over the pencil lines along the outside edges of all the petals, stems, and the vase. The pencil lines can be erased later when the masking fluid is removed. Let dry before applying any paint.

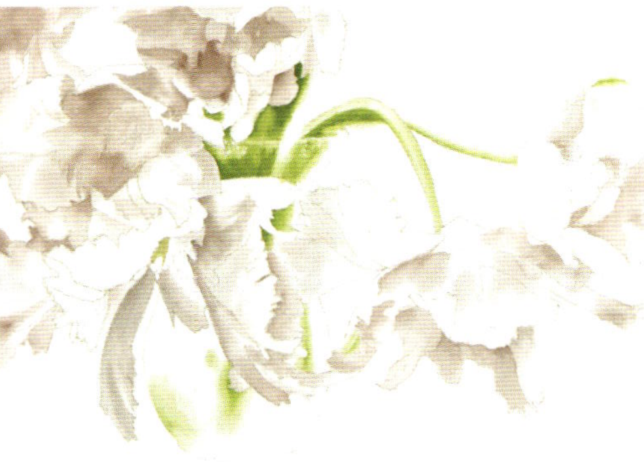

2 Mix phthalo green and scarlet red to make warm grays with a reddish tinge. Using a wet-into-wet technique and a No. 6 brush, apply graded washes of gray in all the shadowed areas of the petals. Let dry between washes. Develop the stems wet-into-wet with sap green.

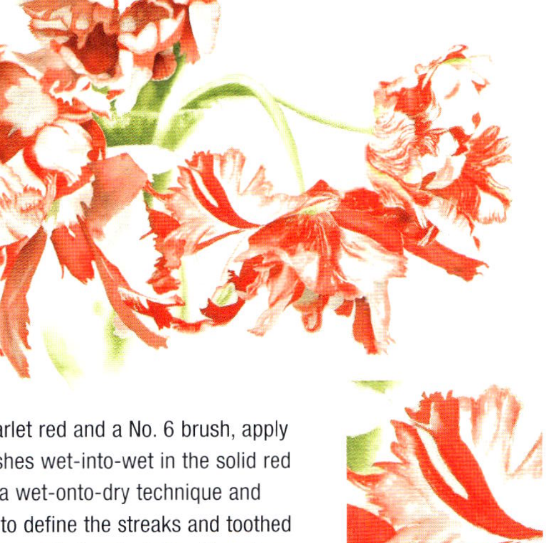

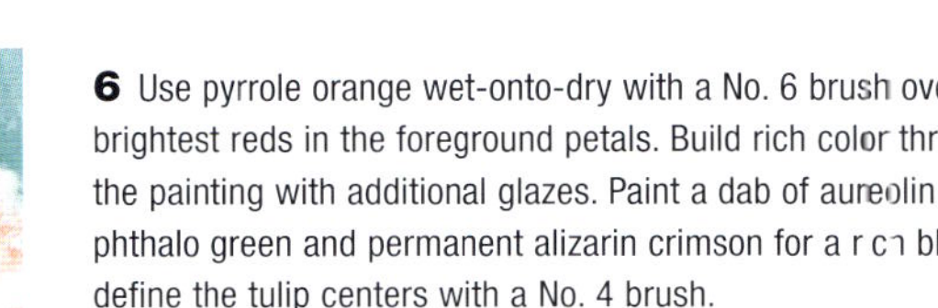

3 With scarlet red and a No. 6 brush, apply graded washes wet-into-wet in the solid red areas. Use a wet-onto-dry technique and scarlet red to define the streaks and toothed edges of the petals (inset). Soften the edges of the dry-brushed paint with a damp brush.

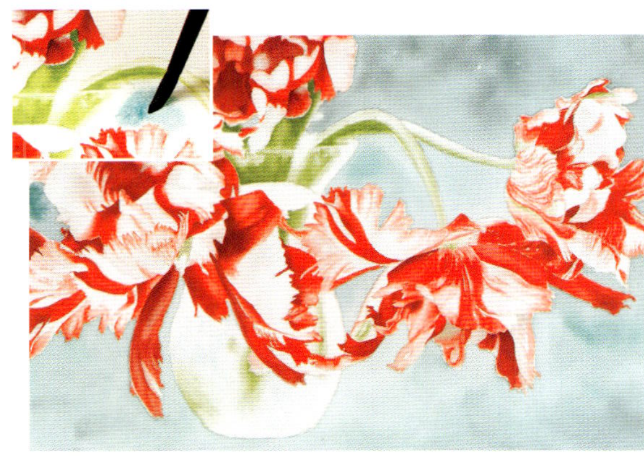

4 Mix phthalo blue and phthalo green and apply wet-into-wet with a No. 8 brush to lay in the first variegated background wash (inset). Strengthen the red in the petals with additional glazes of scarlet red and permanent alizarin crimson.

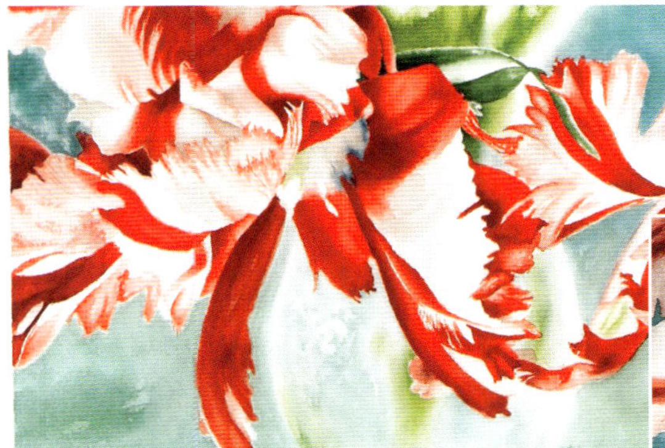

5 Remove the masking fluid. Soften the hard edges with a damp scrubber and blot with tissue. Mix a touch of phthalo blue and phthalo green to permanent alizarin crimson and apply wet-onto-dry with a No. 6 brush for deep reds in the petals.

6 Use pyrrole orange wet-onto-dry with a No. 6 brush over the brightest reds in the foreground petals. Build rich color throughout the painting with additional glazes. Paint a dab of aureolin, then mix phthalo green and permanent alizarin crimson for a rich black, and define the tulip centers with a No. 4 brush.

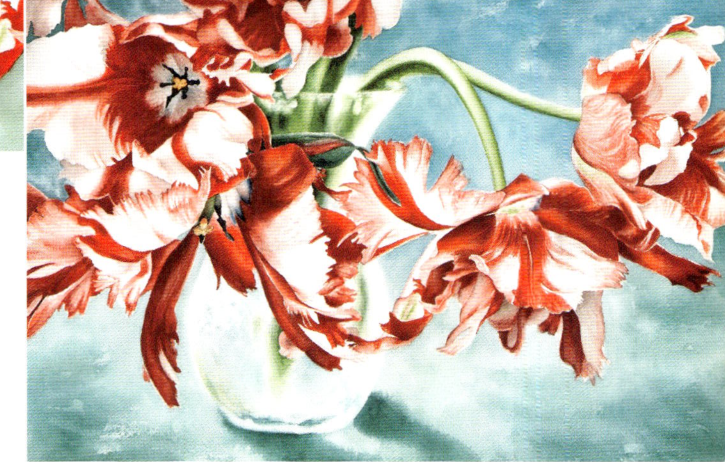

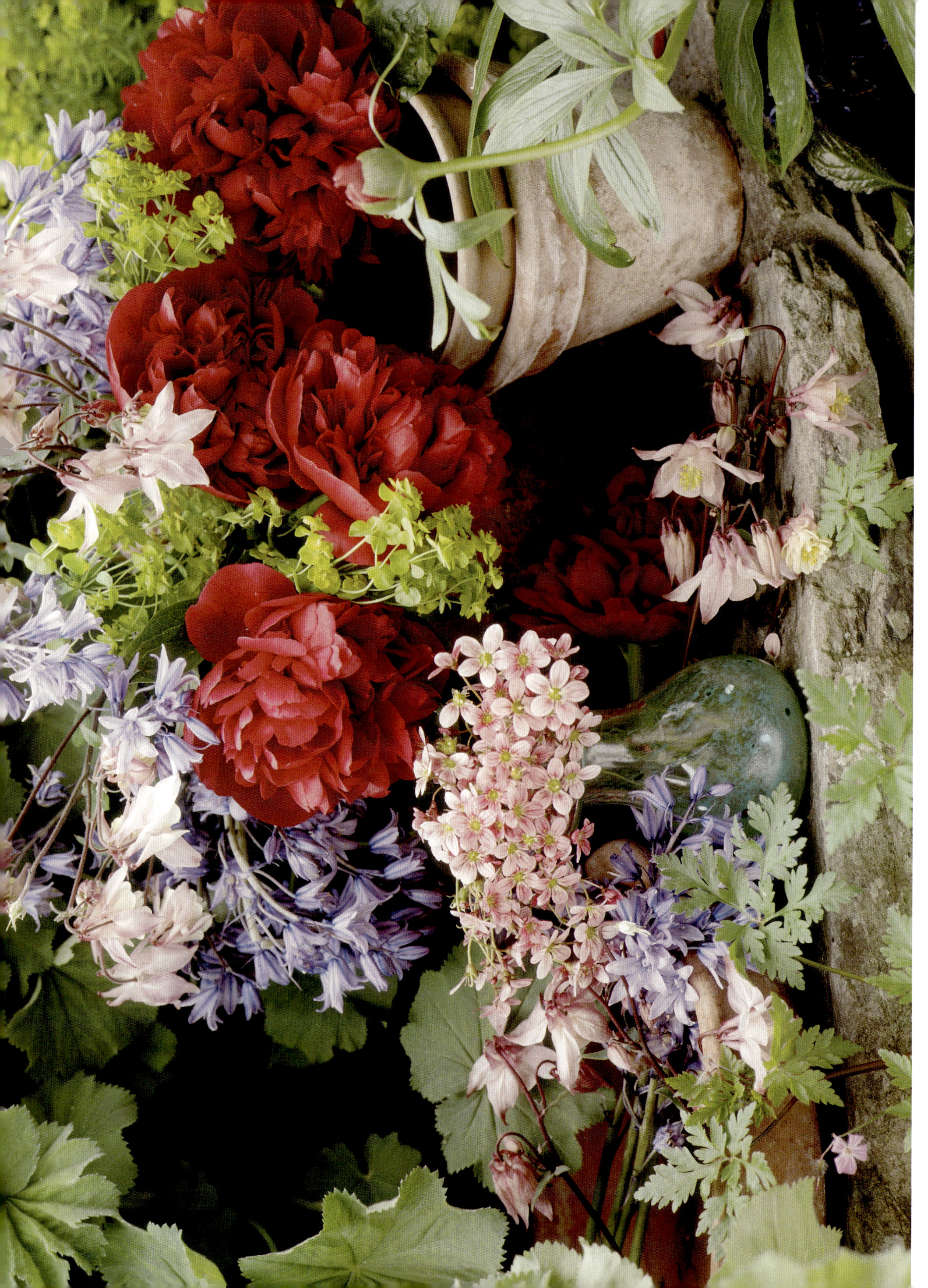

Spring Bouquet

The artist chose to simplify the photograph to fit with a looser, interpretive style. By eliminating some of the detail, more movement is achieved in the painting.

PAINTS
Burnt sienna
Cadmium red light
Cadmium yellow light
Cobalt blue
Cobalt violet
Olive green
Permanent rose
Phthalo green
Ultramarine blue

TOOLS & MATERIALS
Cold-pressed paper, 140 lb. (300 gsm)
HB pencil
1-in. (2.5-cm) flat brush
Mop brushes, Nos. 5 and 8
Round brush, No. 12
Small stiff-bristled brush
Natural sponge

TECHNIQUES USED
Flat wash, *p. 20*
Wet-into-wet, *p. 22*
Paint light to dark, *p. 23*
Lost and found edges, *p. 24*
Adding highlights, *p. 27*
Negative painting, *p. 28*

1 Begin with a very loose line drawing using an HB pencil to get the approximate placement of the major shapes. This sketch should take only a few minutes. It is not a blueprint but a guide.

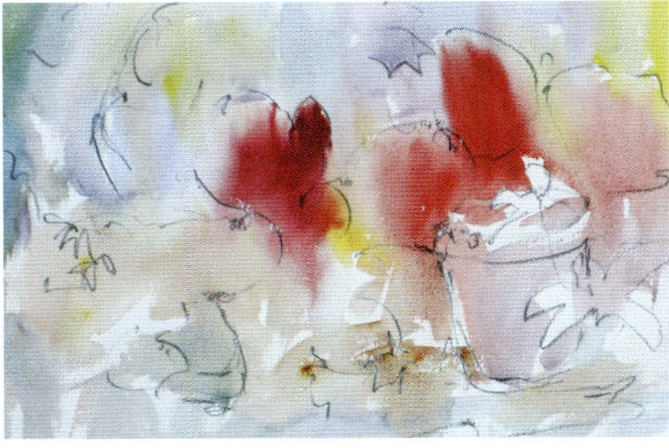

2 Fully charge a 1-in. (2.5-cm) flat brush with water and pigment. Painting wet-into-wet and light to dark, lay down the initial washes using permanent rose, cadmium red, cadmium yellow, cobalt blue, cobalt violet, and olive green to represent the light pattern of the shapes. Even though the washes run together, the color harmonies are established. Also, paint some of the midtones and darker values of the deep red flowers. Be careful not to overmix the colors at any point.

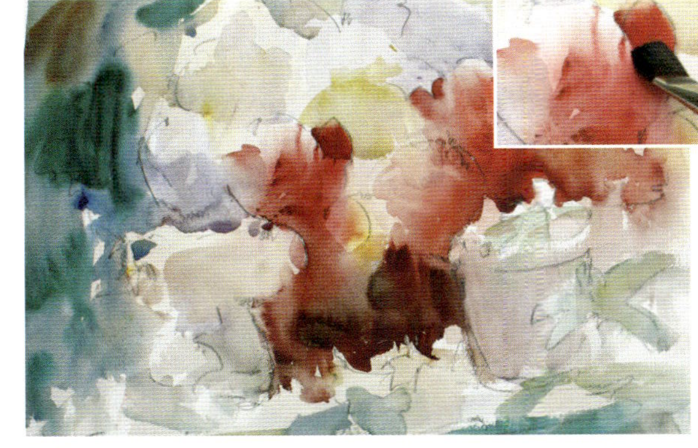

3 Block in the large shadow shapes of the flowers using the No. 8 mop and 1-in. (2.5-cm) flat brush (inset). Begin to introduce some of the darker patterns seen in the lower center. Having a dark pattern introduced early in the painting allows you to judge lights and midtones more easily. Introduce both soft and hard edges at this point. For darker colors, use mixtures of permanent rose, ultramarine blue, phthalo green, and burnt sienna.

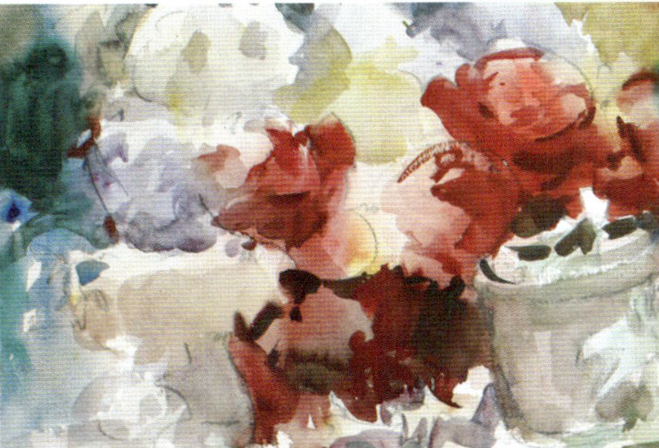

4 Give the flowers definition by positive and negative painting. Begin adding detail within the flowers by breaking down the larger shapes into small ones and using deeper values to bring out the detail and harder edges.

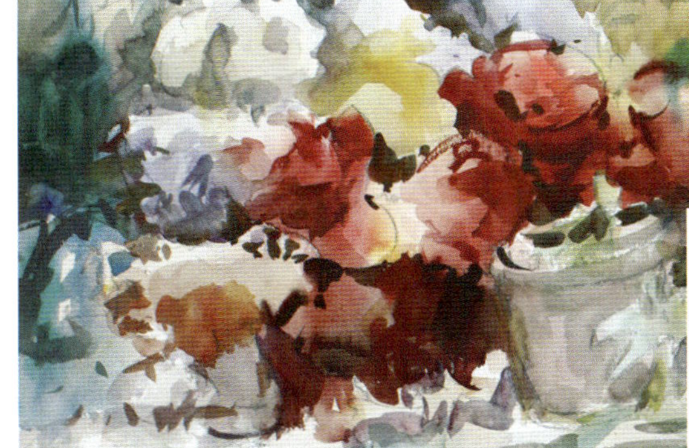

5 Using a No. 5 mop, reinforce the crispest edges in the center of interest near the pot. Gray-out colors that need to be subordinated outside the area of dominance. Continue to break down the negative shapes into smaller pieces. Introduce calligraphic strokes to indicate leaves and stems.

6 Add any final detail to the center of interest with a No. 12 brush. Lift out a few highlights with a stiff-bristled brush and/or sponge.

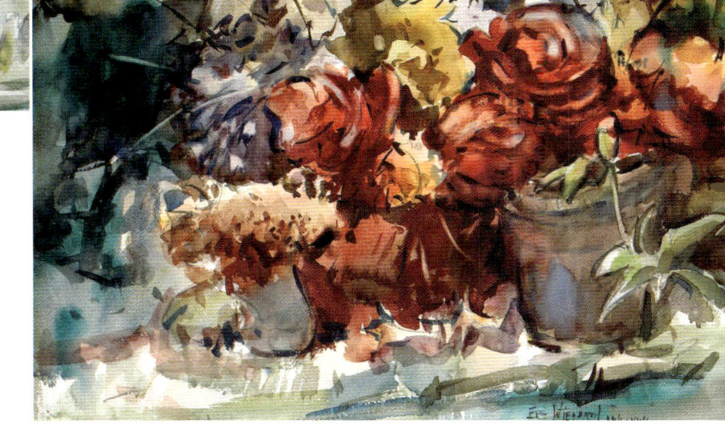

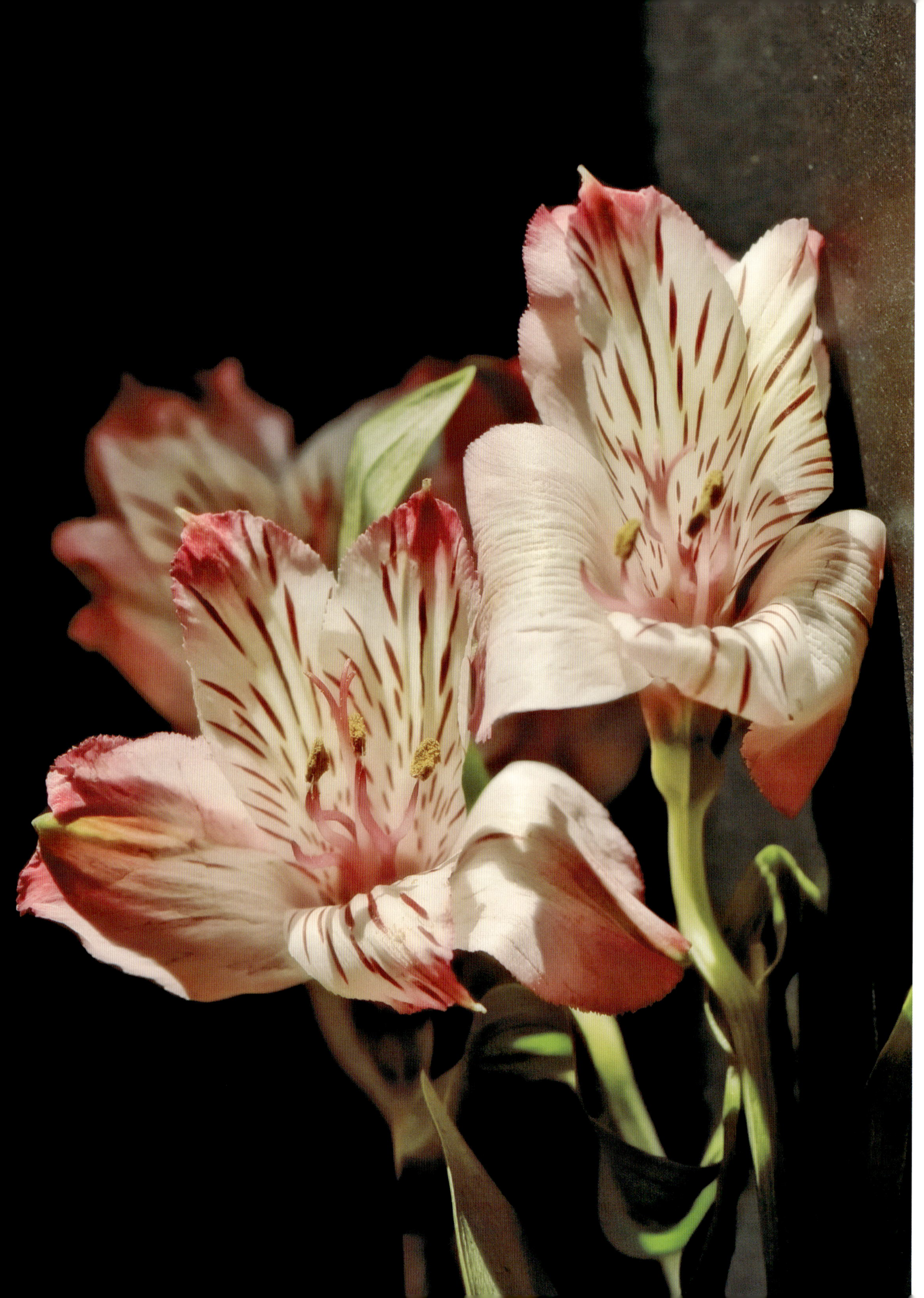

Peruvian Lilies

The artist was compelled to retain the contrast between the actual flowers and the intense dark background. Keeping that sense of drama between the foreground and background meant careful realistic interpretation of the photograph.

PAINTS
Black
Crimson lake
Gamboge
Phthalo green
Quinacridone magenta
Raw umber
Sap green
Ultramarine blue
Venetian brown

TOOLS & MATERIALS
Cold-pressed paper, 140 lb. (300 gsm)
2B pencil
Masking fluid
Incredible Nib
Round brushes, Nos. 1, 4, 8
Old toothbrush
Mat knife

TECHNIQUES USED
Mixing paint in the palette, *p. 21*
Mixing paint on the paper, *p. 21*
Dropping in color, *p. 21*
Wet-onto-dry, *p. 22*
Wet-into-wet, *p. 22*
Glazing, *p. 23*
Softening masked edges, *p. 25*
Blending, *p. 27*
Shadows, *p. 28*

1 Draw the picture with a 2B pencil. Apply masking fluid with an Incredible Nib to any small areas that remain white, such as the edges of the flower or any other highlights. In a palette, mix ultramarine blue, black, and Venetian brown.

2 Apply the mix wet-onto-dry for the dark background, using a No. 8 round brush. After drying, repeat the wet-onto-dry background color to achieve a rich, dark color. Working quickly from side to side or top to bottom will create even color, avoiding puddling. On the paper, mix Venetian brown, dropping in phthalo green and crimson lake for the bright reflection of the flower on the surface of the table.

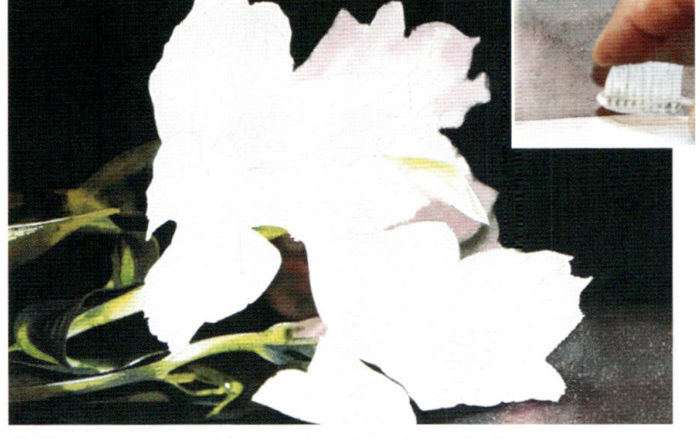

3 Mix sap green and black, and paint the leaves in the darker green area wet-onto-dry, dropping in a mixture of gamboge and sap green to the brighter areas of the leaves and stem wet-into-wet. Soften the edges of the dark background by applying paint with a small brush and pulling the color with a "water only" brush. Add ultramarine blue to the background leaves in the shadowed areas. To achieve the table's texture, protect the white areas and spatter with a tooth brush (inset).

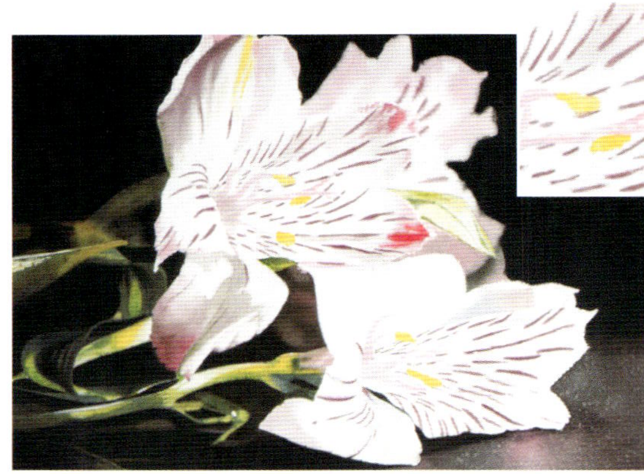

4 Using a No. 1 brush, paint the linear strokes on the inside of the petals using magenta mixed with a little black. Soften edges with a damp No. 4 brush. Keep the brush clean so that the color does not spread. Begin painting gamboge onto the tips of the stamens (inset).

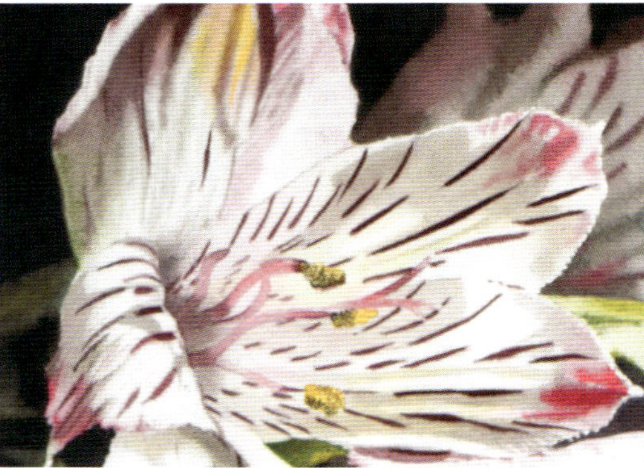

5 Using a No. 1 brush, intensify the magenta on the petal areas as needed and paint the stamens the same color. Glaze a light yellow inside the flowers with a No. 4 brush and, once dry, follow with an ultramarine shadow color. While this is still wet, touch in various reds and gamboge for reflected color.

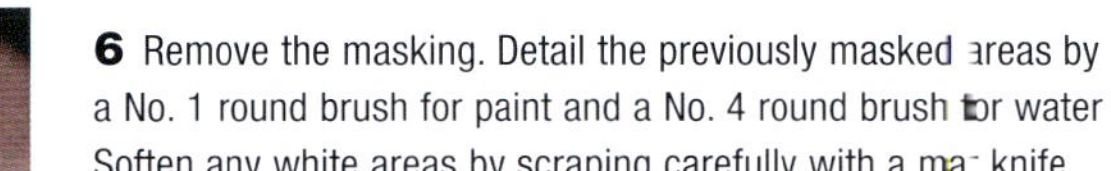

6 Remove the masking. Detail the previously masked areas by using a No. 1 round brush for paint and a No. 4 round brush for water only. Soften any white areas by scraping carefully with a mat knife.

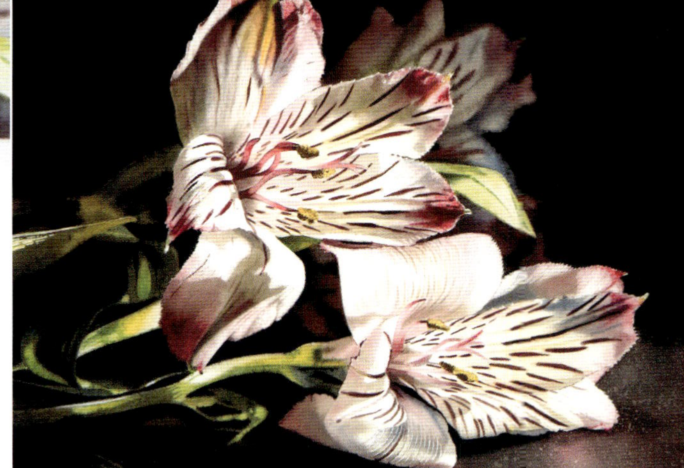

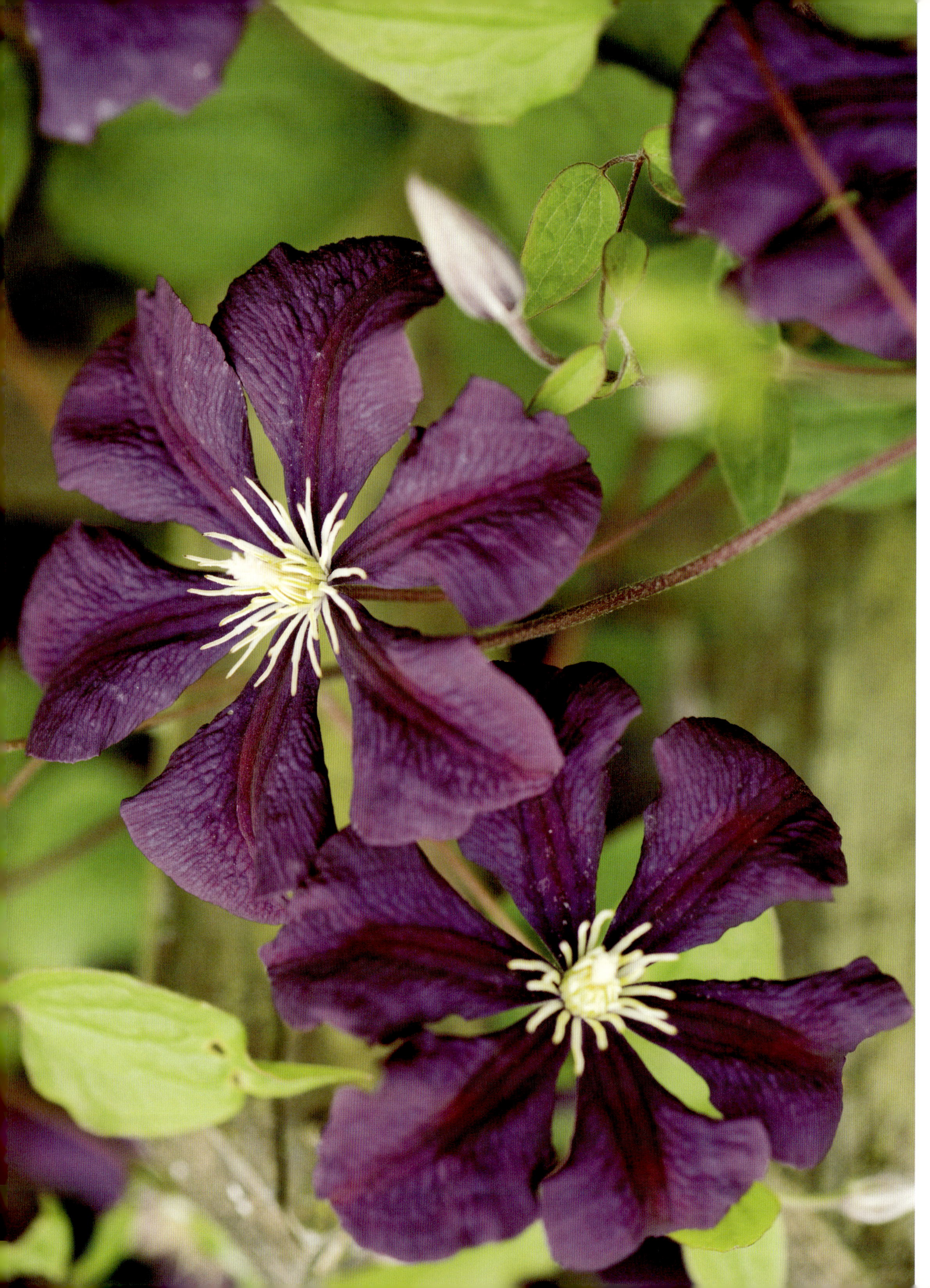

Clematis

The artist liked the soft and sharp areas of focus in the painting. They allowed for working wet-into-wet and blending techniques for the soft-focus areas, contrasting with the hard-edged linear details.

PAINTS
Cadmium yellow
Cobalt blue
Dioxazine violet
French ultramarine blue
Indian red
Quinacridone violet
Raw sienna
Ultramarine violet

TOOLS & MATERIALS
Cold-pressed paper, 140 lb. (300 gsm)
HB pencil
Masking fluid
Old brush
Round brushes, Nos. 5 and 12
Flat brush, No. 10
Rigger

TECHNIQUES USED
Flat wash, *p. 20*
Mixing paint in the palette, *p. 21*
Dropping in color, *p. 21*
Wet-onto-dry, *p. 22*
Wet-into-wet, *p. 22*
Glazing, *p. 23*
Lost and found edges, *p. 24*
Masking to reserve the paper, *p. 25*
Softening masked edges, *p. 25*
Shadows, *p. 28*
Negative painting, *p. 28*

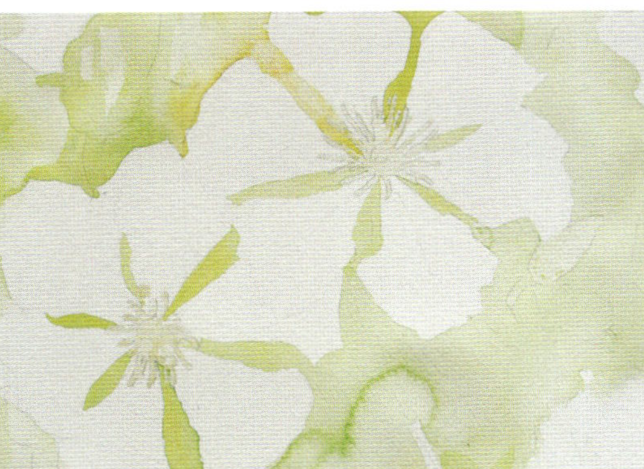

1 Using an HB pencil on watercolor paper, lightly draw in the basic shapes of the flowers and stamens, then mask the stamen shapes with masking fluid and an old brush. Let dry. In the palette, mix cadmium yellow and cobalt blue to make a green. Wet the background foliage area with clean water. With a No. 12 brush, drop the green mixture into the wet areas. Add a touch of raw sienna for variety.

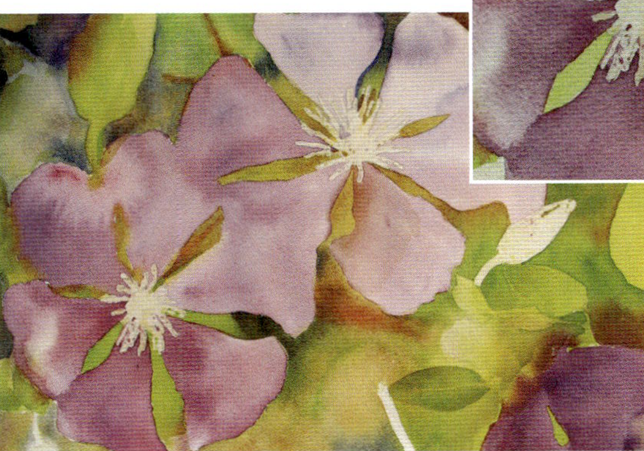

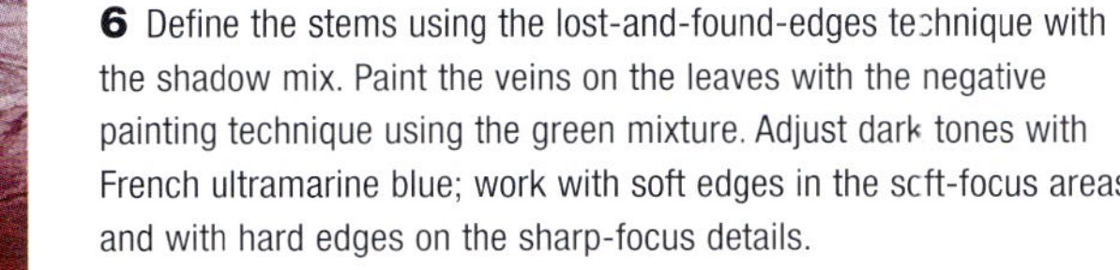

2 Next, still with the No. 12 brush, paint the petals using pale violet washes (inset). Let some areas bleed into the background where the focus is soft. Paint the soft-focus plant stems in Indian red into a just-damp background. Prepare two mixes in the palette using the two violets: Mix more of the quinacridone violet to make a warmer mix and more of the dioxazine violet for a cooler mix. Using a No. 5 brush, wet the petals with clean water.

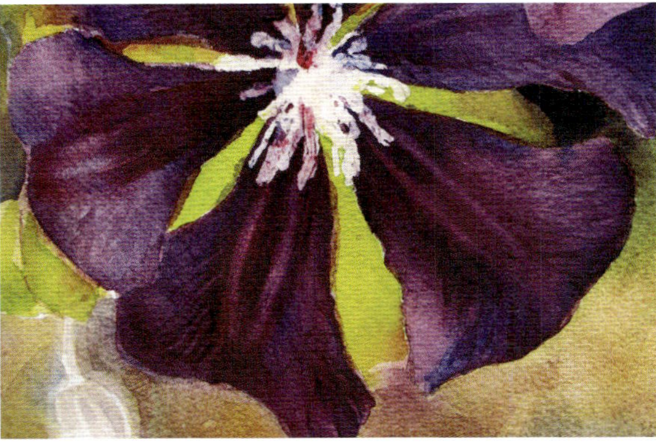

3 Working on the clematis on the left, drop in the warmer mix to the central area and the cooler mix on the outer petal sides; let dry. Using ultramarine violet, loosely paint in the veins of this flower. It is soft-focus so this can be done on damp paper. Using a No. 10 flat brush, rub out the two ridges in the center of each petal. Make a shadow mix of French ultramarine blue and raw sienna to paint the closed buds with successive pale, fading glazes to define form.

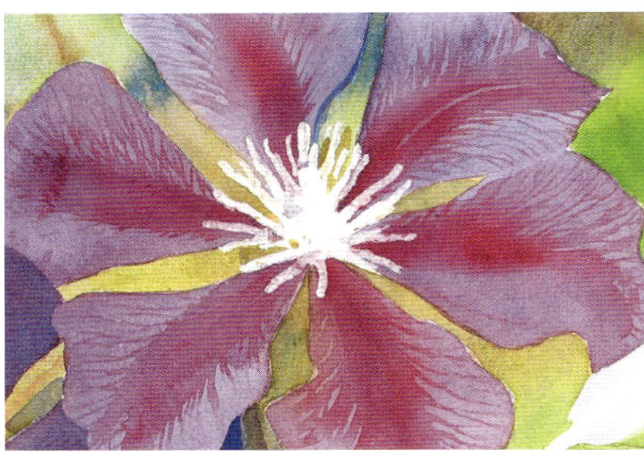

4 For the clematis on the right, using the warm violet mix with the No. 5 brush, paint the central area wet-onto-dry. Then, using a rigger, pull the veins out from the central areas. Drop some clear water onto the edge of some petals and let the vein color bleed into it.

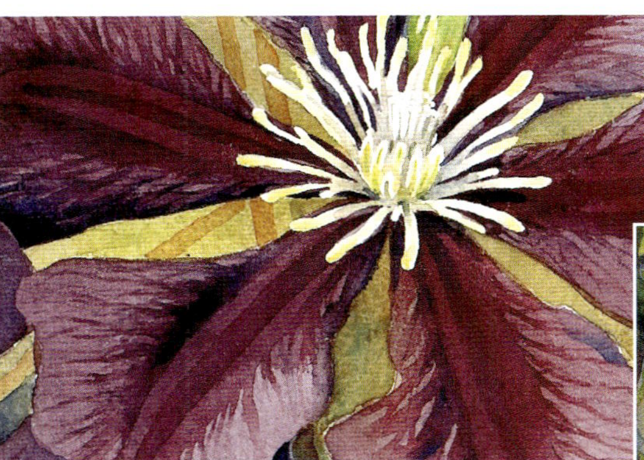

5 For extra detail, use the rigger and paint a criss-cross of clear water following the directions of the veins. Then drop ultramarine violet into the wet strands. Define the shadows and the central ridge areas on both flowers with soft blends of French ultramarine blue. Remove the masking from the stamens and paint with a pale wash of cadmium yellow and the shadow mix from step 3.

6 Define the stems using the lost-and-found-edges technique with the shadow mix. Paint the veins on the leaves with the negative painting technique using the green mixture. Adjust dark tones with French ultramarine blue; work with soft edges in the soft-focus areas, and with hard edges on the sharp-focus details.

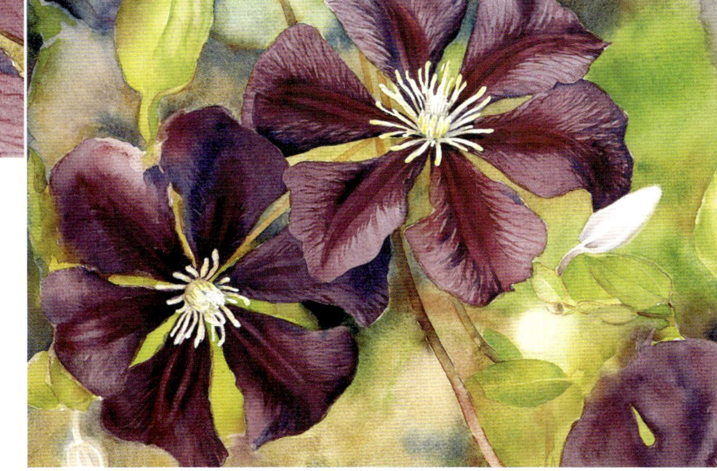

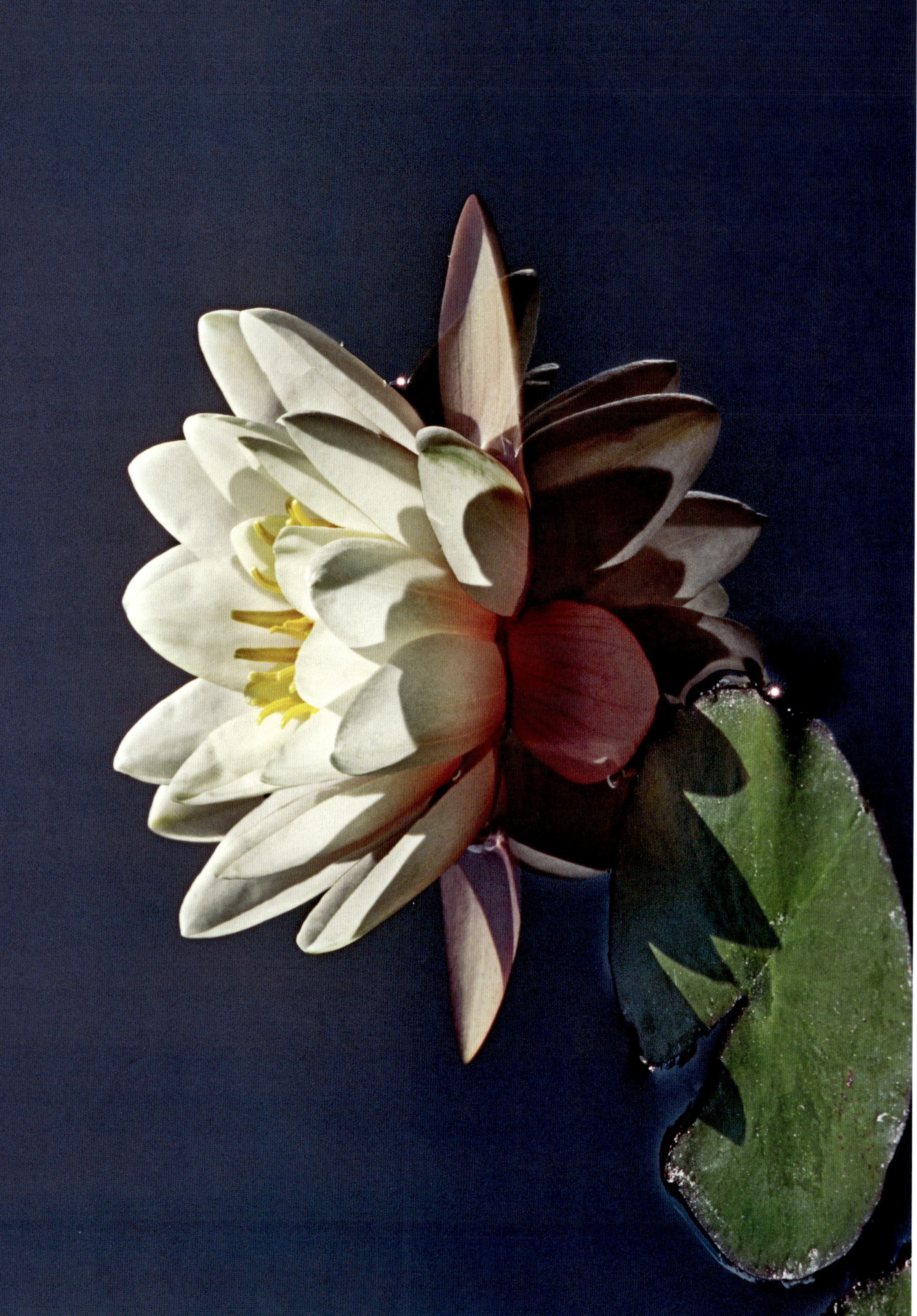

Water Lily

The water here should be depicted strongly to make the image of the flower stand out, but requires that it be painted in one fluid effort to achieve a relatively even appearance.

PAINTS
Alizarin crimson
Indigo
New gamboge

TOOLS & MATERIALS
Cold-pressed paper, 140 lb. (300 gsm)
Masking fluid
Old brush
Round brushes, Nos. 5 or 8 and 10 or 12

TECHNIQUES USED
Flat wash, *p. 20*
Variegated wash, *p. 20*
Mixing paint in the palette, *p. 21*
Dropping in color, *p. 21*
Wet-into-wet, p. *22*
Masking to reserve the paper, *p. 25*
Shadows, *p. 28*

1 Make a detailed drawing of the lily, pads, and reflection (above), and apply masking fluid to the inside edge of the drawing where the image meets the water. Don't forget to mask the reflection. In a palette, mix a large puddle of rich indigo blue. Into the indigo, gradually add alizarin crimson to develop the warm hue of the water.

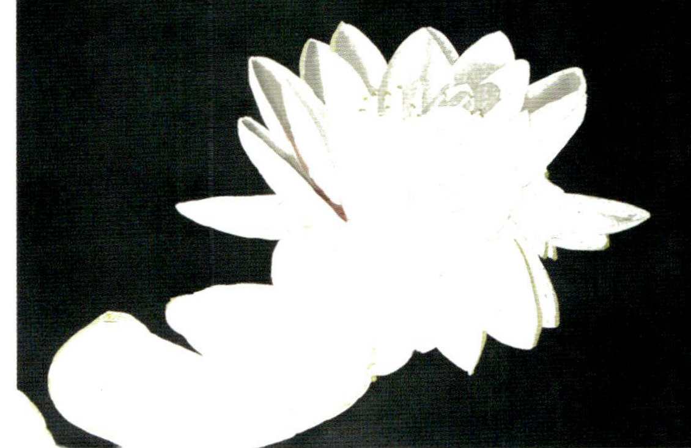

2 Lie the piece flat and, using a No. 10 or No. 12 round brush, apply the color quickly as a flood to the entire water surface in one attempt, keeping it uniformly wet and even. Because these two pigments are sedimentary, they w ll not lend themselves well to a wash. Dry completely. Remove the masking fluid and reapply to those small areas of highlight and sparkle that you wish to preserve.

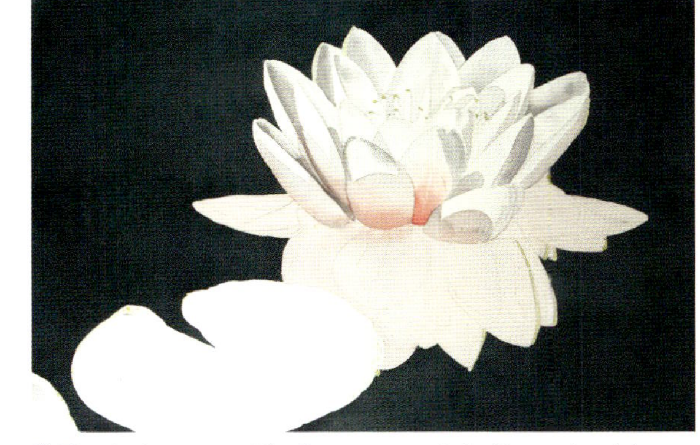

3 The shadow areas of the flower are created with a watered-down version of the same indigo/alizarin mix as the water, adding more indigo or alizarin, as you prefer. While the shadows are still wet, you can drop more indigo or alizarin into the wet and allow it to flow and bleed to add interest to the shadows. Using the same mixture with added alizarin, paint a wash over the reflection of the flower.

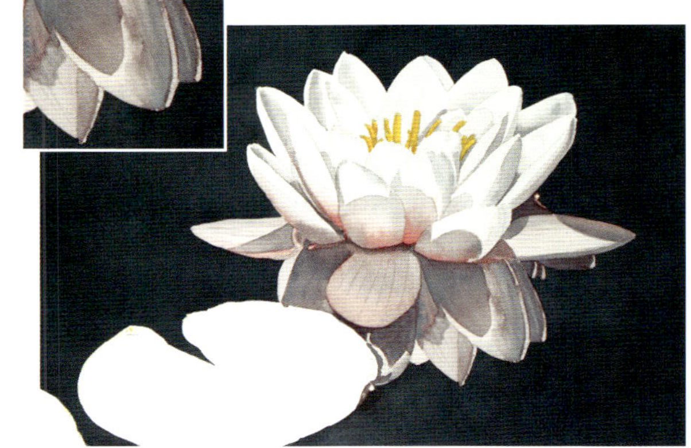

4 Still using indigo and alizarin in varying proportions, paint the shadows in the reflection (inset). Be mindful of the intensity and tone, a reflected image tends to be cooler and darker than the object reflected. Mix a small amount of new gamboge and, using the same brush, paint the pistils. Using the indigo/alizarin mixture, define the pistils by adding shadows. When dry, remove all the remaining masking fluid from the flower and reflection.

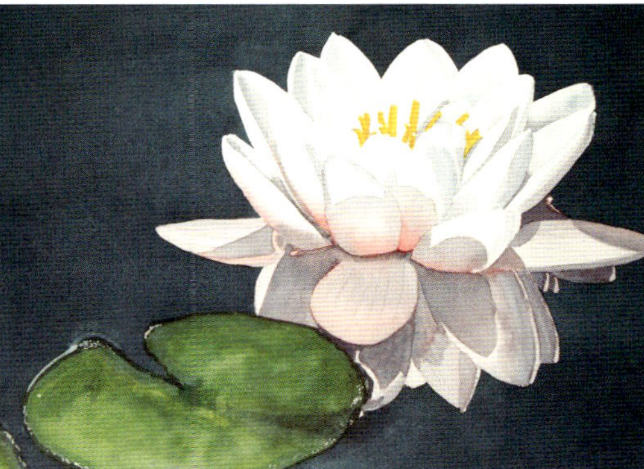

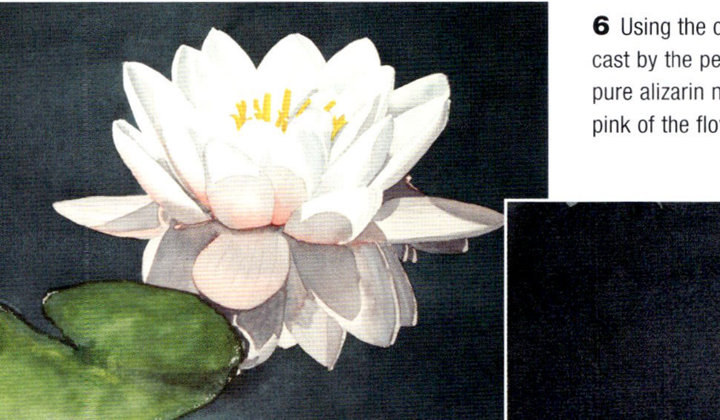

5 Mix a good quant ty of new gamboge and indigo to create a rich green for the l ly pads. Keeping the work flat, paint the pad surface quickly, leaving it evenly wet. Drop in extra indigo or new gamboge to add texture and variation. Remove the remaining masked highlights.

6 Using the original indigo/alizarin mix, add the shadows on the pads cast by the petals of the lily. When the shadows are still wet, drop in pure alizarin near the flower to warm the shadows with the reflected pink of the flower.

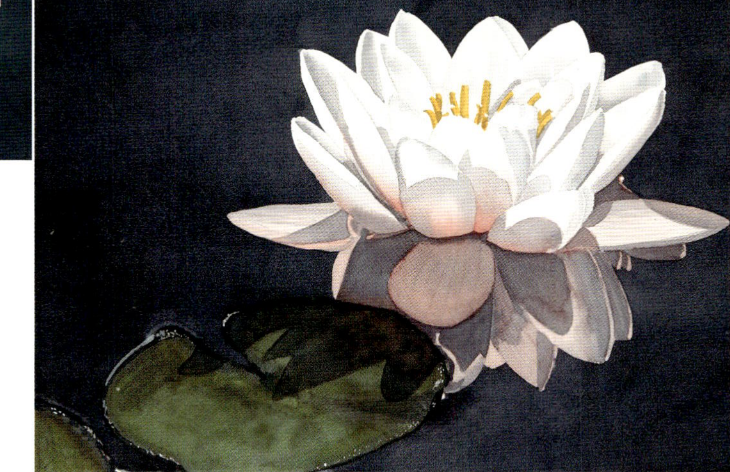

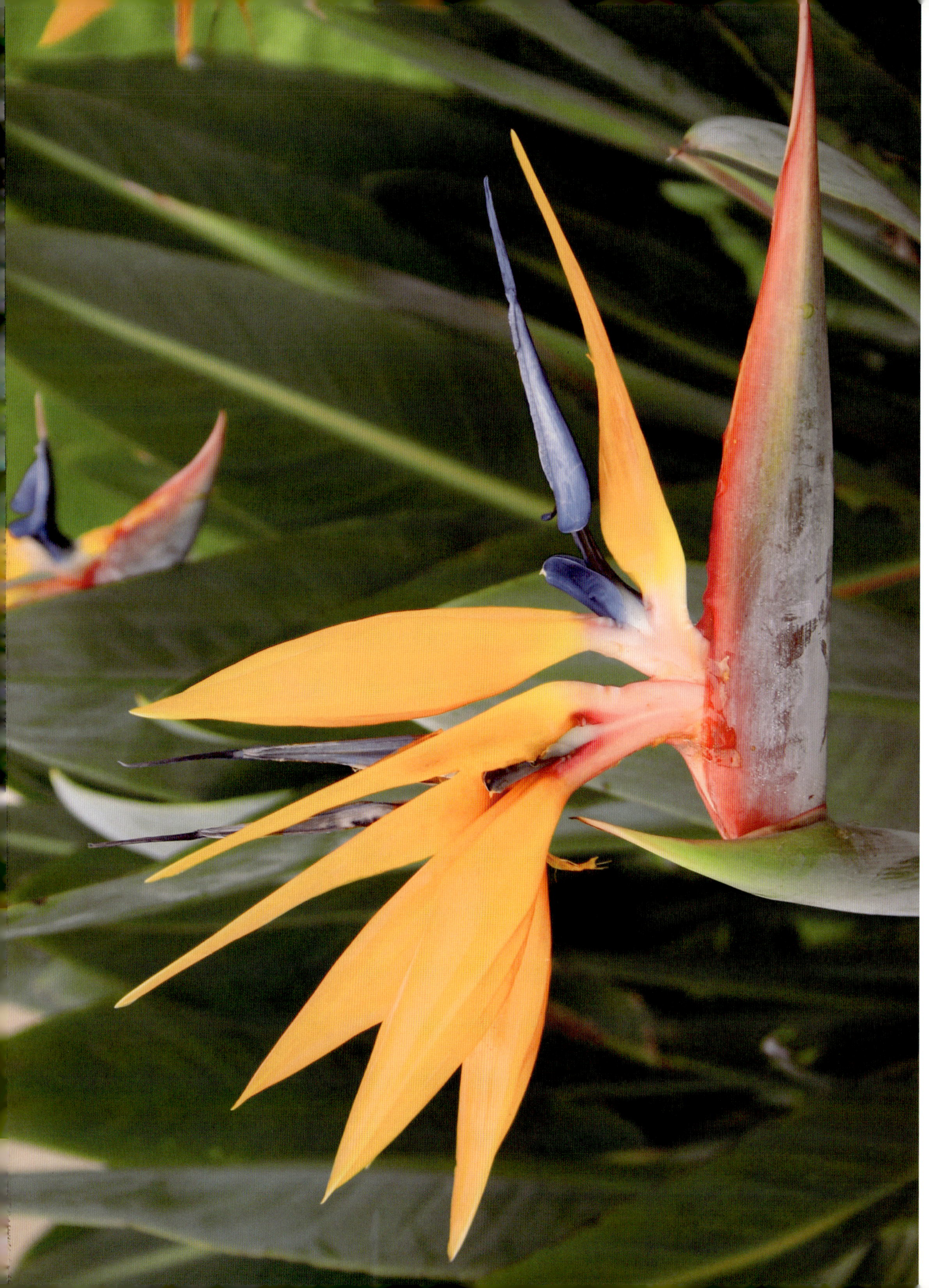

Bird of Paradise

The drama and color of the bird of paradise almost demands that it is the center of attention in the painting. The challenge was to integrate it with other elements in the background.

PAINTS
Alizarin crimson
Brilliant violet
Cadmium scarlet
Cadmium yellow light
Cobalt blue
French ultramarine blue
New gamboge
Permanent rose
Quinacridone gold
Rose madder genuine

TOOLS & MATERIALS
4-ply plate-finish Bristol board
¼-in. (6-mm) plywood
Brown paper tape
Pencil
Staples
Round brush, No. 8
Filbert brush, No. 3

TECHNIQUES USED
Mixing paint in the palette, *p. 21*
Mixing paint on the paper, *p. 21*
Wet-into-wet, *p. 22*

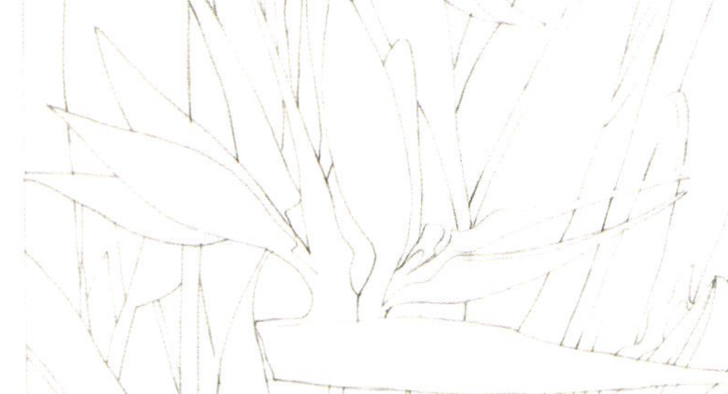

1 Place the Bristol board on a ¼-in. (6-mm) piece of plywood that has been sealed on both sides. Wet the edges of the board paper and plywood. Quickly apply 2-in. (5-cm) gummed brown tape around the edge of the paper and press to seal. Staple in a few places. Don't wet the full sheet of board to avoid stretching the paper. Let the tape dry before working. With a pencil, draw the image outline onto the board.

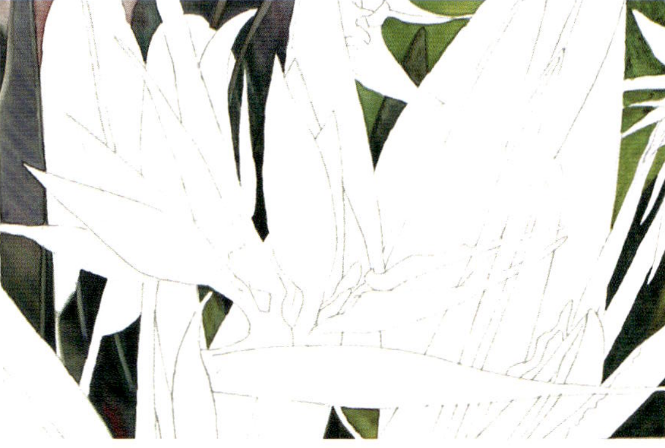

2 With a No. 8 brush, begin painting shapes in the farthest plane with mixtures of cadmium yellow light and French ultramarine blue, as well as brilliant violet and French ultramarine blue, working your way forward. Put the darkest values in early so you can key other values to that. Colors will mix on the surface. Use a lot of paint in each shape for dark colors. Lift out excess paint to lighten areas and to avoid unwanted puddles.

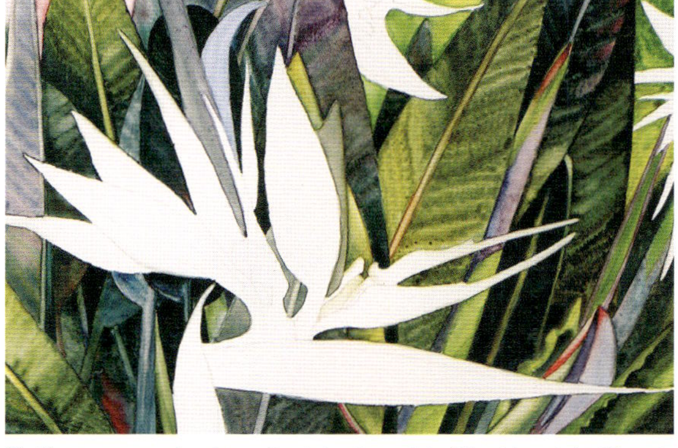

3 Clean any rough edges of paint using a thin filbert brush to lift and blot any extra paint. Continue to paint the leaves in the background, using the same mixtures as in step 2. Think "variety in unity" by keeping the negative space unified but varied in color and value. Leave the partial flowers of the background to paint last, so that you can key them to the main flower to avoid having them too strong.

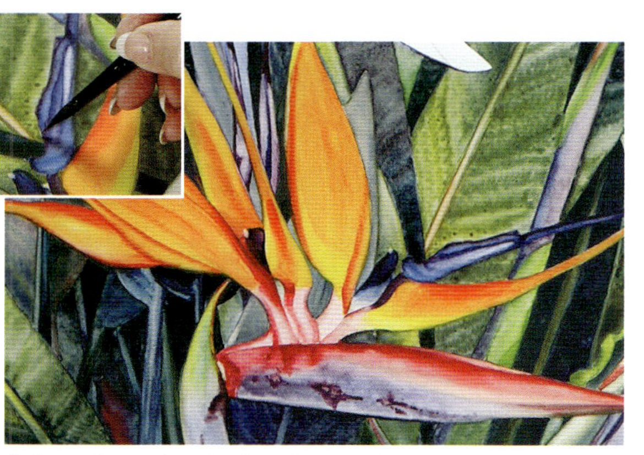

4 Use various reds and yellows in your palette to create the flower color. The petals should be painted smoothly, contrasting with the texture of the leaves (inset). With this paper, it is hard to know how the paint will "lay" when it dries. If you don't like it, you can rewet the area, blot it, or just mix up the color inside the shape and brush it out again until you have something more pleasing.

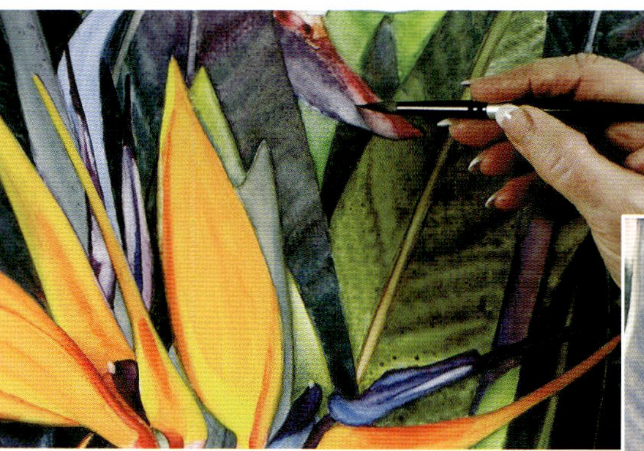

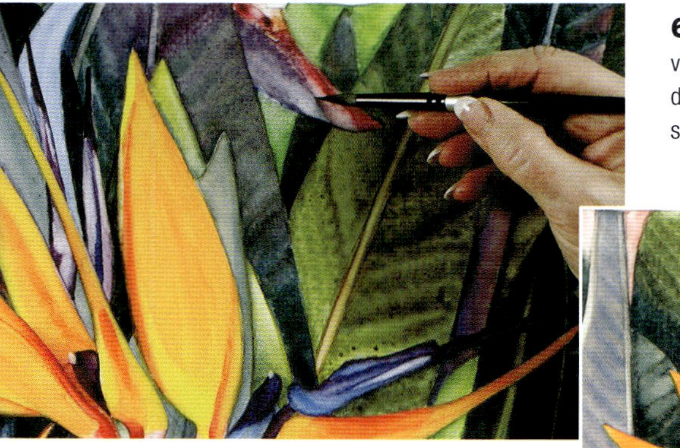

5 Adjust values surrounding the main flower if needed to make it stand out. Next, paint the final flower segments in the background. Slightly gray the colors of those flowers so they won't overpower the main one, yet will still help to move the eye around the painting. Soften the edges of the most distant leaves and petals by using the tip of the wet brush. Color can be added to small areas that are too light or open with the brush tip, as in pointillism.

6 Plate-finish Bristol board produces a painting with energy and vibrant color. The oranges, reds, and purples are strong, but the direction of the leaves, and the texture and touches of related colors successfully pull the eye around the painting.

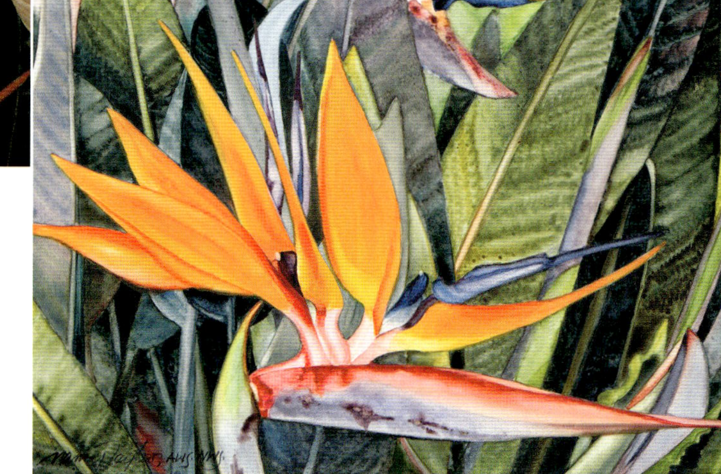

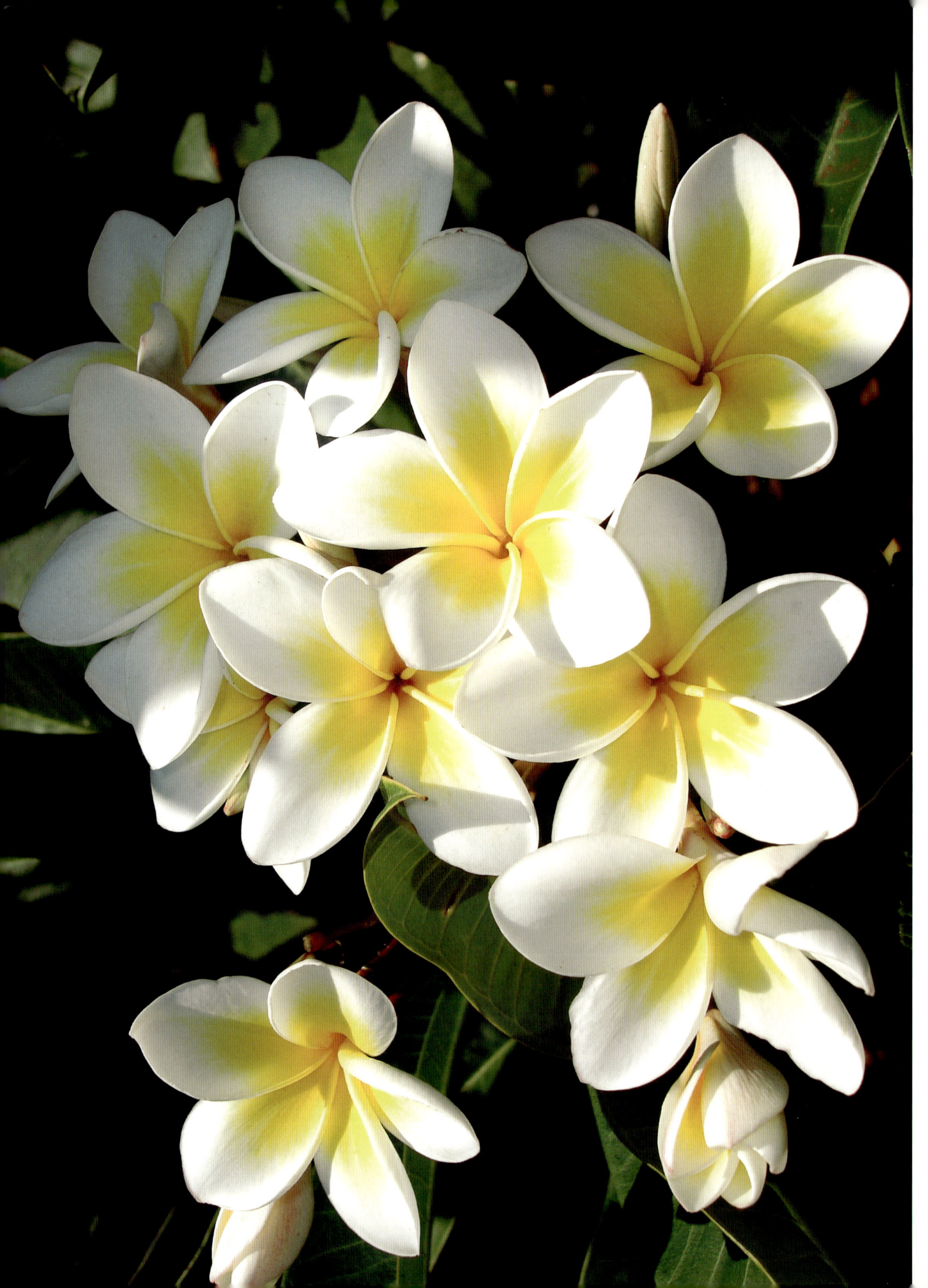

Frangipani

The artist was drawn to the crisp-edged flowers and the value range from white to black. The challenge was to make a very dark background lively without distracting from the simple foreground flowers.

PAINTS
Antwerp blue
Aureolin
Brown madder
Cadmium orange
Cadmium yellow
Cobalt blue
French ultramarine blue
Neutral tint
Phthalo green
Quinacridone coral
Winsor yellow deep

TOOLS & MATERIALS
Cold-pressed paper, 140 lb. (300 gsm)
Mechanical pencil
Eraser
3-in. (7.5-cm) wash brush
Round brushes, Nos. 3, 6, 10
Hair dryer
Tissues

TECHNIQUES USED
Variegated wash, *p. 20*
Mixing paint in the palette, *p. 21*
Dropping in color, *p. 21*
Wet-onto-dry, *p. 22*
Wet-into-wet, *p. 22*
Glazing, *p. 23*
Blending, *p. 24*
Lost and found edges, *p. 24*
White of the paper, *p. 26*
Shadows, *p. 28*

1 Make a detailed drawing of the photograph. Keep your pencil lines fairly light around the flowers and in the center. These will not erase after the paint is applied. They look darker here for demonstration purposes.

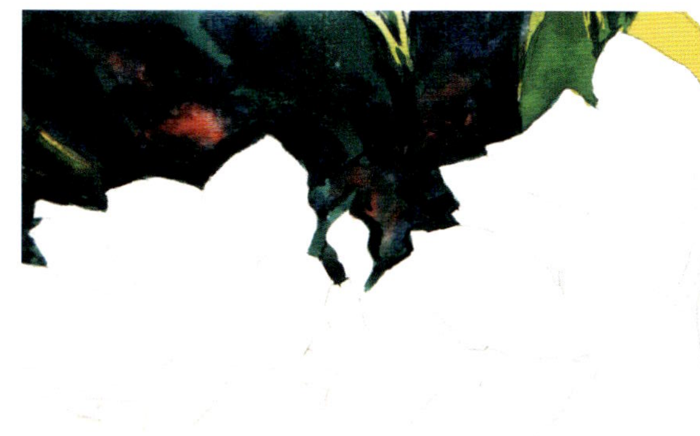

2 Wet some of the area of the upper background using the wash brush, leaving a few dry spots. With a No. 10 round brush, paint around the flowers and any leaves you have drawn in. Then drop in Winsor yellow deep quinacridone coral, brown madder, and cobalt blue. Let the paints spread. With a creamy mixture of phthalo green and neutral tint, paint wet-into-wet around the same area. This strong color will bleed into the other colors. To stop the bleeding, dry with a hair dryer.

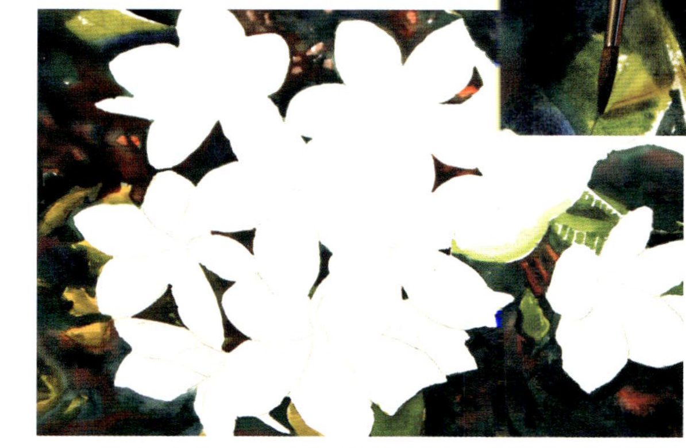

3 Move on to the leaves, using a variegated wash of the yellows and blues from your palette. Observe the many colors of green in the photograph. Some are more yellow, some are more blue, but all have a drop or two of red. Painting a coat of yellow first, then paint the blue or green mixture inside the leaf veins with a No. 6 or No. 3 brush (inset). The leaves can fade (wet-into-wet) in and out of the background dark.

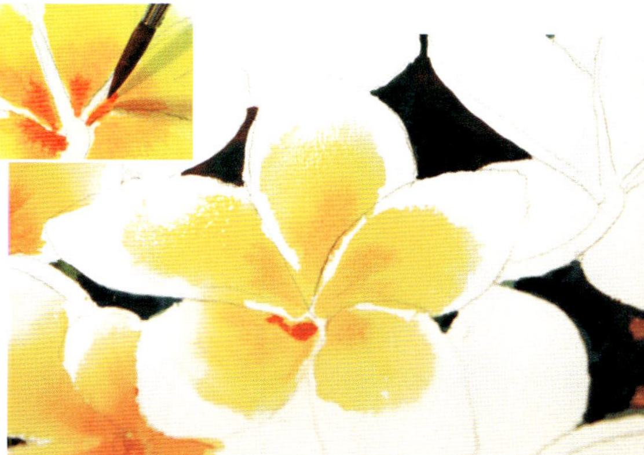

4 Moving through the cluster of flowers one by one and petal by petal, paint water at the top of the yellow area. Working inside the wet area and with a No. 6 round brush, paint aureolin, then cadmium yellow near the center of the flower, and a dot of quinacridone coral at the center (inset). When dry, add a dot of brown madder at the center. With each layer of paint, work in ever-smaller circles into the center of the flower. Paint around the curl in the petal unless indicated otherwise by the photograph.

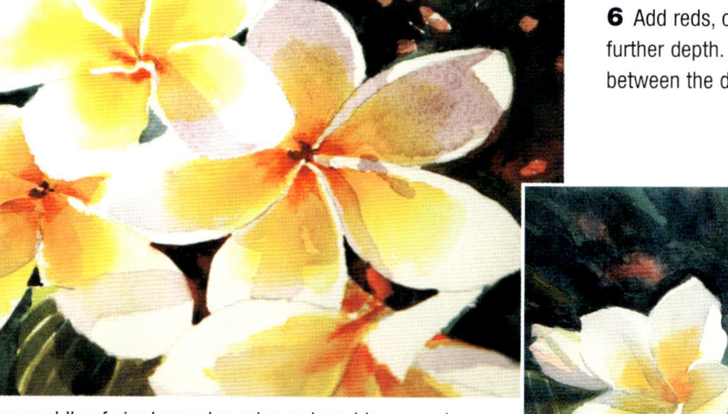

5 Mix a puddle of shadow color using quinacridone coral, brown madder, and Antwerp blue, so that it leans toward violet to set off the yellow flower color. For all areas where the shadow is soft, wet the edge and let the color blend into the wet. You will achieve a smoother shadow if the entire shadow area is damp. You may want to add a dot more brown madder to intensify the center of the flower.

6 Add reds, corals, blues, and yellows to the background to create further depth. The finished painting shows the strong contrast between the dark background and the white and yellow flowers.

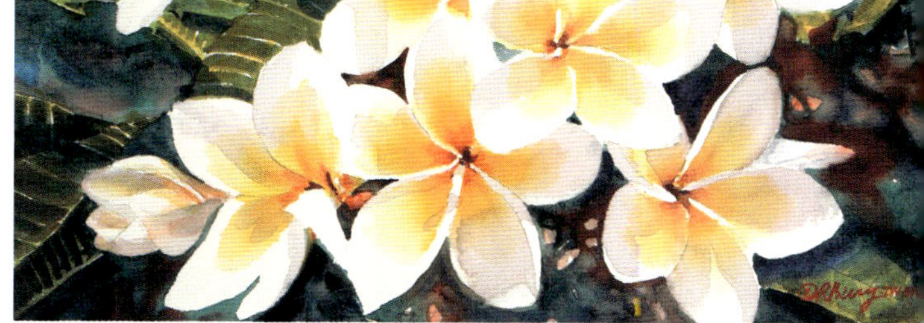

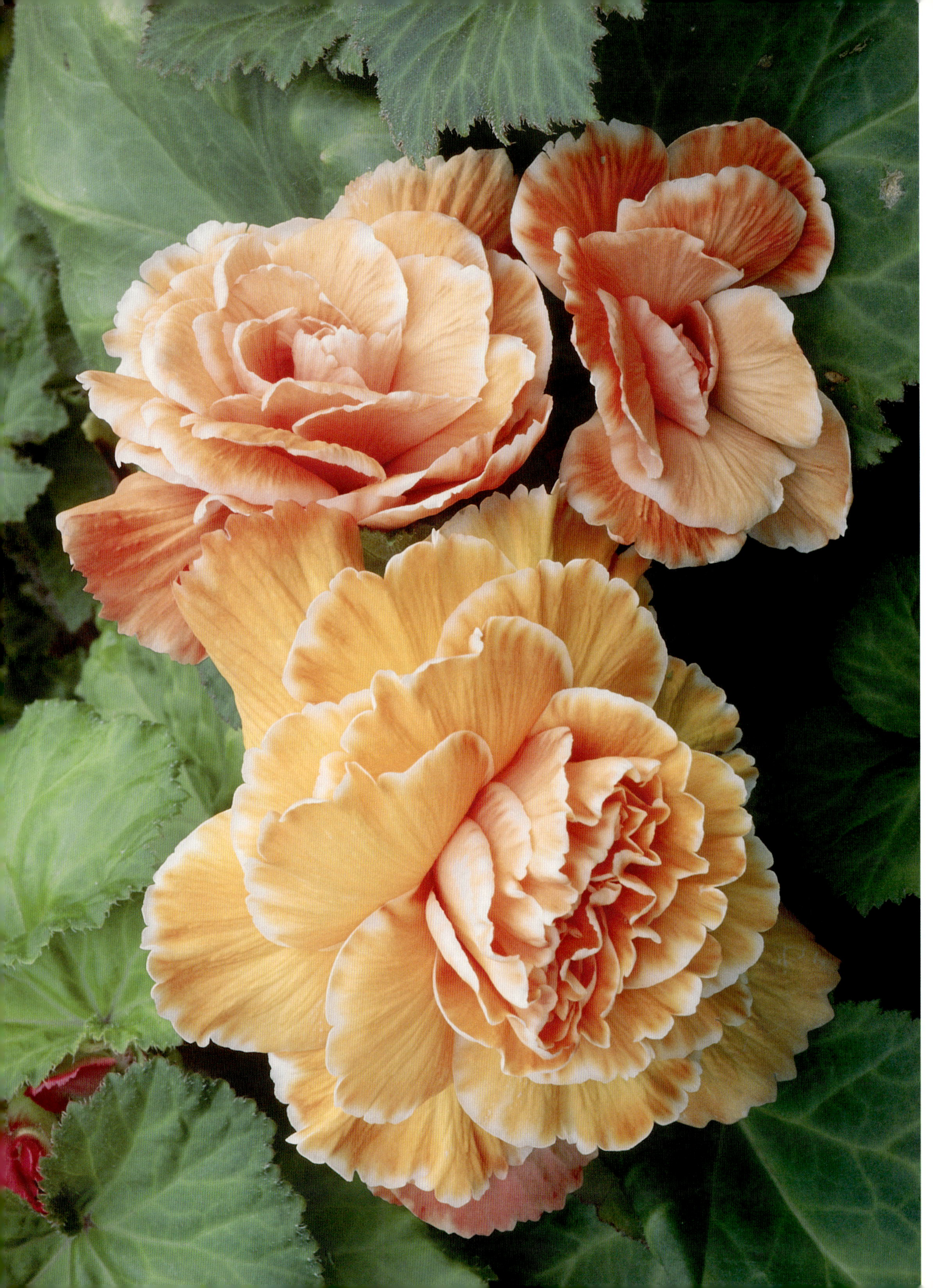

Begonias

The artist was attracted to this image because of the variety of color and interesting details in the flowers and leaves. It was decided that the light should come from upper right and that effect was kept throughout the painting.

PAINTS

Alizarin crimson
Cadmium lemon
Cadmium orange
Naples yellow
New gamboge
Permanent rose
Ultramarine blue
Viridian
Winsor green
Winsor violet

TOOLS & MATERIALS

Cold-pressed paper, 140 lb. (300 gsm)
Transfer paper
Masking tape
Ballpoint pen
Round brushes, Nos. 3 and 5

TECHNIQUES USED

Mixing paint in the palette, *p. 21*
Dropping in color, *p. 21*
Wet-onto-dry, *p. 22*
Wet-into-wet, *p. 22*
Paint light to dark, *p. 23*
Glazing, *p. 23*
Lost and found edges, *p. 24*
White of the paper, *p. 26*
Shadows, *p. 28*
Negative painting, *p. 28*

1 To trace the photograph onto the watercolor paper, place a sheet of transfer paper on top of the watercolor paper and lay the photograph on top of the transfer, taping them together at the top to prevent slipping. Using a ballpoint pen, trace over the shapes of the flowers and leaves (inset) to transfer the lines from the transfer paper onto the watercolor paper.

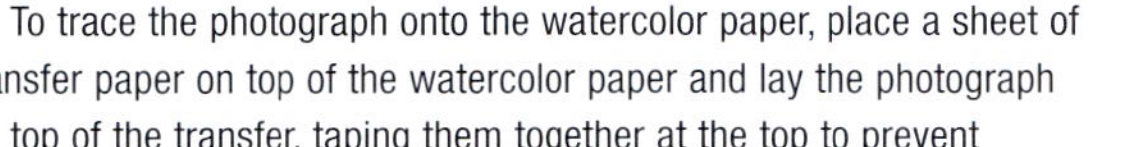

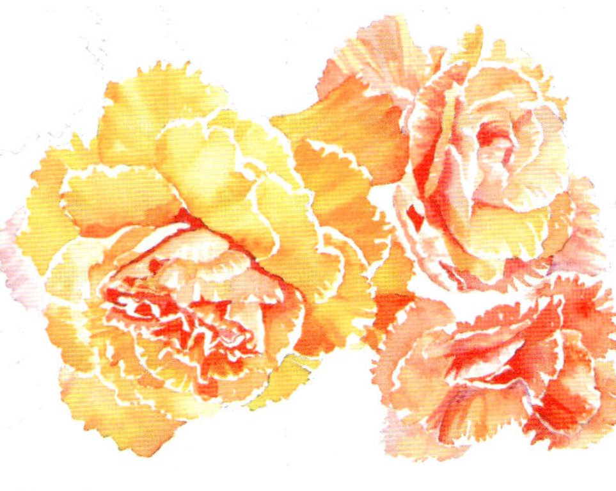

2 With a No. 5 round brush, paint the yellow, pink, and orange flowers, letting each dry before painting the one beside it. Put darker and lighter colors beside each other and let them intermix wet-into-wet on petals that have variegated color or shadows. Be careful to leave the white of the paper on the jagged edges of the flowers and on some turning edges by painting up to the edge. Permanent rose in combination with cadmium orange, Naples yellow, and alizarin crimson are good mixtures for these petals.

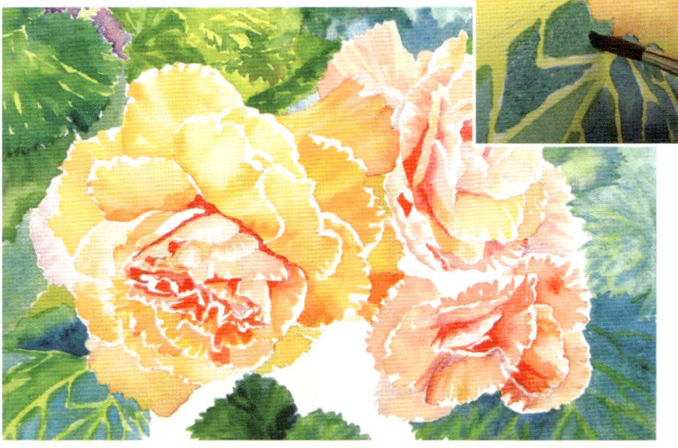

3 Next paint the greens and blues of the leaves. Glaze a layer of cadmium lemon on the leaves that have prominent yellow vein patterns. Dry. Work with negative painting to paint the shapes of the spaces between the veins, using blues and/or greens (inset). Paint less prominent leaves one at a time. Let colors mingle on some and on others wait until the sheen has gone and then paint darker shapes or lines on top, which will have soft edges as the two colors merge. Experiment with hard and soft edges.

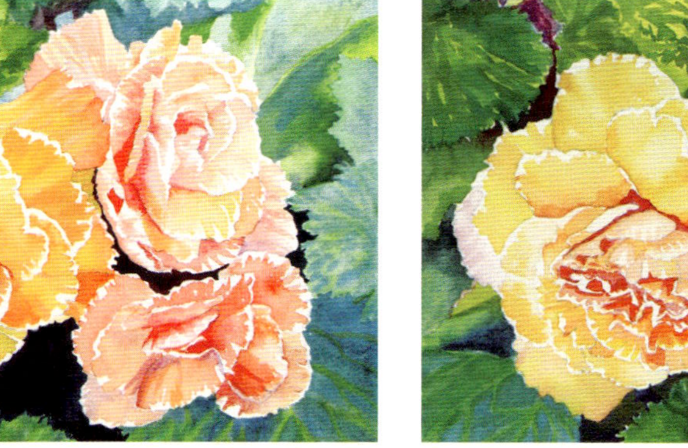

4 Paint the darks between the flowers and leaves, and glaze over leaves as needed to simplify and unify them. Mix dark variations of ultramarine blue, Winsor green, and Winsor violet, and paint the dark shapes between the flowers and leaves. Vary the colors to make the darks more interesting and imply shapes in the shadows.

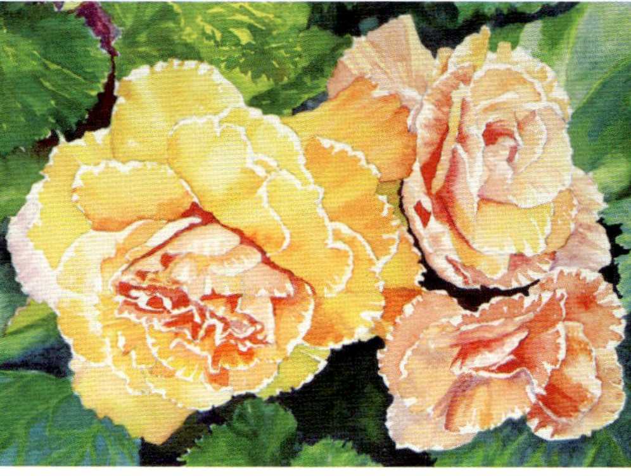

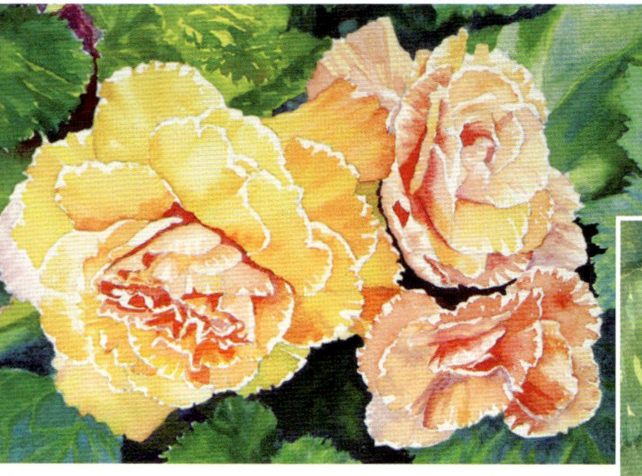

5 Use viridian to glaze over the leaves with bright yellow veins to simplify and subdue them. Use a mixture of viridian and ultramarine blue to glaze shadows on the leaves, being careful to negative paint around the sharp edges of the leaves that are casting the shadow. With a damp brush, feather the edge of the shadow as it moves away from its source.

6 Finally, using a No. 3 round brush and a mixture of cadmium lemon, cadmium orange, and permanent rose, paint the lines on the petals that indicate veins, ridges, and shadows. To add a sunny highlight, use new gamboge for a few of the lines that would be in the sun.

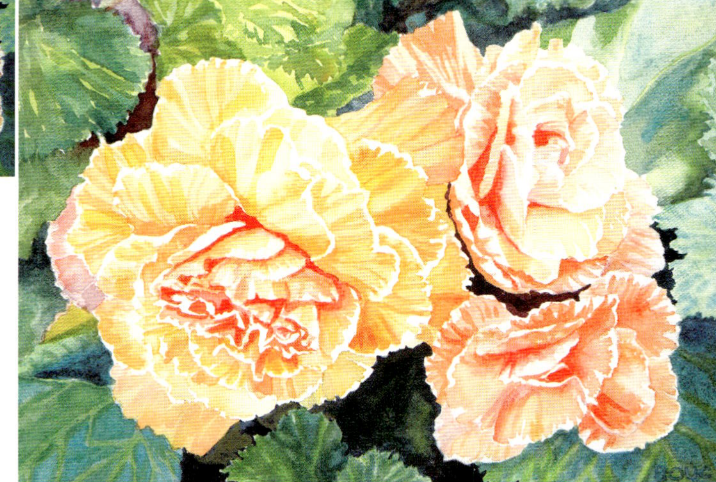

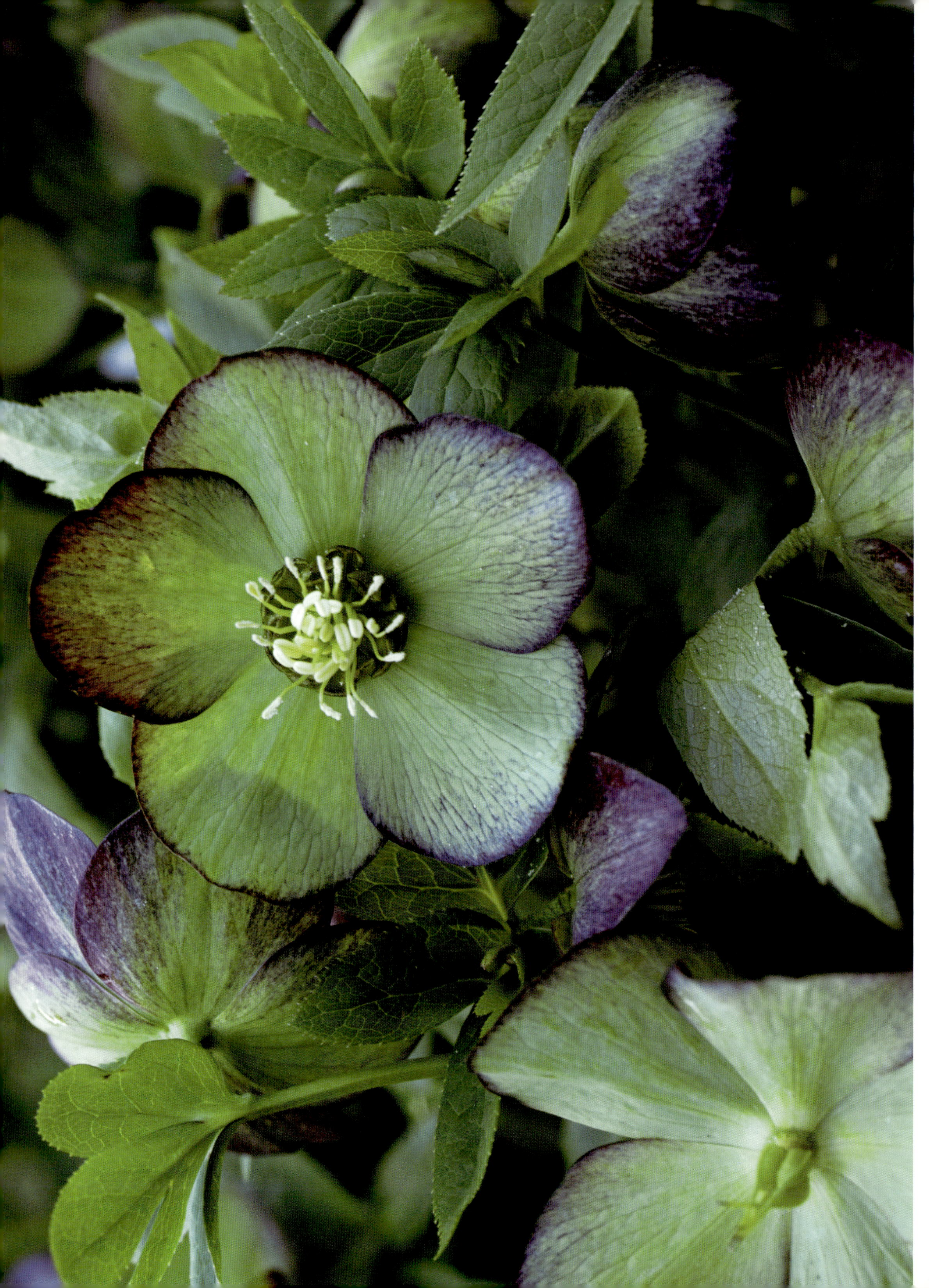

Lenten Rose

The artist was drawn to the way the light shines through the petals of the main flower. The upper half of the rose is warm from the light and the lower half is cool, in shadow.

PAINTS
Alizarin crimson
Bismuth yellow
Burnt sienna
Cobalt blue
French ultramarine blue
Manganese violet
Permanent rose
Quinacridone gold
Winsor blue (red shade)
Winsor green (blue shade)

TOOLS & MATERIALS
Rough paper, 140 lb. (300 gsm)
H pencil
Masquepen
Round brushes, Nos. 4 and 12
Small stiff-bristled brush or scrubber

TECHNIQUES
Dropping in color, *p. 21*
Wet-onto-dry, *p. 22*
Wet-into-wet, *p. 22*
Masking to reserve the paper, *p. 25*
Masking for details, *p. 25*
Softening masked edges, *p. 25*

1 Make a drawing using the pencil on watercolor paper; add interest by paying attention to the wonderful variety of shapes within the photograph. Place the main flower slightly above and to the right of center. Don't forget to indicate the shadows showing through the petals of the center rose. With a Masquepen, mask out the highlights, light on stems and edges, and lightest lights of the foreground shapes. Be precise (inset).

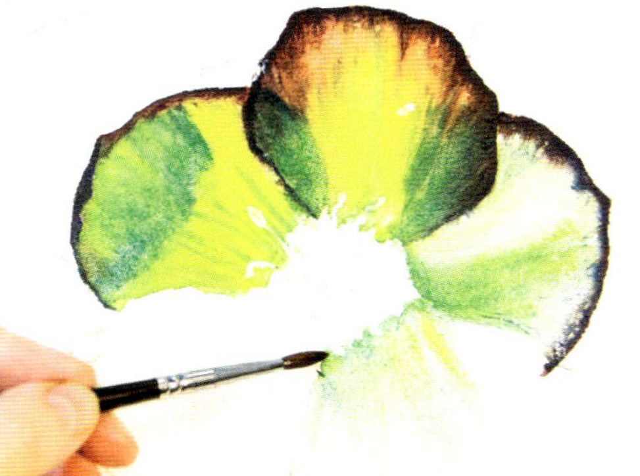

2 With the No. 4 brush, add bismuth yellow and quinacridone gold, and various blues and greens (cobalt blue, Winsor blue—red shade—French ultramarine blue, and Winsor green—blue shade) within the main flower. Put warm yellows on the top where sunlight shows through, and cool blues below, where it doesn't. Green should show at the center. Edge the petals using purples and browns (burnt sienna, alizarin crimson, permanent rose, and manganese violet).

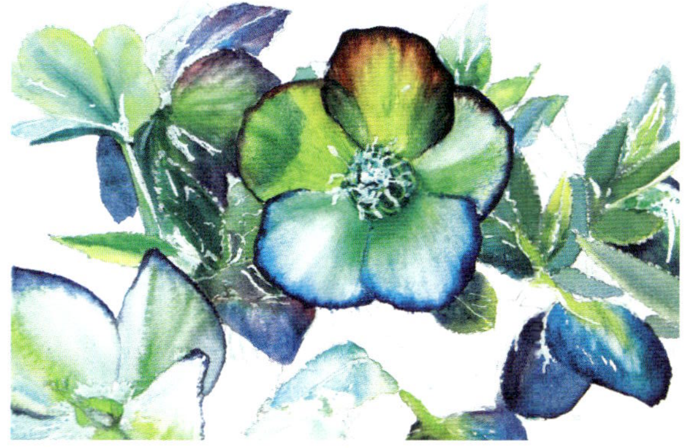

3 Continue painting into the other flower and leaf shapes across the painting. Try not to make everything "green" and the same value. Push some shapes toward yellow and others toward blues and purples. Keep in mind where the light is and be aware of lighter and darker values. When dry, move on to the background.

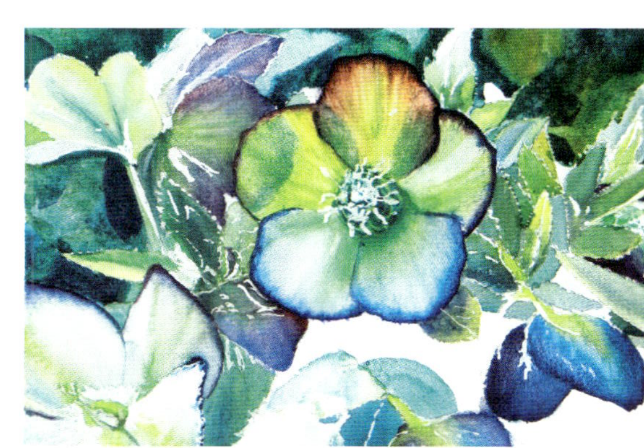

4 Paint into the background with a No. 12 brush using darks. Winsor green, French ultramarine blue, and alizarin crimson in various strengths and combinations will mix and separate into interesting textures and shapes. Load your brush with yellow to drop some leaf shapes here and there into the wet paint.

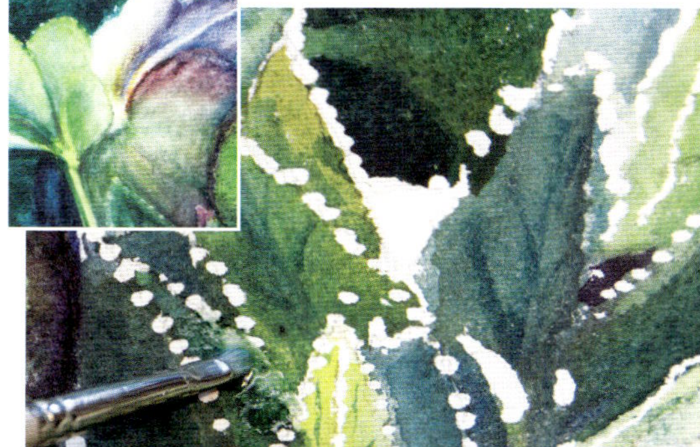

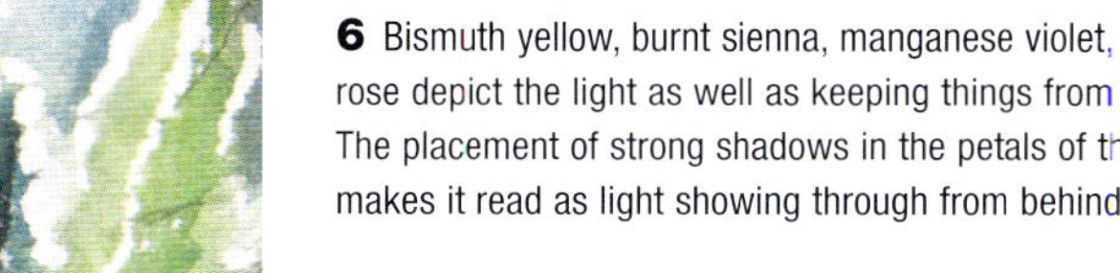

5 Once the paint is dry, remove the mask. With a small, stiff-bristled brush or scrubber, soften some of the edges and paint into others (inset). Try to retain the light. Adjust your color around the painting. To avoid the pitfall of "isolated color," use colors from the main flower in other areas of the painting. Your aim is unity—all of your elements should "play" with one another.

6 Bismuth yellow, burnt sienna, manganese violet, and permanent rose depict the light as well as keeping things from being too green. The placement of strong shadows in the petals of the lead flower makes it read as light showing through from behind.

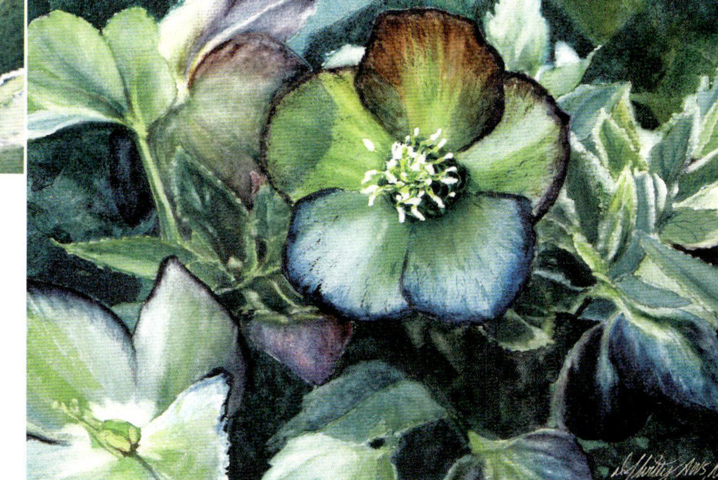

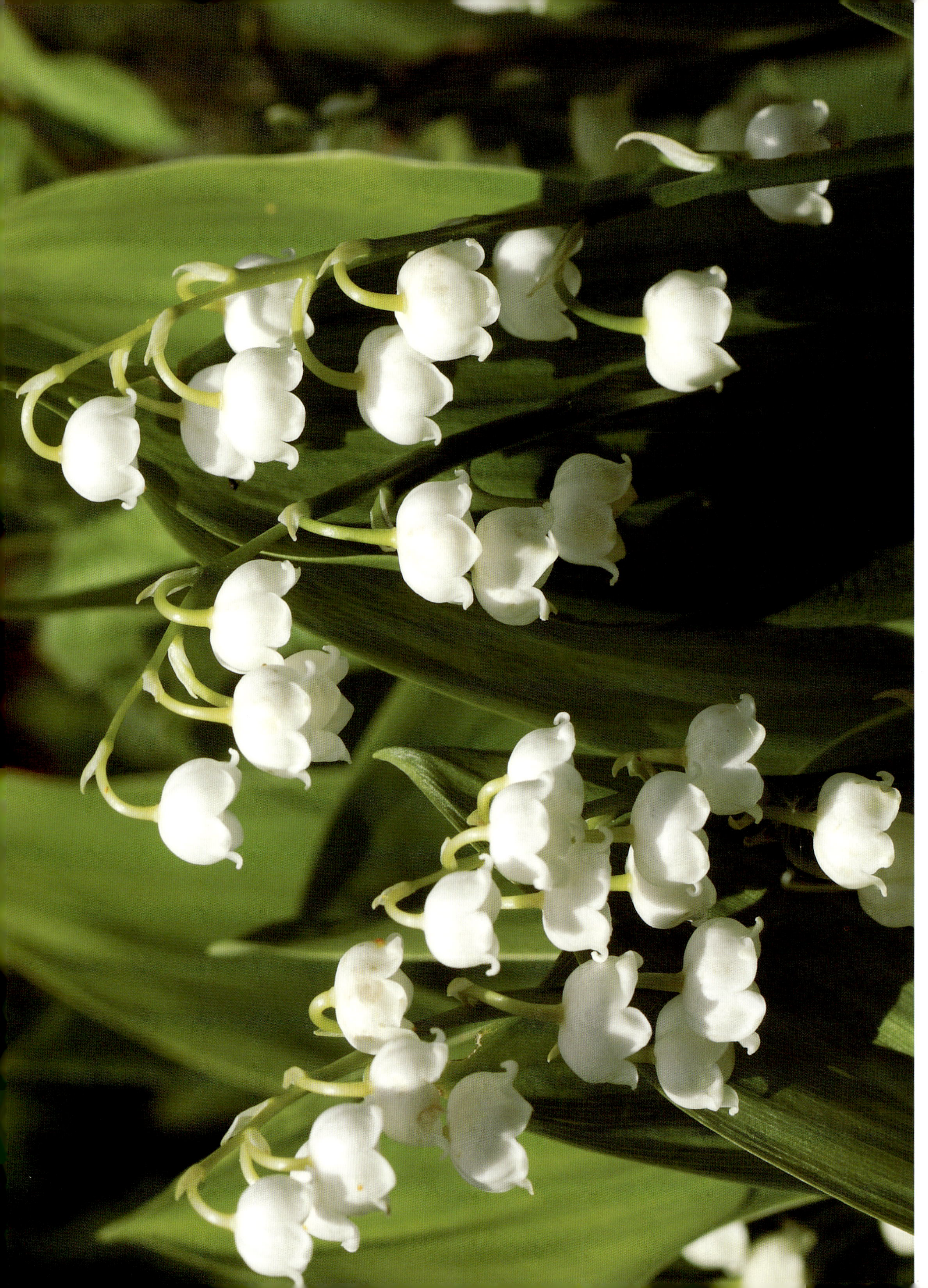

Lily of the Valley

The artist was drawn to the delicate flowers against the simple background. Unifying the white dots into larger shapes was the main challenge.

PAINTS
Aureolin
Cerulean blue
Dioxazine purple
Indigo
Peacock blue
Phthalo blue
Prussian blue
Quinacridone gold
Rich green-gold
Sap green
Viridian

TOOLS & MATERIALS
Cold-pressed paper, 140 lb. (300 gsm)
HB pencil
Invisible tape
Masking fluid
Color shaper, size 0
Round brushes, Nos. 2, 4, 5, 10
Paper towel

TECHNIQUES
Variegated wash, *p. 20*
Mixing paint in the palette, *p. 21*
Wet-onto-dry, *p. 22*
Wet-into-wet, *p. 22*
Lost and found edges, *p. 24*
Masking to reserve the paper, *p. 25*
Softening masked edges, *p. 25*
White-on-white, *p. 27*

1 Draw the image using a sharp pencil on watercolor paper, taking care not to press too hard to avoid indenting the paper. Tape off the edges of the painting to allow you to paint freely up to and over the edges. When the tape is removed, you will be left with crisp edges.

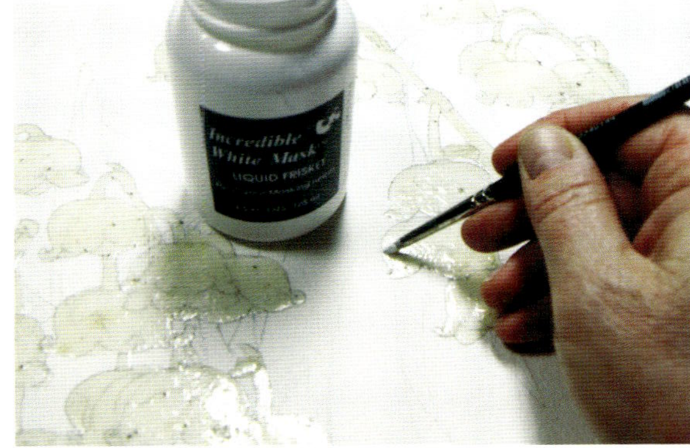

2 After drawing the image, mask the flowers and stems using masking fluid and a color shaper. The white of the flowers is now protected.

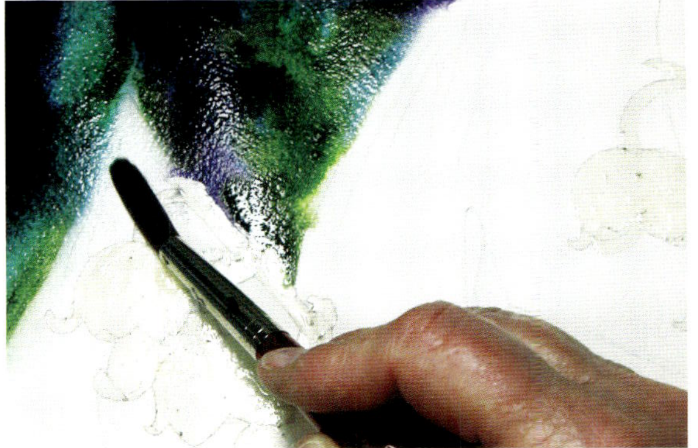

3 Mix several yellow, blue, and green puddles of paint in your palette. With a No. 10 round brush, paint a variegated wash, keeping the foreground leaves lighter by using more aureolin, rich green-gold, and sap green in the mixtures.

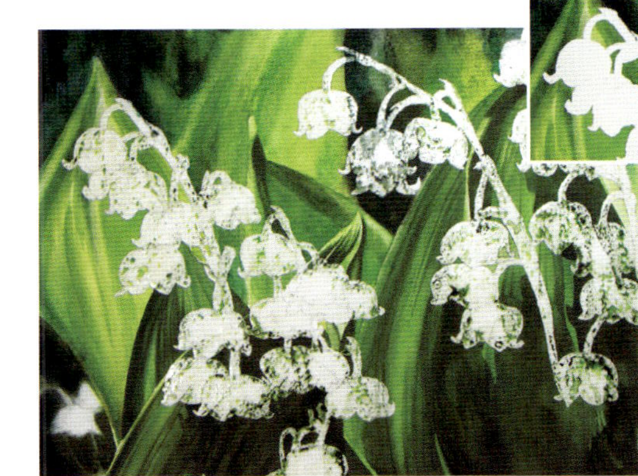

4 Some of the leaves are part of the background, so it is not necessary to call too much attention to them. Keep them soft-edged and let them fade. Paint the middle-ground leaves in more detail, using aureolin, rich green-gold, and sap green. Reserve the dioxazine purple, indigo, and Prussian and phthalo blue for the background darks. When your painting is completely dry, remove the masking (inset).

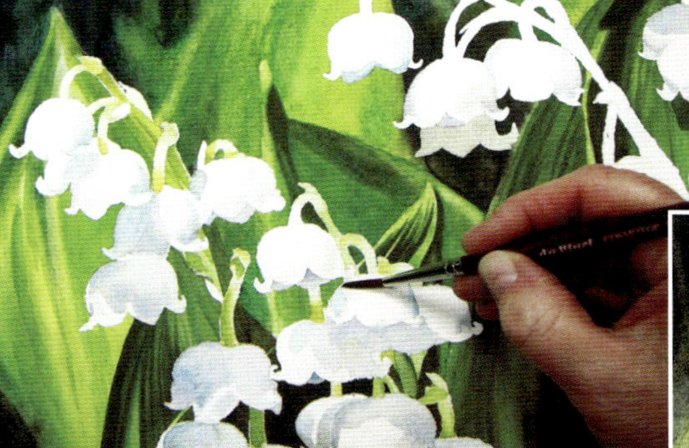

5 Handle the flowers with a gentle touch, since they are small and delicate in nature. Shade the white flowers with various mixtures of cerulean blue, dioxazine purple, and greens—but remember, they are white flowers.

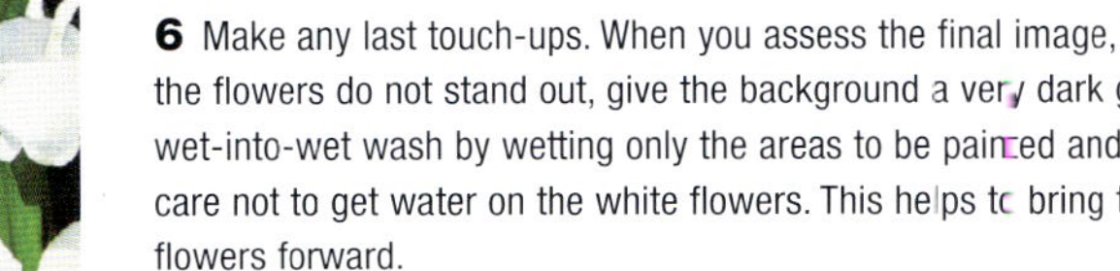

6 Make any last touch-ups. When you assess the final image, if the flowers do not stand out, give the background a very dark green wet-into-wet wash by wetting only the areas to be painted and taking care not to get water on the white flowers. This helps to bring the flowers forward.

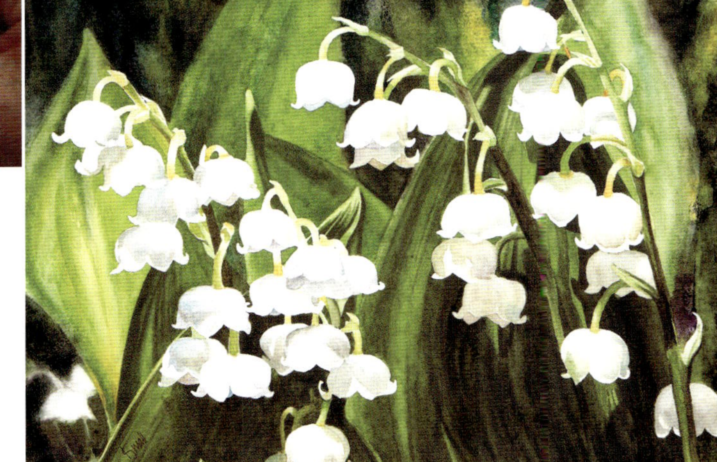

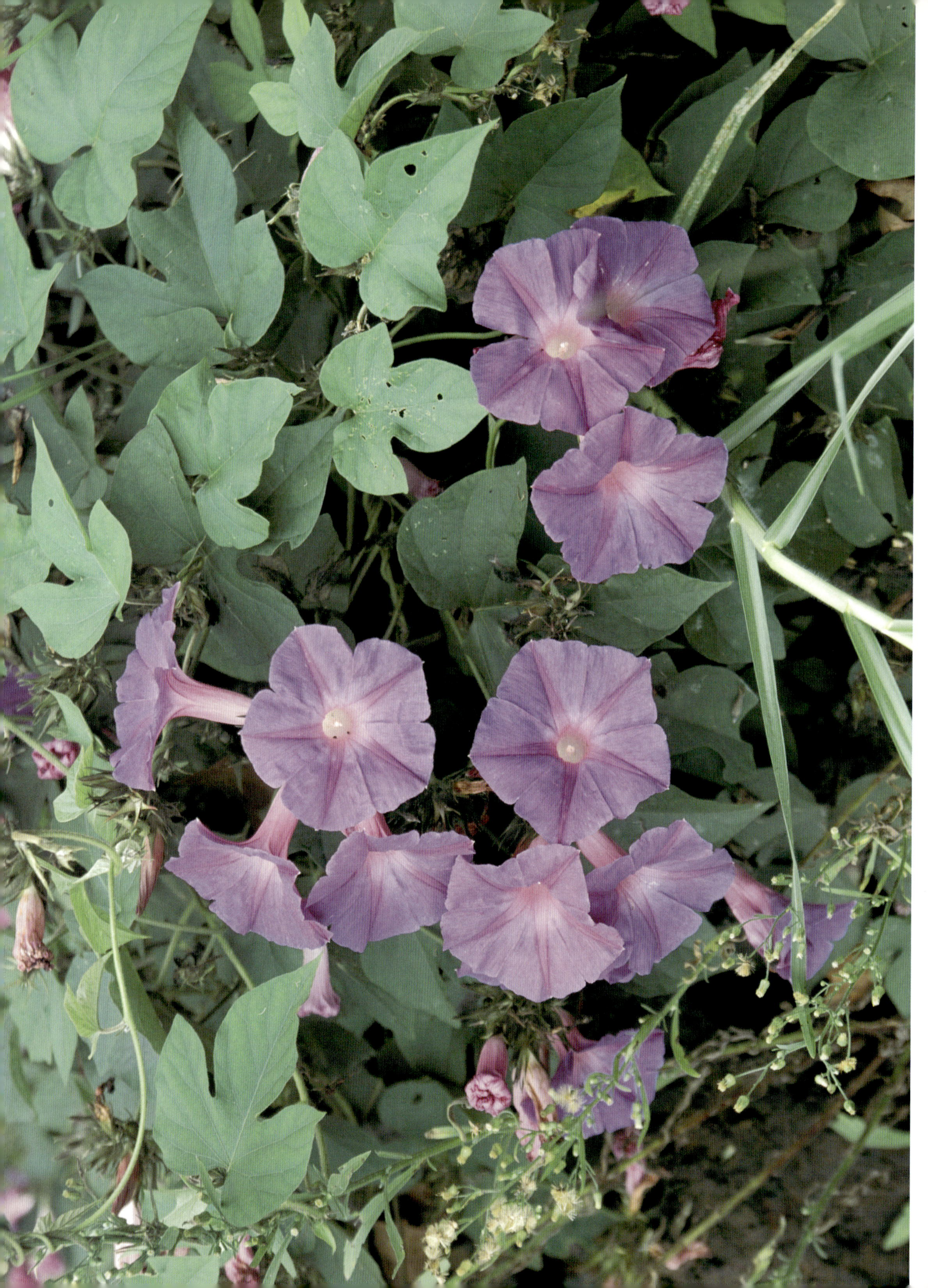

Ipomoea

The artist liked the tangle of flowers and foliage. She used the negative painting method and worked from light to dark to define the leaf shapes and deep rich shadows; this also made the mauve flowers stand out from the background.

PAINTS
Aureolin
Cadmium yellow
Cerulean blue
Cobalt blue
Cobalt violet
French ultramarine blue
Indian red
Phthalo blue
Quinacridone pink
Raw sienna

TOOLS & MATERIALS
Cold-pressed paper, 140 lb. (300 gsm)
HB pencil
Masking fluid
Old brush
Round brushes, Nos. 1, 5, 12
Tissues
1-in. (2.5-cm) flat scrubber

TECHNIQUES
Variegated wash, *p. 20*
Mixing paint in the palette, *p. 21*
Dropping in color, *p. 21*
Wet-onto-dry, *p. 22*
Wet-into-wet, *p. 22*
Paint light to dark, *p. 23*
Lost and found edges, *p. 24*
Masking for details, *p. 25*
Softening masked edges, *p. 25*
Adding highlights, *p. 27*
Negative painting, *p. 28*

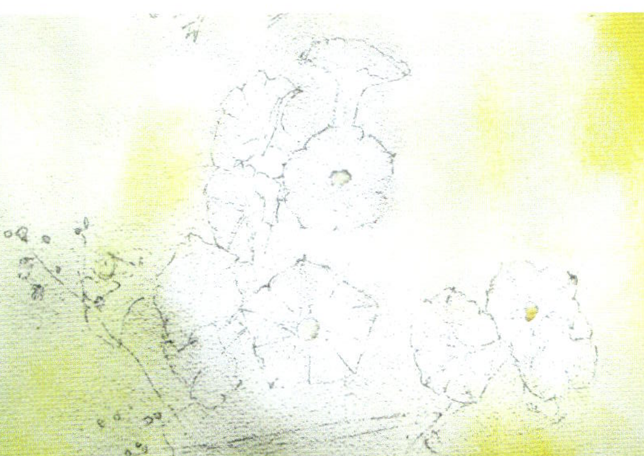

1 Lightly draw in the shapes of flowers on the watercolor paper in pencil. Mask the flower centers and the little white seeds with masking fluid and an old brush. Let dry. Wet the background area with clean water. With a No. 12 brush, paint a pale, variegated wash of aureolin. Leave the flower area white. In preparation for painting the flowers, mix two pale washes—one of cobalt violet and another of quinacridone pink.

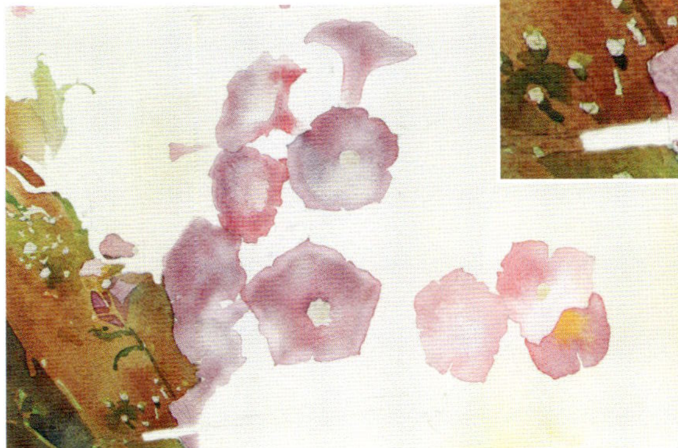

2 When the background is dry, with a No. 5 brush randomly paint the flower mixes into the petal areas. Lift out paint with a tissue to make the soft white blends. Next mix a few different combinations of greens in the palette using blues and yellows. Using a No. 5 brush, paint the yellow-green mix for the seed-head foliage with Indian red and touches of cobalt blue around them (inset).

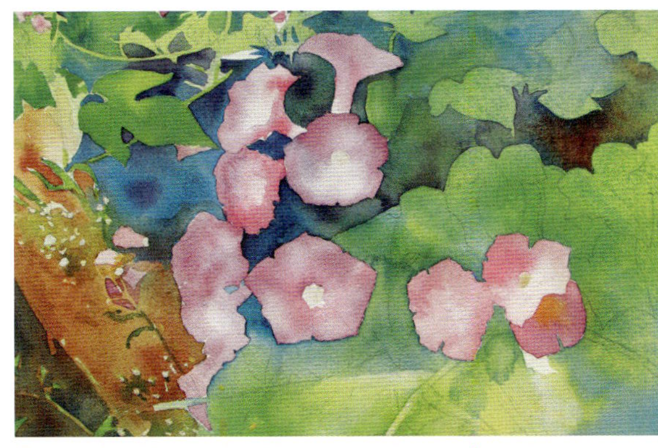

3 Use a No. 12 brush to add a variegated wash of cobalt and cerulean blue to the background. Drop in, wet-into-wet, some of the green mixes in your palette. Let dry. Draw the leaf shapes in pencil. Behind the leaves, paint negative dark shapes of the deep shadows with a variegated wash of phthalo blue, French ultramarine blue, and Indian red. This will give you the positive shapes of the leaves.

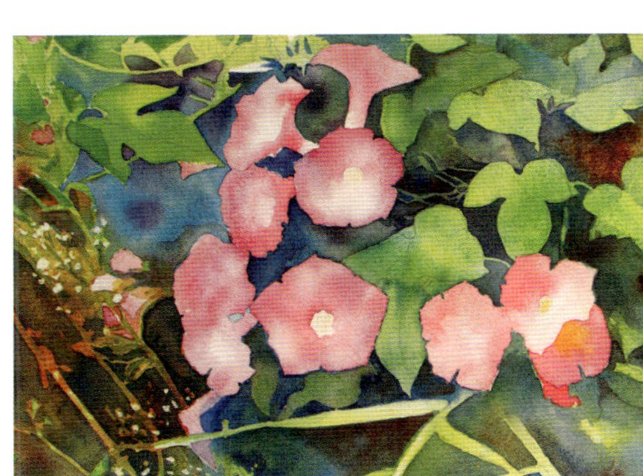

4 Using the same colors, continue to paint the negative shapes, working into the background and painting successively darker washes. Paint hard edges to indicate the crisp fore edge of the leaves and allow the receding edges to blend into the background. Use the same technique to create the veins on the leaves.

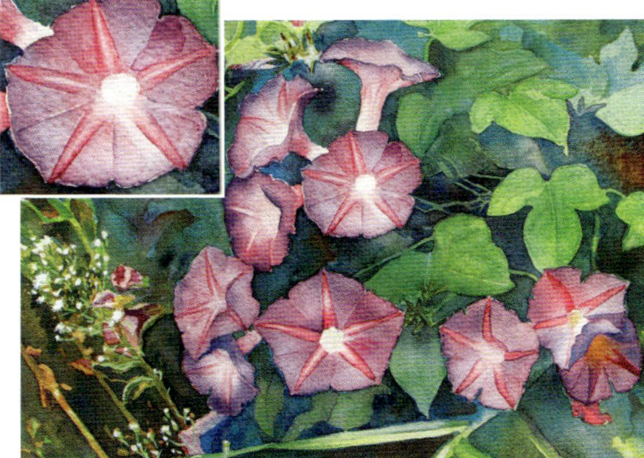

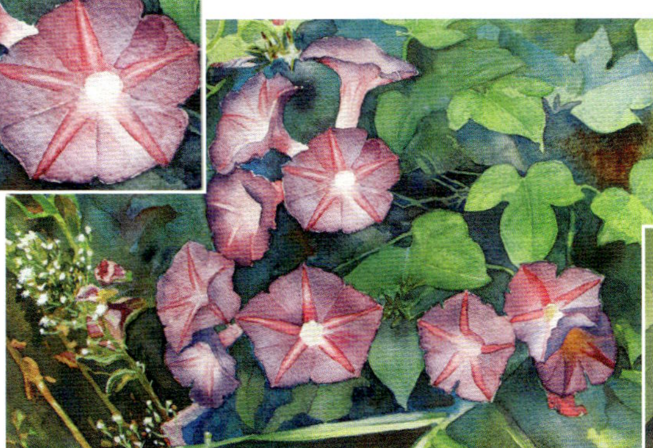

5 Using the No. 5 brush, paint the petal shapes. Use cobalt violet for the main petals, leaving the star shapes. Let dry. Next paint the star shape with the quinacridone pink, allowing the edges of the two colors to overlap. With a flat scrubber, scrub out the highlight lines in the points of the star (inset). Remove the masking fluid.

6 Using a No. 1 brush, paint aureolin around the stamens in the centers of the flowers. Paint cobalt blue thin washes on the petals to describe the form. Tidy up the seed heads and their fine stems with body-color mixes.

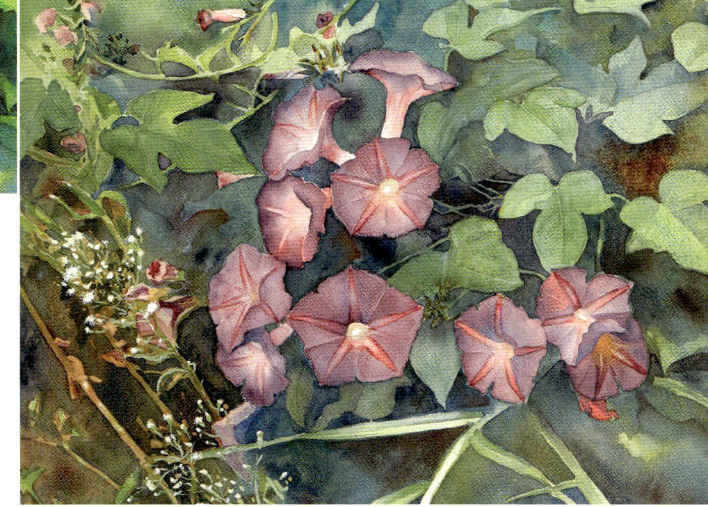

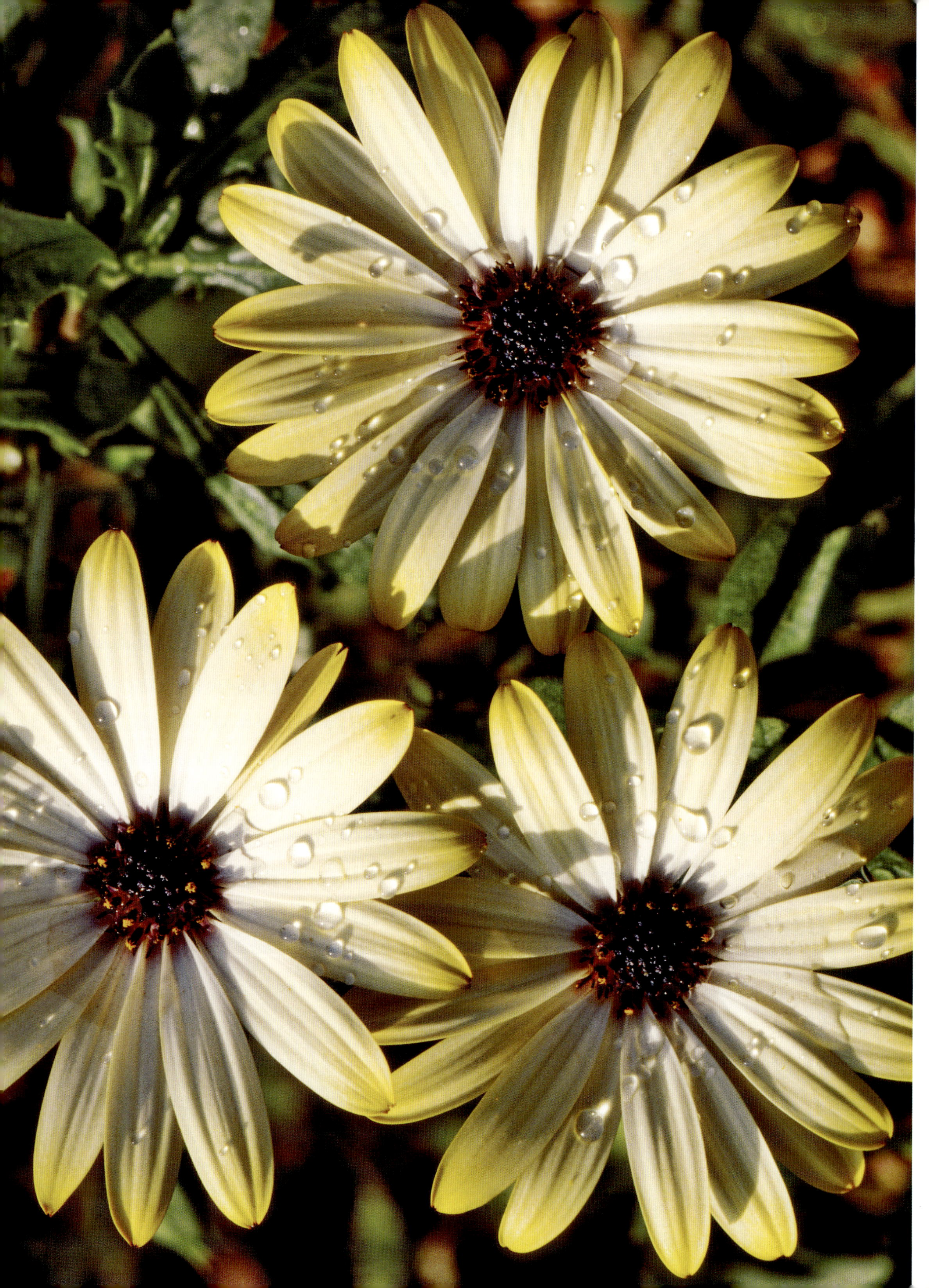

African Daisies

This is a complex image that offers challenges in replicating the details of the flower and the water droplets.

PAINTS
Burnt sienna
Burnt umber
French ultramarine blue
New gamboge
Sap green
Winsor violet

TOOLS & MATERIALS
Cold-pressed paper, 140 lb. (300 gsm)
Mechanical pencil, 5 mm HB lead
Eraser
Round brushes, Nos. 5 or 8 and 10 or 12
Masking fluid
Old brush

TECHNIQUES USED
Mixing paint in the palette, *p. 21*
Dropping in color, *p. 21*
Wet-into-wet, *p. 22*
Paint light to dark, *p. 23*
Lost and found edges, *p. 24*
Masking for details, *p. 25*

1 Make a detailed drawing of the flower to define the light and dark areas. Don't concern yourself with the background since it will be painted last.

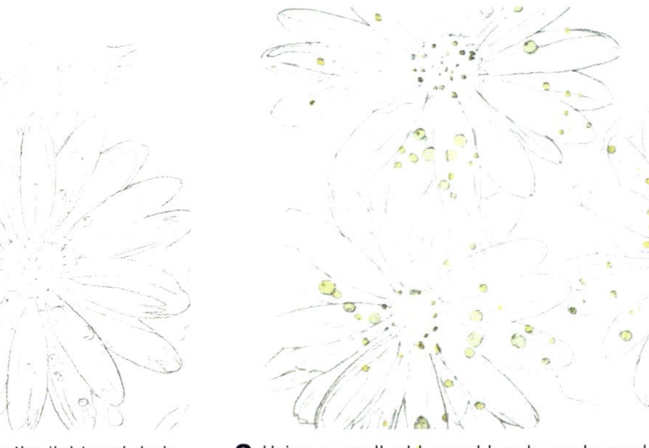

2 Using a small, old round brush, apply masking fluid to each of the water droplets, keeping the edges as smooth as possible. Note that some of the droplets have refracted light spots outside the drop itself, and these must be masked as well. At this time you should also mask the yellow and white points in the flowers' compound centers. These will have more irregular edges.

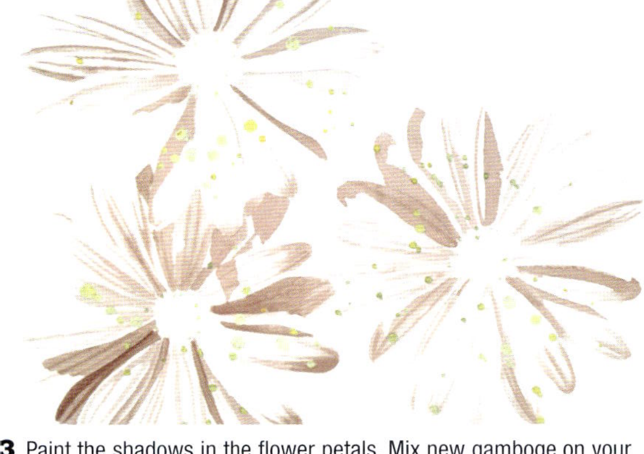

3 Paint the shadows in the flower petals. Mix new gamboge on your palette with Winsor violet to create a fairly large puddle of a tertiary color tending to the violet end. Identify the shadows and crease in the petals and, using a thin mix of this color, paint the markings, petal by petal. If desired, you may soften the edges with a brush wetted with clear water.

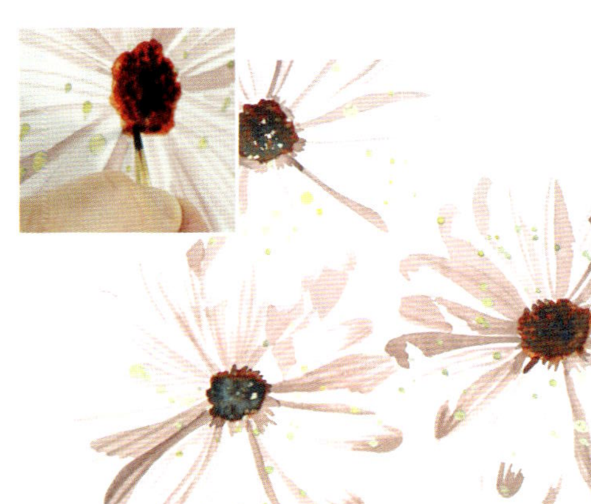

4 Mix a strong puddle of burnt sienna and dab it into the centers of each of the flowers. While still wet, drop in strong French ultramarine blue (inset) and let it spread and flow in irregular patterns. Using the new gamboge and Winsor violet mixture, paint the shadows on the petals that are cast by the centers.

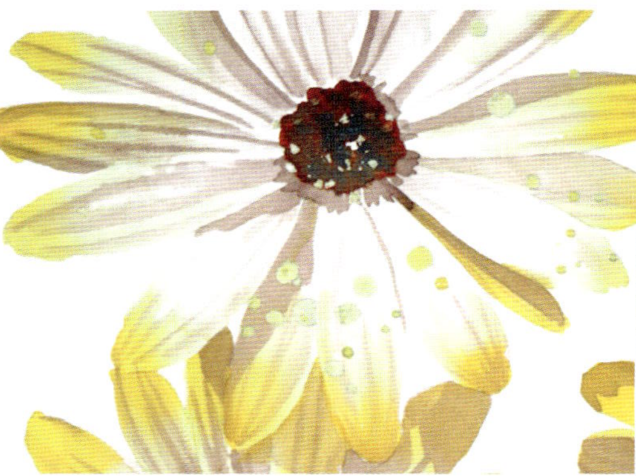

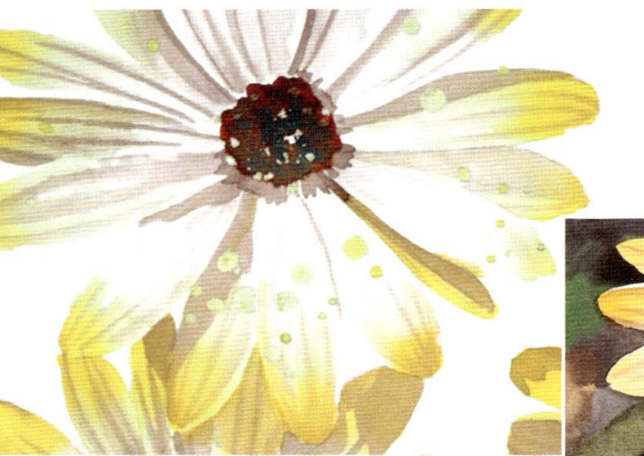

5 Using a rich mixture of new gamboge, draw the yellow from the tips of the petals toward the center. Then, using a brush wetted with water, draw the yellow closer to the center, allowing the color to lighten and fade as you pass the middle of the petal. Remove the masking when dry. Using new gamboge, paint in the yellow stamens in the centers. Reapply masking fluid to the tiny points of light on a few of the water droplets.

6 With a bluish mixture of French ultramarine and burnt umber, paint a crescent and leave a spot of white on the lighter side of the droplet (inset). Apply sap green, French ultramarine blue, yellow, and violet colors to the wet background, painting light to dark. Remove the masking fluid.

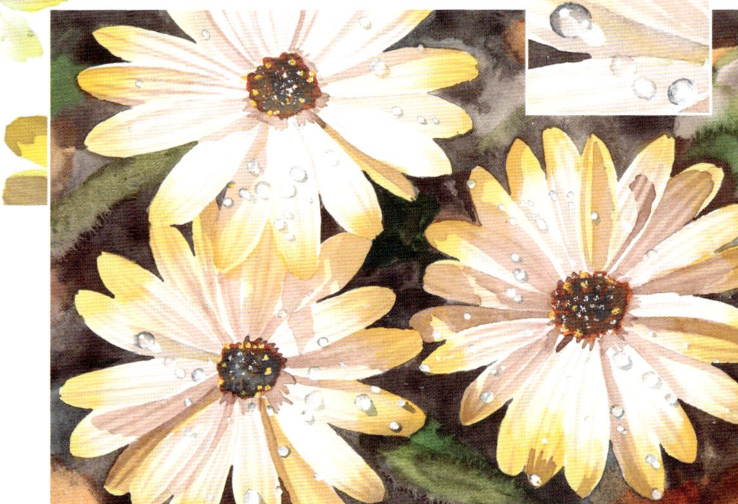

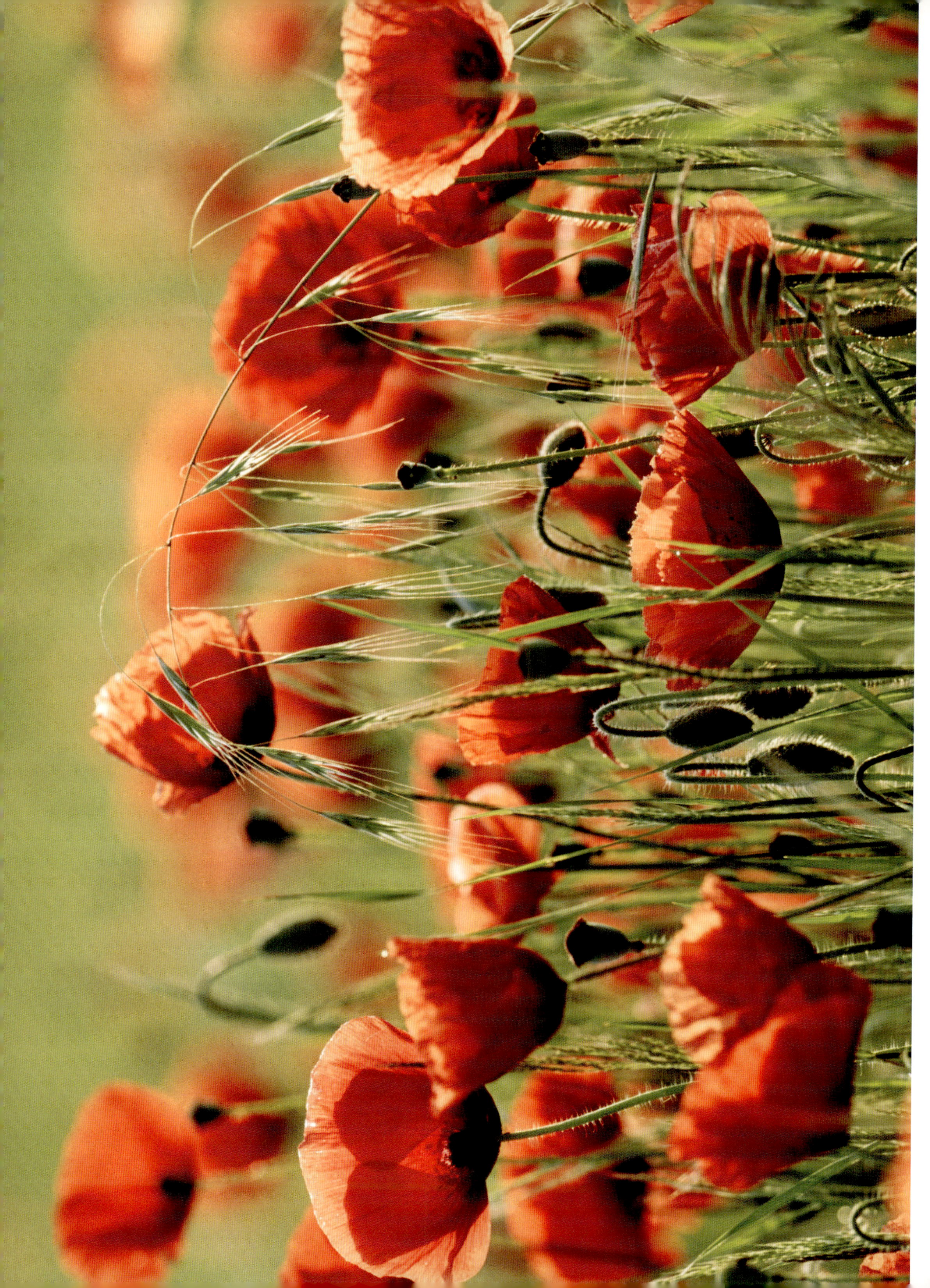

Poppies

The artist was drawn to the wonderful color of the poppies, the quality of light created by the backlighting, and the fuzzy haloes around the seedpods. Careful, precise masking controls the lights, and keeps the background paint layer fresh and colorful.

PAINTS
Azo green
Bismuth yellow
Cerulean blue
Cobalt blue
Permanent alizarin crimson
Prussian blue
Pyrrole red
Sap green
Ultramarine blue
Yellow ocher

TOOLS & MATERIALS
Cold-pressed paper, 140 lb. (300 gsm)
HB pencil
Masquepen
Round brushes, Nos. 4, 8,12
Spray bottle
Fritch scrubber, No. 4

TECHNIQUES USED
Variegated wash, *p. 20*
Mixing paint in the palette, *p. 21*
Dropping in color, *p. 21*
Wet-onto-dry, *p. 22*
Wet-into-wet, *p. 22*
Masking for details, *p. 25*
Softening masked edges, *p. 25*
Adding highlights, *p. 27*

1 Begin with a rough drawing in HB pencil. A pattern of light as well as the major shapes of the poppies and grasses must be given consideration in the design. The drawing needs to portray a natural rhythm as the shapes dance across the paper.

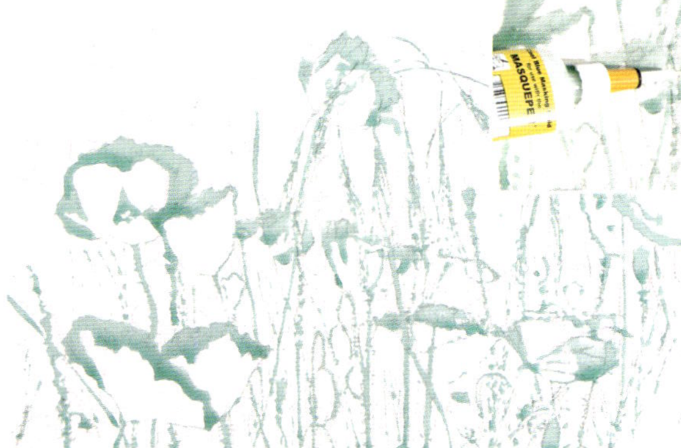

2 The Masquepen (inset) is extremely precise and simple to use. Its blue color is also easy to see against the white of the paper. Mask the shapes of light on the flowers and the shapes of the grasses, stems, and the "fuzzies" on the pods and stalks.

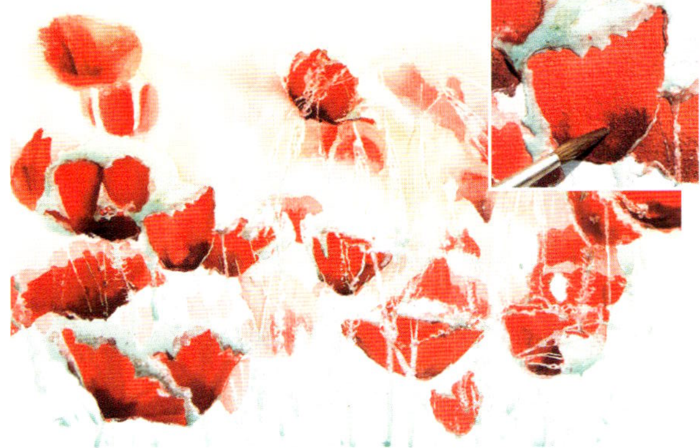

3 With a No. 8 round brush, begin to paint the brilliant red of the poppies (inset). The backlight in each flower is already masked. Use pyrrole red, permanent alizarin crimson, and touches of bismuth yellow to create variety within each shape. Use ultramarine blue and alizarin to create the darks.

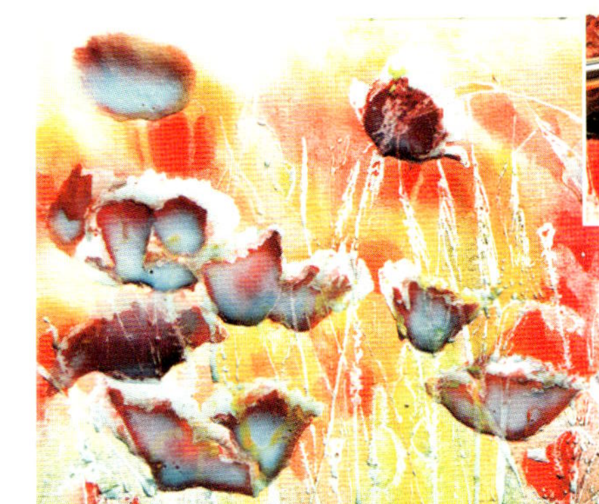

4 Once all is dry, apply more masking over the red flower shapes so that you are able to freely paint "behind" the flowers (inset). When the mask is dry, create a variegated wash by wetting the entire sheet of paper with a spray bottle and, with a No. 12 brush, drop in areas of yellow ocher, pyrrole red, bismuth yellow, and cerulean blue.

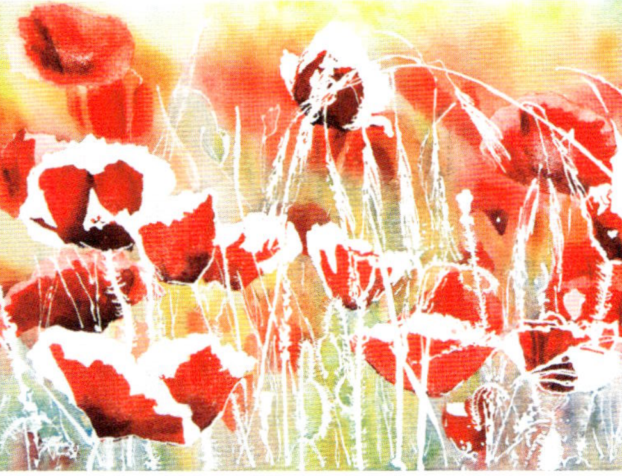

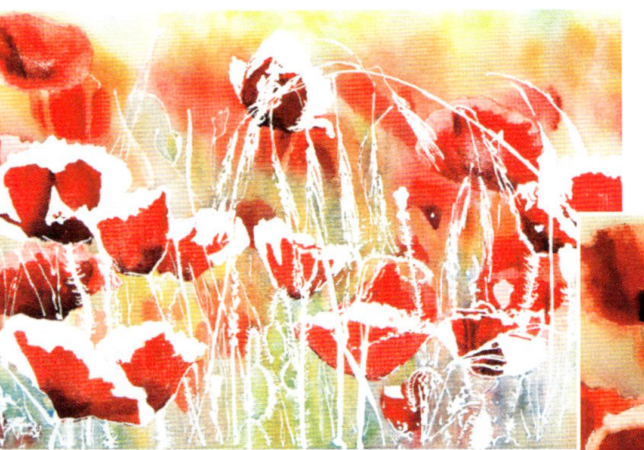

5 After the first background wash has totally dried, go over it once again, rewetting the paper with the spray bottle and reinforcing the color pattern using the No. 12 brush with yellows, oranges, blues, and greens. When dry, remove the masking and begin painting into the shapes with a No. 4 round brush.

6 Continue refining the shapes using a No. 4 sable brush. Use a No. 4 Fritch scrubber to soften the edges and lift lights where needed. Add color and value to the poppies with the two reds. Finally, paint the stems and buds using cobalt blue, Prussian blue, sap green, and azo green.

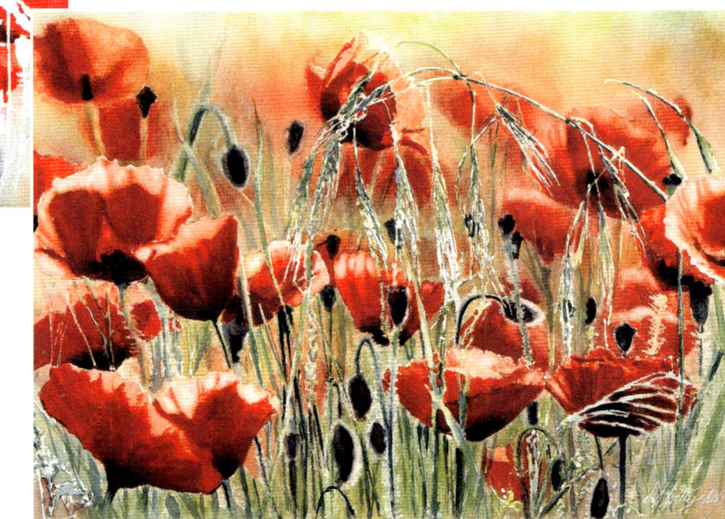

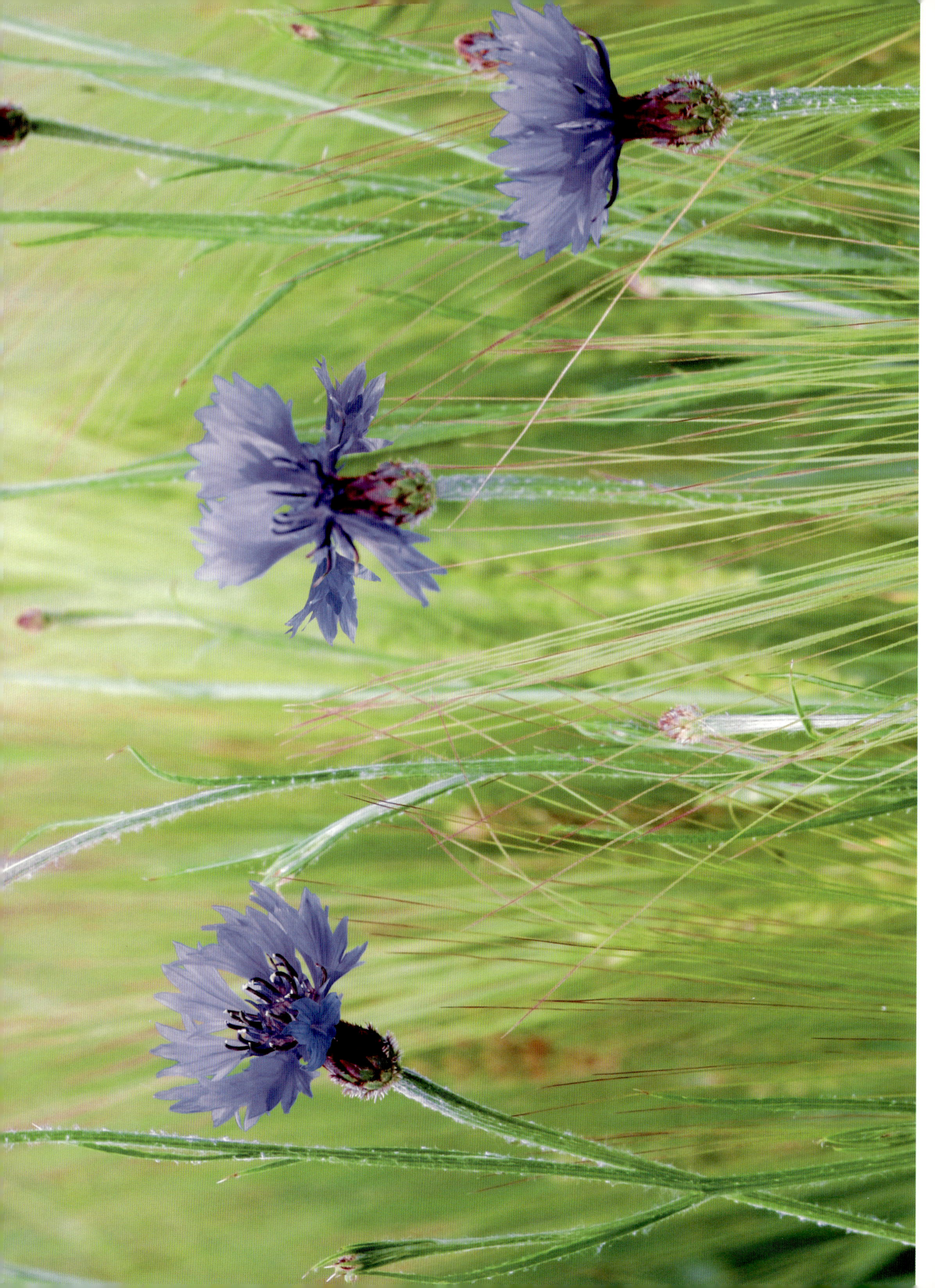

Bachelor's Buttons

The cobalt blue summer-sky-colored bachelor's buttons peep out from the rich textured grasses. The challenge here is to describe the grass shapes in the background without letting them overpower the delicate frilly petals of the flowers.

PAINTS
Aureolin
Burnt sienna
Cadmium yellow
Cerulean blue
Cobalt blue
Indian red
Indigo
Quinacridone pink
Yellow ocher
Zinc white designers' gouache

MATERIALS
Cold-pressed paper, 140 lb. (300 gsm)
HB pencil
Masking fluid
Old brush
Round brushes, Nos. 1, 5, 12
Masking tape
Rigger, No. 0

TECHNIQUES
Variegated wash, *p. 20*
Mixing paint in the palette, *p. 21*
Dropping in color, *p. 21*
Wet-onto-dry, *p. 22*
Wet-into-wet, *p. 22*
Masking to reserve the paper, *p. 25*
Watercolor and gouache, *p. 32*

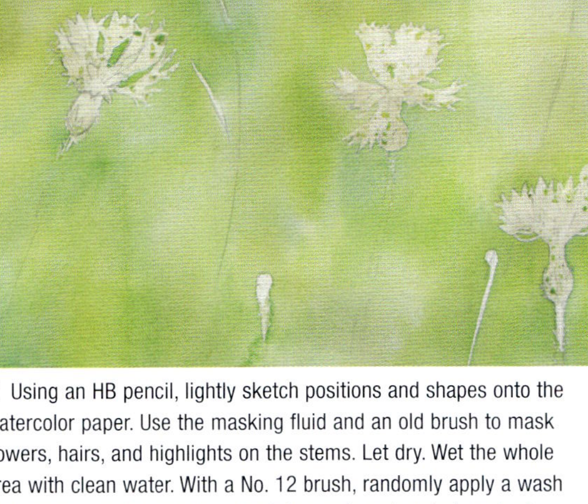
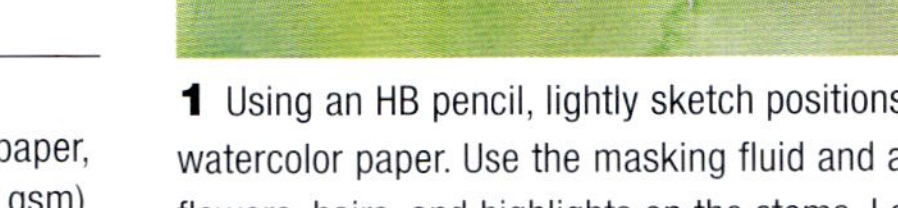

1 Using an HB pencil, lightly sketch positions and shapes onto the watercolor paper. Use the masking fluid and an old brush to mask flowers, hairs, and highlights on the stems. Let dry. Wet the whole area with clean water. With a No. 12 brush, randomly apply a wash of aureolin. Let dry and then wash in a pale variegated wash of cerulean blue and cobalt blue, allowing the paint to create backruns and lively textures. Let dry.

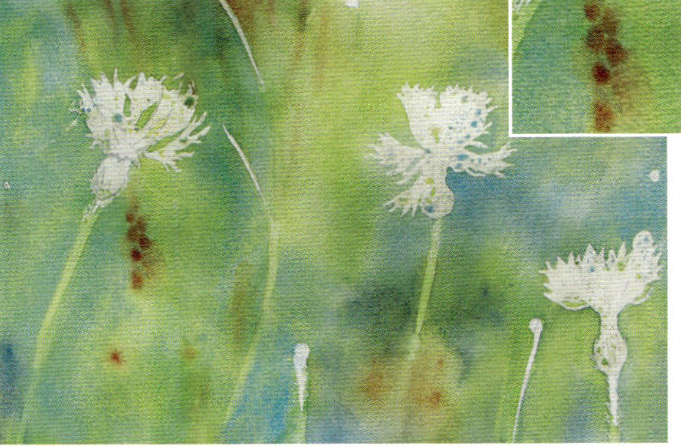

2 Wet the surface again with clean water. Use a No. 5 brush to paint pale washes of cerulean blue, indigo, Indian red, and burnt sienna. Drop in wet-into-wet blots and marks to represent the grass seed heads and background shapes (inset). Avoid painting the stems, which will now start to emerge from the background.

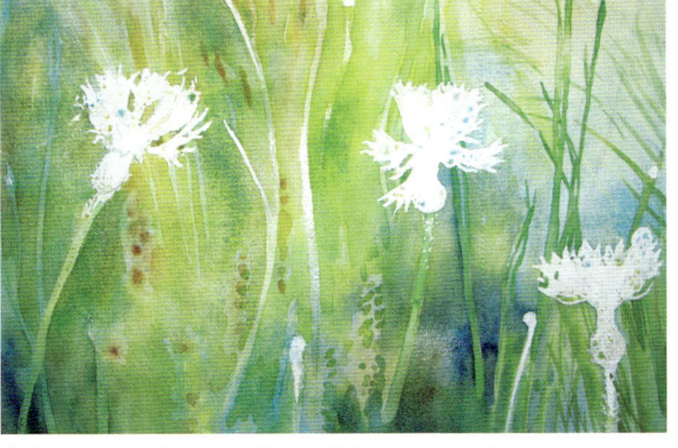

3 Continue to paint the background shapes, using stronger, darker mixes of the different blues and yellows. Paint the more defined shapes with crisp grass-blade edges. Wash in deeper shadow areas using indigo. Let the paint granulate for texture. Lay washes of yellow ocher over the grass area to soften into the background as required.

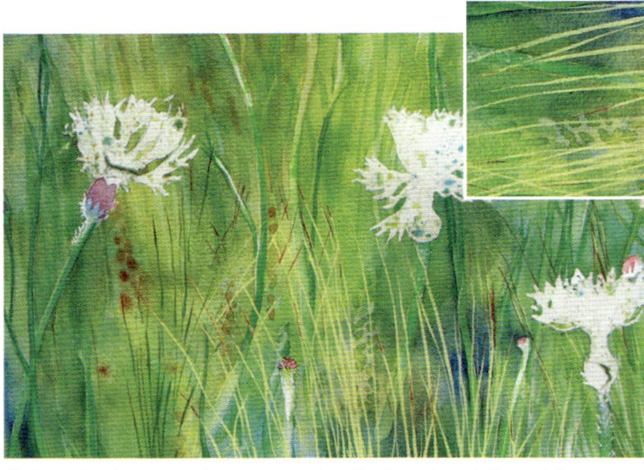

4 To paint foreground grasses, mix a body color of zinc white designers' gouache with yellow ocher. Lay masking tape along the bottom edge of the painting, and turn through 90 degrees. Using the rigger, support your wrist and make sweeping strokes from right to left—lift the rigger at the top end of the stroke to mimic the tip of the grass (inset). When dry, add Indian red to the tip. Remove the masking tape and fluid. With the No. 5 brush, start to paint the buds with quinacridone pink.

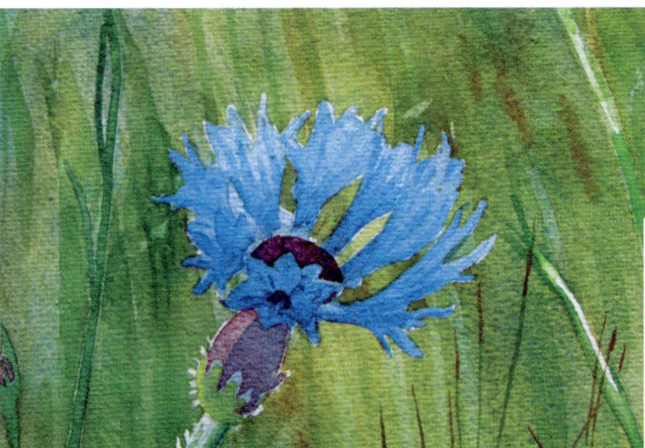
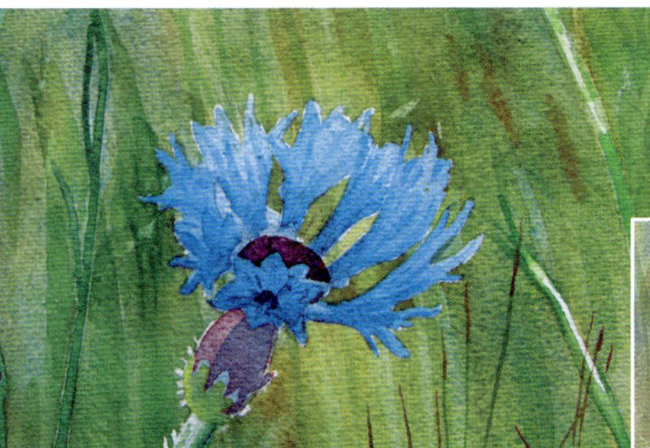

5 Using the No. 5 brush, paint the petal shapes in successive layers of cobalt blue, letting the paint dry between each. Paint the round base shape of the flower with mixes of pink and cobalt blue. Paint the bracts with a yellow-green mix.

6 With a No. 1 brush, paint the filaments with indigo. Drop white gouache on the tip for the anthers. On the bracts, leave touches of the green from step 5. Paint the detail with mixes of pink and indigo.

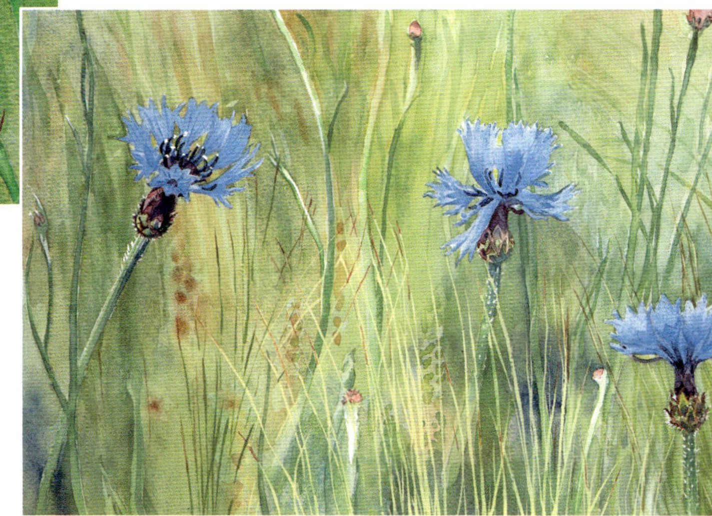

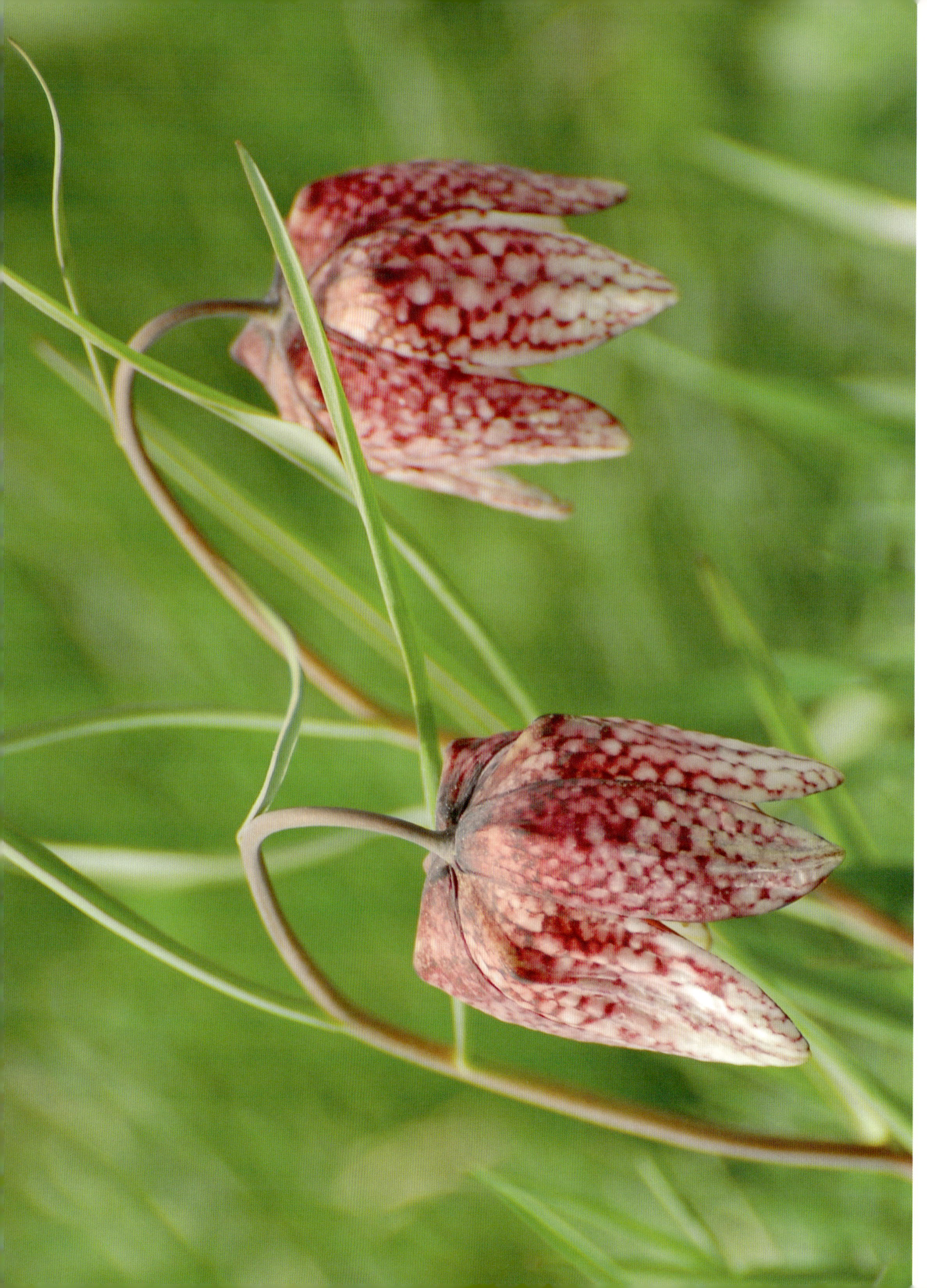

Fritillaria

The pink and magenta colors of the nodding flowers are beautifully complemented by vibrant green hues. Soft-focus leaves and grasses in the background give a strong sense of depth.

PAINTS
Hansa yellow medium
Hooker's green
Phthalo blue
Purple magenta
Quinacridone red

TOOLS & MATERIALS
Cold-pressed paper, 140 lb. (300 gsm)
HB pencil
Masking fluid
Old brush
Round brushes, Nos. 4, 6, 8, 10
½-in. (1.2-cm) angled shader
Scrubber

TECHNIQUES
Graded wash, *p. 20*
Variegated wash, *p. 20*
Mixing paint in the palette, *p. 21*
Wet-onto-dry, *p. 22*
Wet-into-wet, *p. 22*
Glazing, *p. 23*
Blending, *p. 24*
Masking to reserve the paper, *p. 25*
Softening masked edges, *p. 25*
Shadows, *p. 28*
Negative painting, *p. 28*

1 Draw the flower in detail in pencil onto the watercolor paper. Next, apply a thin line of masking fluid along the outside edges of all the petals and stems, and a few leaves. Let dry completely before applying paint.

2 To begin the background, apply Hansa yellow medium wet-into-wet with a No. 10 brush. Create random, overlapping stems, leaves, and blades of grass. Define a few leaves and stems with a very thin glaze of Hooker's green applied to slightly damp paper with a No. 8 brush.

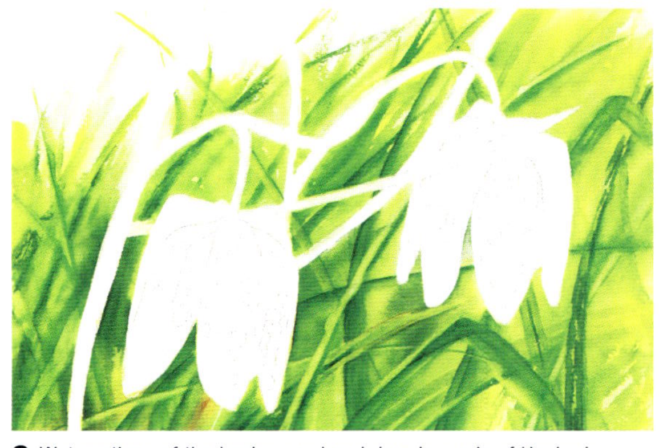

3 Wet sections of the background and drop in a mix of Hooker's green toned down with a touch of purple magenta. When the sheen has disappeared, lift out overlapping leaf and stem patterns with a damp shader. Create darker leaves and stems with the green mix.

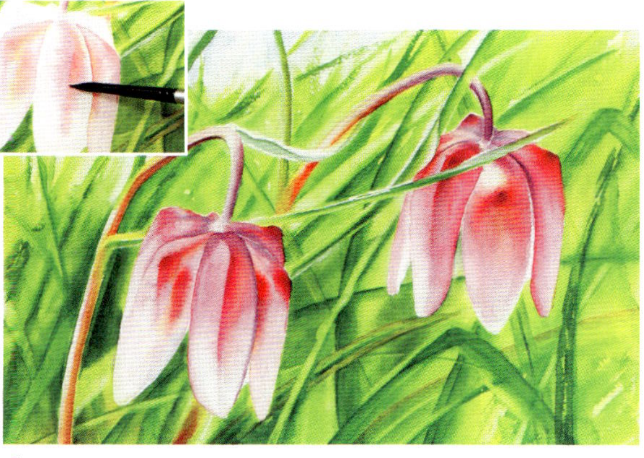

4 Working wet-into-wet, apply Hansa yellow medium, purple magenta, and quinacridone red to the flowers in separate graded washes with a No. 6 brush (inset). Allow the paper to dry thoroughly between glazes. Create flower stems with variegated washes of purple magenta, quinacridone red, and phthalo blue. Remove the masking and soften the edges.

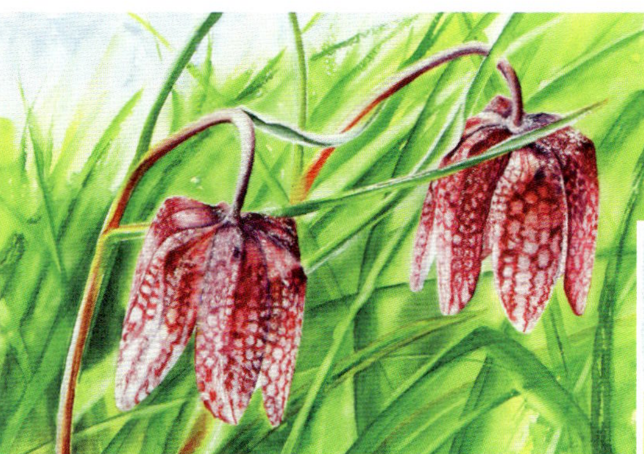

5 Wet each petal individually. When the sheen has disappeared, lightly paint the checkered patterns with purple magenta, quinacridone red, and phthalo blue with a No. 4 brush. When dry, build up rich color in the shadowed areas with several wet-into-wet glazes. Soften hard edges with a damp scrubber.

6 Use phthalo blue wet-into-wet with a No. 6 brush to strengthen the sky in the upper left. Add more purple magenta to the green mix from step 3 and create darker leaves and grasses in the background. Add a few sweeps of green in front of the flowers for a distinct foreground.

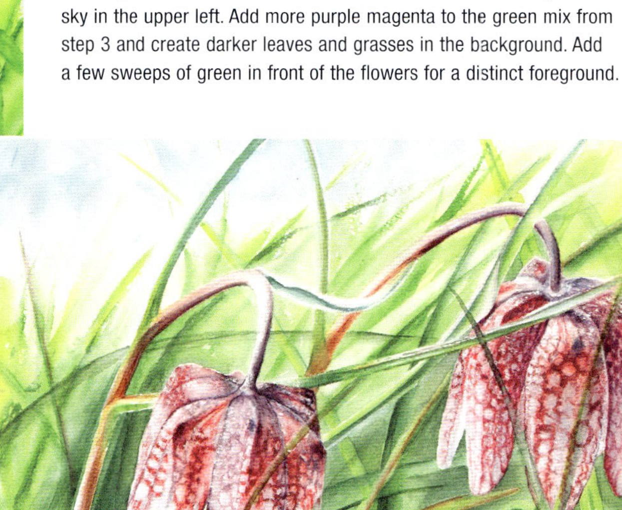

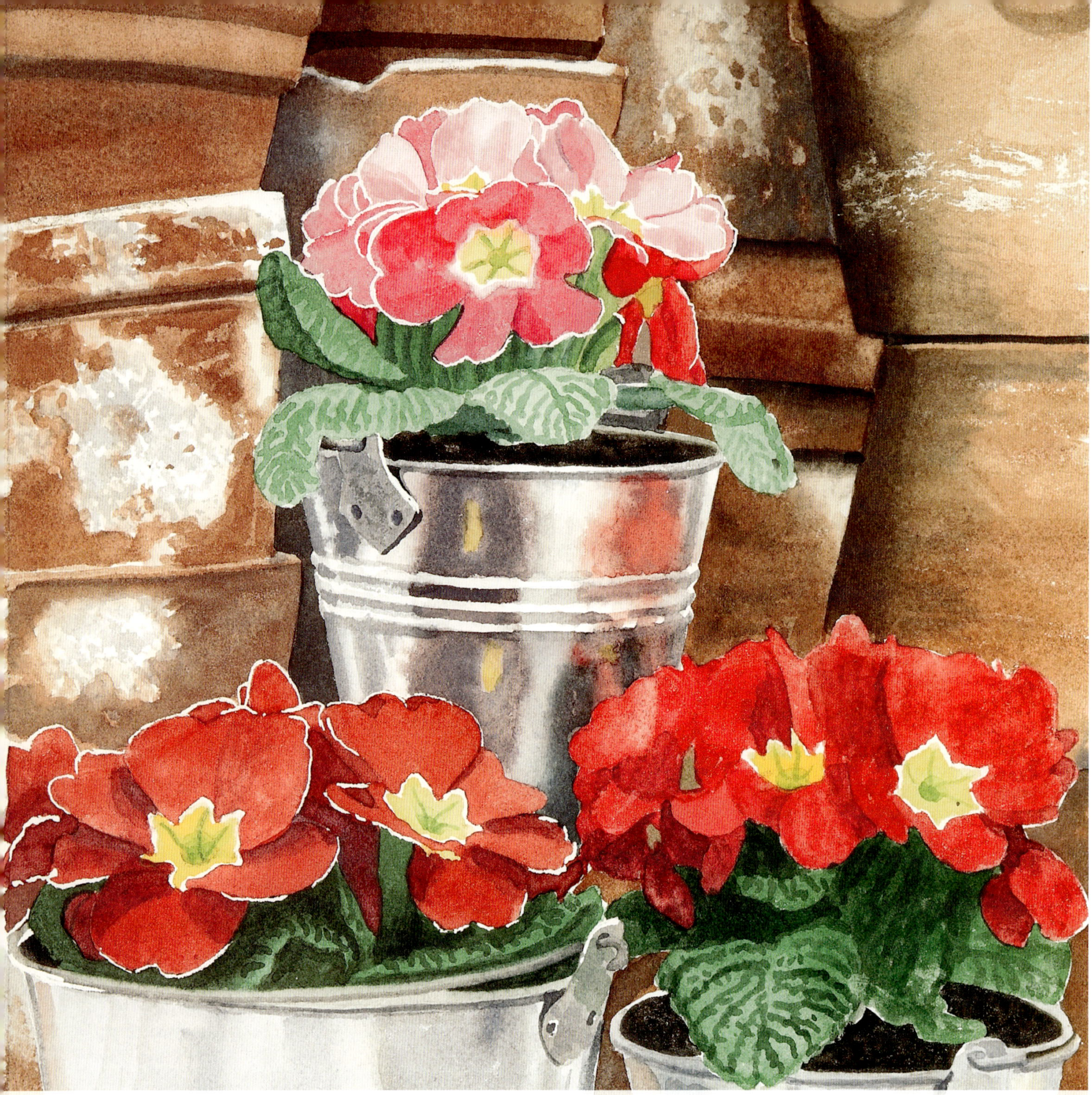

In Detail

In this section, you can view some of the preceding paintings at a larger size, enabling you to examine in detail the effect of the techniques the artists decided to use and how they contributed to the overall exuberance of the finished piece. Smaller images zoom in to the most intriguing parts of the painting, with a professional appraisal of the artist's use of color, light, and technique.

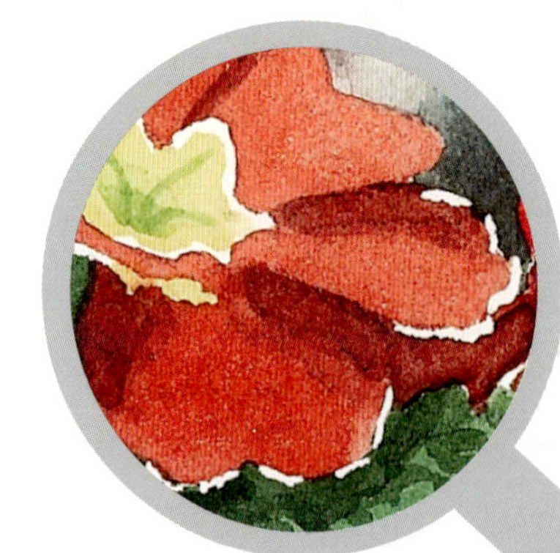

Blue Poppies

Katrina Small (see p. 100)

Katrina achieved this sunny painting of Himalayan blue poppies by using both traditional and nontraditional transparent watercolor techniques. The technique of dropping large blobs of pure color into a wet, variegated wash created the perfect background against which to show the delicate leaf and stem details, painted in white gouache.

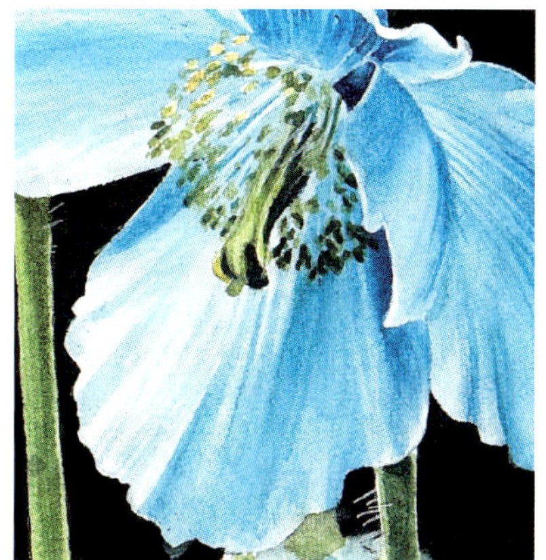

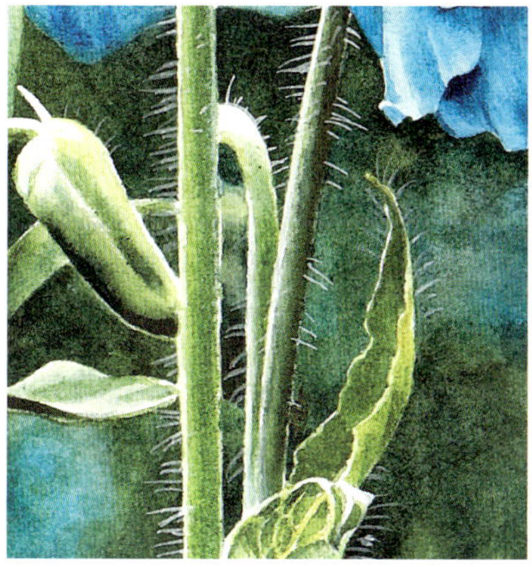

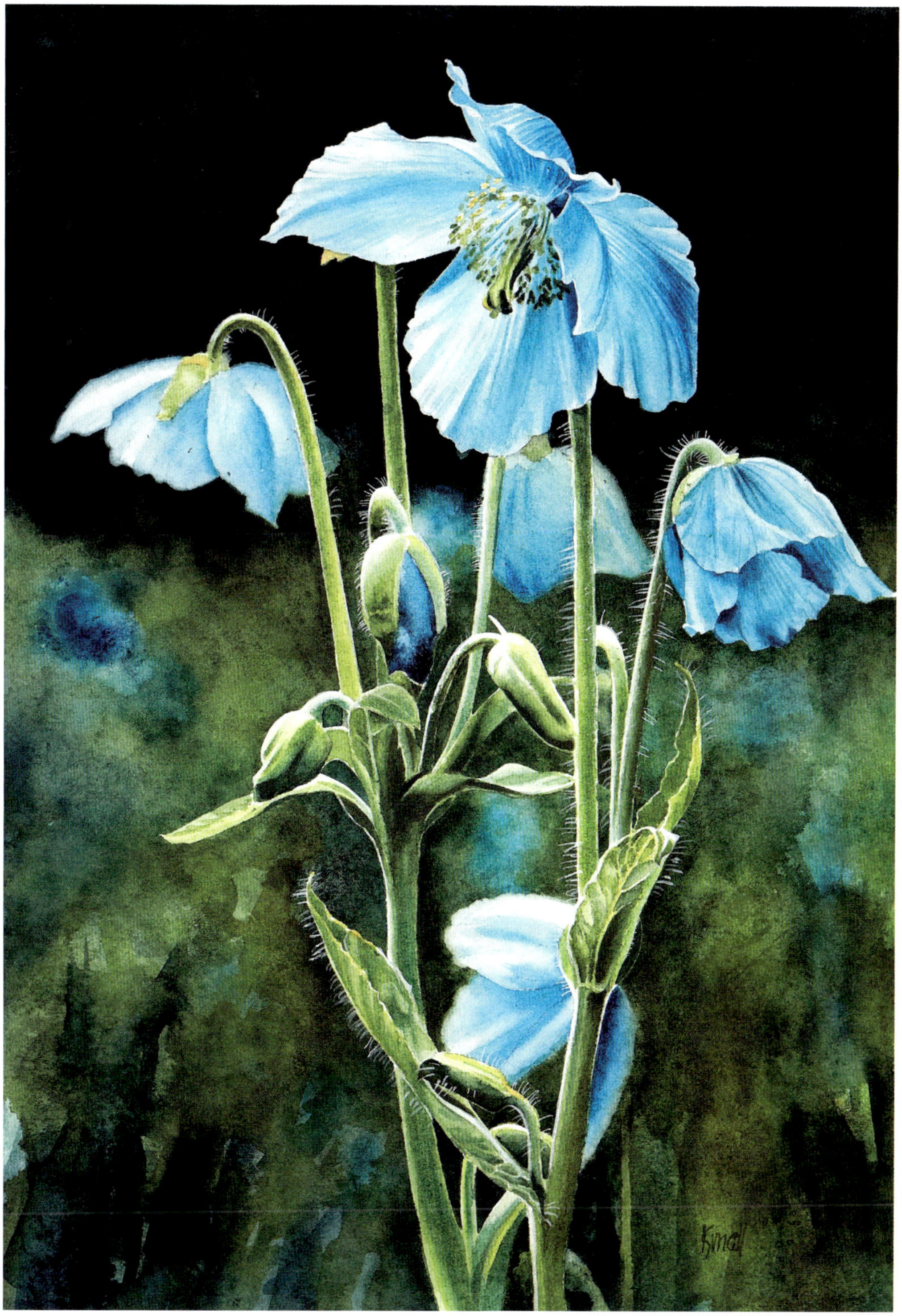

IN DETAIL To make the best possible use of the technique of dropping color into a wet wash, the balance of paint to water had to be just right. The dropped-in color had to have a higher ratio of pigment to water than the color already on the paper, or accidental blooms would have been the result. Katrina showed complete control over this tricky technique.

The viscous nature of most masking fluid can make it difficult to achieve a very fine line, not to mention many fine lines. Also, in the process of painting the complex and very wet background, white could have been lost. In this painting, the artist used a delicate application of white gouache to solve these two problems. The result is a painting in which the fine detail glows against an intense background.

Primroses

Tom Love (see p. 68)

In Tom's tactile painting of primroses, in which there is little doubt the pots are hard or that the petals are soft, two watercolor techniques serve to completely support the main focus—the flowers—and emphasize their softness by convincing the viewer that the pots and buckets are hard. These two techniques were wet-into-wet painting and blending.

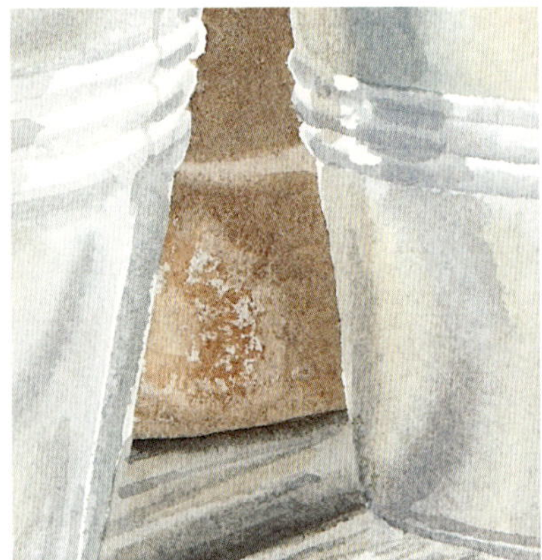

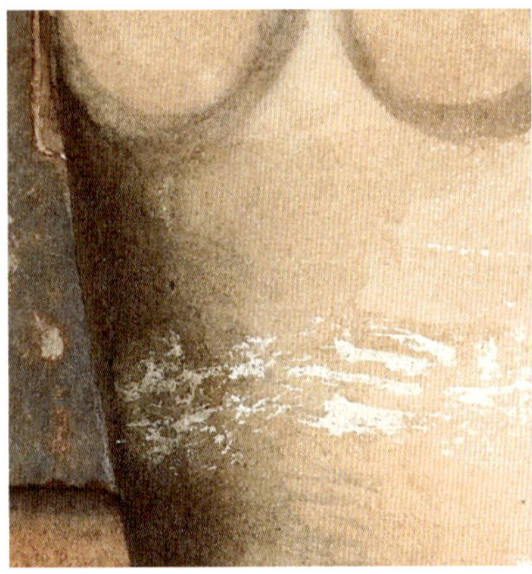

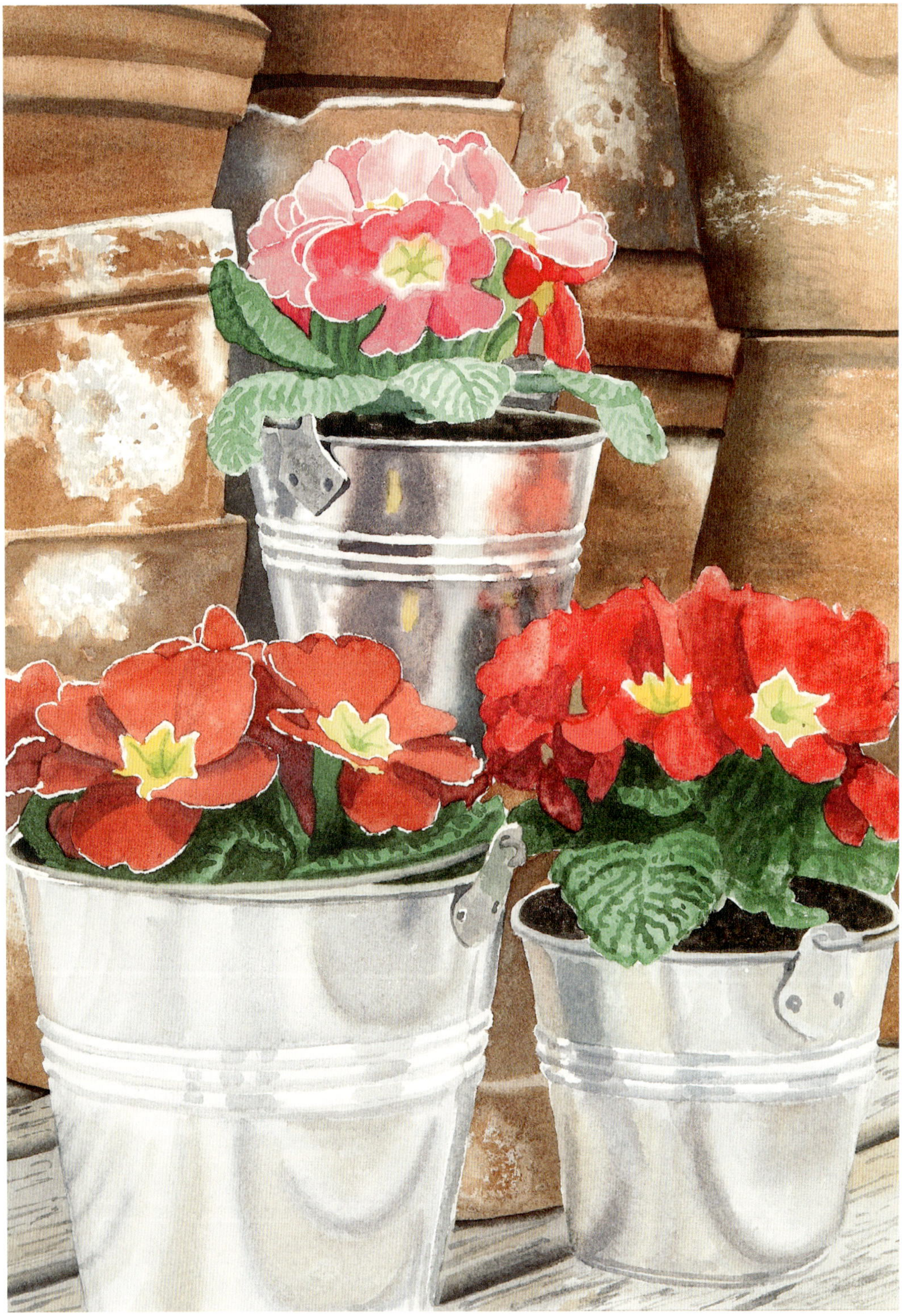

IN DETAIL To paint wet-into-wet, the artist must apply paint to a surface that is already wet. To paint convincing, reflective imagery of pail handles, board slats, and flowers onto that wet surface, the artist here had to have absolute control over a process, which, by design, is not controllable. And he had to understand the exact moment to apply the paint so that it didn't run uncontrollably.

Blending is pulling wet color with a damp brush from an area where it is darker or more intense to an area where it is less intense, creating a seamless transition and a sense of roundness. It is necessary to have the paper wet at the light end of the pull so the color fades into the water.

Heliconia

Connie J. Adams (see p. 78)

Connie's heliconia is an example of two major techniques used together to produce a dramatic effect. Variegated washes—usually used for the background—were here used within the flower petals. In conjunction with this, lifting sharp highlights from some of the petals created areas of focus, since the edges are lost against the light.

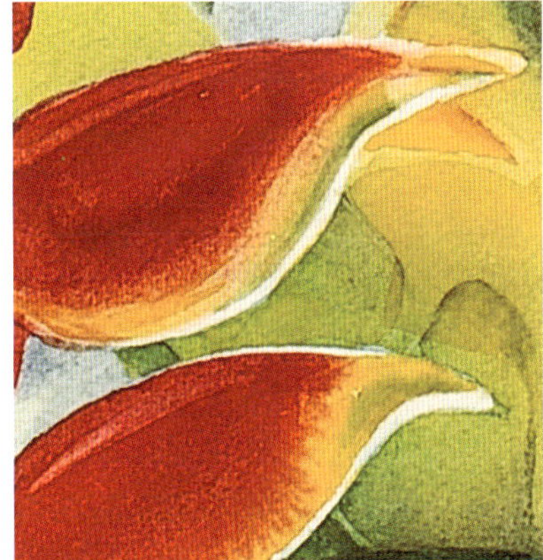

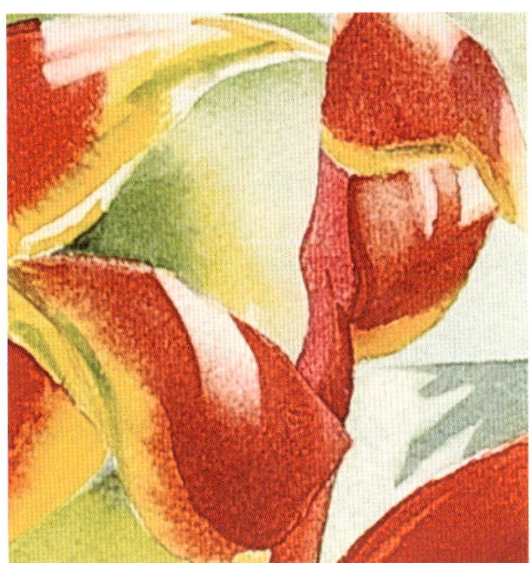

IN DETAIL A variegated wash is often used in flower painting to depict subtle color changes in leaves and petals. The artist made a bold choice and used permanent rose and cadmium red into a wet wash of cadmium yellow. The risk was that the yellow edges would be lost if any of the mixtures contained too much water, but here the results are perfectly controlled heliconia petals that would have been difficult to achieve any other way.

Lifting color is a watercolor technique that can be done in several ways. In this case, the artist chose to mask the area to be lifted with masking tape so that when the color was lifted (by rubbing with a soft sponge or tissue) the result was a hard-edged "shine" on the heliconia petal.

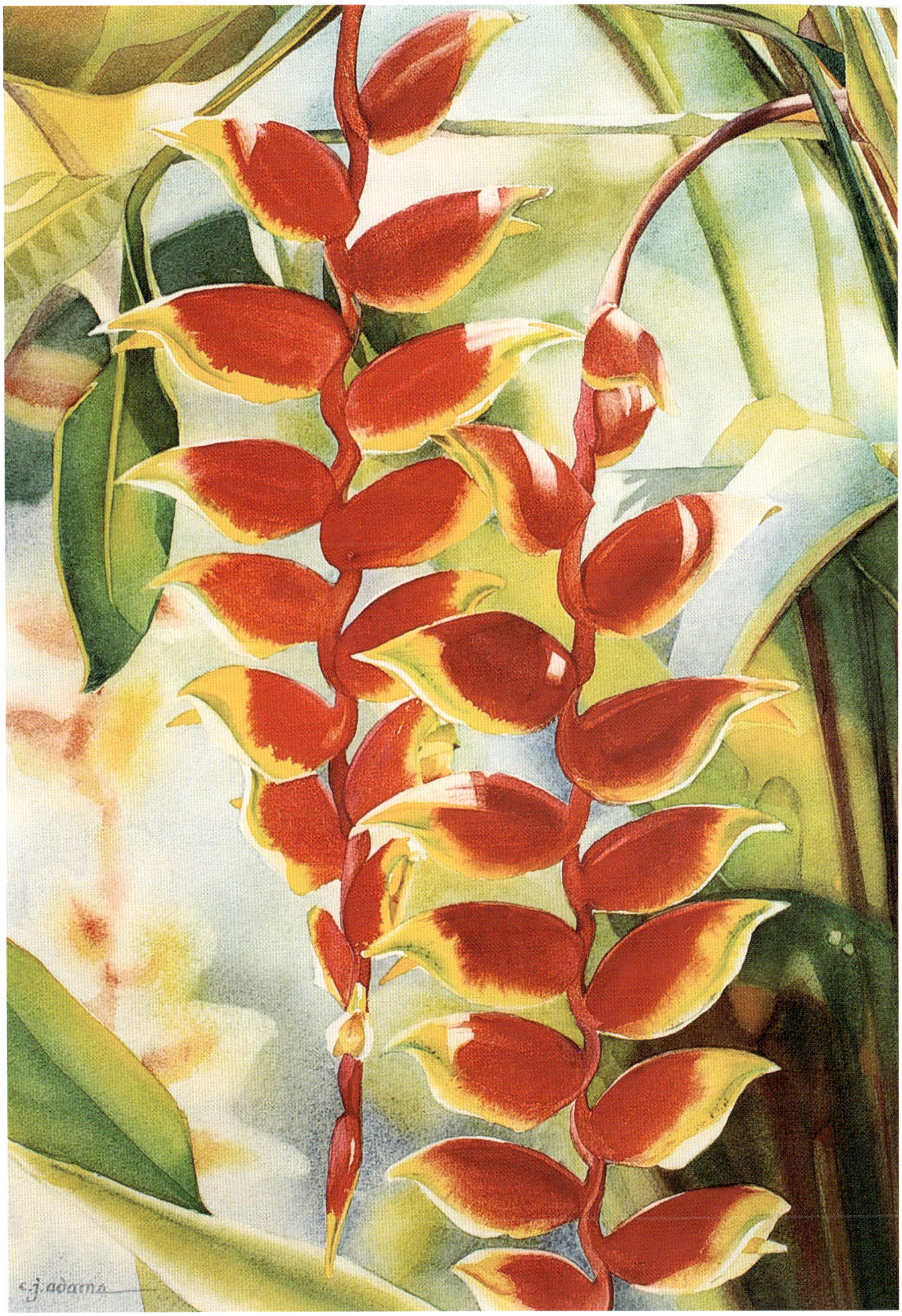

Love in the Mist

Carol Carter (see p. 112)

Carol chose to use two techniques that fit together perfectly—painting wet-into-wet and masking. Covering a paper with flowing water and paint is useful only if the detail to be dealt with at a later stage is protected from the paint. Masking has thus become the tool many artists choose to enable the use of one of watercolor's most cherished techniques.

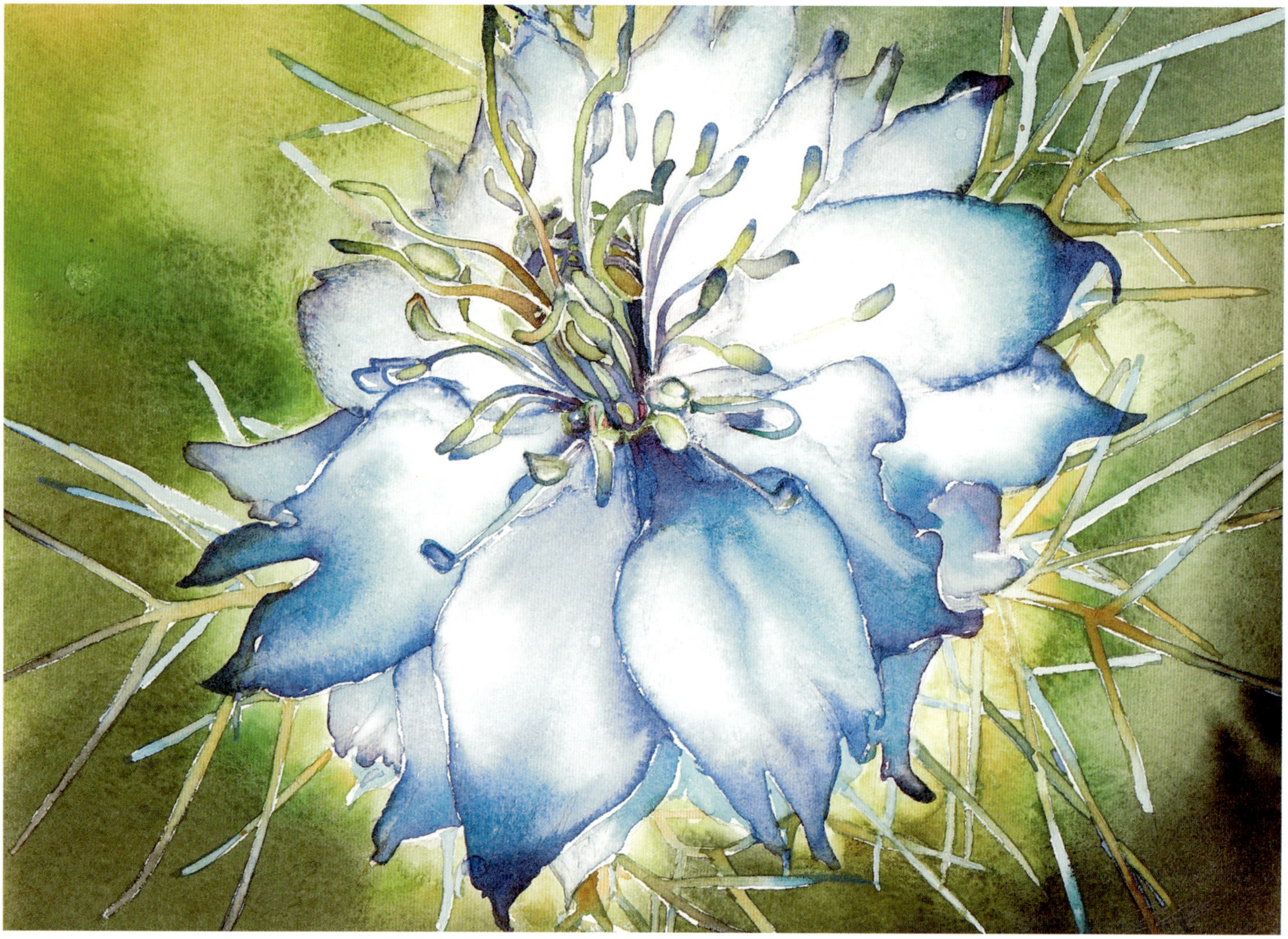

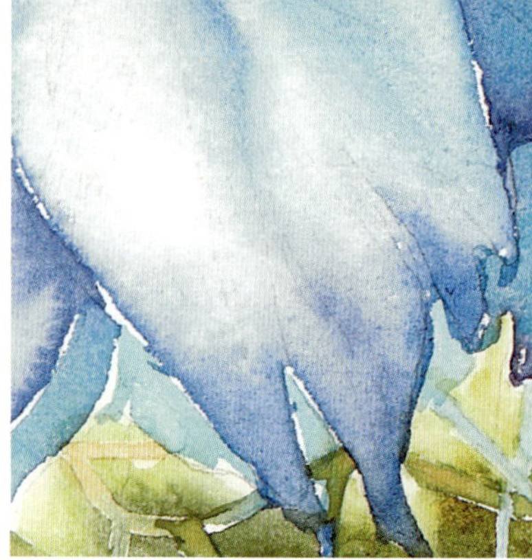

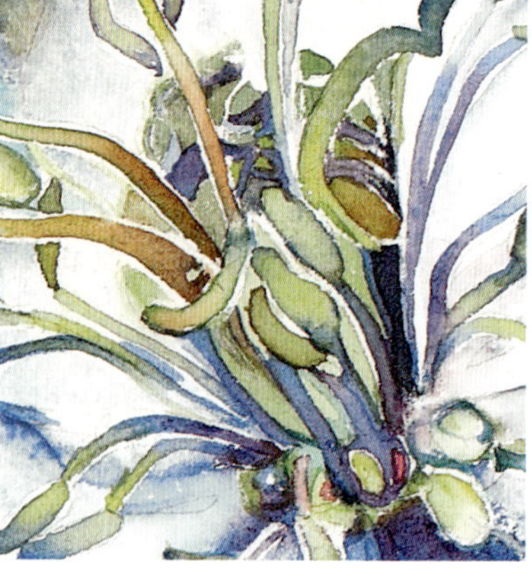

IN DETAIL Painting wet-into-wet can involve the whole sheet of paper or just a small area. In this case, the artist chose to paint one petal at a time using the technique. By wetting the entire petal first, she was able to flow in the subtle, shifting shades of a soft and curving petal; also outlining it at the end to set it apart from the other petals. In this petal you can see how four separate blues flow together seamlessly.

When the rest of the painting was finished, the artist removed the masking and, again, used a wet-into-wet technique to give subtle light and color shifts to the stamens and spines. Using this technique also enabled her to reuse some of the blues from the flower and the greens from the background.

Bluebells

Heather Maunders (see p. 76)

In this beautiful woodland scene, Heather demonstrates the importance of the techniques working together to achieve a unified painting. The two techniques used here achieve the illusion of great depth on a flat surface. The viewer perceives some of these objects as being very close and others as being far away.

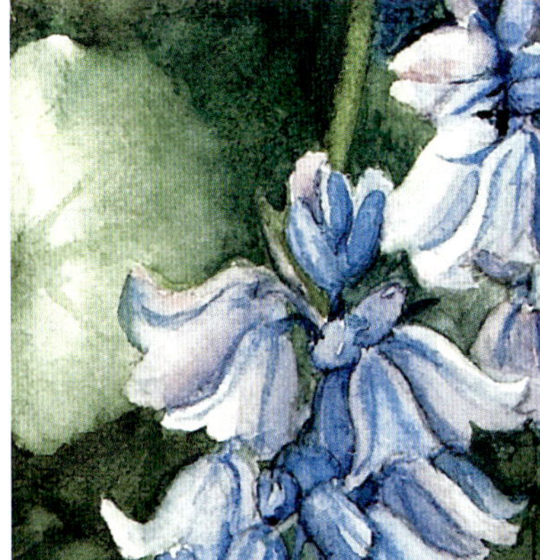

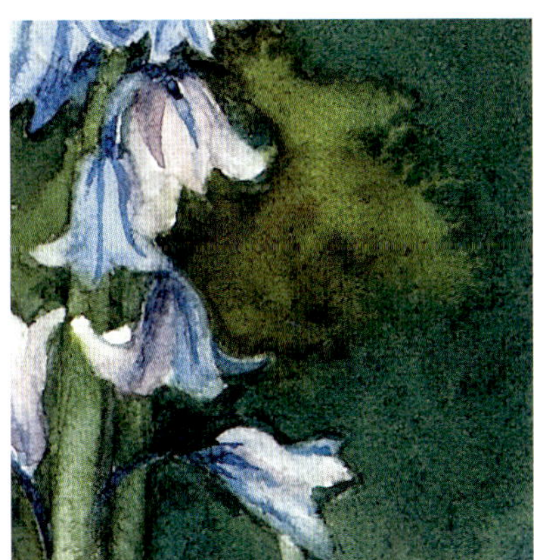

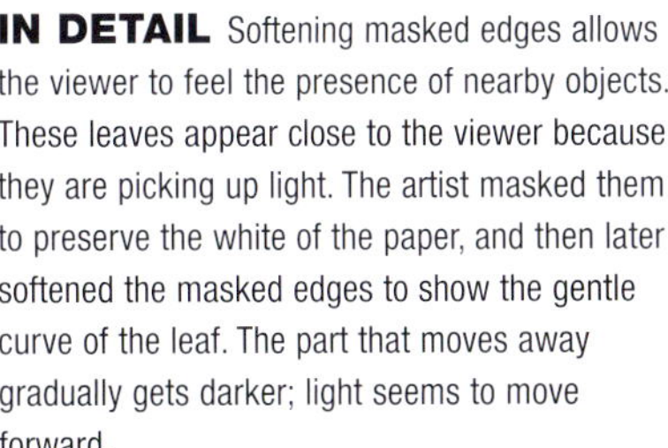

IN DETAIL Softening masked edges allows the viewer to feel the presence of nearby objects. These leaves appear close to the viewer because they are picking up light. The artist masked them to preserve the white of the paper, and then later softened the masked edges to show the gentle curve of the leaf. The part that moves away gradually gets darker; light seems to move forward.

In this intimate scene, the near and the distant are only inches apart on the paper. By employing the technique of charging color into deep, glowing darks, the artist has given the impression that the viewer could reach into the space. Deep, barely discernible shapes and color shifts are perceptible. Into the wet deep green, she charged aureolin, cobalt blue, and ultramarine blue, making the space even deeper and darker.

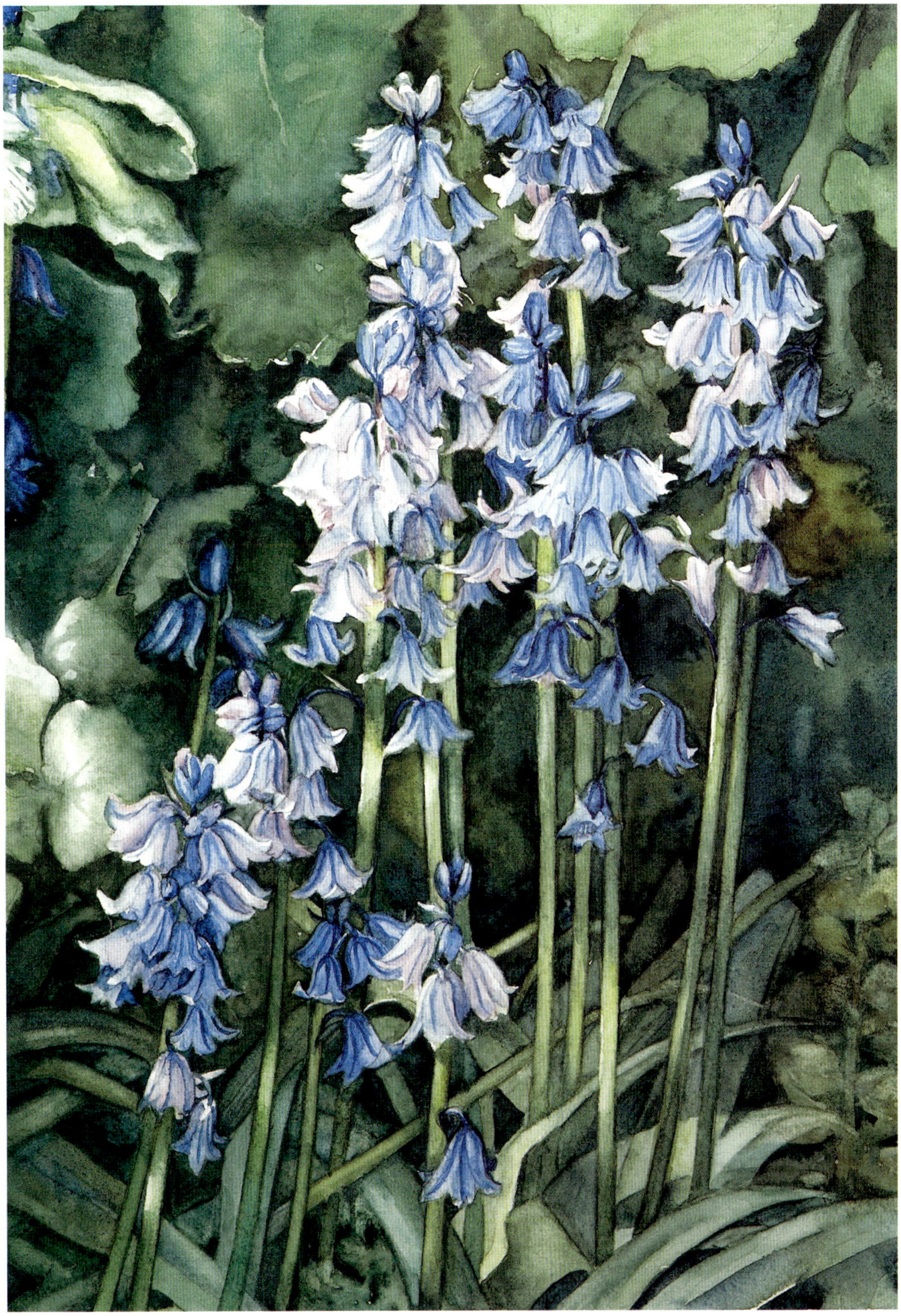

Poppies

Donna Jill Witty (see p. 140)

Crucial to the representation of light in watercolor is the protection of the white of the paper from washes. However, broad juicy washes are also fundamental to watercolor. To accomplish both of these in a single painting, Donna used two signature techniques—the precise masking of areas to remain white and an underpainting of saturated, wet washes.

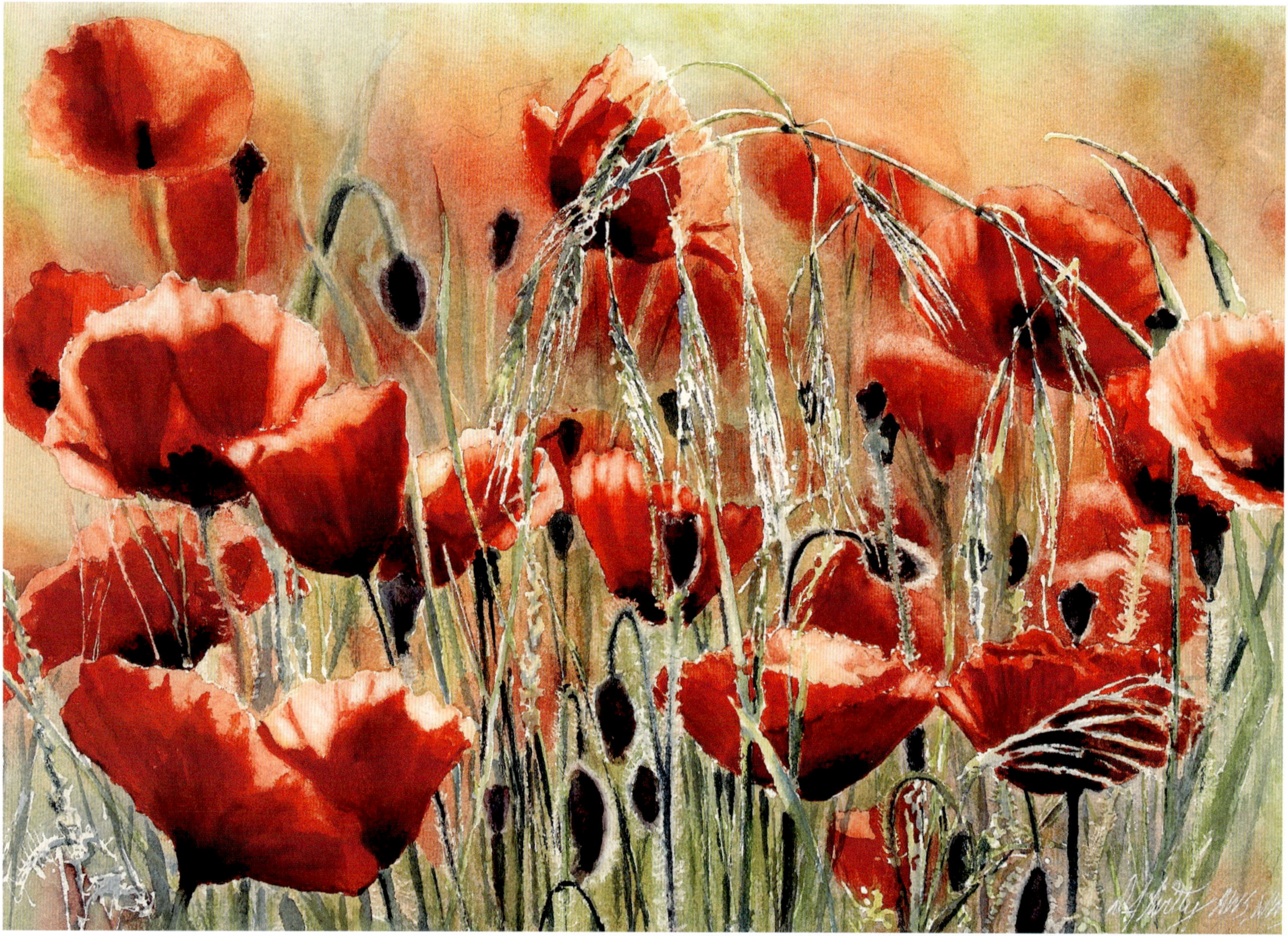

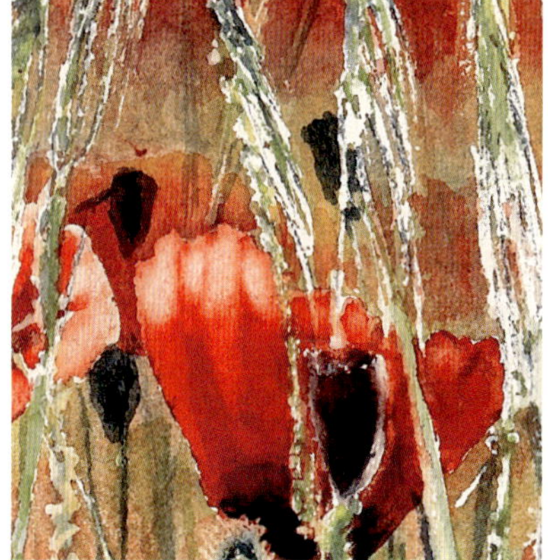

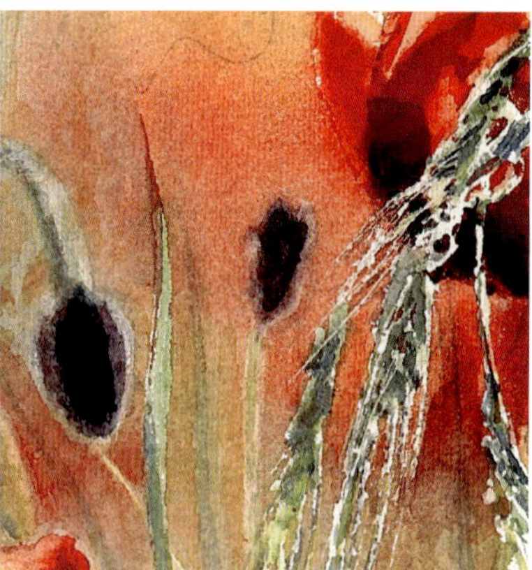

IN DETAIL Masking small and detailed areas in this painting necessitated the use of a special tool—a masking pen. Application of the masking required great patience and thorough drying. This was also the technique that allowed the other critical step to happen easily.

With all the whites protected, the artist freely applied large, juicy washes all over the paper using several colors. The more intense reds of the poppies were also painted at this stage. The pigments were allowed to mix, mingle, and granulate. A unifying underpainting was the result. When the masking was removed, the painting was nearly done.

Calla Lilies

Robin Berry (see p. 62)

Robin chose two complementary techniques to add both glow and dimension to this painting of calla lilies. The use of several layers of transparent washes allowed the color to build while retaining the luminosity of the flower. This set the flower off from the deep background of equally luminous and glowing dark.

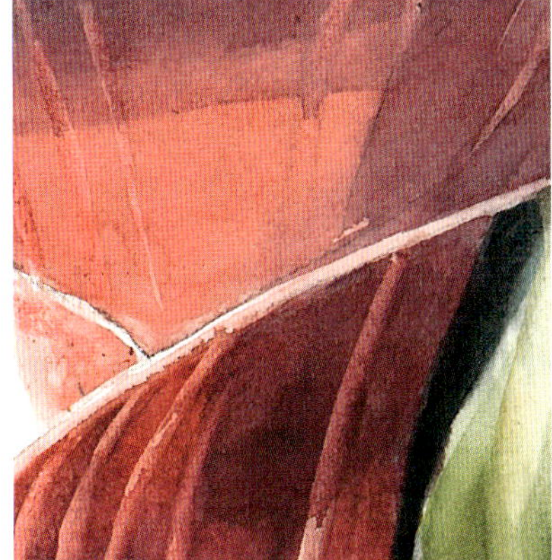

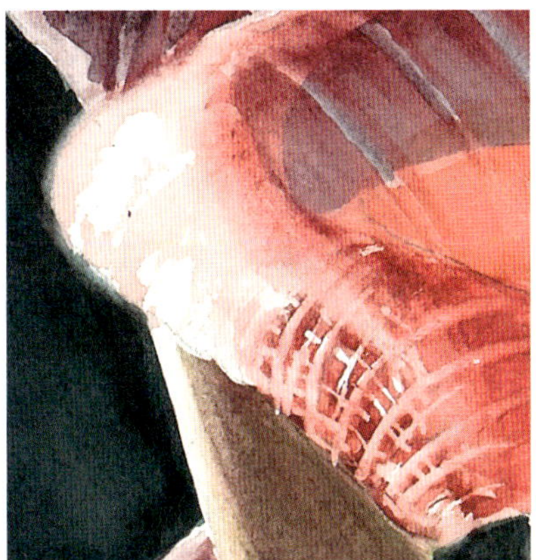

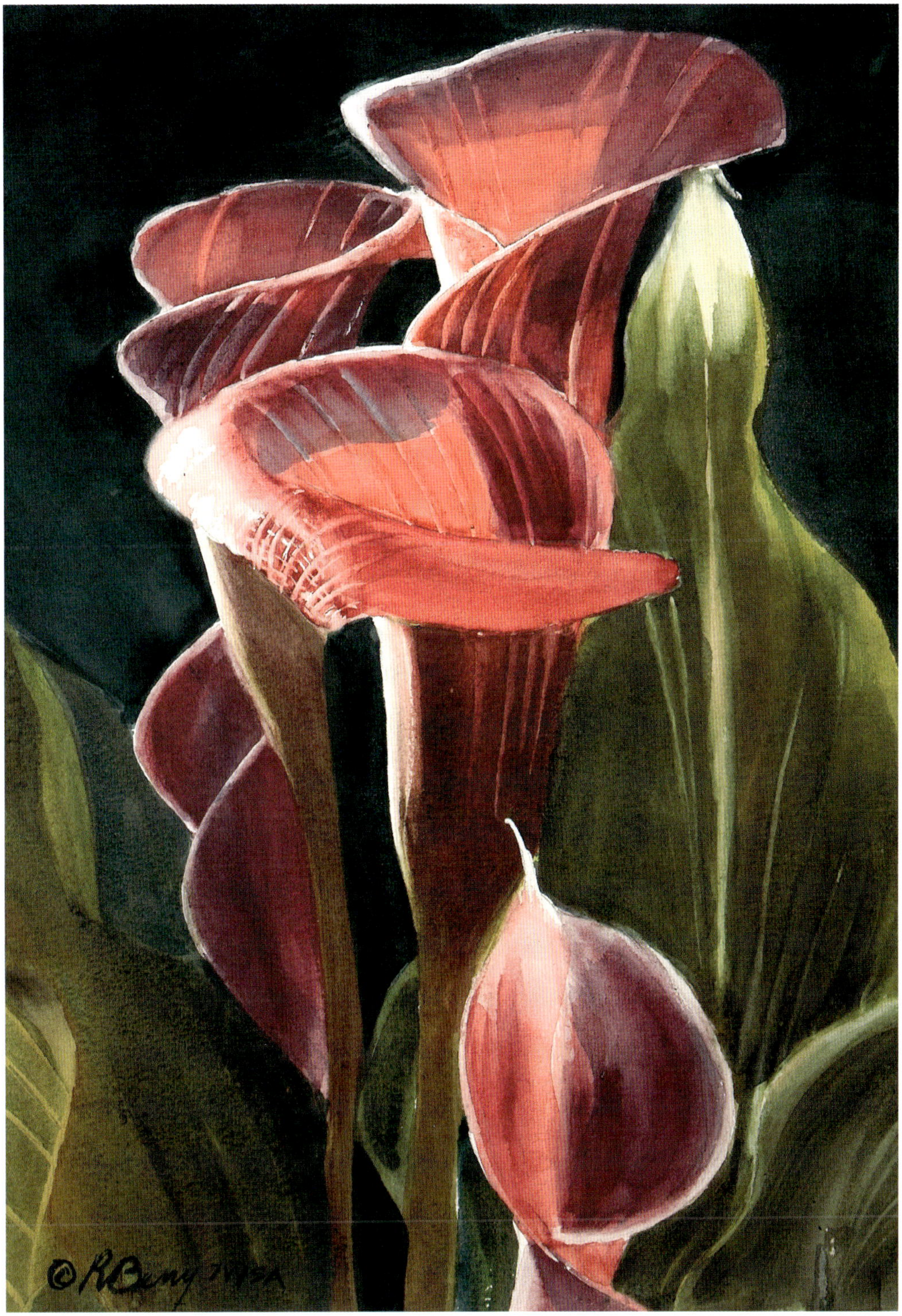

IN DETAIL There are no less than six layers of paint in these flowers, built up light to dark and allowed to dry thoroughly between each layer. It is not always necessary to glaze the whole flower. Shadows showing the rounding of the form or shading by another object can be laid down in certain areas using a different color—in this case, blue.

Had this flower—with its sunlit white edge—been set against a light color, it would not have stood out. And had the background been painted with black paint, it would have been dull and chalky. A glowing dark, like this one, is composed of several transparent colors—in this case, red and deep green, laid down in a single passage, with other colors, such as a deep blue, dropped in. The paper glows through this transparent single layer of dark paint.

Protea

Nancy Taylor (see p. 110)

This was a difficult flower to paint because the photo presented a strong red presence (the closed protea) with a ball of white (the open flower). The issue is balance, since the two flowers lean away from each other. The techniques of dropping in color, especially during the first underpainting, and lifting color at the end helped to create an exciting and balanced painting.

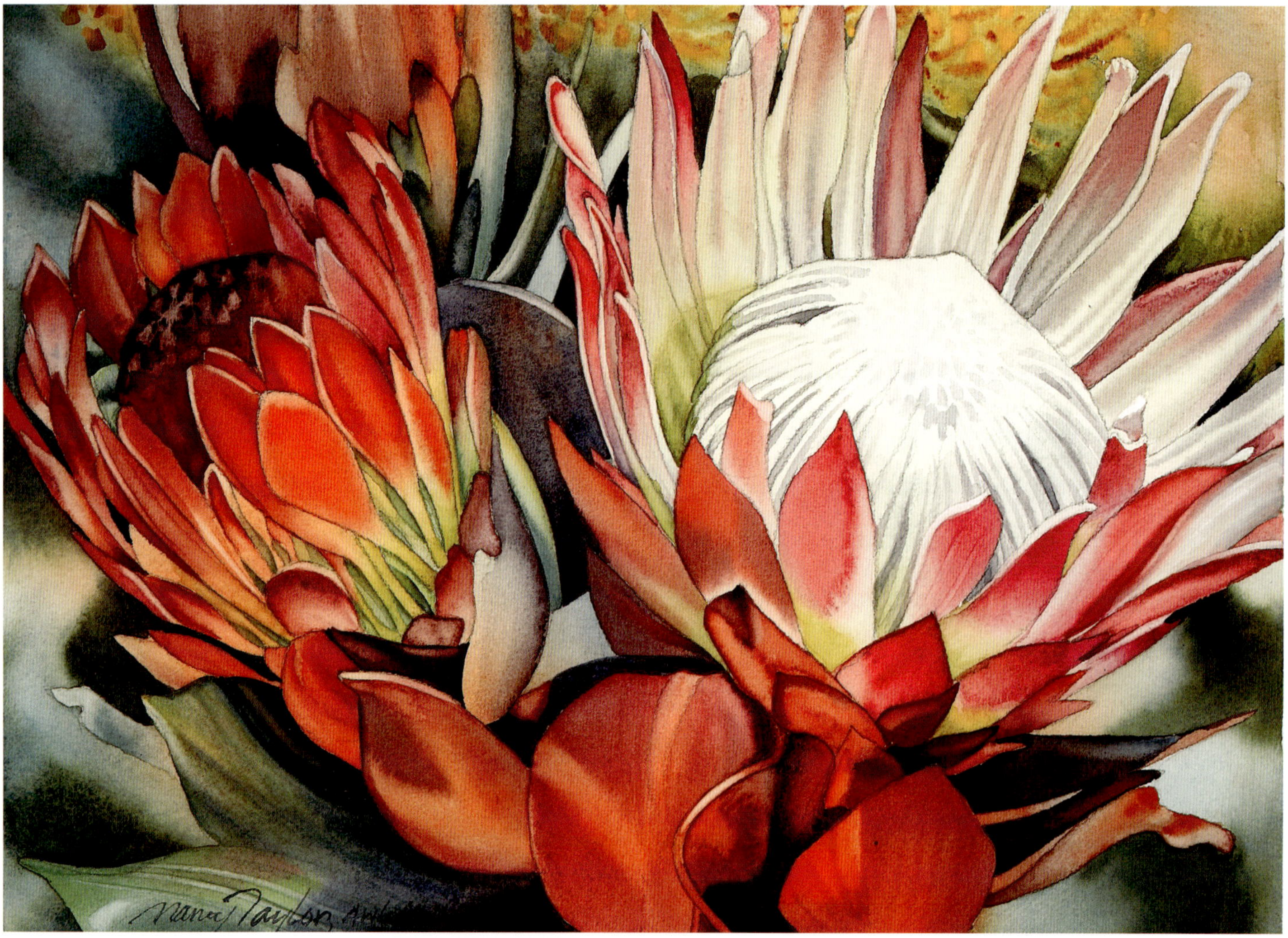

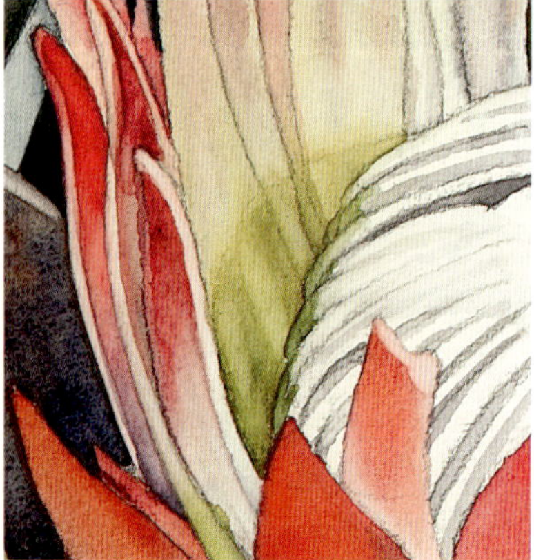

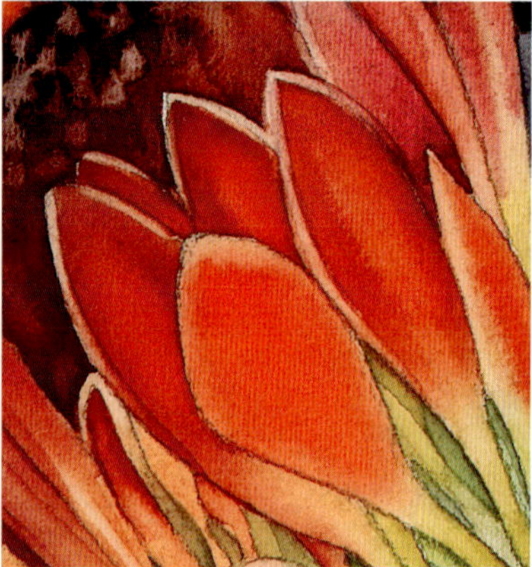

IN DETAIL Underlying the ring of red petals surrounding the white flower is an underpainting of scarlet orange that was dropped in with a wide brush when the paper was first wet and before any detail was added. Although you cannot see it in the finished painting, your eyes can feel its overall unifying power.

A factor in the beautiful balance achieved in Protea was the subtle lifting of red from the tip of each of the petals in the left flower, continuing around the open flower. Although you probably don't notice this as you look at the painting, your eye subconsciously picks it up and this also contributes to the unifying effect.

Parrot Tulips

Lisa Hill (see p.116)

In Lisa's painting, the two techniques that contributed most to the startling beauty of dancing reds across the painting are glazing and the use of rich shadows. The use of glazing unified the painting, while the incorporation of rich shadows both balanced the strong reds (by the use of complementary green) and anchored the vase in space.

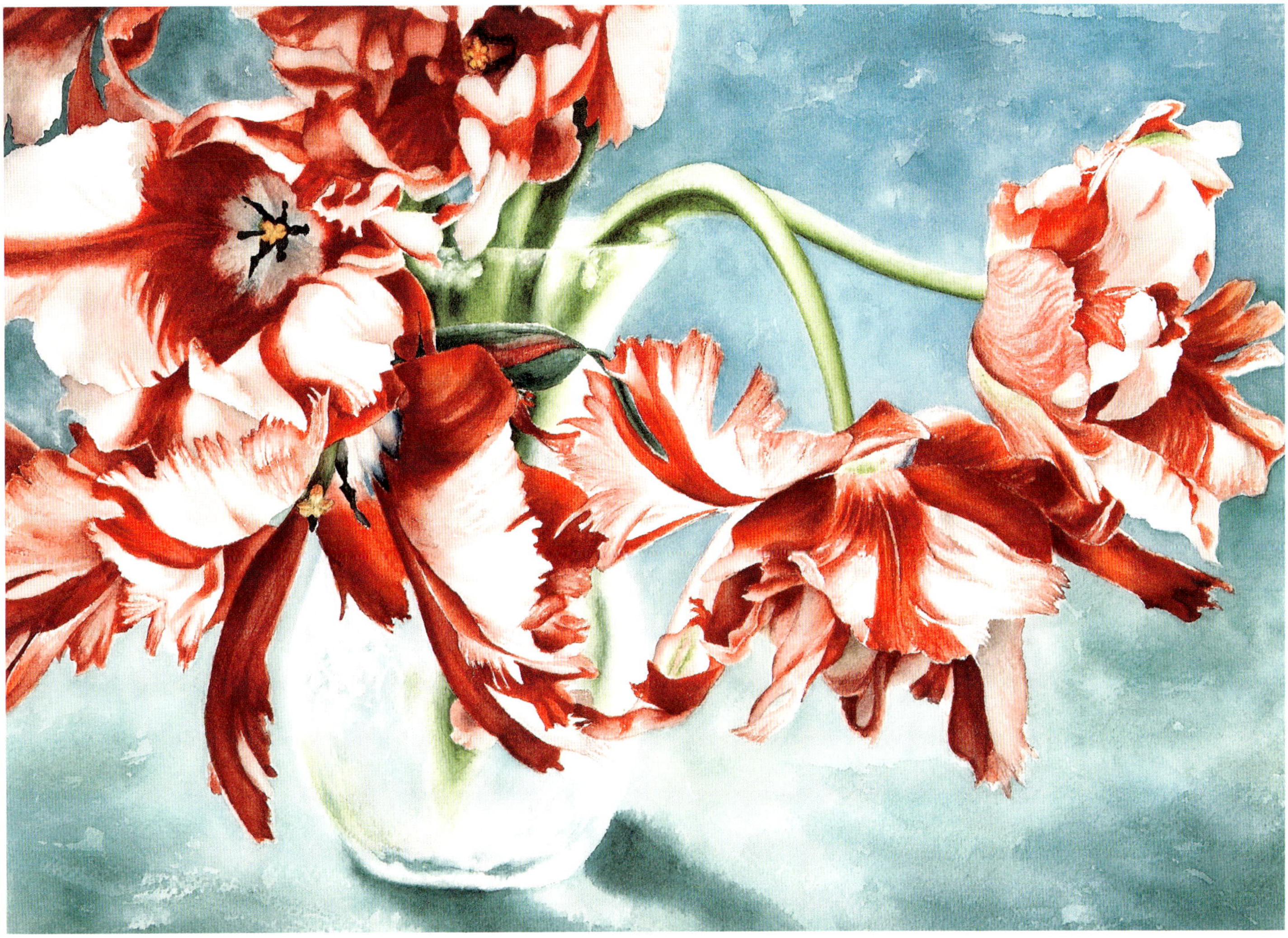

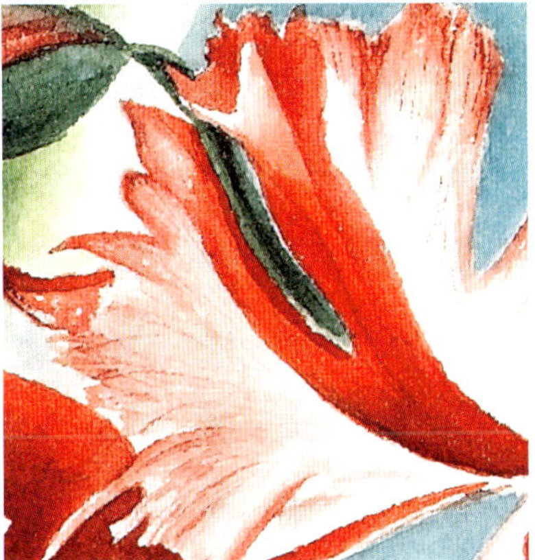

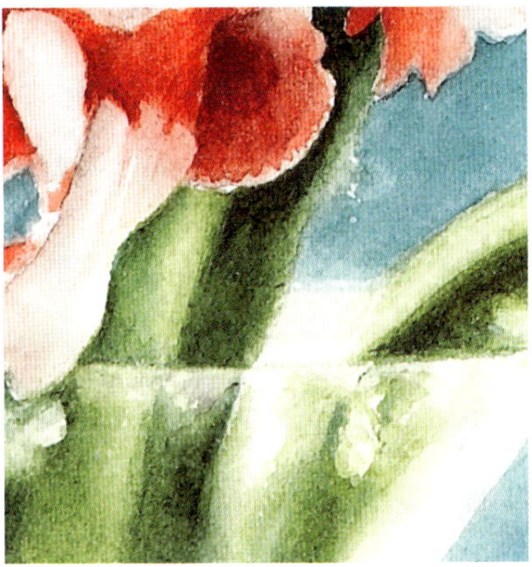

IN DETAIL Glazing is the application of thin layers of color to build up a more intense hue, while still remaining transparent. Each layer affects the one above it. Making sure the paint is completely dry between layers is essential. In Parrot Tulips, the luscious reds you see in the flowers are a result of glazing. Trying to achieve this in a single passage could have resulted in a chalky appearance, while glazing left the colors soft, translucent, and intense.

The tulips are bathed in light and seem about to take flight. The rich shadows at the base of the vase are what give clarity and definition to the light. The choice of the color green was important here, since it is not only the complementary of red—and so sets off the flowers—but provides a dark value in contrast to the white of the paper (the light) of the vase.

Ranunculus

Jana Bouc (see p. 64)

To create this beautiful burst of color and bring to life a complex photograph, Jana used several techniques. Painting wet-into-wet retained the softness of the flowers and leaves, which contrast with strong colors and defining edges. The vase illustrates the use of reflected color both to connect it to the flowers and to show the shiny nature of the surface.

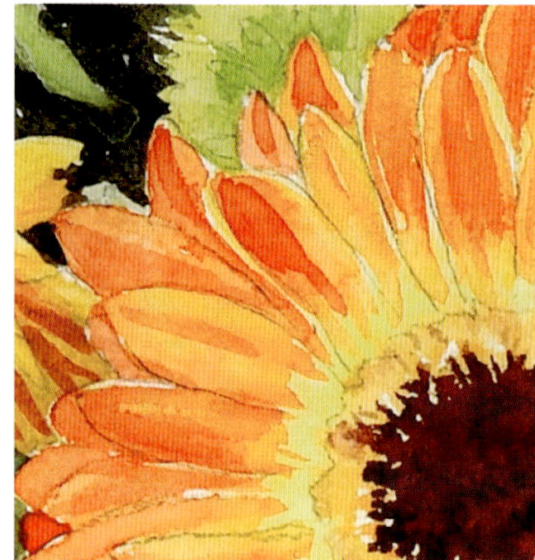

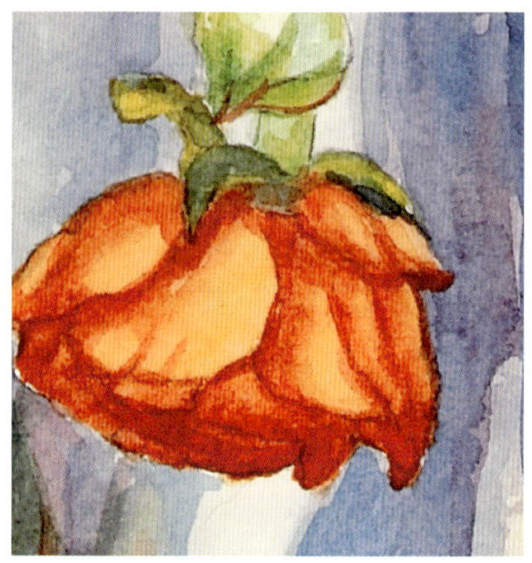

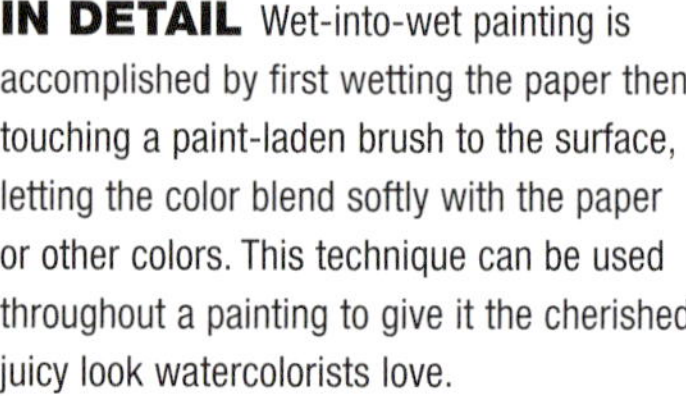

IN DETAIL Wet-into-wet painting is accomplished by first wetting the paper then touching a paint-laden brush to the surface, letting the color blend softly with the paper or other colors. This technique can be used throughout a painting to give it the cherished juicy look watercolorists love.

Wet-into-wet was also used in the vase to show the reflected color. Here the vase was wetted, painted blue, and the colors of the leaves and flowers touched into the surface.

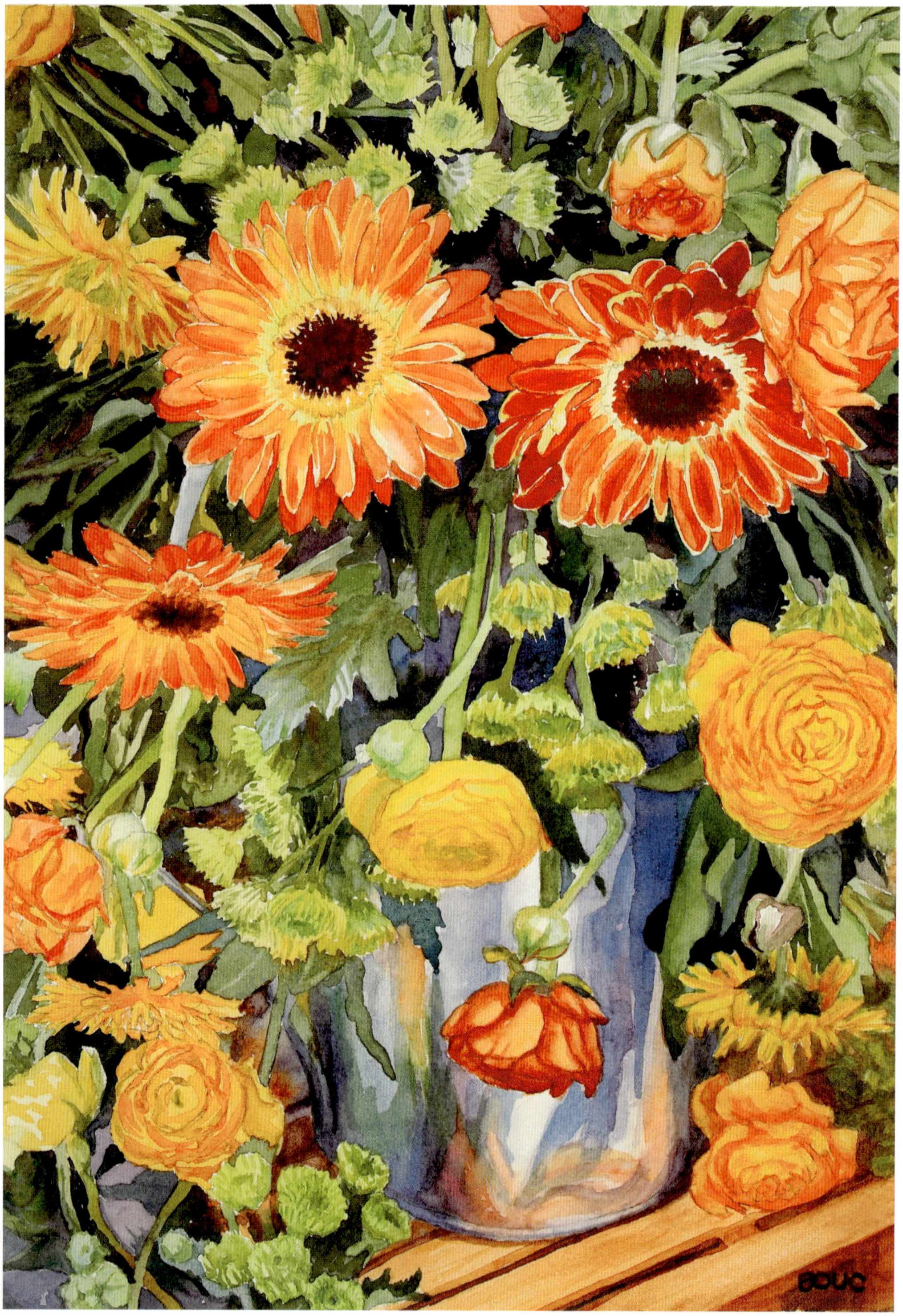

Peruvian Lilies

Denny Bond (see p. 120)

This painting works so well due to Denny's accuracy in replicating the petals of the flowers, both in color and in softness. This was accomplished by glazing, which allows both the colors and the shadows to be applied in a most natural way. To make the liner strokes inside of the flower appear natural, the artist used the technique of blending.

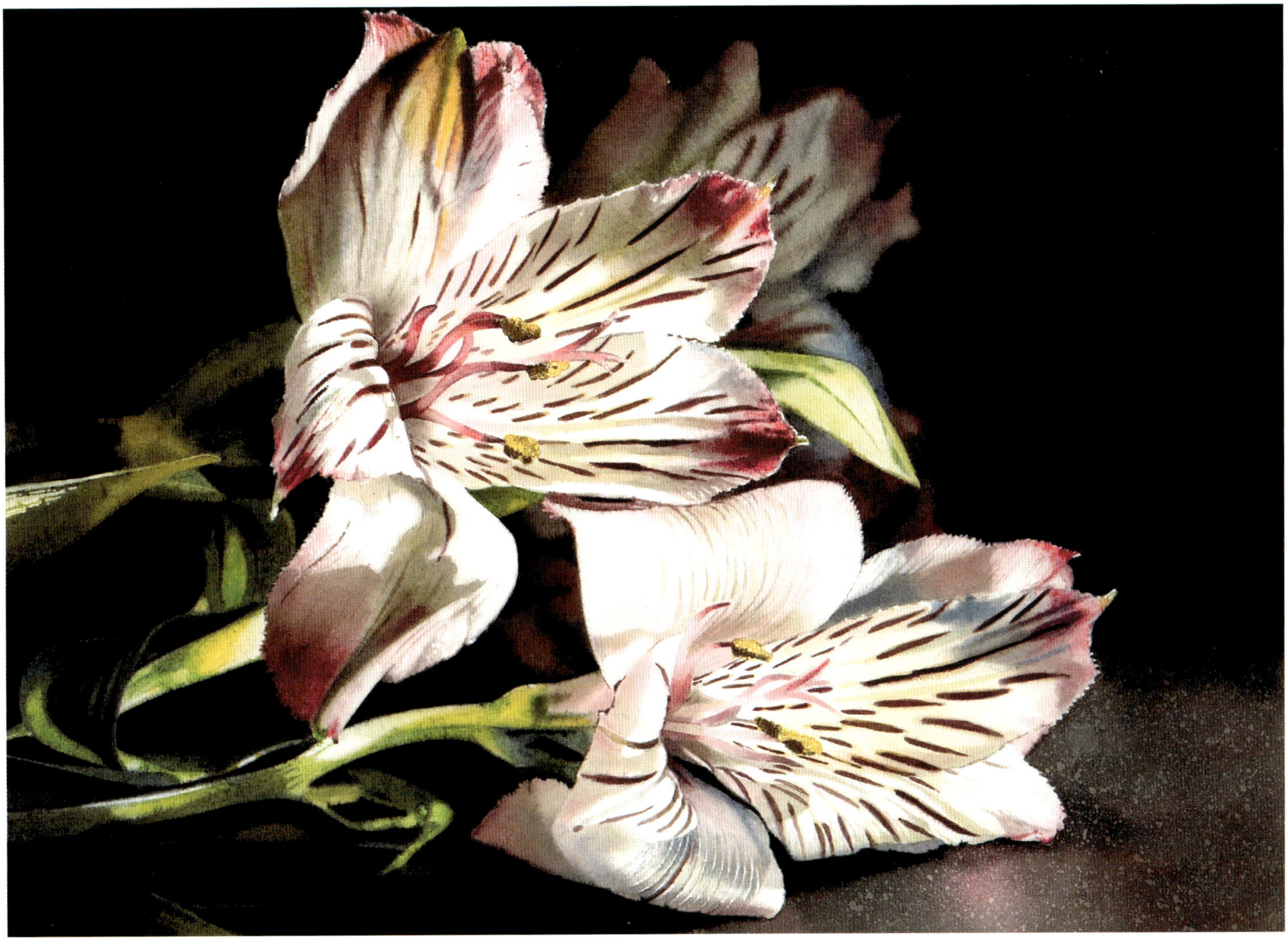

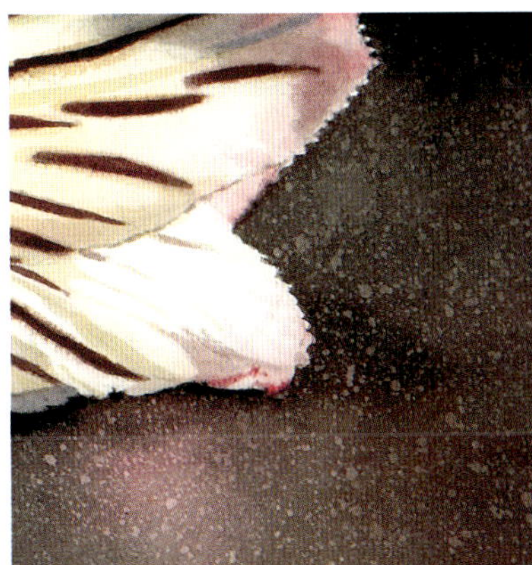

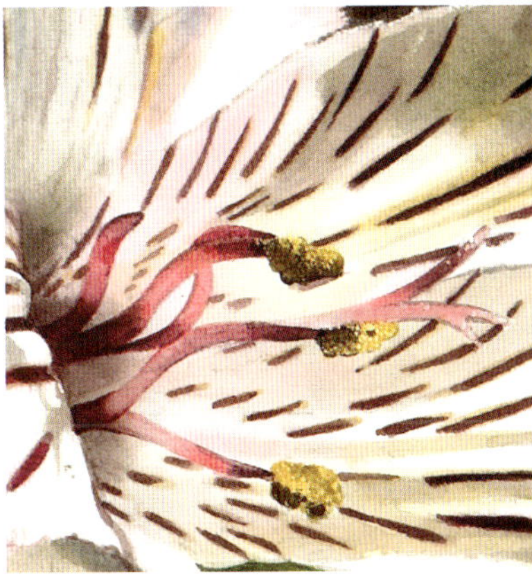

IN DETAIL Glazing is accomplished by applying thin layers of paint over one another, letting the paint dry between applications. The end effect is transparent and allows the white of the paper to reflect light.

To blend the stripes inside the flower, a damp brush was carefully drawn over each stripe, with great care taken not to smear the paint. Blending softens edges and here embedded the stripe deeper into the paper, creating an attractive depth.

About the Artists

Connie J. Adams
www.conniejadams.com
Heliconia **79**
A resident of and teacher in Maui in the Hawaiian Islands, Connie Adams has always been fascinated by the exotic botanical image—a fascination that led her to travel the Caribbean, Bali, and Costa Rica. In 2001 she graduated from the Maryland Institute, College of Art, with an MFA in Painting. Connie has won numerous awards.

Robin Berry
Foxglove **39**
Sunflowers **47**
Sunny Bouquet **57**
Calla Lilies **63**
Tulips **71**
Columbines **81**
Hollyhocks **85**
Blue Thistles **95**
Magnolia Blossoms **103**
Peonies **109**
Frangipani **129**
How To Paint Watercolor Flowers author Robin Berry has been a professional artist for 35 years. After 20 years as a nationally recognized porcelain artist, Robin changed direction to painting, focusing exclusively on transparent watercolor. Today, her flower paintings regularly win awards in national shows. Robin lives and works in Minneapolis, Minnesota.

Denny Bond
Amaryllis **55**
Tiger Lilies **73**
Peruvian Lilies **121**
Denny Bond is an award-winning watercolorist and illustrator residing in East Petersburg, Pennsylvania. Using permanent liquid watercolors, Denny combines several elements in a painting to define the composition. His subject matter ranges from figurative to landscape and nature.

Jana Bouc
Orchids **41**
Ranunculus **65**
Begonias **131**
For over 25 years, Jana Bouc has used watercolor as her primary medium. Flowers are a favorite subject of hers, along with people, still lifes, animals, and landscapes. She carries her sketchbook and watercolors everywhere, and can often be found sketching and painting around the San Francisco Bay Area or in her home studio where she teaches watercolor.

Carol Carter
www.carol-carter.com
Crown Imperial **87**
Love in the Mist **113**
Carol Carter received her MFA from Washington University, St. Louis. She was voted Best St. Louis Artist by The Riverfront Times in 2000. The U.S. Embassy sponsored a solo exhibition of Carol's work at the Teatro del Centro de Arte, in Guayaquil, Ecuador in 2003, and she is the Artist-in-Residence for the Everglades National Park.

Moira Clinch
Clematis **123**
Ipomoea **137**
Bachelor's Buttons **143**
Moira Clinch trained at Central Saint Martins School of Art in London and has exhibited at the Royal Academy's Summer Exhibition in London. She is author of *The Watercolor Artist's Pocket Palette.*

Jan Hart
www.janhart.com
Passion Flowers **93**
Jan Hart, a watercolor artist with a background in science and architecture, has been painting and teaching for over 30 years. Now living in Costa Rica, she is author of *The Watercolor Artist's Guide to Exceptional Color*, and her passion is color and light in all she sees and paints.

Lisa Hill
www.lisahillwatercolorist.com
Indian Reed Lily **37**
Pansies **61**
Rhododendron **97**
Cyclamen **107**
Parrot Tulips **117**
Fritillaria **145**
Lisa Hill lives in Richland, Washington. The only medium she has worked with is watercolor, which she has been studying for four years. Realistic depictions of flowers and foliage are her preferred subjects, and she has a growing portfolio of bird, animal, and butterfly paintings.

Tom Love
www.artincanada.com/thomaslove
Mallows **45**
Primroses **69**
Gerbera Daisy **115**
Water Lily **125**
African Daisies **139**
Tom Love lives in Western Canada and paints, exclusively in watercolor, a broad spectrum of subject matter, primarily the human form. His paintings hang in collections across Canada and in the United States, Europe, and Australia. Tom is a senior member and past president of the Society of Western Canadian Artists in Edmonton.

Heather Maunders
Honeysuckle **53**
Bluebells **77**
After a career in scientific research, Heather Maunders now paints full time from her studio in Cambridgeshire, UK. Her preferred medium is watercolor, with its inspiring versatility in allowing the delicate transparency and bold layers of color necessary to paint flowers.

Katrina Small
Fuchsia **75**
Blue Poppies **101**
Lily of the Valley **135**
Katirna Small is a fine art instructor and demonstrator, as well as a web and graphic designer. She enjoys working in watercolor, losing herself in moving pigment in water, saturating, blending, and glazing. She also paints in pastel, oil, and acrylic.

Nancy Meadows Taylor
www.nancymeadowstaylor.com
Rose **43**
Crocuses **49**
Snowdrops **83**
Protea **111**
Bird of Paradise **127**
Nancy Taylor studied interior design in college, developing skills she has used for 30 years in painting with watercolor and recently oil. She has memberships in the American Watercolor Society, the National Watercolor Society, and the Rocky Mountain National Watermedia Society. She paints images from nature and has a studio in Raleigh, North Carolina.

Naomi Tydeman
Iris **88**
Naomi Tydeman runs her own gallery and studio in Tenby, Wales, where she produces delicate and realistic watercolor paintings. Self-taught, she is a member of the Royal Institute of Painters in Watercolor and the Welsh Watercolor Society.

Karen Vernon
www.karenvernon.com
Hyacinths **59**
Karen Vernon's paintings hang in museum and corporate collections in Europe, the United States, and throughout the rest of the world. She is the founder of ACT (Artists Changing Tomorrow), and is one of only three watercolorists whose works were chosen to tour as part of the national museum exhibition, Sea to Shining Sea.

Eric Wiegardt
Spring Bouquet **119**
Eric Wiegardt has been painting for 25 years, displaying his watercolors at Wiegardt Studio Gallery in Ocean Park, Washington. He is an award-winning watercolorist, author, and juror. Eric has influenced countless artists—who have attended his workshops throughout the United States and Europe—with his loose painting style.

Donna Jill Witty
Chrysanthemums **51**
Peonies and Poppies **67**
Hibiscus **91**
Snapdragon **99**
Lilies of the Nile **105**
Lenten Rose **133**
Poppies **140**
A professional artist for over 30 years, Donna Jill Witty holds signature status in the American Watercolor Society, National Watercolor Society, and Transparent Watercolor Society of America. Her subject matter ranges from landscapes and street scenes, to still life and figures. She runs a studio in Woodstock, Illinois.

Index

Credits

Quarto would like to thank the following agencies for supplying images for inclusion in this book:

Photolibrary: p. 36, 38, 40, 42, 46, 52, 56, 58, 60, 64, 66, 68, 70, 72, 76, 84, 86, 92, 98, 101, 110, 112, 118, 122, 124, 126, 130, 132, 136, 138, 140, 142

Getty Images: p. 50, 88, 90, 116

Clive Nichols: p. 54, 94